AVANT GARD

CHAMBERS

Dictionary of
Spelling
and
Word Division

CHAMBERS

Dictionary of
Spelling
and
Word Division

Edited by
David Edmonds

CHAMBERS

CHAMBERS
An imprint of Larousse plc
43–45 Annandale Street
Edinburgh EH7 4AZ

10 9 8 7 6 5 4 3 2 1

A CIP catalogue record for this book
is available from the British Library

ISBN 0-550-18300-0

Typeset by Hewer Text Composition Services, Edinburgh
Printed and bound in Great Britain
by Cox & Wyman Ltd, Reading, Berkshire

Contents

Preface

This book is designed to help those who know the words they want to write, but are unsure how to spell them. It does not explain what the words mean, which is the job of an ordinary dictionary, except where particular words need to be distinguished (eg *rain, reign, rein*). All the main forms of each word are listed, and for each form I have shown the best places for splitting it at the end of a line of writing or typescript so as to give a smooth and easy read.

Acknowledgement is due to Dr R. E. Allen, Publishing Director of Larousse plc, for unfailing help and encouragement, and to Dr Caroline Fraser for help with some Russian transliterations.

Introduction

1. What the dictionary contains

In this book you will find all the words in common use in the English language. I have also included the names of States and their capitals, and of other towns and cities likely to be of interest to the reader. You will also find all the commonest first names, and a selection of the surnames of famous people from all walks of life: the standard English titles of famous books, films, stage works, and pictures are also included, together with a note of their foreign-language titles where appropriate. I have included those abbreviations which are now thought of as words (eg *radar, won't, Stasi, MIND, FORTRAN*), but not those which are still perceived as a string of initials (eg *BBC, MOT*).

2. How to find spellings

(a) Plural forms are given for all nouns that normally have them, except where they are simply made by adding *s* (ie *cherry, cherries, man, men* are given, but not *door, doors*); alternative plurals are given, with (where possible) a note on their use, eg

> bass
> *in music*
> △ basses
> *fish*
> △ bass *or* basses.

For each verb every part which is spelt differently from the headword (3rd person singular present; past form; present participle) is listed; where it differs from the past form the past participle is given as well, as in

> grow
> △ grows
> △ grew
> △ growing
> △ grown.

Similarly, every adjective and adverb whose comparative and superlative forms involve a change of spelling in standard English is given a full listing:

bad	fast
△ worse	△ faster
△ worst	△ fastest.

Inflections that are considerably different from their headword are also listed at their own alphabetic place; so *worse* also appears as a headword between *worry* and *worsen*, and *worst* (with its inflections, since it is also a verb) between *worshipper* and *worsted*.

(b) Part-of-speech markers (eg *noun*, *adj*.; see abbreviations and symbols list on p.xii below) are only employed to identify inflections of a headword that functions as more than one part of speech; for example, since *worst* functions as both verb and superlative adjective, its verbal inflections are identified:

worst

VERB

△ worsts

△ worsted

△ worsting,

whereas at *worsen*, which is a verb only, they are not.

(c) Where several forms of a spelling exist, only the preferred form is given a full entry. Alternative forms are given in the following way when they are alphabetically remote from the preferred form:

widgeon *see* wigeon.

(d) A number of confusables (mostly words with the same sound but different spellings and meanings) have been cross-referred and their ranges of meaning identified:

storey	story
floor in building	*narrative*
⚠ story	△ stories
	⚠ storey

These entries are printed within frames in the text, for ease of reference. The symbol ⚠ is used to indicate another word that is often confused with the entry-word. Note that the meanings are kept as short as possible for reasons of space; they are intended only to identify the word in question, not to define it fully.

In some cases the part of speech is a sufficient identifier:

teeth	teethe
PL. NOUN	VERB
⚠ teethe	△ teethes
	△ teethed
	△ teething
	⚠ teeth,

while in a few others where the entries adjoin and are spelt the same (ie the only difference being capitalization or hyphenation), the cross reference is omitted:

> Incarnation
> *of Christ*
> incarnation
> *of any spirit etc; person who typifies a quality etc.*

3. How to divide words

Every word in the dictionary is marked to show where it can be split at the end of a line of writing.

(a) The mark | shows the best place to split: other possible places are shown by ⁝.

(b) Words with no mark (generally those of less than 5 letters, and some with awkward spellings or pronunciation) should never be split.

(c) Hyphenated words (eg *ad-lib, airy-fairy*) are best split immediately after the hyphen; since this is always the case, I have not marked them with | each time in the dictionary.

(d) Unhyphenated words that have only ⁝ marks are best left unsplit if possible.

Abbreviations and symbols

adj.	adjective	pl.	plural
adv.	adverb	pron.	pronoun
c	century (19c, etc)	sing.	singular
esp.	especially	⚠	do not confuse with

A

a
Aa|chen
aard|vark
Aarhus *see*
  Århus
Aaron
aback
aba|cus
  △ aba|cu|ses
abaft
Abailard *see*
  Abelard
aba|lone
aban|don
  VERB
  △ aban|dons
  △ aban|doned
  △ aban|don|ing
aban|doned
aban|don|ment
abase
  △ aba|ses
  △ abased
  △ aba|sing
abase|ment
abashed
abate
  △ abates
  △ aba|ted
  △ aba|ting
abate|ment
abat|toir

ab|bacy
  △ ab|ba|cies
Ab|bado
Ab|ba|sid
ab|bess
  △ ab|bes|ses
abbey
abbot
ab|bre|vi|ate
  △ ab|bre|vi|ates
  △ ab|bre|vi|ated
  △ ab|bre|vi|ating
ab|bre|vi|ation
ab|di|cate
  △ ab|di|cates
  △ ab|di|ca|ted
  △ ab|di|ca|ting
ab|di|ca|tion
ab|do|men
ab|dom|inal
ab|duct
  △ ab|ducts
  △ ab|duc|ted
  △ ab|duct|ing
ab|duc|tion
ab|duc|tor
abeam
Abel
Ab|el|ard
Ab|er|deen
Ab|er|fan
ab|er|rance
ab|er|rancy
  △ ab|er|ran|cies

ab|er|rant
ab|er|ra|tion
Ab|er|yst|wyth
abet
  △ abets
  △ abet|ted
  △ abet|ting
abet|ter
abey|ance
abhor
  △ ab|hors
  △ ab|horred
  △ ab|hor|ring
ab|hor|rence
ab|hor|rent
ab|hor|rently
abide
  △ abides
  △ abode *or* abi|
    ded
  △ abi|ding
abi|ding
Abi|gail
abil|ity
  △ abil|it|ies
ab ini|tio
ab|ject
ab|jec|tion
ab|jectly
ab|ject|ness
ab|jur|ation
ab|jure
  △ ab|jures
  △ ab|jured

  △ ab|jur|ing
ab|la|tive
ab|laut
ablaze
able
  △ abler
  △ ablest
able-bod|ied
ab|lu|tion
ably
ab|nega|tion
ab|nor|mal
ab|nor|mal|ity
  △ ab|nor|mal|it|
    ies
ab|nor|mally
Abo
aboard
abode
abol|ish
  △ abol|ishes
  △ abol|ished
  △ abol|ish|ing
abol|ition
abol|ition|ism
abol|ition|ist
A-bomb
abom|in|able
abom|in|ably
abom|in|ate
  △ abom|in|ates
  △ abom|in|ated
  △ abom|in|ating
abom|in|ation

-able / -ible

These endings are derived from Latin endings **-abilis** and **-ibilis**, and form adjectives essentially meaning 'able to be . . .', although some have developed special meanings in their own right, or are less closely tied to a root verb, eg **changeable**, **infallible**.

-able is an active suffix that can be used to make new words (such as **photocopiable** and **microwaveable**), whereas **-ible** is generally more integral with the stem of the word.

Words ending in a silent **-e** often drop the e when adding **-able**, but not when the ending is **-ce** or **-ge**, eg **movable** but **changeable**.

For the most common words in **-ible**, see the panel at **-ible**.

Ab|ori|gi|nal
with reference to
Australia
△ aboriginal
△ aborigine

ab|ori|gi|nal
earliest;
primitive;
indigenous
△ Aboriginal
△ aborigine

ab|ori|gine
one of the
original
inhabitants of a
country
△ Aboriginal
△ aboriginal

abort
△ aborts
△ abor|ted
△ abort|ing
abor|tion
abor|tion|ist
abor|tive
abor|tively
aboulia *see*
abulia
abound
△ abounds
△ aboun|ded
△ abound|ing
abound|ing
about
A Bout de
souffle
(Breath|less)
about-face
VERB
△ about-faces
△ about-faced

△ about-facing
about-turn
VERB
△ about-turns
△ about-turned
△ about-turn|
ing
above
above-board
ab|ra|ca|dabra
ab|rade
△ ab|rades
△ ab|ra|ded
△ ab|ra|ding
Ab|ra|ham
ab|ra|sion
ab|ra|sive
ab|ra|sively
ab|ra|sive|ness
abreast
abridge
△ abrid|ges
△ abridged
△ abrid|ging
abridged
abridge|ment
abroad
ab|ro|gate
△ ab|ro|gates
△ ab|ro|ga|ted
△ ab|ro|ga|ting
ab|ro|ga|tion
ab|rupt
△ ab|rup|ter
△ ab|rupt|est
ab|ruptly
ab|rupt|ness
ab|scess
△ ab|sces|ses
ab|scissa
△ ab|scis|sas *or*
ab|scis|sae
ab|scis|sion
ab|scond

△ ab|sconds
△ ab|scon|ded
△ ab|scond|ing
ab|scon|der
ab|seil
VERB
△ ab|seils
△ ab|seiled
△ ab|seil|ing
ab|seil|ing
ab|sence
ab|sent
VERB
△ ab|sents
△ ab|sen|ted
△ ab|sent|ing
ab|sen|tee
ab|sen|tee|ism
ab|sen|tly
ab|sent-minded
ab|sent-mind|
edly
ab|sent-mind|
ed|ness
ab|sinthe
ab|so|lute
ab|so|lutely
ab|so|lute|ness
ab|so|lu|tion
ab|so|lu|tism
ab|so|lu|tist
ab|solve
△ ab|solves
△ ab|solved
△ ab|sol|ving
ab|sorb
△ ab|sorbs
△ ab|sorbed
△ ab|sorb|ing
ab|sorbed
ab|sor|bedly
ab|sor|bency
△ ab|sor|ben|cies
ab|sor|bent

ab|sorb|ing
ab|sorp|tance
ab|sorp|tion
ab|sorp|tive
ab|stain
△ ab|stains
△ ab|stained
△ ab|stain|ing
ab|stainer
ab|ste|mi|ous
ab|ste|mi|ously
ab|ste|mi|ous|
ness
ab|sten|tion
ab|stin|ence
ab|stin|ent
ab|stract
VERB
△ ab|stracts
△ ab|strac|ted
△ ab|stract|ing
ab|strac|ted
ab|strac|tedly
ab|strac|tion
ab|struse
△ ab|stru|ser
△ ab|stru|sest
ab|strusely
ab|surd
△ ab|sur|der
△ ab|surd|est
ab|surd|ism
ab|surd|ity
△ ab|surd|it|ies
ab|surdly
ab|surd|ness
Abu Dhabi
Abuja
abu|lia
abun|dance
abun|dant
abun|dantly
abuse

VERB
△ abu|ses
△ abused
△ abu|sing
Abu Sim|bel
abu|sive
abu|sively
abu|sive|ness
abut
△ abuts
△ abut|ted
△ abut|ting
abut|ment
Abu Zabi *see*
  Abu Dhabi
abuzz
abys|mal
abys|mally
abyss
△ abys|ses
abys|sal
Abys|sinia
aca|cia
aca|deme
aca|demic
aca|dem|ic|ally
aca|de|mi|cian
acad|emy
△ acad|em|ies
acan|thus
△ acan|thuses
Aca|pulco
ac|cede
△ ac|cedes
△ ac|ceded
△ ac|ced|ing
ac|cel|er|ate
△ ac|cel|er|ates
△ ac|cel|er|ated
△ ac|cel|er|ating
ac|cel|er|ation
ac|cel|er|ator
ac|cent

VERB
△ ac|cents
△ ac|cen|ted
△ ac|cent|ing
ac|cen|tor
ac|cen|tu|ate
△ ac|cen|tu|ates
△ ac|cen|tu|ated
△ ac|cen|tu|ating
ac|cen|tu|ation

---

ac|cept
take; agree to
△ ac|cepts
△ ac|cep|ted
△ ac|cept|ing
⚠ except

---

ac|cep|ta|bil|ity
ac|cept|able
ac|cept|ably
ac|cept|ance
ac|cep|tor

---

ac|cess
*means or right
of approach,
entry, etc; gain
access to*
VERB
△ ac|ces|ses
△ ac|cessed
△ ac|ces|sing
⚠ excess

---

ac|ces|sary
△ ac|ces|sar|ies
ac|ces|si|bil|ity
ac|cess|ible
ac|cess|ibly
ac|ces|sion
ac|ces|sory
△ ac|ces|sor|ies
ac|ci|dent
ac|ci|den|tal
Ac|ci|den|tal

*Death of an
An|ar|chist
(Morte ac|ci|
den|tale di un
an|ar|chico)*
ac|ci|dent|ally
ac|ci|dent-prone
ac|claim
VERB
△ ac|claims
△ ac|claimed
△ ac|claim|ing
ac|clam|ation
ac|cli|ma|ti|za|
tion
ac|cli|ma|tize
△ ac|cli|ma|ti|zes
△ ac|cli|ma|tized
△ ac|cli|ma|ti|
  zing
ac|cliv|ity
△ ac|cliv|it|ies
ac|co|llade
ac|com|mo|date
△ ac|com|mo|
  dates
△ ac|com|mo|da|
  ted
△ ac|com|mo|da|
  ting
ac|com|mo|da|
ting
ac|com|mo|da|
tingly
ac|com|mo|da|
tion
ac|com|pa|ni|
ment
ac|com|pan|ist
ac|com|pany
△ ac|com|pan|ies
△ ac|com|pan|ied
△ ac|com|pany|
  ing

ac|com|plice
ac|com|plish
△ ac|com|pli|
  shes
△ ac|com|
  plished
△ ac|com|plish|
  ing
ac|com|plish|
able
ac|com|plished
ac|com|plish|
ment
ac|cord
VERB
△ ac|cords
△ ac|cor|ded
△ ac|cord|ing
ac|cord|ance
ac|cord|ing
ac|cord|ingly
ac|cor|dion
ac|cor|dion|ist
ac|cost
△ ac|costs
△ ac|cos|ted
△ ac|cost|ing
ac|count
VERB
△ ac|counts
△ ac|coun|ted
△ ac|count|ing
ac|count|abil|ity
ac|count|able
ac|count|ancy
ac|count|ant
ac|count|ing
ac|cou|tre|ment
Accra
ac|credit
△ ac|cred|its
△ ac|cred|ited
△ ac|cred|it|ing
ac|cre|di|ta|tion

ac|cred|ited
ac|cre|tion
ac|crual
ac|crue
△ ac|crues
△ ac|crued
△ ac|cru|ing
ac|cul|tur|ation
ac|cu|mu|late
△ ac|cu|mu|lates
△ ac|cu|mu|lated
△ ac|cu|mu|la|
ting
ac|cu|mu|la|tion
ac|cu|mu|la|tive
ac|cu|mu|la|
tively
ac|cu|mu|la|tor
ac|cu|racy
ac|cu|rate
ac|cu|rately
ac|cur|sed *or* ac|
cursed
according to
pronunciation
ac|cur|sedly *or*
ac|cursedly
according to
pronunciation
ac|cu|sa|tion
ac|cu|sa|tive
ac|cuse
△ ac|cu|ses
△ ac|cused
△ ac|cu|sing
ac|cu|ser
ac|cu|sing
ac|cu|singly
ac|cus|tom
△ ac|cus|toms
△ ac|cus|tomed
△ ac|cus|tom|ing
ac|cus|tomed
ace

acel|lu|lar
acer|bic
acer|bity
ace|sul|fame
acetal
acet|al|de|hyde
acet|ate
acetic
acet|one
acet|yl|cho|line
acety|lene
Achaean
ache
VERB
△ aches
△ ached
△ ach|ing
ach|ene
Ach|eron
Ach|eson
Acheu|lian
achiev|able
achieve
△ achieves
△ achieved
△ achiev|ing
achieve|ment
achiever
Achil|les
achon|dro|pla|
sia
achro|ma|tic
achro|mat|ic|ally
achy
△ ach|ier
△ achi|est
acid
aci|dic
aci|di|fi|ca|tion
acid|ify
△ aci|di|fies
△ aci|di|fied
△ a|ci|di|fy|ing
acid|ity

△ acid|it|ies
acidly
acid|osis
ack–ack
ac|know|ledge
△ ac|know|led|
ges
△ ac|know|ledged
△ ac|know|led|
ging
ac|know|ledge|
ment
acme
acne
aco|lyte
acon|ite
acorn
acous|tic
acous|tic|ally
acous|tics
ac|quaint
△ ac|quaints
△ ac|quain|ted
△ ac|quaint|ing
ac|quaint|ance
ac|quaint|ance|
ship
ac|quain|ted
ac|qui|esce
△ ac|qui|es|ces
△ ac|qui|esced
△ ac|qui|es|cing
ac|qui|es|cence
ac|qui|es|cent
ac|qui|es|cently
ac|quire
△ ac|quires
△ ac|quired
△ ac|quir|ing
ac|quire|ment
ac|qui|si|tion
ac|quis|it|ive
ac|quis|it|ive|
ness

ac|quit
△ ac|quits
△ ac|quit|ted
△ ac|quit|ting
ac|quit|tal
acre
acre|age
acrid
ac|rid|ity
ac|ridly
ac|ri|mo|ni|ous
ac|ri|mo|ni|ously
ac|ri|mony
ac|ro|bat
ac|ro|ba|tic
ac|ro|bat|ic|ally
ac|ro|bat|ics
ac|ro|meg|aly
ac|ro|nym
ac|ro|pho|bia
ac|ro|po|lis
across
acros|tic
ac|rylic
act
VERB
△ acts
△ acted
△ act|ing
Ac|taeon
act|ing
ac|tinic
ac|tin|ide
ac|tin|oid
ac|tin|ium
ac|ti|no|ther|apy
ac|tion
ac|tion|able
ac|tion-packed
ac|ti|vate
△ ac|ti|vates
△ ac|ti|va|ted
△ ac|ti|va|ting
ac|ti|va|tion

act|ive
act|ively
ac|tiv|ist
ac|tiv|ity
△ ac|tiv|it|ies
actor
act|ress
△ act|res|ses
Acts of the
Apostles
act|ual
ac|tu|al|ity
△ ac|tu|al|it|ies
ac|tu|ally
ac|tu|ar|ial
ac|tu|ary
△ ac|tu|ar|ies
ac|tu|ate
△ ac|tu|ates
△ ac|tu|ated
△ ac|tu|at|ing
ac|tu|ation
acu|ity
acu|men
acu|pres|sure
acu|punc|ture
acu|punc|tur|ist
acute
△ acu|ter
△ acu|test
acutely
acute|ness
ad
adage
ada|gio
Adam
ada|mant
ada|mantly
Adam Bede

Adam|nan
Adams
Ad|am|son
adapt
△ ad|apts
△ ad|ap|ted
△ ad|apt|ing
ad|ap|ta|bil|ity
ad|apt|able
ad|ap|ta|tion
ad|ap|tor
add
△ adds
△ added
△ add|ing
added
ad|den|dum
△ ad|denda
adder
ad|dict
ad|dic|ted
ad|dic|tion
ad|dict|ive
Addis Ababa
Ad|di|son
ad|di|tion
ad|di|tional
ad|di|tion|ally
ad|dit|ive
addle
△ addles
△ addled
△ ad|dling
addle-brained
addled
add-on
ad|dress
NOUN
△ ad|dres|ses

VERB
△ ad|dres|ses
△ ad|dressed
△ ad|dres|sing
ad|dres|see
ad|duce
△ ad|du|ces
△ ad|duced
△ ad|du|cing
ad|du|cible
Ad|elaide
Aden
Ad|en|auer
ad|en|ine
ad|en|oi|dal
ad|en|oids
adeno|sine
adept
ad|eptly
ad|equacy
ad|equate
ad|equately
à deux
ad|here
△ ad|heres
△ ad|hered
△ ad|her|ing
ad|her|ence
ad|her|ent
ad|he|sion
ad|he|sive
ad hoc
ad hom|inem
adia|ba|tic
Adie
adieu
△ adieus *or*
adieux
Adi Granth

ad infi|ni|tum
adi|pose
adi|pos|ity
Adis Abeba *see*
Addis Ababa
ad|ja|cent
ad|jec|ti|val
ad|jec|ti|vally
ad|jec|tive
ad|join
△ ad|joins
△ ad|joined
△ ad|join|ing
ad|join|ing
ad|journ
△ ad|journs
△ ad|journed
△ ad|journ|ing
ad|journ|ment
ad|judge
△ ad|jud|ges
△ ad|judged
△ ad|jud|ging
ad|judge|ment
ad|ju|di|cate
△ ad|ju|di|cates
△ ad|ju|di|ca|ted
△ ad|ju|di|ca|
ting
ad|ju|di|ca|tion
ad|ju|di|ca|tor
ad|junct
ad|ju|ra|tion
ad|jure
△ ad|jures
△ ad|jured
△ ad|jur|ing
ad|just
△ ad|justs

-acy / -asy

-acy is a genuine suffix in English, derived from Latin **-acia** and **-atia**, and is found in nouns representing a quality or state, eg **accuracy, literacy, piracy**. There are a few nouns in English ending in **-asy**; these are: **apostasy, ecstasy, fantasy, idiosyncrasy**.

△ ad|jus|ted
△ ad|just|ing
ad|just|able
ad|just|ment
ad|ju|tant
ad-lib
VERB
△ ad-libs
△ ad-libbed
△ ad-lib|bing
ad litem
adman
△ admen
admin
ad|min|is|ter
△ ad|min|is|ters
△ ad|min|is|tered
△ ad|min|is|ter|ing
ad|min|is|trate
△ ad|min|is|trates
△ ad|min|is|tra|ted
△ ad|min|is|tra|ting
ad|min|is|tra|tion
ad|min|is|tra|tive
ad|min|is|tra|tively
ad|min|is|tra|tor
ad|mir|able
ad|mir|ably
ad|mi|ral
Ad|mir|alty
ad|mir|ation
ad|mire
△ ad|mires
△ ad|mired
△ ad|mir|ing
ad|mirer
ad|mir|ing

ad|mir|ingly
ad|mis|si|bil|ity
ad|miss|ible
ad|mis|sion
admit
△ ad|mits
△ ad|mit|ted
△ ad|mit|ting
ad|mit|tance
ad|mit|tedly
ad|mix|ture
ad|mon|ish
△ ad|mon|ishes
△ ad|mon|ished
△ ad|mon|ish|ing
ad|mon|ish|ingly
ad|mon|ition
ad|mon|it|ory
ad nau|seam
ado
adobe
adol|es|cence
adol|es|cent
Ado|nis
adopt
△ ad|opts
△ ad|op|ted
△ ad|opt|ing
ad|op|ted
ad|op|tion
ad|opt|ive
ad|or|able
ad|or|ably
ad|ora|tion
adore
△ ad|ores
△ ad|ored
△ ad|or|ing
ad|orer
ad|or|ing
ad|or|ingly
adorn
△ ad|orns

△ ad|orned
△ ad|orn|ing
ad|orn|ment
ad|renal
ad|ren|al|ine
ad|re|no|cor|ti|
  co|tro|phic
Ad|rian
Ad|ri|atic
adrift
adroit
adroitly
adroit|ness
ad|sorb
△ ad|sorbs
△ ad|sorbed
△ ad|sorb|ing
ad|sorb|ent
ad|sorp|tion
adu|late
△ adu|lates
△ adu|la|ted
△ adu|la|ting
adu|la|tion
adu|la|tory
adult
adul|ter|ate
△ adul|ter|ates
△ adul|ter|ated
△ adul|ter|ating
adul|ter|ation
adul|terer
adul|ter|ess
△ adul|ter|es|ses
adul|ter|ous
adul|ter|ously
adul|tery
adult|hood
ad|um|brate
△ ad|um|brates
△ ad|um|bra|ted
△ ad|um|bra|
  ting
ad|um|bra|tion

Ad|vaita Ve|
  danta
ad|vance
VERB
△ ad|van|ces
△ ad|vanced
△ ad|van|cing
ad|vanced
Ad|vanced-level
ad|vance|ment
ad|vant|age
ad|vant|aged
ad|van|ta|geous
ad|van|ta|
  geously
ad|van|ta|geous|
  ness
Ad|vent
in Christian
context
ad|vent
arrival
Ad|ven|tist
ad|ven|ti|tious
ad|ven|ti|tiously
ad|ven|ture
ad|ven|turer
ad|ven|tur|ess
△ ad|ven|tur|es|
  ses
ad|ven|tur|ous
ad|ven|tur|ously
ad|verb
ad|ver|bial
ad|ver|bi|ally
ad|ver|sar|ial
ad|ver|sary
△ ad|ver|sar|ies

ad|verse
hostile; hurtful
⚠averse

ad|versely
ad|ver|sity

△ ad|ver|si|ties
ad|vert
  VERB
△ ad|verts
△ ad|ver|ted
△ ad|vert|ing
ad|ver|tise
△ ad|ver|ti|ses
△ ad|ver|tised
△ ad|ver|ti|sing
ad|ver|tise|ment
ad|ver|tiser
ad|ver|ti|sing
ad|vice
ad|vi|sa|bil|ity
ad|vis|able
ad|vise
△ ad|vi|ses
△ ad|vised
△ ad|vi|sing
ad|vised
ad|vi|sedly
ad|vi|ser
ad|vi|sory
ad|vo|caat
ad|vo|cacy
ad|vo|cate
  VERB
△ ad|vo|cates
△ ad|vo|ca|ted
△ ad|vo|ca|ting
adze
Ae|gean
Ae|gina
aegis
Ae|gis|thus
Ael|fric
Ae|neas
Ae|neid, The
ae|olian
Ae|olus
aeon *see* eon
aer|ate
△ aer|ates

△ aer|ated
△ aer|ating
aer|ation
aer|en|chyma
aer|ial
aeri|ally
aerie *see* eyrie
aero|batic
aero|bat|ics
aer|obe
aero|bic
aero|bics
aero|drome
aero|dy|namic
aero|dy|nam|ic|ally
aero|dy|nam|ics
aero|foil
aero|gramme
aerom|etry
aero|nau|tic
aero|nau|ti|cal
aero|naut|ics
aero|phone
aero|plane
aero|sol
aero|space
Aes|chy|lus
Aesculapius *see*
  Asclepius
Aesop
aes|thete

af|fixed
af|fix|ing
af|flict
△ af|flicts
△ af|flic|ted
△ af|flict|ing
af|flic|tion
af|flu|ence

> af|flu|ent
> *rich*
> ⚠ effluent

---

aes|thet|ic|ally
aes|thet|ics
aes|ti|va|tion
Aethelred *see*
  Ethelred
aether *see* ether
ae|tio|lo|gi|cal

ae|tio|lo|gic|ally
ae|ti|ol|ogy
afar
af|fa|bil|ity
af|fable
af|fably
af|fair
af \ faire

> af|fect
> *influence; infect;*
> *pretend; make a*
> *show of*
> △ af|fects
> △ af|fec|ted
> △ af|fect|ing
> ⚠ effect

---

af|fec|ta|tion
af|fec|ted
af|fec|tedly
af|fect|ing
af|fec|tion
af|fec|tion|ate
af|fec|tion|ately
af|fect|ive
af|fer|ent
af|fi|anced
af|fi|da|vit
af|fi|li|ate
△ af|fi|li|ates
△ af|fi|li|ated
△ af|fi|li|ating
af|fi|li|ation
af|fin|ity
△ af|fin|it|ies
af|firm
△ af|firms
△ af|firmed
△ af|firm|ing
af|fir|ma|tion
af|firm|at|ive
af|firm|at|ively
affix
△ af|fixes

af|ford
△ af|fords
△ af|for|ded
△ af|ford|ing
af|ford|able
af|for|est
△ af|for|ests
△ af|for|es|ted
△ af|for|est|ing
af|for|es|ta|tion
af|fray
af|front
  VERB
△ af|fronts
△ af|fron|ted
△ af|front|ing
Af|ghan
Af|ghan|is|tan
afi|ci|on|ado
afield
afire
aflame
af|la|toxin
afloat
afoot
afore
afore|men|
  tioned
afore|said
afore|thought
a for|ti|ori
afraid

> aes|thetic
> *tasteful; having*
> *good taste*
> ⚠ ascetic

afresh
Af|rica
Af|ri|can
Af|ri|can Queen,
  The
Af|ri|kaans
Af|rika Corps
Af|ri|kaner
Afro
Afro-Ameri|can
Afro-Asi|atic
Afro-Car|ib|
  bean
aft
after
af|ter|birth
af|ter|burn|ing
af|ter|care
after-effect
af|ter|glow
af|ter|life
af|ter|math
af|ter|noon
af|ters
af|ter|shave
af|ter|taste
af|ter|thought
af|ter|wards
again
against
Aga Khan
Aga|mem|non
aga|mid
aga|pan|thus
agape
agar
aga|ric
Agassi
agate
Aga|tha
agave
age
  VERB
  △ ages

△ aged
△ age|ing
aged
Age d'or, L'
  (The Gol|den
  Age)
age|ing
age|ism
age|ist
age|less
agency
  △ agen|cies
agenda
  △ agen|das
agent
agent pro|vo|ca|
  teur
  △ agents pro|vo|
  ca|teurs
age-old
ag|gior|na|mento
ag|glom|er|ate
  VERB
  △ ag|glom|er|
  ates
  △ ag|glom|er|
  ated
  △ ag|glom|er|
  ating
ag|glom|er|ation
ag|glu|tin|ate
  △ ag|glu|tin|ates
  △ ag|glu|tin|ated
  △ ag|glu|tin|
  ating
ag|glu|tin|ation
ag|glu|tin|ative
ag|grand|ize
  △ ag|grand|izes
  △ ag|grand|ized
  △ ag|grand|iz|
  ing
ag|grand|ize|
  ment

ag|gra|vate
  △ ag|gra|vates
  △ ag|gra|va|ted
  △ ag|gra|va|ting
ag|gra|va|ting
ag|gra|va|tingly
ag|gra|va|tion
ag|gre|gate
  VERB
  △ ag|gre|gates
  △ ag|gre|ga|ted
  △ ag|gre|ga|ting
ag|gre|ga|tion
ag|gres|sion
ag|gres|sive
ag|gres|sively
ag|gres|sive|ness
ag|gres|sor
ag|grieved
aggro
aghast
agile
agilely
agil|ity
agin
Agin|court
aging see ageing
agism see
  ageism
agist see ageist
agi|tate
  △ agi|tates
  △ agi|ta|ted
  △ agi|ta|ting
agi|ta|ted
agi|ta|tedly
agi|ta|tion
agi|ta|tor
agit|prop
aglow
Agnes
Agnew
ag|no|sia
ag|nos|tic

ag|nos|ti|cism
ago
agog
ag|on|ist
ag|on|ize
  △ ag|on|izes
  △ ag|on|ized
  △ ag|on|izing
ag|on|ized
ag|on|izing
ag|on|izingly
agony
  △ ag|on|ies
ago|ra|pho|bia
ago|ra|pho|bic
agouti
Agra
agra|nu|lo|cy|to|
  sis
agra|phia
ag|rar|ian
agree
  △ ag|rees
  △ ag|reed
  △ ag|ree|ing
ag|ree|able
ag|ree|ably
ag|ree|ment
agrichemical see
  agrochemical
ag|ri|cul|tural
ag|ri|cul|tur|al|
  ist
ag|ri|cul|ture
ag|ri|cul|tur|ist
ag|ri|mony
ag|ro|chem|ical
agro-indus|try
ag|ron|omy
aground
ague
ah
aha
ahead

ahem
Ahimsa
ahoy
aid
  VERB
  △ aids
  △ aided
  △ aid|ing
Aida
Aidan
aide
aide-de-camp
  △ aides-de-camp
aide-mémoire
  △ aides-mémoire
AIDS
ai|kido

ail
be ill; trouble
  △ ails
  △ ailed
  △ ail|ing
  ⚠ ale

ail|eron
ail|ing
ail|ment
Ailsa
aim
  VERB
  △ aims
  △ aimed
  △ aim|ing
aim|less
aim|lessly
ain't
Ain|tree
air
  VERB
  △ airs
  △ aired
  △ air|ing
air|bag
air|borne

air|brush
  NOUN
  △ air|bru|shes
  VERB
  △ air|bru|shes
  △ air|brushed
  △ air|brush|ing
Air|bus
air-con|di|tioned
air-con|di|tioner
air-con|di|tion|
  ing
air|craft
  sing. and pl.
air|craft|man
  △ air|craft|men
air|crew
air-drop
  VERB
  △ air-drops
  △ air-dropped
  △ air-drop|ping
air|field
air|gun
air|head
air|ily
airi|ness
air|ing
air|ing-cup|
  board
air|less
air|lift
  VERB
  △ air|lifts
  △ air|lif|ted
  △ air|lift|ing
air|line
air|liner
air|lock
air|mail
air|man
  △ air|men
air|plane
air|port

air-rifle
air|ship
air|sick
air|sick|ness
air|space
air|strip
air|tight
air|time
air-to-air
air|waves
air|way
air|wo|man
  △ air|wo|men
air|wor|thi|ness
air|wor|thy
airy
  △ air|ier
  △ airi|est
airy-fairy

aisle
*passage between
seats etc*
  ⚠ isle

aitch
  △ ait|ches
aitch|bone
Aix-en-Pro|
  vence
Ajac|cio
ajar
Ajax
akimbo
akin
Ak|ka|dian
Ala|bama
ala|bas|ter
à la carte
alac|rity
Alain-Four|nier
Alamo
à la mode
Alan
alan|ine

*À la Re|cherche
du temps perdu
(Re|mem|
brance of
Things Past)*
alarm
  VERB
  △ alarms
  △ alarmed
  △ alarm|ing
alarm|ing
alarm|ingly
alarm|ism
alarm|ist
alas
Alas|dair
Alaska
alb
Al|ba|nia
Al|ba|nian
Al|bany
al|ba|tross
  △ al|ba|tros|ses
Albee
albeit
Al|bé|niz
Al|bert
Al|berta
Al|berti
al|bin|ism
al|bino
Al|bion
album

al|bu|men
*white part of
egg*
  ⚠ albumin

al|bu|min
*protein found in
egg white and
blood*
  ⚠ albumen

al¦bu¦min¦uria
Al¦ces¦tis
Al¦chem¦ist, The
al¦chem¦ist
al¦chemy
Al¦ci¦bi¦ades
Al¦cock
al¦co¦hol
al¦co¦holic
al¦co¦hol¦ic¦ally
al¦co¦hol¦ism
Al¦cott
al¦cove
Al¦cuin
Alde¦burgh
al¦de¦hyde
al dente
alder
al¦der¦man
  △ al¦der¦men
Al¦der¦ney
Al¦der¦shot
Al¦diss
al¦do¦ster¦one
Ald¦wych

> ale
> *beer*
> △ail

aleat¦ory
ale¦house
Aleppo
alert
  VERB
  △ alerts
  △ aler¦ted
  △ alert¦ing
  ADJ.
  △ aler¦ter
  △ alert¦est
alertly
alert¦ness
Aleut
A-level

Alex¦an¦der
Al¦ex¦an¦dria
al¦ex¦an¦drine
alexia
Alexis
al¦falfa
Alf¦red
al¦fresco
alga
  △ algae
Al¦garve
al¦ge¦bra
al¦ge¦braic
al¦ge¦bra¦ic¦ally
Al¦geria
Al¦giers
al¦gin¦ate
ALGOL
Al¦gon¦kian
Al¦gon¦kin
al¦go¦rithm
al¦go¦rith¦mic
Al¦ham¦bra
Ali
alias
  NOUN
  △ ali¦ases
alibi
Ali¦cante
Alice
Alice's Ad¦ven¦
  tures in Won¦
  der¦land
Alice Springs
alien
ali¦en¦able
ali¦en¦ate
  △ ali¦en¦ates
  △ ali¦en¦ated
  △ ali¦en¦ating
ali¦en¦ation
alight
  VERB
  △ alights

△ aligh¦ted
△ alight¦ing
align
  △ aligns
  △ aligned
  △ align¦ing
align¦ment
alike
ali¦ment¦ary
ali¦mony
ali¦pha¦tic
ali¦quot
Ali¦son
alive
al¦kali
al¦ka¦line
al¦ka¦lin¦ity
al¦ka¦loid
al¦ka¦lo¦sis
al¦kane
al¦kene
alkyl
al¦kyne
all
alla breve
all-Ameri¦can
al¦lan¦tois
  △ al¦lan¦toi¦des
allay
  △ allays
  △ al¦layed
  △ al¦lay¦ing
al¦le¦ga¦tion
al¦lege
  △ al¦leges
  △ al¦leged
  △ al¦le¦ging
al¦leged
al¦le¦gedly
al¦le¦giance
al¦le¦gor¦ical
al¦le¦gor¦ic¦ally
al¦leg¦or¦ize
  △ al¦leg¦or¦izes

△ al¦leg¦or¦ized
△ al¦leg¦or¦izing
al¦leg¦ory
  △ al¦leg¦or¦ies
al¦legro
al¦lele
al¦le¦luia
alle¦mande
all-embra¦cing
Allen
Al¦lenby
Al¦lende
al¦ler¦gen
al¦ler¦gic
al¦lergy
  △ al¦ler¦gies
al¦le¦vi¦ate
  △ al¦le¦vi¦ates
  △ al¦le¦vi¦ated
  △ al¦le¦vi¦ating
al¦le¦vi¦ation
alley
All for Love, or
  The World
  Well Lost
al¦li¦ance
al¦lied
al¦li¦ga¦tor
All¦ing¦ham
all-in
al¦lit¦er¦ate
  △ al¦lit¦er¦ates
  △ al¦lit¦er¦ated
  △ al¦lit¦er¦ating
al¦lit¦er¦ation
al¦lit¦er¦at¦ive
al¦lit¦er¦at¦ively
al¦lo¦cate
  △ al¦lo¦cates
  △ al¦lo¦ca¦ted
  △ al¦lo¦ca¦ting
al¦lo¦ca¦tion
al¦lo¦phone
allot

△ al¦lots
△ al¦lot¦ted
△ al¦lot¦ting
al¦lot¦ment
al¦lo¦trope
al¦lo¦tro¦pic
al¦lo¦tropy
all-out
allow
△ al¦lows
△ al¦lowed
△ al¦low¦ing
al¦low¦able
al¦low¦ably
al¦low¦ance
al¦low¦edly
alloy
VERB
△ al¦loys
△ al¦loyed
△ al¦loy¦ing
all-pur¦pose
All Quiet on the West¦ern Front
all-round
all-roun¦der
all¦spice
All's Well that Ends Well
All the Presi¦dent's Men
all-time

al¦lude
refer (to)
△ al¦ludes
△ al¦lu¦ded
△ al¦lu¦ding
⚠elude

al¦lure
VERB
△ al¦lures
△ al¦lured
△ al¦lur¦ing

al¦lure¦ment
al¦lur¦ing
al¦lur¦ingly

al¦lu¦sion
indirect reference
⚠illusion

al¦lu¦sive
al¦lu¦sively
al¦lu¦vial
al¦lu¦vium
△ al¦lu¦via
ally
NOUN
△ al¦lies
VERB
△ al¦lies
△ al¦lied
△ al¦ly¦ing
Alma
Alma-Ata
alma mater
al¦ma¦nac
Alma-Tadema
Al¦mighty
name for God
al¦mighty
having complete power; very great
al¦mond
al¦mond-eyed
al¦moner
al¦most
alms
alms-house
Al¦nico
Aln¦wick
aloe
aloft
alone
along
along¦side
aloof

aloof¦ly
aloof¦ness
alo¦pe¦cia
aloud
Alou¦ette, L' (The Lark)
alp
al¦paca
al¦pen¦horn
alpha
al¦pha¦bet
al¦pha¦betic
al¦pha¦bet¦ical
al¦pha¦bet¦ic¦ally
al¦pha¦bet¦ize
△ al¦pha¦bet¦izes
△ al¦pha¦bet¦ized
△ al¦pha¦bet¦izing
al¦pha¦nu¦meric
al¦pha¦nu¦mer¦ical
al¦pha¦nu¦mer¦ic¦ally
alp¦horn
al¦pine
Alps
al¦ready
al¦right
Al¦sace
Al¦sa¦tian
also
also-ran
Al¦taic

al¦tar
table in church etc
⚠alter

al¦tar¦piece

al¦ter
change
△ al¦ters

△ al¦tered
△ al¦ter¦ing
⚠altar

al¦ter¦able
al¦ter¦ation
al¦ter¦ca¦tion
al¦ter¦nate
VERB
△ al¦ter¦nates
△ al¦ter¦na¦ted
△ al¦ter¦na¦ting
al¦ter¦nately
al¦ter¦na¦ting
al¦ter¦na¦tion
al¦ter¦nat¦ive
al¦ter¦nat¦ively
al¦ter¦na¦tor
al¦though
Alt¦hus¦ser
al¦ti¦meter
al¦ti¦tude
alto
al¦to¦cu¦mu¦lus
△ al¦to¦cu¦muli
al¦to¦gether
al¦to¦stra¦tus
△ al¦to¦strati
al¦tru¦ism
al¦tru¦ist
al¦tru¦is¦tic
al¦tru¦is¦tic¦ally
alum
alu¦mina
alu¦min¦ium
alu¦mi¦no¦sili¦cate
alum¦nus
△ alumni
al¦veo¦lar
al¦veo¦li¦tis
al¦veo¦lus
△ al¦veoli
al¦ways

alys|sum
Alz|hei|mer
am
Ama|deus
Amal
Amal|ek|ite
amal|gam
amal|ga|mate
△ amal|ga|mates
△ amal|ga|ma|
　ted
△ amal|ga|ma|
　ting
amal|ga|ma|tion
Amal|thea
Amanda
ama|nu|en|sis
△ ama|nu|en|ses

ama|ranth
ama|ryl|lis
amass
△ amas|ses
△ amassed
△ amass|ing
ama|teur
ama|teur|ish
ama|teur|ishly
ama|teur|ism
amat|ory
amaze
△ ama|zes
△ amazed
△ ama|zing
amazed
ama|zedly
amaze|ment

ama|zing
ama|zingly
Ama|zon
Ama|zo|nian
am|bas|sa|dor
am|bas|sa|dor|ial
am|bas|sa|dor|
　ship
Am|bas|sa|dors,
　The
am|bas|sa|dress
△ am|bas|sa|
　dres|ses
amber
am|ber|gris
am|bi|dex|trous
am|bi|dex|
　trously

am|bi|ence
am|bi|ent
am|bi|gu|ity
△ am|bi|gu|it|ies
am|bi|gu|ous
am|bi|gu|ously
ambit
am|bi|tion
am|bi|tious
am|bi|tiously
am|bi|tious|ness
am|bi|va|lence
am|bi|va|lent
am|bi|va|lently
am|ble
VERB
△ am|bles
△ am|bled

American spellings

American spelling practice differs in some ways from British, although British usage is increasingly influenced by American. The main features of American spelling are:

- -ae- and -oe- are often reduced to -e-:

  diarrhea, encyclopedia, esthetic, estrogen, eon, gynecologist.

- -ense is often used in nouns instead of -ence:

  defense, license (noun and verb), **offense, pretense.**

- -er is often used to end nouns instead of -re:

  center, fiber, theater. But note **acre, lucre, massacre, ogre** as in British English.

- -or is often used to end nouns instead of -our:

  color, harbor, honor.

- z is sometimes used instead of soft s, especially in the ending -yze:

  analyze, catalyze, cozy, dialyze, electrolyze, hydrolyze.

- A final -l preceded by a single vowel often remains single in inflection, whereas it is doubled in British English:

  counselor, rivaled, teetotaler, traveling.

- The endings -amme and -ogue are often reduced to -am and -og:

  analog, catalog, dialog, program.

- Other common American spellings which differ from British are:

  check (in Banking), **specialty.**

△ am|bling
Am|bler
Am|ble|side
am|bly|gon|ite
Am|brose
am|bro|sia
Am|bro|sian
am|bu|lance
am|bush
  NOUN
△ am|bu|shes
  VERB
△ am|bu|shes
△ am|bushed
△ am|bush|ing
Ame|lia
ameli|or|ate
△ ameli|or|ates
△ ameli|or|ated
△ ameli|or|ating
ameli|or|ation
Amen see
  Amun
amen
amen|able

amend
correct; improve
△ amends
△ amen|ded
△ amend|ing
⚠emend

amend|ment
amen|ity
△ amen|it|ies
amen|or|rhoea
Ameri|can
Ameri|can in
Paris, An
Ameri|can|ism
am|er|icium
Am|er|in|dian
ame|thyst
Am|haric

ami|ab|il|ity
ami|able
ami|ably
ami|ca|bil|ity
am|ic|able
am|ic|ably
amid
amide
amid|ships
Ami|ens
Amin
amine
amino
amir *see* emir
Amis
Amish
amiss
amity
Amman
am|meter
ammo
Ammon *see*
  Amun
am|mo|nia
am|mo|niac
am|mon|ite
Am|mon|ites
am|mo|nium
am|mu|ni|tion
am|ne|sia
am|ne|siac
am|ne|sic
am|nesty
△ am|nes|ties
am|nio|cen|te|sis
△ am|nio|cen|te|
  ses
am|nion
△ amnia
am|ni|otic
amoeba
△ amoe|bae *or*
  amoe|bas
amoe|bic

amok
Amon *see* Amun
among
amongst
amoral
amor|al|ity
Amor|ite
amor|ous
amor|ously
amor|phous
amor|ti|za|tion
amor|tize
△ amor|ti|zes
△ amor|tized
△ amor|ti|zing
Amos, Book of
amount
  VERB
△ amounts
△ amoun|ted
△ amount|ing
amour
amour-propre
amp
am|per|age
am|pere
am|per|sand
am|phet|am|ine
Am|phi|bia
am|phib|ian
am|phi|bi|ous
am|phi|bole
am|phi|pod
am|phi|theatre
am|phora
△ am|phoras *or*
  am|phorae
am|pho|teric
am|ple
△ amp|ler
△ amp|lest
am|pli|fi|ca|tion
am|pli|fier
am|plify

△ am|pli|fies
△ am|pli|fied
△ am|pli|fy|ing
am|pli|tude
amply
am|poule
am|pulla
△ am|pul|lae
am|pu|tate
△ am|pu|tates
△ am|pu|ta|ted
△ am|pu|ta|ting
am|pu|ta|tion
am|pu|tee
Am|rit|sar
Am|ster|dam
amuck *see* amok
amu|let
Amun
Amund|sen
amuse
△ amu|ses
△ amused
△ amu|sing
amused
amu|sedly
amuse|ment
amu|sing
amu|singly
Amy
amy|lase
an
Ana|bap|tism
Ana|bap|tist
ana|ba|tic
ana|bo|lic
ana|bol|ism
ana|chron|ism
ana|chron|is|tic
ana|chron|is|tic|
  ally
ana|conda
an|ae|mia
an|ae|mic

an|ae|mic|ally
an|aer|obe
an|aer|obic
an|aes|the|sia
an|aes|thetic
an|aes|thet|ist
an|aes|thet|ize
△ an|aes|thet|
  izes
△ an|aes|thet|
  ized
△ an|aes|thet|
  izing
ana|glyph
ana|glypta
ana|gram
anal
anal|gesia
an|al|gesic
ana|lo|gi|cal
ana|lo|gic|ally
anal|og|ous
anal|og|ously

ana|logue
anal|ogy
△ anal|ogies
ana|lys|able
ana|lyse
△ ana|ly|ses
△ ana|lysed
△ ana|ly|sing
ana|ly|sis
△ ana|ly|ses
ana|lyst
ana|lytic
ana|lyt|ical
ana|lyt|ic|ally
ana|mor|pho|sis
△ ana|mor|pho|
  ses
ana|paest
ana|paes|tic
ana|phase
ana|phy|laxis
△ ana|phy|laxes
ana|phy|laxy

△ ana|phy|lax|ies
an|ar|chic
an|arch|ic|ally
an|arch|ism
an|arch|ist
an|arch|is|tic
an|arch|is|tic|ally
an|archy
Ana|sta|sia
an|ath|ema
ana|the|ma|tize
△ ana|the|ma|ti|
  zes
△ ana|the|ma|
  tized
△ ana|the|ma|ti|
  zing
Ana|to|lia
Ana|to|lian
ana|tom|ical
ana|tom|ic|ally
anat|om|ist
anat|omy

△ anat|om|ies
Anat|omy of
Mel|an|choly,
The
an|ces|tor
an|ces|tral
an|ces|try
△ an|ces|tries
an|chor
VERB
△ an|chors
△ an|chored
△ an|chor|ing
an|chor|age
an|chor|ite
an|chor|man
△ an|chor|men
an|chor|wo|man
△ an|chor|wo|
  men
an|chovy
△ an|cho|vies
an|cien ré|gime

-ance / -ence

These suffixes form nouns, often corresponding to adjectives in **-ant** and **-ent**.

The most common nouns in **-ance** denoting a state or quality are:

abundance	avoidance	fragrance	observance	substance
acceptance	brilliance	grievance	performance	surveillance
acquaintance	clearance	guidance	perseverance	sustenance
admittance	defiance	hindrance	relevance	temperance
alliance	disappearance	ignorance	reliance	tolerance
allowance	disturbance	importance	reluctance	vengeance
appearance	dominance	insignificance	remittance	vigilance
arrogance	elegance	insurance	resemblance	
assistance	endurance	irrelevance	resistance	
assurance	extravagance	maintenance	semblance	
attendance	exuberance	nuisance	significance	

The most common nouns in **-ence** denoting a state or quality are:

abhorrence	coincidence	existence	permanence	reminiscence
abstinence	competence	imminence	persistence	repellence
acquiescence	convalescence	independence	precedence	subsistence
adherence	correspondence	interference	preference	
adolescence	deterrence	negligence	prevalence	
affluence	difference	obedience	recurrence	
coherence	disobedience	occurrence	reference	

an|cient
an|cil|lary
  NOUN
  △ an|cil|lar|ies
and
An|da|lu|sia
an|da|lu|site
an|dante
An|der|sen
Andes
an|des|ite
And|hra Prad|
  esh
and|iron
An|dorra
An|drea
An|drew
An|drews
and|roe|cium
and|ro|gen
and|ro|gy|nous
and|roid
An|dro|mache
An|dro|maque
An|dro|pov
an|ec|do|tal
an|ec|dote
an|ech|oic
anemia *see*
  anaemia
ane|mom|eter
anem|one
an|er|oid
anesthesia *see*
  anaesthesia
anesthetic *see*
  anaesthetic
An|eurin
an|eurysm
anew
angel
An|gela
an|gel|fish
  sing. and pl.

an|gelic
an|gel|ica
an|gel|ic|ally
an|gelus
An|gelus, The
anger
  VERB
  △ an|gers
  △ an|gered
  △ an|ger|ing
An|ge|vin
an|gina
an|gio|sperm
An|le
an|gle
  VERB
  △ an|gles
  △ an|gled
  △ ang|ling
ang|ler
ang|ler|fish
  sing. and pl.
Angle|sey
An|glia
An|gli|can
An|gli|can|ism
an|gli|cism
an|gli|ci|za|tion
an|gli|cize
  △ an|gli|ci|zes
  △ an|gli|cized
  △ an|gli|ci|zing
ang|ling
An|glo-Cath|olic
An|glo-Cath|oli|
  cism
An|glo-Ind|ian
An|glo-Nor|man
an|glo|phile
an|glo|phobe
an|glo|phone
An|glo-Saxon
An|gola
an|gora

an|gos|tura
an|grily
angry
  △ an|grier
  △ an|gri|est
angst
ang|strom
An|guilla
an|guish
an|guished
an|gu|lar
an|gu|lar|ity
Angus
an|hy|dride
an|hy|drous
an|il|ine
an|im|ad|ver|
  sion
ani|mal
ani|mal|cule
Ani|mal Farm
ani|mal|ism
ani|mal|ity
ani|mal|ize
  △ ani|mal|izes
  △ ani|mal|ized
  △ ani|mal|izing
ani|mate
  VERB
  △ ani|mates
  △ ani|ma|ted
  △ ani|ma|ting
ani|ma|ted
ani|ma|tedly
ani|ma|tion
ani|ma|tor
ani|mat|ron|ics
an|im|ism
an|im|ist
an|im|is|tic
ani|mos|ity
  △ ani|mos|it|ies
ani|mus
anion

anise
ani|seed
Anjou
An|kara
ankh
an|kle
ank|let
an|ky|lo|saur
an|ky|lo|sis
  △ an|ky|lo|ses
Ann
An|na|bel
Anna Ka|ren|ina
an|nal|ist
an|nals
*Anna of the
  Five Towns*
Anne
an|neal
  △ an|neals
  △ an|nealed
  △ an|neal|ing
an|neal|ing
an|nelid
An|nel|ida

annex
  VERB
  △ an|nexes
  △ an|nexed
  △ an|nex|ing
  ⚠annexe

an|nex|ation

an|nexe
  NOUN
  ⚠annex

An|ni|goni
an|ni|hil|ate
  △ an|ni|hil|ates
  △ an|ni|hil|ated
  △ an|ni|hil|ating
an|ni|hil|ation
an|ni|ver|sary

△ an|ni|ver|sar|
ies
Anno Dom|ini
an|no|tate
△ an|no|tates
△ an|no|ta|ted
△ an|no|ta|ting
an|no|ta|tion
an|no|ta|tor
an|nounce
△ an|noun|ces
△ an|nounced
△ an|noun|cing
an|nounce|ment
an|noun|cer
annoy
△ an|noys
△ an|noyed
△ an|noy|ing
an|noy|ance
an|noyed
an|noy|ing
an|noy|ingly
an|nual
an|nu|al|ize
△ an|nu|al|izes
△ an|nu|al|ized
△ an|nu|al|izing
an|nu|ally
an|nu|ity
△ an|nu|it|ies
annul
△ an|nuls
△ an|nulled
△ an|nul|ling
an|nu|lar
an|nu|late
an|nul|ment
an|nu|lus
△ an|nuli
An|nun|ci|ation
annus mi|ra|bi|lis
anode
ano|dize

△ ano|di|zes
△ ano|dized
△ ano|di|zing
ano|dyne
anoint
△ anoints
△ anoin|ted
△ anoint|ing
anoint|ment
an|om|al|ous
an|om|al|ously
an|om|aly
△ an|om|al|ies
ano|mia
ano|mie
anon
ano|nym|ity
an|ony|mous
an|ony|mously
an|orak
an|or|exia
an|or|exic
an|other
Anou|ilh
An|schluss
An|selm
an|ser|ine
an|swer
VERB
△ an|swers
△ an|swered
△ an|swer|ing
an|swer|abil|ity
an|swer|able
ant
ant|acid
ant|ag|on|ism
ant|ag|on|ist
ant|ag|on|is|tic
ant|ag|on|is|tic|
ally
ant|ag|on|ize
△ ant|ag|on|izes
△ ant|ag|on|ized

△ ant|ag|on|izing
An|ta|nan|arivo
Ant|arc|tic
Ant|arc|tica
ant|bird
ante
VERB
△ antes
△ anted
△ an|te|ing
ant|eater
an|te|ce|dence
an|te|ce|dent
an|te|cham|ber
an|te|date
△ an|te|dates
△ an|te|da|ted
△ an|te|da|ting
an|te|di|lu|vian
an|te|lope
△ an|te|lope *or*
an|te|lopes
ante me|rid|iem
an|te|na|tal
an|tenna
insect's feeler
△ an|ten|nae
aerial
△ an|ten|nas
an|te|pen|ul|ti|
mate
an|ter|ior
an|te|room
An|thea
an|them
an|ther
an|the|sis
an|tho|cy|anin
an|thol|ogist
an|thol|ogy
△ an|thol|ogies
An|thony
an|thra|cite
an|thrax

an|thro|po|cen|
tric
an|thro|po|cen|
tric|ally
an|thro|poid
an|thro|poi|dal
an|thro|po|lo|gi|
cal
an|thro|po|lo|gic|
ally
an|thro|pol|ogist
an|thro|pol|ogy
an|thro|po|mor|
phic
an|thro|po|
morph|ism
an|thro|po|
morph|ous
anti
anti-air|craft
An|tibes
an|ti|bi|otic
an|ti|body
△ an|ti|bod|ies
An|ti|christ
an|ti|ci|pate
△ an|ti|ci|pates
△ an|ti|ci|pa|ted
△ an|ti|ci|pa|ting
an|ti|ci|pa|tion
an|ti|ci|pa|tory
an|ti|cler|ical
an|ti|cler|ic|al|ism
an|ti|cli|mac|tic
an|ti|cli|max
△ an|ti|cli|maxes
an|ti|cline
an|ti|clock|wise
an|ti|co|agu|llant
an|ti|con|vul|sant
antic
an|ti|cy|clone
an|ti|de|pres|
sant

an|ti|dote
an|ti|freeze
an|ti|gen
An|ti|gone
An|ti|gua and
Bar|buda
an|ti|hero
△ an|ti|her|oes
an|ti|his|ta|mine
anti-inflam|ma|
tory
an|ti|knock
An|til|les
anti-lock
an|ti|log|ar|ithm
an|ti|ma|cas|sar
an|ti|mat|ter
an|ti|mony
an|ti|node
an|ti|no|mian
an|ti|nomy
△ an|ti|no|mies
an|ti|novel
an|ti|nu|clear
An|ti|och
an|ti|oxid|ant
an|ti|par|ticle
an|ti|pasto
△ an|ti|pasti or
an|ti|pas|tos
an|ti|pa|thetic
an|ti|pa|thet|ic|
ally
an|ti|pa|thy
△ an|ti|pa|thies
anti-per|son|nel
an|ti|per|spir|ant
an|ti|phon
an|ti|po|dean
an|ti|po|des
an|ti|pope
an|ti|py|retic
an|ti|quar|ian
an|ti|quary

△ an|ti|quar|ies
an|ti|qua|ted
an|tique
an|ti|quity
△ an|ti|qui|ties
an|ti|ra|cism
an|ti|ra|cist
an|tir|rhi|num
an|ti|scor|bu|tic
anti-sem|ite
anti-sem|itic
anti-sem|it|ism
an|ti|sep|tic
an|ti|serum
an|ti|sera
an|ti|so|cial
an|ti|so|ci|ally
an|ti|sta|tic
an|ti|tank
an|ti|thesis
△ an|ti|theses
an|ti|thetic
an|ti|thet|ical
an|ti|thet|ic|ally
an|ti|toxin
an|ti|trades
anti-trust
an|ti|vi|ral
anti-vivi|sec|tion
anti-vivi|sec|
tion|ist
ant|ler
An|to|nia
An|to|ni|oni
An|tony
*An|tony and
Cleo|patra*
an|to|nym
ant|ony|mous
ant|onymy
An|trim
ant|rum
△ antra
Ant|werp

Anubis
anus
△ anuses
anvil
anxi|ety
△ anxi|et|ies
anxi|ous
anxi|ously
anxi|ous|ness
any
any|body
any|how
any|one
any|place
any|thing
any|way
any|where
Anzac
aor|ist
aorta
Aou|ita
apace
Apa|che
apart
apart|heid
apart|ment
apa|thetic
apa|thet|ic|ally
apathy
apat|ite
apa|to|sau|rus
ape
VERB
△ apes
△ aped
△ aping
ape|man
△ ape|men
Apen|nines
aperi|ent
aperi|tif
aper|ture
apex
△ apexes *or* api|

ces
apha|sia
aph|el|ion
△ aph|elia
aphid
aphis *see* aphid
apho|nia
aph|or|ism
aph|or|is|tic
aph|ro|di|siac
Aph|ro|dite
api|ar|ist
api|ary
△ api|ar|ies
api|cal
api|cul|ture
apiece
apish
aplomb
ap|noea
apo|ca|lypse
*Apo|ca|lypse
Now*
apo|ca|lyp|tic
Apo|cry|pha
apo|cry|phal
apo|gee
apo|li|ti|cal
apo|li|ti|cally
Apol|li|naire
Apollo
Apol|lo|nius
Rhod|ius
Apol|lyon
apo|lo|getic
apo|lo|get|ic|ally
apo|lo|gia
apo|lo|gist
apo|lo|gize
△ apo|lo|gi|zes
△ apo|lo|gized
△ apo|lo|gi|zing
apo|logy
△ apo|lo|gies

apoph|thegm
apo|plec|tic
apo|plec|tic|ally
apo|plexy
apos|tasy
△ apos|ta|sies
apos|tate
a pos|teri|ori
apos|tle
apos|tolic
apos|tol|ic|ally
apos|tro|phe
apos|tro|phize
△ apos|tro|phi|
zes
△ apo|stro|
phized
△ apo|stro|phi|
zing
apo|the|cary
△ apo|the|car|ies
apo|the|osis
△ apo|the|oses
appal
△ ap|pals
△ ap|palled
△ ap|pal|ling
Ap|pa|la|chian
ap|pal|ling
ap|pal|lingly
ap|pa|rat|chik
ap|par|atus
△ ap|par|atuses
or ap|par|atus
ap|parel
ap|par|ent
ap|par|ently
ap|pari|tion
'Ap|pas|sion|ata'
Sonata
ap|peal
VERB
△ ap|peals
△ ap|pealed

△ ap|peal|ing
ap|peal|ing
ap|peal|ingly
ap|pear
△ ap|pears
△ ap|peared
△ ap|pear|ing
ap|pear|ance
ap|pease
△ ap|pea|ses
△ ap|peased
△ ap|peas|ing
ap|pease|ment
ap|pel|lant
ap|pel|late
ap|pel|la|tion
*ap|pel|la|tion
d'ori|gine con|
trô|lée*
ap|pend
△ ap|pends
△ ap|pen|ded
△ ap|pend|ing
ap|pend|age
ap|pend|ec|tomy
△ ap|pend|ec|
tom|ies
ap|pen|dic|ec|
tomy
△ ap|pen|dic|ec|
tom|ies
ap|pen|di|ci|tis
ap|pen|dix
△ ap|pen|dixes
or ap|pen|di|
ces
ap|per|tain
△ ap|per|tains
△ ap|per|tained
△ ap|per|tain|ing
ap|pet|ite
ap|pet|izer
ap|pet|izing
ap|pet|iz|ingly

Ap|pian
ap|plaud
△ ap|plauds
△ ap|plau|ded
△ ap|plaud|ing
ap|plause
ap|ple
ap|pli|ance
ap|plic|able
ap|plic|ant
ap|pli|ca|tion
ap|pli|ca|tor
ap|plied
ap|pli|qué
apply
△ ap|plies
△ ap|plied
△ ap|ply|ing
ap|point
△ ap|points
△ ap|poin|ted
△ ap|point|ing
ap|poin|tee
ap|point|ment
ap|por|tion
△ ap|por|tions
△ ap|por|tioned
△ ap|por|tion|ing
ap|pos|ite
ap|pos|itely
ap|pos|ite|ness
ap|po|si|tion
ap|prai|sal
ap|praise
△ ap|prai|ses
△ ap|praised
△ ap|prais|ing
ap|prai|ser
ap|pre|ci|able
ap|pre|ci|ably
ap|pre|ci|ate
△ ap|pre|ci|ates
△ ap|pre|ci|ated
△ ap|pre|ci|ating

ap|pre|ci|ation
ap|pre|cia|tive
ap|pre|cia|tively
ap|pre|hend
△ ap|pre|hends
△ ap|pre|hen|
ded
△ ap|pre|hend|
ing
ap|pre|hen|sion
ap|pre|hen|sive
ap|pre|hen|
sively
ap|pren|tice
VERB
△ ap|pren|ti|ces
△ ap|pren|ticed
△ ap|pren|ti|cing
ap|pren|tice|ship
ap|prise
△ ap|pri|ses
△ ap|prised
△ ap|pri|sing
appro
ap|proach
NOUN
△ ap|proa|ches
VERB
△ ap|proa|ches
△ ap|proached
△ ap|proach|ing
ap|proach|able
ap|pro|ba|tion
ap|pro|pri|ate
VERB
△ ap|pro|pri|ates
△ ap|pro|pri|
ated
△ ap|pro|pri|
ating
ap|pro|pri|ately
ap|pro|pri|ate|
ness
ap|pro|pri|ation

ap|pro|val
ap|prove
△ ap|proves
△ ap|proved
△ ap|pro|ving
ap|pro|ving
ap|pro|vingly
ap|proxi|mate
VERB
△ ap|proxi|
mates
△ ap|proxi|ma|
ted
△ ap|proxi|ma|
ting
ap|proxi|mately
ap|proxi|ma|tion
ap|pur|ten|ance
apraxia
après-ski
apri|cot
April
a pri|ori
apron
apro|pos
apse
apsis
△ ap|si|des
apt
△ apter
△ apt|est
ap|teryx
△ ap|teryxes
ap|ti|tude
aptly
apt|ness
Apu|leius
Aqaba
aqua|cul|ture
aqua|fit
aqua for|tis
aqua|lung
aqua|ma|rine
aqua|plane

VERB
△ aqua|planes
△ aqua|planed
△ aqua|pla|ning
aqua regia
Aquar|ian
aquar|ium
△ aquar|iums or
aquaria
Aquar|ius
aqua|tic
aqua|tint
aqua|tube
aqua vitae
aque|duct
aque|ous
aquiculture see
aquaculture
aqui|fer
aqui|le|gia
aqui|line
Aqui|nas
Aqui|taine
Arab
Ara|bella
arab|esque
Ara|bia
Ara|bian
Ara|bian Nights
Ara|bic
Arab|ist
ar|able
arach|nid
arach|noid
Ara|fat
Ara|gon
ara|gon|ite
arak see arrack
Ara|maic

Aran
group of islands
off Ireland
⚠Arran

Ara|rat
ar|bi|ter
ar|bi|trar|ily
ar|bi|trari|ness
ar|bi|trary
ar|bi|trate
△ ar|bi|trates
△ ar|bi|tra|ted
△ ar|bi|tra|ting
ar|bi|tra|tion
ar|bi|tra|tor
arbor
ar|bor|eal
ar|bor|etum
△ ar|bor|eta
ar|bori|cul|ture
ar|bour
Ar|buth|not
arc
VERB
△ arcs
△ arced
△ arc|ing
ar|cade
Ar|ca|dia
Ar|ca|dian
ar|cane
Arc de Tri|
omphe
arch
NOUN
△ ar|ches
VERB
△ ar|ches
△ arched
△ arch|ing
ADJ.
△ ar|cher
△ arch|est
Ar|chaean
Ar|chae|bac|teria
ar|chaeo|lo|gi|cal
ar|chae|olo|gist
ar|chae|ol|ogy

ar|chae|op|teryx
△ ar|chae|op|
teryxes
ar|chaic
ar|cha|ic|ally
ar|cha|ism
Arch|an|gel
arch|an|gel
arch|bi|shop
arch|bish|op|ric
arch|dea|con
arch|dea|conry
△ arch|dea|con|
ries
arch|dio|cese
arch|duch|ess
△ arch|duch|es|
ses
arch|duchy
△ arch|duch|ies
arch|duke
Archean see
Archaean
arched
arch|en|emy
△ arch|en|em|ies
archeology see
archaeology
ar|cher
arch|ery
ar|che|ty|pal
ar|che|typ|ally
ar|che|type
arch|fiend
Ar|chi|bald
ar|chi|di|ac|onal
ar|chi|epis|co|pal
ar|chi|man|drite
Ar|chi|me|des
ar|chi|pel|ago
ar|chi|tect
ar|chi|tec|tural
ar|chi|tec|tur|
ally

ar|chi|tec|ture
ar|chi|trave
ar|chive
ar|chi|vist
archly
arch|way
Arc|tic
Arc|turus
Arden
Ar|dennes
ar|dent
ar|dently
ar|dour
ar|du|ous
ar|du|ously
ar|du|ous|ness
are
area
arena
aren't
ar|eola
  △ areo|lae
Areo|pa|gus
Ares
Ar|gen|tina
ar|gin|ine
Ar|go|lid
argon
Ar|go|nauts
Argos
argot
ar|gu|able
ar|gu|ably
argue
  △ ar|gues
  △ ar|gued
  △ ar|gu|ing
ar|gu|ment
ar|gu|men|ta|
  tion
ar|gu|men|ta|tive
ar|gu|men|ta|
  tively
Argus

Århus
aria
Ari|adne
Ari|adne auf
  Naxos (Ari|
  adne on
  Naxos)
Arian
Ari|an|ism
arid
arid|ity
Ariel
Aries
aright
Ari|osto
arise
  △ ari|ses
  △ arose
  △ ari|sing
  △ arisen
aris|to|cracy
  △ aris|to|cra|cies
aris|to|crat
aris|to|cra|tic
aris|to|crat|ic|
  ally
Aris|to|pha|nes
Aris|to|tel|ian
Aris|totle
arith|metic
arith|met|ic|ally
arith|me|ti|cian
Arius
Ari|zona
ark
Arkan|sas
Arles
Ar|lott
arm
  VERB
  △ arms
  △ armed
  △ arm|ing
ar|mada

ar|ma|dillo
Ar|ma|ged|don
Ar|magh
ar|ma|ment
ar|ma|ture
arm|band
arm|chair
armed
Ar|me|nia
Ar|me|nian
arm|ful
arm|hole
ar|mis|tice
arm|let
ar|mor|ial
ar|mour
ar|moured
ar|mourer
ar|mour-plate
ar|mour-pla|ted
ar|moury
  △ ar|mour|ies
arm|pit
Arm|strong
army
  △ ar|mies
Arne
Arn|hem
Arno
Ar|nold
A-road
aroma
aro|ma|ther|ap|
  ist
aro|ma|ther|apy
aro|ma|tic
aro|mat|ic|ally
arose
around
Around the
  World in
  Eighty Days
arou|sal
arouse

  △ arou|ses
  △ aroused
  △ arous|ing
ar|peg|gio
ar|que|bus
  △ ar|que|buses
ar|rack
ar|raign
  △ ar|raigns
  △ ar|raigned
  △ ar|raign|ing
ar|raign|ment

> Arran
> *island off*
> *Scotland*
>   ⚠ Aran

ar|range
  △ ar|ran|ges
  △ ar|ranged
  △ ar|ran|ging
ar|range|ment
ar|rant
Arras
arras
  △ ar|rases
array
  VERB
  △ ar|rays
  △ ar|rayed
  △ ar|ray|ing
ar|rears
ar|rest
  VERB
  △ ar|rests
  △ ar|res|ted
  △ ar|rest|ing
ar|rest|ing
arris
  △ ar|rises
ar|ri|val
ar|rive
  △ ar|rives
  △ ar|rived

△ ar|ri|ving
ar|ro|gance
ar|ro|gant
ar|ro|gantly
ar|ro|gate
△ ar|ro|gates
△ ar|ro|ga|ted
△ ar|ro|ga|ting
ar|ro|ga|tion
arrow
ar|row|head
ar|row|root
Ars Ama|toria
arse
arse|hole
ar|senal
ar|senic
arson
ar|son|ist
art
Art Deco
ar|te|fact
Ar|te|mis
ar|te|mi|sia
ar|ter|ial
ar|teri|ole
ar|terio|scler|osis
ar|tery
△ ar|ter|ies
ar|tes|ian
art|ful
art|fully
art|ful|ness
arth|ri|tic
arth|ri|tis
arth|ro|pod
Arth|ro|poda
Ar|thur
ar|ti|choke
art|icle
art|icled
ar|ti|cu|lar
ar|ti|cu|late
  VERB

△ ar|ti|cu|lates
△ ar|ti|cu|la|ted
△ ar|ti|cu|la|ting
ar|ti|cu|la|ted
ar|ti|cu|lately
ar|ti|cu|la|tion
ar|ti|fact
ar|ti|fice
ar|ti|ficer
ar|ti|fi|cial
ar|ti|fi|ci|al|ity
ar|ti|fi|ci|ally
ar|til|lery
△ ar|til|ler|ies
art|iness
ar|ti|san

art|ist
  painter; expert
  in some other
  art etc
  ▲artiste

artiste
  performer in
  circus, theatre,
  etc
  ▲artist

ar|tis|tic
ar|tis|tic|ally
ar|tis|try
art|less
art|lessly
art|less|ness
Art Nou|veau
Art of Fugue,
  The (Die Kunst
  der Fuge)
art|work
arty
△ ar|tier
△ ar|ti|est
arum
Arun|del

Aryan
as
asa|foe|tida
as|bes|tos
as|bes|to|sis
as|cend
△ as|cends
△ as|cen|ded
△ as|cend|ing
as|cend|ancy
as|cend|ant
as|cend|ing
as|cen|sion

as|cent
  act of rising;
  upward slope
  ▲assent

as|cer|tain
△ as|cer|tains
△ as|cer|tained
△ as|cer|tain|ing
as|cer|tain|able

as|cetic
  avoiding
  pleasure and
  comfort; one
  who does this
  ▲aesthetic

as|cet|ic|ally
as|ce|ti|cism
As|cle|pius
As|co|my|ce|tes
Ascot
as|crib|able
as|cribe
△ as|cribes
△ as|cribed
△ as|cri|bing
ascus
△ asci
asdic
asep|tic

asex|ual
asexu|al|ity
asexu|ally
ash
△ ashes
ashamed
asha|medly
ash|can
Ash|croft
Ash|down
ashen
Ashes
Ash|kha|bad
Ash|ken|azy
ash|lar
Ash|ley
Ash|mo|lean
ashore
ash|ram
Ash|ton
ash|tray
ashy
△ ash|ier
△ ash|iest
Asia
Asian
Asi|atic
A-side
aside
Asi|mov
as|in|ine
ask
△ asks
△ asked
△ ask|ing
as|kance
askew
as|leep
aso|cial
asp
as|pa|ra|gine
as|pa|ra|gus
as|par|tame
as|par|tic

as|pect
aspen
as|per|gil|losis
as|per|ity
  △ as|per|it|ies
as|per|sion
as|phalt
  VERB
  △ as|phalts
  △ as|phal|ted
  △ as|phalt|ing
as|phyxia
as|phyxi|ate
  △ as|phyxi|ates
  △ as|phyxi|ated
  △ as|phyxi|ating
as|phyxi|ation
aspic
as|pi|dis|tra
as|pir|ant
as|pir|ate
  VERB
  △ as|pir|ates
  △ as|pir|ated
  △ as|pir|ating
as|pir|ation
as|pir|ator
as|pire
  △ as|pires
  △ as|pired
  △ as|pir|ing
as|pi|rin
as|pir|ing
As|quith
ass
  △ asses
Assad
assagai *see*
  assegai
as|sail
  △ as|sails
  △ as|sailed
  △ as|sail|ing
as|sail|ant

Assam
As|sam|ese
as|sas|sin
as|sas|sin|ate
  △ as|sas|sin|ates
  △ as|sas|sin|ated
  △ as|sas|sin|ating
as|sas|sin|ation
as|sault
  VERB
  △ as|saults
  △ as|saul|ted
  △ as|sault|ing

---

assay
*test purity of
metal etc; such
test*
VERB
  △ as|says
  △ as|sayed
  △ as|say|ing
  ⚠ essay

---

as|se|gai
as|sem|blage
as|sem|ble
  △ as|sem|bles
  △ as|sem|bled
  △ as|sem|bling
as|sem|bler
as|sem|bly
  △ as|sem|blies

---

as|sent
*consent or agree
(to)*
VERB
  △ as|sents
  △ as|sen|ted
  △ as|sent|ing
  ⚠ ascent

---

as|sert
  △ as|serts
  △ as|ser|ted

  △ as|sert|ing
as|ser|tion
as|sert|ive
as|sert|ively
as|sert|ive|ness
as|sess
  △ as|ses|ses
  △ as|sessed
  △ as|ses|sing
as|sess|ment
as|ses|sor
asset
asset-strip|ping
as|sev|er|ate
  △ as|sev|er|ates
  △ as|sev|er|ated
  △ as|sev|er|ating
as|si|du|ity
  △ as|si|du|it|ies
as|si|du|ous
as|si|du|ously
as|si|du|ous|ness
as|sign
  △ as|signs
  △ as|signed
  △ as|sign|ing
as|sig|na|tion
as|signee
as|sign|ment
as|signor
as|sim|il|able
as|sim|il|ate
  VERB
  △ as|sim|il|ates
  △ as|sim|il|ated
  △ as|sim|il|ating
as|sim|il|ation
as|sist
  △ as|sists
  △ as|sis|ted
  △ as|sist|ing
as|sist|ance
as|sist|ant
as|size

as|so|ci|ate
  VERB
  △ as|so|ci|ates
  △ as|so|ci|ated
  △ as|so|ci|ating
as|so|ci|ated
as|so|ci|ation
as|so|ci|ative
as|son|ance
as|sor|ted
as|sort|ment
as|suage
  △ as|sua|ges
  △ as|suaged
  △ as|sua|ging
as|sume
  △ as|sumes
  △ as|sumed
  △ as|su|ming
as|sumed
as|su|ming
as|sump|tion
as|sur|ance
as|sure
  △ as|sures
  △ as|sured
  △ as|sur|ing
as|sured
as|sur|edly
As|syria
As|syr|ian
As|taire
as|ta|tine
aster
as|ter|isk
  VERB
  △ as|ter|isks
  △ as|ter|isked
  △ as|ter|isk|ing
astern
as|ter|oid
as|theno|sphere
asthma
asth|ma|tic

asth|mat|ic|ally
astig|ma|tic
astig|mat|ism
astir
as|ton|ish
△ as|ton|ishes
△ as|ton|ished
△ as|ton|ish|ing
as|ton|ished
as|ton|ish|ing
as|ton|ish|ingly
as|ton|ish|ment
Astor
as|tound
△ as|tounds
△ as|toun|ded
△ as|tound|ing
as|toun|ded
as|tound|ing
as|tound|ingly
as|tra|khan
ast|ral
astray
Ast|rid
astride
astrin|gency
astrin|gent
astrin|gently
as|tro|dome
as|tro|labe
as|trol|oger
as|trol|lo|gi|cal
as|trol|lo|gic|ally
as|trol|ogy
as|trom|etry
as|tro|naut
as|tro|naut|ics
as|tron|omer
as|tro|nomic
as|tro|nom|ical
as|tro|nom|ic|ally
as|tron|omy
as|tro|phys|ical

as|tro|phy|si|cist
as|tro|phys|ics
as|tute
as|tutely
as|tute|ness
Asun|ción
asun|der
Aswan
asy|lum
asym|met|ric
asym|met|ri|cal
asym|met|ric|ally
asym|metry
asymp|tote
As You Like It
at
Ata|lante, L'
Ata|tu|rk
atav|ism
atav|is|tic
ataxia
ate
atel|ier
Atha|na|sian
Atha|na|sius
athe|ism
athe|ist
athe|is|tic
athe|is|ti|cal
athe|is|tic|ally
Ath|ena
Ath|ens
athero|scler|osis
athero|scler|otic
ath|lete
ath|letic
ath|let|ics
Athos
athwart
At|lan|tic
At|lan|tis
Atlas
  giant; star

atlas
  map book
  △ at|lases
atman
at|mo|sphere
at|mo|spheric
at|mo|spher|ic|
  ally
at|mo|spher|ics
atoll
atom
atomic
atom|ic|ally
ato|mi|city
atom|ism
atom|ize
  △ atom|izes
  △ atom|ized
  △ atom|izing
atom|izer
ato|nal
ato|nal|ity
atone
  △ atones
  △ atoned
  △ ato|ning
atone|ment
Atreus
atrial
atrium
  △ atria *or* atri|
    ums
at|ro|cious
at|ro|cious|ness
at|ro|city
  △ at|ro|ci|ties
atro|phy
  VERB
  △ atro|phies
  △ atro|phied
  △ atro|phy|ing
atro|pine
at|tach
  △ at|ta|ches

△ at|tached
△ at|tach|ing
at|ta|ché
at|taché-case
at|tached
at|tach|ment
at|tack
  VERB
  △ at|tacks
  △ at|tacked
  △ at|tack|ing
at|tacker
at|tain
  △ at|tains
  △ at|tained
  △ at|tain|ing
at|tain|able
at|tain|ment
attar
at|tempt
  VERB
  △ at|tempts
  △ at|temp|ted
  △ at|tempt|ing
At|ten|bor|ough
at|tend
  △ at|tends
  △ at|ten|ded
  △ at|tend|ing
at|tend|ance
at|tend|ant
at|ten|tion
at|tent|ive
at|tent|ively
at|tent|ive|ness
at|tenu|ate
  △ at|tenu|ates
  △ at|tenu|ated
  △ at|tenu|ating
at|tenu|ated
at|tenu|ation
at|test
  △ at|tests
  △ at|tes|ted

△ at|test|ing
at|tes|ta|tion
at|tes|ted
At|tic
at|tic
At|tica
At|tila
at|tire
at|tired
at|ti|tude
at|ti|tu|din|ize
　△ at|ti|tu|din|
　　izes
　△ at|ti|tu|din|
　　ized
　△ at|ti|tu|din|
　　izing
Att|lee
at|tor|ney
at|tract
　△ at|tracts
　△ at|trac|ted
　△ at|tract|ing
at|trac|tion
at|tract|ive
at|tract|ively
at|tract|ive|ness
at|trib|ut|able
at|trib|ute
　VERB
　△ at|trib|utes
　△ at|trib|uted
　△ at|trib|uting
at|tri|bu|tion
at|trib|utive
at|trib|utively
at|tri|tion
at|tune
　△ at|tunes
　△ at|tuned
　△ at|tu|ning
atyp|ical
au|ber|gine
au|brie|tia

au|burn
Auck|land
auc|tion
　VERB
　△ auc|tions
　△ auc|tioned
　△ auc|tion|ing
auc|tion|eer
au|da|cious
au|da|ciously
au|da|city
Auden
au|di|bil|ity
aud|ible
aud|ibly
au|di|ence
audio
au|dio|gram
au|dio|meter
au|dio-typ|ing
au|dio-typ|ist
au|dio|vis|ual
audit
　VERB
　△ au|dits
　△ au|di|ted
　△ au|dit|ing
au|di|tion
　VERB
　△ au|di|tions
　△ au|di|tioned
　△ au|di|tion|ing
au|di|tor
au|di|tor|ium
　△ au|di|tori|ums
　　or au|di|toria
au|dit|ory
Aud|rey
Au|du|bon
au fait
Au|gean
auger

┌─────────────┐
│ *anything* │
│ ⚠ ought   │
└─────────────┘
aught

┌─────────────┐
│ *anything* │
│ ⚠ ought   │
└─────────────┘
aug|ment
　△ aug|ments
　△ aug|men|ted
　△ aug|ment|ing
aug|men|ta|tion
aug|men|ta|tive
aug|men|ted
au gra|tin
augur
　△ au|gurs
　△ au|gured
　△ au|gur|ing
au|gury
　△ au|gur|ies
Au|gust
au|gust
Au|gus|tine
Au|gus|tin|ian
au|gustly
Au|gus|tus
auk
Auld Lang Syne
aunt
aun|tie
au pair
aura
　△ auras *or* aurae

┌─────────────┐
│ aural   │
│ *of hearing*│
│ ⚠ oral   │
└─────────────┘

aur|ally
au|re|ate
au|re|ole
au revoir
aur|icle
au|ric|ular
au|ri|fer|ous
Au|rig|na|cian
aur|ochs
　sing. and pl.

au|rora
　△ au|roras *or* au|
　　rorae
Ausch|witz
aus|cul|ta|tion
aus|pi|ces
aus|pi|cious
aus|pi|ciously
aus|pi|cious|ness
Aus|sie
Aus|ten
aus|tere
aus|terely
aus|ter|ity
　△ aus|ter|it|ies
Aus|ter|litz
Aus|tin
aus|tral
Aus|tra|la|sia
Aus|tra|la|sian
Aus|tra|lia
Aus|tra|lian
Aus|tra|lo|pi|the|
　cus
Aus|tria
Aus|tria-Hun|
　gary
Aus|tro-Asi|atic
Aus|tro|nes|ian
Aus|tro-Prus|
　sian

┌──────────────────┐
│ aut|ar|chy   │
│ *despotism*   │
│ △ aut|ar|chies   │
│ ⚠ autarky   │
└──────────────────┘

┌──────────────────┐
│ aut|arky   │
│ *economic self-* │
│ *sufficiency*   │
│ △ aut|ar|kies   │
│ ⚠ autarchy   │
└──────────────────┘

au|then|tic
au|then|tic|ally

au|then|ti|cate
△ au|then|ti|
cates
△ au|then|ti|
cated
△ au|then|ti|ca|
ting
au|then|ti|ca|tion
au|then|ti|city
au|thor
au|tho|ri|tar|ian
au|tho|ri|tari|an|
ism
au|thor|it|at|ive
au|thor|it|at|
ively
au|thor|ity
△ au|thor|it|ies
au|thor|iza|tion
au|thor|ize
△ au|thor|izes
△ au|thor|ized
△ au|thor|izing
Au|thor|ized
Ver|sion
au|thor|ship
aut|ism
aut|is|tic
aut|is|tic|ally
auto
au|to|bahn
au|to|bi|og|ra|
pher
au|to|bio|graph|
ical
au|to|bi|og|ra|
phy
au|to|bi|og|raph|
ies
au|to|ca|ta|ly|sis
△ au|to|ca|ta|
lyses
au|to|clave
au|to|cracy

△ au|to|cra|cies
au|to|crat
au|to|cra|tic
au|to|crat|ic|ally
au|to|cross
△ au|to|cros|ses
Au|to|cue
auto-da-fé
△ *autos-da-fé*
au|to|gen|ics
au|to|giro
au|to|graph
VERB
△ au|to|graphs
△ au|to|graphed
△ au|to|graph|
ing
au|to|im|mu|nity
au|to|ly|sis
au|to|mat
au|to|mate
△ au|to|mates
△ au|to|ma|ted
△ au|to|ma|ting
au|to|ma|ted
au|to|ma|tic
au|to|mat|ic|ally
au|to|ma|tion
au|to|ma|ton
△ au|to|mata
au|to|mo|bile
au|to|mo|tive
au|to|no|mic
au|ton|om|ous
au|ton|om|ously
au|ton|omy
△ au|ton|om|ies
auto-oxid|ation
au|to|pi|lot
aut|opsy
△ aut|op|sies
au|to|ra|di|og|ra|
phy
auto-reverse

au|to|route
au|to|some
au|to|strada
auto-sug|ges|
tion
auto-sug|ges|
tive
au|to|tro|phism
au|tumn
au|tum|nal
au|tum|nally
Au|vergne
Aux|erre
aux|ili|ary
NOUN
△ aux|ili|ar|ies
auxin
Ava
avail
VERB
△ avails
△ availed
△ avail|ing
avail|ab|il|ity
avail|able
avail|ably
aval|anche
Ava|lon
avant-garde
avar|ice
ava|ri|cious
ava|ri|ciously
ava|tar
Ave
Ave|bury
Ave Maria
avenge
△ aven|ges
△ avenged
△ aven|ging
aven|ger
aven|ging
av|enue
aver

△ avers
△ averred
△ aver|ring
av|er|age
VERB
△ av|er|ages
△ av|er|aged
△ av|era|ging

┌─────────────────┐
│ averse   │
│ *unwilling*   │
│ ⚠ adverse   │
└─────────────────┘

aver|sion
avert
△ averts
△ aver|ted
△ avert|ing
Aves
avi|ary
△ avi|ar|ies
avi|ation
avi|ator
avid
avid|ity
avidly
Avie|more
Avig|non
avi|on|ics
avo|cado
avo|ca|tion
avo|cet
avoid
△ avoids
△ avoi|ded
△ avoid|ing
avoid|able
avoid|ably
avoid|ance
avoir|du|pois
Avon
avow
△ avows
△ avowed
△ avow|ing

avowal
avowed
avow|edly
Avril
avun|cu|lar
await
△ awaits
△ awai|ted
△ await|ing
awake
VERB
△ awakes
△ awoke
△ awa|king
△ awo|ken
awa|ken
△ awa|kens
△ awa|kened
△ awa|ken|ing
awa|ken|ing
award

VERB
△ awards
△ awar|ded
△ award|ing
aware
aware|ness
awash
away
awe
VERB
△ awes
△ awed
△ awe|ing
aweigh
awe-inspir|ing
awe|some
awe|stricken
awe|struck
awful
aw|fully
aw|ful|ness
awhile

awk|ward
awk|wardly
awk|ward|ness
awl
awn
awn|ing
awoke
awo|ken
awry
axe
VERB
△ axes
△ axed
△ axing
axial
axi|al|ity
axil
axil|lary
axiom
axi|oma|tic
axi|omat|ic|ally
Axis

axis
△ axes
axle
axo|lotl
axo|no|met|ric
ayah
aya|tol|lah
Ayck|bourn
aye
aye-aye
Ayles|bury
Ayl|ward
Ayr
ay|ur|veda
aza|lea
Aza|riah, Prayer
of
Azer|bai|jan
azi|muth
Azores
Azov
Aztec
azure

B

baa
  VERB
△ baas
△ baaed
△ baaing
Baader–Mein|
  hof Group
Baal
Baal|bek
baba
bab|ble
△ bab|bles
△ bab|bled
△ bab|bling
bab|bler
bab|bling
babe
ba|bel
Ba|bel, Tower
  of
ba|boon
baby
  NOUN
△ ba|bies
  VERB
△ ba|bies
△ ba|bied
△ ba|by|ing
ba|by|hood
ba|by|ish
Ba|by|lon
baby-sit
  VERB
△ baby-sits
△ baby-sat
△ baby-sit|ting
baby-sit|ter
baby-sit|ting
baby-walker
Bac|all
bac|ca|laure|ate
bac|ca|rat

Bac|chae, The
bac|cha|nal
Bac|cha|na|lia
bac|cha|na|lian
Bac|chus
baccy
△ bac|cies
Bach
bach|elor
bach|elor|hood
ba|cil|lus
△ ba|cilli
back
  VERB
△ backs
△ backed
△ back|ing
back|ache
back|bench
back|ben|cher
back|bite
△ back|bites
△ back|bit
△ back|bi|ting
back|bi|ting
back|bone
back|break|ing
back|chat
back|cloth
back|comb
△ back|combs
△ back|combed
△ back|comb|ing
back-cross
△ back-cros|ses
back|date
△ back|dates
△ back|da|ted
△ back|da|ting
back|door
back|drop
backer
back|fire
△ back|fires

△ back|fired
△ back|firing
back-for|ma|tion
back|gam|mon
back|ground
back|hand
back|han|ded
back|han|der
back|ing
back|lash
△ back|la|shes
back|less
back|log
back|mar|ker
back|pack
  VERB
△ back|packs
△ back|packed
△ back|pack|ing
back|packer
back|pack|ing
back-pedal
△ back-ped|als
△ back-ped|alled
△ back-ped|al|
  ling
back|room
back|side
back|slide
△ back|slides
△ back|slid
△ back|sli|ding
back|sli|der
back|sli|ding
back|space
  VERB
△ back|spa|ces
△ back|spaced
△ back|spa|cing
back|spin
back|stage
back|street
back|stroke
back|track

△ back|tracks
△ back|tracked
△ back|track|ing
back|up
back|ward
back|ward|ness
back|wards
back|wash
△ back|wa|shes
back|wa|ter
back|woods
back|woods|man
△ back|woods|
  men
baclava see
  baklava
Bacon
bacon
bac|ter|ae|mia
bac|ter|ial
bac|teri|cide
bac|terio|logi|cal
bac|terio|lo|gist
bac|terio|logy
bac|terio|ly|sis
bac|terio|lytic
bac|terio|phage
bac|terio|sta|tic
bac|ter|ium
△ bac|teria
Bac|tria
bad
  ADJ.
△ worse
△ worst
baddy
△ bad|dies
bade
Baden-Powell
Bader
badge
badger
  VERB
△ badgers

△ badgered
△ badger|ing
badly
△ worse
△ worst
bad|min|ton
bad|mouth
△ bad|mouths
△ bad|mouthed
△ bad|mouth|
ing
bad|ness
bad-tem|pered
Bae|deker
Baez
baf|fle
VERB
△ baf|fles
△ baf|fled
△ baf|fling
baffle|ment
baf|fling
baf|flingly
bag
VERB
△ bags
△ bagged
△ bag|ging
ba|ga|telle
Bage|hot
ba|gel
bag|gage
bag|gily
bag|gi|ness
baggy
△ bag|gier
△ bag|gi|est
Bagh|dad
bag|piper
bag|pipes
ba|guette
Ba|guio
bah
Ba|ha'i

Ba|ha|'ism
Ba|ha|mas
Bah|rain
Bai|kal

bail
*money for
release; part of
wicket; scoop or
jump (out)*
VERB
△ bails
△ bailed
△ bail|ing
⚠ bale

bai|ley
Bai|ley bridge
bai|liff
bain-marie
△ bains-marie
Baird
bairn
bait
VERB
△ baits
△ bai|ted
△ bait|ing
baize
bake
△ bakes
△ baked
△ ba|king
bake|house
Ba|ke|lite
Ba|ker
ba|ker
ba|kery
△ ba|ker|ies
ba|king
bak|lava
bak|sheesh
△ bak|shee|shes
Bakst
Baku

Ba|ku|nin
ba|la|clava
ba|la|laika
bal|ance
VERB
△ bal|an|ces
△ bal|anced
△ bal|an|cing
bal|anced
Ba|lan|chine
bal|cony
△ bal|co|nies
bald
△ balder
△ bald|est
bal|dac|chino
Bal|der
bal|der|dash
bald|ing
baldly
bald|ness
bald|ric
Baldur *see*
Balder
Bald|win

bale
*bundle; tie up
into bundle*
VERB
△ bales
△ baled
△ ba|ling
⚠ bail

Ba|learic
ba|leen
bale|ful
bale|fully
bale|ful|ness
Bal|four
Bali
Ba|li|nese
balk
△ balks

△ balked
△ balk|ing
Bal|kan
ball
VERB
△ balls
△ balled
△ bal|ling
bal|lad
bal|lade
bal|last
ball-bear|ing
ball|cock
bal|ler|ina
Bal|les|teros
bal|let
bal|let-dan|cer
bal|letic
bal|let|ic|ally
bal|lis|tic
bal|lis|tics
bal|loon
VERB
△ bal|loons
△ bal|looned
△ bal|loon|ing
bal|loon|ing
bal|loon|ist
bal|lot
VERB
△ bal|lots
△ bal|loted
△ bal|lot|ing
bal|lot-box
△ bal|lot-boxes
bal|lot-paper
ball|park
ball|point
ball|room
balls
VERB
△ ball|ses
△ ballsed
△ balls|ing

bally
△ bal|lier
△ bal|li|est
bal|ly|hoo
balm
Bal|main
balm|ily
balmi|ness
Bal|moral
balmy
△ balm|ier
△ balmi|est
baloney
balsa
bal|sam
balti
Bal|tic
Bal|ti|more
Ba|lu|chis|tan
bal|us|ter
ba|lus|trade
Bal|zac
Bam|ako
bam|boo
bam|boozle
△ bam|boozles
△ bam|boozled
△ bam|booz|ling
bam|boozle|
 ment
ban
 VERB
 △ bans
 △ banned
 △ ban|ning
ba|nal
ba|nal|ity
 △ ba|nal|it|ies
ba|nana
Banares *see*
 Benares
Ban|bury
banc|as|sur|ance
band

VERB
△ bands
△ ban|ded
△ band|ing
Banda
ban|dage
 VERB
 △ ban|dages
 △ ban|daged
 △ ban|daging
ban|dana
Ban|dara|naike
Ban|dar Seri
 Be|ga|wan
band|box
 △ band|boxes
ban|deau
 △ ban|deaux
ban|ded
ban|der|ole
ban|di|coot
ban|dit
band|mas|ter
ban|dog
ban|do|leer
band-saw
bands|man
 △ bands|men
band|stand
band|wagon
band|width
bandy
 VERB
 △ ban|dies
 △ ban|died
 △ ban|dy|ing
 ADJ.
 △ ban|dier
 △ ban|di|est
bandy-legged
bane
bane|ful
Banff
bang

VERB
△ bangs
△ banged
△ bang|ing
Ban|ga|lore
ban|ger
Bang|kok
Bang|la|desh
ban|gle
Ban|gor
Ban|gui
banian *see*
 banyan
ban|ish
 △ ban|ishes
 △ ban|ished
 △ ban|ish|ing
ban|ish|ment
ban|is|ter
banjo
 △ ban|jos *or*
 ban|joes
banjo|ist
Ban|jul
bank
 VERB
 △ banks
 △ banked
 △ bank|ing
ban|ker
bank|ing
bank|note
bank|roll
 VERB
 △ bank|rolls
 △ bank|rolled
 △ bank|rol|ling
bank|rupt
 VERB
 △ bank|rupts
 △ bank|rup|ted
 △ bank|rupt|ing
bank|ruptcy
 △ bank|rupt|cies

bank|sia
ban|ner
bannister *see*
 banister
Ban|nis|ter
ban|nock
Ban|nock|burn
banns
ban|quet
 VERB
 △ ban|quets
 △ ban|queted
 △ ban|quet|ing
ban|shee
ban|tam
ban|tam|weight
ban|ter
 VERB
 △ ban|ters
 △ ban|tered
 △ ban|ter|ing
ban|ter|ing
Bantu
Ban|tu|stan
ban|yan
bao|bab
baptise *see*
 baptize
bap|tism
bap|tis|mal
bap|tist
bap|tis|tery
 △ bap|tis|ter|ies
bap|tize
 △ bap|ti|zes
 △ bap|tized
 △ bap|ti|zing
bar
 VERB
 △ bars
 △ barred
 △ bar|ring
Bar|ab|bas
barb

VERB
△ barbs
△ barbed
△ barb|ing
Bar|ba|dos
Bar|bara
bar|bar|ian
bar|ba|ric
bar|bar|ic|ally
bar|bar|ism
bar|bar|ity
△ bar|bar|it|ies
bar|bar|ous
bar|bar|ously
Bar|bary
bar|becue
VERB
△ bar|becues
△ bar|becued
△ bar|becu|ing
barbed
bar|bel
bar|bell
bar|ber
*Bar|ber of Se|
ville, The (Il
bar|bi|ere di Si|
vi|glia)*
bar|berry
△ bar|ber|ries
bar|ber|shop
bar|bet
bar|bi|can
Bar|bi|rolli
bar|bit|ur|ate
bar|ca|role
Bar|ce|lona
bard
bar|dic
Bar|dot

bare
*uncovered;
empty; uncover*

VERB
△ bares
△ bared
△ baring
ADJ.
△ barer
△ barest
⚠ bear

bare|back
bare|faced
bare|fa|cedly
bare|foot
bare|headed
bare|legged
barely
Bar|en|boim
bare|ness
Bar|ents
bar|gain
VERB
△ bar|gains
△ bar|gained
△ bar|gain|ing
bar|gainer
barge
VERB
△ bar|ges
△ barged
△ bar|ging
bar|gee
barge|pole
bar|ite
ba|ri|tone
bar|ium
bark
VERB
△ barks
△ barked
△ bark|ing
bark
ship see *barque*
bar|ker
bar|ley

bar|ley|corn
bar|maid
bar|man
△ bar|men
bar mitz|vah
barmy
△ bar|mier
△ bar|mi|est
barn
Bar|naby
bar|nacle
Bar|nard
Bar|nardo
bar|ney
Barns|ley
barn|storm
△ barn|storms
△ barn|stormed
△ barn|storm|
ing
barn|stor|mer
Bar|num
barn|yard
baro|graph
ba|ro|meter
ba|ro|met|ric
ba|ro|met|ric|
ally

baron
nobleman
⚠ barren

ba|ron|ess
△ ba|ron|es|ses
ba|ro|net
ba|ro|netcy
△ ba|ro|net|cies
ba|ro|nial
bar|ony
△ bar|on|ies
ba|roque
bar|per|son
barque
bar|rack

VERB
△ bar|racks
△ bar|racked
△ bar|rack|ing
bar|rack|ing
*Bar|rack-Room
Bal|lads*
bar|ra|cuda
△ bar|ra|cuda *or*
bar|ra|cudas
bar|rage
Bar|rault
barre
barred
bar|rel
VERB
△ bar|rels
△ bar|relled
△ bar|rel|ling
bar|rel-chested

bar|ren
unfertile
⚠ baron

bar|ren|ness
bar|ri|cade
VERB
△ bar|ri|cades
△ bar|ri|ca|ded
△ bar|ri|ca|ding
Bar|rie
bar|rier
bar|ring
bar|ris|ter
bar|row
Bar|row-in-Fur|
ness
Barry
Bar|ry|more
Bar|set|shire
nov|els, The
Bart
bar|ten|der
bar|ter

VERB
△ bar|ters
△ bar|tered
△ bar|ter|ing
Bar|tered Bride,
The (Pro|daná
Ne|věhk|sta)
bar|terer
Bar|tho|lo|mew
Bar|tók
ba|ryon
ba|ry|tes
ba|ry|ton
basal
ba|salt
ba|sal|tic

base
bottom; origin;
establish; wicked
VERB
△ bases
△ based
△ ba|sing
ADJ.
△ baser
△ ba|sest
⚠ bass

base|ball
base|less
base|line
basely
base|ment
base|ness
bash
NOUN
△ ba|shes
VERB
△ ba|shes
△ bashed
△ bash|ing
bash|ful
bash|fully
bash|ful|ness

basic
ba|sic|ally
Ba|si|dio|my|ce|
tes
Basie
Basil
basil
ba|sil|ica
bas|ilisk
basin
Ba|sing|stoke
basis
△ bases
bask
△ basks
△ basked
△ bask|ing
bas|ket
bas|ket|ball
bas|ket|ful
bas|ketry
bas|ket|work
Basle
Basque
basque
bas-relief

bass
in music
△ bas|ses
fish
△ bass *or* bas|
ses
⚠ base

bas|set
bas|si|net
bass|ist
bas|soon
bas|soon|ist
bast
bas|tard
bas|tard|iza|tion
bas|tard|ize
△ bas|tard|izes

△ bas|tard|ized
△ bas|tard|izing
bas|tard|ized
bas|tardy
baste
△ bastes
△ bas|ted
△ bast|ing
Bas|tille
bas|ti|nado
NOUN
△ bas|ti|na|does
VERB
△ bas|ti|na|does
△ bas|ti|na|doed
△ bas|ti|na|do|
ing
bas|tion
bat
VERB
△ bats
△ bat|ted
△ bat|ting
batch
VERB
△ bat|ches
△ batched
△ batch|ing
bated
Bates
Bath
bath
VERB
△ baths
△ bathed
△ bath|ing
bath|cube
bathe
VERB
△ bathes
△ bathed
△ bath|ing
bather
ba|thetic

batho|lith
ba|thos
bath|robe
bath|room
bath|tub
ba|thy|metry
ba|thy|scaphe
ba|thy|sphere
batik
Bat|man
bat|man
△ bat|men

ba|ton
stick
⚠ batten

bats
bats|man
△ bats|men
bats|wo|man
△ bats|wo|men
bat|tal|ion
bat|tels

bat|ten
strip of wood;
fasten with this
VERB
△ bat|tens
△ bat|tened
△ bat|ten|ing
⚠ baton

bat|ter
VERB
△ bat|ters
△ bat|tered
△ bat|ter|ing
bat|tered
bat|ter|ing
bat|ter|ing-ram
bat|tery
△ bat|ter|ies
bat|tle

VERB
△ bat¦tles
△ bat¦tled
△ bat¦tling
battle-axe
battle-cruiser
battle-cry
△ battle-cries
battle|dress
△ battle-dres¦ses
battle|ment
battle|ship
Battle|ship Po¦
tem|kin
batty
△ bat|tier
△ bat|ti|est
bau¦ble
Bau¦de|laire
Bau|haus
baulk *see* balk
baux|ite
Ba|va|ria
baw|dily
baw|di|ness
bawdy
△ baw¦dier
△ baw¦di|est
bawl
△ bawls
△ bawled
△ bawl|ing
bay
VERB
△ bays
△ bayed
△ bay|ing
Bay|eux Tap|es¦
try
bayo|net
VERB
△ bayo|nets
△ bayo|neted
△ bayo|net|ing

bayou
Bay|reuth

```
ba¦zaar
   market
      ⚠ bizarre
```

ba|zooka
bazouki *see*
  bouzouki
be
  present tense
△ am
△ are
△ is
  past tense
△ was
△ were
  present participle
△ being
  past participle
△ been

```
beach
   shore; land on
   beach
   NOUN
△ bea¦ches
   VERB
△ bea¦ches
△ beached
△ beach|ing
      ⚠ beech
```

beach|comber
beach|comb|ing
beach|head
bea|con
bead
  VERB
△ beads
△ bea¦ded
△ bead|ing
bea¦ded
bead|ing
bea¦dle

beady
△ bea¦dier
△ bea¦di|est
bea|gle
  VERB
△ bea|gles
△ bea|gled
△ beag|ling
beag|ling
beak
beaked
bea¦ker
bea¦ker|ful
beam
  VERB
△ beams
△ beamed
△ beam|ing

```
bean
   vegetable
      ⚠ been
```

bean|feast
bean|sprout
bean|shoot
bean|stalk

```
bear
   animal; carry
   VERB
△ bears
△ bore
△ bear|ing
   when followed
   by by and
   mother's name
△ borne
   other senses
△ born
      ⚠ bare
```

bear|able
bear|ably
beard

VERB
△ beards
△ bearded
△ beard|ing
bearded
beard|less
Beards|ley
bearer
bear|ing
bear|ish
bear|skin
beast
beast|li|ness
beastly
  ADJ.
△ beast¦lier
△ beast¦li|est

```
beat
   regular stroke;
   route; hit;
   defeat; drive
   VERB
△ beats
△ beat
△ beat|ing
△ bea|ten
      ⚠ beet
```

bea¦ter
be¦ati|fic
be¦ati|fi|ca|tion
be¦atify
△ be¦ati|fies
△ be¦ati|fied
△ be¦ati|fy|ing
beat|ing
be¦ati|tude
Be¦ati|tudes
Bea¦tles
beat|nik
Bea¦ton
Bea¦trice
Beatty
beat-up

beau
△ beaux
Beau|fort
Beau|jo|lais
Beau|mar|chais
Beau|mont
beau|te|ous
beau|te|ously
beau|ti|cian
beau|ti|fi|ca|tion
beau|ti|ful
beau|ti|fully
beau|tify
△ beau|ti|fies
△ beau|ti|fied
△ beau|ti|fy|ing
beauty
△ beau|ties
Beau|vais
Beau|voir
bea|ver
VERB
△ bea|vers
△ bea|vered
△ bea|ver|ing
Bea|ver|brook
bebop
be|calmed
be|came
be|cause
beck
Becker
Becket
*Becket, ou
l' Hon|neur de
Dieu (Becket,
or The Hon|
our of God)*
Beck|ett
beckon
△ beck|ons
△ beck|oned
△ beck|on|ing
be|come

△ be|comes
△ be|came
△ be|com|ing
△ be|come
be|com|ing
be|com|ingly
bec|que|rel
bed
VERB
△ beds
△ bed|ded
△ bed|ding
be|daz|zle
△ be|daz|zles
△ be|daz|zled
△ be|daz|zling
be|dazzled
be|dazzle|ment
bed|bath
bed|bug
bed|clothes
bed|cover
bed|ding
Bede
be|deck
△ be|decks
△ be|decked
△ be|deck|ing
be|devil
△ be|dev|ils
△ be|dev|illed
△ be|dev|il|ling
be|dev|il|ment
bed|fel|low
Bed|ford
Bed|ford|shire
Bed|lam
bed|lam
Bed|ouin
△ Bed|ouin *or*
Bed|ouins
bed|pan
be|drag|gled
bed|rid|den

bed|rock
bed|room
bed|side
bed|sit
bed|sit|ter
bed|sit|ting
bed|sore
bed|spread
bed|stead
bed|straw
bed-wet|ting
bee

---
beech
tree
NOUN
△ bee|ches
⚠ beach

Bee|cham
bee-eater
beef
NOUN
△ beeves
VERB
△ beefs
△ beefed
△ beef|ing
beef|bur|ger
beef|cake
beef|ea|ter
beefi|ness
beef|steak
beefy
△ bee|fier
△ bee|fi|est
bee|hive
bee|keeper
bee|keep|ing
bee|line
Be|el|ze|bub

---
been
*past participle of
be*

⚠ bean
---

beep
VERB
△ beeps
△ beeped
△ beep|ing
bee|per

---
beer
drink
⚠ bier

Beer|bohm
Beer|sheba
beery
△ beer|ier
△ beeri|est
bees|wax

---
beet
vegetable
⚠ beat

Beet|ho|ven
bee|tle
VERB
△ bee|tles
△ bee|tled
△ beet|ling
beetle-browed
beet|ling
Bee|ton
beet|root
be|fall
△ be|falls
△ be|fell
△ be|fal|ling
△ be|fal|len
be|fit
△ be|fits
△ be|fit|ted
△ be|fit|ting
be|fit|ting
be|fit|tingly
be|fore

be¦fore¦hand
be¦friend
△ be¦friends
△ be¦frien¦ded
△ be¦friend¦ing
be¦fuddle
△ be¦fuddles
△ be¦fuddled
△ be¦fud¦dling
be¦fuddled
beg
△ begs
△ begged
△ beg¦ging
be¦gan
be¦get
△ be¦gets
△ be¦got *or* be¦
gat
△ be¦get¦ting
△ be¦got¦ten
beg¦gar
beg¦garly
△ beg¦gar¦lier
△ beg¦gar¦li¦est
*Beg¦gar's Opera,
The*
Begin
begin
△ be¦gins
△ began
△ be¦gin¦ning
△ begun
be¦gin¦ner
be¦gin¦ning
be¦gone
be¦go¦nia
begot
be¦grudge
△ be¦grudges
△ be¦grudged
△ be¦grudging
be¦guile
△ be¦guiles

△ be¦guiled
△ be¦guil¦ing
be¦guile¦ment
be¦guil¦ing
be¦guil¦ingly
begun
be¦half
Behan
be¦have
△ be¦haves
△ be¦haved
△ be¦ha¦ving
be¦ha¦viour
be¦ha¦vioural
be¦ha¦viour¦ally
be¦ha¦viour¦ism
be¦ha¦viour¦ist
be¦head
△ be¦heads
△ be¦headed
△ be¦head¦ing
be¦head¦ing
be¦held
be¦hest
be¦hind
be¦hind¦hand
Behn
be¦hold
△ be¦holds
△ be¦held
△ be¦hold¦ing
be¦hol¦den
be¦hol¦der
be¦hove
△ be¦hoves
△ be¦hoved
△ be¦ho¦ving
beige
beigel *see* bagel
Bei¦jing
being
Bei¦rut
Bé¦jart
be¦jew¦elled

bel
be¦la¦bour
△ be¦la¦bours
△ be¦la¦boured
△ be¦la¦bour¦ing
Belarus *see*
Belorussia
be¦la¦ted
be¦la¦tedly
Belau *see* Palau
be¦lay
VERB
△ be¦lays
△ be¦layed
△ be¦lay¦ing
bel canto
belch
VERB
△ bel¦ches
△ belched
△ belch¦ing
be¦lea¦guer
△ be¦lea¦guers
△ be¦lea¦guered
△ be¦lea¦guer¦ing
be¦lea¦guered
bel¦em¦nite
Bel¦fast
bel¦fry
△ bel¦fries
Bel¦gium
Bel¦grade
Bel¦grano
Be¦lial
be¦lie
△ be¦lies
△ be¦lied
△ be¦ly¦ing
be¦lief
be¦liev¦able
be¦lieve
△ be¦lieves
△ be¦lieved
△ be¦liev¦ing

be¦liever
Bel¦linda
Be¦li¦sha
be¦lit¦tle
△ be¦lit¦tles
△ be¦lit¦tled
△ be¦lit¦tling
be¦little¦ment
be¦lit¦tling
Be¦lize
Bell
bell
bel¦la¦donna
bell-bot¦tomed
bell-bot¦toms
bell-boy
belle
Bel¦lero¦phon
belles-lettres
bell-hop
bel¦li¦cose
bel¦li¦ger¦ence
bel¦li¦ger¦ency
bel¦li¦ger¦ent
bel¦li¦ger¦ently
Bel¦lini
Bel¦loc
Bel¦low
bel¦low
VERB
△ bel¦lows
△ bel¦lowed
△ bel¦low¦ing
bell-pull
bell-push
bell-ringer
bell-ring¦ing
bell¦wether
belly
NOUN
△ bel¦lies
VERB
△ bel¦lies
△ bel¦lied

△ bel|ly|ing
belly|ache
  VERB
△ belly|aches
△ belly|ached
△ belly|aching
belly-dance
  VERB
△ belly-dan|ces
△ belly-danced
△ belly-dan|cing
belly-dan|cer
belly-flop
belly|ful
belly-land|ing
Bel|mo|pan
be|long
△ be|longs
△ be|longed
△ be|long|ing
be|long|ings
Be|lo|rus|sia
be|loved
below
Bel|shaz|zar
belt
  VERB
△ belts
△ bel|ted
△ belt|ing
bel|ted
be|luga
bel|ve|dere
be|moan
△ be|moans
△ be|moaned
△ be|moan|ing
be|muse
△ be|mu|ses
△ be|mused
△ be|mu|sing
be|mused
ben
Be|na|res

bench
bench|mark
bend
  VERB
△ bends
△ bent
△ bend|ing
bendy
△ ben|dier
△ ben|di|est
be|neath
Bene|dict
Bene|dic|tine
bene|dic|tion
bene|dic|tory
bene|fac|tion
bene|fac|tor
bene|fac|tory
bene|fice
bene|ficed
be|ne|fi|cence
be|ne|fi|cent
be|ne|fi|cently
bene|fi|cial
bene|fi|ci|ally
bene|fi|ci|ary
△ bene|fi|ci|ar|ies
bene|fit
  VERB
△ bene|fits
△ bene|fited
△ bene|fit|ing
Bene|lux
bene|vo|lence
bene|vo|lent
bene|vo|lently
Ben|gal
Ben|gali
Ben-Gur|ion
Ben-Hur
Beni|dorm
be|nigh|ted
be|nign

be|nig|nant
be|nig|nity
△ be|nig|ni|ties
be|nignly
Benin
Ben|ja|min
Benn
Ben|nett
Ben Nevis
bent
  ADJ.
△ benter
△ bent|est
Ben|tham
ben|thic
ben|thos
ben|ton|ite
be|numb
△ be|numbs
△ be|numbed
△ be|numb|ing
Benz

ben|zene
*a liquid
hydrocarbon*
⚠benzine

ben|zine
motor fuel
⚠benzene

ben|zo|dia|zep|
ine
ben|zoic
ben|zoin
Beo|wulf
be|queath
△ be|queaths
△ be|queathed
△ be|queath|ing
be|quest
be|rate
△ be|rates
△ be|ra|ted

△ be|ra|ting
Ber|ber
be|reaved
be|reave|ment
be|reft
Be|re|nice
beret
Berg
Ber|gamo
ber|ga|mot
Ber|gen
Berg|man
Beria
be|rib|boned
beri|beri
Ber|ing
Berio
berk
Berke|ley
ber|ke|lium
Berk|shire
Ber|lin
Ber|lioz
Ber|muda
Bern
Ber|na|dette
Ber|nard
Bern|hardt
Ber|nini
Bern|stein
Berry
berry
△ ber|ries
ber|serk

berth
*place to sleep or
for ship etc;
provide this*
  VERB
△ berths
△ berthed
△ berth|ing
⚠birth

Ber|tha
Ber|to|lucci
Bert|ram
Ber|wick-upon-
  Tweed
Beryl
beryl
be|ryl|lium
be|seech
△ be|see|ches
△ be|seeched *or*
  be|sought
△ be|seech|ing
be|seech|ing
be|seech|ingly
beset
△ be|sets
△ beset
△ be|set|ting
be|side
be|sides
be|siege
△ be|sieges
△ be|sieged
△ be|sie|ging
be|smirch
△ be|smir|ches
△ be|smirched
△ be|smirch|ing
besom
be|sot|ted
be|sot|tedly
be|sought
be|span|gle
△ be|span|gles
△ be|span|gled
△ be|spang|ling
be|spat|ter
△ be|spat|ters
△ be|spat|tered
△ be|spat|ter|ing
be|speak
△ be|speaks
△ be|spoke

△ be|speak|ing
△ be|spo|ken
be|spoke
Bes|semer
Best
best
VERB
△ bests
△ bes|ted
△ best|ing
bes|tial
bes|ti|al|ity
bes|ti|ally
bes|ti|ary
△ bes|ti|ar|ies
be|stir
△ be|stirs
△ be|stirred
△ be|stir|ring
be|stow
△ be|stows
△ be|stowed
△ be|stow|ing
be|stowal
be|strewn
be|stride
△ be|strides
△ be|strode
△ be|strid|ing
△ be|strid|den
best-sel|ler
best-sel|ling
bet
△ bets
△ bet
△ bet|ting
beta
beta-blocker
be|take
△ be|takes
△ be|took
△ be|tak|ing
betel
Be|tel|geuse

bête noire
△ *bêtes noires*
Beth|le|hem
be|tide
Bet|je|man
be|to|ken
△ be|to|kens
△ be|to|kened
△ be|to|ken|ing
be|took
be|tray
△ be|trays
△ be|trayed
△ be|tray|ing
be|trayal
be|trayer
be|tro|thal
be|trothed
bet|ter
VERB
△ bet|ters
△ bet|tered
△ bet|ter|ing
bet|ter|ment
bet|ting
bet|ting-shop
be|tween
be|tween|times
be|twixt
Bevan
bevel
VERB
△ bev|els
△ bev|elled
△ bev|el|ling
bev|elled
bev|er|age
Bev|er|idge
Bev|er|ley
Bev|erly Hills
Bevin
bevy
△ bev|ies
be|wail

△ be|wails
△ be|wailed
△ be|wail|ing
be|ware
be|wil|der
△ be|wil|ders
△ be|wil|dered
△ be|wil|der|ing
be|wil|dered
be|wil|der|ing
be|wil|der|ingly
be|wil|der|ment
be|witch
△ be|wit|ches
△ be|witched
△ be|witch|ing
be|witch|ing
be|witch|ingly
Bex|hill
bey
be|yond
be|zique
B-film
Bha|ga|vad|gita
bhaji
bhakti
bhan|gra
Bho|pal
Bhu|tan
Bhutto
bi|an|nual
bi|an|nu|ally
Bi|ar|ritz
bias
VERB
△ bia|ses
△ biased *or*
  biassed
△ bias|ing *or*
  bias|sing
biased
bi|ath|lon
bib
Bi|ble

as an institution
bi¦ble
*a copy of the
book*
bib|li|cal
bib|lio|gra|pher
bib|lio|gra|phic
bib|lio|graph|
 ical
bib|lio|graphy
 △ bib|lio|graph|
 ies
bib|lio|phile
bib|ulous
bi|cam|eral
bi|carb
bi|car¦bon|ate
bi|cen¦ten|ary
 △ bi|cen¦ten|ar¦
 ies
bi|cen¦ten|nial
bi|ceps
sing. and pl.
bicker
 △ bick|ers
 △ bick¦ered
 △ bick¦er|ing
bick¦er|ing
bi|con¦cave
bi|con¦vex
bi|cus¦pid
bi|cy¦cle
 VERB
 △ bi|cy¦cles
 △ bi|cy¦cled
 △ bi|cyc|ling
*Bi|cy¦cle Thieves
(Ladri di bi¦ci¦
clette)*
bi|cyc|list
bid
 offer
 VERB
 △ bids

△ bid
△ bid|ding
bid
 say
 △ bids
 △ bade
 △ bid|ding
 △ bid|den
bid|dable
bid|der
bid|ding
bide
 △ bides
 △ bided *or* bode
 △ bi¦ding
 △ bided
bidet
Bi|en|nale
bi|en|nial
bi|en|ni|ally

bier
 stand for coffin
 ⚠ beer

biff
 VERB
 △ biffs
 △ biffed
 △ bif|fing
bi|fo|cal
bi|fo|cals
bi|fur|cate
 △ bi|fur|cates
 △ bi|fur|ca¦ted
 △ bi|fur|ca¦ting
bi|fur|ca¦ted
bi|fur|ca¦tion
big
 ADJ.
 △ big|ger
 △ big|gest
big¦am|ist
big¦am|ous
big¦am|ously

big|amy
 △ big|am|ies
big|gish
Biggles
Biggs
big|head
big-headed
big-headed|ness
big-hearted
big|horn

bight
 *curve in coast or
rope*
 ⚠ bite

bigot
big|oted
big|otry
Big Sleep, The
big|wig
bijou
 NOUN
 △ bi|joux
bike
 VERB
 △ bikes
 △ biked
 △ bi|king
biker
bike|way
bi|king
Bi|kini
bi|kini
Biko
bi|la|bial
bi|lat|eral
bi|lat¦er|al|ism
bi|lat¦er|ally
bil|berry
 △ bil|ber|ries
Bil|dungs|roman
bile
bilge
bi|lin|gual

bi|lin|gual|ism
bi|lin|guist
bili|ous
bili|ously
bi¦li|ru|bin
bi¦li|ver|din
bilk
 △ bilks
 △ bilked
 △ bilk|ing
bill
 VERB
 △ bills
 △ billed
 △ bil|ling
bil|la|bong
bill|board
bil¦let
 VERB
 △ bil|lets
 △ bil|leted
 △ bil|let|ing
bil¦let-doux
 △ bil¦lets-doux
bil|liards
bil|ling
Bil¦lings|gate
bil|lion
 NOUN
 after a number
 △ bil|lion
 other senses
 △ bil|lions
bil|lion|aire
bil|lion|air¦ess
 △ bil|lion|air|es¦
 ses
bil|lionth
bil|low
 VERB
 △ bil|lows
 △ bil|lowed
 △ bil|low|ing
bil|low|ing

bil|lowy
bill|pos|ter
bill|sticker
billy
△ bil|lies
Billy Budd
bil|ly|can
billy-o
bimbo
bi|met|al|lic
bi|monthly
bin
bi|nary
NOUN
△ bi|nar|ies
bind
VERB
△ binds
△ bound
△ bind|ing
binder
bind|ery
△ bind|er|ies
bind|ing
bind|weed
Bi|net
Bing
binge
VERB
△ bin|ges
△ binged
△ bin|ging
bingo
bin-liner
bin|nacle
bin|ocu|lar
bin|ocu|lars
bi|no|mial
Bin|yon
bio|as|say
bio|chemi|cal
bio|chem|ist
bio|chem|is|try
bio|con|trol

bio|de|grad|able
bio|deg|ra|da|
   tion
bio|di|ver|sity
bio|en|er|get|ics
bio|en|gin|eer|ing
bio|feed|back
bio|gra|pher
bio|gra|phic
bio|graph|ical
bio|graph|ic|ally
bio|gra|phy
△ bio|graph|ies
bio|lin|guis|tics
bio|lo|gi|cal
bio|lo|gic|ally
bio|lo|gist
bio|logy
bio|lu|min|es|
   cence
bio|mass
△ bio|mas|ses
biome
bio|mech|an|ics
bio|mor|phic
bi|onic
bi|onics
bio|phy|si|cist
bio|phys|ics
bi|opsy
△ bi|op|sies
bio|rhythm
bio|sphere
bio|syn|the|sis
△ bio|syn|the|ses
bi|ota
bio|tech|no|logy
△ bio|tech|no|lo|
   gies
bio|tin
bi|par|ti|san
bi|par|tite
bi|ped
bi|pedal

bi|plane
bi|po|lar
birch
   NOUN
△ bir|ches
   VERB
△ bir|ches
△ birched
△ birch|ing
bird
bir|der
bir|die
   VERB
△ bir|dies
△ bir|died
△ bir|dy|ing
bird-lime
Birds|eye
birds|foot
Birds of Amer|ica
bird-wat|cher
bird-watch|ing
bi|reme
bi|retta
bi|ri|ani
Bir|ken|head
Bir|ming|ham
Biro

birth
   being born
   ⚠ berth

birth|day
*Birth|day Party,
   The*
birth|ing
birth|mark
*Birth of a Na|
   tion, The*
*Birth of Venus,
   The*
birth|place
birth|right
Birt|wistle

biryani *see*
   biriani
Bis|cay
bis|cuit
bi|sect
△ bi|sects
△ bi|sec|ted
△ bi|sect|ing
bi|sec|tion
bi|sex|ual
bi|sexu|al|ity
Bish|kek
bi|shop
bish|op|ric
Bishop's Lynn
   see King's
   Lynn
Bis|marck
bis|muth
bi|son
   sing. and pl.
bisque
Bis|sau
bis|tort
bis|tro
bi|sul|phate
bit
bitch
△ bit|ches
bitch|ily
bit|chi|ness
bitchy
△ bit|chier
△ bit|chi|est

bite
   *seize or tear
   with teeth; an
   instance of this*
   VERB
△ bites
△ bit
△ bi|ting
   ⚠ bight

Bi|thynia
bi|ting
bit-map|ping
bit-part
bit|ter
△ bit|terer
△ bit|ter|est
bit|terly
bit|tern
bit|ter|ness
bit|ters
bit|ter|sweet
bit|ti|ness
bitty
△ bit|tier
△ bit|ti|est
bitu|men
bi|tu|min|ous
bi|va|lent
bi|valve
bi|vari|ate
biv|ouac
VERB
△ biv|ou|acs
△ biv|ou|acked
△ biv|ou|ack|ing

bi|zarre
strange
⚠ bazaar

bi|zarrely
Bi|zet
blab
△ blabs
△ blabbed
△ blab|bing
blab|ber
△ blab|bers
△ blab|bered
△ blab|ber|ing
blab|ber|mouth
black
VERB
△ blacks

△ blacked
△ black|ing
ADJ.
△ blacker
△ black|est
blacka|moor
black|ball
△ black|balls
△ black|balled
△ black|bal|ling
Black Beauty
black|berry
△ black|ber|ries
black|bird
black|board
Black|burn
black|cap
black|cock
black|cur|rant
blacken
△ black|ens
△ black|ened
△ black|en|ing
black|guard
black|guardly
△ black|guard|
    lier
△ black|guard|li|
    est
black|head
black|ing
black|jack
black|leg
VERB
△ black|legs
△ black|legged
△ black|leg|ging
black|list
VERB
△ black|lists
△ black|lis|ted
△ black|list|ing
blackly
black|mail

VERB
△ black|mails
△ black|mailed
△ black|mail|ing
black|mailer
black-mar|ket|
    eer
Black|more
black|ness
black|out
Black|pool
Black|shirt
black|smith
black|thorn
black-tie
Black|well
blad|der
blade
Blair
Blake
blame
VERB
△ blames
△ blamed
△ bla|ming
blame|less
blame|lessly
blame|less|ness
blame|wor|thy
△ blame|wor|
    thier
△ blame|wor|thi|
    est
blanch
△ blanches
△ blanched
△ blanch|ing
Blanche
Blanch|flower
blanc|mange
bland
△ blan|der
△ bland|est
blan|dish

△ blan|di|shes
△ blan|dished
△ blan|dish|ing
blan|dish|ments
blan|dly
bland|ness
blank
VERB
△ blanks
△ blanked
△ blank|ing
ADJ.
△ blan|ker
△ blank|est
blan|ket
VERB
△ blan|kets
△ blan|keted
△ blan|ket|ing
blankly
blank|ness
blan|quette
blare
VERB
△ blares
△ blared
△ blar|ing
Blar|ney
blar|ney
VERB
△ blar|neys
△ blar|neyed
△ blar|ney|ing
blasé
blas|pheme
△ blas|phemes
△ blas|phemed
△ blas|phem|ing
blas|phemer
blas|phem|ous
blas|phem|ously
blas|phemy
△ blas|phem|ies
blast

VERB
△ blasts
△ blas¦ted
△ blast¦ing
blas¦ted
blast¦ing
blas¦tula
bla¦tant
bla¦tantly
blather *see*
  blether
blaze
  VERB
  △ bla¦zes
  △ blazed
  △ bla¦zing
bla¦zer
bla¦zing
bla¦zon
  VERB
  △ bla¦zons
  △ bla¦zoned
  △ bla¦zon¦ing
bleach
  NOUN
  △ blea¦ches
  VERB
  △ blea¦ches
  △ bleached
  △ bleach¦ing
bleak
  △ blea¦ker
  △ bleak¦est
Bleak House
bleakly
bleak¦ness
blear¦ily
bleary
  △ blear¦ier
  △ bleari¦est
bleat
  △ bleats
  △ blea¦ted
  △ bleat¦ing

bleed
  △ bleeds
  △ bled
  △ bleed¦ing
bleed¦ing
bleep
  VERB
  △ bleeps
  △ bleeped
  △ bleep¦ing
blee¦per
blem¦ish
  NOUN
  △ blem¦ishes
  VERB
  △ blem¦ishes
  △ blem¦ished
  △ blem¦ish¦ing
blench
  △ blen¦ches
  △ blenched
  △ blench¦ing
blend
  VERB
  △ blends
  △ blen¦ded
  △ blend¦ing
blende
blen¦der
Blen¦heim
blenny
  △ blen¦nies
Blé¦riot
bless
  △ bles¦ses
  △ blessed
  △ bles¦sing
  △ blessed *or*
    blest
blessed *or* bles¦
  sed
  ADJ.
  according to
  pronunciation

bles¦sedly
bles¦sing
ble¦ther
  △ bleth¦ers
  △ bleth¦ered
  △ bleth¦er¦ing
blew
Bligh
blight
  VERB
  △ blights
  △ bligh¦ted
  △ blight¦ing
bligh¦ter
bli¦mey
Blimp
blimp
blimp¦ish
blind
  VERB
  △ blinds
  △ blinded
  △ blind¦ing
  ADJ.
  △ blinder
  △ blind¦est
blind¦fold
  VERB
  △ blind¦folds
  △ blind¦fol¦ded
  △ blind¦fold¦ing
blind¦ing
blindly
blind¦man's-
  buff
blind¦ness
blind¦worm
blink
  VERB
  △ blinks
  △ blinked
  △ blink¦ing
blin¦ker

VERB
△ blin¦kers
△ blin¦kered
△ blin¦ker¦ing
blin¦kered
blink¦ing
blip
  VERB
  △ blips
  △ blipped
  △ blip¦ping
bliss
  △ blis¦ses
bliss¦ful
bliss¦fully
blis¦ter
  VERB
  △ blis¦ters
  △ blis¦tered
  △ blis¦ter¦ing
blis¦tered
blis¦ter¦ing
blithe
  △ bli¦ther
  △ bli¦thest
blithely
blith¦er¦ing
Blithe Spirit
blitz
  NOUN
  △ blit¦zes
  VERB
  △ blit¦zes
  △ blitzed
  △ blitz¦ing
Blixen
bliz¦zard
bloat
  △ bloats
  △ bloa¦ted
  △ bloat¦ing
bloa¦ted
bloa¦ter
blob

bloc

block

 VERB

 △ blocks

 △ blocked

 △ block|ing

block|ade

 VERB

 △ block|ades

 △ block|aded

 △ block|ad|ing

block|age

block|bus|ter

blocked

block|head

block|house

Bloem|fon|tein

Blok

bloke

blond
*used of any
person*
⚠ blonde

blonde
*used of women
only*
⚠ blond

Blon|del

Blon|din

blood

 VERB

 △ bloods

 △ blooded

 △ blood|ing

blood-and-thun|
 der

blood|bath

blood|curd|ling

blood|hound

blood|ily

blood|ness

blood|less

blood|lessly

blood|let|ting

blood-money

 △ blood-mon|ies

blood|shed

blood|shot

blood|stained

blood|stock

blood|stone

blood|stream

blood|sucker

blood|suck|ing

blood|thirs|tily

blood|thirs|ti|
 ness

blood|thir|sty

 △ blood|thirs|
  tier

 △ blood|thirs|ti|
  est

blood-ves|sel

*Blood Wed|ding
 (Bodas de
 San|gre)*

bloody

 VERB

 △ blood|ies

 △ blood|ied

 △ bloody|ing

 ADJ.

 △ blood|ier

 △ bloodi|est

bloody Mary

bloody-minded

bloody-mind|ed|
 ness

bloom

 VERB

 △ blooms

 △ bloomed

 △ bloom|ing

bloo|mer

bloom|ing

blos|som

 VERB

 △ blos|soms

 △ blos|somed

 △ blos|som|ing

blos|som|ing

blot

 VERB

 △ blots

 △ blot|ted

 △ blot|ting

blotch

 NOUN

 △ blot|ches

 VERB

 △ blot|ches

 △ blotched

 △ blotch|ing

blotchy

 △ blotch|ier

 △ blotchi|est

blot|ter

blot|ting-paper

blouse

 VERB

 △ blou|ses

 △ bloused

 △ blous|ing

blou|son

blow

 VERB

 △ blows

 △ blew

 △ blow|ing

 △ blown

blow-by-blow

blow-dry

 NOUN

 △ blow-dries

 VERB

 △ blow-dries

 △ blow-dried

 △ blow-drying

blower

blow|fly

 △ blow|flies

blow|hole

blow|lamp

blown

blow-out

blow|pipe

blowsy *see*
 blowzy

blow|torch

 △ blow|tor|ches

blow-up

blowy

 △ blow|ier

 △ blowi|est

blowzy

 △ blow|zier

 △ blow|zi|est

blub|ber

 VERB

 △ blub|bers

 △ blub|bered

 △ blub|ber|ing

Blü|cher

blud|geon

 VERB

 △ blud|geons

 △ blud|geoned

 △ blud|geon|ing

blue

 VERB

 △ blues

 △ blued

 △ blu|ing *or*
  blue|ing

 ADJ.

 △ bluer

 △ blu|est

*Blue An|gel,
 The (Der
 Blaue En|gel)*

Blue|beard

blue|bell

blue|berry

 △ blue|ber|ries

blue|bird
blue|bot|tle
blue-chip
blue-col|lar
Blue Dan|ube,
The (An der
Schö|nen,
Blauen
Donau)
blue|funk
blue|grass
blue|ness
blue-pen|cil
△ blue-pen|cils
△ blue-pen|
cilled
△ blue-pen|cil|
ling
blue|print
blues
blue|stock|ing
bluff
VERB
△ bluffs
△ bluffed
△ bluf|fing
ADJ.
△ bluf|fer
△ bluf|fest
bluf|fly
bluff|ness
blu|ish
Blun|den
blun|der
VERB
△ blun|ders
△ blun|dered
△ blun|der|ing
blun|der|buss
△ blun|der|bus|
ses
blun|derer
blun|der|ing
Blunt

blunt
VERB
△ blunts
△ blun|ted
△ blunt|ing
ADJ.
△ blun|ter
△ blunt|est
bluntly
blunt|ness
blur
VERB
△ blurs
△ blurred
△ blur|ring
blurb
blurred
blurry
△ blur|rier
△ blur|ri|est
blurt
△ blurts
△ blur|ted
△ blurt|ing
blush
NOUN
△ blushes
VERB
△ blushes
△ blushed
△ blush|ing
blusher
blush|ing
blus|ter
VERB
△ blus|ters
△ blus|tered
△ blus|ter|ing
blus|terer
blus|tery
Blyth
Bly|ton
B-movie
boa

Boa|di|cea

boar
pig
⚠ boor
⚠ bore

board
VERB
△ boards
△ boar|ded
△ board|ing
boar|der
board|ing
board|ing-card
board|ing-house
board|ing-pass
△ board|ing-pas|
ses
board|ing-
school
board|room
boast
VERB
△ boasts
△ boas|ted
△ boast|ing
boast|ful
boast|fully
boast|ful|ness
boast|ing
boat
VERB
△ boats
△ boa|ted
△ boat|ing
boa|ter
boat|hook
boat|house
boat|ing
boat|man
△ boat|men
boat|swain
bob

NOUN
shilling
△ bob
other senses
△ bobs
VERB
△ bobs
△ bobbed
△ bob|bing
bob|bin
bob|ble
bobby
△ bob|bies
bob|sleigh
bob|tail
bob|tailed
Boc|cac|cio
Boche
bod
bo|da|cious
bode
△ bodes
△ boded
△ bo|ding
bodge
△ bod|ges
△ bodged
△ bod|ging
Bod|hi|sat|tva
bod|ice
bod|ily
bod|kin
Bod|leian
body
NOUN
△ bodies
VERB
△ bod|ies
△ bod|ied
△ body|ing
body-bag
body-buil|der
body-build|ing
body|guard

body-pier|cing
body-snat|cher
body|suit
body|work
Boe|ing
Boe|otia
Boer
Bo|ethius
bof|fin
bog
  VERB
  △ bogs
  △ bogged
  △ bog|ging
Bo|garde
Bo|gart
bogey
  evil spirit
  △ bo|geys *or* bo|
    gies
  golf score
  △ bo|geys
bo|gey|man
  △ bo|gey|men
bog|gle
  △ bog|gles
  △ bog|gled
  △ bog|gling
boggy
  △ bog|gier
  △ bog|gi|est
bogie
Bog|nor Regis
Bo|gotá
bogus
bogy
  evil spirit see
  bogey
bogyman *see*
  bogeyman
Bo|hème, La
  (Bo|hemian
  Life)
Bo|hemia

bo|hem|ian
boil
  VERB
  △ boils
  △ boiled
  △ boil|ing
boi|ler
Bois de Bou|
  logne
bois|ter|ous
bois|ter|ously
bold
  △ bol|der
  △ bold|est
bold|face
boldly
bold|ness
bole
Bo|léro
bo|lero
Bol|eyn
Bo|ling|broke
Bo|li|via
boll
bol|lard
bol|locks
boll-wee|vil
Bo|logna
boloney *see*
  baloney
Bol|shevik
Bol|shev|ism
Bol|shev|ist
bol|shie
  ADJ.
  △ bol|shier
  △ bol|shi|est
Bol|shoi
bol|ster
  VERB
  △ bol|sters
  △ bol|stered
  △ bol|ster|ing
Bolt

bolt
  VERB
  △ bolts
  △ bol|ted
  △ bolt|ing
bolt|hole
Bol|ton
bomb
  VERB
  △ bombs
  △ bombed
  △ bomb|ing
bom|bard
  △ bom|bards
  △ bom|bar|ded
  △ bom|bard|ing
bom|bar|dier
bom|bard|ment
bom|bast
bom|bas|tic
bom|bas|tic|ally
Bom|bay
bomber
bomb|ing
bomb|shell
bomb|site
bona fide
  ADJ.
bona fides
  NOUN
bo|nanza
Bo|na|parte
Bo|na|part|ism
Bo|na|ven|ture
bon|bon
Bond
bond
  VERB
  △ bonds
  △ bon|ded
  △ bond|ing
bond|age
Bondi
bond|ing

bone
  VERB
  △ bones
  △ boned
  △ bo|ning
bone-dry
bone|head
bone-headed
bone|less
bone|shaker
bon|fire
bong
  VERB
  △ bongs
  △ bonged
  △ bong|ing
bongo
  △ bongos *or*
    bongoes
bon|homie
Boni|face
Bon|ing|ton
bonk
  VERB
  △ bonks
  △ bonked
  △ bonk|ing
bonk|ers
bon mot
  △ *bons mots*
Bonn
bonne-bouche
  △ *bonne-bouches*
    or bonnes-
    bouches
bon|net
Bon|nie and
  Clyde
bonny
  △ bon|nier
  △ bon|ni|est
bon|sai
  sing. and pl.
bonus

△ bon|uses

bon vi|vant
  △ *bons vi|vants*

bon vi|veur
  △ *bons vi|veurs*

bon voy|age

bony
  △ bo|nier
  △ bo|ni|est

bon|zer

boo
  VERB
  △ boos
  △ booed
  △ boo|ing

boob
  VERB
  △ boobs
  △ boobed
  △ boob|ing

booby
  △ boo|bies

booby-trap
  △ booby-traps
  △ booby-
    trapped
  △ booby-trap|
    ping

boo|dle

boo|gie
  VERB
  △ boo|gies
  △ boo|gied
  △ boo|gie|ing *or*
    boo|gy|ing

book
  VERB
  △ books
  △ booked
  △ book|ing

book|able

book|binder

book|bind|ing

book|case

Booker

bookie

book|ing

book|ish

book|ish|ness

book|kee|per

book|keep|ing

book|let

book|ma|ker

book|mark

Book of Kells,
  The

book|plate

book|sel|ler

book|shelf
  △ book|shelves

book|shop

book|stall

book|worm

boom
  VERB
  △ booms
  △ boomed
  △ boom|ing

boom|er|ang
  VERB
  △ boom|er|angs
  △ boom|er|
    anged
  △ boom|er|ang|
    ing

boon

---

boor
  coarse person
  ⚠ boar
  ⚠ bore

---

boor|ish

boor|ishly

boor|ish|ness

boost
  VERB
  △ boosts
  △ boos|ted

△ boost|ing

boos|ter

boot
  VERB
  △ boots
  △ boo|ted
  △ boot|ing

boo|tee

Bo|ötes

Booth

booth

boot|lace

Bootle

boot|leg
  VERB
  △ boot|legs
  △ boot|legged
  △ boot|leg|ging

boot|leg|ger

boot|leg|ging

boot|licker

boots

boot|strap
  VERB
  △ boot|straps
  △ boot|strapped
  △ boot|strap|
    ping

booty
  △ boot|ies

booze
  VERB
  △ boo|zes
  △ boozed
  △ booz|ing

boo|zer

booze-up

boozy
  △ boo|zier
  △ boo|zi|est

bop
  VERB
  △ bops
  △ bopped

△ bop|ping

Bo|phu|that|
  swana

bop|per

bo|ra|cic

bor|age

borax

Bor|deaux

bor|der
  VERB
  △ bor|ders
  △ bor|dered
  △ bor|der|ing

bor|dered

bor|derer

bor|der|land

bor|der|line

Bor|ders

---

bore
  barrel diameter;
  dull person; high
  wave; drill hole;
  destroy interest
  of
  VERB
  △ bores
  △ bored
  △ bor|ing
    ⚠ boar
    ⚠ boor

---

bor|eal

bored

bore|dom

bore|hole

borer

Borg

Bor|gia

boric

bor|ing

bor|ingly

Boris

Boris Go|du|nov

born

born-again
borne
Bor|neo
Bo|ro|din
boron

bor|ough
English town
⚠ burgh

Bor|row
bor|row
△ bor|rows
△ bor|rowed
△ bor|row|ing
bor|rower
bor|row|ing
bor|stal
bor|zoi
Bosch
bosh
Bosnia-Her|ze|
go|vina
bosom

boson
*subatomic
particle*
⚠ bosun

Bos|po|rus
boss
NOUN
△ bos|ses
VERB
△ bos|ses
△ bossed
△ boss|ing
bossa nova
boss-eyed
boss|ily
bos|si|ness
bossy
△ bos|sier
△ bos|si|est
bossy-boots

Bos|ton
Bos|to|ni|ans,
The

bosun *see*
boatswain
⚠ boson

Bos|well
bo|ta|nic
bot|an|ist
bot|any
botch
VERB
△ bot|ches
△ botched
△ botch|ing
botched
bot|cher
both
Botha
Bo|tham
bother
VERB
△ both|ers
△ both|ered
△ both|er|ing
both|er|ation
both|er|some
Bot|swana
Bot|ti|celli
bot|tle
VERB
△ bot|tles
△ bot|tled
△ bot|tling
bottle-feed
△ bottle-feeds
△ bottle-fed
△ bottle-feed|
ing
bottle-feed|ing
bottle-green
bottle|neck
bot|tom

VERB
△ bot|toms
△ bot|tomed
△ bot|tom|ing
bot|tom|less
botu|lism
bou|clé
Boudicca *see*
Boadicea
bou|doir
bouf|fant
bou|gain|vil|laea
bough
bought
bouil|la|baisse
bouil|lon
boul|der
boules
bou|le|vard
Bou|lez
boulle *see* buhl
Bou|logne
boult *see* bolt
bounce
VERB
△ boun|ces
△ bounced
△ boun|cing
boun|cer
boun|cily
boun|ci|ness
boun|cing
bouncy
△ boun|cier
△ boun|ci|est
bound
VERB
△ bounds
△ boun|ded
△ bound|ing
bound|ary
△ bound|ar|ies
boun|den
boun|der

bound|less
bound|lessly
boun|teous
boun|teously
boun|ti|ful
boun|ti|fully
bounty
△ boun|ties
bou|quet
bou|quet garni
bour|bon
bour|geois
sing. and pl.
bour|geoisie
bourn
Bourne|mouth
bou|stro|phedon
bout
bou|tique
Bout|ros-Ghali
bou|zouki
bo|vine
bow
VERB
△ bows
△ bowed
△ bow|ing
Bowd|ler
bowd|ler|iza|tion
bowd|ler|ize
△ bowd|ler|izes
△ bowd|ler|ized
△ bowd|ler|izing
bowd|ler|ized
bowel
bower
bower-bird
bowie
bowl
VERB
△ bowls
△ bowled
△ bowl|ing
bow-legged

bowler
bowl|ful
bow|line
bowl|ing
bowl|ing-alley
bowl|ing-green
bowls
bow|shot
bow|sprit
bow|string
bow-wow
box
  VERB
  △ boxes
  △ boxed
  △ box|ing
boxed
boxer
box|ful
box|ing
box|ing-glove
box-kite
box|room
box|tree
box|wood
boy
Boy|cott
boy|cott
  VERB
  △ boy|cotts
  △ boy|cot|ted
  △ boy|cot|ting
boy|friend
boy|hood
boy|ish
boy|ishly
boy|ish|ness
Boyle
bra
brace
  NOUN
  of pheasants
  △ brace
  other senses

△ bra|ces
VERB
△ bra|ces
△ braced
△ bra|cing
brace|let
bra|chio|pod
bra|cing
bracken
bracket
  VERB
  △ brack|ets
  △ brack|eted
  △ brack|et|ing
brack|ish
brack|ish|ness
bract
brad
brad|awl
Brad|bury
Brad|ford
Brad|laugh
Brad|ley
Brad|man
bra|dy|car|dia
brae
Brae|mar
brag
  VERB
  △ brags
  △ bragged
  △ brag|ging
brag|gart
brag|gingly
Brahe
Brahma
Brah|man
Brah|man|ism
Brahms
braid
  VERB
  △ braids
  △ brai|ded
  △ braid|ing

brai|ded
braid|ing
Braille
brain
  VERB
  △ brains
  △ brained
  △ brain|ing
brain|child
  △ brain|chil|dren
brain-dead
Braine
brai|ni|ness
brain|less
brain|lessly
brain|stem
brain|storm
brain|storm|ing
brain|teaser
brain|wash
  △ brain|wa|shes
  △ brain|washed
  △ brain|wash|ing
brain|wash|ing
brain|wave
brainy
  △ brai|nier
  △ brai|ni|est
braise
  △ brai|ses
  △ braised
  △ brais|ing
braised

> brake
> *device to stop*
> *vehicle; rough*
> *ground; stop*
> *with brake*
> VERB
> △ brakes
> △ braked
> △ braking
> ⚠ break

bra|less
bram|ble
bram|bling
bran
Bran|agh
branch
  NOUN
  △ bran|ches
  VERB
  △ bran|ches
  △ branched
  △ branch|ing
branched
branch|ing
branch|less
brand
  VERB
  △ brands
  △ bran|ded
  △ brand|ing
Bran|den|burg
bran|dish
  △ bran|di|shes
  △ bran|dished
  △ bran|dish|ing
brand-new
Brando
Brandt
brandy
  △ bran|dies
brandy-snap
Bran|son
Braque
brash
  △ brasher
  △ brash|est
brashly
brash|ness
Bra|sí|lia
brass
  NOUN
  △ bras|ses
bras|serie
bras|sica

bras|si|ère
bras|sily
bras|si|ness
brassy
△ bras|sier
△ bras|si|est
brat
Bratby
Bra|ti|slava
Braun
bra|vado
brave
ADJ.
△ braver
△ bravest
VERB
△ braves
△ braved
△ bra|ving
bravely
*Brave New
World*
bravery
bravo
NOUN
shout
△ bra|vos
ruffian
△ bra|vos *or*
bra|voes
bra|vura
brawl
VERB
△ brawls
△ brawled
△ brawl|ing
braw|ler
brawl|ing
brawn
braw|ni|ness
brawny
△ braw|nier
△ braw|ni|est
bray

VERB
△ brays
△ brayed
△ bray|ing
braze
△ bra|zes
△ brazed
△ bra|zing
bra|zen
VERB
△ bra|zens
△ bra|zened
△ bra|zen|ing
bra|zenly
bra|zen|ness
bra|zier
Bra|zil
state
bra|zil
wood; nut
bra|zing
Braz|za|ville

breach
break
NOUN
△ brea|ches
VERB
△ brea|ches
△ breached
△ breach|ing
⚠ breech

bread
VERB
△ breads
△ breaded
△ bread|ing
bread|board
bread|crumbs
breaded
bread|fruit
bread|line
breadth
breadth|ways

breadth|wise
bread|win|ner

break
*smash;
interruption*
VERB
△ breaks
△ broke
△ break|ing
△ bro|ken
⚠ brake

break|able
break|age
break|away
break|dan|cing
break|down
breaker
break|fast
VERB
△ break|fasts
△ break|fas|ted
△ break|fast|ing
break-in
break|ing-point
break|neck
break|out
break|through
break-up
break|water
Bream
bream
sing. and pl.
breast
VERB
△ breasts
△ breas|ted
△ breast|ing
breast|bone
breast|fed
breast|feed
△ breast|feeds
△ breast|fed
△ breast|feed|ing

breast|feed|ing
breast|plate
breast|stroke
breast|work
breath
breath|alyse
△ breath|aly|ses
△ breath|alysed
△ breath|alys|
ing
Breath|aly|ser
breathe
△ breathes
△ breathed
△ brea|thing
brea|ther
breath|ily
brea|thing
brea|thing-space
breath|less
breath|lessly
breath|less|ness
breath|ta|king
breath|ta|kingly
breathy
△ breath|ier
△ breathi|est
brec|cia
Brecht
Bre|con
bred

breech
*back part of gun
barrel; buttocks*
△ bree|ches
⚠ breach

bree|ches
breed
VERB
△ breeds
△ bred
△ breed|ing
bree|der

breed|ing
breed|ing-
  ground
breeze
  VERB
  △ bree|zes
  △ breezed
  △ breez|ing
breeze|block
bree|zily
bree|zi|ness
breezy
  △ bree|zier
  △ bree|zi|est
Bre|men
Bre|mer|ha|ven
Brenda
Bren|dan
bren
Brest
breth|ren
Bre|ton
Bret|ton Woods
Breu|ghel
breve
bre|vi|ary
  △ bre|vi|ar|ies
brev|ity
brew
  VERB
  △ brews
  △ brewed
  △ brew|ing
brewer
brew|ery
  △ brew|er|ies
brew|ing
Brezh|nev
Brian
briar
bribe
  VERB
  △ bribes
  △ bribed

△ bri|bing
bri|bery
bric-à-brac
brick
  VERB
  △ bricks
  △ bricked
  △ brick|ing
brick|bat
brick|layer
brick|lay|ing
brick|work
brick|yard

> bri|dal
>   △ of a bride
>   ⚠ bridle

Bride
bride
bride|groom
Brides|head Re|
  vi|si|ted
brides|maid
bride|wealth
bridge
  VERB
  △ brid|ges
  △ bridged
  △ brid|ging
bridge-buil|der
bridge|head
Bridge of Sighs
Brid|ges
Brid|get
Bridge|town
bridge|work
Bridgwa|ter
Bri|die

> bri|dle
>   *horse's*
>   *headgear;*
>   *restraint; put*
>   *bridle on horse;*

>   *restrain; show*
>   *resentment*
>   VERB
>   △ bri|dles
>   △ bri|dled
>   △ bri|dling
>   ⚠ bridal

Brid|ling|ton
Brie
brief
  ADJ.
  △ brie|fer
  △ brief|est
  VERB
  △ briefs
  △ briefed
  △ brief|ing
brief|case
Brief En|coun|
  ter
brief|ing
briefly
brief|ness
brier *see* briar
brig
bri|gade
bri|ga|dier
brig|and
brig|an|tine
Bright
bright
  ADJ.
  △ brigh|ter
  △ bright|est
brigh|ten
  △ bright|ens
  △ bright|ened
  △ bright|en|ing
brightly
bright|ness
Brigh|ton
Brigh|ton Rock
brill

△ brill *or* brills
Bril|lat-Sav|arin
bril|li|ance
bril|li|ancy
bril|li|ant
bril|li|an|tine
bril|li|antly
brim
  VERB
  △ brims
  △ brimmed
  △ brim|ming
brim|ful
brim|less
brim|stone
Brin|disi
brin|dled
brine
bring
  △ brings
  △ brought
  △ bring|ing
brink
brink|man|ship
briny
  ADJ.
  △ bri|nier
  △ bri|ni|est
bri|oche
Briony *see*
  Bryony
bri|quette
Bris|bane
brisk
  △ bris|ker
  △ brisk|est
bris|ket
briskly
brisk|ness
bris|ling
bris|tle
  VERB
  △ bris|tles
  △ bris|tled

△ brist|ling
brist|ling
bristly
  △ brist|lier
  △ brist|li|est
Bris|tol
Brit
Brit|ain
Bri|tan|nia
Bri|tan|nic
Brit|ish
Bri|ton
Brit|tain
Brit|tan
Brit|tany
Brit|ten
brit|tle
brittle|ly
brittle|ness
brittle|star
Brno

broach
  boring tool; raise
  topic; pierce
  NOUN
  △ broa|ches
  VERB
  △ broa|ches
  △ broached
  △ broach|ing
  ⚠ brooch

B-road
broad
  ADJ.
  △ broader
  △ broad|est
broad-based
broad|cast
  VERB
  △ broad|casts
  △ broad|cast
  △ broad|cast|ing
broad|cas|ter

broad|cast|ing
broad|cloth
broaden
  △ broad|ens
  △ broad|ened
  △ broad|en|ing
broad|loom
broadly
broad-minded
broad-mind|
  edly
broad-mind|ed|
  ness
Broad|moor
broad|ness
Broads, The
broad|sheet
broad|side
Broad|stairs
broad|sword
Broad|way
Broad|wood
bro|cade
bro|caded
broc|coli
bro|chure
bro|derie ang|
  laise
brogue
broil
  △ broils
  △ broiled
  △ broil|ing
broi|ler
broke
bro|ken
bro|ken-down
bro|ken-hearted
bro|ken-heart|
  edly
bro|ken-in
bro|kenly
bro|ken|ness
bro|ker

bro|ker|age
bro|king
brolly
  △ brol|lies
bro|mel|iad
bro|mide
bro|mine
bron|chial
bron|chi|tic
bron|chi|tis
bron|cho|di|la|
  tor
bron|chus
  △ bron|chi
bronco
Bronte
bron|to|sau|rus
  △ bron|to|sau|
  ruses
Bronx
bronze
  VERB
  △ bron|zes
  △ bronzed
  △ bron|zing
Bronze Age
bronzed

brooch
  clothes-
  decoration
  △ brooches
  ⚠ broach

brood
  VERB
  △ broods
  △ broo|ded
  △ brood|ing
brood|ily
broo|di|ness
brood|ing
brood|ingly
broody
  △ broo|dier

△ broo|di|est
Brook
brook
  VERB
  △ brooks
  △ brooked
  △ brook|ing
Brooke
Brook|lyn
Brooks
broom
broom|rape
broom|stick
broth
bro|thel
bro|ther
  relative; fellow-
  member
  △ brothers
  monk
  △ brothers *or*
    breth|ren
bro|ther|hood
bro|ther-in-law
  △ bro|thers-in-
  law
bro|therly
Bro|thers Ka|ra|
  ma|zov, The
brougham
brought
brou|haha
brow
brow|beat
  △ brow|beats
  △ brow|beat
  △ brow|beat|ing
  △ brow|bea|ten
brow|bea|ten
Brown
brown
  ADJ.
  △ brow|ner
  △ brown|est

VERB
△ browns
△ browned
△ brown|ing
Browne
Brow|nie
member of girls'
organization
brow|nie
goblin; cake
Brown|ing
author; rifle
brown|ing
gravy thickener
Brown|ing Ver|
sion, The
brown|ish
brown|ness
Brown|shirt
browse
VERB
△ brow|ses
△ browsed
△ brow|sing
Bruce
bru|cel|lo|sis
Bruck|ner
Brueghel *see*
Breughel
Bru|ges
bruise
VERB
△ bruises
△ bruised
△ bruis|ing
bruised
bruiser
bruis|ing
bruit
△ bruits
△ bruited
△ bruit|ing
brûlé
Brum|mell

brunch
△ brun|ches
Bru|nei
Bru|nel
bru|nette
Brun|hild
Bruno
Bruns|wick
brunt
brush
NOUN
△ bru|shes
VERB
△ bru|shes
△ brushed
△ brush|ing
brushed
brush-off
brush-up
brush|wood
brush|work
brusque
brusquely
brusque|ness
Brus|sels
bru|tal
Bru|tal|ism
bru|tal|ity
△ bru|tal|it|ies
bru|tal|iza|tion
bru|tal|ize
△ bru|tal|izes
△ bru|tal|ized
△ bru|tal|izing
bru|tally
brute
bru|tish
bru|tishly
bru|tish|ness
Bru|tus
Brynhild *see*
Brunhild
Bry|ony
bry|ony

△ bry|on|ies
Bryo|phyta
bryo|phyte
Bry|thonic
B-side
bub|ble
VERB
△ bub|bles
△ bub|bled
△ bub|bling
bubble-jet
Bub|bles
bub|bly
ADJ.
△ bub|blier
△ bub|bli|est
bubo
△ bu|boes
buc|cal
buc|can|eer
buc|can|eer|ing
Buchan
Bu|char|est
Bu|ch|ner
Buck
buck
VERB
△ bucks
△ bucked
△ buck|ing
bucked
bucket
VERB
△ buck|ets
△ buck|eted
△ buck|et|ing
buck|et|ful
Buck|ing|ham
Buck|ing|ham|
shire
buckle
VERB
△ buckles
△ buckled

△ buck|ling
buckled
buck|ler
buck|min|ster|
ful|ler|ene
buck|ram
buck|shee
buck|shot
buck|skin
buck|thorn
buck|tooth
buck|toothed
buck|wheat
bu|colic
bu|col|ic|ally
bud
VERB
△ buds
△ bud|ded
△ bud|ding
Bu|da|pest
Budd
Bud|dha
Bud|dhism
Bud|dhist
bud|ding
bud|dleia
buddy
NOUN
△ bud|dies
VERB
△ bud|dies
△ bud|died
△ bud|dy|ing
budge
△ bud|ges
△ budged
△ bud|ging
bud|geri|gar
bud|get
VERB
△ bud|gets
△ bud|geted
△ bud|get|ing

bud|get|ary
bud|get|ing
bud|gie
Bue|nos Aires
Buerk
buff
 VERB
 △ buffs
 △ buffed
 △ buf|fing
Buf|falo
buf|falo
 △ buf|falo *or*
 buf|fa|loes
buf|fer
buf|fered
buf|fet
 VERB
 △ buf|fets
 △ buf|feted
 △ buf|fet|ing
buf|fet|ing
buf|foon
buf|foon|ery
bug
 VERB
 △ bugs
 △ bugged
 △ bug|ging
buga|boo
Bu|gatti
bug|bear
bug-eyed
bug|ger
 VERB
 △ bug|gers
 △ bug|gered
 △ bug|ger|ing
bug|gery
buggy
 △ bug|gies
bugle
 VERB
 △ bugles

△ bugled
△ bu|gling
bu|gler
buhl
build
 △ builds
 △ built
 △ build|ing
buil|der
build|ing
build|ing-block
build-up
built-up
Bu|jum|bura
Buk|harin
bulb
bul|bous
Bul|ga|nin
Bul|garia
Bul|gar|ian
Bul|gars
bulge
 VERB
 △ bul|ges
 △ bulged
 △ bul|ging
bul|ghar wheat
bul|ging
bulgy
 △ bul|gier
 △ bul|gi|est
bu|limia
bulk
bulk|head
bulk|ily
bul|ki|ness
bulky
 △ bul|kier
 △ bul|ki|est
Bull
bull
bull|dog
bull|doze
 △ bull|do|zes

△ bull|dozed
△ bull|do|zing
bull|do|zer
bul|let
bul|letin
bul|letin-board
bul|let-proof
bull|fight
bull|figh|ter
bull|fight|ing
bull|finch
bull|frog
bull|head
bul|lion
bul|lish
bul|lishly
bul|lish|ness
bull-mas|tiff
bull-necked
bul|lock
bull|ring
bull's-eye
bull|shit
 VERB
 △ bull|shits
 △ bull|shit|ted
 △ bull|shit|ting
bully
 NOUN
 △ bul|lies
 VERB
 △ bul|lies
 △ bul|lied
 △ bul|ly|ing
bully-boy
bul|ly|ing
Bülow
bul|rush
 △ bul|ru|shes
bul|wark
bum
 VERB
 △ bums
 △ bummed

△ bum|ming
bum|bag
bum|ble
 △ bum|bles
 △ bum|bled
 △ bum|bling
bum|bling
bumf
bum|mer
bump
 VERB
 △ bumps
 △ bumped
 △ bump|ing
bum|per
bump|ily
bum|pi|ness
bump|kin
bump|tious
bump|tiously
bump|tious|ness
bumpy
 △ bum|pier
 △ bum|pi|est
bun
bunch
 NOUN
 △ bun|ches
 VERB
 △ bun|ches
 △ bunched
 △ bunch|ing
bunch|ing
bunchy
 △ bunch|ier
 △ bun|chi|est
Bun|des|bank
Bun|des|tag
bun|dle
 VERB
 △ bun|dles
 △ bun|dled
 △ bund|ling
bung

VERB
△ bungs
△ bunged
△ bung|ing
bun|ga|low
bun|gee
bung|hole
bun|gle
  VERB
  △ bun|gles
  △ bun|gled
  △ bun|gling
bungled
bun|gler
bun|gling
bun|ion
bunk
  VERB
  △ bunks
  △ bunked
  △ bunk|ing
bun|ker
bunk|house
bun|kum
bunny
  △ bun|nies
bun|raku
Bun|sen
bun|sen bur|ner
bun|ting
Buñuel
Bun|yan
buoy
  VERB
  △ buoys
  △ buoyed
  △ buoy|ing
buoy|ancy
buoy|ant
buoy|antly

bur
prickly seedcase
⚠ burr

Bur|bage
bur|ble
  △ bur|bles
  △ bur|bled
  △ bur|bling
bur|bot
  △ bur|bot *or*
    bur|bots
bur|den
  VERB
  △ bur|dens
  △ bur|dened
  △ bur|den|ing
bur|den|some
bur|dock
bur|eau
  △ bur|eaux *or*
    bur|eaus
bur|eau|cracy
  △ bur|eau|cra|cies
bur|eau|crat
bur|eau|cratic
bur|eau|crat|ic|ally
bur|eau de
  change
bur|ette
bur|geon
  △ bur|geons
  △ bur|geoned
  △ bur|geon|ing
bur|geon|ing
bur|ger
Bur|gess
bur|gess
  △ bur|ges|ses

burgh
Scottish town
⚠ borough

bur|gher
Bur|ghers of
  Cal|ais, The
burg|lar
burg|lary

△ burg|lar|ies
bur|gle
  △ bur|gles
  △ bur|gled
  △ bur|gling
bur|go|mas|ter
Bur|gos
Bur|gundy
bur|ial
burin
burk *see* berk
Burke
Bur|kina
bur|lesque
  VERB
  △ bur|lesques
  △ bur|lesqued
  △ bur|les|quing
bur|li|ness
burly
  △ bur|lier
  △ bur|li|est
Burma
Bur|mese
burn
  VERB
  △ burns
  △ burned *or*
    burnt
  △ burn|ing
Burne-Jones
bur|ner
Bur|net
Bur|nett
Bur|ney
burn|ing
bur|nish
  △ bur|ni|shes
  △ bur|nished
  △ bur|nish|ing
bur|nished
bur|nish|ing
Burn|ley
bur|nous

△ bur|nouses
burn-out
Burns
burnt
burp
  VERB
  △ burps
  △ burped
  △ burp|ing

burr
rough sound or
surface; make
this sound
  VERB
  △ burrs
  △ burred
  △ bur|ring
  ⚠ bur

burr
prickly seedcase
see *bur*
bur|rito
Bur|roughs
bur|row
  VERB
  △ bur|rows
  △ bur|rowed
  △ bur|row|ing
bur|sar
bur|sary
  △ bur|sar|ies
burst
  VERB
  △ bursts
  △ burst
  △ burst|ing
burst|ing
burthen *see*
  burden
Bur|ton
bur|ton
Bur|ton-upon-
  Trent

Bur|undi
Bury
bury
△ bur|ies
△ bur|ied
△ bury|ing
Bury St
Edmunds
bus
NOUN
△ buses
VERB
△ buses
△ bused or
bussed
△ bus|ing or
bus|sing
Busby
busby
△ bus|bies
Bush
bush
NOUN
△ bushes
VERB
△ bushes
△ bushed
△ bush|ing
bush|baby
△ bush|ba|bies
bushed
bushel
bu|shido
bush|ily
bushi|ness
Bush|man
S African
tribesman
△ Bush|men
bush|man
Australasian
bush-dweller
△ bush|men
bush|ranger

bush|whack
△ bush|whacks
△ bush|whacked
△ bush|whack|
ing
bush|whacker
bush|whack|ing
bushy
△ bush|ier
△ bushi|est
bus|ily

busi|ness
job
△ busi|nes|ses
⚠ busyness

busi|ness|like
busi|ness|man
△ busi|ness|men
busi|ness|wo|
man
△ busi|ness|wo|
men
busk
△ busks
△ busked
△ busk|ing
busker
busk|ing
bust
VERB
△ busts
△ bust or bus|
ted
△ bust|ing
bus|tard
bus|ter
bus|tle
VERB
△ bus|tles
△ bus|tled
△ bust|ling
bust|ler
bust|ling

bust-up
busty
△ bus|tier
△ bus|ti|est
busy
ADJ.
△ bus|ier
△ busi|est
VERB
△ bus|ies
△ bus|ied
△ busy|ing
busy|body
△ busy|bod|ies

busy|ness
having a lot to do
⚠ business

but
bu|tane
butch
but|cher
VERB
△ but|chers
△ but|chered
△ but|cher|ing
but|chery
△ but|cher|ies
Bute
But|ler
but|ler
But|lin
butt
VERB
△ butts
△ but|ted
△ but|ting
butte
but|ter
VERB
△ but|ters
△ but|tered
△ but|ter|ing
but|ter|cup

but|tered
but|ter|fin|gers
but|ter|fly
△ but|ter|flies
but|ter-knife
△ but|ter-knives
but|ter|milk
but|ter|pat
but|ter|scotch
but|ter|wort
but|tery
NOUN
△ but|ter|ies
but|tock
but|ton
VERB
△ but|tons
△ but|toned
△ but|ton|ing
but|ton|hole
VERB
△ but|ton|holes
△ but|ton|holed
△ but|ton|holing
but|tress
NOUN
△ but|tres|ses
VERB
△ but|tres|ses
△ but|tressed
△ but|tres|sing
butty
△ but|ties
buxom
△ bux|omer
△ bux|om|est
Bux|te|hude
Bux|ton
buy
VERB
△ buys
△ bought
△ buy|ing
buyer

buy|out
buzz
  NOUN
  △ buz|zes
  VERB
  △ buz|zes
  △ buzzed
  △ buz|zing
buz|zard
buz|zer
bwana

by
  NOUN
  use only in

*phrase 'by the
by'*
  △ byes
  ⚠ bye

bye
  *in cricket and in
competitions;
goodbye*
  ⚠ by

bye-bye
Byelarus *see*
  Belorussia

by-elec|tion
by|gone
by-law
by|line
by|name
by|pass
  NOUN
  △ by|pas|ses
  VERB
  △ by|pas|ses
  △ by|passed
  △ by|pas|sing
by-play
by-prod|uct

Byrd
byre
by|road
By|ron
by|stan|der
byte
by|way
by|word
Byz|an|tine *or*
  By|zan|tine
  *according to
pronunciation*

C

cab
cabal
Ca|ballé
cab|aret
cab|bage
cabby
△ cab|bies
caber
cabin
cab|inet
cab|inet-maker
cab|inet-mak|ing
Cab|inet of Dr
Ca|li|gari, The
(Das Ka|bi|
nett des Dr
Ca|li|gari)
ca|ble
VERB
△ ca|bles
△ ca|bled
△ ca|bling
cable|gram
cable|vi|sion
ca|boo|dle
ca|boose
Cabot
cab|ri|ole
cab|rio|let
cacao
cache
VERB
△ ca|ches
△ cached
△ cach|ing
ca|chet
cach|exia
cack-han|ded
cackle
VERB
△ cackles
△ cackled

△ cack|ling
ca|co|phon|ous
ca|co|phony
△ ca|co|phon|ies
cac|tus
△ cacti *or* cac|
tuses
cad
ca|da|ver
ca|da|ver|ous
Cad|bury

---

cad|die
golf assistant;
act as such
VERB
△ cad|dies
△ cad|died
△ cad|dy|ing
⚠ caddy

---

cad|dish

---

caddy
tea container
△ cad|dies
⚠ caddie

Cade
ca|dence
ca|denza
Cader Idris
cadet
cadge
△ cad|ges
△ cadged
△ cad|ging
cad|ger
cadi
Cad|il|lac
Cádiz
cad|mium
Cad|mus
cadre
cae|cal
cae|cil|ian

cae|cum
△ caeca
Caed|mon
Caen
Caenozoic *see*
Cenozoic
Caer|nar|von
Caer|philly
Cae|sar
cae|sar|ean
cae|sium
cae|sura
café
ca|fe|teria
ca|fe|ti|ère
caf|feine
caf|tan
Cage
cage
VERB
△ cages
△ caged
△ ca|ging
cage|bird
caged
cagey
△ ca|gier
△ ca|gi|est
ca|gily
ca|gi|ness
Ca|gli|ari
Cag|ney
ca|goule
ca|hoots
Caia|phas
caiman *see*
cayman
Cain
Caine
Cainozoic *see*
Cenozoic
ca|ique
cairn
cairn|gorm

type of quartz
Cairn|gorms
mountain range
Cairo
cais|son
ca|jole
△ ca|joles
△ ca|joled
△ ca|jo|ling
ca|jo|lery
cake
VERB
△ cakes
△ caked
△ caking
cake|hole
cake|walk
VERB
△ cake|walks
△ cake|walked
△ cake|walk|ing
cala|bash
△ cala|ba|shes
ca|la|boose
cala|brese
Ca|lab|ria
Cal|ais
cala|mine
ca|lam|it|ous
ca|lam|it|ously
ca|lam|ity
△ ca|lam|it|ies
Ca|lam|ity Jane
cal|car|eous
cal|ceo|laria
cal|ci|cole
cal|ci|ferol
cal|ci|fer|ous
cal|ci|fi|ca|tion
cal|ci|fuge
cal|cify
△ cal|ci|fies
△ cal|ci|fied
△ cal|ci|fy|ing

cal|cite
cal|cium
cal|cu|lable
cal|cu|lably
cal|cu|late
△ cal|cu|lates
△ cal|cu|la|ted
△ cal|cu|la|ting
cal|cu|la|ted
cal|cu|la|ting
cal|cu|la|tingly
cal|cu|la|tion
cal|cu|la|tor
cal|cu|lus
△ cal|culi
Cal|cutta
cal|dera
Cal|derón de la
  Barca
Cald|well
Ca|ledo|nian

cal|en|dar
for dates
  ⚠ calender
  ⚠ colander

cal|en|der
press
VERB
△ cal|en|ders
△ cal|en|dered
△ cal|en|der|ing
  ⚠ calendar
  ⚠ colander

cal|ends
calf
△ calves
calf|skin
Cal|gary
cal|ib|rate
△ cal|ib|rates
△ cal|ib|ra|ted
△ cal|ib|ra|ting

cal|ib|ra|tion
cal|ibre
cal|ico
△ cali|coes
Ca|li|for|nia
Ca|li|for|nian
ca|li|for|nium
Ca|lig|ula
ca|liph
ca|liph|ate
call
VERB
△ calls
△ called
△ call|ing
Cal|laghan
Cal|las
cal|ler
cal|li|gra|pher
cal|li|graph|ist
cal|li|gra|phy
call|ing
call|ing-card
cal|li|per
cal|lis|thenic
cal|lis|then|ics
cal|los|ity
△ cal|los|it|ies

cal|lous
hard-hearted
  ⚠ callus

cal|lously
cal|lous|ness
cal|low
△ cal|lower
△ cal|low|est
call-up

cal|lus
pad of skin
△ cal|luses
  ⚠ callous

calm

VERB
△ calms
△ calmed
△ calm|ing
ADJ.
△ calmer
△ calm|est
calmly
calm|ness
cal|orie
cal|or|ific
cal|ori|meter
calque
Calum
ca|lum|ni|ate
△ ca|lum|ni|ates
△ ca|lum|ni|ated
△ ca|lum|ni|
  ating
ca|lum|ni|ator
ca|lum|ni|ous
cal|umny
△ cal|um|nies
Cal|vary
place
cal|vary
*representation of
the Crucifixion*
△ cal|var|ies
calve
△ calves
△ calved
△ calving
Cal|vin
Cal|vin|ism
Cal|vin|ist
Cal|vin|is|tic
calx
△ cal|ces *or*
  calxes
ca|lypso
calyx
△ calyces *or*
  calyxes

cal|zone
cam
ca|ma|rad|erie
Cam|argue
cam|ber
cam|bium
Cam|bo|dia
Cam|brian
cam|bric
Cam|bridge
Cam|bridge|
  shire
cam|cor|der
Cam|den
came
camel
cam|el|hair
ca|mel|lia
Cam|elot
Cam|em|bert
cameo
cam|era
cam|era|man
△ cam|era|men
cam|era-shy
Cam|eron
Cam|er|oon
ca|mi|knick|ers
Ca|milla
ca|mi|sole
Camões
camo|mile
Ca|morra
ca|mou|flage
VERB
△ ca|mou|fla|ges
△ ca|mou|flaged
△ ca|mou|fla|
  ging
camp
VERB
△ camps
△ camped
△ camp|ing

cam|paign
  VERB
  △ cam|paigns
  △ cam|paigned
  △ cam|paign|ing
cam|paigner
cam|pa|nile
cam|pa|no|lo|gist
cam|pa|nol|ogy
cam|pan|ula
Camp|bell
camper
camp-fol|lower
cam|phor
cam|phor|ated
camp|ing
Cam|pion
cam|pion
camp|site
cam|pus
  △ cam|puses
Cam|py|lo|bac|ter
cam|shaft
Camus
can
  VERB
  be able
  △ can
  △ could
can
  VERB
  put into tins
  △ cans
  △ canned
  △ can|ning
Can|aan
Can|ada
Ca|na|dian
canal
Ca|na|letto
ca|nal|iza|tion
ca|nal|ize
  △ ca|nal|izes
  △ ca|nal|ized

△ ca|nal|izing
can|apé
ca|nard *or* can|
  ard
  according to
  pronunciation
ca|nary
  △ ca|nar|ies
Ca|nary Is|lands
can|asta
Ca|na|veral
Can|berra
can|can
can|cel
  △ can|cels
  △ can|celled
  △ can|cel|ling
can|cel|la|tion
Can|cer
  sign of zodiac
can|cer
  disease
Can|cer|ian
can|cer|ous
can|dela
can|de|lab|rum
  △ can|de|labra
    or can|de|lab|
    rums
Can|dice
can|did

Can|dida
by G. B. Shaw
  ⚠ *Candide*

can|di|dacy
  △ can|di|da|cies
can|did|ate
can|di|da|ture

Can|dide
by Voltaire
  ⚠ *Candida*

can|didly

can|did|ness
can|died
can|dle
candle|light
candle|lit
Candle|mas
  △ Candle|mas|ses
candle|stick
candle|wick
can|dour
candy
  NOUN
  △ can|dies
  VERB
  △ can|dies
  △ can|died
  △ can|dy|ing
can|dy|floss
candy-striped
can|dy|tuft
cane
  VERB
  △ canes
  △ caned
  △ caning
cane-sugar
Can|etti
can|ful
can|ine *or* ca|
  nine
  according to
  pronunciation
caning
can|is|ter
can|ker
can|ker|ous
can|na|bis
canned
can|nel|loni
can|nery
  △ can|ner|ies
Cannes
can|ni|bal
can|ni|bal|ism

can|ni|bal|is|tic
can|ni|bal|ize
  △ can|ni|bal|izes
  △ can|ni|bal|ized
  △ can|ni|bal|
    izing
can|nily
can|ni|ness
Can|ning

can|non
  NOUN
  gun
  sing. and pl.
  billiards stroke
  △ can|nons
  VERB
  collide
  △ can|nons
  △ can|noned
  △ can|non|ing
    ⚠ canon

can|non|ade
can|non|ball
can|not
can|nula
  △ can|nu|lae *or*
    can|nu|las
canny
  △ can|nier
  △ can|ni|est
canoe
  VERB
  △ ca|noes
  △ ca|noed
  △ ca|noe|ing
ca|noe|ing
ca|noe|ist

canon
  rule; list;
  clergyman;
  musical form
  ⚠ cannon

ca|non|ical
can|on|iza|tion
can|on|ize
△ can|on|izes
△ can|on|ized
△ can|on|izing
ca|noo|dle
△ ca|noo|dles
△ ca|noo|dled
△ ca|nood|ling
can-opener
cano|pied
can|opy
△ cano|pies
Can|ova
canst
cant
VERB
△ cants
△ can|ted
△ cant|ing
can't
can|ta|bile
can|ta|loup
can|tan|ker|ous
can|tan|ker|
ously
can|tan|ker|ous|
ness
*Can|tar de Mio
Cid (Song of
my Cid)*
can|tata
can|teen
can|ter
VERB
△ can|ters
△ can|tered
△ can|ter|ing
Can|ter|bury
can|ticle
can|ti|lever
cant|ing
cant|ingly

canto
Can|ton
can|ton
Can|ton|ese
can|ton|ment
can|tor
*Can't Pay,
Won't Pay
(Non si paga!
non si paga!)*
canula *see*
cannula
Can|ute

can|vas
*heavy cloth;
painting*
△ can|vases
⚠ canvass

can|vass
*seek votes,
opinions; discuss*
△ can|vas|ses
△ can|vassed
△ can|vas|sing
⚠ canvas

can|vas|ser
can|yon
cap
VERB
△ caps
△ capped
△ cap|ping
ca|pa|bil|ity
△ ca|pa|bil|it|ies
ca|pable
ca|pably
ca|pa|cious
ca|pa|ciously
ca|pa|cious|ness
ca|pa|ci|tance
ca|pa|ci|tor
ca|pa|city

△ ca|pa|ci|ties
ca|pari|son
VERB
△ ca|pari|sons
△ ca|pari|soned
△ ca|pari|son|ing
cape
caper
VERB
△ ca|pers
△ ca|pered
△ ca|per|ing
ca|per|cail|zie
Capet
Ca|pet|ian
Cape Town
Cape Verde
ca|pil|lar|ity
ca|pil|lary
△ ca|pil|lar|ies
cap|ita
cap|ital
cap|ital-inten|
sive
cap|it|al|ism
cap|it|al|ist
cap|it|al|is|tic
cap|it|al|iza|tion
cap|it|al|ize
△ cap|it|al|izes
△ cap|it|al|ized
△ cap|it|al|izing
cap|it|ally
ca|pi|ta|tion
Cap|itol
Ca|pi|to|line
ca|pit|ulate
△ ca|pit|ulates
△ ca|pit|ula|ted
△ ca|pit|ula|ting
ca|pit|ula|tion
ca|pit|ulum
△ ca|pit|ula
Ca|po|di|monte

capon
Ca|pone
Ca|pote
Cap|pa|do|cia
cap|puc|cino
Capra
Capri
cap|ric|cio
△ cap|ricci *or*
cap|ric|cios
cap|rice
Cap|ri|chos, Los
cap|ri|cious
cap|ri|ciously
cap|ri|cious|ness
Cap|ri|corn
Cap|ri|cor|nian
cap|si|cum
cap|siz|able
cap|size
VERB
△ cap|sizes
△ cap|sized
△ cap|sizing
cap|stan
cap|su|lar
cap|sule
cap|sul|ize
△ cap|sul|izes
△ cap|sul|ized
△ cap|sul|izing
cap|tain
VERB
△ cap|tains
△ cap|tained
△ cap|tain|ing
cap|taincy
△ cap|tain|cies
cap|tion
VERB
△ cap|tions
△ cap|tioned
△ cap|tion|ing
cap|tious

cap|tiously
cap|tious|ness
cap|ti|vate
△ cap|ti|vates
△ cap|ti|va|ted
△ cap|ti|va|ting
cap|ti|va|ting
cap|ti|va|tingly
cap|ti|va|tion
cap|tive
cap|tiv|ity
cap|tor
cap|ture
VERB
△ cap|tures
△ cap|tured
△ cap|tur|ing
cap|turer
Ca|pu|chin
monk
ca|pu|chin
monkey
ca|py|bara
car
Ca|ra|cas
Ca|rac|ta|cus
ca|rafe
ca|ram|bola
ca|ra|mel
ca|ra|mel|iza|
tion
ca|ra|mel|ize
△ ca|ra|mel|izes
△ ca|ra|mel|ized
△ ca|ra|mel|izing
ca|ra|pace

ca|rat
jewellers' unit
⚠ caret
⚠ carrot

Caratacus *see*
Caractacus
Ca|ra|vag|gio

ca|ra|van
VERB
△ ca|ra|vans
△ ca|ra|vanned
△ ca|ra|van|ning
ca|ra|van|ette
ca|ra|van|ning
ca|ra|van|serai
ca|ra|vel
ca|ra|way
car|bide
car|bine
car|bo|hy|drate
car|bon
car|bo|na|ceous
car|bon|ate
car|bon|ated
car|bon|ation
car|bonic
car|bon|if|er|ous
car|bon|iza|tion
car|bon|ize
△ car|bon|izes
△ car|bon|ized
△ car|bon|izing
car|bo|run|dum
car|boy
car|bun|cle
car|bu|ret|tor
car|case
Car|cas|sonne
Car|chem|ish
car|ci|no|gen
car|ci|no|genic
car|ci|noma
card
VERB
△ cards
△ car|ded
△ card|ing
car|da|mom
card|board
card-car|ry|ing
car|diac

Car|diff
Car|di|gan
town; famous
soldier
car|di|gan
garment
car|di|nal
car|din|al|ate
card|ing
car|dio|gram
car|dio|graph
car|dio|gra|pher
car|dio|gra|phy
car|di|olo|gist
car|di|ol|ogy
car|dio|pul|mon|
ary
car|dio|vas|cu|lar
card|phone
card-sharp
card-shar|per
care
VERB
△ cares
△ cared
△ caring
ca|reen
△ ca|reens
△ ca|reened
△ ca|reen|ing
ca|reer
VERB
△ ca|reers
△ ca|reered
△ ca|reer|ing
ca|reer|ism
ca|reer|ist
care|free
care|ful
care|fully
care|ful|ness
care|less
care|lessly
care|less|ness

carer
ca|ress
NOUN
△ ca|res|ses
VERB
△ ca|res|ses
△ ca|ressed
△ ca|res|sing

caret
omission sign
⚠ carat
⚠ carrot

care|ta|ker
Care|ta|ker, The
care|worn
cargo
△ car|goes
Carib
Ca|rib|bean
ca|ri|bou
△ ca|ri|bous *or*
ca|ri|bou
ca|ri|ca|ture
VERB
△ ca|ri|ca|tures
△ ca|ri|ca|tured
△ ca|ri|ca|tur|ing
ca|ri|ca|tur|ist
car|ies
ca|ril|lon
caring
car|jack|ing
Carl
Car|lisle
Car|lyle
Car|mar|then
Car|mel
Car|mel|ite
Car|men
Car|mina Bur|ana
car|mine
carn|age
car|nal

car|nal|ity
carn|ally
car|na|tion
Carné
Car|negie
carnelian *see*
  cornelian
car|ni|val
Car|ni|val of the
  Ani|mals, The
  (Car|na|val
  des ani|maux,
  Le)
car|ni|vore
car|ni|vor|ous
carob
Carol
carol
  VERB
  △ car|ols
  △ car|olled
  △ car|ol|ling
Ca|ro|line
Ca|ro|lin|gians
Ca|ro|lyn
carom
ca|ro|tene
ca|ro|ten|oid
ca|ro|tid
ca|rou|sal
ca|rouse
  △ ca|rou|ses
  △ ca|roused
  △ ca|rous|ing
ca|rou|sel
carp
  NOUN
  △ carp *or* carps
  VERB
  △ carps
  △ carped
  △ carp|ing
car|pal
Car|pa|thian

car|pel
car|pen|ter
car|pen|try
carper
car|pet
  VERB
  △ car|pets
  △ car|peted
  △ car|pet|ing
car|pet-bag
car|pet|bag|ger
car|pet|ing
carpet-sweeper
carp|ing
carp|ingly
car|port
car|pus
  △ carpi
car|rel
car|riage
car|riage|way
car|rier
Car|ring|ton
car|rion
Car|roll

car|rot
  vegetable
  ⚠ carat
  ⚠ caret

car|roty
carry
  △ car|ries
  △ car|ried
  △ car|ry|ing
car|ry|cot
car|ry|ing
carry-on
carry-out
car-sick
car-sick|ness
cart
  VERB
  △ carts

△ car|ted
△ cart|ing
Carte
carte blanche
car|tel
Car|ter
Car|tes|ian
Car|thage
cart|horse
Car|thu|sian
Car|tier-Bres|
  son
car|ti|lage
car|ti|la|gin|ous
Cart|land
car|to|gra|pher
car|to|graphic
car|to|gra|phy
car|ton
car|toon
car|toon|ist
car|touche
cart|ridge
cart|wheel
  VERB
  △ cart|wheels
  △ cart|wheeled
  △ cart|wheel|ing
Ca|ruso
carve
  △ carves
  △ carved
  △ car|ving
car|vel-built
car|ver
car|very
  △ car|ver|ies
carve-up
car|ving
car|ving-fork
car|ving-knife
  △ car|ving-
    knives
Cary

ca|ry|atid
  △ ca|ry|at|ids *or*
    ca|ry|at|ides
Ca|sa|blanca
Ca|sals
Ca|sa|nova
cas|cade
  VERB
  △ cas|cades
  △ cas|ca|ded
  △ cas|ca|ding
case
  VERB
  △ cases
  △ cased
  △ ca|sing
case|book
ca|sein
case|ment
case|work
cash
  VERB
  △ ca|shes
  △ cashed
  △ cash|ing
cash-and-carry
  △ cash-and-car|
    ries
cashew *or* ca|
  shew
  according to
  pronunciation
ca|shier
  VERB
  △ ca|shiers
  △ ca|shiered
  △ ca|shier|ing
cash|less
cash|mere
cash|phone
ca|sing
ca|sino
cask
cas|ket

Cas|pian
Cas|san|dra
cas|sava
cas|ser|ole
 VERB
 △ cas|ser|oles
 △ cas|ser|oled
 △ cas|ser|oling
cas|sette
 △ cas|sette-
  player
cas|si|ter|ite
Cas|sius
cas|sock
cas|so|wary
 △ cas|so|war|ies

cast
actors in play;
throw
 VERB
 △ casts
 △ cast
 △ cast|ing
 ⚠ caste

cas|ta|nets
cast|away

caste
social class
 ⚠ cast

cas|tel|lated
cas|tel|la|tion

cas|ter
sugar sprinkler
 ⚠ castor

cas|ti|gate
 △ cas|ti|gates
 △ cas|ti|ga|ted
 △ cas|ti|ga|ting
cas|ti|ga|tion
cas|ting
cast-iron

 ADJ.
cas|tle
 VERB
 △ cas|tles
 △ cas|tled
 △ cast|ling
Cas|tle
Castle|reagh
cast-off

cas|tor
furniture wheel
 ⚠ caster

Cas|tor
cas|trate
 △ cas|trates
 △ cas|tra|ted
 △ cas|tra|ting
cas|tra|ted
cas|tra|tion
cas|trato
 △ cas|trati *or*
  cas|tra|tos
Cas|tro
casual
casu|ally
casu|al|ness
casu|alty
 △ casu|al|ties
casu|ist
casu|is|tic
casu|is|try
cat
ca|ta|bol|ism
ca|ta|clysm
ca|ta|clys|mic
ca|ta|comb
ca|ta|falque
Ca|ta|lan
ca|ta|lepsy
 △ ca|ta|lep|sies
ca|ta|lep|tic
ca|ta|logue

 VERB
 △ ca|ta|logues
 △ ca|ta|logued
 △ ca|ta|loguing
ca|ta|loguer
Ca|ta|lo|nia
ca|ta|lysis
 △ ca|ta|lyses
ca|ta|lyst
ca|ta|lytic
ca|ta|lyse
 △ ca|ta|lyses
 △ ca|ta|lysed
 △ ca|ta|ly|sing
ca|ta|ma|ran
ca|ta|plec|tic
ca|ta|plexis
ca|ta|plexy
 △ ca|ta|plex|ies
ca|ta|pult
 VERB
 △ ca|ta|pults
 △ ca|ta|pul|ted
 △ ca|ta|pult|ing
ca|ta|ract
ca|tarrh
ca|tar|rhal
ca|ta|stro|phe
ca|ta|stro|phic
ca|ta|stroph|ic|
 ally
ca|ta|to|nia
ca|ta|tonic
cat|call
catch
 NOUN
 △ cat|ches
 VERB
 △ cat|ches
 △ caught
 △ catch|ing
Catch-22
catch-22
catch-all

cat|cher
Cat|cher in the
 Rye, The
cat|chi|ness
catch|ing
catch|ment
catch|penny
catch|phrase
catch|word
cat|chy
 △ cat|chier
 △ cat|chi|est
cat|ech|ism
cat|ech|ize
 △ cat|ech|izes
 △ cat|ech|ized
 △ cat|ech|izing
cat|eg|or|ical
cat|eg|or|ic|ally
cat|eg|or|iza|tion
cat|eg|or|ize
 △ cat|eg|or|izes
 △ cat|eg|or|ized
 △ cat|eg|or|izing
cat|eg|ory
 △ cat|eg|or|ies
ca|ten|ary
 △ ca|ten|ar|ies
cater
 △ ca|ters
 △ ca|tered
 △ ca|ter|ing
ca|terer
ca|ter|ing
cat|er|pil|lar
cat|er|waul
 VERB
 △ cat|er|wauls
 △ cat|er|wauled
 △ cat|er|waul|ing
cat|er|waul|ing
Catesby
cat|fish
sing. and pl.

cat|gut
ca|thar|sis
△ ca|thar|ses
ca|thar|tic
ca|thed|ral
Cath|er|ine
cath|eter
cath|ode
cath|olic
ca|tho|li|city
Ca|ti|line
cat|ion
cat|kin
cat|mint
cat|nap
VERB
△ cat|naps
△ cat|napped
△ cat|nap|ping
cat|nip
Cato
Cat on a Hot
Tin Roof
cat-o'-nine-tails
Cat|ri|ona
Cats
cat|suit
cat|tery
△ cat|ter|ies
cat|tily
cat|ti|ness
cattle
cat|tleya
catty
△ cat|tier
△ cat|ti|est

Ca|tul|lus
cat|walk
Cau|ca|sian
Cau|cas|oid
Cau|ca|sus
cau|cus
△ cau|cuses
cau|dal
caud|ate
caught
caul
caul|dron
cauli|flower
caulk
△ caulks
△ caulked
△ caulk|ing
causal
caus|al|ity
caus|ally
caus|ation
caus|at|ive
caus|at|ively
cause
VERB
△ cau|ses
△ caused
△ caus|ing
cause cé|lèbre
△ *causes cé|lèbres*
cause|way
caus|tic
caus|tic|ally
caus|ti|city
cau|ter|iza|tion
cau|ter|ize

△ cau|ter|izes
△ cau|ter|ized
△ cau|ter|izing
cau|tion
VERB
△ cau|tions
△ cau|tioned
△ cau|tion|ing
cau|tion|ary
cau|tious
cau|tiously
cau|tious|ness
ca|val|cade
ca|va|lier
ca|va|lierly
cav|alry
△ cav|al|ries
cav|al|ry|man
△ cav|al|ry|men
cave
cav|eat
cave-dwel|ler
cave-in
Cav|ell
cave|man
△ cave|men
caver
cav|ern
cav|ern|ous
cav|ern|ously
ca|vetto
△ ca|vetti
ca|vi|are
cavil
VERB
△ cav|ils

△ cav|illed
△ cav|il|ling
cav|il|ler
cav|ing
cav|ita|tion
cav|ity
△ cav|it|ies
ca|vort
△ ca|vorts
△ ca|vor|ted
△ ca|vort|ing
Ca|vour
cavy
△ ca|vies
caw
VERB
△ caws
△ cawed
△ caw|ing
Cax|ton
cay *see* key
Cay|enne
cay|enne
cay|man
Cay|man Is|lands
cease
VERB
△ cea|ses
△ ceased
△ ceas|ing
cease-fire
cease|less
cease|lessly
Ceau|sescu
Cecil
Ce|ci|lia

-cede / -ceed / -sede

-cede is derived from Latin **cedo** 'to go', 'to yield'. The following common words end in -cede: **accede, antecede, concede, intercede, precede, recede**.

-ceed is also derived from **cedo**, and is used in: **exceed, proceed, succeed**.

-sede is derived from Latin **sedeo**, 'to sit', and forms part of the word **supersede**.

cedar
ce|dar|wood
cede
△ cedes
△ ceded
△ ce|ding
ce|dilla
Ced|ric
Cee|fax
cei|lidh
ceil|ing
cel|an|dine
cel|eb|rant
cel|eb|rate
△ cel|eb|rates
△ cel|eb|ra|ted
△ cel|eb|ra|ting
cel|eb|ra|ted
cel|eb|ra|tion
cel|eb|ra|tor
cel|eb|ra|tory
ce|leb|rity
△ ce|leb|ri|ties
ce|ler|iac
ce|ler|ity
cel|ery
ce|lesta
ce|les|tial
celiac *see* coeliac
cel|ib|acy
cel|ib|ate
cell

cel|lar
underground
room; store in
this
VERB
△ cel|lars
△ cel|lared
△ cel|lar|ing
⚠ seller

cel|lar|age
Cel|lini

cel|list
cello
Cel|lo|phane
cell|phone
cel|lu|lar
cel|lule
cel|lu|lite
cel|lu|loid
cel|lu|lose
Cel|sius
Celt
Cel|tic
ce|ment
VERB
△ ce|ments
△ ce|men|ted
△ ce|ment|ing
ce|men|ta|tion
cem|et|ery
△ cem|et|er|ies
ceno|taph
Ce|no|zoic

cen|ser
incense container
⚠ censor
⚠ censure

cen|sor
person who
deletes
undesirable
material from
books etc; do
this
VERB
△ cen|sors
△ cen|sored
△ cen|sor|ing
⚠ censer
⚠ censure

cen|sor|ial
cen|sori|ous
cen|sori|ously

cen|sori|ous|ness
cen|sor|ship
cen|sur|able

cen|sure
criticism;
disapproval;
criticize
VERB
△ cen|sures
△ cen|sured
△ cen|sur|ing
⚠ censer
⚠ censor

cen|sus
△ cen|suses

cent
currency unit
⚠ scent
⚠ sent

cen|taur
cen|ten|ar|ian
cen|ten|ary
△ cen|ten|ar|ies
cen|ten|nial
cen|ti|grade
cen|time
cen|ti|metre
cen|ti|pede
Cen|tral
Scottish region
cen|tral
cen|tral|ism
cen|tral|ist
cen|tral|ity
cen|tral|iza|tion
cen|tral|ize
△ cen|tral|izes
△ cen|tral|ized
△ cen|tral|izing
cen|trally
cen|trally-
heated

centre
VERB
△ centres
△ centred
△ cen|tring
centre|board
centre|fold
centre-for|ward
centre-half
△ centre-halfs
or centre-
halves
centre|piece
cen|tri|fu|gal
cen|tri|fuge
VERB
△ cen|tri|fu|ges
△ cen|tri|fuged
△ cen|tri|fu|ging
cen|tri|ole
cen|tri|petal
cen|trism
cen|trist
cen|tro|mere
cen|tur|ion
cen|tury
△ cen|tur|ies
ceph|alic
cepha|lo|pod
Cepha|lo|poda
cer|amic
Cer|berus

cer|eal
breakfast food
⚠ serial

ce|re|bel|lar
ce|re|bel|lum
△ ce|re|bella
cer|eb|ral
ce|reb|rate
△ ce|reb|rates
△ ce|reb|ra|ted
△ ce|reb|ra|ting

ce|reb|ra|tion
ce|reb|ro|spi|nal
ce|reb|rum
△ ce|rebra
ce|re|mo|nial
ce|re|mo|ni|ally
ce|re|mo|ni|ous
ce|re|mo|ni|
  ously
ce|re|mony
△ ce|re|mon|ies
Ce|re|mony of
  Car|ols, A
Ceres
ce|rise
cer|ium
cer|met
ceroc
cert
cer|tain
cer|tainly
cer|tainty
△ cer|tain|ties
cer|ti|fi|able
cer|ti|fi|cate
  VERB
△ cer|ti|fi|cates
△ cer|ti|fi|ca|ted
△ cer|ti|fi|ca|ting
cer|ti|fi|ca|ted
cer|ti|fi|ca|tion
cer|ti|fied
cer|tify
△ cer|ti|fies
△ cer|ti|fied
△ cer|ti|fy|ing
cer|ti|tude
Cer|van|tes
cer|vi|cal
cer|vix
△ cer|vi|ces
cesium *see*
  caesium
ces|sa|tion

ces|sion
cess|pit
cess|pool
ce|ta|cean
ce|tane
Cé|zanne
cha-cha
cha|conne
Chad
cha|dor

chafe
  become warm,
  sore, or
  impatient
  △ chafes
  △ chafed
  △ cha|fing
  ⚠ chaff

cha|fer

chaff
  husks; fodder;
  rubbish; teasing;
  tease
  VERB
  △ chaffs
  △ chaffed
  △ chaf|fing
  ⚠ chafe

chaf|finch
△ chaf|fin|ches
Cha|gall
chag|rin
chain
  VERB
△ chains
△ chained
△ chain|ing
chain|mail
chain|saw
chain-smoke
△ chain-smokes
△ chain-smoked

△ chain-smo|
  king
chain-smo|ker
chair
  VERB
△ chairs
△ chaired
△ chair|ing
chair|lift
chair|man
△ chair|men
chair|per|son
chair|wo|man
△ chair|wo|men
chaise
chaise longue
△ chaises
  longues
cha|laza
Chal|ce|don
chal|ce|dony
Chal|cis
Chal|co|li|thic
chal|co|py|rite
Chal|daean
cha|let
Cha|lia|pin
chal|ice
chalk
  VERB
△ chalks
△ chalked
△ chalk|ing
chalk|board
chalki|ness
chalky
△ chalkier
△ chalki|est
chal|lenge
  VERB
△ chal|len|ges
△ chal|lenged
△ chal|len|ging
chal|lenged

chal|len|ger
chal|len|ging
chal|len|gingly
cha|lu|meau
cham|ber
Cham|ber|lain
cham|ber|lain
cham|ber|maid
cham|ber|pot
Cham|bers
cham|bré
cha|me|leon
cham|fer
  VERB
△ cham|fers
△ cham|fered
△ cham|fer|ing
cham|ois
  sing. and pl.
champ
  VERB
△ champs
△ champed
△ cham|ping
cham|pagne
cham|pers
cham|pion
  VERB
△ cham|pi|ons
△ cham|pi|oned
△ cham|pi|on|
  ing
cham|pi|on|ship
champ|levé
chance
  VERB
△ chan|ces
△ chanced
△ chan|cing
chan|cel
chan|cel|lery
△ chan|cel|ler|ies
chan|cel|lor
chan|cel|lor|ship

chan|cer
chan|cery
  △ chan|cer|ies
chan|ci|ness
chan|cre
chan|crous
chancy
  △ chan|cier
  △ chan|ci|est
chan|de|lier
Chand|ler
chand|ler
chand|lery
  △ chand|ler|ies
Cha|nel
Cha|ney
change
  VERB
  △ chan|ges
  △ changed
  △ chan|ging
change|ab|il|ity
change|able
change|able|ness
change|ably
change|less
change|lessly
change|ling
change-over
change-ring|ing
chan|ging-room
chan|nel
  VERB
  △ chan|nels
  △ chan|nelled
  △ chan|nel|ling
chan|son
chant
  VERB
  △ chants
  △ chan|ted
  △ chant|ing
chan|ter
chan|ter|elle

chant|ing
chan|try
  △ chant|ries
chanty *see*
  shanty
Chanukkah *see*
  Hannukkah
Chaos
  primeval state of
  universe
chaos
  disorder
cha|otic
cha|ot|ic|ally
chap
  VERB
  △ chaps
  △ chapped
  △ chap|ping
cha|par|ral
cha|pati
cha|pel
chap|er|one
  VERB
  △ chap|er|ones
  △ chap|er|oned
  △ chap|ero|ning
chap|lain
chap|laincy
  △ chap|lain|cies
chap|let
Chap|lin
Chap|man
chap|man
  △ chap|men
chapped
chap|pie
chap|ter
char
  NOUN
  fish
  △ char *or* chars
  tea; cleaner
  △ chars

VERB
  △ chars
  △ charred
  △ char|ring
cha|ra|banc
char|ac|ter
char|ac|ter|is|tic
char|ac|ter|is|tic|
  ally
char|ac|ter|iza|
  tion
char|ac|ter|ize
  △ char|ac|ter|
   izes
  △ char|ac|ter|
   ized
  △ char|ac|ter|
   izing
char|ac|ter|less
cha|rade
char|coal
Char|don|nay
charge
  VERB
  △ char|ges
  △ charged
  △ char|ging
charge|able
charged
chargé d'af|
  faires
  △ *char|gés d'af|*
   faires
char|ger
char|ily
chari|ness
char|iot
cha|ri|ot|eer
Cha|ri|ots of
  Fire
cha|risma
  △ cha|ris|mata
cha|ris|ma|tic
char|it|able

char|it|ably
char|ity
  △ char|it|ies
char|lady
  △ char|la|dies
char|la|tan
char|la|tan|ism
Charle|magne
Charles
Charles|ton
char|lie
char|lock
Char|lotte
Charl|ton
charm
  VERB
  △ charms
  △ charmed
  △ charm|ing
charmed
char|mer
charm|ing
charm|ingly
charm|less
charm|lessly
char|nel
Charon
charr *see* char
chart
  VERB
  △ charts
  △ char|ted
  △ chart|ing
char|ter
  VERB
  △ char|ters
  △ char|tered
  △ char|ter|ing
char|tered
char|terer
Char|teris
Chart|ism
Chart|ist
Char|tres

Char|treuse
monastery
char|treuse
liqueur
char|wo|man
△ char|wo|men
chary
△ charier
△ chari|est
Cha|ryb|dis
Chase
chase
VERB
△ cha|ses
△ chased
△ chas|ing
cha|ser
chas|ing
chasm
chassé
VERB
△ chas|sés
△ chas|séd
△ chas|sé|ing
chas|sis
sing. and pl.
chaste
chastely
chas|ten
△ chas|tens
△ chas|tened
△ chas|ten|ing
chaste|ness
chas|tise
△ chas|ti|ses
△ chas|tised
△ chas|tis|ing
chas|tise|ment
chas|tity
chas|uble
chat
VERB
△ chats
△ chat|ted

△ chat|ting
châ|teau
△ châ|teaux
Cha|teau|bri|and
châ|te|laine
Chats|worth
chat|tel
chat|ter
VERB
△ chat|ters
△ chat|tered
△ chat|ter|ing
chat|ter|box
△ chat|ter|boxes
chat|terer
Chat|ter|ton
chat|tily
chat|ti|ness
chatty
△ chat|tier
△ chat|ti|est
Chau|cer
chauf|feur
VERB
△ chauf|feurs
△ chauf|feured
△ chauf|feur|ing
chauf|feuse
chau|vin|ism
chau|vin|ist
chau|vin|is|tic
chau|vin|is|tic|
ally
Cheadle

┌─────────────────┐
│ cheap   │
│ *low-priced*   │
│ △ chea|per   │
│ △ cheap|est   │
│ ⚠ cheep   │
└─────────────────┘

cheapen
△ cheap|ens
△ cheap|ened
△ cheap|en|ing

cheap|jack
cheaply
cheap|ness
Cheap|side
cheap|skate
cheat
VERB
△ cheats
△ chea|ted
△ cheat|ing

┌─────────────────┐
│ check   │
│ *test; stop;*   │
│ *rebuke*   │
│ VERB   │
│ △ checks   │
│ △ checked   │
│ △ check|ing   │
│ ⚠ cheque   │
└─────────────────┘

check|able
checked
checker
one who checks
checker
chessboard
pattern; games
piece see chequer
check-in
check|list
check|mate
VERB
△ check|mates
△ check|ma|ted
△ check|ma|ting
check|out
check|point
check-up
Ched|dar
cheek
cheek|bone
cheek|ily
chee|ki|ness
cheeky
△ chee|kier

△ cheeki|est

┌─────────────────┐
│ cheep   │
│ *bird's cry; make* │
│ *this*   │
│ VERB   │
│ △ cheeps   │
│ △ cheeped   │
│ △ cheep|ing   │
│ ⚠ cheap   │
└─────────────────┘

cheer
VERB
△ cheers
△ cheered
△ cheer|ing
cheer|ful
cheer|fully
cheer|ful|ness
cheer|ily
cheeri|ness
cheer|ing
cheerio
cheer|leader
cheer|less
cheer|lessly
cheer|less|ness
cheers
cheery
△ cheer|ier
△ cheeri|est
cheese
cheese|bur|ger
cheese|cake
cheese|cloth
cheese|par|ing
cheesy
△ chee|sier
△ chee|si|est
chee|tah
chef
chef d'oeuvre
△ *chefs d'oeuvre*
cheirography *see*
  chirography

cheiromancy *see*
  chiromancy
Chek|hov
che|late
Chelms|ford
Chel|sea
Chel|ten|ham
chem|ical
chem|ic|ally
che|min de fer
che|mise
chem|ist
chem|istry
che|mo|re|cep|
  tor
che|mo|taxis
che|mo|thera|
  peu|tic
che|mo|ther|apy
che|nille
Chep|stow

cheque
  in banking
   △ check

cheque|book
che|quer
che|quered
Che|quers
Cher|bourg
cher|ish
  △ cher|ishes
  △ cher|ished
  △ cher|ish|ing
Cher|nenko
Cher|no|byl
cher|no|zem
Che|ro|kee
che|root
Cherry
cherry
  △ cher|ries
Cherry Or|
  chard, The

(Vish|nyovy
  sad)
cherry-pick|ing
chert
cherub
  △ cher|ubs *or*
    cheru|bim
che|ru|bic
che|ru|bic|ally
cher|vil
Che|ryl
Che|shire
chess
chess|board
chess|man
  △ chess|men
chest
Ches|ter
Ches|ter|field
  town
ches|ter|field
  sofa
Ches|ter-le-
  Street
Ches|ter|ton
chest|ily
ches|ti|ness
chest|nut
chesty
  △ ches|tier
  △ ches|ti|est
che|val
Che|val|ier
che|val|ier
Chev|iot
Chev|ro|let
chev|ron
chev|ro|tain
chew
  VERB
  △ chews
  △ chewed
  △ chew|ing
chewi|ness

chew|ing-gum
chewy
  △ chew|ier
  △ chewi|est
Chey|enne
chi *see* qi
Chiang Ch'ing
  see Jiang Qing
Chiang Kai-
  shek *see* Jiang
  Jieshi
Chi|anti
chi|aro|scuro
chi|asma
chic
  ADJ.
  △ chicer
  △ chic|est
Chi|cago
chi|cane
  VERB
  △ chi|canes
  △ chi|caned
  △ chi|can|ing
chi|can|ery
  △ chi|can|er|ies
Chi|chén Itzá
Chi|ches|ter
chick
chicken
  VERB
  △ chick|ens
  △ chick|ened
  △ chick|en|ing
chick|en|feed
chicken-hearted
chicken-liv|ered
chick|en|pox
chick|pea
chick|weed
chicly
chic|ory
chide
  △ chides

△ chided *or* chid
△ chi|ding
△ chided *or*
  chid|den
chi|ding
chief
chiefly
chief|tain
chief|taincy
  △ chief|tain|cies
chief|tain|ship
chiff|chaff
chif|fon
chif|fo|nier
chig|ger
chig|non
chi|hua|hua
chil|blain
child
  △ chil|dren
child|bear|ing
child|birth
Childe Har|old's
  Pil|grim|age
child|hood
child|ish
child|ishly
child|ish|ness
child|less
child|like
child-lock
child|minder
child|proof
child-resis|tant
Chile
chill
  VERB
  △ chills
  △ chilled
  △ chil|ling
chilled
chilli
  △ chil|lis *or* chil|
    lies

chil|li|ness
chil|ling
chil|lingly
chilly
△ chil|lier
△ chil|li|est
Chil|tern
chime
VERB
△ chimes
△ chimed
△ chi|ming
Chi|mera
chi|mer|ical
chim|ney
chim|ney|pot
chim|ney-sweep
chimp
chim|pan|zee
chin
China
china
Chi|na|man
△ Chi|na|men
Chi|na|town
chin|chilla
chine
VERB
△ chines
△ chined
△ chi|ning
Chi|nese
Chink
Chin|kie
Chinky
△ Chin|kies
chink
VERB
△ chinks
△ chinked
△ chink|ing
chin|less
chi|nois|erie
Chi|nook

chin|strap
chintz
△ chint|zes
chintzy
△ chint|zier
△ chint|zi|est
chin|wag
Chios
chip
VERB
△ chips
△ chipped
△ chip|ping
chip|board
chip|munk
chi|po|lata
chipped
Chip|pen|dale
chip|per
chippy
△ chip|pies
Chi|rac
chi|ro|gra|phy
chi|ro|mancy
chi|ro|pod|ist
chi|ro|pody
chi|ro|prac|tic
chirp
VERB
△ chirps
△ chirped
△ chirp|ing
chirp|ily
chir|pi|ness
chirpy
△ chir|pier
△ chir|pi|est
chir|rup
VERB
△ chir|rups
△ chir|ruped
△ chir|rup|ing
chir|rupy
chisel

VERB
△ chis|els
△ chis|elled
△ chis|el|ling
chit
chi|tar|rone
△ chi|tar|roni
chit|chat
VERB
△ chit|chats
△ chit|chat|ted
△ chit|chat|ting
chi|tin
chi|tin|ous
chit|ter|lings
chitty
chi|val|rous
chi|val|rously
chi|val|rous|ness
chiv|alry
chive
chivvy
△ chiv|vies
△ chiv|vied
△ chiv|vy|ing
Chloe
chloral
chlor|ate
chloric
chlor|ide
chlor|in|ate
△ chlor|in|ates
△ chlor|in|ated
△ chlor|in|ating
chlor|in|ated
chlor|in|ation
chlor|ine
chloro|flu|oro|
car|bon
chlo|ro|form
VERB
△ chlo|ro|forms
△ chlo|ro|
formed

△ chlo|ro|form|
ing
chlo|ro|phyll
chloro|plast
choc
choc|aholic
chock
VERB
△ chocks
△ chocked
△ chock|ing
chock-a-block
chock-full
choco|late
choco|late-box
choco|laty
choice
choice|ness

choir
group of singers
⚠ quire

choir|boy
choir|girl
choir|mas|ter
choir|mis|tress
△ choir|mis|tres|
ses
choke
VERB
△ chokes
△ choked
△ cho|king
cho|ker
cho|le|cal|ci|ferol
choler
chol|era
chol|eric
cho|les|terol
cho|line
chomp
VERB
△ chomps
△ chomped

△ chom|ping
Chom|sky
choose
△ choo|ses
△ chose
△ choos|ing
△ cho|sen
choosy
△ choo|sier
△ choo|si|est
chop
VERB
△ chops
△ chopped
△ chop|ping
chop|house
Cho|pin
chop|per
chop|pily
chop|pi|ness
chop|ping-board
choppy
△ chop|pier
△ chop|pi|est
chops
chop|sticks
choral
chor|ale
chor|ally

chord
in music; in
geometry
△ cord

Chor|data
chor|date
chore
cho|rea
choreo|graph
△ choreo|graphs
△ choreo|
graphed
△ choreo|graph|
ing

cho|reo|gra|pher
cho|reo|gra|phic
cho|reo|gra|phy
chori|onic
chor|is|ter
chor|oid
chor|tle
△ chor|tles
△ chor|tled
△ chort|ling
chorus
NOUN
△ chor|uses
VERB
△ chor|uses
△ chor|used
△ chor|us|ing
chose
chosen
Chou En-Lai
see Zhou Enlai
chough
choux
chow
chow|der
Chré|tien de
Troyes
chrism
Christ
Chris|ta|del|
phian
Christ|church
chris|ten
△ chris|tens
△ chris|tened
△ chris|ten|ing
Chris|ten|dom
chris|ten|ing
Chris|tian
Chris|ti|an|ity
Chris|tie
Chris|tina
Chris|tine
Christ|mas

△ Christ|mases
Christ|mas
Carol, A
Christ|massy
Chris|tol|ogy
△ Chris|tol|ogies
Chris|to|pher
chro|ma|key
chro|ma|tic
chro|mat|ic|ally
chro|ma|ti|cism
chro|ma|tid
chro|ma|tin
chro|ma|tog|ra|
phy
chro|ma|to|phore
chro|ma|to|
sphere
chrome
chro|min|ance
chro|mite
chro|mium
chro|mo|phore
chro|mo|plast
chro|mo|so|mal
chro|mo|some
chro|mo|sphere
chro|nic
chron|ic|ally
chro|ni|city
chron|icle
VERB
△ chron|icles
△ chron|icled
△ chron|ic|ling
chron|ic|ler
Chron|icles,
Books of
chro|no|gram
chro|no|lo|gi|cal
chro|no|lo|gic|
ally
chro|nol|ogist
chro|nol|ogy

△ chro|nol|ogies
chro|no|meter
chrys|alis
△ chrys|al|ises
chrys|an|the|mum
Chrys|ler
chry|so|beryl
chry|so|lite
chry|so|prase
Chry|sos|tom
chub
chub|bily
chub|bi|ness
chubby
△ chub|bier
△ chub|bi|est
chuck
VERB
△ chucks
△ chucked
△ chuck|ing
chuckle
VERB
△ chuckles
△ chuckled
△ chuck|ling
chuddar see
chador
chuff
VERB
△ chuffs
△ chuffed
△ chuf|fing
chuffed
chug
VERB
△ chugs
△ chugged
△ chug|ging

chukka
boot; spell of
play in polo
△ chukker

chuk|ker
spell of play in polo
△ chukka

chum
VERB
△ chums
△ chummed
△ chum|ming
chummy
△ chum|mier
△ chum|mi|est
chump
chun|der
VERB
△ chun|ders
△ chun|dered
△ chun|der|ing
chunk
chunky
△ chun|kier
△ chun|ki|est
church
△ chur|ches
church|goer
Chur|chill
church|man
△ church|men
church|war|
den
church|wo|man
△ church|wo|
men
church|yard
churl|ish
churl|ishly
churl|ish|ness
churn
VERB
△ churns
△ churned
△ churn|ing

chute
slide; parachute
△ shoot

chut|ney
chutz|pah
chyle
chyme
cia|batta
ci|cada
ci|ca|trice
ci|ca|trix
△ ci|ca|trixes
ci|cely
Ci|cero

Cid, El
Spanish warrior
△ Cid, Le

cider

Cid, Le
play by
Corneille
△ Cid, El

cigar
ci|gar|ette
ci|gar|ette-
holder
ci|gar|ette-ligh|ter
cigar-shaped
ci|li|ary
ci|li|ate
Ci|li|cia
ci|lium
△ cilia
cim|ba|lom
Cimon
cinch
△ cin|ches
cin|chona
Cin|cin|nati
cinc|ture
cin|der

Cin|der|ella
cin|dery
cine
cin|ema
Cin|ema|Scope
ci|ne|ma|tic
ci|ne|ma|to|
graph
ci|ne|ma|to|gra|
pher
ci|ne|ma|to|gra|
phic
ci|ne|ma|to|
graphy
cinema vérité
Cin|er|ama
cin|er|aria
cin|er|ary
cin|na|bar
cin|na|mon
cin|que|cento
cinque|foil
Cinque Ports
ci|pher
VERB
△ ci|phers
△ ci|phered
△ ci|pher|ing
circa
cir|ca|dian
Cir|cas|sian
Circe
cir|cle
VERB
△ cir|cles
△ cir|cled
△ circ|ling
circ|let
cir|co|therm
cir|cuit
cir|cuit-breaker
cir|cu|it|ous
cir|cu|it|ously
cir|cu|it|ous|ness

cir|cuitry
△ cir|cuit|ries
cir|cu|lar
cir|cu|lar|ity
△ cir|cu|lar|it|ies
cir|cu|lar|ize
△ cir|cu|lar|izes
△ cir|cu|lar|ized
△ cir|cu|lar|izing
cir|cu|larly
cir|cu|late
△ cir|cu|lates
△ cir|cu|la|ted
△ cir|cu|la|ting
cir|cu|la|tion
cir|cu|la|tory
cir|cum|cise
△ cir|cum|ci|ses
△ cir|cum|cised
△ cir|cum|ci|sing
Cir|cum|ci|sion
religious feast
cir|cum|ci|sion
*surgical
operation*
cir|cum|fer|ence
cir|cum|fer|en|
tial
cir|cum|flex
△ cir|cum|flexes
cir|cum|lo|cu|
tion
cir|cum|lo|cu|
tory
cir|cum|na|vi|
gate
△ cir|cum|na|vi|
gates
△ cir|cum|na|vi|
ga|ted
△ cir|cum|na|vi|
ga|ting
cir|cum|na|vi|ga|
tion

cir|cum|na|vi|ga|
tor
cir|cum|scribe
△ cir|cum|
scribes
△ cir|cum|
scribed
△ cir|cum|scri|
bing
cir|cum|scrip|
tion
cir|cum|spect
cir|cum|spec|
tion
cir|cum|spectly
cir|cum|stance
cir|cum|stan|tial
cir|cum|stan|ti|
ally
cir|cum|vent
△ cir|cum|vents
△ cir|cum|ven|
ted
△ cir|cum|vent|
ing
cir|cum|ven|tion
cir|cus
△ cir|cuses
Ci|ren|ces|ter
cirque
cir|rho|sis
cir|ri|ped
cir|ro|cu|mu|lus
△ cir|ro|cu|muli
cir|ro|stra|tus
△ cir|ro|strati
cir|rus
△ cirri
Cis|kei
cissy
△ cis|sies
cist
Cis|ter|cian
cis|tern

cis|tron
ci|ta|del
ci|ta|tion

---
cite
name; mention
△ cites
△ ci|ted
△ ci|ting
⚠ sight
⚠ site
---

cithern *see*
cittern
ci|ti|zen
Ci|ti|zen Kane
ci|ti|zenry
ci|ti|zen|ship
cit|rate
cit|ric
cit|rin
Cit|roën
cit|ron
cit|rus
cit|tern
city
△ cit|ies
City Lights
city-state
civet
civic
civ|ic|ally
civ|ics
civil
ci|vil|ian
ci|vil|ity
△ ci|vil|it|ies
civ|il|iza|tion
civ|il|ize
△ civ|il|izes
△ civ|il|ized
△ civ|il|izing
civ|il|ized
civ|illy
civ|vies

clack
VERB
△ clacks
△ clacked
△ clack|ing
clad
VERB
△ clads
△ clad|ded *or*
clad
△ clad|ding
clad|ding
cla|dis|tics
claim
VERB
△ claims
△ claimed
△ claim|ing
claim|ant
Claire
Clair|vaux
clair|voy|ance
clair|voy|ant
clam
VERB
△ clams
△ clammed
△ clam|ming
clam|ber
VERB
△ clam|bers
△ clam|bered
△ clam|ber|ing
clam|mily
clam|mi|ness
clammy
△ clam|mier
△ clam|mi|est
clam|or|ous
clam|or|ously
clam|or|ous|ness
clam|our
VERB
△ clam|ours

△ clam|oured
△ clam|our|ing
clamp
VERB
△ clamps
△ clamped
△ clamp|ing
clamp|down
clan
clan|des|tine
clan|des|tinely
clang
VERB
△ clangs
△ clanged
△ clang|ing
clanger
clan|gour
clank
VERB
△ clanks
△ clanked
△ clank|ing
clan|nish
clan|nishly
clan|nish|ness
clans|man
△ clans|men
clans|wo|man
△ clans|wo|men
clap
VERB
△ claps
△ clapped
△ clap|ping
clap|per
clap|per|board
Clap|ton
clap|trap
claque
Clara
Clare
Clar|ence
Clar|en|don

claret

cla|ri|fi|ca|tion

clar|ify

△ clar|ifies

△ clar|ified

△ clar|ify|ing

cla|ri|net

cla|ri|net|tist

clar|ion

Cla|rissa

clar|ity

Clark

Clarke

clar|sach

clash

  NOUN

△ cla|shes

  VERB

△ cla|shes

△ clashed

△ clash|ing

clasp

  VERB

△ clasps

△ clasped

△ clasp|ing

class

  NOUN

△ clas|ses

  VERB

△ clas|ses

△ classed

△ clas|sing

class-con|scious

class-con|scious|
ness

clas|sic

clas|si|cal

clas|sic|ally

clas|si|cism

clas|si|cist

Clas|sic

  *famous horse
race*

clas|sics

  *study of ancient
Greece and
Rome*

clas|si|fi|able

clas|si|fi|ca|tion

clas|si|fied

clas|sify

△ clas|si|fies

△ clas|si|fied

△ clas|si|fy|ing

class|less

class|less|ness

class|mate

class|room

classy

△ clas|sier

△ clas|si|est

clat|ter

  VERB

△ clat|ters

△ clat|tered

△ clat|ter|ing

Claude

Claud|ius

clause

Clau|se|witz

claus|tro|pho|bia

claus|tro|pho|bic

cla|vi|chord

clav|icle

claw

  VERB

△ claws

△ clawed

△ claw|ing

claw|back

Clay

clay

clayey

Clay|hanger

clay|ma|tion

clay|more

clean

VERB

△ cleans

△ cleaned

△ clean|ing

ADJ.

△ clea|ner

△ clean|est

clean-cut

clea|ner

clean-limbed

clean|li|ness

clean-liv|ing

cleanly

clean|ness

clean-out

cleanse

△ cleanses

△ cleansed

△ cleans|ing

cleanser

clean-shaven

clean-up

clear

  VERB

△ clears

△ cleared

△ clear|ing

ADJ.

△ clearer

△ clear|est

clear|ance

clear-cut

clear-headed

clear-head|edly

clear|ing

clear|ing-house

clearly

clear|ness

clear-out

clear-sigh|ted

clear-sigh|tedly

clear-sigh|ted|ness

clearstory *see*
  clerestory

clear|way

clea|vage

cleave

△ cleaves

  cut; split

△ clove *or* cleft
  or cleaved

  cling; stick

△ cleaved

△ clea|ving

△ clo|ven *or*
  cleft *or*
  cleaved

clea|ver

Clee|thorpes

clef

cleft

Cle|land

clem|atis *or* cle|
  ma|tis

  *according to
pronunciation*

Cle|men|ceau

clem|ency

Clem|ent

clem|ent

clem|en|tine

clem|ently

clench

  VERB

△ clen|ches

△ clenched

△ clench|ing

Cleon

Cleo|patra

clere|story

△ clere|stor|ies

clergy

△ cler|gies

cler|gy|man

△ cler|gy|men

cler|gy|wo|man

△ cler|gy|wo|
  men

cleric
cler|ical
cleri|hew
clerk
clerk|ess
△ clerk|es|ses
Cleve|don
Cleve|land
clever
△ clev|erer
△ clev|er|est
clev|erly
clev|er|ness

clew
corner of sail;
cords for
hammock; pull
sail
VERB
△ clews
△ clewed
△ clew|ing
⚠clue

cli|ché
cli|chéd
click
VERB
△ clicks
△ clicked
△ click|ing
cli|ent
cli|en|tèle
cliff
cliff|hanger
cliff|hang|ing
Clif|ford
cli|mac|teric
cli|mac|tic
cli|mac|tic|ally
cli|mate
cli|matic
cli|mat|ic|ally
cli|ma|to|lo|gi|cal

cli|ma|tol|ogist
cli|ma|tol|ogy
cli|max
NOUN
△ cli|maxes
VERB
△ cli|maxes
△ cli|maxed
△ cli|max|ing
climb
VERB
△ climbs
△ climbed
△ climb|ing
climb|able
climb-down
climber
climb|ing
climb|ing-frame
clime
clinch
NOUN
△ clin|ches
VERB
△ clin|ches
△ clinched
△ clinch|ing
clin|cher
cline
cling
VERB
△ clings
△ clung
△ cling|ing
clinger
cling|film
clingi|ness
cling|stone
clingy
cli|nic
clin|ical
clin|ic|ally
cli|ni|cian
clink

VERB
△ clinks
△ clinked
△ clink|ing
clin|ker
clin|ker-built
cli|no|meter
clint
Clin|ton
Clio
clip
VERB
△ clips
△ clipped
△ clip|ping
clip|board
clip-on
clipped
clip|per
clip|ping
clique
cli|quey
△ cli|quier
△ cli|qui|est
cli|qui|ness
cli|quish
cli|quish|ness
clit|oral
cli|tor|id|ec|
  tomy
clit|oris
△ clit|or|ises
Clive
clo|aca
cloak
VERB
△ cloaks
△ cloaked
△ cloak|ing
cloak-and-dag|
  ger
cloak|room
clob|ber

VERB
△ clob|bers
△ clob|bered
△ clob|ber|ing
cloche
clock
VERB
△ clocks
△ clocked
△ clock|ing
clock|wat|cher
clock|wise
clock|work
clod
clod|dish
clod|dishly
clod|dish|ness
clod|hop|per
clod|hop|ping
clog
VERB
△ clogs
△ clogged
△ clog|ging
cloi|sonné
clois|ter
VERB
△ clois|ters
△ clois|tered
△ clois|ter|ing
clois|tral
clo|nal
clone
VERB
△ clones
△ cloned
△ clo|ning
clonk
VERB
△ clonks
△ clonked
△ clonk|ing
clop

VERB
△ clops
△ clopped
△ clop|ping
Close
close
VERB
△ clo|ses
△ closed
△ clo|sing
ADJ.
△ clo|ser
△ clo|sest
closed
closed-loop
close-down
close-fis|ted
close-hauled
close-knit
closely
close|ness
closet
VERB
△ clos|ets
△ clos|eted
△ clos|et|ing
close-up
clo|sing-time
clos|trid|ium
△ clos|tri|dia
clo|sure
VERB
△ clo|sures
△ clo|sured
△ clo|sur|ing
clot
VERB
△ clots
△ clot|ted
△ clot|ting
cloth
clothe
△ clothes
△ clothed or

clad
△ clo|thing
clothes
clothes|line
clo|thier
clo|thing
Clo|tho
cloud
VERB
△ clouds
△ clou|ded
△ cloud|ing
cloud|burst
cloud-cuckoo-
land
cloud|ily
clou|di|ness
cloud|less
Clouds, The
cloudy
△ clou|dier
△ clou|di|est
clout
VERB
△ clouts
△ clou|ted
△ clout|ing
clove
clo|ven
clo|ver
clo|ver|leaf
clown
VERB
△ clowns
△ clowned
△ clown|ing
clown|ish
clown|ishly
clown|ish|ness
cloy
△ cloys
△ cloyed
△ cloy|ing
cloy|ing

cloze
club
VERB
△ clubs
△ clubbed
△ club|bing
club|bable
clubbed
club|house
club|root
cluck
VERB
△ clucks
△ clucked
△ cluck|ing

---

clue
  hint; inform
VERB
△ clues
△ clued
△ clu|ing
  ⚠ clew

---

clue|less
clump
VERB
△ clumps
△ clumped
△ clump|ing
clum|pi|ness
clumpy
△ clum|pier
△ clum|pi|est
clum|sily
clum|si|ness
clumsy
△ clum|sier
△ clum|si|est
clung
clunk
VERB
△ clunks
△ clunked
△ clunk|ing

cluster
VERB
△ clus|ters
△ clus|tered
△ clus|ter|ing
clutch
NOUN
△ clut|ches
VERB
△ clut|ches
△ clutched
△ clutch|ing
clut|ter
VERB
△ clut|ters
△ clut|tered
△ clut|ter|ing
Clwyd
Clyde
Clyde|side
Cly|tem|nes|tra
coach
NOUN
△ coa|ches
VERB
△ coa|ches
△ coached
△ coach|ing
coach|buil|der
coach|ing
coach|man
△ coach|men
coach|work
co|agu|lant
co|agu|late
△ co|agu|lates
△ co|agu|la|ted
△ co|agu|la|ting
co|agu|la|tion

---

coal
  black fossil fuel
  ⚠ cole

---

co|alesce

△ co|ales|ces
△ co|alesced
△ co|ales|cing
co|ales|cence
co|ales|cent
coal|face
coal|field
coal-fired
co|ali|tion
coal|mine
coam|ing

coarse
rough; crude
△ coar|ser
△ coar|sest
⚠ course

coarsely
coar|sen
△ coar|sens
△ coar|sened
△ coar|sen|ing
coarse|ness
coast
VERB
△ coasts
△ coas|ted
△ coast|ing
coas|tal
coas|ter
coast|guard
coast|line
coat
VERB
△ coats
△ coa|ted
△ coat|ing
Coat|bridge
Coates
coat-hanger
coati
coat|ing
coat-tails
co-author

VERB
△ co-auth|ors
△ co-auth|ored
△ co-auth|or|ing
coax
△ coaxes
△ coaxed
△ coax|ing
co|axial
coax|ingly
cob
co|balt
co|bal|tic
cob|ber
Cob|bett
cob|ble
VERB
△ cob|bles
△ cob|bled
△ cob|bling
cob|bled
cob|bler
Cob|den
Cob|lenz
cobra
cob|web
cob|webby
coca
co|caine
coc|cus
△ cocci
coc|cyx
△ coc|cy|xes *or*
coc|cy|ges
coch|in|eal
coch|lea
△ coch|leae
coch|lear
cock
VERB
△ cocks
△ cocked
△ cock|ing
cock|ade

cock-a-hoop
cock-a-leekie
cock-and-bull
cocka|too
cocka|trice
cock|cha|fer
cock-crow
cocker
cock|erel
Cock|er|mouth
cock-eyed
cock|fight
cock|fight|ing
cock|ily
cocki|ness
cockle
cockle|shell
cock|ney
cock|pit
cock|roach
△ cock|roa|ches
cocks|comb
cock|sure
cock|tail
cock-up
cocky
△ cock|ier
△ cocki|est

coco
coconut tree
⚠ cocoa

cocoa
drink or powder
⚠ coco

co|co|nut
co|coon
VERB
△ co|coons
△ co|cooned
△ co|coon|ing
co|coon|ing
co|cotte

co-coun|sel|ling
Coc|teau
cod
NOUN
fish
△ cod
hoax
△ cods
VERB
△ cods
△ cod|ded
△ cod|ding
coda
cod|dle
△ cod|dles
△ cod|dled
△ cod|dling
code
VERB
△ codes
△ coded
△ co|ding
co|deine
co-depen|dency
codex
△ co|di|ces
cod|fish
sing. and pl.
cod|ger
co|di|cil
co|di|fi|ca|tion
co|dify
△ co|di|fies
△ co|di|fied
△ co|di|fy|ing
cod|ling
codon
cod|piece
cods|wal|lop
Cody
Coe
co-edu|ca|tion
co-edu|ca|tional
co|ef|fi|cient

coe|la|canth
Coel|en|ter|ata
coel|en|ter|ate
coe|liac
coe|lom
coe|no|bite
coe|no|bi|tic
co-enzyme
co|erce
△ co|er|ces
△ co|erced
△ co|er|cing
co|er|cible
co|er|cion
co|er|cive
co|eval
co-exist
△ co-exists
△ co-exis|ted
△ co-exist|ing
co-exist|ence
co-exist|ent
co-exten|sive
cof|fee
cof|fer
cof|fer|dam
cof|fin
cog
co|gency
co|gen|cies
co|gent
co|gently
co|gi|tate
△ co|gi|tates
△ co|gi|ta|ted
△ co|gi|ta|ting
co|gi|ta|tion
co|gi|ta|tive
cognac
cog|nate
cog|ni|tion
cog|ni|tive
cog|ni|tively
cog|ni|zance

cog|ni|zant
cog|no|men
cogno|scenti
cog|wheel
co|habit
△ co|hab|its
△ co|hab|ited
△ co|hab|it|ing
co|ha|bi|ta|tion
co|hab|iter
co|ha|bi|tee
co|here
△ co|heres
△ co|hered
△ co|her|ing
co|her|ence
co|her|ent
co|her|ently
co|he|sion
co|he|sive
co|hort
coif
VERB
△ coifs
△ coiffed
△ coif|fing
coif|feur
coif|feuse
coif|fure
VERB
△ coif|fures
△ coif|fured
△ coif|fur|ing
coil
VERB
△ coils
△ coiled
△ coil|ing
coin
VERB
△ coins
△ coined
△ coin|ing
coin|age

co|in|cide
△ co|in|cides
△ co|in|cided
△ co|in|ci|ding
co|in|ci|dence
co|in|ci|dent
co|in|ci|den|tal
co|in|ci|den|tally
coin-oper|ated
coir
co|ital
co|ition
co|itus
coke
VERB
△ cokes
△ coked
△ co|king
col
cola

col|an|der
strainer
⚠ calendar
⚠ calender

Col|ches|ter
cold
△ colder
△ cold|est
cold-blooded
cold-blood|edly
cold-blood|ed|
  ness
*Cold Com|fort
  Farm*
cold-hearted
cold-heart|edly
cold-heart|ed|
  ness
coldly
cold|ness
cold-shoul|der
△ cold-shoul|
  ders

△ cold-shoul|
  dered
△ cold-shoul|
  der|ing

cole
sort of cabbage
⚠ coal

col|ec|tomy
△ col|ec|tom|ies
Co|ler|idge
cole|slaw
Co|lette
col|eus
△ col|euses
coley
colic
col|icky
co|li|seum
co|li|tis
col|la|bor|ate
△ col|la|bor|ates
△ col|la|bor|ated
△ col|la|bor|
  ating
col|la|bor|ation
col|la|bor|ation|
  ism
col|la|bor|ation|
  ist
col|la|bor|at|ive
col|la|bor|at|
  ively
col|la|bor|ator

col|lage
artwork
⚠ college

col|la|gen
col|lapse
VERB
△ col|lap|ses
△ col|lapsed
△ col|lap|sing

col|lap|si|bil|ity
col|laps|ible
col|lar
  VERB
  △ col|lars
  △ col|lared
  △ col|lar|ing
col|lar|bone
col|lar|less
col|late
  △ col|lates
  △ col|la|ted
  △ col|la|ting
col|lat|eral
col|lat|er|ally
col|la|tion
col|la|tor
col|league
col|lect
  VERB
  △ col|lects
  △ col|lec|ted
  △ col|lect|ing
col|lect|able
col|lec|ted
col|lec|tedly
col|lec|ted|ness
col|lec|tion
col|lec|tive
col|lec|tively
col|lec|tiv|ism
col|lec|tiv|iza|
  tion
col|lec|tiv|ize
  △ col|lec|tiv|izes
  △ col|lec|tiv|ized
  △ col|lec|tiv|
  izing
col|lec|tor
Col|leen
col|leen

col|lege
  place of
  education
  ⚠ collage

col|legi|ate
col|lide
  △ col|lides
  △ col|li|ded
  △ col|li|ding
col|lie
col|lier
col|liery
  △ col|lier|ies
col|li|ma|tor
col|li|near
Col|lins
col|li|sion
col|lo|cate
  △ col|lo|cates
  △ col|lo|ca|ted
  △ col|lo|ca|ting
col|lo|ca|tion
col|loid
col|lo|quial
col|lo|qui|al|ism
col|lo|qui|ally
col|lo|quium
  △ col|lo|quia
col|lo|quy
  △ col|lo|quies
col|lu|sion
col|lu|sive
col|ly|wobbles
Co|logne
co|logne
Co|lom|bia
Co|lombo
colon
colo|nel
colo|nelcy
  △ colo|nel|cies
colo|nel-in-chief
  △ colo|nels-in-
  chief
co|lo|nial

co|lo|ni|al|ism
co|lo|ni|al|ist
co|lo|ni|ally
co|lonic
col|on|iza|tion
col|on|ize
  △ col|on|izes
  △ col|on|ized
  △ col|on|izing
col|on|nade
col|on|na|ded
col|ony
  △ col|on|ies
colo|phon
Co|lor|ado
col|or|ant
col|or|ation
co|lo|ra|tura
co|lo|ri|meter
co|los|sal
co|los|sally
Co|los|seum
Co|los|si|ans,
  Let|ter of Paul
  to the
co|los|sus
  △ co|lossi *or* co|
  los|suses
co|los|tomy
  △ co|los|tom|ies
co|los|trum
col|our
  VERB
  △ col|ours
  △ col|oured
  △ col|our|ing
col|our-blind|
  ness
col|our-coded
col|oured
col|our-fast
col|our|ful
col|our|fully
col|our|ing

col|our|ist
col|our|iza|tion
col|our|ize
  △ col|our|izes
  △ col|our|ized
  △ col|our|izing
col|our|less
col|our|lessly
col|our|way
Colt
  pistol
colt
  young horse or
  person
colt|ish
colt|ishly
colts|foot
co|lugo
Co|lumba
Co|lum|bia
col|um|bine
co|lum|bium
Co|lum|bus
col|umn
co|lum|nar
col|umn|ist
Col|wyn Bay

coma
  unconscious state
  ⚠ comma

co|ma|tose
comb
  VERB
  △ combs
  △ combed
  △ comb|ing
com|bat
  VERB
  △ com|bats
  △ com|ba|ted
  △ com|bat|ing
com|bat|ant
com|bat|ive

com|bi|na|tion
com|bi|na|tory
com|bine
  VERB
  △ com|bines
  △ com|bined
  △ com|bi|ning
combo
com|bus|ti|bil|ity
com|bust|ible
com|bus|tion
come
  VERB
  △ comes
  △ came
  △ com|ing
  △ come
come|back
co|med|ian
Com|édie-Fran|
çaise
co|medi|enne
com|edo
come|down
com|edy
  △ com|ed|ies
come-hither
come|li|ness
comely
  △ come|lier
  △ come|li|est
come-on
comer
com|est|ible
comet
come-uppance
com|fit
com|fort
  VERB
  △ com|forts
  △ com|for|ted
  △ com|fort|ing
com|fort|able
com|fort|ably

com|for|ter
com|frey
comfy
  △ com|fier
  △ com|fi|est
comic
com|ical
com|ic|al|ity
com|ic|ally
com|ing
com|ity

> comma
> *punctuation*
> *mark*
> ⚠ coma

com|mand
  VERB
  △ com|mands
  △ com|man|ded
  △ com|mand|ing
com|man|dant
com|man|deer
  △ com|man|
    deers
  △ com|man|
    deered
  △ com|man|
    deer|ing
com|man|der
com|man|der-
in-chief
  △ com|man|
    ders-in-chief
com|mand|ing
com|mand|ment
com|mando
com|me|dia
dell'arte
com|mem|or|ate
  △ com|mem|or|
    ates
  △ com|mem|or|
    ated

  △ com|mem|or|
    ating
com|mem|or|
ation
com|mem|or|
ative
com|mence
  △ com|men|ces
  △ com|menced
  △ com|men|cing
com|mence|
ment
com|mend
  △ com|mends
  △ com|men|ded
  △ com|mend|ing
com|mend|able
com|mend|ably
com|men|da|tion
com|men|da|
tory
com|men|sal|ism
com|men|sur|
able
com|men|sur|ate
com|men|sur|
ately
com|ment
  VERB
  △ com|ments
  △ com|men|ted
  △ com|ment|ing
com|men|tary
  △ com|men|tar|
    ies
com|men|tate
  △ com|men|tates
  △ com|men|ta|
    ted
  △ com|men|ta|
    ting
com|men|ta|tor
com|merce
com|mer|cial

com|mer|cial|
ism
com|mer|ci|al|ity
com|mer|cial|iza|
tion
com|mer|cial|ize
  △ com|mer|cial|
    izes
  △ com|mer|cial|
    ized
  △ com|mer|cial|
    izing
com|mer|cially
com|mie
com|mi|nute
  △ com|mi|nutes
  △ com|mi|nu|ted
  △ com|mi|nu|
    ting
com|mi|nu|tion
com|mis
sing. and pl.
com|mis|er|ate
  △ com|mis|er|
    ates
  △ com|mis|er|
    ated
  △ com|mis|er|
    ating
com|mis|er|ation
com|mis|sar
com|mis|sar|ial
com|mis|sar|iat
com|mis|sary
  △ com|mis|sar|
    ies
com|mis|sion
  VERB
  △ com|mis|sions
  △ com|mis|
    sioned
  △ com|mis|sion|
    ing

com|mis|sion|
aire
doorman
⚠ commissioner

com|mis|sioner
government
official
⚠ commis-
sionaire

com|mis|sion|er|
ship
com|mit
△ com|mits
△ com|mit|ted
△ com|mit|ting
com|mit|ment
com|mit|tal
com|mit|tee
com|mode
com|mo|di|ous
com|mo|di|ously
com|mo|di|ous|
ness
com|mod|ity
△ com|mod|it|ies
com|mo|dore
com|mon
ADJ.
△ com|moner
△ com|mon|est
com|moner
com|mon-law
com|monly
com|mon|ness
com|mon-or-
gar|den
com|mon|place
com|mon-riding
com|mon-sense
com|mon|sen|si|
cal
com|mon|wealth

com|mo|tion
com|mu|nal
com|mu|nally
com|mune
VERB
△ com|munes
△ com|muned
△ com|mu|ning
com|mu|nic|able
com|mu|ni|cant
com|mu|ni|cate
△ com|mu|ni|
cates
△ com|mu|ni|ca|
ted
△ com|mu|ni|ca|
ting
com|mu|ni|ca|tion
com|mu|ni|ca|
tive
com|mu|ni|ca|
tively
com|mu|nion
com|mu|ni|qué
com|mu|nism
com|mu|nist
com|mu|nis|tic
com|mu|ni|tar|
ian
com|mu|nity
△ com|mu|ni|
ties
com|mut|able
com|mu|ta|tion
com|mu|ta|tive
com|mu|ta|tor
com|mute
△ com|mutes
△ com|mu|ted
△ com|mu|ting
com|mu|ter
Como
Co|moros
com|pact

VERB
△ com|pacts
△ com|pac|ted
△ com|pact|ing
com|pac|tion
com|pactly
com|pact|ness
com|pan|ion
com|pan|ion|
able
com|pan|ion|
ably
com|pan|ion|
ship
com|pan|ion|
way
com|pany
△ com|pan|ies
com|par|ab|il|ity
com|par|able
com|par|ably
com|par|at|ive
com|par|at|ively

com|pare
make comparison
△ com|pares
△ com|pared
△ com|par|ing
⚠ compère

com|par|ison
com|part|ment
com|part|men|
tal
com|part|men|
tal|iza|tion
com|part|men|
tal|ize
△ com|part|men|
tal|izes
△ com|part|men|
tal|ized
△ com|part|men|
tal|izing

com|pass
△ com|pas|ses
com|pas|sion
com|pas|sion|ate
com|pas|sion|
ately
com|pa|ti|bil|ity
com|pat|ible
com|pat|ibly
com|pat|riot
com|peer
com|pel
△ com|pels
△ com|pelled
△ com|pel|ling
com|pel|ling
com|pel|lingly
com|pen|di|ous
com|pen|di|
ously
com|pen|dium
△ com|pen|di|
ums *or* com|
pen|dia
com|pen|sate
△ com|pen|sates
△ com|pen|sa|
ted
△ com|pen|sa|
ting
com|pen|sa|tion
com|pen|sa|tory

com|père
presenter of
show etc; act as
this
VERB
△ com|pères
△ com|pèred
△ com|père|ing
⚠ compare

com|pete
△ com|petes

△ com|peted
△ com|pet|ing
com|pet|ence
com|pet|ent
com|pet|ently
com|pe|ti|tion
com|pet|it|ive
com|pet|it|ively
com|pet|it|ive|ness
com|pet|itor
com|pil|lation
com|pile
△ com|piles
△ com|piled
△ com|pi|ling
com|pi|ler

com|pla|cence
self-satisfaction
⚠ complaisance

com|pla|cency
com|pla|cent
com|pla|cently
com|plain
△ com|plains
△ com|plained
△ com|plain|ing
com|plain|ant
com|plai|ner
com|plaint

com|plai|sance
desire to please
⚠ complacence

com|plai|sant
com|plai|santly
Com|pleat Ang|ler, The

com|ple|ment
thing that completes

VERB
△ com|ple|ments
△ com|ple|men|ted
△ com|ple|ment|ing
⚠ compliment

com|ple|ment|ar|ily

com|ple|ment|ary
completing
⚠ complimentary

com|plete
VERB
△ com|pletes
△ com|ple|ted
△ com|ple|ting
com|pletely
com|plete|ness
com|ple|tion
com|plex
NOUN
△ com|plexes
com|plex|ion
com|plex|ity
△ com|plex|it|ies
com|pli|ance
com|pli|ant
com|pli|antly
com|pli|cate
△ com|pli|cates
△ com|pli|ca|ted
△ com|pli|ca|ting
com|pli|ca|ted
com|pli|ca|tion
com|pli|city

com|pli|ment
praise
VERB
△ com|pli|ments

△ com|pli|men|ted
△ com|pli|men|ting
⚠ complement

com|pli|ment|ary
praising
⚠ complementary

com|pline
com|ply
△ com|plies
△ com|plied
△ com|ply|ing
com|po|nent
com|port
△ com|ports
△ com|por|ted
△ com|port|ing
com|port|ment
com|pose
△ com|poses
△ com|posed
△ com|po|sing
com|posed
com|po|sedly
com|poser
com|po|site
com|po|si|tion
com|pos|itor
com|pos men|tis
com|post
com|po|sure
com|pound
VERB
△ com|pounds
△ com|poun|ded
△ com|pound|ing
com|pre|hend
△ com|pre|hends

△ com|pre|hen|ded
△ com|pre|hend|ing
com|pre|hen|si|bil|ity
com|pre|hens|ible
com|pre|hens|ibly
com|pre|hen|sion
com|pre|hen|sive
com|pre|hen|sively
com|pre|hen|sive|ness
com|press
NOUN
△ com|pres|ses
VERB
△ com|pres|ses
△ com|pressed
△ com|pres|sing
com|pres|si|bil|ity
com|press|ible
com|pres|sion
com|pres|sor
com|prise
△ com|pri|ses
△ com|prised
△ com|pri|sing
com|pro|mise
VERB
△ com|pro|mi|ses
△ com|pro|mised
△ com|pro|mi|sing
Comp|ton
Comp|ton-Bur|nett

com|pul|sion
com|pul|sive
com|pul|sively
com|pul|sor|ily
com|pul|sory
com|punc|tion
com|pu|table
com|pu|ta|tion
com|pu|ta|tional
com|pu|ta|tion|
ally
com|pute
△ com|putes
△ com|pu|ted
△ com|pu|ting
com|pu|ter
com|pu|ter|iza|
tion
com|pu|ter|ize
△ com|pu|ter|
izes
△ com|pu|ter|
ized
△ com|pu|ter|
izing
com|rade
com|rade-in-arms
△ com|rades-in-
arms
com|radely
com|rade|ship
Comte
con
VERB
△ cons
△ conned
△ con|ning
Con|akry
con|cat|en|ate
△ con|cat|en|ates
△ con|cat|en|
ated
△ con|cat|en|
ating

con|cat|en|ation
con|cave
con|cav|ity
△ con|cav|it|ies
con|ceal
△ con|ceals
△ con|cealed
△ con|ceal|ing
con|ceal|ment
con|cede
△ con|cedes
△ con|ceded
△ con|ced|ing
con|ceit
con|cei|ted
con|ceit|edly
con|ceiv|abil|ity
con|ceiv|able
con|ceiv|ably
con|ceive
△ con|ceives
△ con|ceived
△ con|ceiv|ing
con|cen|trate
VERB
△ con|cen|trates
△ con|cen|tra|ted
△ con|cen|tra|
ting
con|cen|tra|ted
con|cen|tra|tion
con|cen|tric
con|cen|tric|ally
con|cen|tri|city
Con|cep|ción
con|cept
con|cep|tion
con|cep|tual
con|cep|tu|al|ism
con|cep|tu|al|iza|
tion
con|cep|tu|al|ize
△ con|cep|tu|al|
izes

△ con|cep|tu|al|
ized
△ con|cep|tu|al|
izing
con|cep|tu|ally
con|cern
VERB
△ con|cerns
△ con|cerned
△ con|cern|ing
con|cerned
con|cern|edly
con|cern|ed|ness
con|cern|ing
con|cern|ment

con|cert
*musical
performance; do
in co-operation*
VERB
△ con|certs
△ con|cer|ted
△ con|cert|ing
⚠ consort

con|cer|ted
Con|cert|ge|
bouw
con|cer|tina
VERB
△ con|cer|ti|nas
△ con|cer|ti|naed
△ con|cer|ti|na|
ing
con|cer|tino
con|certo
△ con|cer|tos *or*
con|certi
con|certo grosso
△ con|certi
grossi
con|ces|sion
con|ces|sion|aire
con|ces|sion|ary

con|ces|sive
conch
△ conchs *or*
con|ches
conch|olo|gist
conch|ol|ogy
con|ci|li|ate
△ con|ci|li|ates
△ con|ci|li|ated
△ con|ci|li|ating
con|ci|li|ation
con|ci|li|ator
con|ci|li|atory
con|cise
con|cisely
con|ci|sion
con|cise|ness
con|clave
con|clude
△ con|cludes
△ con|clu|ded
△ con|clu|ding
con|clu|sion
con|clu|sive
con|clu|sively
con|clu|sive|ness
con|coct
△ con|cocts
△ con|coc|ted
△ con|coct|ing
con|coc|tion
con|com|it|ant
con|com|it|antly
con|cord
con|cor|dance
con|cor|dant
con|cor|dat
Con|corde
con|course
con|crete
VERB
△ con|cretes
△ con|cre|ted
△ con|cre|ting

con|cretely
con|crete|ness
con|cre|tion
con|cu|bin|age
con|cu|bine
con|cu|pis|cence
con|cu|pis|cent
con|cur
△ con|curs
△ con|curred
△ con|cur|ring
con|cur|rence
con|cur|rent
con|cur|rently
con|cuss
△ con|cus|ses
△ con|cussed
△ con|cus|sing
con|cus|sion
con|demn
△ con|demns
△ con|demned
△ con|demn|ing
con|dem|na|tion
con|dem|na|tory
con|den|sa|tion
con|dense
△ con|den|ses
△ con|densed
△ con|den|sing
con|den|ser
con|des|cend
△ con|des|cends
△ con|des|cen|ded
△ con|des|cend|ing
con|des|cend|ing
con|des|cend|ingly
con|des|cen|sion
con|dign
con|di|ment
con|di|tion

VERB
△ con|di|tions
△ con|di|tioned
△ con|di|tion|ing
con|di|tional
con|di|tion|ally
con|di|tioner
con|di|tion|ing
con|dole
△ con|doles
△ con|doled
△ con|do|ling
con|do|lence
con|dom
con|do|min|ium
con|don|able
con|done
△ con|dones
△ con|doned
△ con|do|ning
con|dor
con|duce
△ con|du|ces
△ con|duced
△ con|du|cing
con|du|cive
con|duct
VERB
△ con|ducts
△ con|duc|ted
△ con|duct|ing
con|duct|ance
con|duc|tion
con|duc|tiv|ity
con|duc|tor
con|duc|tress
△ con|duc|tres|ses
con|duit
cone
con|fab
VERB
△ con|fabs
△ con|fabbed

△ con|fab|bing
con|fa|bu|late
△ con|fa|bu|lates
△ con|fa|bu|la|ted
△ con|fa|bu|la|ting
con|fa|bu|la|tion
con|fec|tion
con|fec|tioner
con|fec|tion|ery
con|fed|er|acy
△ con|fed|er|acies
con|fed|er|ate
VERB
△ con|fed|er|ates
△ con|fed|er|ated
△ con|fed|er|ating
con|fed|er|ation
con|fer
△ con|fers
△ con|ferred
△ con|fer|ring
con|fer|ence
con|fer|en|cing
con|fer|ment
con|fess
△ con|fes|ses
△ con|fessed
△ con|fes|sing
con|fes|sed
con|fes|sedly
con|fes|sion
con|fes|sional
con|fes|sor
con|fetti

con|fi|dant
*man in whom
one confides*
⚠ confidante
⚠ confident

con|fi|dante
*woman in whom
one confides*
⚠ confidant
⚠ confident

con|fide
△ con|fides
△ con|fi|ded
△ con|fi|ding
con|fid|ence

con|fid|ent
self-assured
⚠ confidant
⚠ confidante

con|fi|den|tial
con|fi|den|ti|al|ity
con|fi|den|ti|ally
con|fi|ding
con|fi|dingly
con|fi|gur|ation
con|fine
VERB
△ con|fines
△ con|fined
△ con|fi|ning
con|fined
con|fine|ment
con|firm
△ con|firms
△ con|firmed
△ con|firm|ing
con|fir|ma|tion
con|firm|at|ory
con|firmed
con|fis|cate
△ con|fis|cates
△ con|fis|ca|ted
△ con|fis|ca|ting
con|fis|ca|tion
con|fla|gra|tion
con|flate

△ con|flates
△ con|fla|ted
△ con|fla|ting
con|fla|tion
con|flict
VERB
△ con|flicts
△ con|flic|ted
△ con|flict|ing
con|flu|ence
con|flu|ent
con|form
△ con|forms
△ con|formed
△ con|form|ing
con|form|able
con|for|ma|tion
con|form|ist
con|form|ity
con|found
△ con|founds
△ con|foun|ded
△ con|found|ing
con|foun|ded
con|foun|dedly
con|frère
con|front
△ con|fronts
△ con|fron|ted
△ con|front|ing
con|fron|ta|tion
Con|fu|cian
Con|fu|cian|ism
Con|fu|cian|ist
Con|fu|cius
con|fuse
△ con|fu|ses
△ con|fused
△ con|fu|sing
con|fused
con|fu|sedly
con|fu|sing
con|fu|singly

con|fu|sion
con|fu|ta|tion
con|fute
△ con|futes
△ con|fu|ted
△ con|fu|ting
conga
VERB
△ con|gas
△ con|gaed
△ con|ga|ing
cong
con|geal
△ con|geals
△ con|gealed
△ con|geal|ing
con|geal|ment
con|gela|tion
con|gener
con|gen|ial
con|geni|al|ity
con|geni|ally
con|gen|ital
con|gen|it|ally
con|ger
con|ger|ies
sing. and pl.
con|ges|ted
con|ges|tion
con|glom|er|ate
VERB
△ con|glom|er|
ates
△ con|glom|er|
ated
△ con|glom|er|
ating
con|glom|er|
ation
Congo
con|grats
con|gra|tu|late
△ con|gra|tu|
lates

△ con|gra|tu|la|
ted
△ con|gra|tu|la|
ting
con|gra|tu|la|
tion
con|gra|tu|la|
tory
con|greg|ate
△ con|greg|ates
△ con|greg|ated
△ con|greg|ating
con|grega|tion
con|grega|tional
Con|grega|tion|
al|ism
Con|grega|tion|
al|ist
Con|gress
state law-making
body (US etc)
con|gress
assembly
con|gres|sional
con|gress|man
△ con|gress|men
con|gress|wo|
man
△ con|gress|wo|
men
Con|greve
con|gru|ence
con|gru|ency
con|gru|ent
con|gru|ently
con|gru|ity
con|gru|ous
con|gru|ously
conic
con|ical
coni|fer
con|if|er|ous
Con|is|ton
con|jec|tural

con|jec|tur|ally
con|jec|ture
VERB
△ con|jec|tures
△ con|jec|tured
△ con|jec|tur|ing
con|join
△ con|joins
△ con|joined
△ con|join|ing
con|joint
con|jointly
con|ju|gal
con|ju|gal|ity
con|ju|gally
con|ju|gate
VERB
△ con|ju|gates
△ con|ju|ga|ted
△ con|ju|ga|ting
con|ju|ga|tion
con|junc|tion
con|junc|tiva
△ con|junc|ti|vas
or con|junc|ti|
vae
con|junc|ti|val
con|junct|ive
con|junct|ively
con|junc|ti|vi|tis
con|junc|ture
con|jure
△ con|jures
△ con|jured
△ con|jur|ing
con|jurer
con|jur|ing
conk
VERB
△ conks
△ conked
△ conk|ing
con|ker
Con|nacht

con|nect
△ con|nects
△ con|nec|ted
△ con|nect|ing
con|nect|able
Con|nec|ti|cut
con|nect|ing-rod
con|nec|tion
con|nect|ive
con|nec|tor
Con|ne|mara
Con|nery
con|ning-tower
con|ni|vance
con|nive
△ con|nives
△ con|nived
△ con|ni|ving
con|ni|ver
con|nois|seur
Con|nor
Con|nors
con|no|ta|tion
con|no|ta|tive
con|note
△ con|notes
△ con|no|ted
△ con|no|ting
con|nu|bial
con|nu|bi|ally
con|quer
△ con|quers
△ con|quered
△ con|quer|ing
con|quer|ing
con|queror
con|quest
con|quis|ta|dor
△ con|quis|ta|
dores *or* con|
quis|ta|dors
Con|rad
Con|ran
con|san|guin|eous

con|san|guin|ity
con|sci|ence
con|sci|ence-
stricken
con|sci|en|tious
con|sci|en|
tiously
con|sci|en|tious|
ness
con|scious
con|sciously
con|scious|ness
con|script
VERB
△ con|scripts
△ con|scrip|ted
△ con|script|ing
con|scrip|tion
con|sec|rate
△ con|sec|rates
△ con|sec|ra|ted
△ con|sec|ra|ting
con|sec|ra|tion
con|secu|tive
con|secu|tively
con|sen|sus
con|sent
VERB
△ con|sents
△ con|sen|ted
△ con|sent|ing
con|se|quence
con|se|quent
con|se|quen|tial
con|se|quently
con|serv|able
con|ser|vancy
con|ser|va|tion
con|ser|va|tion|
ist
con|serv|at|ism
Con|ser|va|tive
politics
con|ser|va|tive

disliking change
con|ser|va|tively
con|ser|va|toire
con|ser|va|tory
△ con|ser|va|tor|
ies
con|serve
VERB
△ con|serves
△ con|served
△ con|ser|ving
con|si|der
△ con|sid|ers
△ con|sid|ered
△ con|sid|er|ing
con|sid|er|able
con|sid|er|ably
con|sid|er|ate
con|sid|er|ately
con|sid|er|ate|
ness
con|sid|era|tion
con|sid|ered
con|sid|er|ing
con|sign
△ con|signs
△ con|signed
△ con|sign|ing
con|signee
con|sign|ment
con|signor
con|sist
△ con|sists
△ con|sis|ted
△ con|sist|ing
con|sis|tency
△ con|sis|ten|
cies
con|sis|tent
con|sis|tently
con|sis|tory
△ con|sis|tor|ies
con|sol|able
con|so|la|tion

con|sol|at|ory
con|sole
VERB
△ con|soles
△ con|soled
△ con|so|ling
con|sol|id|ate
△ con|sol|id|ates
△ con|sol|id|ated
△ con|sol|id|
ating
con|sol|id|ation
con|sol|id|ator
con|sols
con|sommé
con|son|ance
con|son|ant
con|son|an|tal

---

con|sort
*spouse; group of
musicians; keep
company with*
VERB
△ con|sorts
△ con|sor|ted
△ con|sort|ing
⚠ concert

---

con|sor|tium
△ con|sor|tia *or*
con|sor|ti|ums
con|spec|tus
△ con|spec|tuses
con|spicu|ous
con|spicu|ously
con|spicu|ous|
ness
con|spir|acy
△ con|spir|acies
con|spir|ator
con|spira|tor|ial
con|spira|tori|
ally
con|spire

△ con|spires
△ con|spired
△ con|spir|ing
Con|stable
con|stable
con|stab|ulary
△ con|stab|ular|ies
Con|stance
con|stancy
con|stant
Con|stan|tine
Con|stan|ti|nople
con|stantly
con|stel|la|tion
con|ster|na|tion
con|sti|pate
△ con|sti|pates
△ con|sti|pa|ted
△ con|sti|pa|ting
con|sti|pa|ted
con|sti|pa|tion
con|stitu|ency
△ con|stitu|en|cies
con|stitu|ent
con|sti|tute
△ con|sti|tutes
△ con|sti|tu|ted
△ con|sti|tu|ting
con|sti|tu|tion
con|sti|tu|tional
con|sti|tu|tion|ally
con|strain
△ con|strains
△ con|strained
△ con|strain|ing
con|strained
con|straint
con|strict
△ con|stricts
△ con|stric|ted

△ con|strict|ing
con|stric|tion
con|strict|ive
con|stric|tor
con|struct
VERB
△ con|structs
△ con|struc|ted
△ con|struct|ing
con|struc|tion
con|struc|tional
con|struct|ive
con|struct|ively
Con|struct|iv|ism
con|struc|tor
con|strue
△ con|strues
△ con|strued
△ con|stru|ing
con|sub|stan|ti|ation
con|sul
con|su|lar
con|su|late
con|sul|ship
con|sult
△ con|sults
△ con|sul|ted
△ con|sult|ing
con|sult|ancy
△ con|sult|an|cies
con|sult|ant
con|sul|ta|tion
con|sul|ta|tive
con|sult|ing
con|su|mable
con|sume
△ con|sumes
△ con|sumed
△ con|su|ming
con|sumer
con|su|mer|ism

con|su|ming
con|sum|mate
VERB
△ con|sum|mates
△ con|sum|ma|ted
△ con|sum|ma|ting
con|sum|mately
con|sum|ma|tion
con|sump|tion
con|sumpt|ive
con|tact
VERB
△ con|tacts
△ con|tac|ted
△ con|tact|ing
con|tact|able
con|ta|gion
con|ta|gious
con|tain
△ con|tains
△ con|tained
△ con|tain|ing
con|tain|able
con|tainer
con|tain|er|iza|tion
con|tain|er|ize
△ con|tain|er|izes
△ con|tain|er|ized
△ con|tain|er|izing
con|tain|ment
con|tam|in|ant
con|tam|in|ate
△ con|tam|in|ates
△ con|tam|in|ated
△ con|tam|in|ating

con|tam|in|ation
con|temn
△ con|temns
△ con|temned
△ con|tem|ning
con|tem|plate
△ con|tem|plates
△ con|tem|pla|ted
△ con|tem|pla|ting
con|tem|pla|tion
con|tem|pla|tive
con|tem|pla|tively
con|tem|por|an|eity
con|tem|pora|ne|ous
con|tem|pora|ne|ously
con|tem|por|ary
NOUN
△ con|tem|por|ar|ies
con|tempt
con|tempt|ible
con|tempt|ibly
con|temp|tu|ous
con|temp|tu|ously
con|tend
△ con|tends
△ con|ten|ded
△ con|tend|ing
con|ten|der
con|tent
VERB
△ con|tents
△ con|ten|ted
△ con|tent|ing
con|ten|ted
con|ten|tedly
con|ten|ted|ness

con|ten|tion
con|ten|tious
con|ten|tiously
con|tent|ment
con|test
  VERB
△ con|tests
△ con|tes|ted
△ con|test|ing
con|test|able
con|test|ant
con|text
con|tex|tual
con|ti|gu|ity
con|ti|gu|ous
con|ti|gu|ously
con|tin|ence
con|tin|ent
con|tin|en|tal
con|tin|gency
△ con|tin|gen|
  cies
con|tin|gent

> con|tin|ual
> *frequent;*
> *unceasing*
> ⚠ continuous

con|tinu|ally
con|tinu|ance
con|tinu|ation
con|tinue
△ con|tin|ues
△ con|tin|ued
△ con|tinu|ing
con|ti|nu|ity
con|tinuo

> con|tinu|ous
> *unceasing;*
> *unbroken*
> ⚠ continual

con|tinu|ously
con|tinuum

△ con|tinua *or*
  con|tinu|ums
con|tort
△ con|torts
△ con|tor|ted
△ con|tort|ing
con|tor|tion
con|tor|tion|ist
con|tour
  VERB
△ con|tours
△ con|toured
△ con|tour|ing
con|tra|band
con|tra|bass
△ con|tra|bas|ses
con|tra|cep|tion
con|tra|cept|ive
con|tract
  VERB
△ con|tracts
△ con|trac|ted
△ con|tract|ing

> con|tract|able
> *able to be caught*
> ⚠ contractible

> con|tract|ible
> *that can be*
> *made smaller*
> ⚠ contractable

con|tract|ile
con|trac|tion
con|trac|tor
con|tract|ual
con|trac|tu|ally
con|tra|dict
△ con|tra|dicts
△ con|tra|dic|ted
△ con|tra|dict|
  ing
con|tra|dic|tion
con|tra|dict|ory

con|tra|dis|tinc|
  tion
con|tra|flow
con|tra|in|di|cate
△ con|tra|in|di|
  cates
△ con|tra|in|di|
  ca|ted
△ con|tra|in|di|
  ca|ting
con|tra|in|di|ca|
  tion
con|tralto
con|trap|tion
con|tra|pun|tal
con|tra|punt|ally
con|tra|ri|ety
con|tra|ri|ness
con|tra|ri|ly
con|tra|ri|wise
con|trary
  NOUN
△ con|trar|ies
con|trast
  VERB
△ con|trasts
△ con|tras|ted
△ con|trast|ing
con|tra|vene
△ con|tra|venes
△ con|tra|vened
△ con|tra|ven|
  ing
con|tra|ven|tion
con|tre|temps
con|tri|bute
△ con|tri|butes
△ con|tri|bu|ted
△ con|tri|bu|ting
con|tri|bu|tion
con|tri|bu|tor
con|tri|bu|tory
con|trite
con|tritely

con|tri|tion
con|tri|vance
con|trive
△ con|trives
△ con|trived
△ con|tri|ving
con|trived
con|trol
  VERB
△ con|trols
△ con|trolled
△ con|trol|ling
con|trol|la|bil|ity
con|trol|lable
con|trol|ler
con|tro|ver|sial
con|tro|ver|si|
  ally
con|tro|versy
△ con|tro|ver|
  sies
con|tu|ma|cious
con|tu|ma|
  ciously
con|tu|macy
con|tu|me|li|ous
con|tumely
△ con|tume|lies
con|tuse
△ con|tu|ses
△ con|tused
△ con|tu|sing
con|tu|sion
co|nun|drum
con|ur|ba|tion
con|va|lesce
△ con|va|les|ces
△ con|va|lesced
△ con|va|les|cing
con|va|les|cence
con|va|les|cent
con|vec|tion
con|vec|tor
con|vene

△ con|venes
△ con|vened
△ con|ven|ing
con|vener
con|veni|ence
con|veni|ent
con|veni|ently
con|vent
con|ven|ticle
con|ven|tion
con|ven|tional
con|ven|tion|al|
  ity
△ con|ven|tion|
  al|it|ies
con|ven|tion|al|
  ize
△ con|ven|tion|
  al|izes
△ con|ven|tion|
  al|ized
△ con|ven|tion|
  al|izing
con|ven|tion|ally
con|verge
△ con|ver|ges
△ con|verged
△ con|ver|ging
con|ver|gence
con|ver|gent
con|ver|sant
con|ver|sa|tion
con|ver|sa|tional
con|ver|sa|tion|
  al|ist
con|verse
  VERB
△ con|ver|ses
△ con|versed
△ con|ver|sing
con|versely
con|ver|sion
con|vert

  VERB
△ con|verts
△ con|ver|ted
△ con|vert|ing
con|ver|ter
con|vert|ible
con|vex
con|vex|ity
△ con|vex|it|ies
con|vey
△ con|veys
△ con|veyed
△ con|vey|ing
con|vey|able
con|vey|ance
con|vey|an|cer
con|vey|an|cing
con|veyer
con|vict
  VERB
△ con|victs
△ con|vic|ted
△ con|vict|ing
con|vic|tion
con|vince
△ con|vin|ces
△ con|vinced
△ con|vin|cing
con|vinced
con|vin|cing
con|vin|cingly
con|viv|ial
con|vi|vi|al|ity
con|vi|vi|ally
Con|vo|ca|tion
  Church of
  England
  governing body
con|vo|ca|tion
  assembly; act of
  summoning
con|voke
△ con|vokes
△ con|voked

△ con|vo|king
con|vo|lu|ted
con|vo|lu|tion
con|vol|vu|lus
con|vol|vu|luses
con|voy
  VERB
△ con|voys
△ con|voyed
△ con|voy|ing
con|vulse
△ con|vul|ses
△ con|vulsed
△ con|vul|sing
con|vul|sion
con|vul|sive
con|vul|sively
Conwy
cony
△ co|nies
coo
  VERB
△ coos
△ cooed
△ coo|ing
coo|ee
  VERB
△ coo|ees
△ coo|eed
△ coo|ee|ing
Cook
cook
  VERB
△ cooks
△ cooked
△ cook|ing
cook–chill
Cooke
cooker
cook|ery
cook|book
cookie
Cook|son
cool

  VERB
△ cools
△ cooled
△ cool|ing
  ADJ.
△ cooler
△ cool|est
cool|ant
cooler
coo|lie
coolly
cool|ness
coomb
coon
coop
co–op
Cooper
coo|per
co–oper|ate
△ co–oper|ates
△ co–oper|ated
△ co–oper|ating
co–oper|ation
co–oper|ative
co–oper|atively
co–oper|ator
co–opt
△ co–opts
△ co–opted
△ co–opt|ing
co–option
co–opt|ive
co–ordi|nate
  VERB
△ co–ordi|nates
△ co–ordi|na|ted
△ co–ordi|na|
  ting
co–ordi|na|tion
co–ordi|na|tor
coot
cop
  VERB
△ cops

△ copped
△ cop|ping
cope
  VERB
  △ copes
  △ coped
  △ co|ping
Co|pen|ha|gen
Co|per|ni|cus
cop|ier
co-pilot
co|ping
co|ping-stone
co|pi|ous
co|pi|ously
Cop|land
cop-out
Cop|pé|lia
cop|per
cop|per-bot|
  tomed
cop|per|head
cop|per|plate
cop|pery
cop|pice
  VERB
  △ cop|pi|ces
  △ cop|piced
  △ cop|pi|cing
Cop|pola
copra
cop|ro|la|lia
copse
Copt
Cop|tic
cop|ula
copu|late
  △ copu|lates
  △ copu|la|ted
  △ copu|la|ting
copu|la|tion
copy
  NOUN
  △ cop|ies

VERB
  △ cop|ies
  △ cop|ied
  △ copy|ing
copy|book
copy|cat
copy|ist
copy|right
copy|wri|ter
co|que|try
co|quette
co|quet|tish
co|quet|tishly
co|quet|tish|ness
Cora
cor|acle

coral
  sea animal;
  pinkish colour
  ⚠ corral

Coral Is|land,
  The
cor|al|line
cor ang|lais
  △ cors ang|lais
cor|bel
cor|belled
cor|bel|ling
Cor|bi|ères
Cor|bu|sier

cord
  string; electric
  cable; sort of
  cloth; wood
  measurement
  ⚠ chord

cor|ded
cor|dial
cor|di|al|ity
cor|di|ally
cor|dite
cord|less

Cór|doba
cor|don
  VERB
  △ cor|dons
  △ cor|doned
  △ cor|don|ing
cor|don bleu
  NOUN
  △ cor|dons bleus
cor|du|roy
core
  VERB
  △ cores
  △ cored
  △ cor|ing
Cor|elli
corer

co-res|pon|dent
  adulterer
  ⚠ correspondent

Corfu
corgi
co|ri|an|der
Cor|inne
Cor|inth
Cor|in|thian
Cor|in|thi|ans,
  Let|ters of
  Paul to the
Co|rio|la|nus
Cork
cork
  VERB
  △ corks
  △ corked
  △ cork|ing
cork|age
corked
cor|ker
cork|screw
  VERB
  △ cork|screws
  △ cork|screwed

△ cork|screw|ing
corm
cor|mor|ant
corn
corn|cob
corn|crake
cor|nea
cor|neal
corned
Cor|neille
cor|ne|lian
Cor|nell
cor|ner
  VERB
  △ cor|ners
  △ cor|nered
  △ cor|ner|ing
cor|ner|stone
cor|net
cor|net|ist
corn|flakes

corn|flour
  maize flour
  ⚠ cornflower

corn|flower
  plant with blue
  flowers
  ⚠ cornflour

cor|nice
corn|ily
cor|ni|ness
Corn|ish
cor|nu|co|pia
cor|nu|co|pian
Corn|wall
corny
  △ cor|nier
  △ cor|ni|est
co|rolla
co|rol|lary
  △ co|rol|lar|ies
Co|ro|man|del

co|rona
△ co|ro|nae *or*
co|ro|nas
cor|on|ary
 NOUN
 △ cor|on|ar|ies
cor|on|ation
cor|oner
coro|net
co|ro|no|graph
Corot
cor|pora
cor|poral
cor|por|ate
cor|por|ately
cor|pora|tion
cor|por|at|ism
cor|por|at|iv|ism
cor|por|eal
cor|pore|al|ity
cor|por|eally
corps
 sing. and pl.
corpse
cor|pu|lence
cor|pu|lent
cor|pus
 △ cor|pora
cor|pus cal|lo|
 sum
 △ cor|pora cal|
 losa
Cor|pus Christi
cor|pus|cle
cor|pus|cu|lar
cor|pus lu|teum
 △ cor|pora lu|tea

cor|ral
 pen for animals;
 put into this
 VERB
 △ cor|rals
 △ cor|ralled

△ cor|ral|ling
 ⚠ coral

cor|rect
 VERB
 △ cor|rects
 △ cor|rec|ted
 △ cor|rect|ing
cor|rec|tion
cor|rect|ive
cor|rectly
cor|rect|ness
cor|rec|tor
Cor|reg|gio
cor|re|late
 △ cor|re|lates
 △ cor|re|la|ted
 △ cor|re|la|ting
cor|re|la|tion
cor|rel|at|ive
cor|res|pond
 △ cor|res|ponds
 △ cor|res|pon|
 ded
 △ cor|res|pond|
 ing
cor|res|pon|
 dence

cor|res|pon|dent
 writer
 ⚠ co-respondent

cor|ri|dor
cor|rie
Cor|ri|gan-
 Maguire
cor|ri|gen|dum
 △ cor|ri|genda
cor|ro|bor|ate
 △ cor|ro|bor|ates
 △ cor|ro|bor|
 ated
 △ cor|ro|bor|
 ating

cor|ro|bor|ation
cor|ro|bor|at|ive
cor|ro|bor|ator
cor|ro|bo|ree
cor|rode
 △ cor|rodes
 △ cor|ro|ded
 △ cor|ro|ding
cor|ro|sion
cor|ro|sive
cor|ru|gate
 △ cor|ru|gates
 △ cor|ru|ga|ted
 △ cor|ru|ga|ting
cor|ru|ga|tion
cor|rupt
 VERB
 △ cor|rupts
 △ cor|rup|ted
 △ cor|rupt|ing
 ADJ.
 △ cor|rup|ter
 △ cor|rupt|est
cor|rup|ti|bil|ity
cor|rup|tible
cor|rup|tion
cor|rupt|ive
cor|ruptly
cor|sage
cor|sair
corse|let
cor|set
 VERB
 △ cor|sets
 △ cor|seted
 △ cor|set|ing
cor|setry
Cor|sica
cor|tège
Cor|tes
 Spanish
 parliament
Cor|tés
 Spanish explorer

cor|tex
 △ cor|ti|ces
cor|ti|cal
cor|tic|oid
cor|ti|co|ster|oid
cor|ti|sone
co|run|dum
Co|runna
cor|us|cate
 △ cor|us|cates
 △ cor|us|ca|ted
 △ cor|us|ca|ting
cor|us|ca|tion
cor|vette
Cos
 island
cos
 lettuce
 △ cos|ses
co|sec|ant
Cos|grave
cosh
 NOUN
 △ coshes
 VERB
 △ coshes
 △ coshed
 △ cosh|ing
Così fan tutte
 (Wo|men are
 Like That)
co|sily
co|sine
co|si|ness
cos|metic
cos|met|ic|ally
cos|mic
cos|mic|ally
cos|mog|ony
 △ cos|mog|on|ies
cos|mo|lo|gi|cal
cos|mol|ogist
cos|mol|ogy
 △ cos|mol|ogies

cos|mo|naut
cos|mo|pol|itan
cos|mo|pol|itan|
  ism
cos|mos
Cos|sack
cos|set
  △ cos|sets
  △ cos|seted
  △ cos|set|ing
cost
  VERB
  △ costs
  estimate price
  △ costed
  other senses
  △ cost
  △ cost|ing
cost-account|ing
cos|tal
co-star
  VERB
  △ co-stars
  △ co-starred
  △ co-star|ring
Costa Rica
cost-effect|ive
cos|ter|mon|ger
cos|tive
cost|li|ness
costly
  △ cost|lier
  △ cost|li|est
Cost|ner
cos|tume
cos|tu|mier
cosy
  NOUN
  △ co|sies
  ADJ.
  △ co|sier
  △ co|si|est
cot
co|tan|gent

cote
co|terie
co|ter|min|ous
co|tinga
co|to|ne|as|ter
Co|to|paxi
Cots|wold
cot|tage
cot|ta|ger
cot|tar
Cot|tian Alps
cot|ton
  VERB
  △ cot|tons
  △ cot|toned
  △ cot|ton|ing
cot|ton|grass
cot|ton|wool
cot|tony
co|ty|le|don
couch
  NOUN
  △ cou|ches
  VERB
  △ cou|ches
  △ couched
  △ couch|ing
couch|ette
cou|gar
cough
  VERB
  △ coughs
  △ coughed
  △ cough|ing
could
couldn't
couldst
cou|lomb

coun|cil
body of rulers,
advisers, etc
⚠ counsel

coun|cil|lor
council member
⚠ counsellor

coun|sel
advice; lawyer;
advise
NOUN
lawyer
△ coun|sel
other senses
△ coun|sels
VERB
△ coun|sels
△ coun|selled
△ coun|sel|ling
⚠ council

coun|sel|lor
adviser
⚠ councillor

count
  VERB
  △ counts
  △ coun|ted
  △ count|ing
count|able
count|down
coun|ten|ance
  VERB
  △ coun|ten|an|
    ces
  △ coun|ten|
    anced
  △ coun|ten|an|
    cing
coun|ter
  VERB
  △ coun|ters
  △ coun|tered
  △ coun|ter|ing
coun|ter|act
  △ coun|ter|acts

  △ coun|ter|ac|ted
  △ coun|ter|act|
    ing
coun|ter|ac|tion
coun|ter|act|ive
coun|ter-attack
  VERB
  △ coun|ter-
    attacks
  △ coun|ter-
    attacked
  △ coun|ter-
    attack|ing
coun|ter-attrac|
  tion
coun|ter|bal|
  ance
  VERB
  △ coun|ter|bal|
    an|ces
  △ coun|ter|bal|
    anced
  △ coun|ter|bal|
    an|cing
coun|ter|blast
coun|ter-charge
coun|ter-claim
coun|ter-clock|
  wise
coun|ter-cul|
  ture
coun|ter-espi|
  on|age
coun|ter|feit
  VERB
  △ coun|ter|feits
  △ coun|ter|feited
  △ coun|ter|feit|
    ing
coun|ter|foil
coun|ter-insur|
  gency
coun|ter-intel|li|
  gence

coun|ter|mand
  △ coun|ter| mands
  △ coun|ter|man| ded
  △ coun|ter| mand|ing
coun|ter-meas| ure
coun|ter-offen| sive
coun|ter|pane
coun|ter|part
coun|ter|point
coun|ter|poise
coun|ter-pro| duc|tive
Coun|ter-Refor| ma|tion
coun|ter-revo|lu| tion
coun|ter-revo|lu| tion|ary
NOUN
  △ coun|ter-revo| lu|tion|ar|ies
coun|ter|sign
VERB
  △ coun|ter|signs
  △ coun|ter| signed
  △ coun|ter|sign| ing
coun|ter-sig|na| ture
coun|ter|sink
  △ coun|ter|sinks
  △ coun|ter|sank
  △ coun|ter|sink| ing
  △ coun|ter|sunk
coun|ter-tenor
coun|ter|weight
count|ess

△ count|es|ses
count|less
coun|tri|fied
coun|trify
  △ coun|tri|fies
  △ coun|tri|fied
  △ coun|tri|fy|ing
coun|try
  △ coun|tries
coun|try-and- wes|tern
coun|try|man
  △ coun|try|men
coun|try|wo| man
  △ coun|try|wo| men
coun|try|side
coun|try|wide
Coun|try Wife, The
county
NOUN
  △ coun|ties

coup
successful move
⚠ coupe
⚠ coupé

coup de grâce
  △ *coups de grâce*
coup d'état
  △ *coups d'état*

coupe
sort of pudding
⚠ coup
⚠ coupé

coupé
sort of car
⚠ coup
⚠ coupe

cou|ple

VERB
  △ cou|ples
  △ cou|pled
  △ coup|ling
coup|let
coup|ling
cou|pon
cour|age
cour|age|ous
cour|age|ously
cour|age|ous| ness
cour|ante
cour|gette
cour|ier
Cour|règes

course
path; series;
flow; hunt
VERB
△ cour|ses
△ coursed
△ cour|sing
⚠ coarse

course|book
cour|ser
cours|ing
court
VERB
  △ courts
  △ cour|ted
  △ court|ing
Cour|tauld
cour|te|ous
cour|te|ously
cour|te|ous|ness
cour|tesan
court|esy
  △ court|es|ies
court|house
court|ier
court|li|ness
court|ly

court-mar|tial
NOUN
  △ courts-mar| tial *or* court- mar|tials
VERB
  △ court-mar| tials
  △ court-mar| tialled
  △ court-mar|tial| ling
Court|ney
court|room
court|ship
court|yard
cous|cous
cousin
Cous|teau
cou|ture
cou|tu|rier
  male fashion designer
cou|tu|ri|ère
  female fashion designer
co|va|ri|ance
cove
coven
cov|en|ant
VERB
  △ cov|en|ants
  △ cov|en|an|ted
  △ cov|en|ant|ing
cov|en|an|ter
Cov|ent Gar| den
Cov|en|try
cover
VERB
  △ cov|ers
  △ cov|ered
  △ cov|er|ing
cov|er|age

cov¦er¦all
Cov¦er¦dale
cov¦er¦ing
cov¦er¦let
cov¦ert
cov¦ertly
cover-up
covet
△ cov¦ets
△ cov¦eted
△ cov¦et¦ing
cov¦et¦ous
cov¦et¦ously
cov¦et¦ous¦ness
covey
cow
VERB
△ cows
△ cowed
△ cow¦ing
Cow¦ard
cow¦ard
cow¦ard¦ice
cow¦ard¦li¦ness
cow¦ardly
cow¦bell
cow¦berry
△ cow¦ber¦ries
cow¦boy
cow¦cat¦cher
cower
△ cow¦ers
△ cow¦ered
△ cow¦er¦ing
Cowes
cow¦girl
cow¦hand
cow¦herd
cow¦hide
cow¦house
cowl
cow¦lick
cowl¦ing
cow¦man

△ cow¦men
co-wor¦ker
cow¦pat
Cow¦per
cow¦pox
cow¦rie
cow¦shed
cow¦slip
cox
NOUN
△ coxes
VERB
△ coxes
△ coxed
△ cox¦ing
cox¦comb
cox¦less
cox¦swain
coy
△ coyer
△ coy¦est
coyly
coy¦ness
coy¦ote
△ coy¦ote or
coy¦otes
coypu
△ coypu or coy¦
pus
crab
Crabbe
crab¦bed
crab¦bedly
crab¦bed¦ness
crabby
△ crab¦bier
△ crab¦bi¦est
crab¦wise
crack
VERB
△ cracks
△ cracked
△ crack¦ing
crack¦brained

crack¦down
cracked
cracker
crack¦ers
crack¦ing
crackle
VERB
△ crackles
△ crackled
△ crack¦ling
crack¦ling
crackly
crack¦nel
crack¦pot
Cracow *see*
Kraków
cra¦dle
VERB
△ cra¦dles
△ cra¦dled
△ cra¦dling
cradle-snat¦cher
craft
NOUN
boat; aircraft
△ craft
skill; handiwork
△ crafts
VERB
△ crafts
△ craf¦ted
△ craft¦ing
craf¦tily
craf¦ti¦ness
crafts¦man
△ crafts¦men
crafts¦wo¦man
△ crafts¦wo¦men
crafts¦man¦ship
crafty
△ craf¦tier
△ craf¦ti¦est
crag
crag¦gi¦ness

craggy
△ crag¦gier
△ crag¦gi¦est
Craig
Cram
cram
VERB
△ crams
△ crammed
△ cram¦ming
cram-full
cram¦mer
cramp
VERB
△ cramps
△ cramped
△ cramp¦ing
cramped
cram¦pon
cran¦berry
△ cran¦ber¦ries
crane
VERB
△ cranes
△ craned
△ cra¦ning
crane¦fly
△ crane¦flies
cranes¦bill
Cran¦ford
cra¦nial
cra¦nium
△ cra¦nia or cra¦
ni¦ums
crank
VERB
△ cranks
△ cranked
△ crank¦ing
crank¦shaft
cranky
△ cran¦kier
△ cran¦ki¦est
Cran¦mer

cran|nied
cranny
△ cran|nies
crap
VERB
△ craps
△ crapped
△ crap|ping
crape *see* crèpe
craps
cra|pu|lence
cra|pu|lent
cra|pu|lous
crash
NOUN
△ cra|shes
VERB
△ cra|shes
△ crashed
△ crash|ing
crash dive
NOUN
crash-dive
VERB
△ crash-dives
△ crash-dived
△ crash-diving
crash|ing
crash-land
△ crash-lands
△ crash-lan|ded
△ crash-land|ing
crash-land|ing
crass
△ cras|ser
△ cras|sest
cras|sly
crass|ness
Cras|sus
crate
VERB
△ crates
△ crated
△ cra|ting

crater
cra|ton
cra|vat
crave
△ craves
△ craved
△ cra|ving
cra|ven
cra|venly
cra|ven|ness
cra|ving
craw
craw|fish
sing. and pl.
Craw|ford
crawl
VERB
△ crawls
△ crawled
△ crawl|ing
crawler
Craw|ley
Craxi
cray|fish
sing. and pl.
crayon
VERB
△ cray|ons
△ cray|oned
△ cray|on|ing
craze
VERB
△ cra|zes
△ crazed
△ cra|zing
cra|zily
cra|zi|ness
crazy
△ cra|zier
△ cra|zi|est
Crazy Horse

creak
noise

VERB
△ creaks
△ creaked
△ creak|ing
⚠ creek

creak|ily
crea|ki|ness
creaky
△ creak|ier
△ crea|ki|est
cream
VERB
△ creams
△ creamed
△ cream|ing
creamer
cream|ery
△ cream|er|ies
cream|ware
creamy
△ cream|ier
△ crea|mi|est
crease
VERB
△ crea|ses
△ creased
△ creas|ing
cre|ate
△ cre|ates
△ cre|ated
△ cre|ating
cre|at|ine
cre|ation
*Cre|ation, The (Die
  Schöp|fung)*
cre|at|ive
cre|at|ively
cre|ativ|ity
cre|ator
crea|ture
crèche
cred
cre|dence

cre|den|tials
cre|di|bil|ity
cred|ible
cred|ibly
credit
VERB
△ cred|its
△ cred|ited
△ cred|it|ing
cred|it|able
cred|it|ably
cred|itor
cred|it|wor|thi|
  ness
cred|it|wor|thy
credo
cre|du|lity
credu|lous
credu|lously
creed

creek
inlet; stream
⚠ creak

creel
creep
VERB
△ creeps
△ crept
△ creep|ing
cree|per
creep|ily
cree|pi|ness
creepy
△ cree|pier
△ cree|pi|est
creepy-crawly
△ creepy-crawl|
  ies
cre|mate
VERB
△ cre|mates
△ cre|ma|ted
△ cre|ma|ting

cre|ma|tion
cre|ma|tor|ium
△ cre|ma|toria
or cre|ma|tori|
ums
crème
crème caramel
crème de la
crème
crème de
menthe
crème fraîche
cren|el|lated
cre|ole
Creon
creo|sote
crêpe
crept
cre|pus|cu|lar
crêpy
△ crê|pier
△ crê|pi|est
cres|cendo
cres|cent
cress
△ cres|ses
Cres|sida
crest
cres|ted
crest|fal|len
Cre|ta|ceous
Crete
cretin
cret|in|ism
cret|in|ous
cre|tonne

cre|vasse
crack in glacier
⚠crevice

crev|ice
narrow opening
⚠crevasse

crew
VERB
△ crews
△ crewed
△ crew|ing
crew *see* crow
crew|cut
Crewe
crewel
crew|el|work
crew-necked
crib
VERB
△ cribs
△ cribbed
△ crib|bing
crib|bage
crick
VERB
△ cricks
△ cricked
△ crick|ing
cricket
crick|eter
cri de coeur
△ *cris de coeur*
crier
cri|key
crime
Cri|mea
*Crime and Pun|
ish|ment*
crim|inal
crim|in|al|ity
crim|in|ally
cri|min|olo|gist
cri|min|ology
crimp
VERB
△ crimps
△ crimped
△ crimp|ing
Crimp|lene
crim|son

VERB
△ crim|sons
△ crim|soned
△ crim|son|ing
cringe
VERB
△ crin|ges
△ cringed
△ crin|ging
crin|ger
crin|kle
VERB
△ crin|kles
△ crin|kled
△ crink|ling
crinkly
△ crink|lier
△ crink|li|est
cri|no|line
crip|ple
VERB
△ crip|ples
△ crip|pled
△ crip|pling
Cripps
cri|sis
△ cri|ses
crisp
△ cris|per
△ crisp|est
crisp|bread
crisply
crispy
△ cris|pier
△ cris|pi|est
criss-cross
NOUN
△ criss-cros|ses
VERB
△ criss-cros|ses
△ criss-crossed
△ criss-cros|sing
cri|ter|ion
△ cri|teria

critic
crit|ical
crit|ic|ally
cri|ti|cism
cri|ti|cize
△ cri|ti|ci|zes
△ cri|ti|cized
△ cri|ti|ci|zing
cri|tique
croak
VERB
△ croaks
△ croaked
△ croak|ing
Cro|atia

cro|chet
*decorative
threadwork;
make this*
VERB
△ cro|chets
△ cro|cheted
△ cro|chet|ing
⚠crotchet

crock
crock|ery
crocket
Crock|ett
cro|co|dile
cro|cus
△ cro|cuses
Croe|sus
croft
VERB
△ crofts
△ crof|ted
△ croft|ing
crof|ter
crois|sant
Cro-Mag|non
crom|lech
Cromp|ton
Crom|well

crone
Cro|nin
Cronus
crony
△ cro|nies
crook
  VERB
  △ crooks
  △ crooked
  △ crook|ing
croo|ked
crook|edly
crook|ed|ness
croon
  VERB
  △ croons
  △ crooned
  △ croon|ing
croo|ner
crop
  VERB
  △ crops
  △ cropped
  △ crop|ping
crop|per
cro|quet
cro|quette
Crosby
cro|sier
Cros|land
cross
  NOUN
  △ cros|ses
  VERB
  △ cros|ses
  △ crossed
  △ cross|ing
  ADJ.
  △ cros|ser
  △ cros|sest
cross|bar
cross|bench
  △ cross|ben|ches
cross|ben|cher

cross|bill
cross|bones
cross|bow
cross-breed
  VERB
  △ cross-breeds
  △ cross-bred
  △ cross-breed|ing
cross-check
  VERB
  △ cross-checks
  △ cross-checked
  △ cross-check|ing
cross-coun|try
crosse
cross-exam|ina|tion
cross-exam|ine
  △ cross-exam|ines
  △ cross-exam|ined
  △ cross-exam|in|ing
cross-exam|iner
cross-eyed
cross-fer|til|iza|tion
cross-fer|til|ize
  △ cross-fer|til|izes
  △ cross-fer|til|ized
  △ cross-fer|til|izing
cross|fire
cross-grained
cross|hatch
  △ cross|hat|ches
  △ cross|hatched
  △ cross|hatch|ing
cros|sing

cross-legged or
cross-leg|ged
  according to
  pronunciation
Cross|man
cross|patch
  △ cross|pat|ches
cross-ply
cross-pol|lin|ation
cross-ques|tion
  △ cross-ques|tions
  △ cross-ques|tioned
  △ cross-ques|tion|ing
cross-refer
  △ cross-refers
  △ cross-referred
  △ cross-refer|ring
cross-ref|er|ence
  VERB
  △ cross-ref|er|en|ces
  △ cross-ref|er|enced
  △ cross-ref|er|en|cing
cross|roads
cross-sec|tional
cross-stitch
  △ cross-stit|ches
cross-talk
cross-train|ing
cross|wind
cross|wise
cross|word
crotch
  △ crot|ches

crot|chet
musical note
⚠crochet

crot|cheti|ness
crot|chety
crouch
  NOUN
  △ crou|ches
  VERB
  △ crou|ches
  △ crouched
  △ crouch|ing
croup
crou|pier
croupy
  △ crou|pier
  △ crou|pi|est
croû|ton
crow
  VERB
  △ crows
  △ crowed or crew
  △ crow|ing
crow|bar
crowd
  VERB
  △ crowds
  △ crow|ded
  △ crowd|ing
crow|ded
Crow|ley
Crown
  sovereign as head
  of state
crown
  royal headdress,
  etc
  VERB
  △ crowns
  △ crowned
  △ crown|ing
crown|ing
cro|zier
cru|ces
cru|cial
cru|cially
cru|cible

Cru|cible, The

cru|ci|fix
△ cru|ci|fixes

Cru|ci|fix|ion
of Christ

cru|ci|fix|ion
execution by
crucifying

cru|ci|form

cru|cify
△ cru|ci|fies
△ cru|ci|fied
△ cru|ci|fy|ing

crude
△ cru|der
△ cru|dest

crudely

cru|dity

cruel
△ cru|el|ler
△ cru|el|lest

cru|elly

cru|elty
△ cru|el|ties

cruet

Cruise

cruise
VERB
△ crui|ses
△ cruised
△ cruis|ing

crui|ser

cruis|er|weight

crumb
VERB
△ crumbs
△ crumbed

△ crumb|ing

crum|ble
VERB
△ crum|bles
△ crum|bled
△ crum|bling

crum|bly
△ crum|blier
△ crum|bli|est

---
crumby
full of crumbs
△ crumb|ier
△ crumbi|est
⚠ crummy
---

crum|mi|ness

---
crummy
dirty; no good
△ crum|mier
△ crum|mi|est
⚠ crumby
---

crum|pet

crum|ple
△ crum|ples
△ crum|pled
△ crump|ling

crunch
NOUN
△ crun|ches
VERB
△ crun|ches
△ crunched
△ crunch|ing

crun|chy
△ crun|chier
△ crun|chi|est

cru|sade
VERB
△ cru|sades
△ cru|sa|ded
△ cru|sa|ding

cru|sa|der

crush
NOUN
△ cru|shes
VERB
△ cru|shes
△ crushed
△ crush|ing

cru|sher

crust
VERB
△ crusts
△ crus|ted
△ crust|ing

Crus|ta|cea

crus|ta|cean

crus|tie

crust|ily

crusty
△ crus|tier
△ crus|ti|est

crutch
△ crut|ches

crux
△ cruxes *or* cru|
ces

cry
NOUN
△ cries
VERB
△ cries
△ cried

△ cry|ing

cry|baby
△ cry|ba|bies

cry|ing

cryo|gen|ics

cryo|lite

cryo|pre|ser|va|
tion

crypt

crypt|ana|ly|sis
△ crypt|ana|ly|
ses

cryp|tic

cryp|tic|ally

cryp|to|gam

cryp|to|gram

cryp|to|gra|pher

cryp|to|gra|phic

cryp|to|gra|phy

Crys|tal

crys|tal

crys|tal–gazer

crys|tal–gazing

crys|tal|line

cry|stal|liza|tion

crys|tal|lize
△ crys|tal|li|zes
△ crys|tal|lized
△ crys|tal|li|zing

crys|tal|log|ra|
pher

crys|tal|log|ra|
phy

crys|tal|loid

Cry, the Be|
loved Coun|try

cub

-ction / -xion

These suffixes are derived from a Latin ending **-tio, -tionis**, and form nouns denoting a condition or action, eg: **conjunction, connection, deflection, extinction, inflection, inspection, reflection, section**.

A few words are spelt **-xion**. The most common are **complexion** and **crucifixion**.

VERB
△ cubs
△ cubbed
△ cub|bing
Cuba
cub|by|hole
cube
VERB
△ cubes
△ cubed
△ cu|bing
cubic
cu|bi|cal
cu|bi|cle
Cu|bism
Cu|bist
cubit
cuck|old
VERB
△ cuck|olds
△ cuck|ol|ded
△ cuck|old|ing
cuck|oldry
cuckoo
cu|cum|ber
cud
cud|dle
△ cud|dles
△ cud|dled
△ cud|dling
cuddle|some
cud|dly
△ cud|dlier
△ cud|dli|est
cud|gel
VERB
△ cud|gels
△ cud|gelled
△ cud|gel|ling

cue
*signal; billiards
stick; give or use
these*

VERB
△ cues
△ cued
△ cue|ing
⚠ queue

cuff
VERB
△ cuffs
△ cuffed
△ cuf|fing
cuff|link
cuir|ass
△ cuir|as|ses
cuis|ine
Cukor
cul-de-sac
△ culs-de-sac
cu|lin|ary
Cul|kin
cull
VERB
△ culls
△ culled
△ cull|ing
Cul|loden
culm
cul|min|ate
△ cul|min|ates
△ cul|min|ated
△ cul|min|ating
cul|min|ation
cu|lottes
cul|pa|bil|ity
culp|able
cul|pably
cul|prit
cult
cul|ti|vate
△ cul|ti|vates
△ cul|ti|va|ted
△ cul|ti|va|ting
cul|ti|va|ted
cul|ti|va|tion

cul|ti|va|tor
cul|tural
cul|tur|ally
cul|ture
VERB
△ cul|tures
△ cul|tured
△ cul|tur|ing
cul|tured
cul|vert
Cum|ber|land
Cum|ber|nauld
cum|ber|some
Cum|bria
cum|brous
cumin
cum|mer|bund
cu|mu|la|tive
cu|mu|la|tively
cu|mu|lo|nim|
bus
cu|mu|lus
△ cu|muli
cu|nei|form
cun|ni|lin|gus
cun|ning
Cun|ning|ham
*Cun|ning Little
Vixen, The
(Pří|hody
Lišky Bys|trou|
šky)*
cun|ningly
cunt
cup
VERB
△ cups
△ cupped
△ cup|ping
cup|board
cup|ful
Cupid
*Roman god of
Love*

cupid
*representation of
Cupid*
cu|pid|ity
cu|pola
cuppa
cup|ping
cup|ric
cup|rite
cupro-nickel
cup|rous
cur
cur|ab|il|ity
cur|able
Cu|ra|çao
cur|acy
△ cu|ra|cies
cu|rare
cur|ate
cur|at|ive
cur|ator

curb
*restraint; raised
edge; control*
VERB
△ curbs
△ curbed
△ curb|ing
⚠ kerb

curd
cur|dle
△ cur|dles
△ cur|dled
△ curd|ling
cure
VERB
△ cures
△ cured
△ cur|ing
cure-all
cu|ret|tage
cur|ette

VERB
△ cur|ettes
△ cur|et|ted
△ cur|et|ting
cur|few
Curie
curie
curio
cu|ri|os|ity
△ cu|ri|os|it|ies
cu|ri|ous
cu|ri|ously
cu|rium
curl
VERB
△ curls
△ curled
△ curl|ing
curler
cur|lew
cur|li|cue
cur|li|ness
curl|ing
curly
△ cur|lier
△ cur|li|est
cur|mud|geon
cur|mud|geonly

cur|rant
fruit
⚠ current

cur|rency
△ cur|ren|cies

cur|rent
*flow; belonging
to the present, etc*
⚠ currant

cur|rently
cur|ri|cu|lum
△ cur|ri|cula
cur|ri|cu|lum
vitae

△ cur|ri|cula
vitae
curry
NOUN
△ cur|ries
VERB
△ cur|ries
△ cur|ried
△ cur|ry|ing
curse
VERB
△ cur|ses
△ cursed
△ curs|ing
cur|sed *or*
cursed
*according to
pronunciation*
cur|sive
cur|sively
cur|sor
cur|sor|ily
cur|sory
curt
cur|tail
△ cur|tails
△ cur|tailed
△ cur|tail|ing
cur|tail|ment
cur|tain
VERB
△ cur|tains
△ cur|tained
△ cur|tain|ing
cur|tain-raiser
curtly
curt|ness
curtsy
NOUN
△ curt|sies
VERB
△ curt|sies
△ curt|sied
△ curt|sy|ing

cur|va|ceous
cur|va|ture
curve
VERB
△ curves
△ curved
△ cur|ving
cur|vi|lin|ear
curvy
△ cur|vier
△ cur|vi|est
Cur|zon
cushi|ness
cush|ion
VERB
△ cush|ions
△ cush|ioned
△ cush|ion|ing
cushy
△ cush|ier
△ cushi|est
cusp
cuss
NOUN
△ cus|ses
VERB
△ cus|ses
△ cussed
△ cuss|ing
cus|sed
cus|sedly
cus|sed|ness
cus|tard
Cus|ter
cus|to|dial
cus|to|dian
cus|to|dian|ship
cus|tody
cus|tom
cus|tom|ar|ily
cus|tom|ary
cus|tom-built
cus|tomer
cus|tom-made

cus|toms
cut
VERB
△ cuts
△ cut
△ cut|ting
cut|away
cut|back
cute
△ cuter
△ cu|test
cutely
cute|ness
Cuth|bert
cu|ti|cle
cut|lass
△ cut|las|ses
cut|ler
cut|lery
cut|let
cut-off
cut-out
cut|ter
cut-throat
cut|ting
cuttle|fish
△ cuttle|fish *or*
cuttle|fi|shes
Cutty Sark
cut|wa|ter
cwm
cy|an|ide
cy|ano|bac|teria
cy|ano|co|bal|
amin
cy|ano|gen
cy|an|osed
cy|an|osis
Cy|bele
cy|ber|netic
cy|ber|net|ics
cy|ber|punk
cy|ber|space
cycad

Cyc|la|des
cyc|la|mate
cyc|la|men
cy|cle
　VERB
　△ cy|cles
　△ cy|cled
　△ cyc|ling
cyc|lic
cyc|li|cal
cyc|lic|ally
cyc|list
cyclo-cross
　△ cyclo-cros|ses
cyc|lo|meter
cyc|lone
cy|clonic
cyc|lo|pedia
Cyc|lops
cyc|lo|style
　VERB
　△ cyc|lo|styles

△ cyc|lo|styled
△ cyc|lo|styl|ing
cyc|lo|tron

cyg|net
　young swan
　⚠ signet

cyl|in|der
cy|lin|dri|cal
cyma
cy|mat|ium

cym|bal
　*percussion
　instrument*
　⚠ symbol

cym|bal|ist
Cym|bel|ine
cym|bid|ium
cyme
cy|mose
Cym|ric

cynic
cyn|ical
cyn|ic|ally
cyni|cism
cy|no|sure
Cyn|thia
cypher *see*
　cipher
cy|press
　△ cy|pres|ses
Cyp|riot
Cy|prus
Cy|rano de Ber|
　gerac
Cy|rene
Cyril
Cy|ril|lic
Cyrus
cyst
cys|teine
cys|tic
cys|tine

cys|ti|tis
cy|to|chrome
cy|to|gen|et|ics
cy|to|kin|esis
cy|to|ki|nin
cy|to|lo|gi|cal
cy|tol|ogist
cy|tol|ogy
cy|to|plasm
cy|to|sine
cy|to|ske|le|ton
cy|to|sol
cy|to|toxic
czar *see* tsar
czarevitch *see*
　tsarevitch
czarina *see*
　tsarina
Czech
Cze|cho|slo|va|
　kia

D

dab
  VERB
  △ dabs
  △ dabbed
  △ dab|bing
dab|ble
  △ dab|bles
  △ dab|bled
  △ dab|bling
dab|bler
dab|chick
da capo
Dacca *see*
  Dhaka
dace
  △ daces *or* dace
dacha
dachs|hund
da|coit
dac|tyl
dac|tylic
dad
Dada
Dada|ism
daddy
  △ dad|dies
daddy-long-legs
  sing. and pl.
dado
  △ dados *or* da|
  does
dae|mon
daf|fo|dil
daft
  △ dafter
  △ daft|est
daftly
daft|ness
dag|ger
dago
  △ da|goes
da|guerre|otype

Dahl
dahl *see* dal
dah|lia
Dáil
daily
  NOUN
  △ dai|lies
Daim|ler
dain|tily
dain|ti|ness
dainty
  NOUN
  △ dain|ties
  ADJ.
  △ dain|tier
  △ dain|ti|est
dai|quiri
dairy
  △ dair|ies
dairy|maid
dairy|man
  △ dairy|men
dairy|wo|man
  △ dairy|wo|men
dais
  △ daises
Daisy
daisy
  △ dai|sies
Daisy Mil|ler
daisy-wheel
Dakar
dakoit *see* dacoit
dal
Dalai Lama
Dale
dale
Dali
Dalit
Dal|las
dal|li|ance
Dal|lo|way, Mrs
dally
  △ dal|lies

△ dal|lied
△ dal|ly|ing
Dal|ma|tia
Dal|ma|tian
dal segno
Dal|ton
dal|ton

---

dam
  water barrier;
  animal's mother
  VERB
  △ dams
  △ dammed
  △ dam|ming
  ⚠damn

---

dam|age
  VERB
  △ dam|ages
  △ dam|aged
  △ dam|aging
dam|aged
dam|aging
Da|mas|cus
dam|ask
dame
Da|mian

---

damn
  curse; condemn
  VERB
  △ damns
  △ damned
  △ damn|ing
  ⚠dam

---

dam|nable
dam|nably
dam|na|tion
damned
damn|ing
Dam|ocles
damp
  VERB
  △ damps

△ damped
△ damp|ing
ADJ.
△ dam|per
△ damp|est
damp-course
dam|pen
  △ dam|pens
  △ dam|pened
  △ dam|pen|ing
damp|ener
dam|per
damply
damp|ness
damp-proof
  VERB
  △ damp-proofs
  △ damp-proofed
  △ damp-proof|
  ing
dam|sel
dam|sel|fly
  △ dam|sel|flies
dam|son
Dan
  Israelite tribe
dan
  judo, etc grade
dance
  VERB
  △ dan|ces
  △ danced
  △ dan|cing
Dance of Death,
  The
dan|cer
Dan|ces with
  Wolves
Dance to the
  Music of Time,
  A
dan|cing
dan|de|lion
dan|der

dan¦dle
 △ dan¦dles
 △ dan¦dled
 △ dand¦ling
dan¦druff
dandy
 NOUN
 △ dan¦dies
 ADJ.
 △ dan¦dier
 △ dan¦di¦est
Dane
Dane¦geld
Dane¦law
dan¦ger
dan¦ger¦ous
dan¦ger¦ously
dan¦gle
 △ dan¦gles
 △ dan¦gled
 △ dan¦gling
Dan¦iel
Dan¦iel, Book
 of
Dan¦iel Der¦
 onda
Da¦nish
dank
 △ dan¦ker
 △ dank¦est
dank¦ness
Dante
Dan¦ton
Dan¦ube
Danzig *see*
 Gdańsk
Daphne
Daph¦nia
Da Ponte
dap¦per
dap¦pled
dapple-grey
Darby and Joan
Dar¦da¦nelles

dare
 VERB
 △ dares
 △ dared
 △ dar¦ing
dare-devil
Dar es Sa¦laam
Dar¦ién
dar¦ing
dar¦ingly
Dar¦jee¦ling
dark
 ADJ.
 △ dar¦ker
 △ dark¦est
dar¦ken
 △ dark¦ens
 △ dark¦ened
 △ dark¦en¦ing
dark¦ened
darkly
dark¦ness
dark¦room
darky
 △ dark¦ies
dar¦ling
Dar¦ling¦ton
darn
 VERB
 △ darns
 △ darned
 △ darn¦ing
darned
darn¦ing
Darn¦ley
Dar¦rell
Dar¦ren
dart
 VERB
 △ darts
 △ dar¦ted
 △ dart¦ing
dart¦board
dar¦ter

Dart¦ford
dart¦ing
Dart¦moor
Dart¦mouth
darts
Dar¦win
Dar¦win¦ism
dash
 NOUN
 △ da¦shes
 VERB
 △ da¦shes
 △ dashed
 △ dash¦ing
dash¦board
dash¦ing
dash¦ingly
das¦tardly
data
 sing. and pl.
da¦ta¦bank
da¦ta¦base
da¦ta¦glove
date
 VERB
 △ dates
 △ dated
 △ da¦ting
dated
Date Line
 boundary of date
 change
dateline
 time and place of
 newspaper report
date-stamp
 VERB
 △ date-stamps
 △ date-stamped
 △ date-stamp¦
 ing
da¦tive
datum
 △ data

daub
 VERB
 △ daubs
 △ daubed
 △ daub¦ing
dau¦ber
daugh¦ter
daugh¦ter¦board
daugh¦ter-in-
 law
 △ daugh¦ters-in-
 law
daugh¦terly
daunt
 △ daunts
 △ daun¦ted
 △ daunt¦ing
daunt¦ing
daunt¦ingly
daunt¦less
Dau¦phin
Dau¦phine
Dav¦en¦ant
dav¦en¦port
David
Dav¦ina
Da Vinci
Davis
davit
Davos
Davy
daw¦dle
 △ daw¦dles
 △ daw¦dled
 △ daw¦dling
daw¦dler
Dawn
dawn
 VERB
 △ dawns
 △ dawned
 △ dawn¦ing
Day
day

Dayak
Dayan
day|break
day|dream
  VERB
  △ day|dreams
  △ day|dreamed
  △ day|dream|ing
day|drea|mer
Day-Lewis
day|light
day-release
day|time
daze
  VERB
  △ dazes
  △ dazed
  △ da|zing
dazed
daz|zle
  VERB
  △ daz|zles
  △ daz|zled
  △ daz|zling
daz|zling
daz|zlingly
D-Day
dea|con
dea|con|ess
  △ dea|con|es|ses
de|ac|ti|vate
  △ de|ac|ti|vates
  △ de|ac|ti|va|ted
  △ de|ac|ti|va|ting
de|ac|ti|va|tion
dead
dead-beat
deaden
  △ dead|ens
  △ dead|ened
  △ dead|en|ing
dead-head
  △ dead-heads
  △ dead-headed

△ dead-head|ing
dead|line
dead|li|ness
dead|lock
  VERB
  △ dead|locks
  △ dead|locked
  △ dead|lock|ing
deadly
dead|ness
dead-nettle
dead|pan
dead|weight
deaf
  △ deafer
  △ deaf|est
deaf-aid
deafen
  △ deaf|ens
  △ deaf|ened
  △ deaf|en|ing
deaf|en|ing
deaf|en|ingly
deaf-mute
deaf|ness
Deal
deal
  VERB
  △ deals
  △ dealt
  △ deal|ing
dealer
deal|er|ship
deal|ings
dealt
Dean
dean
dean|ery
  △ dean|er|ies

dear
expensive;
beloved; loved
one

ADJ.
△ dearer
△ dear|est
⚠ deer

dearly
dear|ness
dearth
death
death-bed
death-knell
death|less
deathly
death-mask
Death of a
Sales|man
death-rate
death's-head
death|trap
death-war|rant
death|watch
  beetle
deb
de|bacle
debar
  △ debars
  △ de|barred
  △ de|bar|ring
de|bar|ment
de|base
  △ de|ba|ses
  △ de|based
  △ de|ba|sing
de|based
de|base|ment
de|bat|able
de|bate
  VERB
  △ de|bates
  △ de|ba|ted
  △ de|ba|ting
de|ba|ter
de|ba|ting
de|bauch

NOUN
△ de|bau|ches
VERB
△ de|bau|ches
△ de|bauched
△ de|bauch|ing
de|bauched
de|bau|chee
de|bauch|ery
deb|en|ture
de|bi|li|tate
  △ de|bi|li|tates
  △ de|bi|li|ta|ted
  △ de|bi|li|ta|ting
de|bi|li|ta|ting
de|bi|li|ta|tion
de|bil|ity
debit
  VERB
  △ deb|its
  △ deb|ited
  △ deb|it|ing
de|bon|air
de|bon|airly
De Bono
Deb|orah
de|bouch
  △ de|bou|ches
  △ de|bouched
  △ de|bouch|ing
de|bouch|ment
Deb|rett's Peer|
age
de|brief
  △ de|briefs
  △ de|briefed
  △ de|brief|ing
de|brief|ing
deb|ris
debt
debtor
debug
  △ de|bugs
  △ de|bugged

△ de|bug|ging
de|bunk
△ de|bunks
△ de|bunked
△ de|bunk|ing
De|bussy
début
dé|bu|tante
dec|ade
dec|ad|ence
dec|ad|ent
dec|ad|ently
de|caff
de|caf|fein|ate
△ de|caf|fein|ates
△ de|caf|fein|ated
△ de|caf|fein|ating
de|caf|fein|ated
deca|gon
de|ca|gonal
de|ca|hed|ral
de|ca|hed|ron
De|ca|logue
De|cam|eron
de|camp
△ de|camps
△ de|camped
△ de|camp|ing
de|ca|nal
de|cant
△ de|cants
△ de|can|ted
△ de|cant|ing
de|can|ter
de|cap|it|ate
△ de|cap|it|ates
△ de|cap|it|ated
△ de|cap|it|ating
de|cap|it|ation
de|ca|pod
De|ca|poda

de|car|bon|iza|tion
de|car|bon|ize
△ de|car|bon|izes
△ de|car|bon|ized
△ de|car|bon|izing
dec|ath|lete
dec|ath|lon
decay
VERB
△ de|cays
△ de|cayed
△ de|cay|ing
de|cease
de|ceased
de|ceit
de|ceit|ful
de|ceit|fully
de|ceive
△ de|ceives
△ de|ceived
△ de|ceiv|ing
de|ceiver
de|cel|er|ate
△ de|cel|er|ates
△ de|cel|er|ated
△ de|cel|er|ating
de|cel|er|ation
De|cem|ber
de|cency
△ de|cen|cies
de|cen|nial
de|cent
de|cently
de|cen|tral|iza|tion
de|cen|tral|ize
△ de|cen|tral|izes
△ de|cen|tral|ized

△ de|cen|tral|izing
de|cep|tion
de|cep|tive
de|cep|tively
de|ci|bel
de|cide
△ de|cides
△ de|ci|ded
△ de|ci|ding
de|ci|ded
de|ci|dedly
de|ci|der
de|ci|du|ous
de|ci|litre
de|ci|mal
de|ci|mal|iza|tion
de|ci|mal|ize
△ de|ci|mal|izes
△ de|ci|mal|ized
△ de|ci|mal|izing
de|ci|mate
△ de|ci|mates
△ de|ci|ma|ted
△ de|ci|ma|ting
de|ci|ma|tion
de|ci|pher
△ de|ci|phers
△ de|ci|phered
△ de|ci|pher|ing
de|ci|pher|able
de|ci|pher|ment
de|cis|ion
de|ci|sive
de|ci|sively
de|ci|sive|ness
deck
VERB
△ decks
△ decked
△ deck|ing
deck-chair
decko *see* dekko

de|claim
△ de|claims
△ de|claimed
△ de|claim|ing
dec|la|ma|tion
de|clam|at|ory
Dec|lan
dec|lar|ation
de|clar|at|ive
de|clare
△ de|clares
△ de|clared
△ de|clar|ing
de|clas|si|fi|ca|tion
de|clas|sify
△ de|clas|si|fies
△ de|clas|si|fied
△ de|clas|si|fy|ing
de|clen|sion
dec|li|na|tion
de|cline
VERB
△ de|clines
△ de|clined
△ de|cli|ning
De|cline and Fall of the Roman Em|pire, The
de|cliv|ity
△ de|cliv|it|ies
de|clutch
△ de|clut|ches
△ de|clutched
△ de|clutch|ing
de|coc|tion
de|code
△ de|codes
△ de|co|ded
△ de|co|ding
de|co|der
dé|col|let|age

dé|col|leté
of low-cut dress
dé|col|letée
*of woman wearing
low-cut dress*
de|com|mis|sion
△ de|com|mis|
 sions
△ de|com|mis|
 sioned
△ de|com|mis|
 sion|ing
de|com|pose
△ de|com|po|ses
△ de|com|posed
△ de|com|po|
 sing
de|com|po|si|tion
de|com|press
△ de|com|pres|
 ses
△ de|com|
 pressed
△ de|com|pres|
 sing
de|com|pres|sion
de|con|gest|ant
de|con|struc|tion
de|con|tam|in|
 ate
△ de|con|tam|in|
 ates
△ de|con|tam|in|
 ated
△ de|con|tam|
 ina|ting
de|con|tam|ina|
 tion
décor
dec|or|ate
△ dec|or|ates
△ dec|or|ated
△ dec|or|ating
dec|or|ating

dec|or|ation
dec|or|at|ive
dec|or|ator
dec|or|ous
dec|or|ously
de|corum
decoy
VERB
△ de|coys
△ de|coyed
△ de|coy|ing
de|crease
VERB
△ de|crea|ses
△ de|creased
△ de|creas|ing
de|creas|ingly
de|cree
VERB
△ de|crees
△ de|creed
△ de|cree|ing
de|crepit
de|crepi|tude
de|cre|tal

decry
 criticize
△ de|cries
△ de|cried
△ de|cry|ing
⚠ descry

dedi|cate
△ dedi|cates
△ dedi|ca|ted
△ dedi|ca|ting
dedi|ca|ted
dedi|ca|tion
dedi|ca|tor
dedi|ca|tory
de|duce
△ de|duces
△ de|duced
△ de|du|cing

de|du|cible
de|duct
△ de|ducts
△ de|duc|ted
△ de|duct|ing
de|duct|ible
de|duc|tion
de|duc|tive
deed
dee-jay
deem
△ deems
△ deemed
△ deem|ing
deep
ADJ.
△ deeper
△ deep|est
dee|pen
△ deep|ens
△ deep|ened
△ deep|en|ing
deep-freeze
VERB
△ deep-free|zes
△ deep-froze
△ deep-freez|ing
△ deep-fro|zen
deep-fry
△ deep-fries
△ deep-fried
△ deep-fry|ing
deeply
deep-roo|ted
deep-sea
deep-sea|ted
deep-set

deer
 *animal with
 antlers etc
 sing. and pl.*
⚠ dear

deer|hound

deer|skin
deer|stal|ker
de|face
△ de|fa|ces
△ de|faced
△ de|fa|cing
de|face|ment
de facto
de|fa|ma|tion
de|fam|at|ory
de|fame
△ de|fames
△ de|famed
△ de|fa|ming
de|fault
VERB
△ de|faults
△ de|faul|ted
△ de|fault|ing
de|faul|ter
de|feat
VERB
△ de|feats
△ de|fea|ted
△ de|feat|ing
de|feat|ism
de|feat|ist
de|fec|ate
△ de|fec|ates
△ de|fec|ated
△ de|fec|ating
de|fec|ation
de|fect
VERB
△ de|fects
△ de|fec|ted
△ de|fect|ing
de|fec|tion
de|fect|ive
de|fec|tor
de|fence
de|fence|less
de|fend
△ de|fends

△ de|fen|ded
△ de|fend|ing
de|fend|ant
de|fen|der
de|fens|ible
de|fens|ibly
de|fen|sive
de|fen|sively
de|fen|sive|ness
defer
  △ de|fers
  △ de|ferred
  △ de|fer|ring
def|er|ence
def|er|en|tial
def|er|en|tially
de|fer|ment
de|fer|ral
de|fi|ance
de|fi|ant
de|fi|antly
de|fi|ci|ency
  △ de|fi|ci|en|cies
de|fi|ci|ent
de|fi|cit
de|file
  VERB
  △ de|files
  △ de|filed
  △ de|fi|ling
de|file|ment
de|fi|ler
de|fin|able
de|fine
  △ de|fines
  △ de|fined
  △ de|fi|ning
def|in|ite
def|in|itely
def|in|ite|ness
de|fi|ni|tion
de|fin|it|ive
de|fin|it|ively
de|flate

△ de|flates
△ de|fla|ted
△ de|fla|ting
de|fla|ted
de|fla|tion
de|fla|tion|ary
de|flect
△ de|flects
△ de|flec|ted
△ de|flect|ing
de|flec|tion
de|flower
△ de|flowers
△ de|flowered
△ de|flower|ing
Defoe
de|fo|li|ant
de|fo|li|ate
△ de|fo|li|ates
△ de|fo|li|ated
△ de|fo|li|ating
de|fo|li|ation
de|for|est
△ de|for|ests
△ de|for|es|ted
△ de|for|est|ing
de|for|es|ta|tion
de|form
△ de|forms
△ de|formed
△ de|form|ing
de|formed
de|form|ity
△ de|form|it|ies
de|fraud
△ de|frauds
△ de|frau|ded
△ de|fraud|ing
de|fray
△ de|frays
△ de|frayed
△ de|fray|ing
de|frayal
de|fray|ment

de|frock
△ de|frocks
△ de|frocked
△ de|frock|ing
de|frost
△ de|frosts
△ de|fros|ted
△ de|frost|ing
deft
△ def|ter
△ deft|est
deftly
deft|ness
de|funct
de|fuse
△ de|fu|ses
△ de|fused
△ de|fu|sing
defy
△ de|fies
△ de|fied
△ de|fy|ing
Degas
de Gaulle
de|gaus|sing
de|gen|er|acy
de|gen|er|ate
  VERB
△ de|gen|er|ates
△ de|gen|er|ated
△ de|gen|er|ating
de|gen|er|ation
de|gen|er|at|ive
de|grad|able
deg|ra|da|tion
de|grade
△ de|grades
△ de|gra|ded
△ de|gra|ding
de|gra|ding
de|gree
De Hav|il|land
de|his|cent

de|hu|man|ize
△ de|hu|man|
  izes
△ de|hu|man|
  ized
△ de|hu|man|
  izing
de|hy|drate
△ de|hy|drates
△ de|hy|dra|ted
△ de|hy|dra|ting
de|hy|dra|ted
de|hy|dra|tion
de-ice
△ de-ices
△ de-iced
△ de-icing
de-icer
dei|fi|ca|tion
deify
△ dei|fies
△ dei|fied
△ dei|fy|ing
deign
△ deigns
△ deigned
△ deign|ing
de|ion|iza|tion
Deir|dre
deism
deist
deity
△ dei|ties
déjà vu
de|jec|ted
de|jec|tedly
de|jec|tion
Dé|jeuner sur
  l'herbe, Le
de jure
Dek|ker
dekko
De|la|croix
De La Mare

De La Roche
delay
  VERB
  △ de¦lays
  △ de¦layed
  △ de¦lay¦ing
de¦lect¦able
de¦lect¦ably
de¦lec¦ta¦tion
dele¦gate
  VERB
  △ dele¦gates
  △ dele¦ga¦ted
  △ dele¦ga¦ting
dele¦ga¦tion
de¦lete
  △ de¦letes
  △ de¦le¦ted
  △ de¦let¦ing
de¦le¦teri¦ous
de¦le¦teri¦ously
de¦le¦tion
delf
Delft
Delft¦ware
Delhi
Delia
de¦lib¦er¦ate
  VERB
  △ de¦lib¦er¦ates
  △ de¦lib¦er¦ated
  △ de¦lib¦er¦ating
de¦lib¦er¦ately
de¦lib¦er¦ation
De¦libes
deli¦cacy
  △ deli¦ca¦cies
deli¦cate
deli¦cately
deli¦ca¦tes¦sen
de¦li¦cious
de¦li¦ciously
de¦light

VERB
△ de¦lights
△ de¦ligh¦ted
△ de¦light¦ing
de¦ligh¦ted
de¦ligh¦tedly
de¦light¦ful
de¦light¦fully
De¦li¦lah
de¦limit
△ de¦lim¦its
△ de¦lim¦ited
△ de¦lim¦it¦ing
de¦li¦mi¦ta¦tion
de¦lin¦eate
△ de¦lin¦eates
△ de¦lin¦ea¦ted
△ de¦lin¦ea¦ting
de¦lin¦ea¦tion
de¦lin¦quency
de¦lin¦quent
de¦li¦quesce
△ de¦li¦ques¦ces
△ de¦li¦quesced
△ de¦li¦ques¦cing
de¦li¦ques¦cence
de¦li¦ques¦cent
de¦liri¦ous
de¦liri¦ously
de¦lir¦ium
De¦lius
de¦liver
△ de¦liv¦ers
△ de¦liv¦ered
△ de¦liv¦er¦ing
de¦liv¦er¦ance
de¦liv¦erer
de¦liv¦ery
△ de¦liv¦er¦ies
dell
Delos
De Los An¦ge¦
  les
delph *see* delf

Del¦phi
Del¦phine
del¦phin¦ium
  △ del¦phin¦iums
  or del¦phinia
delta
de¦lude
  △ de¦ludes
  △ de¦lu¦ded
  △ de¦lu¦ding
de¦luge
  VERB
  △ de¦lu¦ges
  △ de¦luged
  △ de¦lu¦ging
de¦lu¦sion
de¦lu¦sive
de¦lu¦sory
de luxe
delve
  △ delves
  △ delved
  △ del¦ving
de¦mag¦net¦ize
  △ de¦mag¦net¦
    izes
  △ de¦mag¦net¦
    ized
  △ de¦mag¦net¦
    izing
dem¦ago¦gic
dem¦agogue
dem¦agoguery
dem¦agogy
de¦mand
  VERB
  △ de¦mands
  △ de¦man¦ded
  △ de¦mand¦ing
de¦mand¦ing
de¦mar¦cate
  △ de¦mar¦cates
  △ de¦mar¦ca¦ted
  △ de¦mar¦ca¦ting

de¦mar¦ca¦tion
de¦mean
  △ de¦means
  △ de¦meaned
  △ de¦mean¦ing
de¦mean¦ing
de¦mean¦our
de¦men¦ted
de¦men¦tedly
de¦men¦tia
dem¦er¦ara
de¦merit
De¦me¦ter
demi¦god
demi¦john
de¦mil¦it¦ar¦iza¦
  tion
de¦mil¦it¦ar¦¦ize
  △ de¦mil¦it¦ar¦
    izes
  △ de¦mil¦it¦ar¦
    ized
  △ de¦mil¦it¦ar¦
    izing
De Mille
de¦mise
demi¦semi¦qua¦
  ver
de¦mist
  △ de¦mists
  △ de¦mis¦ted
  △ de¦mist¦ing
de¦mis¦ter
demo
demob
  VERB
  △ de¦mobs
  △ de¦mobbed
  △ de¦mob¦bing
de¦mo¦bil¦iza¦
  tion
de¦mo¦bil¦ize
  △ de¦mo¦bil¦izes
  △ de¦mo¦bil¦ized

△ de|mo|bil|
  izing
de|mo|cracy
  △ de|mo|cra|cies
demo|crat
demo|cra|tic
de|mo|crat|ic|
  ally
De|moc|ri|tus
de|modu|late
  △ de|modu|lates
  △ de|modu|la|
    ted
  △ de|modu|la|
    ting
de|modu|la|tor
de|mo|gra|pher
de|mo|gra|phic
de|mo|gra|phy
De|moi|selles
  d'Avig|non,
  Les
de|mol|ish
  △ de|mol|ishes
  △ de|mol|ished
  △ de|mol|ish|ing
de|mo|li|tion
demon
de|mo|niac
de|mo|ni|acal
de|monic
de|mon|ic|ally
dem|on|strable
dem|on|strably
dem|on|strate
  △ dem|on|strates
  △ dem|on|stra|
    ted
  △ dem|on|stra|
    ting
de|mon|stra|tion
de|mon|stra|tive
de|mon|stra|
  tively

dem|on|stra|tor
de|mor|al|iza|
  tion
de|mor|al|ize
  △ de|mor|al|izes
  △ de|mor|al|ized
  △ de|mor|al|
    izing
De|mos|thenes
de|mote
  △ de|motes
  △ de|mo|ted
  △ de|mo|ting
de|motic
de|mo|tion
demur
  VERB
  △ de|murs
  △ de|murred
  △ de|mur|ring
de|mure
de|murely
de|mure|ness
de|mur|ral
de|mys|ti|fi|ca|
  tion
de|mys|tify
  △ de|mys|ti|fies
  △ de|mys|ti|fied
  △ de|mys|ti|fy|
    ing
den
den|ar|ius
  △ den|arii
de|na|tion|al|iza|
  tion
de|na|tion|al|ize
  △ de|na|tion|al|
    izes
  △ de|na|tion|al|
    ized
  △ de|na|tion|al|
    izing
de|na|ture

△ de|na|tures
△ de|na|tured
△ de|na|tur|ing
den|drite
den|dro|chron|
  ol|ogy
den|drol|ogist
den|drol|ogy
den|dron
Deng Xiao|ping
de|nial
den|ier
de|nig|rate
  △ de|nig|rates
  △ de|nig|ra|ted
  △ de|nig|ra|ting
de|nig|ra|tion
de|nig|ra|tor
denim
De Niro
Denis, St
Denis
den|izen
Den|mark
Den|ning
Den|nis
de|nom|in|ate
  △ de|nom|in|ates
  △ de|nom|in|
    ated
  △ de|nom|in|
    ating
de|no|mi|na|tion
de|no|mi|na|
  tional
de|nom|in|ator
de|no|ta|tion
de|note
  △ de|notes
  △ de|no|ted
  △ de|no|ting
dé|noue|ment
de|nounce
  △ de|noun|ces

△ de|nounced
△ de|noun|cing
dense
  △ den|ser
  △ den|sest
densely
dense|ness
den|sity
  △ den|si|ties
dent
  VERB
  △ dents
  △ den|ted
  △ dent|ing
den|tal
den|tate
den|ti|frice
den|til
den|tine
den|tist
den|tis|try
den|ti|tion
den|ture
de|nu|da|tion
de|nude
  △ de|nudes
  △ de|nu|ded
  △ de|nu|ding
de|nun|ci|ation
Den|ver
deny
  △ de|nies
  △ de|nied
  △ de|ny|ing
Denys, St *see*
  Denis, St
de|odor|ant
de|odor|iza|tion
de|odor|ize
  △ de|odor|izes
  △ de|odor|ized
  △ de|odor|izing
de|oxy|ri|bo|nu|
  cleic

de|paato
De|par|dieu
de|part
△ de|parts
△ de|par|ted
△ de|part|ing
de|par|ted
de|part|ment
de|part|men|tal
de|par|ture
de|pend
△ de|pends
△ de|pen|ded
△ de|pend|ing
de|pend|abil|ity
de|pend|able
de|pend|ably

de|pend|ant
NOUN
⚠ dependent

de|pend|ence
de|pend|ency
△ de|pend|en|
cies

de|pend|ent
ADJ.
⚠ dependant

de|per|son|al|iza|
tion
de|per|son|al|ize
△ de|per|son|al|
izes
△ de|per|son|al|
ized
△ de|per|son|al|
izing
de|pict
△ de|picts
△ de|pic|ted
△ de|pict|ing
de|pic|tion
de|pil|at|ory

NOUN
△ de|pil|at|or|ies
de|plete
△ de|pletes
△ de|ple|ted
△ de|ple|ting
de|ple|tion
de|plor|able
de|plor|ably
de|plore
△ de|plores
△ de|plored
△ de|plor|ing
de|ploy
△ de|ploys
△ de|ployed
△ de|ploy|ing
de|ploy|ment
de|po|lar|iza|
tion
de|popu|late
△ de|popu|lates
△ de|popu|la|ted
△ de|popu|la|
ting
de|popu|la|ted
de|popu|la|tion
de|port
△ de|ports
△ de|por|ted
△ de|port|ing
de|por|ta|tion
de|por|tee
de|port|ment
de|pose
△ de|po|ses
△ de|posed
△ de|po|sing
de|posit
VERB
△ de|pos|its
△ de|pos|ited
△ de|pos|it|ing

de|pos|it|ary
person entrusted
△ de|pos|it|ar|ies
⚠ depository

de|pos|ition
de|pos|itor

de|pos|it|ory
store; depositary
△ de|pos|it|or|
ies
⚠ depositary

depot
de|prave
△ de|praves
△ de|praved
△ de|pra|ving
de|praved
de|prav|ity

de|pre|cate
deplore
△ de|pre|cates
△ de|pre|ca|ted
△ de|pre|ca|ting
⚠ depreciate

de|pre|ca|ting
de|pre|ca|tingly
de|pre|ca|tion
de|pre|ca|tory

de|pre|ci|ate
*become or make
of less value;
belittle*
△ de|pre|ci|ates
△ de|pre|ci|ated
△ de|pre|ci|ating
⚠ deprecate

de|pre|ci|ation
de|pre|ci|at|ory
de|pre|da|tion
de|press

△ de|pres|ses
△ de|pressed
△ de|pres|sing
de|pres|sant
de|pressed
de|pres|sing
de|pres|singly
de|pres|sion
de|pres|sive
de|pri|va|tion
de|prive
△ de|prives
△ de|prived
△ de|pri|ving
de|prived
depth
de|pu|ta|tion
de|pute
△ de|putes
△ de|pu|ted
△ de|pu|ting
depu|tize
△ depu|ti|zes
△ depu|tized
△ depu|ti|zing
dep|uty
NOUN
△ depu|ties
De Quin|cey
de|rail
△ de|rails
△ de|railed
△ de|rail|ing
de|rail|ment
de|range
△ de|ran|ges
△ de|ranged
△ de|ran|ging
de|ranged
de|range|ment
Derby
derby
△ der|bies
Der|by|shire

de|regu|late
△ de|regu|lates
△ de|regu|la|ted
△ de|regu|la|ting
de|regu|la|tion
de|re|lict
de|re|lic|tion
de|res|trict
△ de|res|tricts
, △ de|res|tric|ted
△ de|res|trict|ing
de|res|tric|tion
de|ride
△ de|rides
△ de|ri|ded
△ de|ri|ding
de ri|gueur
de|ri|sion
de|ri|sive
de|ri|sively
de|ri|sory
de|ri|va|tion
de|riv|ative
de|rive
△ de|rives
△ de|rived
△ de|ri|ving
der|ma|ti|tis
der|ma|tol|ogist
der|ma|tol|ogy
der|mis
Der|mot
de|ro|gate
△ de|ro|gates
△ de|ro|ga|ted
△ de|ro|ga|ting
de|ro|ga|tion
de|ro|ga|tor|ily
de|rog|at|ory
der|rick
Der|rida
der|ring-do
der|ris
Derry

derv
der|vish
△ der|vi|shes
Der|went
de|sa|lin|ate
△ de|sa|lin|ates
△ de|sa|lin|ated
△ de|sa|lin|ating
de|sa|lin|ation
des|cant
Des|cartes
des|cend
△ des|cends
△ des|cen|ded
△ des|cend|ing

---
des|cend|ant
NOUN
⚠ descendent

---
des|cend|ent
ADJ.
⚠ descendant
---

des|cend|ing
des|cent
des|cribe
△ des|cribes
△ des|cribed
△ des|cri|bing
des|crip|tion
des|crip|tive
des|crip|tively

---
des|cry
catch sight of
△ des|cries
△ des|cried
△ des|cry|ing
⚠ decry
---

de|se|crate
△ de|se|crates
△ de|se|cra|ted
△ de|se|cra|ting
de|se|cra|tion

de|se|cra|tor
de|seg|re|gate
△ de|seg|re|gates
△ de|seg|re|ga|ted
△ de|seg|re|ga|ting
de|se|gre|ga|tion
de|sel|ect
△ de|sel|ects
△ de|sel|ec|ted
△ de|sel|ect|ing
de|sel|ec|tion
de|sen|si|ti|za|tion
de|sen|si|tize
△ de|sen|si|ti|zes
△ de|sen|si|tized
△ de|sen|si|ti|zing

---
des|ert
arid area
⚠ dessert

---
de|sert
abandon
△ de|serts
△ des|er|ted
△ des|ert|ing
⚠ dessert
---

des|er|ted
Des|er|ted Vil|lage, The
des|er|ter
des|er|ti|fi|ca|tion
des|er|tion
des|erts
de|serve
△ de|serves
△ de|served
△ de|ser|ving
de|ser|vedly

de|ser|ving
dés|ha|billé
De Sica
des|ic|cant
des|ic|cate
△ des|ic|cates
△ des|ic|ca|ted
△ des|ic|ca|ting
des|ic|ca|ted
des|ic|ca|tion
des|ic|ca|tor
de|si|der|atum
△ de|si|der|ata
de|sign
VERB
△ de|signs
△ de|signed
△ de|sign|ing
des|ig|nate
VERB
△ des|ig|nates
△ des|ig|na|ted
△ des|ig|na|ting
des|ig|na|tion
de|sign|edly
de|signer
de|sign|ing
de|sir|ab|il|ity
de|sir|able
de|sir|ably
de|sire
VERB
△ de|sires
△ de|sired
△ de|sir|ing
De|sire Under the Elms
de|sir|ous
de|sist
△ de|sists
△ de|sis|ted
△ de|sist|ing
desk
de|skil|ling

desk-top
Des Moines
Des|mond
Des|mou|lins
deso|late
   VERB
   △ deso|lates
   △ deso|la|ted
   △ deso|la|ting
deso|la|ted
deso|la|tion
des|pair
   VERB
   △ des|pairs
   △ des|paired
   △ des|pair|ing
des|pair|ing
des|pair|ingly
despatch *see*
   dispatch
des|per|ado
   △ des|per|ados
   or des|per|
   adoes
des|per|ate
des|per|ately
des|per|ation
des|pic|able
des|pic|ably
des|pise
   △ des|pi|ses
   △ des|pised
   △ des|pi|sing
de|spite
de|spoil
   △ de|spoils
   △ de|spoiled
   △ de|spoil|ing
de|spoiler
de|spo|li|ation
des|pon|dency
des|pon|dent
des|pon|dently
des|pot

des|po|tic
des|pot|ic|ally
des|po|tism

| des|sert |
| *pudding etc* |
| ⚠ desert |

des|sert|spoon
des|sert|spoon|
   ful
de|sta|bil|iza|
   tion
de|sta|bil|ize
   △ de|sta|bil|izes
   △ de|sta|bil|ized
   △ de|sta|bil|izing
De Stijl
des|ti|na|tion
des|tine
   △ des|tines
   △ des|tined
   △ des|tin|ing
des|tiny
   △ des|tin|ies
des|ti|tute
des|ti|tu|tion
des|troy
   △ des|troys
   △ des|troyed
   △ des|troy|ing
des|troyer
de|struct
   △ de|structs
   △ de|struc|ted
   △ de|struct|ing
de|struc|ti|bil|ity
de|struct|ible
de|struc|tion
de|struc|tive
de|struc|tively
de|sul|tor|ily
des|ul|tory
de|tach
   △ de|ta|ches

△ de|tached
△ de|tach|ing
de|tach|able
de|tached
de|tach|edly
de|tach|ment
de|tail
   VERB
   △ de|tails
   △ de|tailed
   △ de|tail|ing
de|tailed
de|tain
   △ de|tains
   △ de|tained
   △ de|tain|ing
de|tainee
de|tect
   △ de|tects
   △ de|tec|ted
   △ de|tect|ing
de|tect|able
de|tec|tion
de|tect|ive
de|tec|tor
dé|tente
de|ten|tion
deter
   △ de|ters
   △ de|terred
   △ de|ter|ring
de|ter|gent
de|teri|or|ate
   △ de|teri|or|ates
   △ de|teri|or|ated
   △ de|teri|or|
   ating
de|teri|or|ation
de|ter|min|ant
de|ter|min|ate
de|ter|min|ation
de|ter|min|at|ive
de|ter|mine
   △ de|ter|mines

△ de|ter|mined
△ de|ter|min|ing
de|ter|mined
de|ter|mi|ner
de|ter|min|ism
de|ter|min|ist
de|ter|rence
de|ter|rent
de|test
   △ de|tests
   △ de|tes|ted
   △ de|test|ing
de|test|able
de|test|ably
de|tes|ta|tion
de|throne
   △ de|thrones
   △ de|throned
   △ de|thro|ning
de|throne|ment
det|on|ate
   △ det|on|ates
   △ det|on|ated
   △ det|on|ating
det|on|ation
det|on|ator
de|tour
   VERB
   △ de|tours
   △ de|toured
   △ de|tour|ing
de|toxi|fi|ca|tion
de|tox|ify
   △ de|toxi|fies
   △ de|toxi|fied
   △ de|toxi|fy|ing
de|tract
   △ de|tracts
   △ de|trac|ted
   △ de|tract|ing
de|trac|tion
de|trac|tor
det|ri|ment
det|ri|men|tal

det¦ri¦men¦tally
det¦ri¦tus
De¦troit
de trop
deuce
deus ex mach\ina
deu¦ter¦ium
deu¦teron
Deu¦ter¦on¦omy,
 Book of
Deutsch\mark
de Val¦era
De Val¦ois
de¦va¦lu¦ation
de¦value
 △ de¦values
 △ de¦valued
 △ de¦valu¦ing
dev¦as¦tate
 △ dev¦as¦tates
 △ dev¦as¦ta¦ted
 △ dev¦as¦ta¦ting
dev¦as¦ta¦ted
dev¦as¦ta¦ting
dev¦as¦ta¦tingly
dev¦as¦ta¦tion
de¦velop
 △ de¦vel¦ops
 △ de¦vel¦oped
 △ de¦vel¦op¦ing
de¦vel¦oper
de¦vel¦op¦ing
de¦vel¦op¦ment
de¦vel¦op¦men¦
 tal
de¦vel¦op¦men¦
 tally
de¦vi¦ance
de¦vi¦ant
de¦vi¦ate
 △ de¦vi¦ates
 △ de¦vi¦ated
 △ de¦vi¦ating
de¦vi¦ation

de¦vi¦ation¦ism
de¦vi¦ation¦ist
de¦vice
devil
 VERB
 △ dev¦ils
 △ dev¦illed
 △ dev¦il¦ling
dev¦il¦ish
dev¦il¦ishly
devil-may-care
dev¦il¦ment
dev¦ilry
 △ dev¦il¦ries
*Devil's Dis\ciple,
 The*
De¦vine
de¦vi¦ous
de¦vi¦ously
de¦vi¦ous¦ness
de¦vise
 △ de¦vi¦ses
 △ de¦vised
 △ de¦vi¦sing
De¦vizes
Dev¦lin
de¦void
de¦vo¦lu¦tion
de¦vo¦lu¦tion¦ist
de¦volve
 △ de¦volves
 △ de¦volved
 △ de¦vol¦ving
Devon
De¦vo¦nian
de¦vote
 △ de¦votes
 △ de¦vo¦ted
 △ de¦vo¦ting
de¦vo¦ted
de¦vo¦tedly
de¦vo¦ted¦ness
de¦vo¦tee
de¦vo¦tion

de¦vo¦tional
de¦vour
 △ de¦vours
 △ de¦voured
 △ de¦vour¦ing
de¦vout
de¦voutly
de¦vout¦ness

> dew
> *water droplets*
> △ due

dew¦claw
dew¦drop
Dewey
dew¦lap
dewy
 △ dew¦ier
 △ dewi¦est
dewy-eyed
dex¦ter¦ity
dex¦ter¦ous
dex¦ter¦ously
dex¦tral
dex¦trin
dex¦trose
Dhaka
dhal *see* dal
dharma
dhobi
dhoti
dhow
dia¦be¦tes
dia¦betic
dia¦bolic
dia¦bol¦ical
dia¦bol¦ic¦ally
di¦ab¦ol¦ism
dia¦chronic
dia¦chron¦ical
di¦ac¦on¦ate
dia¦cri¦tic
dia¦crit¦ical
dia¦dem

di¦aere¦sis
 △ di¦aere¦ses
dia¦gen¦esis
Diag¦hi¦lev
di¦ag¦nose
 △ di¦ag¦no¦ses
 △ di¦ag¦nosed
 △ di¦ag¦no¦sing
di¦ag¦no¦sis
 △ di¦ag¦no¦ses
di¦ag¦nos¦tic
di¦agonal
di¦ag¦on¦ally
dia¦gram
dia¦gram¦matic
dia¦gram¦mat¦ic¦
 ally
dia¦ki¦ne¦sis
dial
 VERB
 △ d¦als
 △ dialled
 △ dial¦ling
dia¦lect
dia¦lec¦tal
dia¦lec¦tic
dia¦lec¦ti¦cal
dia¦logue
dia¦lyse
 △ dia¦ly¦ses
 △ dia¦lysed
 △ dia¦ly¦sing
di¦aly¦sis
 △ di¦aly¦ses
dia¦manté
di¦am¦eter
dia¦met¦ric
dia¦met¦ri¦cal
dia¦met¦ric¦ally
dia¦mond
Diana
di¦an¦thus
dia¦pause
dia¦per

di｜aph｜an｜ous
dia｜phragm
di｜ar｜ist
diar｜rhoea
diary
△ di｜ar｜ies
Diary of a No｜
body, The
Dias *see* Diaz
Di｜as｜pora
dia｜stase
dia｜stole
dia｜stolic
di｜atom
di｜atomic
di｜atom｜ite
dia｜tonic
dia｜toni｜cism
dia｜tribe
Diaz
dia｜ze｜pam
diazo
di｜ba｜sic
dib｜ber
dibble
dice
　NOUN
　sing. and pl.
　VERB
　△ dices
　△ diced
　△ di｜cing
dicey
　△ di｜cier
　△ di｜ci｜est
di｜chot｜om｜ous
di｜chot｜omy
　△ di｜chot｜om｜ies
di｜chro｜ism
dick
Dick｜ens
dick｜ens
Dick｜en｜sian
dicker

△ dick｜ers
△ dick｜ered
△ dick｜er｜ing
Dick｜in｜son
dicky
　NOUN
△ dick｜ies
　ADJ.
△ dick｜ier
△ dicki｜est
dicky-bird
di｜co｜ty｜le｜don
dicta
Dic｜ta｜phone
dic｜tate
　VERB
△ dic｜tates
△ dic｜ta｜ted
△ dic｜ta｜ting
dic｜ta｜tion
dic｜ta｜tor
dic｜ta｜tor｜ial
dic｜ta｜tori｜ally
dic｜ta｜tor｜ship
dic｜tion
dic｜tion｜ary
△ dic｜tion｜ar｜ies
dic｜tum
△ dic｜tums *or*
　　dicta
did
di｜dac｜tic
di｜dac｜tic｜ally
di｜dac｜ti｜cism
did｜dle
△ did｜dles
△ did｜dled
△ did｜dling
did｜dler
Did｜erot
did｜geri｜doo
didn't
Dido
Dido and Ae｜neas

---

die
　NOUN
　metal stamp
　△ dies
　a dice
　△ dice
　VERB
　cease living
　△ dies
　△ died
　△ dying
　△ dye

---

die｜back
die｜hard
di｜elec｜tric
Di｜eppe
dieresis *see*
　diaeresis
die｜sel
diet
　VERB
　△ diets
　△ di｜eted
　△ di｜et｜ing
di｜et｜ary
di｜eter
di｜et｜etic
di｜et｜et｜ics
di｜ethyl｜am｜ide
di｜eti｜cian
Diet｜rich
dif｜fer
△ dif｜fers
△ dif｜fered
△ dif｜fer｜ing
dif｜fer｜ence
dif｜fer｜ent
dif｜fer｜en｜tial
dif｜fer｜en｜ti｜ate
△ dif｜fer｜en｜ti｜
　ates
△ dif｜fer｜en｜ti｜
　ated

△ dif｜fer｜en｜ti｜
　ating
dif｜fer｜en｜ti｜ation
dif｜fer｜ently
dif｜fi｜cult
dif｜fi｜culty
△ dif｜fi｜cul｜ties
dif｜fi｜dence
dif｜fi｜dent
dif｜fi｜dently
dif｜fract
△ dif｜fracts
△ dif｜frac｜ted
△ dif｜fract｜ing
dif｜frac｜tion
dif｜frac｜tive
dif｜fuse
△ dif｜fu｜ses
△ dif｜fused
△ dif｜fu｜sing
dif｜fused
dif｜fusely
dif｜fuse｜ness
dif｜fu｜sion
dig
　VERB
△ digs
△ dug
△ dig｜ging
di｜gest
　VERB
△ di｜gests
△ di｜ges｜ted
△ di｜gest｜ing
di｜gest｜ible
di｜ges｜tion
di｜ges｜tive
dig｜ger
dig｜gings
digit
digi｜tal
di｜gi｜ta｜lis
di｜git｜iza｜tion
digit｜ize

△ digit|izes
△ digit|ized
△ digit|izing
di|git|izer
dig|ni|fied
dig|nify
△ dig|ni|fies
△ dig|ni|fied
△ dig|ni|fy|ing
dig|nit|ary
△ dig|nit|ar|ies
dig|nity
di|graph
di|gress
△ di|gres|ses
△ di|gressed
△ di|gres|sing
di|gres|sion
digs
di|hed|ral
Dijon
dike *see* dyke
dik|tat
di|lap|id|ated
di|lap|id|ation
di|la|ta|tion
di|la|tion
di|late
△ di|lates
△ di|la|ted
△ di|la|ting
di|la|tor|ily
di|la|tori|ness
di|la|tory
dildo
di|lemma
di|let|tante
△ di|let|tan|tes
or di|let|tanti
di|let|tant|ism
di|li|gence
di|li|gent
di|li|gently
dill

dilly-dally
△ dilly-dal|lies
△ dilly-dal|lied
△ dilly-dal|ly|
ing
di|lu|ent
di|lute
VERB
△ di|lutes
△ di|lu|ted
△ di|lu|ting
di|lu|tion
di|lu|vial
di|lu|vian
Dilys
dim
VERB
△ dims
△ dimmed
△ dim|ming
ADJ.
△ dim|mer
△ dim|mest
Dim|bleby
dime
di|men|sion
dimer
di|min|ish
△ di|min|ishes
△ di|min|ished
△ di|min|ish|ing
di|min|ished
di|minu|endo
di|mi|nu|tion
di|minu|tive
dimly
dim|mer
dim|ness
di|morph|ism
dim|ple
dim|pled
dim|wit
dim-wit|ted
din

VERB
△ dins
△ dinned
△ din|ning
dinar
D'Indy
dine
△ dines
△ dined
△ di|ning
diner
ding
VERB
△ dings
△ dinged
△ ding|ing
ding-dong
dinghy
△ din|ghies
din|gi|ness
dingo
△ din|goes
dingy
△ din|gier
△ din|gi|est
di|ning-car
di|ning-room
di|ni|tro|gen
din|kum
dinky
△ din|kier
△ din|ki|est
din|ner
din|ner-dance
din|ner-jacket
din|ner-service
din|ner-set
di|no|saur
dint
di|ocesan
di|ocese
Dio|cle|tian
diode
di|oe|cious

Dio|ny|sus
di|optre
Dior
di|oxide
di|oxin
dip
VERB
△ dips
△ dipped
△ dip|ping
diph|theria
diph|thong
dip|loid
dip|loma
dip|lo|macy
dip|lo|mat
dip|lo|matic
dip|lo|mat|ic|ally
di|pole
dip|per
dip|so|ma|nia
dip|so|ma|niac
dip|stick
dip|switch
△ dip|swit|ches
dip|tych
dire
di|rect
VERB
△ di|rects
△ di|rec|ted
△ di|rect|ing
di|rec|tion
di|rec|tional
di|rec|tion-
finder
di|rect|ive
di|rectly
di|rect|ness
Di|rec|toire
di|rec|tor
di|rec|tor|ate
di|rec|tor|ial
di|rec|tor|ship

di|rect|ory
△ di|rect|or|ies
dirge
di|ri|gible
dirk
dirndl
dirt
dirt-cheap
dirt|ily
dir|ti|ness
dirty
  VERB
△ dir|ties
△ dir|tied
△ dir|ty|ing
  ADJ.
△ dir|tier
△ dir|ti|est
dis|abil|ity
△ dis|abil|it|ies
dis|able
△ dis|ables
△ dis|abled
△ dis|ab|ling
dis|abled
dis|able|ment
dis|abuse
△ dis|abu|ses
△ dis|abused
△ dis|abu|sing
di|sac|char|ide
dis|ad|van|tage
  VERB
△ dis|ad|van|ta|ges
△ dis|ad|van|taged
△ dis|ad|van|ta|ging
dis|ad|van|taged
dis|ad|van|ta|geous
dis|af|fec|ted
dis|af|fec|tion

dis|ag|ree
△ dis|ag|rees
△ dis|ag|reed
△ dis|ag|ree|ing
dis|ag|ree|able
dis|ag|ree|ably
dis|ag|ree|ment
dis|al|low
△ dis|al|lows
△ dis|al|lowed
△ dis|al|low|ing
dis|al|low|ance
dis|ap|pear
△ dis|ap|pears
△ dis|ap|peared
△ dis|ap|pear|ing
dis|ap|pear|ance
dis|ap|point
△ dis|ap|points
△ dis|ap|poin|ted
△ dis|ap|point|ing
dis|ap|poin|ted
dis|ap|point|ing
dis|ap|point|ment
dis|ap|pro|ba|tion
dis|ap|pro|val
dis|ap|prove
△ dis|ap|proves
△ dis|ap|proved
△ dis|ap|prov|ing
dis|ap|prov|ing
dis|arm
△ dis|arms
△ dis|armed
△ dis|arm|ing
dis|ar|ma|ment
dis|arm|ing
dis|arm|ingly
dis|ar|range

△ dis|ar|ran|ges
△ dis|ar|ranged
△ dis|ar|ran|ging
dis|ar|range|ment
dis|ar|ray
  VERB
△ dis|ar|rays
△ dis|ar|rayed
△ dis|ar|ray|ing
dis|as|so|ci|ate
△ dis|as|so|ci|ates
△ dis|as|so|ci|ated
△ dis|as|so|ci|ating
dis|as|ter
dis|as|trous
dis|avow
△ dis|avows
△ dis|avowed
△ dis|avow|ing
dis|avowal
dis|band
△ dis|bands
△ dis|ban|ded
△ dis|band|ing
dis|band|ment
dis|be|lief
dis|be|lieve
△ dis|be|lieves
△ dis|be|lieved
△ dis|be|liev|ing
dis|burse
△ dis|bur|ses
△ dis|bursed
△ dis|bur|sing
dis|burse|ment
disc
dis|card
△ dis|cards
△ dis|car|ded
△ dis|card|ing

dis|cern
△ dis|cerns
△ dis|cerned
△ dis|cern|ing
dis|cern|ible
dis|cern|ing
dis|cern|ment
dis|charge
  VERB
△ dis|char|ges
△ dis|charged
△ dis|char|ging
dis|ci|ple
dis|ci|plin|ar|ian
dis|ci|plin|ary
dis|ci|pline
  VERB
△ dis|ci|plines
△ dis|ci|plined
△ dis|ci|plin|ing
dis|claim
△ dis|claims
△ dis|claimed
△ dis|claim|ing
dis|claimer
dis|close
△ dis|clo|ses
△ dis|closed
△ dis|clo|sing
dis|clo|sure
disco
*Dis|co|bo|lus
(Dis|cus
Thrower)*
dis|col|or|ation
dis|col|our
△ dis|col|ours
△ dis|col|oured
△ dis|col|our|ing
dis|com|fit
△ dis|com|fits
△ dis|com|fi|ted
△ dis|com|fit|ling
dis|com|fi|ture

dis|com|fort
  VERB
  △ dis|com|forts
  △ dis|com|for|
    ted
  △ dis|com|fort|
    ing
dis|com|pose
  △ dis|com|po|ses
  △ dis|com|posed
  △ dis|com|po|
    sing
dis|com|po|sure
dis|con|cert
  △ dis|con|certs
  △ dis|con|cer|ted
  △ dis|con|cert|
    ing
dis|con|cert|ing
dis|con|nect
  △ dis|con|nects
  △ dis|con|nec|ted
  △ dis|con|nect|
    ing
dis|con|nec|ted
dis|con|nec|tion
dis|con|so|late
dis|con|so|lately
dis|con|tent
dis|con|ten|ted
dis|con|tinu|
  ance
dis|con|tinu|
  ation
dis|con|tinue
  △ dis|con|tin|ues
  △ dis|con|tin|ued
  △ dis|con|tinu|
    ing
dis|con|ti|nu|ity
dis|con|tinu|ous
dis|cord
dis|cord|ant
dis|co|theque

dis|count
  VERB
  △ dis|counts
  △ dis|coun|ted
  △ dis|count|ing
dis|cour|age
  △ dis|cour|ages
  △ dis|cour|aged
  △ dis|cour|aging
dis|cour|age|
  ment
dis|cour|aging
dis|course
  VERB
  △ dis|cour|ses
  △ dis|coursed
  △ dis|cour|sing
dis|cour|te|ous
dis|cour|te|ously
dis|cour|tesy
dis|cover
  △ dis|cov|ers
  △ dis|cov|ered
  △ dis|cov|er|ing
dis|cov|ery
  △ dis|cov|er|ies
dis|credit
  VERB
  △ dis|cred|its
  △ dis|cred|ited
  △ dis|cred|it|ing
dis|cred|it|able

┌─────────────────┐
│ dis|creet   │
│ *socially careful* │
│ ⚠ discrete   │
└─────────────────┘

dis|crep|ancy
  △ dis|crep|an|
    cies
dis|crep|ant

┌─────────────────┐
│ dis|crete   │
│ *separate*   │
│ ⚠ discreet   │
└─────────────────┘

dis|cretely
dis|crete|ness
dis|cre|tion
dis|cre|tion|ary
dis|crim|in|ate
  △ dis|crim|in|
    ates
  △ dis|crim|in|
    ated
  △ dis|crim|in|
    ating
dis|crim|in|ating
dis|crim|in|ation
dis|crim|in|at|
  ory
dis|cur|sive
dis|cus
  △ dis|cuses
dis|cuss
  △ dis|cus|ses
  △ dis|cussed
  △ dis|cuss|ing
dis|cus|sion
dis|dain
  VERB
  △ dis|dains
  △ dis|dained
  △ dis|dain|ing
dis|dain|ful
dis|dain|fully
dis|ease
dis|eased
dis|econ|omy
  △ dis|econ|om|
    ies
dis|em|bark
  △ dis|em|barks
  △ dis|em|barked
  △ dis|em|bark|
    ing
dis|em|bark|
  ation
dis|em|bod|ied
dis|em|bowel

△ dis|em|bowels
△ dis|em|
  bowelled
△ dis|em|bowel|
  ling
dis|em|bowel|
  ment
dis|en|chant
  △ dis|en|chants
  △ dis|en|chan|
    ted
  △ dis|en|chant|
    ing
dis|en|chan|ted
dis|en|chant|
  ment
dis|en|fran|chise
  △ dis|en|fran|
    chi|ses
  △ dis|en|fran|
    chised
  △ dis|en|fran|
    chi|sing
dis|en|fran|chise|
  ment
dis|en|gage
  △ dis|en|ga|ges
  △ dis|en|gaged
  △ dis|en|ga|ging
dis|en|gage|ment
dis|en|tangle
  △ dis|en|tangles
  △ dis|en|tangled
  △ dis|en|tan|
    gling
dis|en|tangle|
  ment
dis|es|tab|lish
  △ dis|es|tab|li|
    shes
  △ dis|es|tab|
    lished
  △ dis|es|tab|lish|
    ing

dis|es|tab|lish|
ment
dis|fa|vour
dis|fig|ure
 △ dis|fig|ures
 △ dis|fig|ured
 △ dis|fig|ur|ing
dis|fig|ure|ment
dis|fran|chise
 △ dis|fran|chi|
 ses
 △ dis|fran|chised
 △ dis|fran|chi|
 sing
dis|fran|chise|
ment
dis|gorge
 △ dis|gor|ges
 △ dis|gorged
 △ dis|gor|ging
dis|grace
 VERB
 △ dis|gra|ces
 △ dis|graced
 △ dis|gra|cing
dis|grace|ful
dis|gruntled
dis|guise
 VERB
 △ dis|gui|ses
 △ dis|guised
 △ dis|guis|ing
dis|gust
 VERB
 △ dis|gusts
 △ dis|gus|ted
 △ dis|gust|ing
dis|gus|ted
dis|gust|ing
dish
 NOUN
 △ di|shes
 VERB
 △ di|shes

△ dished
△ dish|ing
dishabille *see*
 déshabillé
dis|har|mo|ni|
 ous
dis|har|mony
dis|hearten
 △ dis|heart|ens
 △ dis|heart|ened
 △ dis|heart|en|
 ing
dis|heart|en|ing
dis|heart|en|
ment
dishev|elled
dishev|el|ment
dis|hon|est
dis|hon|estly
dis|hon|esty
dis|hon|our
 VERB
 △ dis|hon|ours
 △ dis|hon|oured
 △ dis|hon|our|
 ing
dis|hon|our|able
dish|washer
dish|wa|ter
dishy
 △ dish|ier
 △ dishi|est
dis|il|lu|sion
 △ dis|il|lu|sions
 △ dis|il|lu|sioned
 △ dis|il|lu|sion|
 ing
dis|il|lu|sioned
dis|il|lu|sion|
 ment
dis|in|cen|tive
dis|in|clin|ation
dis|in|clined
dis|in|fect

△ dis|in|fects
△ dis|in|fec|ted
△ dis|in|fect|ing
dis|in|fect|ant
dis|in|for|ma|
 tion
dis|in|genu|ous
dis|in|genu|
 ously
dis|in|genu|ous|
 ness
dis|in|herit
 △ dis|in|her|its
 △ dis|in|her|ited
 △ dis|in|her|it|
 ing
dis|in|her|it|ance
dis|in|teg|rate
 △ dis|in|teg|rates
 △ dis|in|teg|ra|
 ted
 △ dis|in|teg|ra|
 ting
dis|in|teg|ra|tion
dis|in|ter
 △ dis|in|ters
 △ dis|in|terred
 △ dis|in|ter|ring
dis|in|ter|est
dis|in|ter|es|ted
dis|in|ter|es|ted|
 ness
dis|in|ter|ment
dis|join|ted
dis|junc|tive
disk
disk|ette
dis|like
 VERB
 △ dis|likes
 △ dis|liked
 △ dis|li|king
dis|lo|cate
 △ dis|lo|cates

△ dis|lo|ca|ted
△ dis|lo|ca|ting
dis|lo|ca|tion
dis|lodge
 △ dis|lod|ges
 △ dis|lodged
 △ dis|lod|ging
dis|lodge|ment
dis|loyal
dis|loy|alty
dis|mal
dis|mally
dis|mantle
 △ dis|mantles
 △ dis|mantled
 △ dis|mant|ling
dis|may
 VERB
 △ dis|mays
 △ dis|mayed
 △ dis|may|ing
dis|mem|ber
 △ dis|mem|bers
 △ dis|mem|
 bered
 △ dis|mem|ber|
 ing
dis|mem|ber|
 ment
dis|miss
 △ dis|mis|ses
 △ dis|missed
 △ dis|miss|ing
dis|mis|sal
dis|miss|ive
dis|mount
 △ dis|mounts
 △ dis|moun|ted
 △ dis|mount|ing
Dis|ney
dis|obedi|ence
dis|obedi|ent
dis|obey
 △ dis|obeys

△ dis|obeyed
△ dis|obey|ing
dis|ob|li|ging
dis|or|der
dis|or|dered
dis|or|derly
dis|or|gan|iza|
tion
dis|or|gan|ize
△ dis|or|gan|izes
△ dis|or|gan|ized
△ dis|or|gan|
izing
dis|ori|ent
△ dis|ori|ents
△ dis|ori|en|ted
△ dis|ori|ent|ing
dis|ori|en|tate
△ dis|ori|en|tates
△ dis|ori|en|ta|
ted
△ dis|ori|en|ta|
ting
dis|ori|en|ta|tion
dis|own
△ dis|owns
△ dis|owned
△ dis|own|ing
dis|own|ment
dis|par|age
△ dis|par|ages
△ dis|par|aged
△ dis|par|aging
dis|par|age|ment
dis|par|aging
dis|par|ate
dis|par|ity
△ dis|par|it|ies
dis|pas|sion|ate
dis|patch
NOUN
△ dis|pat|ches
VERB
△ dis|pat|ches

△ dis|patched
△ dis|patch|ing
dis|pel
△ dis|pels
△ dis|pelled
△ dis|pel|ling
dis|pen|sable
dis|pen|sary
△ dis|pen|sar|ies
dis|pen|sa|tion
dis|pense
△ dis|pen|ses
△ dis|pensed
△ dis|pen|sing
dis|per|sal
dis|perse
△ dis|per|ses
△ dis|persed
△ dis|per|sing
dis|per|sion
dis|pirit
△ dis|pir|its
△ dis|pir|ited
△ dis|pir|it|ing
dis|place
△ dis|pla|ces
△ dis|placed
△ dis|pla|cing
dis|place|ment
dis|play
VERB
△ dis|plays
△ dis|played
△ dis|play|ing
dis|please
△ dis|plea|ses
△ dis|pleased
△ dis|pleas|ing
dis|pleas|ure
dis|port
△ dis|ports
△ dis|por|ted
△ dis|port|ing
dis|po|sable

dis|po|sal
dis|pose
△ dis|po|ses
△ dis|posed
△ dis|po|sing
dis|po|si|tion
dis|pos|sess
△ dis|pos|ses|ses
△ dis|pos|sessed
△ dis|pos|sess|
ing
dis|pos|ses|sion
dis|proof
dis|pro|por|tion
dis|pro|por|tion|
ate
dis|pro|por|tion|
ately
dis|prove
△ dis|proves
△ dis|proved
△ dis|pro|ving
dis|pu|table
dis|pu|ta|tion
dis|pu|ta|tious
dis|pute
VERB
△ dis|putes
△ dis|pu|ted
△ dis|pu|ting
dis|quali|fi|ca|
tion
dis|qual|ify
△ dis|quali|fies
△ dis|quali|fied
△ dis|quali|fy|
ing
dis|quiet
VERB
△ dis|qui|ets
△ dis|qui|eted
△ dis|qui|et|ing
dis|qui|et|ing
dis|qui|et|ude

dis|qui|si|tion
Dis|raeli
dis|re|gard
VERB
△ dis|re|gards
△ dis|re|gar|ded
△ dis|re|gard|ing
dis|re|pair
dis|rep|ut|able
dis|rep|ut|ably
dis|re|pute
dis|res|pect
dis|res|pect|ful
dis|res|pect|fully
dis|robe
△ dis|robes
△ dis|robed
△ dis|ro|bing
dis|rupt
△ dis|rupts
△ dis|rup|ted
△ dis|rupt|ing
dis|rup|tion
dis|rup|tive
dis|sa|tis|fac|tion
dis|sat|is|fied
dis|sat|isfy
△ dis|sat|is|fies
△ dis|sat|is|fied
△ dis|sat|is|fy|
ing
dis|sect
△ dis|sects
△ dis|sec|ted
△ dis|sect|ing
dis|sec|tion
dis|sem|ble
△ dis|sem|bles
△ dis|sem|bled
△ dis|sem|bling
dis|sem|in|ate
△ dis|sem|in|ates
△ dis|sem|in|
ated

△ dis|sem|in|
ating
dis|sem|in|ation
dis|sen|sion
dis|sent
VERB
△ dis|sents
△ dis|sen|ted
△ dis|sent|ing
dis|sen|ter
dis|sen|tient
dis|sent|ing
dis|ser|ta|tion
dis|ser|vice
dis|si|dence
dis|si|dent
dis|si|mi|lar
dis|si|mi|lar|ity
dis|si|mu|late
△ dis|si|mu|lates
△ dis|si|mu|la|
ted
△ dis|si|mu|la|
ting
dis|si|mu|la|tion
dis|si|pate
△ dis|si|pates
△ dis|si|pa|ted
△ dis|si|pa|ting
dis|si|pa|ted
dis|si|pa|tion
dis|so|ci|ate
△ dis|so|ci|ates
△ dis|so|ci|ated
△ dis|so|ci|ating
dis|so|ci|ation
dis|sol|uble
dis|so|lute
dis|so|lute|ness
dis|so|lu|tion
dis|solve
△ dis|solves
△ dis|solved
△ dis|sol|ving

dis|son|ance
dis|son|ant
dis|suade
△ dis|suades
△ dis|sua|ded
△ dis|sua|ding
dis|sua|sion
dis|syl|lable
dis|taff
dis|tance
VERB
△ dis|tan|ces
△ dis|tanced
△ dis|tan|cing
dis|tant
dis|tantly
dis|taste
dis|taste|ful
dis|tem|per
VERB
△ dis|tem|pers
△ dis|tem|pered
△ dis|tem|per|
ing
dis|tend
△ dis|tends
△ dis|ten|ded
△ dis|tend|ing
dis|tens|ible
dis|ten|sion
dis|til
△ dis|tils
△ dis|tilled
△ dis|til|ling
dis|til|late
dis|til|la|tion
dis|til|ler
dis|til|lery
△ dis|til|ler|ies
dis|tinct
dis|tinc|tion
dis|tinc|tive
dis|tinc|tive|ness
dis|tinctly

dis|tin|guish
△ dis|tin|gui|
shes
△ dis|tin|
guished
△ dis|tin|guish|
ing
dis|tin|guish|
able
dis|tin|guished
dis|tin|guish|ing
dis|tort
△ dis|torts
△ dis|tor|ted
△ dis|tort|ing
dis|tor|ted
dis|tor|tion
dis|tract
△ dis|tracts
△ dis|trac|ted
△ dis|tract|ing
dis|trac|ted
dis|tract|ing
dis|trac|tion
dis|train
△ dis|trains
△ dis|trained
△ dis|train|ing
dis|traint
dis|trait
dis|traught
dis|tress
NOUN
△ dis|tres|ses
VERB
△ dis|tres|ses
△ dis|tressed
△ dis|tress|ing
dis|tressed
dis|tress|ing
dis|tri|bute
△ dis|tri|butes
△ dis|tri|bu|ted
△ dis|tri|bu|ting

dis|tri|bu|tion
dis|tri|bu|tive
dis|tri|bu|tor
dis|trict
dis|trust
VERB
△ dis|trusts
△ dis|trus|ted
△ dis|trust|ing
dis|trust|ful
dis|turb
△ dis|turbs
△ dis|turbed
△ dis|turb|ing
dis|turb|ance
dis|turbed
dis|turb|ing
dis|unite
△ dis|unites
△ dis|uni|ted
△ dis|uni|ting
dis|unity
dis|use
dis|used
di|syl|la|bic
di|syl|lable
ditch
NOUN
△ dit|ches
VERB
△ dit|ches
△ ditched
△ ditch|ing
dither
VERB
△ dith|ers
△ dith|ered
△ dith|er|ing
dith|erer
dith|ery
ditsy
ditto
ditty
△ dit|ties

di|ur|etic
di|ur|nal
di|ur|nally
diva
di|va|lent
Di|vali
divan
dive
　VERB
　△ dives
　△ dived
　△ di|ving
dive-bomb
　△ dive-bombs
　△ dive-bombed
　△ dive-bomb|
　　ing
dive-bomber
dive-bomb|ing
diver
di|verge
　△ di|ver|ges
　△ di|verged
　△ di|ver|ging
di|ver|gence
di|ver|gent

di|vers
many different
　⚠diverse

di|verse
assorted;
dissimilar
　⚠divers

di|ver|si|fi|ca|
　tion
di|ver|sify
　△ di|ver|si|fies
　△ di|ver|si|fied
　△ di|ver|si|fy|ing
di|ver|sion
di|ver|sion|ary
di|ver|sity

di|vert
　△ di|verts
　△ di|ver|ted
　△ di|vert|ing
di|ver|ti|cu|lar
di|ver|ti|cu|li|tis
di|ver|ti|cu|lum
　△ di|ver|ti|cula
di|ver|ti|mento
　△ di|ver|ti|menti
　　or di|ver|
　　timen|tos
di|vest
　△ di|vests
　△ di|ves|ted
　△ di|vest|ing
di|vest|ment
di|vide
　VERB
　△ di|vides
　△ di|vi|ded
　△ di|vi|ding
di|vi|dend
di|vi|ders
div|in|ation
di|vine
　VERB
　△ di|vines
　△ di|vined
　△ di|vi|ning
Di|vine Com|
edy, The (di|
vina com|me|
dia, La)
di|vinely
di|ving
di|ving-bell
di|ving-board
di|ving-suit
di|vi|ning-rod
di|vin|ity
　△ di|vin|it|ies
di|vis|ible
di|vi|sion

di|vi|sional
Di|vi|sion|ism
di|vi|sive
di|vi|sive|ness
di|vi|sor
di|vorce
　VERB
　△ di|vor|ces
　△ di|vorced
　△ di|vor|cing
di|vorcé
　divorced man
di|vorced
di|vor|cée
　divorced woman
divot
di|vulge
　△ di|vul|ges
　△ di|vulged
　△ di|vul|ging
di|vul|gence
divvy
　NOUN
　△ div|vies
　VERB
　△ div|vies
　△ div|vied
　△ div|vy|ing
Diwali *see*
　Divali
Dixie
　area in America
dixie
　cooking pot
Dixie|land
diz|zily
diz|zi|ness
dizzy
　ADJ.
　△ diz|zier
　△ diz|zi|est
　VERB
　△ diz|zies
　△ diz|zied

△ diz|zy|ing
Djakarta *see*
　Jakarta
Dji|bouti
djinn *see* jinni
djinni *see* jinni
D-notice
do
　NOUN
　△ dos *or* do's
　VERB
　△ does
　△ did
　△ doing
　△ done
do
　sol-fa symbol
　see doh
do|able
Do|ber|man pin|
　scher
doc
do|cile
do|cilely
do|cil|ity
dock
　VERB
　△ docks
　△ docked
　△ dock|ing
docker
docket
　VERB
　△ dock|ets
　△ dock|eted
　△ dock|et|ing
dock|yard
Doc Mar|tens
doc|tor
　VERB
　△ doc|tors
　△ doc|tored
　△ doc|tor|ing
doc|toral

doc|tor|ate
Doc|tor Faus|tus,
The Tra|gi|cal
His|tory of
Doc|tor Zhi|vago
doc|trin|aire
doc|tri|nal
doc|trine
docu|drama
docu|ment
  VERB
  △ docu|ments
  △ do|cu|men|ted
  △ do|cu|ment|
    ing
do|cu|men|tary
  △ do|cu|men|tar|
    ies
do|cu|men|ta|
  tion
dod|der
  △ dod|ders
  △ dod|dered
  △ dod|der|ing
dod|derer
dod|dery
dod|dle
do|deca|gon
do|deca|hed|ron
Do|deca|nese
dodge
  VERB
  △ dod|ges
  △ dodged
  △ dodge|ing
Dod|gems
dod|ger
dodgy
  △ dod|gier
  △ dod|gi|est
dodo
  △ dodos *or* do|
    does
Do|doma

doe
  female deer,
  rabbit, etc
  △ does *or* doe
  ⚠ dough

doer
does
doesn't
doff
  △ doffs
  △ doffed
  △ doff|ing
dog
  VERB
  △ dogs
  △ dogged
  △ dog|ging
dog|cart
dog-col|lar
doge
dog-eared
dog-end
dog|fight
dog|fish
  △ dog|fish *or*
    dog|fi|shes
dog|ged
dog|gedly
dog|ged|ness
Dog|ger
dog|gerel
doggo
doggy
  NOUN
  △ dog|gies
  ADJ.
  △ dog|gier
  △ dog|gi|est
doggy-bag
doggy-paddle
  VERB
  △ doggy-
    paddles

  △ doggy-
    paddled
  △ doggy-pad|
    dling
dog|house
dog|leg
dogma
dog|ma|tic
dog|ma|tism
dog|ma|tist
dog|ma|tize
  △ dog|ma|ti|zes
  △ dog|ma|tized
  △ dog|ma|ti|zing
do-gooder
dog-paddle *see*
  doggy-paddle
dogs|body
  △ dogs|bo|dies
dog-tired
dog|trot
dog|wood
doh
Doha
doily
  △ doil|ies
do|ings
do-it-your|self
Dolby
dolce
dolce vita, La
  (The Sweet
  Life)
dol|drums
dole
  VERB
  △ doles
  △ doled
  △ dol|ing
dole|ful
dole|fully
dole|ful|ness
doll

  VERB
  △ dolls
  △ dolled
  △ doll|ing
dol|lar
dol|lar|iza|tion
dol|lop
Doll's House, A
  (Et Duk|ke|
  hjem)
Dolly
dolly
  △ dol|lies
dol|men
Dol|metsch
dolo|mite
  mineral; rock
  containing it
Dolo|mites
  mountain range
Do|lores
dol|or|ous
dol|our
dol|phin
dol|phin|ar|ium
dolt
dolt|ish
do|main
dome
domed
Domes|day
  Book
do|mes|tic
do|mes|tic|ally
do|mes|ti|cate
  △ do|mes|ti|cates
  △ do|mes|ti|ca|
    ted
  △ do|mes|ti|ca|
    ting
do|mes|ti|ca|tion
do|mes|ti|city
do|mi|cile

VERB
△ do|mi|ciles
△ do|mi|ciled
△ do|mi|ci|ling
do|mi|cili|ary
dom|in|ance
dom|in|ant
dom|in|ate
△ dom|in|ates
△ dom|in|ated
△ dom|in|ating
dom|in|ating
dom|in|ation
dom|in|eer
△ dom|in|eers
△ dom|in|eered
△ dom|in|eer|ing
dom|in|eer|ing
Do|mingo
Dom|inic
Do|min|ica
republic in
Windward
Islands
Do|min|ican
Do|min|ican Re|
pub|lic
republic in West
Indies
do|min|ion
dom|ino
△ do|mi|noes
Do|mi|tian
Don
river; Spanish
title
don
university
lecturer; put on
(clothes)
VERB
△ dons
△ donned
△ don|ning

Don|ald
do|nate
△ do|nates
△ do|na|ted
△ do|na|ting
Do|na|tello
do|na|tion
Donau
Don|cas|ter
done
Don|egal

doner
kebab
⚠ donor

dong
VERB
△ dongs
△ donged
△ dong|ing
Don Gio|vanni
Doni|zetti
don|jon
Don Juan
don|key
don|key-work
Don|leavy
Donna
Donne
don|nish

donor
giver
⚠ doner

Don Quix|ote
don't
don't-know
donut *see*
doughnut
doo|dah
doo|dle
VERB
△ doo|dles
△ doo|dled

△ dood|ling
doom
VERB
△ dooms
△ doomed
△ doom|ing
Doomsday
Book *see*
Domesday
Book
dooms|day
door
door|bell
door|knocker
door|man
△ door|men
door|mat
door|step
door|stop
door-to-door
door|way
dopa
do|pa|mine
dope
VERB
△ dopes
△ doped
△ doping
dopey
△ do|pier
△ do|pi|est
do|pily
do|pi|ness
doping
dop|pel|gän|ger
Dop|pler
Dor|ches|ter
Dor|dogne
Dord|recht
Dor|ian
Doric
Doris
dorm
dor|mancy

dor|mant
dor|mer
dor|mi|tory
△ dor|mi|tor|ies
Dor|mo|bile
dor|mouse
△ dor|mice
Dor|othy
dor|sal
Dor|set
Dort *see*
Dordrecht
Dort|mund
dory
△ dor|ies
dos|age
dose
VERB
△ doses
△ dosed
△ dos|ing
dosh
do|si|meter
doss
△ dos|ses
△ dossed
△ doss|ing
dos|ser
doss-house
dos|sier
dost
Dos|to|ev|sky
dot
VERB
△ dots
△ dot|ted
△ dot|ting
do|tage
do|tard
dote
△ dotes
△ doted
△ do|ting
doth

do¦ting
dot¦tily
dot¦ti¦ness
dotty
△ dot¦tier
△ dot¦ti¦est
Douai
dou¦ble
VERB
△ dou¦bles
△ dou¦bled
△ doub¦ling
double-bar¦relled
double-breas¦ted
double-check
△ double-checks
△ double-checked
△ double-check¦ing
double-cross
NOUN
△ double-cros¦ses
VERB
△ double-cros¦ses
△ double-crossed
△ double-cross¦ing
double-cros¦ser
double-dealer
double-deal¦ing
double-decker
double-edged
double-glazed
double-gla¦zing
double-join¦ted
double-park
△ double-parks
△ double-parked
△ double-park¦ing
double-quick
dou¦bles

doub¦let
double-talk
double¦think
doub¦loon
doubly
doubt
VERB
△ doubts
△ doubted
△ doubt¦ing
doubter
doubt¦ful
doubt¦fully
doubt¦less
douche
NOUN
△ dou¦ches
VERB
△ dou¦ches
△ douched
△ douch¦ing
Dou¦gal

---

dough
*flour mixture;
money*
△ doe

---

dough¦nut
VERB
△ dough¦nuts
△ dough¦nut¦ted
△ dough¦nut¦ting
dough¦nut¦ting
doughtily
dough¦ti¦ness
doughty
△ dough¦tier
△ dough¦ti¦est
doughy
△ dough¦ier
△ doughi¦est
Doug¦las
Doug¦las-Home
Doul¦ton

Doun¦reay
dour
△ dourer
△ dour¦est
Douro
douse
△ dou¦ses
△ doused
△ dous¦ing
dove
dove¦cote
Dover
dove¦tail
VERB
△ dove¦tails
△ dove¦tailed
△ dove¦tail¦ing
dow¦ager
dow¦dily
dow¦di¦ness
dowdy
△ dow¦dier
△ dow¦di¦est
dowel
dower
Dow¦land
Down
down
VERB
△ downs
△ downed
△ down¦ing
down-and-out
down-at-heel
down¦beat
down¦cast
downer
down¦fall
down¦grade
△ down¦grades
△ down¦gra¦ded
△ down¦gra¦ding
down¦hearted
down¦hill

Down¦ing
down-in-the-
mouth
down¦load
△ down¦loads
△ down¦loaded
△ down¦load¦ing
down-mar¦ket
Down¦pat¦rick
down¦pour
down¦right
Downs
down¦side
down¦si¦zing
down¦stage
down¦stairs
down¦stream
down¦time
down-to-earth
down¦town
down¦trod¦den
down¦turn
down¦ward
down¦wardly
down¦wards
down¦wind
downy
△ dow¦nier
△ dow¦ni¦est
dowry
△ dow¦ries
dowse
*search for hidden
water*
△ dow¦ses
△ dowsed
△ dow¦sing
dowse
*pour water over;
extinguish*
see douse
dow¦ser
dox¦ology
doyen

Doyle
doyley *see* doily
doze
  VERB
  △ dozes
  △ dozed
  △ doz|ing
dozen
  after number
  △ dozen
  other uses
  △ dozens
doz|enth
do|zily
do|zi|ness
dozy
  △ do|zier
  △ do|zi|est
drab
  △ drab|ber
  △ drab|best
Drab|ble
drably
drab|ness
drachm
drachma
  △ drach|mas *or*
    drach|mae
dra|co|nian
Drac|ula

draft
  plan; sketch;
  banker's order;
  make these
  VERB
  △ drafts
  △ draf|ted
  △ draft|ing
    ⚠ draught

draft-dodger
drag
  VERB
  △ drags

  △ dragged
  △ drag|ging
drag|gle
  △ drag|gles
  △ drag|gled
  △ drag|gling
drag|net
dragon
drag|on|fly
  △ drag|on|flies
dra|goon
  VERB
  △ dra|goons
  △ dra|gooned
  △ dra|goon|ing
drag-racing
drag|ster
drain
  VERB
  △ drains
  △ drained
  △ drain|ing
drain|age
drain|ing-board
drain|pipe
Drake
drake
dram
drama
dra|ma|ther|apy
dra|matic
dra|mat|ic|ally
dra|mat|ics
dra|ma|tis per|
  so|nae
dram|at|ist
dra|ma|ti|za|tion
dram|at|ize
  △ dram|at|izes
  △ dram|at|ized
  △ dram|at|izing
drank
drape
  △ drapes

  △ draped
  △ dra|ping
dra|per
dra|pery
  △ dra|per|ies
drapes
dras|tic
dras|tic|ally
drat
drat|ted

draught
  air current;
  amount of
  liquid; playing
  piece; drawn
  from the cask;
  used to pull
  carts etc
    ⚠ draft

draughts
draughts|man
  △ draughts|men
draughts|man|
  ship
draughty
  △ draugh|tier
  △ draugh|ti|est
Dra|vid|ian
draw
  VERB
  △ draws
  △ drew
  △ draw|ing
  △ drawn
draw|back
draw|bridge
drawer
draw|ing
draw|ing-board
draw|ing-pin
draw|ing-room
drawl

  VERB
  △ drawls
  △ drawled
  △ drawl|ing
drawn
drawn-out
draw|string
dray
  heavy cart
dray
  squirrel's nest
see drey
dread
  VERB
  △ dreads
  △ dreaded
  △ dread|ing
dreaded
dread|ful
dread|fully
dread|locks
dread|nought
dream
  VERB
  △ dreams
  △ dreamed *or*
    dreamt
  △ dream|ing
dream|boat
dreamer
dream|ily
dreami|ness
dreamy
  △ dream|ier
  △ dreami|est
drear|ily
dreari|ness
dreary
  △ drear|ier
  △ dreari|est
dredge
  VERB
  △ dred|ges
  △ dredged

△ dred¦ging
dred¦ger
dregs
drench
  NOUN
△ dren¦ches
  VERB
△ dren¦ches
△ drenched
△ drench|ing
Dres|den
dress
  NOUN
△ dres¦ses
  VERB
△ dres¦ses
△ dressed
△ dress|ing
dres|sage
dres|ser
dres|sily
dress|ing
dress¦ing-down
dress¦ing-gown
dress¦ing-table
dress|ma¦ker
dress|ma¦king
dressy
△ dres¦sier
△ dres¦si|est
drew
drey
Drey|fus
drib¦ble
  VERB
△ drib¦bles
△ drib¦bled
△ drib|bling
drib|let
drier
drift
  VERB
△ drifts
△ drif¦ted

△ drift|ing
drif¦ter
drift-net
drift|wood
drill
  VERB
△ drills
△ drilled
△ drill|ing
drily
drink
  VERB
△ drinks
△ drank
△ drink|ing
△ drunk
drink|able
drink-dri¦ver
drink-dri¦ving
drin¦ker
drip
  VERB
△ drips
△ dripped
△ drip|ping
drip-dry
  VERB
△ drip-dries
△ drip-dried
△ drip-dry¦ing
drip-feed
  VERB
△ drip-feeds
△ drip-fed
△ drip-feed|ing
drip|ping
drive
  VERB
△ drives
△ drove
△ dri¦ving
△ driven
drive-in
dri¦vel

  VERB
△ driv|els
△ driv|elled
△ driv¦el|ling
dri¦ver
dri¦ving
driz¦zle
  VERB
△ driz¦zles
△ driz¦zled
△ driz¦zling
driz¦zly
Dr Jekyll and
  Mr Hyde, The
  Strange Case
  of
Drog|heda
droit de sei¦gneur
droll
drol|lery
drolly
drom|ed¦ary
△ drom|ed¦ar|ies
drone
  VERB
△ drones
△ droned
△ dro¦ning
drool
△ drools
△ drooled
△ drool|ing
droop
△ droops
△ drooped
△ droop|ing
droopy
△ droo¦pier
△ droo¦pi|est
drop
  VERB
△ drops
△ dropped
△ drop|ping

drop-kick
  VERB
△ drop-kicks
△ drop-kicked
△ drop-kick¦ing
drop|let
drop|out
  person
drop-out
  in electronics
drop|per
drop|pings
drop|si¦cal
dropsy
dross
drought
drove
dro¦ver
drown
△ drowns
△ drowned
△ drown|ing
drowse
△ drow¦ses
△ drowsed
△ drows|ing
drow|sily
drow¦si|ness
drowsy
△ drow¦sier
△ drow¦si|est
drub
△ drubs
△ drubbed
△ drub|bing
drub|bing
drudge
  VERB
△ drud¦ges
△ drudged
△ drud¦ging
drud¦gery
drug

VERB
△ drugs
△ drugged
△ drug|ging
drug|get
drug|gist
drug|store
druid
dru|idic
dru|id|ical
drum
  VERB
  △ drums
  △ drummed
  △ drum|ming
drum|head
drum|lin
drum|mer
Drum|mond
drum|stick
drunk
drunk|ard
drun|ken
drunk|enly
drunk|en|ness
drupe
Drury
Druze
dry
  NOUN
  △ dries
  VERB
  △ dries
  △ dried
  △ dry|ing
  ADJ.
  △ drier
  △ dri|est
dryad
dry-clean
  △ dry-cleans
  △ dry-cleaned
  △ dry-clean|ing
dry-cleaner

dry-clean|ing
Dry|den
dryer
dry|ness
dry|point
dry-stone

dual
  double
  ⚠ duel

du|al|ism
du|al|ity
dub
  VERB
  △ dubs
  △ dubbed
  △ dub|bing
Dubai
Du Barry
dub|bin
Dub|ček
du|bi|ety
du|bi|ous
du|bi|ously
Dub|lin
Dub|rov|nik
ducal
ducat
duch|ess
  △ duch|es|ses
*Duch|ess of
  Malfi, The*
duchy
  △ duch|ies
duck
  VERB
  △ ducks
  △ ducked
  △ duck|ing
duck|board
duck|ing
duck|ing-stool
duck|ling
duck|weed

ducky
  NOUN
  △ duck|ies
  ADJ.
  △ duck|ier
  △ ducki|est
duct
duc|tile
duc|til|ity
dud
dude

dud|geon
  annoyance
  ⚠ dungeon

Dud|ley

due
  owed, etc
  ⚠ dew

duel
  fight
  VERB
  △ duels
  △ du|elled
  △ du|el|ling
  ⚠ dual

duel|list
du|enna
duet
du|et|tist
Dufay
duff
  VERB
  △ duffs
  △ duffed
  △ duff|ing
duf|fel
duf|fer
dug
du|gong
dug|out
Dukas

duke
duke|dom
dul|cet
dul|ci|mer
dull
  VERB
  △ dulls
  △ dulled
  △ dull|ing
  ADJ.
  △ dul|ler
  △ dul|lest
dul|lard
Dul|les
dull|ness
dully
dulse
duly
Dumas
du Maur|ier
dumb
  △ dumber
  △ dumb|est
Dum|bar|ton
dumb|bell
dumb|found
  △ dumb|founds
  △ dumb|foun|
  ded
  △ dumb|found|
  ing
dumbly
dumb|ness
dumbo
dumb|struck
dumb|waiter
dum|dum
dumfound *see*
  dumbfound
Dum|fries
dummy
  NOUN
  △ dum|mies

VERB
△ dum|mies
△ dum|mied
△ dum|my|ing

dump
VERB
△ dumps
△ dumped
△ dump|ing

dump|ing
dump|ling
dumpy
△ dum|pier
△ dum|pi|est

dun
VERB
△ duns
△ dunned
△ dun|ning

Dun|bar
Dun|can
dunce
Dun|ciad, The
dun|der|head
dun|der|headed
dune
Dun|edin
Dun|ferm|line
dung
dun|gar|ees
dung-beetle
Dunge|ness
  Head

dun|geon
  underground cell
  ⚠ dudgeon

dunk
△ dunks
△ dunked
△ dunk|ing

Dun|kirk
Dun Laog|haire
dun|lin

Dun|lop
Duns Sco|tus
Dun|stable
Dun|stan
duo
duo|de|ci|mal
duo|de|cimo
duo|de|nal
duo|de|num
  △ duo|dena *or*
    duo|de|nums
duo|logue
dupe
VERB
△ dupes
△ duped
△ du|ping

du|ple
du|plex
NOUN
△ du|plexes
du|pli|cate
VERB
△ du|pli|cates
△ du|pli|ca|ted
△ du|pli|ca|ting
du|pli|ca|tion
du|pli|ca|tor
du|pli|cit|ous
du|pli|city
du Pré
dur|ab|il|ity
dur|able
dur|ably
dura mater
dur|ation
Dur|ban
Dur|bar
Dü|rer
dur|ess
Dur|ham
dur|ing
Dur|rell
Duse

Du|shanbe
dusk
dus|ki|ness
dusky
△ dus|kier
△ dus|ki|est
Du|s|sel|dorf
dust
VERB
△ dusts
△ dus|ted
△ dust|ing
dust|bin
dust|cart
dus|ter
dust|ily
dust|man
△ dust|men
dust|pan
dust-storm
dust-up
dusty
△ dus|tier
△ dus|ti|est
Dutch
Dutch|man
△ Dutch|men
Dutch New
  Guinea *see*
  Irian Jaya
Dutch|wo|man
△ Dutch|wo|
  men
du|teous
du|ti|able
du|ti|ful
du|ti|fully
duty
△ du|ties
duty-bound
duty-free
Du|val|lier
duvet
Dvořák

dwarf
NOUN
△ dwarfs *or*
  dwarves
VERB
△ dwarfs
△ dwarfed
△ dwarf|ing
dwarf|ish
dweeb
dwell
△ dwells
△ dwelled *or*
  dwelt
△ dwell|ing
dwel|ler
dwell|ing
dwin|dle
△ dwin|dles
△ dwin|dled
△ dwind|ling
Dyak *see* Dayak
dyb|buk

dye
  stain
  VERB
  △ dyes
  △ dyed
  △ dye|ing
  ⚠ die

dyed-in-the-
  wool
dyer
Dyfed
dying
dyke
VERB
△ dykes
△ dyked
△ dyk|ing
Dylan
dy|namic
dy|nam|ic|ally

dy¦nam|ics
dy¦nam|ism
dy¦na|mite
  VERB
  △ dy¦na|mites
  △ dy¦na|mi¦ted
  △ dy¦na|mi¦ting

dy|namo
dy¦na|mo¦meter
dy¦nas|tic
dy|nasty
  △ dy¦nas|ties
dyne
dys|arth¦ria

dys|en¦tery
dys|lexia
dys|lexic
dys|men¦or|
  rhoea
dys|pep¦sia
dys|pep¦tic

dys|pla¦sia
dys|pnoea
dys|pro¦sium
dys|tro¦phy

E

each
eager
ea|gerly
ea|ger|ness
eagle
eagle-eyed
eag|let
Ea|monn
ear
ear|ache
ear|drum
ear|ful
earl
earl|dom
earli|ness
ear|lobe
early
△ earlier
△ earli|est
ear|mark
△ ear|marks
△ ear|marked
△ ear|mark|ing
ear|muff
earn
△ earns
△ earned
△ earn|ing
earner
earn|est
earn|estly
earn|est|ness
earn|ings
ear|phone
ear|piece
ear-pier|cing
ear|plug
ear|ring
ear|shot
ear-split|ting
earth
earth|bound

earthen
earth|en|ware
earth|ily
earthi|ness
earth|light
earth|ling

earthly
of this world
⚠ earthy

earth|quake
earth-sha|king
earth-sha|kingly
earth-shat|tering
earth-shat|ter|ing
earth|shine
earth|star
earth|work
earth|worm

earthy
like soil; crude
△ earthi|ier
△ earthi|est
⚠ earthly

ear-trum|pet
ear|wig
ease
VERB
△ eases
△ eased
△ eas|ing
easel
ease|ment
eas|ily
easi|ness
east
east|bound
East|bourne
East|en|der
Eas|ter
east|erly
NOUN

△ east|er|lies
east|ern
east|erner
east|ern|most
East|leigh
East|man
east|ward
East|wood
easy
ADJ.
△ eas|ier
△ easi|est
easy-care
easy-going
eat
△ eats
△ ate
△ eat|ing
△ eaten
eat|able
eater
eat|ery
△ eat|er|ies
eau-de-cologne
eaves
eaves|drop
△ eaves|drops
△ eaves|dropped
△ eaves|drop|
ping
eaves|drop|per
eaves|drop|ping
ebb
VERB
△ ebbs
△ ebbed
△ eb|bing
Ebbw Vale
ebony
ebul|li|ence
ebul|li|ency
ebul|li|ent
ebul|li|ently
ec|cen|tric

ec|cen|tric|ally
ec|cen|tri|city
△ ec|cen|tri|cit|
ies
Ec|cle|si|as|tes,
Book of
ec|cle|si|as|tic
ec|cle|si|as|ti|cal
ec|cle|si|as|tic|
ally
Ec|cle|si|as|ti|
cus, Book of
ec|cle|si|ol|ogy
ec|dysis
Ece|vit
ech|elon
ech|idna
ech|ino|derm
Ech|ino|der|
mata
echo
NOUN
△ echoes
VERB
△ echoes
△ echoed
△ echo|ing
echo|car|di|og|
ra|phy
echoic
echo|lo|ca|tion
echo-soun|der
echo-sound|ing
éclair
ec|lamp|sia
éclat
ec|lec|tic
ec|lec|tic|ally
ec|lec|ti|cism

ec|lipse
*darkening of sun
etc; cause this;
outshine*

VERB
- △ ec|lip|ses
- △ ec|lipsed
- △ ec|lip|sing
- ⚠ ellipse

ec|lip|tic
ec|logue
Ec|logues, The
Eco
eco-frien|dly
eco|lo|gi|cal
eco|lo|gic|ally
ecol|ogist
ecol|ogy
eco|no|met|rics
eco|no|mic
eco|nom|ical
eco|nom|ic|ally
eco|nom|ics
econ|om|ist
econ|om|iza|tion
econ|om|ize
- △ econ|om|izes
- △ econ|om|ized
- △ econ|om|izing

econ|omy
NOUN
- △ econ|om|ies

eco|so|cial|ism
eco|sphere
eco|sys|tem
eco|tour|ism
eco|type

ec|stasy
- △ ec|sta|sies

ec|sta|tic
ec|stat|ic|ally
ec|to|derm
ec|to|morph
ec|to|pic
ec|to|plasm
ecu
Ecua|dor
ecu|men|ical
ecu|men|ic|al|ism
ecu|men|ic|ally
ecu|men|ism
ec|zema
Edam
ed|aph|ol|ogy
Ed|berg
Edda
Eddy
eddy
NOUN
- △ ed|dies

VERB
- △ ed|dies
- △ ed|died
- △ ed|dy|ing

edel|weiss
Eden
edent|ate
Ed|gar
Edg|bas|ton
edge

VERB
- △ edges
- △ edged
- △ ed|ging

edge|ways
edge|wise
Edge|worth
ed|gily
ed|gi|ness
ed|ging
edgy
- △ ed|gier
- △ ed|gi|est

ed|ib|il|ity
ed|ible
edict
edi|fi|ca|tion
edi|fice
edify
- △ edi|fies
- △ edi|fied
- △ edi|fy|ing

edi|fy|ing
Ed|in|burgh
Edi|son
edit
VERB
- △ edits
- △ ed|ited
- △ ed|it|ing

ed|ited
Edith
edi|tion
edi|tor

edi|tor|ial
edi|tori|al|ize
- △ edi|tori|al|izes
- △ edi|tori|al|ized
- △ edi|tori|al|izing

edi|tori|ally
edi|tor|ship
Ed|mon|ton
Ed|mund
Edna
Edom
edu|cable
edu|cat|able
edu|cate
- △ edu|cates
- △ edu|ca|ted
- △ edu|ca|ting

edu|ca|ted
edu|ca|tion
edu|ca|tional
edu|ca|tion|al|ist
edu|ca|tion|ally
edu|ca|tion|ist
edu|ca|tive
edu|ca|tor
educe
- △ edu|ces
- △ educed
- △ edu|cing

edu|cible
educ|tion
edu|tain|ment
Edward

-ed / -t

Many verbs ending in **-l, -m, -n** and **-p** form past tenses and past participles in both **-ed** and **-t: burned / burnt, spilled / spilt.**

In current English these are often interchangeable, although **-ed** is more common in the past tense (*we burned the cakes*), and **-t** is more common as a participial adjective (*the cakes are burnt*).

Other common words of this type are: **dream, lean, leap, smell, spell, spoil.**
Note: **earn** forms **earned** only, not **earnt.**

Ed|war|dian
Edward II
Ed|win
eel
e'en
e'er

eerie
frightening
△ eer|ier
△ eeri|est
⚠eyrie

eer|ily
eeri|ness
ef|face
△ ef|fa|ces
△ ef|faced
△ ef|fa|cing
ef|face|ment

ef|fect
result; bring
about
VERB
△ ef|fects
△ ef|fec|ted
△ ef|fect|ing
⚠affect

ef|fect|ive
ef|fect|ively
ef|fect|ive|ness
ef|fec|tor
ef|fec|tual
ef|fec|tu|ally
ef|fec|tu|ate
△ ef|fec|tu|ates
△ ef|fec|tu|ated
△ ef|fec|tu|ating
ef|fec|tu|ation
ef|fem|in|acy

ef|fem|in|ate
ef|fem|in|ately
ef|fer|ent
ef|fer|vesce
△ ef|fer|ves|ces
△ ef|fer|vesced
△ ef|fer|ves|cing
ef|fer|ves|cence
ef|fer|ves|cent
ef|fete
ef|fete|ness
ef|fi|ca|cious
ef|fi|ca|ciously
ef|fic|acy
ef|fi|ciency
ef|fi|cient
ef|fi|ciently
ef|figy
△ ef|fi|gies
ef|flor|esce
△ ef|flor|es|ces
△ ef|flor|esced
△ ef|flor|es|cing
ef|flor|es|cence
ef|flor|es|cent

ef|flu|ent
outflow; flowing
out
⚠affluent

ef|flu|vium
△ ef|flu|via
ef|flux
△ ef|fluxes
ef|fort
ef|fort|less
ef|fort|lessly
ef|front|ery
△ ef|front|er|ies
ef|ful|gence

ef|ful|gent
ef|ful|gently
ef|fu|sion
ef|fu|sive
ef|fu|sively
ef|fu|sive|ness
egal|it|ar|ian
egal|it|ar|ian|ism
egg
VERB
△ eggs
△ egged
△ egg|ing
egg-cup
egg-flip
egg|head
egg-nog
egg|plant
egg|shell
egg-timer
eg|lan|tine
ego
ego|cen|tric
ego|cen|tric|ally
ego|cen|tri|city
ego|ism
ego|ist
ego|is|tic
ego|is|ti|cal
ego|is|tic|ally
ego|ma|nia
ego|ma|niac
ego|tism
ego|tist
ego|tis|tic
ego|tis|ti|cal
ego|tis|tic|ally
egre|gi|ous
egre|gi|ously
egre|gi|ous|ness

egress
△ egres|ses
egret
Egypt
Egyp|tian
Egyp|tol|ogist
Egyp|tol|ogy
Eich|mann
eider
ei|der|down
Eif|fel
Eiger
Eigg
eight
eigh|teen
eigh|teenth
eight|fold
eighth
eighthly
eight|ies
eight|ieth
eighty
NOUN
△ eight|ies
Ei|leen
Eine Kleine
Nacht|mu|sik
(A Little
Night-Music)
Ein|stein
ein|stein|ium
Éire
Eis|en|hower
Ei|sen|stein
eis|tedd|fod
△ eis|tedd|fods
or eis|tedd|fo|
dau
ei|ther
ejac|ulate

-efy
See panel at **-ify**.

△ ejac|ulates
△ ejac|ula|ted
△ ejac|ula|ting
ejac|ula|tion
ejacu|la|tory
eject
△ ejects
△ ejec|ted
△ eject|ing
ejec|tion
eject|ive
ejec|tor
eke
△ ekes
△ eked
△ eking
elab|or|ate
VERB
△ elab|or|ates
△ elab|or|ated
△ elab|or|ating
elab|or|ately
elab|or|ation
Elaine
El Ala|mein
élan
eland
△ elands or
eland
elapse
△ elap|ses
△ elapsed

△ elap|sing
elas|tic
elas|tic|ally
elas|tic|ated
elas|ti|city
elas|ti|cize
△ elas|ti|ci|zes
△ elas|ti|cized
△ elas|ti|ci|zing
elas|to|mer
elate
△ elates
△ ela|ted
△ ela|ting
ela|ted
ela|tedly
ela|tion
Elba
Elbe
el|bow
VERB
△ el|bows
△ el|bowed
△ el|bow|ing
el|bow-grease
el|bow-room
El|brus
el|der
el|der|berry
△ el|der|ber|ries
el|der|li|ness
el|derly

eld|est
El Dor|ado
Elea|nor
elect
VERB
△ elects
△ elec|ted
△ elect|ing
elect|ab|il|ity
elect|able
elec|ted
elec|tion
elec|tion|eer
△ elec|tion|eers
△ elec|tion|eered
△ elec|tion|eer|
ing
elec|tion|eer|ing
elect|ive
elect|ively
elec|tor
elec|toral
elec|tor|ally
elec|tor|ate
Elec|tra
elec|tric
elec|tri|cal
elec|tric|ally
elec|tri|cian
elec|tri|city
elec|tri|fi|ca|tion
elec|trify

△ elec|tri|fies
△ elec|tri|fied
△ elec|tri|fy|ing
elec|tri|fy|ing
elec|tri|fy|ingly
elec|tro-acu|
punc|ture
elec|tro|car|dio|
gram
elec|tro|car|dio|
graph
elec|tro|car|di|
og|ra|phy
elec|tro|chem|is|
try
elec|tro-con|vul|
sive
elec|tro|cute
△ elec|tro|cutes
△ elec|tro|cu|ted
△ elec|tro|cu|
ting
elec|tro|cu|tion
elec|trode
elec|tro|en|
cepha|lo|gram
elec|tro|en|
cepha|lo|graph
elec|tro|lysis
elec|tro|lyte
elec|tro|lytic
elec|tro|mag|net

-ei- / -ie-

The rule 'I before e except after c' is generally valid when the sound is -ee- as in
receive and **achieve**.

Exceptions to this rule are:

either[1]	neither[1]	protein	seizure	weir
heinous	plebeian	seize	species	weird

Other words spelt with -ei- are:

beige	forfeit	geisha	heifer

[1] pronounced **eye-** or **ee-**

elec|tro|mag|
netic

elec|tro|mag|net|
ism

elec|tro|mo|tive

elec|tron

elec|tro|nega|tiv|
ity

elec|tronic

elec|tron|ic|ally

elec|tron|ics

elec|tro|pa|la|
tog|ra|phy

elec|tro|phor|
esis

elec|tro|plate

  VERB

△ elec|tro|plates

△ elec|tro|pla|
ted

△ elec|tro|pla|
ting

elec|tro|pla|ted

elec|tro|pla|ting

elec|tro|scope

elec|tro|stat|ics

el|eg|ance

el|eg|ant

el|eg|antly

ele|giac

ele|gi|ac|ally

ele|gize

△ ele|gi|zes

△ ele|gized

△ ele|gi|zing

elegy

△ ele|gies

*Elegy Writ|ten
in a Coun|try
Church|yard*

ele|ment

ele|men|tal

ele|ment|ary

ele|phant

△ ele|phants *or*
ele|phant

ele|phan|ti|asis

ele|phan|tine

ele|vate

△ ele|vates

△ ele|va|ted

△ ele|va|ting

ele|va|ted

ele|va|ting

ele|va|tion

ele|va|tor

ele|va|tory

eleven

eleven-plus

eleven|ses

elev|enth

elf

△ elves

elfin

elf|ish

Elgar

Elgin

El Greco

eli|cit
  get from
  △ eli|cits
  △ eli|ci|ted
  △ eli|cit|ing
  ⚠illicit

eli|ci|ta|tion

eli|ci|tor

elide

△ elides

△ eli|ded

△ eli|ding

eli|gi|bil|ity

eli|gible

Eli|jah

elim|in|able

elim|in|ate

△ elim|in|ates

△ elim|in|ated

△ elim|in|ating

elim|in|ation

elim|in|ator

Elint

Eliot

Eli|sha

eli|sion

elite

eli|tism

eli|tist

elixir

Eli|za|beth

Eli|za|bethan

elk

△ elks *or* elk

Ellen

El|les|mere

El|ling|ton

el|lipse
  oval
  ⚠eclipse

el|lip|sis

△ el|lip|ses

el|lip|soid

el|lip|tic

el|lip|ti|cal

el|lip|tic|ally

elm

elo|cu|tion

elo|cu|tion|ary

elo|cu|tion|ist

Elo|him

elon|gate

△ elon|gates

△ elon|ga|ted

△ elon|ga|ting

elon|ga|ted

elon|ga|tion

elope

△ elopes

△ eloped

△ elo|ping

elope|ment

eloper

elo|quence

elo|quent

elo|quently

El Sal|va|dor

else

else|where

El|si|nore

El|speth

Elton

elu|ci|date

△ elu|ci|dates

△ elu|ci|da|ted

△ elu|ci|da|ting

elu|ci|da|tion

elu|ci|da|tory

elude
  escape capture
  △ eludes
  △ elu|ded
  △ elu|ding
  ⚠allude

elu|sive

elu|sively

elu|sive|ness

elu|tion

elver

elves

Elvis

elvish *see* elfish

Ely

Ely|sée

Elys|ian

Elys|ium

ema|ci|ate

△ ema|ci|ates

△ ema|ci|ated

△ ema|ci|ating

ema|ci|ated

ema|ci|ation

eman|ate

△ eman|ates

△ eman|ated

△ eman|ating
eman|ation
eman|ci|pate
△ eman|ci|pates
△ eman|ci|pa|ted
△ eman|ci|pa|
ting
eman|ci|pa|ted
eman|ci|pa|tion
Eman|uel
emas|cu|late
△ emas|cu|lates
△ emas|cu|la|ted
△ emas|cu|la|
ting
emas|cu|la|ted
emas|cu|la|tion
emas|cu|la|tory
em|balm
△ em|balms
△ em|balmed
△ em|balm|ing
em|balmer
em|balm|ment
em|bank|ment
em|bargo
NOUN
△ em|bar|goes
VERB
△ em|bar|goes
△ em|bargoed
△ em|bar|go|ing
em|bark
△ em|barks
△ em|barked
△ em|bark|ing
em|bar|ka|tion
em|bar|rass
△ em|bar|ras|ses
△ em|bar|rassed
△ em|bar|ras|
sing
em|bar|rassed
em|bar|ras|sing

em|bar|ras|
singly
em|bar|rass|
ment
em|bassy
△ em|bas|sies
em|bat|tled
embed
△ em|beds
△ em|bed|ded
△ em|bed|ding
em|bel|lish
△ em|bel|li|shes
△ em|bel|lished
△ em|bel|lish|ing
em|bel|lished
em|bel|lish|ment
ember
em|bez|zle
△ em|bez|zles
△ em|bez|zled
△ em|bez|zling
em|bezzle|ment
em|bez|zler
em|bit|ter
△ em|bit|ters
△ em|bit|tered
△ em|bit|ter|ing
em|bit|tered
em|bit|ter|ing
em|bit|ter|ment
em|bla|zon
△ em|bla|zons
△ em|bla|zoned
△ em|bla|zon|ing
em|bla|zon|ment
em|blem
em|blem|atic
em|bo|di|ment
em|body
△ em|bod|ies
△ em|bod|ied
△ em|body|ing
em|bol|den

△ em|bold|ens
△ em|bold|ened
△ em|bold|en|
ing
em|bol|ism
em|bolus
△ em|boli
em|boss
△ em|bos|ses
△ em|bossed
△ em|bos|sing
em|bossed
em|brace
VERB
△ em|bra|ces
△ em|braced
△ em|bra|cing
em|bra|sure
em|bro|ca|tion
em|broi|der
△ em|broi|ders
△ em|broi|dered
△ em|broi|der|
ing
em|broi|derer
em|broi|dery
em|broil
△ em|broils
△ em|broiled
△ em|broil|ing
em|broil|ment
em|bryo
em|bry|olo|gi|cal
em|bry|olo|gist
em|bry|ol|ogy
em|bry|onic

emend
alter (a text)
△ emends
△ emen|ded
△ emend|ing
△ **amend**

emen|da|tion

em|er|ald
emerge
△ emer|ges
△ emerged
△ emer|ging
emer|gence
emer|gency
△ emer|gen|cies
emer|gent
emer|itus
Emer|son
emery
emetic

emig|rant
one who
emigrates
△ **immigrant**

emi|grate
go to live in
another country
△ emi|grates
△ emi|gra|ted
△ emi|gra|ting
△ **immigrate**

emi|gra|tion
leaving one's
country
△ **immigration**

émi|gré
Emily
em|in|ence
émi|nence grise
△ *émi|nences*
grises
em|in|ent
em|in|ently
emir
em|ir|ate
em|is|sary
△ em|is|sar|ies

emis|sion
something (eg gas) let out
⚠ omission

emis|sive
emit
  VERB
  △ emits
  △ emit|ted
  △ emit|ting
Emlyn
Emma
Emma
Emmanuel *see* Immanuel
Em|men|tal
emol|li|ent
emolu|ment
emote
  △ emotes
  △ emo|ted
  △ emo|ting
emo|tion
emo|tional
emo|tion|al|ism
emo|tion|ally
emo|tion|less
emo|tive
emo|tively
em|panel
  △ em|pan|els
  △ em|pan|elled
  △ em|panel|ling
em|pa|thetic
em|path|ize
  △ em|path|izes
  △ em|path|ized
  △ em|path|izing
em|pathy
Em|pedo|cles
em|peror
'Em|peror' Con|certo, The

em|pha|sis
  △ em|pha|ses
em|pha|size
  △ em|pha|si|zes
  △ em|pha|sized
  △ em|pha|si|zing
em|pha|tic
em|phat|ic|ally
em|phys|ema
em|pire
em|pire-buil|der
em|pire-build|ing
em|pi|ric
em|pir|ical
em|pi|ric|ally
em|pi|ri|cism
em|pi|ri|cist
em|place|ment
em|ploy
  VERB
  △ em|ploys
  △ em|ployed
  △ em|ploy|ing
em|ploy|able
em|ployed
em|ployee
em|ployer
em|ploy|ment
em|por|ium
  △ em|pori|ums
  or em|poria
em|power
  △ em|powers
  △ em|powered
  △ em|power|ing
emp|ress
  △ emp|res|ses
Emp|son
emp|tily
emp|ti|ness
empty
  NOUN
  △ emp|ties

  VERB
  △ emp|ties
  △ emp|tied
  △ emp|ty|ing
  ADJ.
  △ emp|tier
  △ emp|ti|est
empty-han|ded
empty-headed
em|py|real *or* em|pyr|eal
  according to pronunciation
em|py|rean *or* em|pyr|ean
  according to pronunciation
emu
em|ulate
  △ em|ulates
  △ em|ula|ted
  △ em|ula|ting
emu|la|tion
emul|si|fier
emul|sify
  △ emul|si|fies
  △ emul|si|fied
  △ emul|si|fy|ing
emul|sion
  VERB
  △ emul|sions
  △ emul|sioned
  △ emul|sion|ing
en|able
  △ en|ables
  △ en|abled
  △ en|abling
enact
  △ en|acts
  △ en|ac|ted
  △ en|act|ing
en|act|ment
enamel

  VERB
  △ enam|els
  △ enam|elled
  △ enam|el|ling
en|amoured
en bloc
en|camp
  △ en|camps
  △ en|camped
  △ en|camp|ing
en|camp|ment
en|cap|su|late
  △ en|cap|su|lates
  △ en|cap|su|la|ted
  △ en|cap|su|la|ting
en|cap|su|la|tion
en|case
  △ en|ca|ses
  △ en|cased
  △ en|ca|sing
en|case|ment
en|cash
  △ en|ca|shes
  △ en|cashed
  △ en|cash|ing
en|caus|tic
en|ceph|alin
en|ceph|al|itis
en|ceph|alo|gram
en|ceph|alo|graph
en|chain
  △ en|chains
  △ en|chained
  △ en|chain|ing
en|chant
  △ en|chants
  △ en|chan|ted
  △ en|chant|ing
en|chan|ted
en|chan|ter

en|chant|ress
△ en|chant|res|
ses
en|chant|ing
en|chant|ingly
en|chant|ment
en|chi|lada
en|cir|cle
△ en|cir|cles
△ en|cir|cled
△ en|circ|ling
en|circle|ment
en|clave
en|close
△ en|clo|ses
△ en|closed
△ en|clo|sing
en|closed
en|clo|sure
en|code
△ en|codes
△ en|co|ded
△ en|co|ding
en|co|mi|as|tic
en|co|mium
△ en|co|mi|ums
en|com|pass
△ en|com|pas|ses
△ en|com|passed
△ en|com|pas|
sing
en|core
VERB
△ en|cores
△ en|cored
△ en|cor|ing
en|coun|ter
VERB
△ en|coun|ters
△ en|coun|tered
△ en|coun|ter|
ing
en|cour|age
△ en|cour|ages

△ en|cour|aged
△ en|cour|aging
en|cour|age|
ment
en|cour|aging
en|cour|agingly
en|croach
△ en|croa|ches
△ en|croached
△ en|croach|ing
en|croach|ment
en|crust
△ en|crusts
△ en|crus|ted
△ en|crust|ing
en|crus|ta|tion
en|cum|ber
△ en|cum|bers
△ en|cum|bered
△ en|cum|ber|
ing
en|cum|brance
en|cyc|li|cal
En|cyc|lo|pae|dia
Bri|tan|nica
en|cyc|lo|pedia
en|cyc|lo|pedic
en|cyc|lo|ped|ist
end
VERB
△ ends
△ ended
△ end|ing
en|dan|ger
△ en|dan|gers
△ en|dan|gered
△ en|dan|ger|ing
en|dear
△ en|dears
△ en|deared
△ en|dear|ing
en|dear|ing
en|dear|ingly
en|dear|ment

en|deav|our
VERB
△ en|deav|ours
△ en|deav|oured
△ en|deav|our|
ing
en|demic
end|ing
en|dive
end|less
end|lessly
end|less|ness
end|most
en|do|car|di|tis
en|do|crine
en|do|crin|ol|ogy
en|do|cy|to|sis
en|do|derm
en|do|der|mis
end|od|ont|ics
en|do|gamy
en|do|met|ri|osis
en|do|morph
en|do|plasm
en|dor|phin
en|dorse
△ en|dor|ses
△ en|dorsed
△ en|dor|sing
en|dorse|ment
en|do|scope
en|do|scopic
en|do|scopy
en|do|skel|eton
en|do|sperm
en|do|the|lium
△ en|do|the|lia
en|do|ther|mic
endow
△ en|dows
△ en|dowed
△ en|dow|ing
en|dow|ment
end|pa|per

end-prod|uct
endue
△ en|dues
△ en|dued
△ en|du|ing
en|dur|able
en|dur|ance
en|dure
△ en|dures
△ en|dured
△ en|dur|ing
en|dur|ing
end-user
end|ways
enema
enemy
NOUN
△ en|em|ies
en|er|getic
en|er|get|ic|ally
en|er|gize
△ en|er|gi|zes
△ en|er|gized
△ en|er|gi|zing
en|ergy
△ en|er|gies
en|er|vate
△ en|er|vates
△ en|er|va|ted
△ en|er|va|ting
en|er|va|ting
en|er|va|tion
En|fants du Pa|
ra|dis, Les
(Chil|dren of
Pa|ra|dise)
en|fant ter|rible
△ *en|fants ter|*
ribles
en|fee|ble
△ en|fee|bles
△ en|fee|bled
△ en|feeb|ling
en|fee|bled

en|feeble|ment
en|fi|lade
  VERB
△ en|fi|lades
△ en|fi|la|ded
△ en|fi|la|ding
en|fold
△ en|folds
△ en|fol|ded
△ en|fold|ing
en|force
△ en|for|ces
△ en|forced
△ en|for|cing
en|force|able
en|forced
en|force|ment
en|fran|chise
△ en|fran|chi|ses
△ en|fran|chised
△ en|fran|chi|
  sing
en|fran|chise|
  ment
en|gage
△ en|ga|ges
△ en|gaged
△ en|ga|ging
en|gagé
en|gaged
en|gage|ment
en|ga|ging
en|ga|gingly
En|gels
en|gen|der
△ en|gen|ders
△ en|gen|dered
△ en|gen|der|ing
en|gine
en|gine-dri|ver
en|gin|eer
  VERB
△ en|gin|eers
△ en|gin|eered

△ en|gin|eer|ing
en|gin|eer|ing
Eng|land
Eng|lish
Eng|lish|man
△ Eng|lish|men
Eng|lish|wo|man
△ Eng|lish|wo|
  men
en|gorged
en|grave
△ en|graves
△ en|graved
△ en|gra|ving
en|gra|ver
en|gra|ving
en|gross
△ en|gros|ses
△ en|grossed
△ en|gros|sing
en|grossed
en|gros|sing
en|gulf
△ en|gulfs
△ en|gulfed
△ en|gulf|ing
en|hance
△ en|han|ces
△ en|hanced
△ en|han|cing
en|hance|ment
en|igma
en|ig|ma|tic
en|ig|mat|ic|ally
'Enigma' Vari|
  ations
en|join
△ en|joins
△ en|joined
△ en|join|ing
en|joy
△ en|joys
△ en|joyed
△ en|joy|ing

en|joy|able
en|joy|ably
en|joy|ment
en|ke|pha|lin
en|kindle
△ en|kindles
△ en|kindled
△ en|kind|ling
en|large
△ en|lar|ges
△ en|larged
△ en|lar|ging
en|large|ment
en|ligh|ten
△ en|ligh|tens
△ en|ligh|tened
△ en|ligh|ten|ing
en|ligh|tened
en|ligh|ten|ing
en|ligh|ten|ment
en|list
△ en|lists
△ en|lis|ted
△ en|list|ing
en|list|ment
en|li|ven
△ en|li|vens
△ en|li|vened
△ en|li|ven|ing
en|li|ven|ment
en masse
en|mesh
△ en|meshes
△ en|meshed
△ en|mesh|ing
en|mity
En|nius
en|noble
△ en|nobles
△ en|nobled
△ en|no|bling
en|noble|ment
ennui
Enoch

enor|mity
△ enor|mit|ies
enor|mous
enor|mously
enor|mous|ness
enough
en pas|sant
enquire *see*
  inquire
enquiry *see*
  inquiry
en|rage
△ en|ra|ges
△ en|raged
△ en|ra|ging
en|raged
en|rapt
en|rap|ture
△ en|rap|tures
△ en|rap|tured
△ en|rap|tur|ing
en|rap|tured
en|rich
△ en|ri|ches
△ en|riched
△ en|rich|ing
en|riched
en|rich|ment
enrol
△ en|rols
△ en|rolled
△ en|rol|ling
en|rol|ment
en route
en|sconce
△ en|scon|ces
△ en|sconced
△ en|scon|cing
en|sem|ble
en|shrine
△ en|shrines
△ en|shrined
△ en|shri|ning
en|shroud

△ en|shrouds
△ en|shrou|ded
△ en|shroud|ing
en|sign
en|si|lage
en|slave
△ en|slaves
△ en|slaved
△ en|sla|ving
en|slave|ment
en|snare
△ en|snares
△ en|snared
△ en|snar|ing
ensue
△ en|sues
△ en|sued
△ en|su|ing
en|su|ing
en suite

en|sure
make certain or safe
△ en|sures
△ en|sured
△ en|sur|ing
⚠ insure

en|tab|la|ture
en|tail
VERB
△ en|tails
△ en|tailed
△ en|tail|ing
en|tail|ment
en|tan|gle
△ en|tan|gles
△ en|tan|gled
△ en|tan|gling
en|tangle|ment
en|ta|sis
En|tebbe
enter
△ en|ters

△ en|tered
△ en|ter|ing
en|teric
en|ter|itis
en|ter|prise
en|ter|pri|sing
en|ter|pri|singly
en|ter|tain
△ en|ter|tains
△ en|ter|tained
△ en|ter|tain|ing
en|ter|tainer
En|ter|tainer, The
en|ter|tain|ing
en|ter|tain|ment
en|thalpy
en|thral
△ en|thrals
△ en|thralled
△ en|thral|ling
en|thralled
en|thral|ling
en|thral|ment
en|throne
△ en|thrones
△ en|throned
△ en|thro|ning
en|throne|ment
en|thuse
△ en|thu|ses
△ en|thused
△ en|thu|sing
en|thu|si|asm
en|thu|si|ast
en|thu|si|as|tic
en|thu|si|as|tic|ally
en|tice
△ en|ti|ces
△ en|ticed
△ en|ti|cing
en|tice|ment
en|ti|cing

en|ti|cingly
en|tire
en|tirely
en|tirety
△ en|tire|ties
en|ti|tle
△ en|ti|tles
△ en|ti|tled
△ en|ti|tling
en|title|ment
en|tity
△ en|ti|ties
en|tomb
△ en|tombs
△ en|tombed
△ en|tomb|ing
en|tomb|ment
en|to|mo|lo|gi|cal
en|to|mol|ogist
en|to|mol|ogy
en|tour|age
entr'|acte
en|trails
en|trance
VERB
△ en|tran|ces
△ en|tranced
△ en|tran|cing
en|trance|ment
en|tran|cing
en|trant
en|trap
△ en|traps
△ en|trapped
△ en|trap|ping
en|trap|ment
en|treat
△ en|treats
△ en|trea|ted
△ en|treat|ing
en|treaty
△ en|treat|ies
en|tre|côte

en|trée
en|trench
△ en|tren|ches
△ en|trenched
△ en|trench|ing
en|trench|ment
en|tre|pôt
en|tre|pren|eur
en|tre|pren|eur|ial
en|tropy
△ en|tro|pies
en|trust
△ en|trusts
△ en|trus|ted
△ en|trust|ing
en|try
△ ent|ries
ent|ry|ism
ent|ry|ist
Ent|ry|phone
en|twine
△ en|twines
△ en|twined
△ en|twi|ning
E-num|ber
enu|mer|ate
△ enu|mer|ates
△ enu|mer|ated
△ enu|mer|ating
enu|mer|ation
enu|mer|at|ive
enun|ci|ate
△ enun|ci|ates
△ enun|ci|ated
△ enun|ci|ating
enun|ci|ation
en|ur|esis
en|ur|etic

en|velop
VERB
△ en|vel|ops
△ en|vel|oped

△ en|vel|op|ing
△ envelope

en|vel|ope
NOUN
△ envelop

en|vel|op|ment
en|vi|able
en|vi|ably
en|vi|ous
en|vi|ously
en|vi|ron|ment
en|vi|ron|men|
tal
en|vi|ron|men|
tal|ism
en|vi|ron|men|
tal|ist
en|vi|ron|men|
tally
en|vi|rons
en|vis|age
△ en|vis|ages
△ en|vis|aged
△ en|vis|aging
en|voy
envy
VERB
△ en|vies
△ en|vied
△ en|vy|ing
en|zyme
Eo|cene
Eo|hip|pus
eo|lian
eo|li|thic
eon
eosin
epaul|ette
épée
eph|ed|rine
eph|em|era
eph|em|eral

eph|em|eris
△ eph|em|er|ides
Ephe|sians, Let|
ter of Paul to
the
Eph|esus
Eph|raim
epi|blast
epic
epi|cene
epi|cen|tre
epi|cure
Epi|cur|ean
Epi|cur|ean|ism
epi|cur|ism
Epi|curus
epi|cy|cle
Epi|dau|rus
epi|demic
epi|demi|ol|ogy
epi|der|mal
epi|der|mis
epi|di|dy|mis
△ epi|di|dy|mi|des
epi|du|ral
epi|geal
epi|glot|tal
epi|glot|tis
△ epi|glot|tises
epi|gram
epi|gram|ma|tic
epi|graph
epi|gra|phy
epi|lepsy
epi|lep|tic
epi|logue
epi|phany
△ epi|phan|ies
epi|physis
△ epi|physes
epi|phyte
epis|co|pacy
△ epis|co|pa|cies
epis|co|pal

epis|co|pa|lian
epis|co|pa|li|an|
ism
epis|co|pate
epi|si|ot|omy
△ epi|si|ot|om|
ies
epi|sode
epi|sodic
epi|sod|ic|ally
epis|te|mo|lo|gi|
cal
epis|te|mol|ogy
epis|tle
epis|tol|ary
epi|taph
epi|the|lial
epi|the|lium
△ epi|the|lia
epi|thet
epi|tome
epi|tom|ize
△ epi|tom|izes
△ epi|tom|ized
△ epi|tom|izing
epoch
epo|chal
epoch-mak|ing
epo|nym
ep|ony|mous
epoxy
Ep|stein
equa|bil|ity
equable
equably
equal
VERB
△ equals
△ equalled
△ equal|ling
equal|ity
equal|iza|tion
equal|ize
△ equal|izes

△ equal|ized
△ equal|izing
equal|izer
equally
equa|nim|ity
equate
△ equates
△ equa|ted
△ equa|ting
equa|tion
equa|tor
equa|tor|ial
Equa|tor|ial
Guinea
equerry
△ equer|ries
eques|trian
equi|an|gu|lar
equi|dis|tance
equi|dis|tant
equi|lat|eral
equi|lib|rium
equine
equi|noc|tial
equi|nox
△ equi|noxes
equip
△ equips
△ equipped
△ equip|ping
equip|age
equip|ment
equi|poise
equit|able
equi|ta|tion
equity
△ equit|ies
equiv|al|ence
equiv|al|ent
equiv|al|ently
equi|vo|cal
equi|vo|cally
equi|vo|cate
△ equi|vo|cates

△ equi|vo|ca|ted
△ equi|vo|ca|ting
equi|vo|ca|tion
Equus
era
era|di|cate
  △ era|di|cates
  △ era|di|ca|ted
  △ era|di|ca|ting
era|di|ca|tion
erase
  △ era|ses
  △ erased
  △ eras|ing
era|ser
Eras|mus
era|sure
er|bium
ere
erect
  VERB
  △ erects
  △ erec|ted
  △ erect|ing
erect|ile
erec|tion
erectly
erect|ness
Ere|whon
erg

ergo
er|go|nomic
er|go|nom|ic|ally
er|go|nom|ics
er|gon|om|ist
ergot
er|got|ism
Eric
Erica
Erik the Red
Erin
Eri|nyes
Eris
Erit|rea
er|mine
Ernie
erode
  △ erodes
  △ ero|ded
  △ ero|ding
ero|gen|ous
'Ero|ica' Sym|
  phony
Eros
ero|sion
ero|sive

> ero|tic
> *sexually*
> *arousing*
> ⚠ erratic

erot|ica
erot|ic|ally
ero|ti|cism
err
  △ errs
  △ erred
  △ err|ing
err|and
er|rant
er|rantry
er|rata

> er|ra|tic
> *inconsistent;*
> *irregular*
> ⚠ erotic

er|ra|tic|ally
er|ra|tum
  △ er|rata
Errol
er|ro|ne|ous
er|ro|ne|ously
error
er|satz
Erse
erst|while
eruc|ta|tion
eru|dite
eru|ditely
eru|di|tion

erupt
  △ erupts
  △ erup|ted
  △ erupt|ing
erup|tion
ery|si|pelas
eryth|ema
eryth|ro|cyte
eryth|ro|my|cin
eryth|ro|poi|etin
Esau
es|ca|late
  △ es|ca|lates
  △ es|ca|la|ted
  △ es|ca|la|ting
es|ca|la|tion
es|ca|la|tor

> es|cal|lop
> *shellfish*
> ⚠ escalope

> es|ca|lope
> *slice of meat*
> ⚠ escallop

es|ca|pade
es|cape
  VERB
  △ es|capes
  △ es|caped

-er, -est

The comparative and superlative of adjectives are formed by adding **-er** and **-est**, when the adjective is of one syllable, or of two syllables ending in **-y** or **-le** preceded by a consonant (eg **gentle, supple**). When the word ends in **-y** or **-ey**, this usually changes to **-ier** and **-iest**: **empty, emptier, emptiest; pricey, pricier, priciest**. Note that **clever, common, demure, handsome, hollow, mature, narrow, obscure, pleasant, polite, remote, shallow**, and **stupid** also add **-er** and **-est**.

Words of one syllable ending in a single consonant preceded by a single vowel usually double the consonant: **big, bigger, biggest; mad, madder, maddest**, but **cheap, cheaper, cheapest**.

Words of more than one syllable, other than those mentioned above, do not normally inflect in this way. You say instead (eg) **more beautiful, most welcome**.

△ es|ca|ping
es|capee
es|cape|ment
es|cap|ism
es|cap|ist
es|ca|pol|ogist
es|ca|pol|ogy
es|carp|ment
es|cha|to|lo|gi|cal
es|cha|tol|ogy
es|cheat
   VERB
   △ es|cheats
   △ es|chea|ted
   △ es|cheat|ing
Es|cheri|chia
   coli
es|chew
   △ es|chews
   △ es|chewed
   △ es|chew|ing
es|chewal
Es|cof|fier
Es|cor|ial
es|cort
   VERB
   △ es|corts
   △ es|cor|ted
   △ es|cort|ing
es|cri|toire
es|cudo
es|cu|lent
es|cut|cheon
esker
Esk|imo
esophagus *see*
   oesophagus

eso|teric
eso|ter|ic|ally
es|pa|drille
es|pa|lier
es|parto
es|pe|cial
es|pe|ci|ally
Es|per|anto
es|pi|on|age
es|plan|ade
es|pou|sal
es|pouse
   △ es|pou|ses
   △ es|poused
   △ es|pous|ing
es|presso
es|prit
es|prit de corps
espy
   △ es|pies
   △ es|pied
   △ espy|ing
es|quire
es|quisse

essay
   short piece of
   writing; attempt
   VERB
   △ es|says
   △ es|sayed
   △ es|say|ing
   ⚠ assay

es|say|ist
Es|says of Elia,
   The
es|sence

Es|sene
es|sen|tial
es|sen|tial|ism
es|sen|ti|al|ity
es|sen|tially
Essex
es|tab|lish
   △ es|tab|li|shes
   △ es|tab|lished
   △ es|tab|lish|ing
es|tab|lished
es|tab|lish|ment
es|tan|cia
es|tate
es|teem
   VERB
   △ es|teems
   △ es|teemed
   △ es|teem|ing
Es|telle
ester
Es|ter|házy
Es|ther
Es|ther, Book of
esthetic *see*
   aesthetic
es|tim|able
es|ti|mate
   VERB
   △ es|ti|mates
   △ es|ti|ma|ted
   △ es|ti|ma|ting
es|ti|ma|tion
es|ti|ma|tor
Es|to|nia
Es|to|nian
estradiol *see*

oestradiol
es|trange
   △ es|tranges
   △ es|tranged
   △ es|tranging
es|tranged
es|trange|ment
es|tu|ary
   △ es|tu|ar|ies
et cet|era
   and so on
et|cet|era
   extra item
etch
   △ et|ches
   △ etched
   △ etch|ing
etcher
etch|ing
eter|nal
etern|ally
etern|ity
   △ etern|it|ies
ethane *or* eth|
   ane
   according to
   pronunciation
ethane|diol *or*
   eth|ane|diol
   according to
   pronunciation
eth|anol
Ethel
Eth|el|bert
Eth|el|red
eth|ene
ether

-erous / -rous

-erous is usual for adjectives formed from nouns ending in **-er**: **murderous, slanderous, thunderous.**

Except: **disastrous, leprous, monstrous, wondrous.**

Note also: **ambidextrous, cumbrous.**

ether|eal
ether|eally
ethic
eth|ical
eth|ic|ally
eth|ics
Ethi|opia
Ethi|opi|an|ism
eth|nic
eth|nic|ally
eth|ni|city
eth|no|cen|tric
eth|no|cen|tri|
city
eth|no|cen|trism
eth|nog|raphy
eth|no|lin|guis|
tics
eth|no|lo|gi|cal
eth|nol|ogist
eth|nol|ogy
eth|no|mu|si|col|
ogy
eth|no|sci|ence
ethol|ogy
ethos
△ ethoses
ethyl
ethyl|ene
eth|yne
etio|la|ted
etio|la|tion
eti|ol|ogy
eti|quette
Etna
Eton
Et|ruria
Et|rus|can
étude
ety|mo|lo|gi|cal
ety|mo|lo|gic|
ally
ety|mol|ogist
ety|mol|ogy

△ ety|mol|ogies
Eu|boea
eu|ca|lyp|tus
△ eu|ca|lyp|tuses
  or eu|ca|lypti
Eu|char|ist
Eu|char|is|tic
eu|ca|ry|ote
eu|chre
Eu|clid
Eu|clid|ean
Eu|gene
Eu|gene On|egin
eu|genic
eu|gen|ic|ally
eu|gen|ics
eu|glena
eu|ka|ry|ote
eu|lo|gis|tic
eu|lo|gis|tic|ally
eu|lo|gize
△ eu|lo|gi|zes
△ eu|lo|gized
△ eu|lo|gi|zing
eu|logy
△ eu|lo|gies
Eu|men|ides
eu|nuch
eu|phem|ism
eu|phem|is|tic
eu|phem|is|tic|
ally
eu|pho|ni|ous
eu|pho|ni|ously
eu|pho|nium
eu|phony
△ eu|phon|ies
eu|phoria
eu|phoric
eu|phor|ic|ally
Eu|phra|tes
Eu|phues
eu|phu|ism
eu|phu|is|tic

eu|phu|is|tic|ally
Eur|asian
eur|eka
eu|rhyth|mic
eu|rhyth|mics
Eu|rip|ides
Eu|ro|cheque
Eu|ro|com|mu|
nism
Eu|ro|crat
Eu|ro|cur|rency
△ Eu|ro|cur|ren|
cies
Eu|ro|dol|lar
Eu|ro|figh|ter
Eu|ro|mo|ney
Eu|ropa
Eur|ope
Eu|ro|pean
eu|ro|pium
Eu|ro|vi|sion
Eu|ry|dice
Eu|se|bio
Eus|ta|chian
eu|stasy
eu|tha|na|sia
eu|tro|phic
eu|tro|phic|ation
eva|cu|ate
△ eva|cu|ates
△ eva|cu|ated
△ eva|cu|ating
eva|cu|ation
eva|cuee
evade
△ evades
△ eva|ded
△ eva|ding
evalu|ate
△ evalu|ates
△ evalu|ated
△ evalu|ating
evalu|ation
evan|esce

△ evan|es|ces
△ evan|esced
△ evan|es|cing
evan|es|cence
evan|es|cent
evan|gel|ical
evan|gel|ic|al|
ism
evan|gel|ic|ally
evan|gel|ism
evan|gel|ist
evan|gel|is|tic
evan|gel|iza|tion
evan|gel|ize
△ evan|gel|izes
△ evan|gel|ized
△ evan|gel|izing
Evans
evap|or|ate
△ evap|or|ates
△ evap|or|ated
△ evap|or|ating
eva|por|ation
eva|por|ite
eva|po|tran|spi|
ra|tion
eva|sion
eva|sive
eva|sively
eva|sive|ness
Eve
eve
Eve|lyn
even
  VERB
△ evens
△ evened
△ even|ing
even
even-han|ded
even-han|dedly
even-han|ded|
ness
even|ing

Ev|enki
evenly
even|ness
even|song
event
even|ter
event|ful
event|fully
even|tide
event|ing
even|tual
even|tu|al|ity
△ even|tu|al|it|
ies
even|tu|ally
even|tu|ate
△ even|tu|ates
△ even|tu|ated
△ even|tu|ating
ever
Ever|est
ever|glade
ever|green
ever|last|ing
ever|last|ingly
ever|more
Evert
every
every|body
every|day
Every|man
every|one
every|thing
every|where
Eve|sham
evict
△ evicts
△ evic|ted
△ evict|ing
evic|tion
evi|dence
VERB
△ evi|den|ces
△ evi|denced

△ evi|den|cing
evi|dent
evi|den|tial
evi|den|tially
evi|dently
evil
evil|doer
evilly
evince
△ evin|ces
△ evinced
△ evin|cing
evis|cer|ate
△ evis|cer|ates
△ evis|cer|ated
△ evis|cer|ating
evis|cer|ation
evo|ca|tion
evoc|at|ive
evoke
△ evokes
△ evoked
△ evo|king
evo|lu|tion
evo|lu|tion|ary
evo|lu|tion|ism
evo|lu|tion|ist
evolve
△ evolves
△ evolved
△ evol|ving
Ewan

ewe
female sheep
⚠yew

ewer
ex
NOUN
△ ex's *or* exes
ex|acer|bate
△ ex|acer|bates
△ ex|acer|ba|ted
△ ex|acer|ba|ting

ex|acer|ba|tion
exact
VERB
△ exacts
△ ex|ac|ted
△ ex|act|ing
ex|act|ing
ex|act|ingly
ex|ac|tion
ex|ac|ti|tude
ex|actly
ex|act|ness
ex|ag|ger|ate
△ ex|ag|ger|ates
△ ex|ag|ger|ated
△ ex|ag|ger|ating
ex|ag|ger|ation
ex|ag|ger|ator
exalt
△ exalts
△ ex|al|ted
△ ex|alt|ing
ex|al|ta|tion
ex|al|ted
ex|al|tedly
exam
ex|am|ina|tion
ex|am|ine
△ ex|am|ines
△ ex|am|ined
△ ex|am|in|ing
ex|am|inee
ex|am|iner
ex|am|ple
ex|as|per|ate
△ ex|as|per|ates
△ ex|as|per|ated
△ ex|as|per|ating
ex|as|per|ation
Ex|ca|li|bur
ex cath|edra
ex|ca|vate
△ ex|ca|vates
△ ex|ca|va|ted

△ ex|ca|va|ting
ex|ca|va|tion
ex|ca|va|tor
ex|ceed
△ ex|ceeds
△ ex|cee|ded
△ ex|ceed|ing
ex|ceed|ingly
excel
△ ex|cels
△ ex|celled
△ ex|cel|ling
ex|cel|lence
Ex|cel|lency
△ Ex|cel|len|cies
ex|cel|lent
ex|cel|lently

ex|cept
leaving out;
leave out
VERB
△ ex|cepts
△ ex|cep|ted
△ ex|cept|ing
⚠accept

ex|cept|ing
ex|cep|tion
ex|cep|tion|able
ex|cep|tional
ex|cep|tion|ally
ex|cerpt
VERB
△ ex|cerpts
△ ex|cerp|ted
△ ex|cerpt|ing
ex|cerp|tion

ex|cess
going beyond
normal limits
NOUN
△ ex|ces|ses
⚠access

ex|ces|sive
ex|cess|ively
ex|change
  VERB
  △ ex|changes
  △ ex|changed
  △ ex|changing
ex|change|able
ex|chequer
ex|cise
  VERB
  △ ex|ci|ses
  △ ex|cised
  △ ex|ci|sing
ex|ci|sion
ex|ci|ta|bil|ity
ex|cit|able
ex|ci|tably
ex|ci|ta|tion
ex|cite
  △ ex|cites
  △ ex|ci|ted
  △ ex|ci|ting
ex|ci|ted
ex|ci|tedly
ex|cite|ment
ex|ci|ting
ex|ci|tingly
ex|claim
  △ ex|claims
  △ ex|claimed
  △ ex|claim|ing
ex|cla|ma|tion
ex|clam|at|ory
ex|clude
  △ ex|cludes
  △ ex|clu|ded
  △ ex|clu|ding
ex|clu|ding
ex|clu|sion
ex|clu|sive
ex|clu|sively
ex|clu|sive|ness
ex|com|mu|ni|

cate
△ ex|com|mu|ni|
  cates
△ ex|com|mu|ni|
  ca|ted
△ ex|com|mu|ni|
  ca|ting
ex|com|mu|ni|ca|
  tion
ex|co|ri|ate
  △ ex|co|ri|ates
  △ ex|co|ri|ated
  △ ex|co|ri|ating
ex|co|ri|ation
ex|cre|ment
ex|cre|men|tal
ex|cres|cence
ex|creta
ex|crete
  △ ex|cretes
  △ ex|cre|ted
  △ ex|cre|ting
ex|cre|tion
ex|cre|tory
ex|cru|ci|ating
ex|cru|ci|atingly
ex|cul|pate
  △ ex|cul|pates
  △ ex|cul|pa|ted
  △ ex|cul|pa|ting
ex|cul|pa|tion
ex|cur|sion
ex|cur|sive
ex|cus|able
ex|cus|ably
ex|cuse
  VERB
  △ ex|cu|ses
  △ ex|cused
  △ ex|cu|sing
ex-dir|ec|tory
exe|crable
exe|crably
exe|crate

△ exe|crates
△ exe|cra|ted
△ exe|cra|ting
exe|cra|tion
exe|cute
  △ exe|cutes
  △ exe|cu|ted
  △ exe|cu|ting
exe|cu|tion
exe|cu|tioner
exe|cu|tive
exe|cu|tor
exe|cu|trix
  △ exe|cu|tri|ces
  or exe|cu|
    trixes
exe|ge|sis
  △ exe|ge|ses
exe|getic
exe|get|ical
ex|em|plar
ex|em|plary
ex|em|pli|fi|ca|
  tion
ex|em|plify
  △ ex|em|pli|fies
  △ ex|em|pli|fied
  △ ex|em|pli|fy|
    ing
ex|empt
  VERB
  △ ex|empts
  △ ex|emp|ted
  △ ex|empt|ing
ex|emp|tion

ex|er|cise
  practice;
  activity;
  practise; make
  active
  VERB
  △ ex|er|ci|ses
  △ ex|er|cised

△ ex|er|ci|sing
⚠ exorcize

exert
  △ ex|erts
  △ ex|er|ted
  △ ex|ert|ing
ex|er|tion
Ex|eter
ex|eunt
ex gra|tia
ex|ha|la|tion
ex|hale
  △ ex|hales
  △ ex|haled
  △ ex|ha|ling
ex|haust
  VERB
  △ ex|hausts
  △ ex|haus|ted
  △ ex|haust|ing
ex|haus|ted
ex|haust|ible
ex|haust|ing
ex|haus|tion
ex|haust|ive
ex|haust|ively
ex|hi|bit
  VERB
  △ ex|hib|its
  △ ex|hib|ited
  △ ex|hib|it|ing
ex|hi|bi|tion
ex|hi|bi|tioner
ex|hi|bi|tion|ism
ex|hi|bi|tion|ist
ex|hi|bi|tion|is|
  tic
ex|hib|itor
ex|hil|ar|ate
  △ ex|hil|ar|ates
  △ ex|hil|ar|ated
  △ ex|hil|ar|ating
ex|hil|ar|ation

ex|hort
△ ex|horts
△ ex|hor|ted
△ ex|hort|ing
ex|hor|ta|tion
ex|hu|ma|tion
ex|hume
△ ex|humes
△ ex|humed
△ ex|hu|ming
exi|gency
△ exi|gen|cies
exi|gent
exi|gu|ity
ex|igu|ous
ex|igu|ously
ex|igu|ous|ness
exile
VERB
△ ex|iles
△ ex|iled
△ exi|ling
exist
△ ex|ists
△ ex|is|ted
△ ex|ist|ing
ex|ist|ence
ex|ist|ent
ex|is|ten|tial
ex|is|ten|tial|ism
ex|is|ten|tial|ist
exit
VERB
△ exits
△ ex|ited
△ ex|it|ing
Ex|moor
Ex|mouth
exo|bi|ol|ogy
Exo|cet
exo|crine
exo|cy|to|sis
ex|odus
△ ex|od|uses

Ex|odus, Book
of
ex of|fi|cio
exo|gamy
exo|gen|ous
ex|on|er|ate
△ ex|on|er|ates
△ ex|on|er|ated
△ ex|on|er|ating
ex|on|er|ation
ex|or|bit|ance
ex|or|bit|ant
ex|or|bit|antly
ex|or|cism
ex|or|cist
┌─────────────────┐
│ ex|or|cize   │
│ △ ex|or|ci|zes │
│ △ ex|or|cized   │
│ △ ex|or|ci|zing │
│ △ exercise   │
└─────────────────┘
ex|or|dium
△ ex|or|di|ums
or ex|or|dia
exo|skel|eton
exo|sphere
exo|therm
ex|otic
ex|ot|ica
ex|ot|ic|ally
ex|pand
△ ex|pands
△ ex|pan|ded
△ ex|pand|ing
ex|pand|able
ex|panse
ex|pan|sible
ex|pan|sion
ex|pan|sion|ism
ex|pan|sion|ist
ex|pan|sive
ex|pan|sively
ex|pan|sive|ness
expat

ex|pa|ti|ate
△ ex|pa|ti|ates
△ ex|pa|ti|ated
△ ex|pa|ti|ating
ex|pa|ti|ation
ex|pat|ri|ate
VERB
△ ex|pat|ri|ates
△ ex|pat|ri|ated
△ ex|pat|ri|ating
ex|pect
△ ex|pects
△ ex|pec|ted
△ ex|pect|ing
ex|pect|ancy
△ ex|pect|an|cies
ex|pect|ant
ex|pect|antly
ex|pec|ta|tion
ex|pec|tor|ant
ex|pec|tor|ate
△ ex|pec|tor|ates
△ ex|pec|tor|ated
△ ex|pec|tor|
ating
ex|pe|di|ence
ex|pe|di|ency
△ ex|pe|di|en|
cies
ex|pe|di|ent
ex|pe|di|ently
ex|ped|ite
△ ex|ped|ites
△ ex|ped|ited
△ ex|ped|iting
ex|ped|ition
ex|ped|ition|ary
ex|ped|itious
ex|ped|itiously
expel
△ ex|pels
△ ex|pelled
△ ex|pel|ling
ex|pend

△ ex|pends
△ ex|pen|ded
△ ex|pend|ing
ex|pend|able
ex|pen|di|ture
ex|pense
ex|pen|sive
ex|pen|sively
ex|peri|ence
VERB
△ ex|peri|en|ces
△ ex|peri|enced
△ ex|peri|en|cing
ex|peri|enced
ex|peri|en|tial
ex|peri|en|tially
ex|peri|ment
VERB
△ ex|peri|ments
△ ex|peri|men|
ted
△ ex|peri|ment|
ing
ex|peri|men|tal
ex|peri|ment|ally
ex|peri|men|ta|
tion
ex|peri|men|ter
Ex|peri|ment
with the Air
Pump
ex|pert
ex|per|tise
ex|pertly
ex|pi|ate
△ ex|pi|ates
△ ex|pi|ated
△ ex|pi|ating
ex|pi|ation
ex|pir|ation
ex|pire
△ ex|pires
△ ex|pired
△ ex|pir|ing

ex|piry
△ ex|pir|ies
ex|plain
△ ex|plains
△ ex|plained
△ ex|plain|ing
ex|plan|ation
ex|plan|at|ory
ex|ple|tive
ex|plic|able
ex|pli|cate
△ ex|pli|cates
△ ex|pli|ca|ted
△ ex|pli|ca|ting
ex|pli|ca|tion
ex|pli|cit
ex|pli|citly
ex|pli|cit|ness
ex|plode
△ ex|plodes
△ ex|plo|ded
△ ex|plo|ding
ex|plo|ded
ex|ploit
VERB
△ ex|ploits
△ ex|ploi|ted
△ ex|ploit|ing
ex|ploi|ta|tion
ex|plor|ation
ex|plor|at|ory
ex|plore
△ ex|plores
△ ex|plored
△ ex|plor|ing
ex|plorer
ex|plo|sion
ex|plo|sive
ex|plo|sively
expo
ex|po|nent
ex|po|nen|tial
ex|po|nen|ti|ally
ex|port

VERB
△ ex|ports
△ ex|por|ted
△ ex|port|ing
ex|por|ta|tion
ex|por|ter
ex|pose
△ ex|po|ses
△ ex|posed
△ ex|po|sing
ex|posé
ex|po|si|tion
ex|pos|tu|late
△ ex|pos|tu|lates
△ ex|pos|tu|la|ted
△ ex|pos|tu|
lating
ex|pos|tu|la|tion
ex|po|sure
ex|pound
△ ex|pounds
△ ex|poun|ded
△ ex|pound|ing
ex|press
NOUN
△ ex|pres|ses
VERB
△ ex|pres|ses
△ ex|pressed
△ ex|pres|sing
ex|press|ible
ex|pres|sion
Ex|pres|sion|ism
Ex|pres|sion|ist
ex|pres|sion|less
ex|pres|sive
ex|pres|sively
ex|pres|sive|ness
ex|pressly
ex|pro|pri|ate
△ ex|pro|pri|ates
△ ex|pro|pri|ated
△ ex|pro|pri|
ating

ex|pro|pri|ation
ex|pro|pri|ator
ex|pul|sion
ex|pul|sive
ex|punge
△ ex|pun|ges
△ ex|punged
△ ex|pun|ging
ex|pur|gate
△ ex|pur|gates
△ ex|pur|ga|ted
△ ex|pur|ga|ting
ex|pur|ga|tion
ex|quis|ite
ex|quis|itely
ex-ser|vice|man
△ ex-ser|vice|
men
ex-ser|vice|wo|
man
△ ex-ser|vice|
wo|men
ex|tant
ex|tem|por|
aneous
ex|tem|por|
aneously
ex|tem|por|ary
ex|tem|por|ar|ily
ex|tem|pore
ex|tem|por|iza|
tion
ex|tem|por|ize
△ ex|tem|por|
izes
△ ex|tem|por|
ized
△ ex|tem|por|
izing
ex|tend
△ ex|tends
△ ex|ten|ded
△ ex|tend|ing
ex|tend|able

ex|ten|ded-play
ex|tend|ible
ex|tens|ible
ex|ten|si|fi|ca|
tion
ex|ten|sion
ex|ten|sive
ex|ten|sively
ex|ten|sor
ex|tent
ex|tenu|ate
△ ex|tenu|ates
△ ex|tenu|ated
△ ex|tenu|ating
ex|tenu|ating
ex|tenu|ation
ex|ter|ior
ex|ter|min|ate
△ ex|ter|min|ates
△ ex|ter|min|
ated
△ ex|ter|min|
ating
ex|ter|min|ation
ex|ter|min|ator
ex|ter|nal
ex|ter|nal|ize
△ ex|ter|nal|izes
△ ex|ter|nal|ized
△ ex|ter|nal|
izing
ex|ter|nally
ex|tinct
ex|tinc|tion
ex|tin|guish
△ ex|tin|gui|shes
△ ex|tin|guished
△ ex|tin|guish|
ing
ex|tin|gui|sher
ex|tir|pate
△ ex|tir|pates
△ ex|tir|pa|ted
△ ex|tir|pa|ting

ex|tir|pa|tion
extol
  △ ex|tols
  △ ex|tolled
  △ ex|tol|ling
ex|tol|ment
ex|tort
  △ ex|torts
  △ ex|tor|ted
  △ ex|tort|ing
ex|tor|tion
ex|tor|tion|ate
ex|tor|tion|ately
ex|tor|tion|ist
extra
ex|tra|cel|lu|lar
ex|tract
  VERB
  △ ex|tracts
  △ ex|trac|ted
  △ ex|tract|ing
ex|trac|tion
ex|trac|tor
ex|tra-cur|ri|cu|lar
ex|tra|dit|able
ex|tra|dite
  △ ex|tra|dites
  △ ex|tra|di|ted
  △ ex|tra|di|ting
ex|tra|di|tion

ex|tra|mar|ital
ex|tra|mu|ral
ex|tra|neous
ex|tra|neously
ex|tra|or|din|ar|ily
ex|tra|or|din|ary
ex|tra|po|late
  △ ex|tra|po|lates
  △ ex|tra|po|la|ted
  △ ex|tra|po|la|ting
ex|tra|po|la|tion
ex|tra|sen|sory
ex|tra|ter|res|trial
ex|tra|va|gance
ex|tra|va|gant
ex|tra|va|gantly
ex|tra|va|ganza
ex|tra|ver|sion
ex|tra|vert
ex|treme
ex|tremely
ex|trem|ism
ex|trem|ist
ex|trem|ity
  △ ex|trem|it|ies
ex|tric|able
ex|tri|cate

  △ ex|tri|cates
  △ ex|tri|ca|ted
  △ ex|tri|ca|ting
ex|tri|ca|tion
ex|tro|ver|sion
ex|tro|vert
ex|tro|ver|ted
ex|trude
  △ ex|trudes
  △ ex|tru|ded
  △ ex|tru|ding
ex|tru|sion
ex|tru|sive
ex|uber|ance
ex|uber|ant
ex|uber|antly
ex|udate
exu|da|tion
exude
  △ ex|udes
  △ ex|uded
  △ ex|uding
exult
  △ ex|ults
  △ ex|ul|ted
  △ ex|ult|ing
ex|ult|ant
ex|ul|ta|tion
Eyck
eye

  VERB
  △ eyes
  △ eyed
  △ eye|ing
eye|ball
eye|bright
eye|brow
eye-cat|cher
eye-catch|ing
eye|ful
eye|glass
  △ eye|glas|ses
eye|lash
  △ eye|la|shes
eye|let
eye|lid
eye-opener
eye|piece
eye|sight
eye|sore
eye|wash
  △ eye|wa|shes
eye|wit|ness
  △ eye|wit|nes|ses

---

eyrie
  nest of eagle etc
  ⚠ eerie

Ey|senck
Ezek|iel
Ezra, Book of

F

fa
Fa|berg
Fa|bian
fa|ble
fa|bled
fab|liau
△ fab|li|aux
fab|ric
fab|ri|cate
△ fab|ri|cates
△ fab|ri|ca|ted
△ fab|ri|ca|ting
fab|ri|ca|tion
fab|ri|ca|tor
fa|bu|lous
fa|bu|lously
Fa|çade
fa|çade
face
  VERB
  △ faces
  △ faced
  △ fa|cing
face|less
face|lift
facer
face-saving
facet
fa|ceti|ous
fa|ceti|ously
fa|ceti|ous|ness
facia
fa|cial
fa|cile
fa|cilely
fa|ci|li|tate
△ fa|ci|li|tates
△ fa|ci|li|ta|ted
△ fa|ci|li|ta|ting
fa|ci|li|ta|tion
fa|cil|ity
△ fa|cil|it|ies

fa|cing
fac|sim|ile
fact
fac|tion
fac|tional
fac|ti|tious
fac|tor
fac|tor|ial
fac|tor|ing
fac|tor|iza|tion
fac|tor|ize
△ fac|tor|izes
△ fac|tor|ized
△ fac|tor|izing
fac|tory
△ fac|tor|ies
fac|to|tum
fac|tual
fac|tu|ally
fac|ul|ta|tive
fac|ulty
△ fac|ul|ties
fad
fad|di|ness
fad|dish
fad|dish|ness
faddy
△ fad|dier
△ fad|di|est
fade
△ fades
△ faded
△ fa|ding
fade-in
fade-out
fae|cal
fae|ces

Faerie Queene,
The
poem by Spenser
⚠ *Fairy Queen,*
The

Faeroes *see*

Faroes
faff
△ faffs
△ faffed
△ faf|fing
fag
  VERB
  △ fags
  △ fagged
  △ fag|ging
fag|got
fah
Fah|ren|heit
fai|ence
fail
  △ fails
  △ failed
  △ fail|ing
fail|ing
fail-safe
fail|ure

fain
  gladly
  ⚠ *feign*

faint
  pale; weak;
  collapse
  VERB
  △ faints
  △ fain|ted
  △ faint|ing
  ADJ.
  △ fain|ter
  △ faint|est
  ⚠ *feint*

faint-hearted
faintly
faint|ness

fair
  market;
  amusements;

  honest; light-
  haired; beautiful
  ADJ.
  △ fairer
  △ fair|est
  ⚠ *fare*

Fair|banks
fair|ground
fair|ing
fairly
fair|ness
fair|way
fairy
  △ fair|ies
fairy|land

Fairy Queen, The
opera by Purcell
⚠ *Faerie*
Queene, The

fait ac|com|pli
  △ faits ac|com|plis
Faith
faith
faith|ful
faith|fully
faith|ful|ness
faith|less
faith|lessly
faith|less|ness
fa|ji|tas
fake
  VERB
  △ fakes
  △ faked
  △ fa|king
faker
fa|kery
fakir
Fa|lange
fal|con
fal|coner
fal|conry

Faldo
Fal|kirk
Falk|land Is|
　lands
fall
　VERB
　△ falls
　△ fal|ling
　△ fal|len
Falla
fal|la|cious
fal|la|ciously
fal|lacy
　△ fal|la|cies
fal|len
fall|ible
fal|ling-off
Fal|lo|pian
fall|out
fal|low
Fal|mouth
false
　△ fal|ser
　△ fals|est
false|hood
falsely
false|ness
fal|setto
fal|si|fi|ca|tion
fal|sify
　△ fal|si|fies
　△ fal|si|fied
　△ fal|si|fy|ing
fal|sity
Fal|staff
fal|ter
　△ fal|ters
　△ fal|tered
　△ fal|ter|ing
fal|ter|ingly
fame
famed
fa|mil|ial
fa|mil|iar

fa|mi|li|ar|ity
　△ fa|mi|li|ar|it|
　　ies
fa|mi|li|ar|iza|
　tion
fa|mi|li|ar|ize
　△ fa|mi|li|ar|izes
　△ fa|mi|li|ar|ized
　△ fa|mi|li|ar|
　　izing
fa|mi|li|arly
fam|ily
　△ fam|il|ies
fam|ine
fam|ished
fam|ish|ing
fa|mous
fa|mously
fan
　VERB
　△ fans
　△ fanned
　△ fan|ning
fa|na|tic
fa|nat|ical
fa|nat|ic|ally
fa|na|ti|cism
fan|cier
fan|ci|ful
fan|ci|fully
fan|cily
fancy
　NOUN
　△ fan|cies
　VERB
　△ fan|cies
　△ fan|cied
　△ fan|cy|ing
　ADJ.
　△ fan|cier
　△ fan|ci|est
fancy-free
fan|cy|work
fan|dango

Fan|fani
fan|fare
fang
Fan|gio
fan|light
fanny
　△ fan|nies
Fanny and
　Alex|an|der
　(Fanny och
　Alex|an|der)
fan|tail
Fan|ta|sia
fan|ta|sia
Fan|ta|sia on a
　Theme by
　Thomas Tal|lis
fan|ta|size
　△ fan|ta|si|zes
　△ fan|ta|sized
　△ fan|ta|si|zing
fan|tas|tic
fan|tas|tic|ally
fan|tasy
　△ fan|ta|sies
Fan|tin-Latour
fan|zine
far
　△ far|ther or
　　fur|ther
　△ far|thest or
　　fur|thest
farad
fa|ra|day
fa|ran|dole
far|away
farce
far|ci|cal
far|ci|cally

fare
　passenger's fee;
　food; get on
　VERB

△ fares
△ fared
△ faring
⚠ fair

Far East
Far-East|ern
Fare|ham
fare|well
Fare|well to
　Arms, A
far-fetched
far-flung
Far from the
　Mad|ding
　Crowd
fa|ri|na|ceous
farm
　VERB
　△ farms
　△ farmed
　△ farm|ing
far|mer
farm|house
farm|ing
farm|stead
farm|yard
Farn|bor|ough
Far|oes
Faro|ese
far-off
far-out
far|rago
　△ far|ra|gos or
　　far|ra|goes
far-reach|ing
far|rier
far|row
　VERB
　△ far|rows
　△ far|rowed
　△ far|row|ing
Farsi
far-sigh|ted

far-sigh|ted|ness
fart
  VERB
  △ farts
  △ far|ted
  △ fart|ing
far|ther
far|thest
far|thing
fas|ces
Fasch|ing
fas|cia
fas|cial
fas|cin|ate
  △ fas|cin|ates
  △ fas|cin|ated
  △ fas|cin|ating
fas|cin|ating
fas|cin|atingly
fas|cin|ation
fas|cio|li|asis
fas|cism
fas|cist
fash|ion
  VERB
  △ fash|ions
  △ fash|ioned
  △ fash|ion|ing
fash|ion|able
fash|ion|ably
Fass|bin|der
Fas|sett
fast
  VERB
  △ fasts
  △ fas|ted
  △ fast|ing
  ADJ.
  △ fas|ter
  △ fast|est
  ADV.
  △ fas|ter
  △ fast|est
fas|ten

△ fas|tens
△ fas|tened
△ fas|ten|ing
fas|tener
fas|ten|ing
fast-for|ward
  VERB
  △ fast-for|wards
  △ fast-for|war|
    ded
  △ fast-for|ward|
    ing
fas|ti|di|ous
fas|ti|di|ously
fas|ti|di|ous|ness
fast|ness
  △ fast|nes|ses
fast-track
  VERB
  △ fast-tracks
  △ fast-tracked
  △ fast-track|ing
fat
  VERB
  △ fats
  △ fat|ted
  △ fat|ting
  ADJ.
  △ fat|ter
  △ fat|test
fatal
fa|tal|ism
fa|tal|ist
fa|tal|is|tic
fa|tal|is|tic|ally
fa|tal|ity
  △ fa|tal|it|ies
fa|tally

> fate
> *destiny; doom*
> ⚠ fête

fated
fate|ful

fate|fully
Fates
fat|head
fat-headed
fa|ther
  VERB
  △ fa|thers
  △ fa|thered
  △ fa|ther|ing
fa|ther|hood
fa|ther-in-law
  △ fa|thers-in-law
fa|ther|land
fa|ther|less
fa|ther|li|ness
fa|therly
fa|thom
  VERB
  △ fa|thoms
  △ fa|thomed
  △ fa|thom|ing
fa|thom|less
fa|tigue
  VERB
  △ fa|tigues
  △ fa|tigued
  △ fa|tiguing
Fat|ima
fat|ness
fat|ten
  △ fat|tens
  △ fat|tened
  △ fat|ten|ing
fat|ten|ing
fat|ti|ness
fatty
  NOUN
  △ fat|ties
  ADJ.
  △ fat|tier
  △ fat|ti|est
fa|tu|ity
  △ fa|tu|it|ies
fatu|ous

fatu|ously
fatu|ous|ness
fatwa
fau|cet
Faulk|ner
fault
fault|less
fault|lessly
faulty
  △ fault|ier
  △ faulti|est

> faun
> *mythical*
> *creature*
> ⚠ fawn

fauna
  △ faunas *or*
    faunae
Faure
  politician
Fauré
  composer
Faust
Faus|tus
Fauv|ism
faux pas
  sing. and pl.
fa|vour
  VERB
  △ fa|vours
  △ fa|voured
  △ fa|vour|ing
fa|vour|able
fa|vour|ably
fa|vour|ite
fa|vour|it|ism
Fawkes

> fawn
> *young deer;*
> *beige; flatter*
> VERB
> △ fawns

△ fawned
△ fawn|ing
⚠ faun

fawn|ing
fawn|ingly
fax
NOUN
△ faxes
VERB
△ faxes
△ faxed
△ fax|ing
Fay
Faye
fay
fealty
fear
VERB
△ fears
△ feared
△ fear|ing
fear|ful
fear|fully
fear|ful|ness
fear|less
fear|lessly
fear|less|ness
fear|some
fea|si|bil|ity
feas|ible
feas|ibly
feast
VERB
△ feasts
△ feas|ted
△ feast|ling

feat
remarkable deed
⚠ feet

feather
VERB
△ feath|ers

△ feath|ered
△ feath|er|ing
feather-bed
VERB
△ feather-beds
△ feather-bed|
ded
△ feather-bed|
ding
feather-brained
feath|ered
feath|er|weight
feath|ery
fea|ture
fea|ture|less
feb|rile
Feb|ru|ary
△ Feb|ru|ar|ies
feck|less
feck|lessly
feck|less|ness
fec|und
fe|cun|dity
fed
Fe|day|een
fed|eral
fed|er|al|ism
fed|er|al|ist
fed|er|al|ize
△ fed|er|al|izes
△ fed|er|al|ized
△ fed|er|al|izing
fed|er|ate
△ fed|er|ates
△ fed|er|ated
△ fed|er|ating
fed|er|ation
Fé|dér|ation In|
ter|na|tion|ale
de Foot|ball
As|soci|ation
fed|er|at|ive
fee
fee|ble

△ feeb|ler
△ feeb|lest
feeble-minded
feeble-mind|ed|
ness
feeble|ness
fee|bly
feed
VERB
△ feeds
△ fed
△ feed|ing
feed|back
feeder
feel
VERB
△ feels
△ felt
△ feel|ing
feeler
feel|good
feel|ing
feel|ingly

feet
pl. of foot
⚠ feat

feign
pretend
△ feigns
△ feigned
△ feign|ing
⚠ fain

feigned

feint
*distracting
movement; ruled
with faint lines*
⚠ faint

feisty
△ feis|tier
△ feis|ti|est

feld|spar
feld|spa|thic
fe|li|ci|tate
△ fe|li|ci|tates
△ fe|li|ci|ta|ted
△ fe|li|ci|ta|ting
fe|li|ci|ta|tion
fe|li|ci|tous
fe|li|ci|tously
fe|li|ci|tous|ness
Fe|li|city
fe|li|city
△ fe|li|ci|ties
fe|line
Felix
Fe|lix|stowe
fell
VERB
△ fells
△ felled
△ fell|ing
also past tense of
fall
fel|la|tio
Fel|lini
fel|low
fel|low|ship
felon
fe|lo|ni|ous
fel|ony
△ fel|on|ies
felspar *see*
feldspar
felt
VERB
△ felts
△ fel|ted
△ felt|ing
also past tense of
feel
fe|male
fem|in|ine
fem|in|in|ity
fem|in|ism

fem|in|ist
femme fa|tale
△ *femmes fa|tales*
fe|moral
femur
fen
fence
VERB
△ fen|ces
△ fenced
△ fen|cing
fen|cer
fen|cing
fend
△ fends
△ fen|ded
△ fend|ing
fen|der
Fen|ella
Fénelon
Fe|nian
fen|nel
Fens
fe|nu|greek
feoff
feral
fer-de-lance
Fer|di|nand
Fer|gus
Fer|man|agh
fer|mata

fer|ment
fermentation;
excitement;
cause these
VERB
△ fer|ments
△ fer|men|ted
△ fer|ment|ing
⚠ foment

fer|men|ta|tion
fer|mium
fern

Fer|nan|del
ferny
△ fer|nier
△ fer|ni|est
fe|ro|cious
fe|ro|ciously
fe|ro|city
fe|ro|cious|ness
Fer|ranti
Fer|rara
city
Fer|rari
car
fer|ret
VERB
△ fer|rets
△ fer|re|ted
△ fer|ret|ing
fer|ric
Fer|rier
Fer|ris
fer|rite
fer|rous
fer|rule
ferry
NOUN
△ fer|ries
VERB
△ fer|ries
△ fer|ried
△ fer|ry|ing
fer|ry|man
△ fer|ry|men
fer|tile
fer|til|ity
fer|til|iza|tion
fer|til|ize
△ fer|til|izes
△ fer|til|lized
△ fer|til|izing
fer|til|izer
fer|vent
fer|vently
fer|vid

fer|vidly
fer|vour
fes|cue
fes|tal
fes|ter
△ fes|ters
△ fes|tered
△ fes|ter|ing
fes|ti|val
fes|tive
fes|tiv|ity
△ fes|tiv|it|ies
fes|toon
VERB
△ fes|toons
△ fes|tooned
△ fes|toon|ing
feta
fetal
fetch
NOUN
△ fet|ches
VERB
△ fet|ches
△ fetched
△ fetch|ing
fetch|ing
fetch|ingly

fête
outdoor
entertainment;
entertain
lavishly
VERB
△ fêtes
△ fêted
△ fêting
⚠ fate

fetid
fet|ish
△ fet|ishes
fet|ish|ism
fet|ish|ist

fet|ish|is|tic
fet|lock
fet|ter
VERB
△ fet|ters
△ fet|tered
△ fet|ter|ing
fet|tle
fet|tuc|cine
fetus
△ fe|tuses
fetwa see *fatwa*
feud
VERB
△ feuds
△ feu|ded
△ feud|ing
feu|dal
feu|dal|ism
fever
fe|vered
fe|ver|few
fe|ver|ish
fe|ver|ishly
few
ADJ.
△ fewer
△ few|est
fey
△ feyer
△ fey|est
fey|ness
Fez
city
fez
hat
△ fez|zes
fi|acre
fi|ancé
betrothed man
fi|an|cée
betrothed woman
Fi|anna Fáil
fi|asco

△ fi|as|cos *or* fi|
as|coes

fiat

fib

VERB

△ fibs

△ fibbed

△ fib|bing

fib|ber

Fi|bo|nacci

fibre

fi|bre|board

fi|bre|glass

fi|bre-optic
ADJ.
▲ fibre optics

fi|bre op|tics
NOUN
▲ fibre-optic

fi|bril

fi|bril|late

△ fi|bril|lates

△ fi|bril|la|ted

△ fi|bril|la|ting

fi|bril|la|tion

fi|brin

fi|brin|ogen

fi|broid

fi|bro|sis

fi|bro|si|tis

fi|brous

fib|ula

△ fib|ulae *or* fib|
ulas

fiche

fickle

△ fick|ler

△ fick|lest

fickle|ness

fic|tion

fic|tional

fic|tion|ally

fic|ti|tious

fic|ti|tiously

fid|dle

VERB

△ fid|dles

△ fid|dled

△ fid|dling

fid|dler

fiddle|sticks

fid|dling

fid|dly

△ fid|dlier

△ fid|dli|est

Fi|dei De|fen|
sor

fi|deism

Fi|delio

fi|del|ity

fid|get

VERB

△ fid|gets

△ fid|ge|ted

△ fid|get|ing

fid|gety

fi|du|ciary

NOUN

△ fi|du|ciar|ies

fie

fief

field

VERB

△ fields

△ fiel|ded

△ field|ing

fiel|der

Field|ing

field|mouse

△ field|mice

Fields

field|work

field|wor|ker

fiend

fiend|ish

fiend|ishly

Fiennes

fierce

△ fier|cer

△ fier|cest

fiercely

fierce|ness

fier|ily

fiery

△ fier|ier

△ fieri|est

fi|esta

Fife

fife

fif|teen

fif|teenth

fifth

fifthly

fif|ties

fif|tieth

fifty

NOUN

△ fif|ties

fifty-fifty

fig

fight

VERB

△ fights

△ fought

△ fight|ing

figh|ter

*Fight|ing Tê|mé|
raire, The*

fig|ment

fig|ur|at|ive

fig|ur|at|ively

fig|ure

VERB

△ fig|ures

△ fig|ured

△ fig|ur|ing

fig|ure|head

fi|gur|ine

Fiji

fil|ament

filch

△ fil|ches

△ filched

△ filch|ing

file

VERB

△ files

△ filed

△ fi|ling

file-ser|ver

fi|lial

fi|li|bus|ter

VERB

△ fi|li|bus|ters

△ fi|li|bus|tered

△ fi|li|bus|ter|
ing

fi|li|gree

fi|ling

Fi|lio|que

fill

VERB

△ fills

△ filled

△ fill|ing

fil|ler

fil|let

VERB

△ fil|lets

△ fil|leted

△ fil|let|ing

fill|ing

fill|ing-sta|tion

fil|lip

filly

△ fil|lies

film

VERB

△ films

△ filmed

△ film|ing

fil|mi|ness

film|set|ting

filmy

△ fil|mier
△ fil|mi|est
filo
Fi|lo|fax
△ Fi|lo|faxes
fi|lo|plume
fil|ter
  VERB
  △ fil|ters
  △ fil|tered
  △ fil|ter|ing
fil|ter-tipped
filth
fil|thily
fil|thi|ness
fil|thy
  ADJ.
  △ fil|thier
  △ fil|thi|est
fil|trate
  VERB
  △ fil|trates
  △ fil|tra|ted
  △ fil|tra|ting
fil|tra|tion
fin
final
fi|nale
fi|nal|ist
fi|nal|ity
fi|nal|iza|tion
fi|nal|ize
  △ fi|nal|izes
  △ fi|nal|ized
  △ fi|nal|izing
fi|nally
fi|nance
  VERB
  △ fi|nan|ces
  △ fi|nanced
  △ fi|nan|cing
fi|nan|cial
fi|nan|cially
fi|nan|cier

finch
  △ fin|ches
find
  VERB
  △ finds
  △ found
  △ find|ing
finder
find|ing
fine
  VERB
  △ fines
  △ fined
  △ fi|ning
  ADJ.
  △ finer
  △ fi|nest
Fine Gael
finely
fine|ness
fi|nery
fines herbes
fine|spun
fin|esse
fine-tooth
fine-tune
  △ fine-tunes
  △ fine-tuned
  △ fine-tuning
Fin|gal's Cave
fin|ger
  VERB
  △ fin|gers
  △ fin|gered
  △ fin|ger|ing
fin|ger|board
fin|ger|bowl
fin|ger|ing
fin|ger|mark
fin|ger|nail
fin|ger|print
  VERB
  △ fin|ger|prints
  △ fin|ger|prin|ted

△ fin|ger|print|
  ing
fin|ger|stall
fin|ger|tip
fin|ial
fin|icky
fin|ish
  NOUN
  △ fin|ishes
  VERB
  △ fin|ishes
  △ fin|ished
  △ fin|ish|ing
fin|ished
fin|isher
fin|ish|ing
fin|ish|ing-
  school
Fin|is|terre
fi|nite
Fin|land
Fin|lan|dia
Fin|lay
Finn
fin|nan
Fin|ne|gans
  Wake
Fin|nish
Fiona
fiord
fip|ple

fir
  tree
  ⚠ fur

fire
  VERB
  △ fires
  △ fired
  △ firing
fire|arm
fire|ball
Fire|bird, The
fire-bomb

fire|brand
fire|break
fire|brick
fire|bug
fire|clay
fire|cracker
fire|damp
fire|dog
fire-eater
fire-extin|gui|
  sher
fire-figh|ter
fire-fight|ing
fire|fly
  △ fire|flies
fire|guard
fire|ligh|ter
fire|man
  △ fire|men
fire|place
fire-power
fire|proof
  VERB
  △ fire|proofs
  △ fire|proofed
  △ fire|proof|ing
fire-rai|ser
fire-rais|ing
fire|side
Fire|stone
fire|trap
fire|wa|ter
fire|wood
fire|work
firm
  VERB
  △ firms
  △ firmed
  △ firm|ing
  ADJ.
  △ fir|mer
  △ firm|est
fir|ma|ment
firmly

firm|ness
firm|ware
first
first-born
first-class
first-degree
first-foot
△ first-foots
△ first-footed
△ first-foot|ing
first-hand
firstly
first-past-the-
post
first-rate
firth
fis|cal
fis|cally
Fis|cher
Fis|cher-Dies|
kau
fish
NOUN
△ fish *or* fi|shes
VERB
△ fi|shes
△ fished
△ fish|ing
Fish|bourne
fish|cake
fi|sher
fish|er|man
△ fish|er|men
fish|ery
△ fish|er|ies
fish-eye
Fish|guard
fish|ing
fish|ing-line
fish|ing-rod
fish|mon|ger
fish|net
fish|wife
△ fish|wives

fishy
△ fish|ier
△ fishi|est
fis|sile
fis|sion
fis|sion|able
fis|sure
fist
fist|ful
fis|ti|cuffs
fis|tula
fit
VERB
△ fits
△ fit|ted
△ fit|ting
ADJ.
△ fit|ter
△ fit|test
fit|ful
fit|fully
fitly
fit|ment
fit|ness
Fitt
fit|ted
fit|ter
fit|ting
fit|tingly
Fitz|Gerald
19c poet and
translator
Fitz|gerald
jazz singer;
novelist;
politician
five
five|fold
fiver
fix
NOUN
△ fixes
VERB
△ fixes

fixed
△ fix|ing
fix|ated
fix|ation
fix|at|ive
fixed
fix|edly
fixer
fix|ity
fix|ture
fizz
NOUN
△ fiz|zes
VERB
△ fiz|zes
△ fizzed
△ fiz|zing
fiz|zi|ness
fiz|zle
VERB
△ fiz|zles
△ fiz|zled
△ fiz|zling
fizzy
△ fiz|zier
△ fiz|zi|est
fjord
flab
flab|ber|gast
△ flab|ber|gasts
△ flab|ber|gas|
ted
△ flab|ber|gast|
ing
flab|bily
flab|bi|ness
flabby
△ flab|bier
△ flab|bi|est
flac|cid
flac|cid|ity
flac|cidly
flag

VERB
△ flags
△ flagged
△ flag|ging
fla|gel|lant
fla|gel|late
VERB
△ fla|gel|lates
△ fla|gel|la|ted
△ fla|gel|la|ting
fla|gel|la|tion
fla|gel|lum
△ fla|gella
fla|geo|let
flagon
flag|pole
fla|grancy
fla|grant
fla|grantly
flag|ship
Flag|stad
flag|staff
flag|stone
flag-waving
Fla|herty
flail
VERB
△ flails
△ flailed
△ flail|ing

flair
aptitude;
stylishness
△ flare

flak
flake
VERB
△ flakes
△ flaked
△ fla|king
flaky
△ fla|kier
△ fla|ki|est

flambé
VERB
△ flam¦bés
△ flam¦béed
△ flam¦bé¦ing
flam|boy¦ance
flam|boy¦ant
flam|boy¦antly
flame
VERB
△ flames
△ flamed
△ fla¦ming
fla|menco
flame|proof
flame-thrower
fla|ming
fla|mingo
△ fla|min¦gos *or*
fla|min¦goes
flam|mable
Flam|steed
flan
Fland|ers
flange
flank
VERB
△ flanks
△ flanked
△ flank|ing
flan|nel
VERB
△ flan|nels
△ flan|nelled
△ flan¦nel|ling
flan¦nel|ette
flap
VERB
△ flaps
△ flapped
△ flap|ping
flap|jack
flap|per
flappy

△ flap|pier
△ flap|pi¦est

flare
bright light;
burn brightly
VERB
△ flares
△ flared
△ flar¦ing
⚠ flair

flare-up
flash
NOUN
△ fla¦shes
VERB
△ fla¦shes
△ flashed
△ flash|ing
flash|back
flash|bulb
fla¦sher
flash|gun
flash|ily
fla¦shi|ness
flash|light
flash|point
fla¦shy
△ fla¦shier
△ fla¦shi|est
flask
flat
ADJ.
△ flat|ter
△ flat|test
flat|fish
sing. and pl.
flat-footed
flat|iron
flat|let
flatly
flat|ness
flat|ten
△ flat|tens

△ flat|tened
△ flat|ten|ing
flat|ter
△ flat|ters
△ flat|tered
△ flat|ter|ing
flat|terer
flat|tery
△ flat|ter¦ies
flat|ulence
flat|ulent
flat|worm
Flau|bert
flaunt
△ flaunts
△ flaun|ted
△ flaunt|ing
flaut|ist
fla|vo|noid
fla|vour
fla|vour|ing
fla|vour|less
fla|vour|some
flaw
flawed
flaw|less
flaw|lessly
flax
flaxen
flay
△ flays
△ flayed
△ flay|ing
F-layer

flea
parasite
⚠ flee

flea|bane
flea-bit|ten
fleck
flecked
Flecker
fled

Fle|der|maus,
Die (The Bat)
fledged
fledgling

flee
run away
△ flees
△ fled
△ flee|ing
⚠ flea

fleece
VERB
△ flee¦ces
△ fleeced
△ flee¦cing
fleecy
△ flee¦cier
△ flee¦ci|est
fleet
ADJ.
△ flee¦ter
△ fleet|est
fleet|ing
fleet|ingly
fleet|ness
Fleet|wood
Flem|ing
Flem|ish
flesh
flesh-col¦oured
fle¦shi|ness
fleshly
flesh|pots
fleshy
△ flesh¦ier
△ fle¦shi|est
Flet|cher
fleur-de-lis
△ fleurs-de-lis
flew
flex
NOUN
△ flexes

VERB
△ flexes
△ flexed
△ flex|ing
flexi|bil|ity
flex|ible
flex|ibly
flexi|time
flexor
flib|ber|ti|gib|bet
flick
  VERB
△ flicks
△ flicked
△ flick|ing
flicker
  VERB
△ flick|ers
△ flick|ered
△ flick|er|ing
flier
flight
Flight into
  Egypt, The
flight|less
flim|sily
flim|si|ness
flimsy
△ flim|sier
△ flim|si|est
flinch
△ flin|ches
△ flinched
△ flinch|ing
fling
  VERB
△ flings
△ flung
△ fling|ing
flint
flint|lock
flinty
△ flin|tier
△ flin|ti|est

flip
  VERB
△ flips
△ flipped
△ flip|ping
flip-flop
flip|pancy
△ flip|pan|cies
flip|pant
flip|pantly
flip|per
flip|ping
flirt
  VERB
△ flirts
△ flir|ted
△ flirt|ing
flir|ta|tion
flir|ta|tious
flit
  VERB
△ flits
△ flit|ted
△ flit|ting
flitch
△ flit|ches
float
  VERB
△ floats
△ floa|ted
△ float|ing
floatation *see*
  flotation
float|ing
flock
  VERB
△ flocks
△ flocked
△ flock|ing
Flod|den

floe
ice sheet
⚠ flow

flog
△ flogs
△ flogged
△ flog|ging
flo|kati
flood
  VERB
△ floods
△ flooded
△ flood|ing
flood|gate
flood|light
  VERB
△ flood|lights
△ flood|lit
△ flood|light|ing
flood|lit
floor
  VERB
△ floors
△ floored
△ floor|ing
floor|board
floor|ing
floo|sie
flop
  VERB
△ flops
△ flopped
△ flop|ping
flop|pily
flop|pi|ness
floppy
△ flop|pier
△ flop|pi|est
Flora
flora
△ floras *or*
  florae
floral
flor|ally
Flor|ence
floret
florid

Flor|ida
flor|idly
florin
flor|ist
floss
  NOUN
△ flos|ses
  VERB
△ flos|ses
△ flossed
△ floss|ing
flossy
△ flos|sier
△ flos|si|est
flo|ta|tion
flo|tilla
flot|sam
flounce
  VERB
△ floun|ces
△ flounced
△ floun|cing
floun|der
  VERB
△ floun|ders
△ floun|dered
△ floun|der|ing
flour
  VERB
△ flours
△ floured
△ flour|ing
flour|ish
  NOUN
△ flour|ishes
  VERB
△ flour|ishes
△ flourished
△ flour|ish|ing

floury
with or like
flour
△ flour|ier

△ flouri|est
△ flowery

flout
△ flouts
△ flou|ted
△ flout|ing

flow
move like water;
this action
VERB
△ flows
△ flowed
△ flow|ing
△ floe

flower
VERB
△ flowers
△ flowered
△ flower|ing
flower|pecker
flower|pot

flowery
with flowers;
fancy
△ floury

flown

flu
influenza
△ flue

fluc|tu|ate
△ fluc|tu|ates
△ fluc|tu|ated
△ fluc|tu|ating
fluc|tu|ation

flue
chimney; duct
△ flu

flu|ency
flu|ent

flu|ently
fluff
VERB
△ fluffs
△ fluffed
△ fluf|fing
fluf|fi|ness
fluffy
△ fluf|fier
△ fluf|fi|est
flu|gel|horn
fluid
flu|id|ics
flu|id|ity
fluke
fluky
△ flu|kier
△ flu|ki|est
flume
flum|mery
△ flum|mer|ies
flum|mox
△ flum|moxes
△ flum|moxed
△ flum|mox|ing
flung
flunk
△ flunks
△ flunked
△ flunk|ing
flun|key
fluor *see*
fluorspar
fluor|esce
△ fluor|es|ces
△ fluor|esced
△ fluor|es|cing
fluor|es|cence
fluor|es|cent
fluor|id|ate
△ fluor|id|ates
△ fluor|id|ated
△ fluor|id|ating
fluor|id|ation

fluor|ide
fluor|id|iza|tion
fluor|id|ize
△ fluor|id|izes
△ fluor|id|ized
△ fluor|id|izing
fluor|ine
fluor|ite
fluoro|car|bon
fluor|spar
flurry
NOUN
△ flur|ries
VERB
△ flur|ries
△ flur|ried
△ flurry|ing
flush
NOUN
△ flu|shes
VERB
△ flu|shes
△ flushed
△ flush|ing
Flush|ing
flus|ter
VERB
△ flus|ters
△ flus|tered
△ flus|ter|ing
flute
VERB
△ flutes
△ flu|ted
△ flu|ting
flu|ting
flut|ter
VERB
△ flut|ters
△ flut|tered
△ flut|ter|ing
fluty
△ flu|tier
△ flu|ti|est

flu|vial
flux
△ fluxes
fly
NOUN
△ flies
VERB
△ flies
△ flew
△ fly|ing
△ flown
fly|blown
fly-by-night
fly|cat|cher
flyer
fly-fish
△ fly-fishes
△ fly-fished
△ fly-fish|ing
fly-fish|ing
fly|ing
Fly|ing Dutch|
man, The (Der
Flie|gende Hol|
län|der)
fly|leaf
△ fly|leaves
Flymo
Flynn
fly|over
fly|pa|per
fly|past
fly|sheet
fly|spray
fly-tip|ping
fly|weight
fly|wheel
f-num|ber
Fo
foal
VERB
△ foals
△ foaled
△ foal|ing

foam

foamy

△ foam|ier

△ foami|est

fob

VERB

△ fobs

△ fobbed

△ fob|bing

fo|cac|cia

focal

Foch

fo'c'sle

focus

NOUN

△ fo|cuses *or* foci

VERB

△ fo|cuses

△ fo|cused *or* fo|cussed

△ fo|cus|ing *or* fo|cus|sing

fod|der

foe

foe|tal

foe|tid

foe|tus

△ foe|tuses

fog

VERB

△ fogs

△ fogged

△ fog|ging

fog|bound

fogey

foggy

△ fog|gier

△ fog|gi|est

fog|horn

fogy

△ fo|gies

Fo|hn

foi|ble

foil

VERB

△ foils

△ foiled

△ foil|ing

foist

△ foists

△ fois|ted

△ foist|ing

Fo|kine

Fok|ker

fold

VERB

△ folds

△ folded

△ fold|ing

fol|der

Fol|ger

fo|li|aceous

fo|li|age

fo|li|ate

fo|li|ation

Fo|lies-Ber|gère

folio

folk

Folke|stone

folk|lore

folksy

△ folk|sier

△ folk|si|est

fol|licle

fol|low

△ fol|lows

△ fol|lowed

△ fol|low|ing

fol|lower

fol|low|ing

fol|low-on

fol|low-through

fol|low-up

folly

△ fol|lies

fo|ment

foster

△ fo|ments

△ fo|men|ted

△ fo|ment|ing

⚠ ferment

fo|men|ta|tion

fond

△ fon|der

△ fond|est

Fonda

fon|dant

fon|dle

△ fon|dles

△ fon|dled

△ fond|ling

fondly

fond|ness

fon|due

font

baptismal basin

⚠ fount

Fon|taine|bleau

fon|tan|elle

Fon|teyn

food

foo|die

food|ism

food|stuff

fool

VERB

△ fools

△ fooled

△ fool|ing

fool|ery

△ fool|er|ies

fool|har|di|ness

fool|hardy

fool|ish

fool|ishly

fool|ish|ness

fool|proof

fools|cap

Foot

foot

unit of length

△ feet *or* foot

other senses

△ feet

foot|age

foot-and-mouth

foot|ball

foot|bridge

foot|fall

foot|hill

foot|hold

foot|ing

foot|lights

foot|loose

foot|man

△ foot|men

foot|note

foot|path

foot|plate

foot|print

foot|sie

foot|slog

△ foot|slogs

△ foot|slogged

△ foot|slog|ging

foot|sore

foot|step

foot|stool

foot|way

foot|wear

foot|work

fop

fop|pery

△ fop|per|ies

fop|pish

fop|pish|ness

for

for|age

VERB

△ for|ages

△ for|aged

△ for|aging

for|as|much

foray
for|bade

for|bear
refrain (from)
△ for|bears
△ for|bore
△ for|bear|ing
△ for|borne
⚠ forebear

for|bear|ance
for|bear|ing
for|bid
△ for|bids
△ for|bade *or*
for|bad
△ for|bid|ding
△ for|bid|den
for|bid|ding
for|bid|dingly
for|bore
force
VERB
△ for|ces
△ forced
△ for|cing
forced
force-feed
△ force-feeds
△ force-fed
△ force-feed|ing
force|ful
force|fully
force|ful|ness
force ma|jeure
force|meat

for|ceps
sing. and pl.
for|cible
for|cibly
Ford
ford
VERB
△ fords
△ for|ded
△ ford|ing
ford|able

fore
front
⚠ four

fore-and-aft
fore|arm
VERB
△ fore|arms
△ fore|armed
△ fore|arm|ing

fore|bear
ancestor
⚠ forbear

fore|bode
△ fore|bodes
△ fore|bo|ded
△ fore|bo|ding
fore|bo|ding
fore|brain
fore|cast
VERB
△ fore|casts
△ fore|cast *or*
fore|cas|ted

△ fore|cast|ing
fore|castle
fore|close
△ fore|clo|ses
△ fore|closed
△ fore|clo|sing
fore|clo|sure
fore|court
fore|fa|ther
fore|fin|ger
fore|foot
△ fore|feet
fore|front
fore|ga|ther
△ fore|gath|ers
△ fore|gath|ered
△ fore|gath|er|
ing

forego
*go before; give
up*
△ fore|goes
△ fore|went
△ fore|go|ing
△ fore|gone
⚠ forgo

fore|go|ing
fore|gone
fore|ground
fore|hand
fore|head
for|eign
for|eigner
fore|know|ledge
fore|leg

fore|lock
fore|man
△ fore|men
fore|most
fore|noon
for|en|sic
for|en|sic|ally
fore|or|dain
△ fore|or|dains
△ fore|or|dained
△ fore|or|dain|
ing
fore|play
fore|run|ner
fore|see
△ fore|sees
△ fore|saw
△ fore|see|ing
△ fore|seen
fore|see|able
fore|sha|dow
△ fore|sha|dows
△ fore|sha|
dowed
△ fore|sha|dow|
ing
fore|shore
fore|shor|ten
△ fore|shor|tens
△ fore|shor|
tened
△ fore|shor|ten|
ing
fore|sight
fore|skin
for|est

fore- / for-

fore- has the meaning 'before', 'beforehand', 'in front': **forearm** (= arm in advance),
forecast (= predict), **foresight** (= advance knowledge), **foreword** (= short piece at
the front of a book).

The most common words beginning in **for-** and not **fore-** are: **forbid, forfeit, forget,
forgo** (= go without), **forlorn, forsake, forward** (= towards the front).

Foreign words

Some words borrowed directly from other languages are regarded as non-naturalized, and often appear in italics in print. In these cases, plurals are usually formed according to the rules of the source language. The same is also true of some naturalized words, especially words used in technical contexts, words ending in **-is**, and words in which the addition of **-es** would produce a difficult sound, eg:

analysis	analyses	narcissus	narcissi
antithesis	antitheses		(also sometimes
apex	apices		narcissuses)
appendix	appendices	nebulus	nebulae
axis	axes		(also sometimes
bacillus	bacilli		nebuluses)
basis	bases	nucleus	nuclei
beau	beaux	oasis	oases
bureau	bureaux	parenthesis	parentheses
cactus	cacti	phenomenon	phenomena
crematorium	crematoria	radius	radii
crisis	crises		(also sometimes
criterion	criteria		radiuses)
crux	cruces	stimulus	stimuli
curriculum	curricula	stratum	strata
ellipsis	ellipses	synopsis	synopses
fungus	fungi	tableau	tableaux
genus	genera	terminus	termini
hypothesis	hypotheses		(also sometimes
matrix	matrices		terminuses)
	(also sometimes	thesis	theses
	matrixes)		

Other words, however, usually follow the rules of English spelling:

agenda[1]	agendas	mausoleum	mausoleums
apparatus	apparatuses	medium	mediums
crocus	crocuses		(but media with
encomium	encomiums		reference to
equinox	equinoxes		journalism and
focus	focuses		broadcasting)
	(but foci in technical	minimum	minimums
	usage)		(but minima in technical
formula	formulas		usage)
	(but formulae in	octopus	octopuses
	technical usage)	referendum	referendums
genius	geniuses		(but referenda is also
	(but genii is sometimes		used)
	used)	sanatorium	sanatoriums
gymnasium	gymnasiums		(but sanatoria is
	(but gymnasia is		sometimes used)
	sometimes used)	stamen	stamens
hiatus	hiatuses	syllabus	syllabuses
hippopotamus	hippopotamuses		(but syllabi is
	(but hippopotami is		sometimes used)
	sometimes used)	ultimatum	ultimatums
index	indexes		(but ultimata is
	(but indices in technical		sometimes used)
	usage)	virus	viruses
lacuna	lacunas		
	(but lacunae in		
	technical usage)		

[1] note that agenda is originally a Latin plural, now naturalized as a singular form in English

fore|stall
△ fore|stalls
△ fore|stalled
△ fore|stal|ling
for|est|ation
for|es|ted
for|es|ter
for|es|try
fore|taste
fore|tell
△ fore|tells
△ fore|told
△ fore|tel|ling
fore|thought
fore|told
for|ever
fore|warn
△ fore|warns
△ fore|warned
△ fore|warn|ing
fore|wo|man
△ fore|wo|men

fore|word
book's
introduction
⚠ forward

for|feit
VERB
△ for|feits
△ for|feited
△ for|feit|ing
for|feit|ure
for|gave
forge
VERB
△ for|ges
△ forged
△ for|ging
for|gery
△ for|ger|ies
for|get
△ for|gets
△ for|got

△ for|get|ting
△ for|got|ten
for|get|ful
for|get|fully
for|get|ful|ness
for|get-me-not
for|giv|able
for|giv|ably
for|give
△ for|gives
△ for|gave
△ for|giv|ing
△ for|gi|ven
for|give|ness
for|giv|ing

forgo
give up
△ for|goes
△ for|went
△ for|gone
⚠ forego

for|got
fork
VERB
△ forks
△ forked
△ fork|ing
forked
for|lorn
for|lornly
for|lorn|ness
form
VERB
△ forms
△ formed
△ form|ing
for|mal
for|mal|de|hyde
for|ma|lin
for|mal|ism
for|mal|ist
for|mal|ity
△ for|mal|it|ies

for|mal|iza|tion
for|mal|ize
△ for|mal|izes
△ for|mal|ized
△ for|mal|izing
for|mally
For|man
form|ant
for|mat
VERB
△ for|mats
△ for|mat|ted
△ for|mat|ting
for|ma|tion
for|mat|ive
for|mer
for|merly
For|mica
for|mid|able
for|mid|ably
form|less
form|lessly
form|less|ness
for|mula
△ for|mu|las *or*
   for|mu|lae
for|mu|laic
for|mu|lary
△ for|mu|lar|ies
for|mu|late
△ for|mu|lates
△ for|mu|la|ted
△ for|mu|la|ting
for|mu|la|tion
for|ni|cate
△ for|ni|cates
△ for|ni|ca|ted
△ for|ni|ca|ting
for|ni|ca|tion
for|sake
△ for|sakes
△ for|sook
△ for|sa|king
△ for|sa|ken

For|ster
for|swear
△ for|swears
△ for|swore
△ for|swear|ing
△ for|sworn
For|syte Saga
For|syth
for|sy|thia
fort
Forte
forte
Forth

forth
forwards
⚠ fourth

forth|com|ing
forth|right
forth|right|ness
forth|with
for|ties
for|ti|eth
for|ti|fi|ca|tion
for|tify
△ for|ti|fies
△ for|ti|fied
△ for|ti|fy|ing
for|tis|simo
for|ti|tude
fort|night
fort|nightly
FOR|TRAN
fort|ress
△ fort|res|ses
for|tu|it|ous
for|tu|it|ously
for|tu|it|ous|ness
For|tuna
for|tu|nate
for|tu|nately
for|tune
for|tune-tel|ler
forty

NOUN

△ for|ties

forum

---

for|ward

onward; ahead

VERB

△ for|wards

△ for|war|ded

△ for|ward|ing

⚠ foreword

---

for|ward-look|
ing

for|wardly

for|ward|ness

for|went

*For Whom the
Bell Tolls*

fos|sil

fos|sil|iza|tion

fos|sil|ize

△ fos|sil|izes

△ fos|sil|ized

△ fos|sil|izing

Fos|ter

foster

VERB

△ fos|ters

△ fos|tered

△ fos|ter|ing

Fou|cault

fought

---

foul

*dirty or nasty;
breach of rule*

VERB

△ fouls

△ fouled

△ foul|ing

ADJ.

△ fouler

△ foul|est

⚠ fowl

---

foul-mouthed

foul|ness

foul-up

found

△ founds

△ foun|ded

△ found|ing

foun|da|tion

foun|der

VERB

△ foun|ders

△ foun|dered

△ foun|der|ing

found|ling

foun|dry

△ foun|dries

---

fount

*source of water
etc; set of
printing type*

⚠ font

---

foun|tain

foun|tain|head

Foun|tains

---

four

number

⚠ fore

---

four|fold

four-poster

Four Quartets

four|score

*Four Seas|ons,
The*

four|some

four-square

four|teen

four|teenth

---

fourth

next after third

⚠ forth

---

four|thly

---

fovea

△ fo|veae

---

fowl

bird

NOUN

△ fowls *or* fowl

VERB

△ fowls

△ fowled

△ fowl|ing

⚠ foul

---

fow|ler

Fowles

Fox

fox

NOUN

△ foxes

VERB

△ foxes

△ foxed

△ fox|ing

fox|glove

fox|hole

fox|hound

fox|hunt|ing

fox|ily

fox|iness

fox|ing

fox|trot

VERB

△ fox|trots

△ fox|trot|ted

△ fox|trot|ting

foxy

△ fox|ier

△ foxi|est

foyer

fra|cas

sing. and pl.

frac|tal

frac|tion

frac|tional

frac|tion|ally

---

frac|tion|ation

frac|tious

frac|tiously

frac|tious|ness

frac|ture

VERB

△ frac|tures

△ frac|tured

△ frac|tur|ing

fra|gile

fra|gil|ity

frag|ment

VERB

△ frag|ments

△ frag|men|ted

△ frag|ment|ing

frag|men|tar|ily

frag|men|tari|
ness

frag|ment|ary

frag|men|ta|tion

Fra|go|nard

fra|grance

fra|grant

fra|grantly

frail

△ frailer

△ frail|est

frail|ness

frailty

△ frail|ties

frame

VERB

△ frames

△ framed

△ fra|ming

frame-up

frame|work

---

franc

currency unit

⚠ frank

France

Fran|ces

fran|chise
 VERB
 △ fran|chi|ses
 △ fran|chised
 △ fran|chi|sing
Fran|cis
Fran|cis|can
fran|cium
Franck
Franco
fran|co|phone
fran|gi|pani
Frank

> frank
> *plain-spoken;*
> *stamp letter*
> VERB
> △ franks
> △ franked
> △ frank|ing
> ADJ.
> △ fran|ker
> △ frank|est
> ⚠ franc

Fran|ken|stein
Frank|fort
 USA
Frank|furt
 Germany
frank|fur|ter
frank|in|cense
Frank|ish
Frank|lin
frankly
frank|ness
fran|tic
fran|tic|ally
Fra|ser
fra|ter|nal
fra|ter|nally
fra|ter|nity
 △ fra|ter|ni|ties
fra|ter|niza|tion

fra|ter|nize
 △ fra|ter|nizes
 △ fra|ter|nized
 △ fra|ter|ni|zing
frat|ri|ci|dal
frat|ri|cide
fraud
frau|du|lence
frau|du|lent
frau|du|lently
fraught
fray
 VERB
 △ frays
 △ frayed
 △ fray|ing
fraz|zle
 VERB
 △ fraz|zles
 △ fraz|zled
 △ fraz|zling
freak
 VERB
 △ freaks
 △ freaked
 △ freak|ing
freak|ish
freaky
 △ freak|ier
 △ freaki|est
freckle
 VERB
 △ freckles
 △ freckled
 △ freck|ling
freckly
Fred|er|ick
free
 VERB
 △ frees
 △ freed
 △ free|ing
 ADJ.
 △ freer

 △ freest
free|base
 VERB
 △ free|ba|ses
 △ free|based
 △ free|ba|sing
free|bie
free|board
free|boo|ter
free|born
freed|man
 △ freed|men
free|dom
freed|wo|man
 △ freed|wo|men
free-fal|ling
Free|fone
free-for-all
free|hand
free|hold
free|hol|der
free|lance
 VERB
 △ free|lan|ces
 △ free|lanced
 △ free|lan|cing
free|lan|cer
free|load
 △ free|loads
 △ free|loa|ded
 △ free|load|ing
free|loa|der
freely
free|man
 △ free|men
Free|ma|son
Free|ma|sonry
Free|post
free-range
free|sia
free-stand|ing
free|style
free|thin|ker
Free|town

free|ware
free|way
free|wheel
 △ free|wheels
 △ free|wheeled
 △ free|wheel|ing

> freeze
> *turn into ice, etc*
> VERB
> △ free|zes
> △ froze
> △ freez|ing
> △ fro|zen
> ⚠ frieze

freeze-dry
 △ freeze-dries
 △ freeze-dried
 △ freeze-dry|ing
freeze-frame
free|zer
Frege
freight
 VERB
 △ freights
 △ freigh|ted
 △ freight|ing
freigh|ter
freight|li|ner
Frei|schu|tz, Der
(The Free|
shooter)
French
French|man
 △ French|men
French-pol|ish
 △ French-pol|
 ishes
 △ French-pol|
 ished
 △ French-pol|
 ish|ing
French|wo|man
 △ French|wo|men

fre|netic
fre|net|ic|ally
fren|zied
frenzy
△ fren|zies
fre|quency
△ fre|quen|cies
fre|quent
VERB
△ fre|quents
△ fre|quen|ted
△ fre|quent|ing
fre|quently
fresco
△ fres|cos *or*
fres|coes
Fres|co|baldi
fresh
ADJ.
△ fresher
△ fresh|est
freshen
△ fresh|ens
△ fresh|ened
△ fresh|en|ing
fresher
fresh|man
△ fresh|men
freshet
freshly
fresh|ness
fresh|wa|ter
fret
VERB
△ frets
△ fret|ted
△ fret|ting
fret|ful
fret|fully
fret|ful|ness
fret|saw
fret|work
Freud
Freud|ian

Freya
fri|ab|il|ity
fri|able

> friar
> *monk*
> ⚠ frier

fri|ary
△ fri|ar|ies
Fri|bourg
fri|cas|see
fric|at|ive
Fricker
fric|tion
fric|tional
Fri|day
fridge
Fried|man
friend
friend|less
friend|li|ness
friendly
NOUN
△ friend|lies
ADJ.
△ friend|lier
△ friend|li|est
friend|ship

> frier
> *person or thing*
> *that fries*
> ⚠ friar

Frie|sian
Fries|land

> frieze
> *decorative band*
> *on wall*
> ⚠ freeze

frig|ate
Frigg
fright
frigh|ten

△ frigh|tens
△ frigh|tened
△ frigh|ten|ing
frigh|tened
fright|ful
fright|fully
fright|ful|ness
fri|gid
fri|gid|ity
frill
frilly
△ fril|lier
△ fril|li|est
Fringe
of theatrical
performances
fringe
other senses
VERB
△ frin|ges
△ fringed
△ frin|ging
frip|pery
△ frip|per|ies
Fris|bee
Fri|sian
frisk
VERB
△ frisks
△ frisked
△ frisk|ing
frisk|ily
fris|ki|ness
frisky
△ fris|kier
△ fris|ki|est
fris|son
fri|til|lary
△ fri|til|lar|ies
frit|ter
VERB
△ frit|ters
△ frit|tered
△ frit|ter|ing

fri|vol|ity
△ fri|vol|it|ies
fri|vol|ous
fri|vol|ously
frizz
NOUN
△ friz|zes
VERB
△ friz|zes
△ frizzed
△ friz|zing
friz|zle
VERB
△ friz|zles
△ friz|zled
△ friz|zling
frizzy
△ friz|zier
△ friz|zi|est
fro
Fro|bi|sher
frock
frock-coat
Froe|bel
frog
frog|ging
frog|hop|per
frog|man
△ frog|men
frog-march
NOUN
△ frog-mar|ches
VERB
△ frog-mar|ches
△ frog-marched
△ frog-march|
ing
Frogs, The
frog|spawn
Frois|sart
frolic
VERB
△ frol|ics
△ frol|icked

△ fro|lick|ing
fro|lic|some
from
fro|mage frais
Frome
frond
front

 VERB

 △ fronts
 △ fronted
 △ front|ing

front|age
frontal
front|bench
front|ben|cher
Front de Li|
 béra|tion Na|
 tion|ale
fron|tier
fron|tis|piece
front-run|ner
frost

 VERB

 △ frosts
 △ fros|ted
 △ frost|ing

frost|bite
frost|bit|ten
fros|ted
frost|ily
fros|ti|ness
frost|ing
frosty

△ fros|tier
△ fros|ti|est
froth

 VERB

 △ froths
 △ frothed
 △ froth|ing

frothy

 △ froth|ier
 △ frothi|est

frot|tage
frown

 VERB

 △ frowns
 △ frowned
 △ frown|ing

frown|ingly
frow|si|ness
frows|ti|ness

---

frowsty
 stuffy; stale-
 smelling
 △ frows|tier
 △ frows|ti|est
 ⚠frowsy

---

frowsy
 untidy; stuffy;
 stale-smelling
 △ frow|sier
 △ frow|si|est
 ⚠frowsty

---

froze
fruc|ti|fi|ca|tion
fruc|tose
fru|gal
fru|gal|ity
fru|gally
fruit

 VERB

 △ fruits
 △ fruited
 △ fruit|ing

fruit|cake
fruit|erer
fruit|ful
fruit|fully
fruit|ful|ness
fruit|ily
fruiti|ness
fru|ition
fruit|less
fruit|lessly
fruit|less|ness
fruity

 △ fruit|ier
 △ fruiti|est

frump
frump|ish
frumpy

 △ frump|ier
 △ frum|pi|est

frus|trate

 △ frus|trates
 △ frus|tra|ted

△ frus|tra|ting
frus|tra|ted
frus|tra|tion
Fry
fry

 NOUN

 △ fries

 VERB

 △ fries
 △ fried
 △ fry|ing

fryer
fry|ing-pan
fry-pan
f-stop
Fuchs
fuch|sia
fuck

 VERB

 △ fucks
 △ fucked
 △ fuck|ing

fuck|ing
fuck-up
fud|dle

 VERB

 △ fud|dles
 △ fud|dled
 △ fud|dling

fuddy-duddy

 NOUN

 △ fuddy-dud|
  dies

-ful

This suffix means essentially 'full of ...', and is used to form adjectives, eg **beautiful,
careful, hateful**, and nouns, eg **cupful, handful**.
Note that the spelling is never *-full*.

Plurals of words like **cupful, handful**, and **spoonful** are formed by adding **-s** to the
ending: **cupfuls, handfuls, spoonfuls**.

Note the difference between **a cup full of water** (referring to the container) and **a
cupful of water** (referring to the contents).

fudge
VERB
△ fud|ges
△ fudged
△ fud|ging
fuel
VERB
△ fuels
△ fu|elled
△ fu|el|ling
fug
fuggy
△ fug|gier
△ fug|gi|est
fu|gi|tive
fugue
Fuji
Ful|bright
ful|crum
△ ful|crums *or*
ful|cra
ful|fil
△ ful|fils
△ ful|filled
△ ful|fil|ling
ful|fil|ment
full
VERB
△ fulls
△ fulled
△ full|ing
ADJ.
△ ful|ler
△ ful|lest
full-blooded
full-blood|ed|
ness
full-blown
full-bod|ied
full-dress
Ful|ler
ful|ler
full-fron|tal
full-length

full|ness
full-scale
full-time
fully
fully-fashioned
fully-fledged
ful|mar
ful|min|ate
△ ful|min|ates
△ ful|min|ated
△ ful|min|ating
ful|min|ation
ful|some
ful|somely
ful|some|ness
fum|ble
VERB
△ fum|bles
△ fum|bled
△ fum|bling
fume
VERB
△ fumes
△ fumed
△ fu|ming
fu|mi|gant
fu|mi|gate
△ fu|mi|gates
△ fu|mi|ga|ted
△ fu|mi|ga|ting
fu|mi|ga|tion
fu|mi|tory
fun
func|tion
VERB
△ func|tions
△ func|tioned
△ func|tion|ing
func|tional
func|tion|al|ism
func|tion|al|ity
func|tion|ally
func|tion|ary
△ func|tion|ar|ies

fund
VERB
△ funds
△ fun|ded
△ fund|ing
fun|da|men|tal
fun|da|men|tal|
ism
fun|da|men|tal|
ist
fun|da|ment|ally
fu|neral

fu|ner|ary
used at funerals
⚠ funereal

fu|ner|eal
*dismal; slow; fit
for a funeral*
⚠ funerary

fu|ner|eally
fun|fair
fun|gal
fun|gi|ci|dal
fun|gi|cide
fun|goid

fun|gous
ADJ.
⚠ fungus

fun|gus
NOUN
△ fungi
⚠ fungous

fu|ni|cu|lar
funk
VERB
△ funks
△ funked
△ funk|ing
funky
△ fun|kier

△ fun|ki|est
fun|nel
VERB
△ fun|nels
△ fun|nelled
△ fun|nel|ling
fun|nily
funny
△ fun|nier
△ fun|ni|est

fur
animal's hair
VERB
△ furs
△ furred
△ fur|ring
⚠ fir

fur|be|low
fur|bish
△ fur|bi|shes
△ fur|bished
△ fur|bish|ing
fur|cate
VERB
△ fur|cates
△ fur|ca|ted
△ fur|ca|ting
fur|ca|tion
fu|ri|oso
fu|ri|ous
fu|ri|ously
furl
△ furls
△ furled
△ furl|ing
fur|long
fur|lough
fur|nace
fur|nish
△ fur|ni|shes
△ fur|nished
△ fur|nish|ing
fur|nish|ings

fur|ni|ture
fu|rore
fur|rier
fur|row
  VERB
  △ fur|rows
  △ fur|rowed
  △ fur|row|ing
furry
  △ fur|rier
  △ fur|ri|est
fur|ther
  VERB
  △ fur|thers
  △ fur|thered
  △ fur|ther|ing
fur|ther|ance
fur|ther|more

fur|ther|most
fur|thest
fur|tive
fur|tively
fur|tive|ness
Furt|wän|gler
fury
  △ fu|ries
furze
fuse
  VERB
  △ fuses
  △ fused
  △ fu|sing
fu|sel|age
fu|si|lier
fu|sil|lade
fu|silli

fu|sion
fuss
  NOUN
  △ fus|ses
  VERB
  △ fus|ses
  △ fussed
  △ fuss|ing
fuss|ily
fus|si|ness
fuss|pot
fussy
  △ fus|sier
  △ fus|si|est
fus|ti|ness
fusty
  △ fus|tier
  △ fus|ti|est

fu|thark
fu|tile
fu|tilely
fu|til|ity
futon
fu|ture
Fu|tur|ism
fu|tur|ist
fu|tur|is|tic
fu|tur|is|tic|ally
fu|tur|ity
  △ fu|tur|it|ies
fu|tur|ol|ogy
fuzz
fuz|zily
fuzzy
  △ fuz|zier
  △ fuz|zi|est

G

gab
VERB
△ gabs
△ gabbed
△ gab|bing
ga|bar|dine
gab|ble
VERB
△ gab|bles
△ gab|bled
△ gab|bling
gab|bro
gaberdine *see*
  gabardine
Ga|ble
ga|ble
ga|bled
Ga|bon
Ga|bo|rone
Ga|briel
Gad
gad
△ gads
△ gad|ded
△ gad|ding
gad|about
Gad|dafi
gad|fly
△ gad|flies
gad|get
gad|getry
ga|do|lin|ium
gad|wall
Gael
Gae|lic

gaff
pole; secret;
seize with gaff
VERB
△ gaffs
△ gaffed

△ gaf|fing
⚠ gaffe

gaffe
embarrassing
mistake
⚠ gaff

gaf|fer
gag
VERB
△ gags
△ gagged
△ gag|ging
gaga
Ga|garin
gage
gag|gle
gai|ety
Gail
gaily
gain
VERB
△ gains
△ gained
△ gain|ing
gain|ful
gain|fully
gain|say
△ gain|says
△ gain|said
△ gain|say|ing
Gains|bor|ough

gait
way of walking
etc
⚠ gate

gai|ter
Gait|skell
gal
gala
ga|lac|tic
ga|lac|tos|ae|mia

ga|lac|tose
Ga|la|had
gal|an|tine
Ga|la|shiels
Ga|la|tians, Let|
  ter of Paul to
  the
gal|axy
△ gal|ax|ies
gale
ga|lena
Gal|ilee
Ga|li|leo
Ga|li|leo, The
  Life of (Le|ben
  des Ga|li|lei)
gall
VERB
△ galls
△ galled
△ gall|ing
gal|lant
gal|lantly
gal|lan|try
△ gal|lan|tries
gall-blad|der
gal|leon
gal|lery
△ gal|ler|ies
gal|ley
gal|li|ard
Gal|lic
Gal|li|cism
gal|li|na|ceous
gall|ing
gal|lin|ule
Gal|li|poli
gal|lium
gal|li|vant
△ gal|li|vants
△ gal|li|van|ted
△ gal|li|vant|ing
gal|lon
gal|lop

VERB
△ gal|lops
△ gal|loped
△ gal|lop|ing
Gal|lo|way
gal|lows
gall|stone
Gal|lup
galop
ga|lore
ga|losh
△ ga|lo|shes
Gals|wor|thy
ga|lumph
△ ga|lumphs
△ ga|lumphed
△ ga|lumph|ing
gal|vanic
gal|van|ism
gal|van|iza|tion
gal|van|ize
△ gal|van|izes
△ gal|van|ized
△ gal|van|izing
gal|van|ized
gal|va|nom|eter
Gal|way
Gama
Gam|bia
gam|bit

gam|ble
bet
VERB
△ gam|bles
△ gam|bled
△ gam|bling
⚠ gambol

gam|bler
gam|bling
gam|boge

gam|bol
dance about

VERB
△ gam|bols
△ gam|bolled
△ gam|bol|ling
⚠gamble

gam|brel
game
VERB
△ games
△ gamed
△ ga|ming
game|cock
game|kee|per
gam|elan
gamely
games|man|ship
gam|ete
ga|meto|phyte
gamey *see* gamy
gam|ine
ga|mi|ness
gamma
gam|mon

gammy
lame
△ gam|mier
△ gam|mi|est
⚠gamy

gamp
gamut

gamy
strong-smelling
△ ga|mier
△ ga|mi|est
⚠gammy

gan|der
Gan|dhi
gang
VERB
△ gangs
△ ganged

△ gang|ing
gang-bang
ganger
Gan|ges
gang|land
gan|gling
gan|glion
△ gan|glia *or*
gan|gli|ons
gangly
△ gan|gl|ier
△ gan|gli|est
gang|plank
gan|grene
gan|gren|ous

gang|sta
music
⚠gangster

gang|ster
criminal
⚠gangsta

gangue
gang|way
ganja
gan|net
gan|try
△ gan|tries
Ga|ny|mede
gaol *see* jail
gaoler *see* jailer
gap
gape
VERB
△ gapes
△ gaped
△ ga|ping
ga|ping
gappy
△ gap|pier
△ gap|pi|est
gar|age
garam ma|sala

garb
VERB
△ garbs
△ garbed
△ garb|ing
gar|bage
gar|ble
△ gar|bles
△ gar|bled
△ gar|bling
Garbo
gar|çon
Gard, Pont du
garda
△ gar|dai
Garda, Lake
gar|den
VERB
△ gar|dens
△ gar|dened
△ gar|den|ing
gar|dener
gar|de|nia
gar|den|ing
Gar|eth
Gar|gan|tua
gar|gan|tuan
gar|gle
VERB
△ gar|gles
△ gar|gled
△ garg|ling
gar|goyle
Ga|ri|baldi
gar|ish
gar|ishly
gar|ish|ness
Gar|land
gar|land
VERB
△ gar|lands
△ gar|lan|ded
△ gar|land|ing
gar|lic

gar|licky
gar|ment
gar|ner
△ gar|ners
△ gar|nered
△ gar|ner|ing
gar|net
gar|nish
NOUN
△ gar|ni|shes
VERB
△ gar|ni|shes
△ gar|nished
△ gar|nish|ing
gar|ret
Gar|rick
gar|ri|son
gar|rotte
VERB
△ gar|rottes
△ gar|rot|ted
△ gar|rot|ting
gar|ru|lity
gar|ru|lous
gar|ru|lous|ness
gar|ter
Gary
gas
NOUN
△ gases
VERB
△ gas|ses
△ gassed
△ gas|sing
gasahol *see*
gasohol
gas|bag
Gas|coigne
Gas|cony
gas|eous
gash
NOUN
△ ga|shes

VERB
△ ga¦shes
△ gashed
△ gash¦ing
ga¦si¦fi¦ca¦tion
gas¦ify
△ gasi¦fies
△ gasi¦fied
△ gasi¦fy¦ing
Gas¦kell
gas¦ket
gas¦light
gaso¦hol
gaso¦line
gas¦om¦eter
gasp
VERB
△ gasps
△ gasped
△ gasp¦ing
gas¦si¦ness
gassy
△ gas¦sier
△ gas¦si¦est
gast¦ar¦beï¦ter
gasteropod *see*
gastropod
Gasteropoda *see*
Gastropoda
gas¦trec¦tomy
△ gas¦trec¦tom¦ies
gas¦tric
gas¦tri¦tis
gas¦tro¦en¦ter¦itis
gas¦tro¦nome
gas¦tron¦omer
gas¦tro¦nomic
gas¦tron¦om¦ist
gas¦tron¦omy
gas¦tro¦pod
Gas¦tro¦poda
gas¦tro¦scope
gast¦rula
gas¦works

---

gate
door etc; confine
VERB
△ gates
△ gated
△ ga¦ting
⚠ gait

---

gat¦eau
△ gat¦eaux *or*
gat¦eaus
gate¦crash
△ gate¦cra¦shes
△ gate¦crashed
△ gate¦crash¦ing
gate¦cra¦sher
gate¦house
gate¦leg
Gates¦head
gate¦way
ga¦ther
VERB
△ gath¦ers
△ gath¦ered
△ gath¦er¦ing
gath¦er¦ing
gat¦to¦pardo, Il
(The Leo¦pard)
gauche
gauchely
gauch¦erie
gaucho
Gaudí
gaud¦ily
gau¦di¦ness
gaudy
△ gau¦dier
△ gau¦di¦est
gauge
VERB
△ gauges
△ gauged
△ gauging
Gau¦guin

Gaul
Gaul¦ish
Gaul¦list
Gau¦mont
gaunt
△ gaun¦ter
△ gaunt¦est
gaunt¦let
gaunt¦ness
gauss
△ gauss *or* gaus¦
ses
Gau¦tier
gauze
gauzy
△ gauz¦ier
△ gau¦zi¦est
gave
gavel
ga¦vial
Gavin
ga¦votte
Ga¦wain
Ga¦wain and the
Green Knight,
Sir
gawk
VERB
△ gawks
△ gawked
△ gawk¦ing
gaw¦ki¦ness
gawky
△ gaw¦kier
△ gaw¦ki¦est
gawp
△ gawps
△ gawped
△ gawp¦ing
Gay
gay
ADJ.
△ gayer
△ gay¦est

Gay-Lus¦sac
gay¦ness
Gay¦nor
Gaza
Gaz¦an¦kulu
gaze
VERB
△ gazes
△ gazed
△ gaz¦ing
ga¦zebo
△ ga¦zebos *or*
ga¦zeboes
ga¦zelle
△ ga¦zelles *or*
ga¦zelle
ga¦zette
VERB
△ ga¦zettes
△ ga¦zet¦ted
△ ga¦zet¦ting
ga¦zet¦teer
gaz¦pacho
ga¦zump
△ ga¦zumps
△ ga¦zumped
△ ga¦zump¦ing
ga¦zum¦per
ga¦zump¦ing
ga¦zun¦der
△ ga¦zun¦ders
△ ga¦zun¦dered
△ ga¦zun¦der¦ing
Gdańsk
gear
VERB
△ gears
△ geared
△ gear¦ing
gear¦box
△ gear¦boxes
gecko
△ geckos *or*
geck¦oes

gee
gee-gee
geese
gee-string *see*
  G-string
gee¦zer
ge¦gen\schein
Ge¦henna
Gei¦ger
gei¦sha
  △ gei¦sha *or* gei¦
    shas

gel
  *colloid; become
  this*
  VERB
  △ gels
  △ gelled
  △ gel\ling
  ⚠jell

gela¦tine
ge¦la¦tin¦ize
  △ ge¦la¦tin¦izes
  △ ge¦la¦tin¦ized
  △ ge¦la¦tin¦iz¦ing
ge¦la¦tin¦ous
geld
  △ gelds
  △ gel¦ded
  △ geld¦ing
geld¦ing
gel¦ig¦nite
gem
gem¦in¦ate
  VERB
  △ gem¦in¦ates
  △ gem¦in¦ated
  △ gem¦in¦ating
gem¦in¦ation
Gemi¦nean
Gem¦ini
Gemma
gem¦stone

gen
  VERB
  △ gens
  △ genned
  △ gen¦ning
gen¦darme
gen¦der
gen¦der-ben¦der
gene
gen¦ea¦lo¦gi¦cal
ge¦ne¦al¦ogist
ge¦ne¦al¦ogy
  △ ge¦ne¦al¦ogies
gen¦era
gen¦eral
Gen¦eral, The
gen¦er¦al¦is¦simo
gen¦er¦al¦ity
  △ gen¦er¦al¦it¦ies
gen¦er¦al¦iza¦tion
gen¦er¦al¦ize
  △ gen¦er¦al¦izes
  △ gen¦er¦al¦ized
  △ gen¦er¦al¦iz¦ing
gen¦er¦ally
gen¦er¦ate
  △ gen¦er¦ates
  △ gen¦er¦ated
  △ gen¦er¦ating
gen¦era¦tion
gen¦era¦tive
gen¦er¦ator
ge¦neric
gen¦er¦os¦ity
gen¦er¦ous
gen¦er¦ously
gen¦esis
  △ gen¦eses
Gen¦esis, Book
  of
Genet
gen¦etic
gen¦etic¦ally
gen¦eti¦cist

gen¦et¦ics
Gen¦eva
Gen¦ghis Khan
ge¦nial
ge¦ni¦al¦ity
ge¦ni¦ally
genie
  △ ge¦nies *or*
    genii
gen¦ital
geni¦ta¦lia
gen¦it¦als
gen¦it¦ive
ge¦nius
  guardian spirit
  △ genii
  other senses
  △ ge¦ni¦uses
Genoa
geno¦ci¦dal
geno¦cide
ge¦nome
geno¦type
genre
gent

gen¦teel
  *refined; upper-
  class*
  ⚠gentle

gen¦teelly
gen¦tian
Gentile
  *non-Jew; not
  Jewish*
gentile
  *concerning
  nationality;
  word indicating
  this*
gen¦til¦ity

gen¦tle
  not rough

  △ gent¦ler
  △ gent¦lest
  ⚠genteel

gentle¦folk
gentle¦man
  △ gentle¦men
gentle¦manly
gentle¦ness
gentle¦wo¦man
  △ gentle¦women
gently
gen¦tri¦fi¦ca¦tion
gen¦trify
  △ gen¦tri¦fies
  △ gen¦tri¦fied
  △ gen¦tri¦fy¦ing
gen¦try
genu¦flect
  △ genu¦flects
  △ genu¦flec¦ted
  △ genu¦flect¦ing
genu¦flec¦tion
genu¦ine
genu¦inely
genu¦ine¦ness
genus
  △ gen¦era
geo¦cen¦tric
geo¦chem¦is¦try
geode
geo¦desic
geo¦desy
Geof¦frey
geog¦ra¦pher
geo¦graph¦ical
geo¦graph¦ic¦ally
geog¦raphy
geo¦lo¦gi¦cal
geo¦lo¦gic¦ally
ge¦ol¦ogist
ge¦ol¦ogy
geo¦mag¦net¦ism
geo¦met¦ric

geo|met|ri|cal
geom|etry
geo|mor|phol|
ogy
geo|phys|ics
geo|pol|it|ics
Geor|die
George
George-Brown
George|town
geor|gette
Geor|gia
Geor|gian
Geor|gics
Geor|gina
geo|sphere
geo|sta|tion|ary
geo|syn|chron|
ous
geo|taxis
geo|ther|mal
geo|tro|pism
Ger|ald
gera|nium
Ger|ard
ger|bil
geri|at|ric
geri|at|ri|cian
Géri|cault
germ

Ger|man
of Germany
⚠ german
⚠ germane

---

ger|man
having the same
parents etc as
oneself
⚠ German
⚠ germane

---

ger|mane

relevant
⚠ German
⚠ german

Ger|manic
ger|ma|nium
Ger|many
ger|mi|ci|dal
ger|mi|cide
Ger|mi|nal
ger|mi|nal
ger|mi|nate
△ ger|mi|nates
△ ger|mi|na|ted
△ ger|mi|na|ting
ger|mi|na|tion
ger|on|to|lo|gi|
cal
ger|on|tol|ogist
ger|on|tol|ogy
ger|ry|man|der
VERB
△ ger|ry|man|
ders
△ ger|ry|man|
dered
△ ger|ry|man|
der|ing
ger|ry|man|der|
ing
Ger|shwin
Gert|rude
ger|und
Ge|samt|kunst|
werk
gesso
△ ges|soes
ges|talt
Ges|tapo
ges|tate
△ ges|tates
△ ges|ta|ted
△ ges|ta|ting
ges|ta|tion

ges|ti|cu|late
△ ges|ti|cu|lates
△ ges|ti|cu|la|ted
△ ges|ti|cu|la|
ting
ges|ti|cu|la|tion
ges|tural
ges|ture
VERB
△ ges|tures
△ ges|tured
△ ges|tur|ing
get
VERB
△ gets
△ got
△ get|ting
get-at-able
get|away
Geth|sem|ane
get-together
Getty
Get|tys|burg
get-up
get-up-and-go
geum
gew|gaw
Ge|würtz|tra|mi|
ner
gey|ser
Ghana
ghar|ial
ghas|tli|ness
ghastly
ADJ.
△ ghast|lier
△ ghast|li|est
ghat
ghee
Ghent
gher|kin
ghetto
△ ghet|tos *or*
ghet|toes

ghetto-blas|ter
ghillie *see* gillie
ghost
VERB
△ ghosts
△ ghos|ted
△ ghost|ing
ghostly
ghoul
ghoul|ish
ghyll *see* gill
giant
giant|ess
△ giant|es|ses
giant-kil|ler
gib|ber
△ gib|bers
△ gib|bered
△ gib|ber|ing
gib|ber|el|lin
gib|ber|ing
gib|ber|ish
gib|bet
VERB
△ gib|bets
△ gib|beted
△ gib|bet|ing
Gib|bon
gib|bon
Gib|bons
gib|bous
gibe
mock; jeer
VERB
△ gibes
△ gibed
△ gi|bing
gibe
swing (of boat or
sail) see gybe
gib|lets
Gib|ral|tar
Gib|son
gid|dily

gid|di|ness
giddy
△ gid|dier
△ gid|di|est
Gide
Gid|eon
Giel|gud
Gif|fard
gift
VERB
△ gifts
△ gif|ted
△ gift|ing
gif|ted
gif|ted|ness
gift-wrap
△ gift-wraps
△ gift-wrapped
△ gift-wrap|ping
gig
VERB
△ gigs
△ gigged
△ gig|ging
gi|gan|tic
gi|gan|tic|ally
gig|gle
VERB
△ gig|gles
△ gig|gled
△ gig|gling
gig|gly
△ gig|glier
△ gig|gli|est
Gigli
gi|golo
gigot
gigue
Gil|bert

gild
cover with gold
△ gilds
△ gil|ded
△ gild|ing
△ gilt
△ guild

gil|der
Giles
Gil|ga|mesh
Gill
gill
Gil|les|pie
Gil|lian
gil|lie
Gil|ling|ham

gilt
gold covering;
sort of share;
young female pig
△ guilt

gim|bals
gim|crack
gim|let
gim|let-eyed
gim|mick
gim|mickry
gim|micky
gimp
gin
VERB
△ gins
△ ginned
△ gin|ning
gin|ger
VERB
△ gin|gers
△ gin|gered
△ gin|ger|ing
gin|ger|bread
gin|gerly
gin|gery
ging|ham
gin|gi|vi|tis
ginkgo
gi|nor|mous

Gins|berg
gin|seng
gin|trap
Gi|otto
gip *see* gyp
gippy
Gipsy *see*
  Gypsy
gi|raffe
Gi|rau|doux
gird
△ girds
△ girded
△ gird|ing
△ girt
girder
gir|dle
belt etc
VERB
△ gir|dles
△ gir|dled
△ gird|ling
girdle
cooking plate see
griddle
girl
girl|friend
girl|hood
gir|lie
girl|ish
giro
girt
girth
Gis|card d'Es|
  taing
Gis|elle
Gis|sing
gist
git
git|tern
give
VERB
△ gives
△ gave

△ giv|ing
△ given
give-and-take
give-away
given
giz|zard
glacé
gla|cial
gla|ci|ally
gla|ci|ate
△ gla|ci|ates
△ gla|ci|ated
△ gla|ci|ating
gla|ci|ation
gla|cier
glad
△ glad|der
△ glad|dest
glad|den
△ glad|dens
△ glad|dened
△ glad|den|ing
glade
gla|di|ator
gla|di|ator|ial
gla|di|olus
△ gla|di|oli *or*
  gla|di|oluses
gladly
glad|ness
Glad|stone
Gladys
glair
Gla|mor|gan
glam|or|ize
△ glam|or|izes
△ glam|or|ized
△ glam|or|izing
glam|or|ous
glam|our
glance
VERB
△ glan|ces
△ glanced

△ glan|cing
gland
glan|ders
glan|du|lar
glare
  VERB
  △ glares
  △ glared
  △ glar|ing
glar|ing
glar|ingly
Glas|gow
glas|nost
glass
  NOUN
  △ glas|ses
  VERB
  △ glas|ses
  △ glassed
  △ glass|ing
glass-blower
glass-blow|ing
glass|house
glass|pa|per
glass|wort
glassy
  △ glas|sier
  △ glas|si|est
Glas|ton|bury
Glas|we|gian
glau|coma
glau|cous
glaze
  VERB
  △ gla|zes
  △ glazed
  △ gla|zing
glazed
gla|zier
gleam
  VERB
  △ gleams
  △ gleamed
  △ gleam|ing

gleam|ing
glean
  △ gleans
  △ gleaned
  △ glean|ing
Glean|ers, The
glebe
glee
glee|ful
glee|fully
Glen
glen
Glenda
Glen|dower
glen|garry
  △ glen|gar|ries
Glenn
Glen|ro|thes
glib
  △ glib|ber
  △ glib|best
glibly
glib|ness
glide
  VERB
  △ glides
  △ gli|ded
  △ gli|ding
gli|der
glim|mer
  VERB
  △ glim|mers
  △ glim|mered
  △ glim|mer|ing
glimpse
  VERB
  △ glimp|ses
  △ glimpsed
  △ glimps|ing
Glinka
glint
  VERB
  △ glints
  △ glin|ted

△ glint|ing
glis|sade
  VERB
  △ glis|sades
  △ glis|sa|ded
  △ glis|sa|ding
glis|sando
  △ glis|sandi *or*
  glis|san|dos
glis|ten
  △ glis|tens
  △ glis|tened
  △ glis|ten|ing
glitch
  △ glit|ches
glit|ter
  VERB
  △ glit|ters
  △ glit|tered
  △ glit|ter|ing
glit|ter|ati
glit|ter|ing
glitz
glitzy
  △ glit|zier
  △ glit|zi|est
gloam|ing
gloat
  VERB
  △ gloats
  △ gloa|ted
  △ gloat|ing
glob
glo|bal
glo|bally
globe
globe|flower
globe|trot|ter
globe|trot|ting
glo|bin
glob|ular
glob|ule
glob|ulin
glock|en|spiel

glom|eru|lus
  △ glom|eruli
gloom
  VERB
  △ glooms
  △ gloomed
  △ gloom|ing
gloom|ily
gloomy
  △ gloo|mier
  △ gloo|mi|est
Gloria
glori|fi|ca|tion
glori|fied
glor|ify
  △ glori|fies
  △ glori|fied
  △ glori|fy|ing
glori|ous
glori|ously
glory
  NOUN
  △ glor|ies
  VERB
  △ glor|ies
  △ glor|ied
  △ glory|ing
glory-hole
gloss
  NOUN
  △ glos|ses
  VERB
  △ glos|ses
  △ glossed
  △ gloss|ing
glos|sary
  △ glos|sar|ies
glos|sily
glos|si|ness
glos|so|la|lia
glos|so|pha|ryn|
  geal
glossy
  △ glos|sier

△ glos|si|est
glot|tal
glot|tis
  △ glot|tises *or*
    glot|ti|des
glot|to|chron|ol|
  ogy
Glou|ces|ter
Glou|ces|ter|
  shire
glove
  VERB
  △ gloves
  △ gloved
  △ glov|ing
glover
glow
  VERB
  △ glows
  △ glowed
  △ glow|ing
glower
  VERB
  △ glowers
  △ glow|ered
  △ glow|er|ing
glow|ing
glow-worm
glox|inia
glu|ca|gon
Gluck
glu|cose
glu|cos|ide
glue
  VERB
  △ glues
  △ glued
  △ glu|ing
glue-snif|fer
glue-snif|fing
gluey
  △ glu|ier
  △ glui|est
glum

△ glum|mer
△ glum|mest
glume
glumly
glum|ness
gluon
glut
  VERB
  △ gluts
  △ glut|ted
  △ glut|ting
glu|tam|ate
glu|ta|mine
glu|ten
glu|tin|ous
glut|ton
glut|ton|ous
glut|tony
gly|cer|ide
gly|cer|ine
gly|cerol
gly|cine
gly|co|gen
gly|co|genic
gly|co|ly|sis
Glynde|bourne
Glyndwr *see*
  Glendower
Glynis
gnarled
gnarly
gnash
  △ gna|shes
  △ gnashed
  △ gnash|ing
gnash|ers
gnat
gnaw
  △ gnaws
  △ gnawed
  △ gnaw|ing
  △ gnawed *or*
    gnawn
gnaw|ing

gneiss
gnoc|chi
gnome
gno|mic
gno|mish
Gnos|tic
  believer in
  Gnosticism
gnos|tic
  relating to
  knowledge
Gnos|ti|cism
gnu
  △ gnus *or* gnu
go
  NOUN
  △ goes
  VERB
  △ goes
  △ went
  △ going
  △ gone
Goa
goad
  VERB
  △ goads
  △ goa|ded
  △ goad|ing
go-ahead
goal
goalie
goal|kee|per
goal-line
goal|post
goat
goa|tee
goat|herd
goat|ish
gob
  VERB
  △ gobs
  △ gobbed
  △ gob|bing
gob|bet

gob|ble
  VERB
  △ gob|bles
  △ gob|bled
  △ gob|bling
gobble|dy|gook
gob|bler
go-bet|ween
Go-Bet|ween,
  The
Gobi
gob|let
gob|lin
gob|smacked
gob|stop|per
goby
  △ go|bies
go-by
God
  supreme being in
  Christian,
  Jewish, etc
  religions
god
  divine being;
  greatly admired
  person or thing
God|ard
god|child
  △ god|chil|dren
god|daugh|ter
god|dess
  △ god|des|ses
god|fa|ther
Godfather, The
God-fear|ing
God-for|sa|ken
God|frey
god|head
Go|diva
god|less
god|less|ness
god|like
god|li|ness

godly
△ god|lier
△ god|li|est
god|mo|ther
god|par|ent
god|send
god|son
God|speed
god|wit
Goeb|bels
goer
Goer|ing
Goe|the
gofer
Gog
go-get|ter
go-get|ting
gog|gle
VERB
△ gog|gles
△ gog|gled
△ gog|gling
goggle-box
△ goggle-boxes
goggles
Gogol
go|ing
go|ing-over
go|ings-on
goi|tre
go-kart
Golan
gold
Gold|berg
gold-dig|ger
gol|den
Gol|den Ass, The
Gol|den Bough,
The
Gol|den Bowl,
The
Gol|den Cock|erel,
The (Zo|lo|toy
Pe|tu|shok)

gol|den|rod
gold|field
gold|finch
△ gold|fin|ches
gold|fish
△ gold|fi|shes *or*
gold|fish
Gold|ing
gold-plate
△ gold-plates
△ gold-pla|ted
△ gold-pla|ting
gold-pla|ted
Gold Rush, The
Gold|smith
gold|smith
Gold|wa|ter
Gold|wyn
golem
golf
VERB
△ golfs
△ golfed
△ golf|ing
gol|fer
gol|iard
Go|li|ath
biblical giant
go|li|ath
large or
influential person
or thing
Gol|lancz
gol|li|wog
golly
NOUN
△ gol|lies
golosh *see*
galosh
Go|mor|rah
gonad
gon|ado|tro|phic
gon|ado|tro|phin
Gon|court

gon|dola
gon|do|lier
gone
goner
Gone with the
Wind
gon|fa|lon
gong
go|nor|rhoea
goo
Gooch
good
ADJ.
△ bet|ter
△ best
good|bye
Good|bye, Mr
Chips
good-for-noth|
ing
good|ies
good|li|ness
goodly
△ good|lier
△ good|li|est
Good|man
good|ness
good|will
goody
△ good|ies
goody-goody
NOUN
△ goody-good|
ies
gooey
△ goo|ier
△ goo|iest
goof
VERB
△ goofs
△ goofed
△ goof|ing
goofy
△ goo|fier

△ goo|fi|est
googly
△ goog|lies
goon
Goons, The
goos|ander
goose
NOUN
pinch on the
bottom
△ gooses
other senses
△ geese
VERB
△ goo|ses
△ goosed
△ goos|ing
goose|berry
△ goose|ber|ries
goose|fish
sing. and pl.
goose-step
VERB
△ goose-steps
△ goose-stepped
△ goose-step|
ping
Goos|sens
go|pher
Gor|azde
Gor|ba|chev
Gor|bals
Gor|bo|duc
Gor|dian
Gor|di|mer
Gor|don
gore
VERB
△ gores
△ gored
△ gor|ing
gorge
VERB
△ gor|ges

△ gorged
△ gor|ging
gor|geous
gor|geously
gor|geous|ness
gor|gon
Gor|gon|zola

gor|illa
ape
⚠ guerrilla

Göring *see*
Goering
Gorky
gorm|less
gorm|lessly
gorse
gorsy
gory
△ gor|ier
△ gori|est
gosh
gos|hawk
gos|ling
go-slow
Gos|pel
*New-Testament
book*
gos|pel
*truth; principle;
sort of Black
religious music*
Gos|port
Gos|saert
gos|sa|mer
gos|sip
VERB
△ gossips
△ gos|siped
△ gos|sip|ing
gos|sipy
got
Goth
Goth|en|burg

Gothic
got|ten
*Göt|ter|däm|mer|
ung (The Twi|
light of the
Gods)*
gou|ache
Gouda
gouge
VERB
△ gou|ges
△ gouged
△ gou|ging
gou|jon
gou|lash
△ gou|la|shes
Gou|nod
gourd

gour|mand
glutton
⚠ gourmet

gour|man|dise
gour|mand|ism

gour|met
food expert
⚠ gourmand

gout
gouty
△ gout|ier
△ gou|ti|est
gov|ern
△ gov|erns
△ gov|erned
△ gov|ern|ing
gov|ern|able
gov|ern|ance
gov|er|ness
△ gov|er|nes|
ses
gov|ern|ing
gov|ern|ment
gov|ern|men|tal

*Gov|ern|ment In|
spec|tor, The*
gov|er|nor
Gov|er|nor-
Gen|eral
△ Gov|er|nors-
Gen|eral *or*
Gov|er|nor-
Gen|erals

Gower
medieval poet
⚠ Gowers

Gowers
*writer on
English style*
⚠ Gower

gown
goy
△ goys *or* goyim
Goya
grab
VERB
△ grabs
△ grabbed
△ grab|bing
gra|ben
Grac|chus
△ Grac|chi
Grace
grace
VERB
△ gra|ces
△ graced
△ gra|cing
grace-and-
favour
grace|ful
grace|fully
grace|ful|ness
grace|less
grace|lessly
grace|less|ness

gra|cious
gra|ciously
gra|cious|ness
gra|date
△ gra|dates
△ gra|da|ted
△ gra|da|ting

gra|da|tion
gradual change
⚠ graduation

gra|da|tional
Grade
grade
VERB
△ grades
△ gra|ded
△ gra|ding
gra|di|ent
grad|ual
gradu|al|ism
gradu|al|ist
gradu|ally
gradu|and
gradu|ate
VERB
△ gradu|ates
△ gradu|ated
△ gradu|ating

gradu|ation
*taking an
academic degree;
scale on
thermometer etc*
⚠ gradation

Graf
graf|fito
△ graf|fiti
graft
VERB
△ grafts
△ graf|ted
△ graft|ing

graf|ter
Gra|ham
Gra|hame
Grail
grain
  VERB
  △ grains
  △ grained
  △ grain|ing
Grain|ger
grainy
  △ grai|nier
  △ grai|ni|est
gram
Gra|mi|nae
gram|mar
gram|mar|ian
gram|mat|ical
gram|mat|ic|ally
gramme *see*
  gram
gra|mo|phone
Gram|pian
gram|pus
  △ gram|puses
gran
Gra|nada
gran|ary
  NOUN
  △ gran|ar|ies
grand
  NOUN
  money
  △ grand
  piano
  △ grands
  ADJ.
  △ gran|der
  △ grand|est
gran|dad
grand|child
  △ grand|chil|
  dren
grand|daugh|ter

gran|dee
gran|deur
grand|fa|ther
Grand Gui|gnol
gran|di|lo|
  quence
gran|di|lo|quent
gran|di|lo|
  quently
gran|di|ose
grandly
grandma
grand|mother
grandpa
grand|par|ent
grand|son
grand|stand
grange
Grange|mouth
gran|ite
granny
  △ gran|nies
Grant
grant
  VERB
  △ grants
  △ gran|ted
  △ grant|ing
Granth
Gran|tham
gran|ular
granu|lar|ity
granu|late
  △ granu|lates
  △ granu|la|ted
  △ granu|la|ting
granu|la|tion
gran|ule
Gran|ville-Bar|
  ker
grape
grape|fruit
  △ grape|fruit *or*
  grape|fruits

Gra|pelli
grape|shot
Grapes of
  Wrath, The
grape|vine
graph
  VERB
  △ graphs
  △ graphed
  △ graph|ing
gra|phic
graph|ic|ally
graph|ics
  sing. and pl.
graph|ite
graph|olo|gist
graph|ol|ogy
grap|nel
grappa
grap|ple
  VERB
  △ grap|ples
  △ grap|pled
  △ grap|pling
grap|pling-hook
grap|pling-iron
grap|to|lite
Gras|mere
grasp
  VERB
  △ grasps
  △ grasped
  △ grasp|ing
grasp|ing
Grass
grass
  NOUN
  △ gras|ses
  VERB
  △ gras|ses
  △ grassed
  △ grass|ing
grass|hop|per
grassy

  △ gras|sier
  △ gras|si|est

grate
  fireplace; grind;
  make grinding
  noise; annoy
  VERB
  △ grates
  △ gra|ted
  △ gra|ting
  △great

grate|ful
grate|fully
gra|ter
gra|ti|fi|ca|tion
grat|ify
  △ grat|ifies
  △ grat|ified
  △ grat|ify|ing
gra|ting
gra|tis
grat|it|ude
gra|tu|it|ous
gra|tu|it|ously
gra|tu|ity
  △ gra|tu|it|ies
gravadlax *see*
  gravlax
grave
  ADJ.
  △ gra|ver
  △ gra|vest
gra|vel
  VERB
  △ grav|els
  △ grav|elled
  △ grav|el|ling
grav|elly
gravely
gra|ven
Graves
Graves|end
grave|stone

Gra|vet|tian
grave|yard
gra|vid
gra|vim|eter
gra|vi|met|ric
gra|vim|etry
grav|itas
gra|vi|tate
△ gra|vi|tates
△ gra|vi|ta|ted
△ gra|vi|ta|ting
gra|vi|ta|tion
gra|vi|ta|tional
gra|vi|ton
grav|ity
grav|lax
△ grav|laxes
gra|vure
gravy
△ gra|vies
Gray
gray
　colour see grey
gray
　unit of radiation
gray|ling
△ gray|ling or
　gray|lings
graywacke see
　greywacke
Graz
graze
　VERB
△ gra|zes
△ grazed
△ gra|zing
gra|zing
grease
　VERB
△ grea|ses
△ greased
△ greas|ing
grease|paint
grea|ser

grea|si|ness
greasy
△ grea|sier
△ grea|si|est

> great
> big; splendid
> ADJ.
> △ greater
> △ great|est
> ⚠grate

great-aunt
great|coat
Great Ex|pec|ta|
　tions
Great Gatsby,
　The
greatly
great-nephew
great|ness
great-niece
great-uncle
greave
grebe
Gre|cian
Greece
greed
greed|ily
greedy
△ gree|dier
△ gree|di|est
Greek
green
　VERB
△ greens
△ greened
△ green|ing
　ADJ.
△ greener
△ green|est
Green|away
green|back
Greene
green|ery

green-eyed
green|finch
△ green|fin|ches
green|fly
△ green|fly or
　green|flies
green|gage
green|gro|cer
green|gro|cery
Green|ham
green|horn
green|house
green|kee|per
Green|land
green|mail
Green|mantle
Green|ock
Green|peace
green|room
Green|sleeves
green|stick
Green|wich
Greer
greet
　VERB
　welcome
△ greets
△ gree|ted
△ greet|ing
　cry
△ greets
△ grat
△ greet|ing
△ grut|ten
greet|ing
gre|gari|ous
gre|gari|ous|
　ness
Gre|gor|ian
Greg|ory
grem|lin
Gre|nada
gre|nade
gre|na|dier

gre|na|dine
Gre|noble
Gretna
grew
Grey
grey
　VERB
△ greys
△ greyed
△ grey|ing
　ADJ.
△ greyer
△ grey|est
grey|hound
grey|lag
grey|ness
grey|wacke
grid
grid|dle
grid|iron
grief
Grieg
grie|vance
grieve
△ grieves
△ grieved
△ grie|ving
grie|vous
grif|fin
Grif|fith
grif|fon
Grig|son
grike see gryke

> grill
> cook under
> radiated heat;
> food so cooked;
> interrogate
> VERB
> △ grills
> △ grilled
> △ gril|ling
> ⚠grille

grill
metal framework
see *grille*

grille
metal framework
△grill

gril|ling
grilse
  △ grilse *or* gril|ses
grim
  △ grim|mer
  △ grim|mest
gri|mace
  VERB
  △ gri|ma|ces
  △ gri|maced
  △ gri|ma|cing
Gri|maldi
grime
  VERB
  △ grimes
  △ grimed
  △ gri|ming
gri|mi|ness
grimly
Grimm
grim|ness
Grim|ond
Grimsby
grimy
  △ gri|mier
  △ gri|mi|est
grin
  VERB
  △ grins
  △ grinned
  △ grin|ning
grind
  VERB
  △ grinds
  △ ground
  △ grind|ing
grinder

grind|stone
gringo
grin|ningly
grip
  VERB
  △ grips
  △ gripped
  △ grip|ping
gripe
  VERB
  △ gripes
  △ griped
  △ gri|ping
grip|ping
gris|aille
gri|seo|ful|vin
gris|li|ness

grisly
horrible
  △ gris|lier
  △ gris|li|est
  △grizzly

grist
gris|tle

gris|tly
full of gristle
  △grisly
  △grizzly

grit
bit of stone;
courage; clench
(teeth)
  VERB
  △ grits
  △ grit|ted
  △ grit|ting
  △grits

grits
ground oats;

dish of this
sing. and pl.
  △grit

gritty
  △ grit|tier
  △ grit|ti|est
Gri|vas
griz|zle
  VERB
  △ griz|zles
  △ griz|zled
  △ griz|zling
griz|zled

grizzly
grey; sort of
bear
  NOUN
  △ griz|zlies
  ADJ.
  △ griz|zlier
  △ griz|zli|est
  △grisly
  △gristly

groan
  VERB
  △ groans
  △ groaned
  △ groan|ing

groat
coin
  △groats

groats
crushed oats
  △groat

gro|cer
gro|cery
  △ gro|cer|ies
grog
grog|gily
grog|gi|ness

groggy
  △ grog|gier
  △ grog|gi|est
grog|ram
groin
  VERB
  △ groins
  △ groined
  △ groin|ing
grommet *see*
  grummet
Gro|myko
groom
  VERB
  △ grooms
  △ groomed
  △ groom|ing
groove
  VERB
  △ grooves
  △ grooved
  △ groo|ving
groovy
  △ groo|vier
  △ groo|vi|est
grope
  VERB
  △ gropes
  △ groped
  △ gro|ping
Gro|pius
gros|beak
gross
  NOUN
  set of 144
  △ gross
  total amount etc
  △ gros|ses
  VERB
  △ gros|ses
  △ grossed
  △ gross|ing
  ADJ.
  △ gros|ser

△ gros|sest
grossly
Gros|smith
gross|ness
Grosz
gro|tesque
gro|tesquely
gro|tesque|ness
grot|ti|ness
grotto
△ grot|tos *or*
grot|toes
grotty
△ grot|tier
△ grot|ti|est
grouch
NOUN
△ grou|ches
VERB
△ grou|ches
△ grouched
△ grouch|ing
grouchy
△ grou|chier
△ grou|chi|est
ground
VERB
△ grounds
△ groun|ded
△ ground|ing
also past tense of
grind
ground|ing
ground|less
ground|ling
ground|nut
ground|sel
ground|sheet
grounds|man
△ grounds|men
ground|swell
ground|wa|ter
ground|work
group

VERB
△ groups
△ grouped
△ group|ing
grou|pie
grouse
NOUN
bird
△ grouse *or*
grou|ses
complaint
△ grou|ses
VERB
△ grou|ses
△ groused
△ grous|ing
grout
VERB
△ grouts
△ grou|ted
△ grout|ing
Grove
grove
grovel
△ grov|els
△ grov|elled
△ grov|el|ling
grov|el|ler
grow
△ grows
△ grew
△ grow|ing
△ grown
growl
VERB
△ growls
△ growled
△ growl|ing
grown
grown-up
growth
groyne
grub

VERB
△ grubs
△ grubbed
△ grub|bing
grub|bily
grub|bi|ness
grubby
△ grub|bier
△ grub|bi|est
grudge
VERB
△ grud|ges
△ grudged
△ grud|ging
grud|ging
grud|gingly
gruel
gru|el|ling
grue|some
gruff
△ gruf|fer
△ gruf|fest
gruf|fly
gruff|ness
grum|ble
VERB
△ grum|bles
△ grum|bled
△ grum|bling
grum|bler
grum|bling
grum|met
grump
grum|pily
grum|pi|ness
grumpy
△ grum|pier
△ grum|pi|est
grunge
grunt
VERB
△ grunts
△ grun|ted
△ grunt|ing

Gruy|ère
gryke
gryphon *see*
griffin
G-string
G-suit
gua|ca|mole
guan|ine
guano

guar|an|tee
promise to repair
etc faulty
article; person
making this;
give guarantee;
promise; ensure
VERB
△ guar|an|tees
△ guar|an|teed
△ guar|an|tee|
ing
⚠guaranty

guar|an|tor

guar|anty
agreement to
take
responsibility if
another person
fails to pay his
debts etc;
security given
for this
△ guar|an|ties
⚠guarantee

guard
VERB
△ guards
△ guarded
△ guard|ing
guarded
guard|edly
guard|ed|ness

guard|house
guard|ian
guard|ian|ship
guards|man
  △ guards|men
guard|room
Guar|es|chi
Guar|ni|eri
Gua|te|mala
guava
gub|bins
  △ gub|bin|ses
guber|na|tor|ial
gud|geon
Guer|nica
Guern|sey
guern|sey

guer|rilla
fighter
  ⚠gorilla

guess
  NOUN
  △ gues|ses
  VERB
  △ gues|ses
  △ guessed
  △ guess|ing
guess|ti|mate
  VERB
  △ guess|ti|mates
  △ guess|ti|ma|
    ted
  △ guess|ti|ma|
    ting
guess|work
guest
  VERB
  △ guests
  △ gues|ted
  △ guest|ing
guest|house
Gue|vara
guff

guf|faw
  VERB
  △ guf|faws
  △ guf|fawed
  △ guf|faw|ing
Gug|gen|heim
Gui|ana
guid|ance
guide
  VERB
  △ guides
  △ guided
  △ guid|ing
guide|book
guide|line

guild
association of
tradesmen etc
  ⚠gild

guil|der
Dutch currency
unit
  △ guil|der *or*
    guil|ders
former German
and Dutch gold
coin
  △ guil|ders
Guild|ford
guild|hall
guile
guile|ful
guile|less
guille|mot
guil|loche
guil|lo|tine
  VERB
  △ guil|lo|tines
  △ guil|lo|tined
  △ guil|lo|ti|ning

guilt
having done

wrong;
awareness of this
  ⚠gilt

guilt|ily
guil|ti|ness
guilt|less
guilty
  △ guil|tier
  △ guil|ti|est
Gui|nea
gui|nea
Gui|nea-Bis|sau
Gui|ne|vere
Guin|ness
gui|pure
Guis|bor|ough
guise
guiser
gui|tar
gui|tar|ist

Gu|ja|rat
state in India
  ⚠Gujrat

Gu|ja|rati

Guj|rat
city in Pakistan
  ⚠Gujarat

gulag
Gul|ben|kian
gulch
  △ gul|ches
gulden *see*
  guilder
gulf
gull
  VERB
  △ gulls
  △ gulled
  △ gull|ing
gul|let
gul|li|bil|ity

gul|lible
Gul|li|ver's
Trav|els
gully
  △ gul|lies
gulp
  VERB
  △ gulps
  △ gulped
  △ gulp|ing
gum
  VERB
  △ gums
  △ gummed
  △ gum|ming
gumbo
gum|boil
gum|boot
gum|drop
gummy
  △ gum|mier
  △ gum|mi|est
gump|tion
gum|shoe
gun
  VERB
  △ guns
  △ gunned
  △ gun|ning
gun|boat
gun|fire
gunge
  VERB
  △ gun|ges
  △ gunged
  △ gun|ging
gung-ho
gungy
  △ gun|gier
  △ gun|gi|est
gunk
gun|man
  △ gun|men
gun|metal

gunnel *see*
  gunwale
gun|ner
gun|nery
gunny
  △ gun|nies
gun|point
gun|pow|der
gun|run|ner
gun|run|ning
gun|shot
gun|slinger
gun|wale
guppy
  △ gup|pies
gurd|wara
gur|gle
  VERB
  △ gur|gles
  △ gur|gled
  △ gurg|ling
Gurkha
Gurk|hali
Gur|ney
guru
gush
  NOUN
  △ gushes
  VERB
  △ gushes
  △ gushed

△ gush|ing
gusher
gush|ing
gus|set
gust
  VERB
  △ gusts
  △ gus|ted
  △ gust|ing
gusto
gusty
  △ gus|tier
  △ gus|ti|est
gut
  VERB
  △ guts
  △ gut|ted
  △ gut|ting
Gu|ten|berg
Guth|rie
gut|less
gutsy
  △ gut|sier
  △ gut|si|est
gutta-per|cha
gut|ted
gut|ter
  VERB
  △ gut|ters
  △ gut|tered
  △ gut|ter|ing

gut|ter|ing
gut|ter|snipe
gut|tural
gut|tur|ally
guv
Guy
guy
  VERB
  △ guys
  △ guyed
  △ guy|ing
Guy|ana
guz|zle
  △ guz|zles
  △ guz|zled
  △ guz|zling
guz|zler
Gwen|do|len
Gwent
Gwyn
Gwyn|edd
Gwyn|eth
gybe
  VERB
  △ gybes
  △ gybed
  △ gy|bing
gym
gym|khana
gym|na|sium
  △ gym|na|si|ums

  or gym|na|sia
gym|nast
gym|nas|tic
gym|nas|tics
gy|nae|cium
gy|nae|co|lo|gi|
  cal
gy|nae|colo|gist
gy|nae|col|ogy
gyp
  VERB
  △ gyps
  △ gypped
  △ gyp|ping
gyp|soph|ila
gyp|sum
Gypsy
  △ Gyp|sies
gy|rate
  △ gy|rates
  △ gy|ra|ted
  △ gy|ra|ting
gy|ra|tion
gyre
gyr|fal|con
gy|ro|com|pass
  △ gy|ro|com|pas|
  ses
gy|ro|scope
gy|ro|scopic

H

ha
Ha|bak|kuk
hab|eas cor|pus
  △ hab|eas cor|
    puses
hab|er|da|sher
hab|er|dash|ery
  △ hab|er|dash|
    er|ies
habit
ha|bit|ab|il|ity
hab|it|able
hab|itat
ha|bi|ta|tion
habit-form|ing
ha|bit|ual
ha|bi|tu|ally
ha|bi|tu|ate
  △ ha|bi|tu|ates
  △ ha|bi|tu|ated
  △ ha|bi|tu|ating
ha|bi|tu|ation
ha|bi|tué
Habs|burg
ha|chure
ha|ci|enda
hack
  VERB
  △ hacks
  △ hacked
  △ hack|ing
hacker
hack|ing
hackles
hack|ney
hack|neyed
hack|saw
had
Had|ding|ton
had|dock
  sing. and pl.
Hades

Had|ith
hadj see hajj
hadji see hajji
hadn't
Ha|drian
had|ron
hadst
haem
haem|at|ite
hae|ma|tol|ogy
hae|ma|turia
hae|mo|di|aly|sis
hae|mo|glo|bin
hae|mo|ly|sis
hae|mo|phi|lia
hae|mo|phil|iac
hae|mor|rhage
  VERB
  △ hae|mor|
    rhages
  △ hae|mor|
    rhaged
  △ hae|mor|rha|
    ging
hae|mor|rhoid
haf|nium
haft
hag
hag|fish
  sing. and pl.
Hag|gai
Hag|gard
hag|gard
hag|gis
  △ hag|gises
hag|gish
hag|gle
  VERB
  △ hag|gles
  △ hag|gled
  △ hag|gling
hag|gler
Hagia So|phia
ha|gi|og|ra|pher

ha|gi|og|ra|phy
ha|gi|ol|ogy
  △ ha|gi|ol|ogies
hag-rid|den
Hague, The
ha-ha
Haig
haiku
  sing. and pl.

> hail
> *frozen rain; fall*
> *as or like this;*
> *shout to; greet*
> VERB
>   △ hails
>   △ hailed
>   △ hail|ing
>   ⚠ hale

Haile Se|las|sie
hail-fel|low-
  well-met
Hail|sham
hail|stone
hail|storm
Hair

> hair
> *growth on head*
> *etc*
>   ⚠ hare

hair|brush
  △ hair|bru|shes
hair|cut
hairdo
hair|dres|ser
hair|dres|sing
hair|drier
hair|dryer
hair-grip
hairi|ness
hair|less
hair|line
hair|net

hair-piece
hair|pin
hair-rais|ing
hair's-breadth
hair-slide
hair-split|ting
hair|spray
hair-spring
hair|style
hairy
  △ hair|ier
  △ hairi|est
Haiti
Hajj
  the pilgrimage to
  Mecca
hajj
  a pilgrim's trip
  to Mecca
  △ haj|jes
hajji
  one who has
  made the
  pilgrimage to
  Mecca
hake
  △ hakes *or* hake
Hak|luyt
Ha|lak|hah
halal
ha|la|tion
hal|berd
hal|cyon

> hale
> *strong and healthy*
>   ⚠ hail

half
  NOUN
  all senses
  △ halves
  all senses except
  maths
  △ halfs

half-and-half
half-a-crown
half|back
half-baked
half-board
half-breed
half-bro|ther
half-caste
half-cell
half-crown
half-cut
half-day
half-hearted
half-heart|edly
half-heart|ed|
  ness
half-hitch
  △ half-hit|ches
half-hour
half-hourly
half-life
  △ half-lives
half-light
half-mara|thon
half-moon
half|penny
  △ half|pen|nies
  or half|pence
half|pen|ny|
  worth
half-price
half-sis|ter
half-term
half-tim|bered
half-time
half-tone
half-track
half-truth
half|way
half|wit
half|wit|ted
half|wit|tedly
half-yearly
ha|li|but

sing. and pl.
ha|lide
Ha|li|fax
hal|ite
ha|li|to|sis
Hall
hall

Halle
German town
⚠Hallé

Hallé
conductor
⚠Halle

hallelujah *see*
  alleluia
Halles, Les
Hal|ley
hal|liard
hall|mark
VERB
  △ hall|marks
  △ hall|marked
  △ hall|mark|ing

hallo
greeting see
hello
⚠hallow

hal|loo
VERB
  △ hal|loos
  △ hal|looed
  △ hal|loo|ing

hal|low
saint; make or
consider holy
VERB
  △ hal|lows
  △ hal|lowed
  △ hal|low|ing
  ⚠hallo

hal|lowed
Hal|low|e'en
hall|stand
hal|lu|cin|ate
  △ hal|lu|cin|ates
  △ hal|lu|cin|ated
  △ hal|lu|cin|
  ating
hal|lu|cin|ation
hal|lu|cin|atory
hal|lu|cin|ogen
hal|lu|ci|no|
  genic
hall|way
halma
halo
NOUN
  △ halos *or* ha|
  loes
VERB
  △ ha|loes
  △ ha|loed
  △ ha|lo|ing
ha|lo|gen
ha|lo|gen|ation
ha|lo|phyte
Hals
halt
VERB
  △ halts
  △ hal|ted
  △ halt|ing
hal|ter
VERB
  △ hal|ters
  △ hal|tered
  △ hal|ter|ing
hal|ter|neck
halt|ing
halt|ingly
halva
halve
  △ halves
  △ halved

  △ halv|ing
hal|yard
Ham
ham
VERB
  △ hams
  △ hammed
  △ ham|ming

ha|ma|dryad
nymph; cobra
⚠hamadryas

ha|ma|dryas
baboon
⚠hamadryad

Ham|burg
ham|bur|ger
ham-fis|ted
ham-han|ded
Ham|il|ton
Ha|mish
Ham|itic
ham|let
Ham|let, Prince
of Den|mark
Ham|mar|skjo|ld
ham|mer
VERB
  △ ham|mers
  △ ham|mered
  △ ham|mer|ing
ham|mer-beam
ham|mer|head
ham|mer|ing
'Ham|mer|kla|
  vier' Son|ata
Ham|mer|stein
ham|mer-toe
Ham|mett
ham|mock
Ham|mond
Hamp|den
ham|per

VERB
△ ham|pers
△ ham|pered
△ ham|per|ing
Hamp|shire
Hamp|ton
ham|ster
ham|string
  VERB
  △ ham|strings
  △ ham|stringed
    or ham|strung
  △ ham|string|ing
hand
  VERB
  △ hands
  △ han|ded
  △ hand|ing
hand|bag
hand|ball
hand|bill
hand|book
hand|brake
hand|cart
hand|clap
hand|craf|ted
hand|cuff
  VERB
  △ hand|cuffs
  △ hand|cuffed
  △ hand|cuf|fing
Han|del
hand|ful
hand-gren|ade
hand|gun
han|di|cap
  VERB
  △ han|di|caps
  △ han|di|capped
  △ han|di|cap|
    ping
han|di|capped
han|di|craft
hand|ily

han|di|ness
han|di|work
hand|ker|chief
  △ hand|ker|
    chiefs *or*
    hand|ker|
    chieves
han|dle
  VERB
  △ han|dles
  △ han|dled
  △ hand|ling
handle|bar
hand|ler
hand|less
Hand|ley
hand|ling

┌─────────────────────┐
│ hand|made   │
│ *made by hand*   │
│ ⚠ handmaid   │
└─────────────────────┘

┌─────────────────────┐
│ hand|maid   │
│ *female servant*   │
│ ⚠ handmade   │
└─────────────────────┘

hand|mai|den
hand-me-down
hand|out
hand|over
hand-pick
  △ hand-picks
  △ hand-picked
  △ hand-pick|ing
hand-picked
hand|rail
hand|saw
hand|set
hand|shake
hands-off

┌─────────────────────┐
│ hand|some   │
│ *good-looking*   │
│ ⚠ hansom   │
└─────────────────────┘

hand|somely

hand|some|ness
hands-on
hand|spring
hand|stand
hand-to-hand
hand|wri|ting
hand|writ|ten
handy
  △ han|dier
  △ han|di|est
han|dy|man
  △ han|dy|men
hang
  VERB
  △ hangs
  kill by rope;
  curse
  △ hanged
  other senses
  △ hung
  △ hang|ing

┌─────────────────────┐
│ hangar   │
│ *for aircraft*   │
│ ⚠ hanger   │
└─────────────────────┘

hang|dog

┌─────────────────────┐
│ hanger   │
│ *for clothes*   │
│ ⚠ hangar   │
└─────────────────────┘

hanger-on
  △ hang|ers-on
hang-gli|der
hang-gli|ding
hang|ing
hang|man
  △ hang|men
hang|nail
hang-out
hang|over
hang-up
hank
han|ker
  △ han|kers

△ han|kered
△ han|ker|ing
han|ker|ing
han|kie
hanky
  △ han|kies
hanky-panky
Han|nah
Han|ni|bal
Hanoi
Han|over
Ha|no|ver|ian
Han|sard
Han|sel and
  Gretel (Hän|
  sel und Gre|
  tel)

┌─────────────────────┐
│ han|som   │
│ *horse-cab*   │
│ ⚠ handsome   │
└─────────────────────┘

Han|uk|kah
ha'penny *see*
  halfpenny
hap|haz|ard
hap|haz|ardly
hap|less
hap|loid
hap'orth *see*
  halfpennyworth
hap|pen
  VERB
  △ hap|pens
  △ hap|pened
  △ hap|pen|ing
hap|pen|ing
hap|pily
hap|pi|ness
happy
  △ hap|pier
  △ hap|pi|est
happy-go-lucky
hara-kiri
ha|rangue

VERB
△ ha|rangues
△ ha|rangued
△ ha|ran|guing
Har|are
har|ass
△ har|as|ses
△ har|assed
△ har|as|sing
har|assed
har|ass|ment
har|bin|ger
har|bour
VERB
△ har|bours
△ har|boured
△ har|bour|ing
hard
ADJ.
△ har|der
△ hard|est
hard-and-fast
hard|back
hard-bit|ten
hard|board
hard-boiled
hard|core
NOUN
hard-core
ADJ.
har|den
△ hard|ens
△ hard|ened
△ hard|en|ing
hard|ened
hard-headed
hard-hearted
hard-heart|edly
hard-heart|ed|ness
hard-hit|ting
Har|di|ca|nute

Har|die

politician
⚠Hardy

har|di|hood
har|di|ness
hard|line
ADJ.
hard line
NOUN
hard|li|ner
hardly
hard|ness
hard-nosed
hard-on
hard|pad
hard-pressed
hard-pushed
hard|ship
hard|tack
hard|top
hard|ware
hard-wear|ing
hard-wired
hard|wood

Hardy
writer
⚠Hardie

hardy
△ har|dier
△ har|di|est
Hare

hare
sort of rabbit;
run fast
VERB
△ hares
△ hared
△ har|ing
⚠hair

hare|bell
hare-brained
Hare Krishna

hare-lipped
harem
Hare|wood
ha|ri|cot
hark
△ harks
△ harked
△ hark|ing
harken *see*
hearken
Har|lech
Har|lem
har|le|quin
Har|ley
har|lot
har|lotry
Har|low
harm
VERB
△ harms
△ harmed
△ harm|ing
harm|ful
harm|fully
harm|ful|ness
harm|less
harm|lessly
harm|less|ness
har|monic
har|mon|ica
har|mon|ics
har|mo|ni|ous
har|mo|ni|ously
har|mo|ni|ous|
ness
har|mo|nium
har|mon|iza|tion
har|mon|ize
△ har|mon|izes
△ har|mon|ized
△ har|mon|izing
har|mony
△ har|mon|ies
Harms|worth

har|ness
NOUN
△ har|nes|ses
VERB
△ har|nes|ses
△ har|nessed
△ har|nes|sing
Har|old
harp
VERB
△ harps
△ harped
△ harp|ing
harp|ist
har|poon
VERB
△ har|poons
△ har|pooned
△ har|poon|ing
harp|si|chord
Harpy
mythological
creature
△ Har|pies
harpy
nasty woman
△ har|pies
har|ri|dan
har|rier
Har|riet
Har|ris
Har|ri|son
Har|ro|gate
har|row
VERB
△ har|rows
△ har|rowed
△ har|row|ing
har|row|ing
Harry
harry
△ har|ries
△ har|ried
△ har|ry|ing

harsh
△ har|sher
△ harsh|est
harshly
harsh|ness

hart
male deer
⚠ heart

Harte
har|te|beest

Hart|ford
American city
⚠ Hertford

Hart|le|pool
Hart|ley
Hart|nell
harum-scarum
ha|ru|spex
△ ha|ru|spi|ces
Har|vard
har|vest
  VERB
△ har|vests
△ har|ves|ted
△ har|vest|ing
har|ves|ter
har|vest|man
△ har|vest|men
Har|wich
has
has-been
Has|dru|bal
hash
  NOUN
△ ha|shes
  VERB
△ ha|shes
△ hashed
△ hash|ing
hash|ish
Hašek
Hasle|mere

Hasid
△ Ha|si|dim
Has|id|ism
hasn't
hasp
has|sle
  VERB
△ has|sles
△ has|sled
△ has|sling
has|sock
hast
haste
has|ten
△ has|tens
△ has|tened
△ has|ten|ing
hast|ily
hasti|ness
Hast|ings
hasty
△ hast|ier
△ hasti|est
hat
hat|band
hat|box
△ hat|boxes
hatch
  NOUN
△ hat|ches
  VERB
△ hat|ches
△ hatched
△ hatch|ing
hatch|back
hatch|ery
△ hatch|er|ies
hat|chet
hat|chet-faced
hatch|ing
hatch|way
hate
  VERB
△ hates

△ hated
△ ha|ting
hate|ful
hate|fully
hate|ful|ness
hat|pin
hat|red
hat|stand
hat|ter
Hat|ters|ley
hau|berk
Haughey
haugh|tily
haugh|ti|ness
haughty
△ haugh|tier
△ haugh|ti|est
haul
  VERB
△ hauls
△ hauled
△ haul|ing
haul|age
haul|ier
haulm
haunch
△ haun|ches
haunt
  VERB
△ haunts
△ haun|ted
△ haunt|ing
haun|ted
haunt|ing
haunt|ingly
Haupt|mann
Hauss|mann
haut|boy
haute couture
haute cuisine
haut|eur
Ha|vana
have

  VERB
△ has
△ had
△ hav|ing
Havel
haven
haven't
ha|ver|sack
havoc
haw
  VERB
△ haws
△ hawed
△ haw|ing
Ha|waii
Ha|wai|ian
haw|finch
△ haw|fin|ches
hawk
  VERB
△ hawks
△ hawked
△ hawk|ing
haw|ker
hawk-eyed
Hawk|ing
hawk|ish
hawk|ish|ness
Hawks
hawk|weed
haw|ser
haw|thorn
Haw|thorne
hay
hay|cock
Haydn
Hay Fever
hay|fork
Hay|ley
hay|rick
hay|stack
Hay Wain, The
hay|wire
haz|ard

VERB
△ haz|ards
△ haz|ar|ded
△ haz|ard|ing
haz|ard|ous
haz|ard|ously
haz|ard|ous|ness
haze
VERB
△ hazes
△ hazed
△ ha|zing
Hazel
hazel
ha|zel|nut
ha|zily
ha|zi|ness
Haz|litt
hazy
△ ha|zier
△ ha|zi|est
H-bomb
he
head
NOUN
unit
△ head
other senses
△ heads
VERB
△ heads
△ headed
△ head|ing
head|ache
head|achy
head|band
head|banger
head|board
head|dress
△ head|dres|ses
headed
header
head|first
head|gear

head|hun|ter
head|hunt|ing
head|ing
Head|ing|ley
head|lamp
head|land
head|less
head|light
head|line
head|long
head|man
△ head|men
head|mas|ter
head|mis|tress
△ head|mis|tres|
ses
head-on
head|phone
head|quar|ters
head|rest
head|room
head|scarf
△ head|scarves
head|set
head|ship
head|shrin|ker
head|stall
head|stone
head|strong
head|wa|ters
head|way
head|wind
head|word
heady
△ head|ier
△ headi|est

heal
make well
△ heals
△ healed
△ heal|ing
⚠ heel

hea|ler

Hea|ley
heal|ing
health
health|ful
health|ily
health|iness
healthy
△ health|ier
△ healthi|est
Hea|ney
heap
VERB
△ heaps
△ heaped
△ heap|ing
heaped
heaps

hear
perceive sounds
△ hears
△ heard
△ hear|ing
⚠ here

hearer
hear|ing
hearken
△ hark|ens
△ hark|ened
△ hark|en|ing
hear|say
hearse

heart
*organ; centre of
emotions*
⚠ hart

heart|ache
heart|beat
heart|break
*Heart|break
House*
heart|break|ing
heart|bro|ken

heart|burn
hearten
△ heart|ens
△ heart|ened
△ heart|en|ing
heart|en|ing
heart|en|ingly
heart|felt
hearth
hearth|rug
heart|ily
hearti|ness
heart|land
heart|less
heart|lessly
heart|less|ness
*Heart of Dark|
ness, The
Heart of Mid|lo|
thian, The
Heart of the
Mat|ter, The*
heart-rend|ing
heart-rend|ingly
heart-search|ing
hearts|ease
heart|sick
heart|strings
heart-throb
heart-to-heart
heart-warm|ing
heart|wood
hearty
△ heart|ier
△ hearti|est
heat
VERB
△ heats
△ hea|ted
△ heat|ing
hea|ted
heat|edly
heat|ed|ness
hea|ter

Heath
heath
hea|then
hea|then|ish
Heather
heather
Heath-Rob|in|
  son
heat|ing
heat-seek|ing
heat|stroke
heat|wave
heave
  VERB
  △ heaves
  of ship
  △ hove
  other senses
  △ heaved
  △ hea|ving
heaven
heaven|li|ness
heavenly
heavens
heaven-sent
heavily
heavi|ness
Heavi|side
heavy
  NOUN
  △ heavies
  ADJ
  △ heavier
  △ heavi|est
heavy-duty
heavy-han|ded
heavy-hand|edly
heavy-hand|ed|
  ness
heavy-hearted
heavy|weight
heb|do|ma|dal
heb|do|mad|ally
Hebe

He|braic
He|brew
He|brews, Let|
  ter to the
Heb|ri|des
'Heb|ri|des'
  Over|ture
He|bron
Hec|ate
heck
heckle
  △ heckles
  △ heckled
  △ heck|ling
heck|ler
hec|tare
hec|tic
hec|tic|ally
Hec|tor
hec|tor
  VERB
  △ hec|tors
  △ hec|tored
  △ hec|tor|ing
Hec|uba
he'd
Hedda Gab|ler
hedge
  VERB
  △ hed|ges
  △ hedged
  △ hed|ging
hedge|hog
hedge-hop
  △ hedge-hops
  △ hedge-hopped
  △ hedge-hop|
    ping
hedge|row
hedge-spar|row
he|don|ism
he|don|ist
he|don|is|tic
hee|bie-jee|bies

heed
  VERB
  △ heeds
  △ hee|ded
  △ heed|ing
heed|ful
heed|less
heed|lessly
heed|less|ness
hee-haw
  VERB
  △ hee-haws
  △ hee-hawed
  △ hee-haw|ing

> heel
> *back of foot,
> sock, etc; nasty
> person; touch,
> kick, or press in
> with heel; follow
> at someone's
> heels; lean over*
> VERB
> △ heels
> △ heeled
> △ heel|ing
> ⚠ heal

heel|ball
Hee|nan
hef|tily
hef|ti|ness
hefty
  △ hef|tier
  △ hef|ti|est
Hegel
He|geli|an|ism
he|gem|ony
  △ he|gem|on|ies
He|gira
Hei|deg|ger
Hei|del|berg
heifer
Hei|fetz

height
heigh|ten
  △ heigh|tens
  △ heigh|tened
  △ heigh|ten|ing
Heine
hein|ous
hein|ously
hein|ous|ness
Heinz
heir
heir|ess
  △ heir|es|ses
heir|loom
heist
Hejira *see*
  Hegira
held
*Hel|den|leben, Ein
  (A Hero's Life)*
Helen
Helga
he|li|cal
heli|cop|ter
Hel|igo|land
he|lio|cen|tric
he|lio|graph
He|lios
he|lio|sphere
he|lio|trope
heli|pad
heli|port
he|lium
helix
  △ he|li|ces *or* he|
    lixes
hell
he'll
hell-bent
hel|le|bore
Hel|lene
Hel|lenic
Hel|len|ism
Hel|len|ist

Hel|len|is|tic
Hel|len|iza|tion
Hel|ler
Hel|les|pont
hell-fire
hell|ish
hell|ishly
hell|ish|ness
hello
helm
hel|met
Helm|holtz
helms|man
  △ helms|men
helot
help
  VERB
  △ helps
  △ helped
  △ help|ing
helper
help|ful
help|fully
help|ful|ness
help|ing
help|less
help|lessly
help|less|ness
Help|mann
help|mate
Hel|sinki
hel|ter-skel|ter
Hel|vel|lyn
hem
  VERB
  △ hems
  △ hemmed
  △ hem|ming
he-man
  △ he-men
hematite *see*
  haematite
Hemel Hemp|
  stead

Hem|ing|way
Hem|ip|tera
hem|ip|ter|ous
hemi|sphere
hemi|spher|ical
hem|line
hem|lock
hemp
hem|stitch
  △ hem|stit|ches
hen
hen|bane
hence
hence|forth
hence|for|ward
hench|man
  △ hench|men
Hen|drix
henge
Hen|gist
Hen|ley-on-
  Thames
henna
  VERB
  △ hen|nas
  △ hen|naed
  △ hen|na|ing
hen|pecked
Hen|ri|etta
Henry
  △ Hen|ries
henry
  △ hen|ries
Henry IV,
  Parts I and II
Hens|lowe
hep|arin
hep|atic
hepa|ti|tis
Hep|burn
Hep|ple|white
hep|ta|gon
hep|ta|gonal
hept|ar|chy

△ hept|ar|chies
hept|ath|lon
Hep|worth
her
Hera
Heracles *see*
  Hercules
Hera|cli|tus
her|ald
  VERB
  △ her|alds
  △ her|al|ded
  △ her|ald|ing
her|al|dic
her|al|dry
herb
her|ba|ceous
herb|age
her|bal
her|bal|ism
her|bal|ist
her|bar|ium
  △ her|baria
Her|bert
her|bi|cide
her|bi|vore
her|bi|vor|ous
Her|cu|la|neum
her|cu|lean
Her|cu|les
herd
  VERB
  △ herds
  △ her|ded
  △ herd|ing
herds|man
  △ herds|men

> here
> *this place; at*
> *this place; call*
> *for attention*
> ⚠ hear

here|abouts

here|af|ter
here|by
her|ed|it|able
her|ed|it|ar|ily
her|ed|it|ary
her|ed|ity
  △ her|ed|it|ies
He|re|ford
here|in
here|in|af|ter
hereof
her|esy
  △ her|es|ies
her|etic
her|et|ical
hereto
here|to|fore
here|upon
He|re|ward
here|with
her|it|able
her|it|age
her|ma|phro|dite
her|ma|phro|
  ditic
her|me|neut|ics
Her|mes
her|metic
her|met|ic|ally
her|mit
Her|mit|age
  St Petersburg
  palace and art
  gallery
her|mit|age
  hermit's dwelling
her|nia
hero
  △ her|oes
Herod
He|rod|otus
he|roic
he|ro|ic|ally

her|oin
drug
⚠ heroine

he|ro|ine
brave etc woman
⚠ heroin

he|ro|ism
heron
hero-wor|ship
  VERB
  △ hero-wor|
    ships
  △ hero-wor|
    shipped
  △ hero-wor|
    ship|ping
her|pes
Her|rick
her|ring
  △ her|ring *or*
    her|rings
her|ring|bone
hers
Her|schel
her|self

Hert|ford
English town
⚠ Hartford

Hert|ford|shire
hertz
  sing. and pl.
Her|zog
film director
Her|zog
novel
he's
Hes|el|tine
He|siod
hes|it|ance
hes|it|ancy
hes|it|ant

hes|it|antly
hes|it|ate
  △ hes|it|ates
  △ hes|it|ated
  △ hes|it|ating
he|si|ta|tion
Hes|per|ides

Hess
*pianist; Nazi
politician*
⚠ Hesse

Hesse
novelist
⚠ Hess

hes|sian
Hes|ter
Hes|ton
het
het|ero|dox
het|ero|gen|eity
het|ero|ge|ne|ous
het|ero|mor|phic
het|ero|mor|
  phism
het|ero|sex|ual
het|ero|sexual|
  ity
het|ero|tro|phic
het|ero|zy|gous
heur|is|tic
heur|is|tic|ally

hew
cut
  △ hews
  △ hewed
  △ hew|ing
  △ hewn
  ⚠ hue

hexa|deci|mal
hexa|gon
hex|ag|onal

hexa|gram
hex|am|eter
hex|ane
hex|ose
hey
hey|day
Hey|er|dahl
Hey|sel
Hezbollah *see*
  Hizbollah
hi
hi|atus
  △ hi|atuses
*Hia|wa|tha,
  Song of*
hi|ber|nate
  △ hi|ber|nates
  △ hi|ber|na|ted
  △ hi|ber|na|ting
hi|ber|na|tion
Hi|ber|nia
Hi|ber|nian
hi|bis|cus
  △ hi|bis|cuses
hiccough *see*
  hiccup
hic|cup
  VERB
  △ hic|cups
  △ hic|cuped
  △ hic|cup|ing
hick
hick|ory
  △ hick|or|ies
hid|den
hide
  VERB
  △ hides
  △ hid
  △ hi|ding
  △ hid|den
hide-and-seek
hide|away
hide|bound

hid|eous
hid|eously
hid|eous|ness
hide|out
hi|ding
hi|ding-place
hie
  △ hies
  △ hied
  △ hie|ing *or*
    hying
hi|er|ar|chi|cal
hi|er|archy
  △ hi|er|ar|chies
hi|ero|glyph
hi|ero|gly|phic
hi|ero|glyph|ics
hi-fi
higgledy-
  piggledy
high
  △ higher
  △ high|est
high|ball
high-born
high|brow
high-chair
high-class
high-defi|ni|tion
Higher
  NOUN
  Scottish exam
higher
  ADJ.
  *further up;
  superior*
high-falu|tin
high-five
high-flier
high-flown
high-flyer
high-fly|ing
high-han|ded
high-hand|edly

high-hand|ed|
ness
highjack *see*
hijack

High|land
*Scottish
administrative
region*
⚠highland
⚠Highlands,
the

high|land
*mountainous
area; belonging
to this*
⚠Highland
⚠Highlands,
the

High|lan|der
*dweller in the
Highlands*
⚠highlander

high|lan|der
highland dweller
⚠Highlander

High|lands, the
*mountainous
area of N and
W Scotland*
⚠Highland
⚠highland

high-level
high|light
VERB
△ high|lights
△ high|ligh|ted
△ high|light|ing
high|ligh|ter
highly

highly-strung
high-minded
high-mind|ed|
ness
High|ness
*title of royalty
etc*
△ High|nes|ses
high|ness
being high
High Noon
high-octane
high-pitched
high-powered
high-pres|sure
high-rise
high-risk
High|smith
high-sound|ing
high-spir|ited
hi-tech
high-ten|sion
high|way
High|way Code
high|way|man
△ high|way|men
High Wy|
combe
hi|jack
△ hi|jacks
△ hi|jacked
△ hi|jack|ing
hi|jacker
hi|jack|ing
hike
VERB
△ hikes
△ hiked
△ hi|king
hiker
hi|lari|ous
hi|lari|ously
hi|lari|ous|ness
hi|lar|ity

Hil|ary
*Christian name;
French bishop*
⚠Hillary

Hilda
Hill
hill

Hil|lary
mountaineer
⚠Hilary

hill|billy
△ hill|bil|lies
hil|li|ness
hil|lock
Hills|bor|ough
hill|side
hilly
△ hil|lier
△ hil|li|est
hilt
Hil|ton
hilum
△ hila
Hil|ver|sum
him
Hi|ma|layas
Him|mler
him|self
hind
Hin|de|mith
Hin|den|burg
hin|der
VERB
△ hin|ders
△ hin|dered
△ hin|der|ing
Hindi
Hind|lish
hind|most
hind|quar|ters
hin|drance
hind|sight

Hindu
Hin|du|ism
Hin|du|stani
hinge
VERB
△ hin|ges
△ hinged
△ hin|ging
hinged
Hinglish *see*
Hindlish
Hink|ley
hinny
△ hin|nies
hint
VERB
△ hints
△ hin|ted
△ hint|ing
hin|ter|land
hip
ADJ.
△ hip|per
△ hip|pest
hip-hop
hippie *see* hippy
hippo
hip|po|cam|pus
△ hip|po|campi
Hip|poc|ra|tes
hip|po|drome
hip|po|pot|amus
△ hip|po|pot|am|
uses *or* hip|
po|pot|ami
hippy
△ hip|pies
hip|sters
hi|ra|gana
hire
VERB
△ hires
△ hired
△ hir|ing

hire|ling
Hire|ling, The
hire-pur|chase
Hi|ro|hito
Hi|ro|shima *or*
  Hi|rosh|ima
  according to
  pronunciation
hir|sute
his
His|panic
hiss
  NOUN
  △ his|ses
  VERB
  △ his|ses
  △ hissed
  △ hiss|ing
his|ta|mine
his|ti|dine
his|to|gram
his|tol|ogy
his|tone
his|tor|ian
his|tori|ated
his|toric
his|tor|ical
his|tor|ic|ally
his|tori|cism
his|tori|city
his|tori|og|ra|
  pher
his|tori|og|ra|
  phy
his|tory
  △ his|tor|ies
his|tri|onic
his|tri|on|ic|ally
hit
  VERB
  △ hits
  △ hit
  △ hit|ting
hit-and-miss

hit-and-run
hitch
  NOUN
  △ hit|ches
  VERB
  △ hit|ches
  △ hitched
  △ hitch|ing
Hitch|cock
hitch|hike
  △ hitch|hikes
  △ hitch|hiked
  △ hitch|hi|king
hitch|hi|ker
hi-tech
hi|ther
hi|therto
Hit|ler
hit-or-miss
Hit|tite
hive
Hiz|bol|lah

┌─────────────────┐
│ hoar   │
│   *whitish*   │
│   ⚠ whore   │
└─────────────────┘

┌─────────────────┐
│ hoard   │
│   *secret store;*│
│   *make this*   │
│   VERB   │
│   △ hoards   │
│   △ hoar|ded   │
│   △ hoard|ing   │
│   ⚠ horde   │
└─────────────────┘

hoar|der
hoard|ing
hoar-frost
hoari|ness

┌─────────────────┐
│ hoarse   │
│   *having a rough*│
│   *voice*   │
│   ⚠ horse   │
└─────────────────┘

hoarsely
hoarse|ness
hoary
  △ hoar|ier
  △ hoari|est
hoax
  NOUN
  △ hoaxes
  VERB
  △ hoaxes
  △ hoaxed
  △ hoax|ing
hoaxer
hob
Ho|bart
Hob|bema
Hobbes
Hob|bit, The
hob|ble
  △ hob|bles
  △ hob|bled
  △ hob|bling
hobby
  △ hob|bies
hobby-horse
hob|gob|lin
hob|nail
hob|nailed
hob|nob
  △ hob|nobs
  △ hob|nobbed
  △ hob|nob|bing
hobo
  △ hobos *or* ho|
    boes
Hob|son
Hoch|huth
Ho Chi Minh
hock
  VERB
  △ hocks
  △ hocked
  △ hock|ing
hockey

Hock|ney
hocus-pocus
hod
hodge|podge
Hodja *see*
  Hoxha
hoe
  VERB
  △ hoes
  △ hoed
  △ hoe|ing
Hof|burg

┌─────────────────┐
│ Hoff|man   │
│   *film star*   │
│   ⚠ Hoffmann   │
└─────────────────┘

┌─────────────────┐
│ Hoff|mann   │
│   *writer and* │
│   *composer*   │
│   ⚠ Hoffman   │
└─────────────────┘

Hof|manns|thal
hog
  VERB
  △ hogs
  △ hogged
  △ hog|ging
Ho|garth
Hogg
Hog|ma|nay
hogs|head
hog|wash
hog|weed
Ho|hen|stau|fen
Ho|hen|zol|lern
hoi *see* hoy
hoick
  △ hoicks
  △ hoicked
  △ hoick|ing
hoi pol|loi
hoi|sin
hoist

VERB
△ hoists
△ hois|ted
△ hoist|ing
hoity-toity
hokum
Hol|bein
hold
  VERB
△ holds
△ held
△ hold|ing
hold|all
holder
Höl|der|lin
hold|ing
hold-up

> hole
>   *gap; difficult*
>   *situation;*
>   *mistake; make*
>   *or put into hole*
>   VERB
> △ holes
> △ holed
> △ ho|ling
>   ⚠ whole

hole-and-cor|
ner

> holey
>   *full of holes*
> △ ho|lier
> △ ho|li|est
>   ⚠ holy

Holi
Holi|day
holi|day
  VERB
△ holi|days
△ holi|dayed
△ holi|day|ing
holi|day|ma|ker

ho|lier-than-
thou
ho|lily
ho|li|ness
Hol|in|shed
hol|ism
hol|is|tic
hol|is|tic|ally
Hol|land
  country
hol|land
  cloth
hol|ler
  VERB
△ hol|lers
△ hol|lered
△ hol|ler|ing
hol|low
  VERB
△ hol|lows
△ hol|lowed
△ hol|low|ing
  ADJ.
△ hol|lower
△ hol|low|est
hol|low-eyed
hol|lowly
hol|low|ness
Holly
holly
△ hol|lies
hol|ly|hock
Hol|ly|wood
hol|mium
Holo|caust
  Nazi persecution
  of European
  Jews
holo|caust
  large-scale
  destruction
holo|gram
holo|graph

VERB
△ holo|graphs
△ holo|graphed
△ holo|graph|ing
ho|lo|gra|phic
ho|lo|graph|ic|
  ally
ho|log|ra|phy
holo|phrase
ho|lo|phy|tic
hols
Holst
hol|ster
holt

> holy
>   *sacred*
> △ ho|lier
> △ ho|li|est
>   ⚠ holey

Holy|head
hom|age
home
  VERB
△ homes
△ homed
△ hom|ing
home-com|ing
home|land
home|less
home|less|ness
home|li|ness
homely
△ home|lier
△ home|li|est
home-made
Home
hom|eo|path *or*
ho|meo|path
  according to
  pronunciation
hom|eo|pa|thic
  or ho|meo|pa|
thic

according to
pronunciation
hom|eo|pa|thic|
ally *or* ho|meo|
pa|thic|ally
  according to
  pronunciation
hom|eo|pa|thy
  or ho|meo|pa|
thy
  according to
  pronunciation
hom|eo|sta|sis *or*
ho|meo|sta|sis
  according to
  pronunciation
Homer
Ho|meric
home|sick
home|sick|ness
home|spun
home|stead
home|ward
home|work
hom|ici|dal
hom|icide
ho|mi|letic
hom|ily
△ hom|il|ies
ho|ming
hom|inid
hom|in|oid
hom|iny
homoeopath *see*
  homeopath
homoeopathic
  see
  homeopathic
homoeopathically
  see
  homeopathically
homoeopathy
  see
  homeopathy

homoeostasis *see*
   homeostasis
ho|mo|gen|eity
ho|mo|gen|eous
ho|mo|gen|
   eously
ho|mo|gen|ize
   △ ho|mo|gen|
      izes
   △ ho|mo|gen|
      ized
   △ ho|mo|gen|
      izing
ho|mo|gen|ous
ho|mo|geny
homo|graph
ho|moio|ther|
   mic
ho|mol|og|ous
ho|mol|ogy
hom|onym
ho|mo|pho|bia
ho|mo|phone
ho|mo|phony
ho|mo|sex|ual
ho|mo|sexu|al|
   ity
ho|mo|zy|go|sis
ho|mo|zy|gous
homy
   △ ho|mier
   △ ho|mi|est
Honda
Hon|duras
hone
   VERB
   △ hones
   △ honed
   △ ho|ning
Hon|ecker
Hon|eg|ger
hon|est
hon|estly
hon|esty

honey
hon|ey|comb
hon|eyed
hon|ey|moon
   VERB
   △ hon|ey|moons
   △ hon|ey|
      mooned
   △ hon|ey|moon|
      ing
hon|ey|mooner
hon|ey|suckle
Hong Kong
Honi|ara
honk
   VERB
   △ honks
   △ honked
   △ honk|ing
honky
   △ hon|kies
honky-tonk
Ho|no|lulu
hon|or|ar|ium
   △ hon|or|ari|ums
      or hon|or|aria
hon|or|ary
hon|or|ific
hon|our
   VERB
   △ hon|ours
   △ hon|oured
   △ hon|our|ing
hon|our|able
hon|our|ably
hon|our-bound
hooch
Hood
hood
hooded
hood|lum
hoo|doo
   VERB
   △ hoo|doos

   △ hoo|dooed
   △ hoo|doo|ing
hood|wink
   △ hood|winks
   △ hood|winked
   △ hood|wink|ing
hooey
hoof
   NOUN
   △ hoofs *or*
      hooves
   VERB
   △ hoofs
   △ hoofed
   △ hoof|ing
hoo-ha
hook
   VERB
   △ hooks
   △ hooked
   △ hook|ing
hookah
Hooke
hooked
hooker
hookey
Hook of Hol|
   land
hook-up
hook|worm
hoo|li|gan
hoo|li|gan|ism

┌─────────────────────┐
│ hoop   │
│ *large ring to*   │
│ *bind casks or as* │
│ *plaything; bind*   │
│ *with this*   │
│ VERB   │
│ △ hoops   │
│ △ hooped   │
│ △ hoop|ing   │
│ ⚠ whoop   │
└─────────────────────┘

hoop-la

hoo|poe
hoo|ray
hoot
   VERB
   △ hoots
   △ hoo|ted
   △ hoot|ing
hoo|ter
Hoo|ver
   NOUN
hoo|ver
   VERB
   △ hoo|vers
   △ hoo|vered
   △ hoo|ver|ing
hooves
hop
   VERB
   △ hops
   △ hopped
   △ hop|ping
Hope
hope
   VERB
   △ hopes
   △ hoped
   △ ho|ping
hope|ful
hope|fully
hope|ful|ness
hope|less
hope|lessly
hope|less|ness
Hop|kins
hop|per
hop|scotch
Hor|ace

┌─────────────────────┐
│ horde   │
│ *crowd*   │
│ ⚠ hoard   │
└─────────────────────┘

Hore-Beli|sha
hori|zon
ho|ri|zon|tal

ho|ri|zon|tally
hor|mo|nal
hor|mone
Hor|muz
horn
  VERB
  △ horns
  △ horned
  △ horn|ing
horn|beam
horn|bill
horn|blende
Horn|blower
horned
hor|net
horn|fels
horn|pipe
horn|tail
horny
  △ hor|nier
  △ hor|ni|est
ho|ro|lo|gi|cal
ho|rol|ogist
ho|rol|ogy
horo|scope
Horo|witz
hor|ren|dous
hor|ren|dously
hor|ren|dous|
  ness
hor|rible
hor|ribly
hor|rid
hor|ridly
hor|rid|ness
hor|ri|fic
hor|rif|ic|ally
hor|rify
  △ hor|ri|fies
  △ hor|ri|fied
  △ hor|ri|fy|ing
hor|ri|fy|ing
hor|ri|fy|ingly
hor|ror

hor|ror-stricken
hor|ror-struck
Horsa
hors d'oeuvre

| horse |
| *animal* |
| ⚠ hoarse |

horse|back
horse-box
  △ horse-boxes
horse|flesh
horse|fly
  △ horse|flies
horse|man
  △ horse|men
horse|man|ship
horse|play
horse|power
horse-racing
horse|rad|ish
  △ horse|rad|
  ishes
horse|shoe
horse|tail
horse-tra|ding
horse|whip
  VERB
  △ horse|whips
  △ horse|
  whipped
  △ horse|whip|
  ping
horse|wo|man
  △ horse|wo|men
*Horst-Wes|sel-
Lied*
horsy
  △ hor|sier
  △ hor|si|est
hor|ta|tive
hor|ta|tory
hor|ti|cul|tural
hor|ti|cul|ture

hor|ti|cul|tur|ist
Horus
hos|anna
hose
  VERB
  △ hoses
  △ hosed
  △ ho|sing
Hosea, Book of
hose|pipe
ho|sier
ho|si|ery
hos|pice
hos|pit|able
hos|pit|ably
hos|pi|tal
hos|pi|tal|ity
hos|pi|tal|iza|
  tion
hos|pit|al|ize
  △ hos|pit|al|izes
  △ hos|pit|al|ized
  △ hos|pit|al|izing
hos|pit|al|ler
host
  VERB
  △ hosts
  △ hosted
  △ host|ing
hosta
hos|tage
hos|tel
hos|telry
  △ hos|tel|ries
host|ess
  △ host|es|ses
hos|tile
hos|til|ity
  △ hos|til|it|ies
hot
  VERB
  △ hots
  △ hot|ted
  △ hot|ting

  ADJ.
  △ hot|ter
  △ hot|test
hot|bed
hot-blooded
hotch|potch
  △ hotch|pot|ches
hotel
ho|tel|ier
hot|foot
  VERB
  △ hot|foots
  △ hot|footed
  △ hot|foot|ing
hot|head
hot|headed
hot|head|ed|ness
hot|house
  VERB
  △ hot|hou|ses
  △ hot|housed
  △ hot|hous|ing
hotly
hot|plate
hot|pot
hot-tem|pered
Hot|ten|tot
hot|ting
hot-wire
  △ hot-wires
  △ hot-wired
  △ hot-wiring
Hou|dini
hoummos *see*
  hummus
houmus *see*
  hummus
hound
  VERB
  △ hounds
  △ houn|ded
  △ hound|ing
hour
hour|glass

△ hour|glas|ses
houri
hourly
house
 VERB
△ hou|ses
△ housed
△ hous|ing
house|boat
house|bound
house|breaker
house|break|ing
house|coat
house|fly
△ house|flies
house|hold
house|hol|der
house|kee|per
house|keep|ing
house|maid
house|man
△ house|men
house|mas|ter
house|mis|tress
△ house|mis|
 tres|ses
*House of Ber|
 narda Alba,
 The (La Casa
 de Ber|narda
 Alba)*
house-proud
house|top
house|train
△ house|trains
△ house|trained
△ house|train|
 ing
house-warm|ing
house|wife
△ house|wives
house|wifely
house|work
hous|ing

Hous|man
Hous|ton
Hove
hove
hovel
hover
 VERB
△ hov|ers
△ hov|ered
△ hov|er|ing
hov|er|craft
 sing. and pl.
hov|er|fly
△ hov|er|flies
how
How|ard
How|ards End
how|dah
howdy
Howe
how|ever
how|it|zer
howl
 VERB
△ howls
△ howled
△ howl|ing
how|ler
howl|ing
how|so|ever
how|zat
Hoxha
hoy
hoy|den
hoy|den|ish
Hoyle
hub
Hub|bard
hubble-bubble
hub|bub
hubby
△ hub|bies
hub-cap
hu|bris

huckle|berry
△ huckle|ber|
 ries
*Huckle\berry
 Finn, The Ad|
 ven|tures of*
huck|ster
Hud|ders|field
hud|dle
 VERB
△ hud|dles
△ hud|dled
△ hud|dling
Hud|dles|ton
Hud|son

| hue |
| colour; shout |
| ⚠ hew |

huff
 VERB
△ huffs
△ huffed
△ huf|fing
huf|fily
huf|fi|ness
huf|fish
huffy
△ huf|fier
△ huf|fi|est
hug
 VERB
△ hugs
△ hugged
△ hug|ging
huge
△ huger
△ hu|gest
hugely
huge|ness
hug|ger-mug|
 ger
Hugh
Hughes

Hu|gue|not
huh
*Huis clos (In
 Cam|era; Vi|
 cious Circle;
 No Exit)*
hula
hulk
hulk|ing
Hull
hull
 VERB
△ hulls
△ hulled
△ hul|ling
hul|la|ba|loo
hullo *see* hello
Hul|ton
hum
 VERB
△ hums
△ hummed
△ hum|ming

| human |
| belonging to |
| persons |
| ⚠ humane |

| hu|mane |
| kind; civilised |
| ⚠ human |

hu|manely
hu|mane|ness
hu|man|ism
hu|man|ist
hu|man|is|tic
hu|man|it|ar|ian
hu|man|it|ar|ian|
 ism
hu|man|ity
△ hu|man|it|ies
hu|man|iza|tion
hu|man|ize

△ hu|man|izes
△ hu|man|ized
△ hu|man|izing
hu|man|kind
hu|manly
hu|man|oid
Hum|ber
Hum|ber|side
hum|ble
VERB
△ hum|bles
△ hum|bled
△ hum|bling
ADJ.
△ hum|bler
△ hum|blest
humble|ness
hum|bly
hum|bug
hum|dinger
hum|drum
Hume
hu|meral

| hu|merus |
| *arm-bone* |
| △ hu|meri |
| ⚠ humorous |

humid
hu|mi|di|fier
hu|mid|ify
△ hu|mid|ifies
△ hu|mid|ified
△ hu|mid|ify|ing
hu|mid|ity
hu|mi|li|ate
△ hu|mi|li|ates
△ hu|mi|li|ated
△ hu|mi|li|ating
hu|mi|li|ating
hu|mi|li|atingly
hu|mi|li|ation
hu|mil|ity
hum|ming|bird

hum|mock

| hum|mus |
| *paste of* |
| *chickpeas and* |
| *tahini* |
| ⚠ humus |

hu|mon|gous
hu|mor|ist

| hu|mor|ous |
| *comic* |
| ⚠ humerus |

hu|mor|ously
hu|mor|ous|ness
hu|mour
VERB
△ hu|mours
△ hu|moured
△ hu|mour|ing
hu|mour|less
hump
VERB
△ humps
△ humped
△ hump|ing
hump|back
Hum|per|dinck
humph
Hum|phrey
Hum|phry Clin|
ker, The Ex|
pe|di|tion of
humungous *see*
humongous

| humus |
| *soil* |
| ⚠ hummus |

Hun
hunch
NOUN
△ hun|ches

VERB
△ hun|ches
△ hunched
△ hunch|ing
hunch|back
hunch|backed
Hunch|back of
Notre Dame,
The
hun|dred
after a number
△ hun|dred
other uses
△ hun|dreds
hun|dred|fold
hun|dredth
hun|dred|weight
after a number
△ hun|dred|
weight
other uses
△ hun|dred|
weights
hung
Hun|gar|ian
Hun|gary
hun|ger
VERB
△ hun|gers
△ hun|gered
△ hun|ger|ing
hun|grily
hun|gri|ness
hun|gry
△ hun|grier
△ hun|gri|est
hunk
hunky
△ hun|kier
△ hun|ki|est
hunky-dory
Hunt
hunt

VERB
△ hunts
△ hun|ted
△ hunt|ing
hun|ter
Hun|ters|ton
hunt|ing
Hun|ting|don
Hun|ting|don|
shire
Hunt
hunt|ress
△ hunt|res|ses
hunts|man
△ hunts|men
Hurd
hur|dle
VERB
△ hur|dles
△ hur|dled
△ hurd|ling
hurd|ler
hurd|ling
hurdy-gurdy
△ hurdy-gur|
dies
hurl
VERB
△ hurls
△ hurled
△ hurl|ing
hur|ley
hurl|ing
hurly-burly
Huron
hur|rah
hur|ri|cane
hur|ried
hur|riedly
hur|ried|ness
hurry
NOUN
VERB
△ hur|ries

△ hur|ried
△ hur|ry|ing
hurt
  VERB
△ hurts
△ hurt
△ hurt|ing
△ hurt
hurt|ful
hurt|fully
hurt|ful|ness
hur|tle
△ hur|tles
△ hur|tled
△ hur|tling
Husain *see*
Hussein
hus|band
  VERB
△ hus|bands
△ hus|ban|ded
△ hus|band|ing
hus|ban|dry
hush
  NOUN
△ hushes
  VERB
△ hushes
△ hushed
△ hush|ing
hushed
hush–hush
hush|kit
husk
  VERB
△ husks
△ husked
△ husk|ing
husk|ily
hus|ki|ness
husky
  NOUN
△ hus|kies

ADJ.
△ hus|kier
△ hus|ki|est
Huss
hus|sar
Hus|sein
Huss|ite
hussy
△ hus|sies
hust|ings
hus|tle
  VERB
△ hus|tles
△ hus|tled
△ hust|ling
hust|ler
Hu|ston
hut
hutch
△ hut|ches
Hut|ton
Huw
Hux|ley
Huys|mans
hya|cinth
hyaena *see*
hyena
hy|brid
hy|brid|ism
hy|brid|iza|tion
hy|brid|ize
△ hy|brid|izes
△ hy|brid|ized
△ hy|brid|izing
Hyde
Hydra
  Greek island;
  mythical monster
hydra
  freshwater
  polyp; something
  hard to get rid
  of or destroy
hy|dran|gea

hy|drant
hy|drate
  VERB
△ hy|drates
△ hy|dra|ted
△ hy|dra|ting
hy|dra|tion
hy|draulic
hy|draul|ic|ally
hy|draul|ics
hy|dride
hydro
hy|dro|car|bon
hy|dro|ceph|alic
hy|dro|ceph|alus
hy|dro|chloric
hy|dro|dy|nam|
ics
hy|dro|elec|tric
hy|dro|elec|tric|
ally
hy|dro|elec|tri|
city
hy|dro|foil
hy|dro|gen
hy|dro|gen|ate
△ hy|dro|gen|
ates
△ hy|dro|gen|
ated
△ hy|dro|gen|
ating
hy|dro|gen|ation
hy|dro|gen|car|
bon|ate
hy|dro|gen|ous
hy|drog|ra|pher
hy|dro|gra|phic
hy|drog|ra|phy
hy|drol|ogy
hy|dro|lyse
△ hy|dro|ly|ses
△ hy|dro|lysed
△ hy|dro|ly|sing

hy|dro|ly|sis
hy|drom|eter
hy|dro|pa|thic
hy|dro|pathy
hy|dro|phi|lic
hy|dro|pho|bia
hy|dro|pho|bic
hy|dro|plane
hy|dro|po|nic
hy|dro|po|nics
hy|dro|sphere
hy|dro|sta|tic
hy|dro|stat|ics
hy|dro|ther|apy
hy|drous
hy|drox|ide
hy|droxyl
hyena
hy|giene
hy|gienic
hy|gien|ic|ally
hy|grom|eter
hy|gro|scope
hy|gro|sco|pic
Hymen
  Greek god of
  marriage
hymen
  vaginal
  membrane
Hy|men|op|tera
hy|men|op|ter|ous
hymn
hym|nal
hym|nary
△ hym|nar|ies
hym|nody
hym|nol|ogist
hym|nol|ogy
hype
  VERB
△ hypes
△ hyped
△ hyp|ing

hyper
hy|per|ac|tive
hy|per|ac|tiv|ity
hy|per|bola
  △ hy|per|bo|las
  or hy|per|bo|
  lae
hy|per|bole
hy|per|bo|lic
hy|per|bol|ical
hy|per|crit|ical
hy|per|crit|ic|
  ally
hy|per|gly|cae|
  mia
hy|per|mar|ket
hy|peron
hy|per|sen|si|tive
hy|per|sen|si|tiv|
  ity
hy|per|sonic
hy|per|ten|sion
hy|per|text
hy|per|thy|roid|
  ism

hy|per|tonic
hy|per|tro|phy
  △ hy|per|tro|
  phies
hy|per|ven|ti|la|
  tion
hypha
hy|phen
VERB
  △ hy|phens
  △ hy|phened
  △ hy|phen|ing
hy|phen|ate
  △ hy|phen|ates
  △ hy|phen|ated
  △ hy|phen|ating
hy|phen|ation
hyp|no|sis
  △ hyp|no|ses
hyp|no|ther|apy
hyp|notic
hyp|not|ic|ally
hyp|no|tism
hyp|no|tist
hyp|no|tize

  △ hyp|no|ti|zes
  △ hyp|no|tized
  △ hyp|no|ti|zing
hypo
hy|po|caust
hy|po|chlor|ite
hy|po|chon|dria
hy|po|chon|driac
hy|po|chon|dri|
  acal
hy|poc|risy
  △ hy|poc|ri|sies
hy|po|crite
hy|po|cri|ti|cal
hy|po|cri|ti|cally
hy|po|der|mic
hy|po|gly|cae|
  mia
hy|po|nym
hy|po|ten|sion
hy|po|ten|use
hy|po|tha|la|mus
hy|po|ther|mia
hy|po|the|sis
  △ hy|po|the|ses

hy|po|thes|ize
  △ hy|po|thes|izes
  △ hy|po|thes|
  ized
  △ hy|po|thes|
  izing
hy|po|thet|ical
hy|po|thet|ic|ally
hy|po|thy|roid|
  ism
hy|po|tonic
hyp|som|eter
Hy|ra|co|ther|
  ium
hyrax
  △ hy|raxes
hys|sop
hys|ter|ec|tomy
  △ hys|ter|ec|
  tom|ies
hys|ter|esis
hys|teria
hys|teric
hys|ter|ical
hys|ter|ic|ally

Hyphenation

The hyphen has three main functions in written English:

- To link words that go together as a feature of their spelling, eg **come-uppance, house-proud** and **jack-of-all-trades**. In this role use of the hyphen is highly inconsistent and unstable in general usage, and in different sources you will readily find occurrences of (for example) **house boat, house-boat** and **houseboat**. It is also used to link word elements such as **re-, non-,** and **Anglo-,** when the formations call for it, eg **re-entry** (because of the two es), **non-Christian, Anglo-American**.

- To link words that go together in particular contexts, as a feature of syntax rather than spelling. In this role the hyphen is meant to clarify, and in some cases avoid ambiguity, eg there were **twenty-odd** people; they all met up at the **filling-station**; a **well-known** woman.

- To indicate the breaking off of a word at the end of a line of print, when there is not room for the whole word. In this dictionary suitable word divisions are indicated in the headwords, as explained in the book's introduction.

I

iamb
iam|bic
iam|bus
  △ iam|buses *or*
    iambi
Ian
Ibá|ñez
Iber|ian
ibex
  △ ibex *or* ibexes
    or ibi|ces
ibi|dem
ibis
  △ ibis *or* ibises
Ibiza
Ibsen
Ica|rus
ice
  VERB
  △ ices
  △ iced
  △ icing
ice-axe
ice|berg
ice|box
  △ ice|boxes
ice|breaker
ice-bucket
ice|cap
iced

Ice|land
Ice|lan|dic
Ice|man Com|
  eth, The
ice-skate
  △ ice-skates
  △ ice-ska|ted
  △ ice-ska|ting
ice-ska|ter
ice-ska|ting
ich|neu|mon
ich|thy|olo|gi|
  cal
ich|thy|ol|ogist
ich|thy|ol|ogy
icicle
icily
ici|ness
icing
Ick|nield
icon
ico|no|clasm
ico|no|clast
ico|no|clas|tic
icon|og|ra|phy
icon|ol|ogy
ico|no|sta|sis
  △ ico|no|sta|ses
ico|sa|hed|ron
  △ ico|sa|hed|
    rons *or* ico|sa|
    hedra

icy
  △ icier
  △ ici|est
I'd
id
Idaho
idea
ideal
ideal|ism
ideal|ist
ideal|is|tic
ideal|is|tic|ally
ideal|iza|tion
ideal|ize
  △ ideal|izes
  △ ideal|ized
  △ ideal|izing
ideally
idée fixe
  △ *idées fixes*
idem
iden|ti|cal
iden|tic|ally
iden|ti|fi|able
iden|ti|fi|ca|tion
iden|tify
  △ iden|ti|fies
  △ iden|ti|fied
  △ iden|ti|fy|ing
Iden|ti|kit
iden|tity
  △ iden|ti|ties

ideo|gram
ideo|graph
ideo|gra|phic
ideo|graph|ic|
  ally
ideo|lo|gi|cal
ideo|lo|gic|ally
ideol|ogist
ideol|ogy
  △ ideol|ogies
Ides
idi|ocy
  △ idi|ocies
idio|lect
idiom
idio|ma|tic
idio|mat|ic|ally
idio|syn|crasy
  △ idio|syn|cra|
    sies
idio|syn|cra|tic
idio|syn|crat|ic|
  ally
idiot
Idiot, The
idi|otic
idi|ot|ic|ally

idle
not at work; *lazy; futile; do* *no work*

-ible

For the difference between **-able** and **-ible**, see the panel at **-able**.

The most common words in **-ible** are:

accessible	digestible	flexible	intangible	persuasible
admissible	dirigible	gullible	irascible	(*there is also*
audible	discernible	impassible	irresistible	*persuadable*)
collapsible	divisible	(= unfeeling)	legible	plausible
comprehensible	eligible	incorrigible	negligible	responsible
contemptible	expressible	incredible	ostensible	reversible
convertible	extendible (*also*	indelible	perceptible	risible
defensible	extendable)	indigestible	permissible	susceptible
destructible	feasible	infallible		

VERB
△ idles
△ idled
△ idling
ADJ.
△ idler
△ idlest
⚠ idol

idle|ness
idler
idly

idol
image etc set up
for worship
⚠ idle

idol|ater
idol|at|ress
△ idol|at|res|ses
idol|at|rous
idol|at|rously
idol|atry
△ idol|at|ries
idol|iza|tion
idol|ize
△ idol|izes
△ idol|ized
△ idol|izing
idol|izer
idyll
idyl|lic
idyl|lic|ally
Idylls of the
King
Ieper *see* Ypres
if

iffy
△ if|fier
△ if|fi|est
igloo
Ig|na|tius Loy|
ola
ig|ne|ous
ignis fat|uus
△ ignes fatui
ig|ni|table
ignite
△ ig|nites
△ ig|ni|ted
△ ig|ni|ting
ig|ni|tion
ig|no|bil|ity
ig|no|ble
ig|noble|ness
ig|nobly
ig|no|mi|ni|ous
ig|no|mi|ni|ously
ig|no|mi|ni|ous|
ness
ig|nom|iny
ig|nor|amus
△ ig|nor|amuses
ig|nor|ance
ig|nor|ant
·ig|nor|antly
ig|nore
△ ig|nores
△ ig|nored
△ ig|nor|ing
igu|ana
△ igua|nas *or*
igu|ana

ike|bana
ikon *see* icon
ileo|stomy
△ ileo|sto|mies

ileum
lower part of
small intestine
△ ilea
⚠ ilium

iliac
Iliad, The

ilium
hip bone
△ ilia
⚠ ileum

ilk
I'll
ill
ADJ.
△ worse
△ worst
ADV.
△ worse
△ worst
ill-advised
ill-assor|ted
ill-bred
ill-con|si|dered
ill-dis|posed
il|legal
il|le|gal|ity
△ il|le|gal|it|ies
il|le|gally
il|le|gi|bil|ity

il|legible
il|legibly
il|le|git|im|acy
il|le|git|im|ate
il|le|git|im|ately
ill-equipped
ill-fated
ill-favoured
ill-feel|ing
ill-foun|ded
ill-got|ten
ill-humoured
il|lib|eral
il|li|ber|al|ity
il|lib|er|ally

il|li|cit
not allowed
⚠ elicit

il|li|citly
il|li|cit|ness
ill-in|formed
Il|li|nois
il|lit|er|acy
il|lit|er|ate
il|lit|er|ately
ill-judged
ill-man|nered
ill-natured
ill|ness
△ ill|nes|ses
il|lo|gi|cal
il|lo|gi|cal|ity
△ il|lo|gi|cal|it|
ies
il|lo|gi|cally

-ify / -efy

-ify is the more common spelling: **amplify, certify, clarify, countrify, dignify, gentrify, terrify.**

-efy is used in: **liquefy, putrefy, rarefy, stupefy.**
Note also: **ladyfy.**

The corresponding adjectival forms are **-ified** (**countrified**) and **-efied** (**rarefied**).

ill-omened
ill-starred
ill-tem¦pered
ill-timed
ill-treat
△ ill-treats
△ ill-trea¦ted
△ ill-treat¦ing
ill-treat¦ment
il¦lu¦min¦ant
il¦lu¦min¦ate
△ il¦lu¦min¦ates
△ il¦lu¦min¦ated
△ il¦lu¦min¦ating
il¦lu¦min¦ating
il¦lu¦min¦ation
il¦lu¦min¦at¦ive
il¦lu¦mine
△ il¦lu¦mines
△ il¦lu¦mined
△ il¦lu¦min¦ing

il¦lu¦sion
false idea etc
⚠allusion

il¦lu¦sion¦ism
il¦lu¦sion¦ist
il¦lu¦sive
il¦lu¦sory
il¦lus¦trate
△ il¦lus¦trates
△ il¦lus¦tra¦ted
△ il¦lus¦tra¦ting
il¦lus¦tra¦ted
il¦lus¦tra¦tion
il¦lus¦tra¦tive
il¦lus¦tra¦tively
il¦lus¦tra¦tor
il¦lus¦tri¦ous
il¦lus¦tri¦ously
ill-will
Il¦lyria
il¦men¦ite
Il¦yu¦shin

I'm
image
VERB
△ ima¦ges
△ imaged
△ ima¦ging
ima¦gery
△ ima¦ger¦ies
ima¦gin¦able
ima¦gin¦ary
ima¦gin¦ation
ima¦gin¦at¦ive
ima¦gin¦at¦ively
ima¦gin¦at¦ive¦
   ness
ima¦gine
△ ima¦gines
△ ima¦gined
△ ima¦gin¦ing
ima¦gin¦ings
Ima¦gism
imago
△ ima¦gos *or*
   ima¦gi¦nes
Imam
*leader of certain
Muslin sects*
imam
*mosque prayer-
leader*
im¦bal¦ance
im¦be¦cile
im¦be¦cil¦ity
△ im¦be¦cil¦it¦ies
imbed
△ im¦beds
△ im¦bed¦ded
△ im¦bed¦ding
im¦bibe
△ im¦bibes
△ im¦bibed
△ im¦bi¦bing
im¦bri¦cate
im¦broglio

imbue
△ im¦bues
△ im¦bued
△ im¦bu¦ing
im¦it¦able
imi¦tate
△ imi¦tates
△ imi¦ta¦ted
△ imi¦ta¦ting
imi¦ta¦tion
*Imi¦ta¦tion of
Christ, The
(De Imi¦ta¦
tione Christi)*
imi¦tat¦ive
imi¦tat¦ively
imi¦tat¦ive¦ness
imi¦ta¦tor
im¦ma¦cu¦late
im¦ma¦cu¦lately
im¦man¦ence
im¦man¦ency
im¦man¦ent
Im¦man¦uel
im¦ma¦ter¦ial
im¦ma¦ture
im¦ma¦turely
im¦ma¦tur¦ity
im¦meas¦ur¦able
im¦meas¦ur¦ably
im¦me¦di¦acy
△ im¦me¦di¦acies
im¦me¦di¦ate
im¦me¦di¦ately
im¦me¦mor¦ial
im¦me¦mori¦ally
im¦mense
im¦mensely
im¦mense¦ness
im¦men¦sity
im¦merse
△ im¦mer¦ses
△ im¦mersed
△ im¦mer¦sing

im¦mers¦ible
im¦mer¦sion

im¦mig¦rant
*one who enters a
foreign country
to settle there*
⚠emigrant

im¦mig¦rate
*enter a foreign
country to settle
there*
△ im¦mig¦rates
△ im¦mig¦ra¦ted
△ im¦mig¦ra¦ting
⚠emigrate

im¦mig¦ra¦tion
*entering a
foreign country
to settle there*
⚠emigration

im¦min¦ence
im¦min¦ent
Im¦ming¦ham
im¦mis¦cible
im¦mo¦bile
im¦mo¦bil¦ity
im¦mo¦bil¦iza¦
   tion
im¦mo¦bil¦ize
△ im¦mo¦bil¦izes
△ im¦mo¦bil¦ized
△ im¦mo¦bil¦
   izing
im¦mod¦er¦acy
im¦mod¦er¦ate
im¦mod¦er¦ately
im¦mod¦er¦ate¦
   ness
im¦mod¦est
im¦mod¦estly
im¦mod¦esty

im|mo|late
△ im|mo|lates
△ im|mo|la|ted
△ im|mo|la|ting
im|mo|la|tion
im|moral

im|mor|al|ity
wickedness
△ im|mor|al|it|
ies
⚠immortality

im|mor|ally
im|mor|tal

im|mor|tal|ity
deathlessness
⚠immorality

im|mor|tal|ize
△ im|mor|tal|
izes
△ im|mor|tal|
ized
△ im|mor|tal|
izing
im|mov|abil|ity
im|mov|able
im|mov|ably
im|mune
im|mu|nity
△ im|mu|ni|ties
im|mun|iza|tion
im|mun|ize
△ im|mun|izes
△ im|mun|ized
△ im|mun|izing
im|mu|no|de|fi|
ciency
△ im|mu|no|de|
fi|cien|cies
im|mu|no|glob|
ulin
im|mu|no|lo|gi|
cal

im|mu|nol|ogist
im|mu|nol|ogy
im|mu|no|sup|
pres|sant
im|mu|no|sup|
pres|sive
im|mure
△ im|mures
△ im|mured
△ im|mur|ing
im|mu|ta|bil|ity
im|mut|able
im|mut|ably
Imo|gen
imp
im|pact
VERB
△ im|pacts
△ im|pac|ted
△ im|pact|ing
im|pac|ted
im|pair
△ im|pairs
△ im|paired
△ im|pair|ing
im|pair|ment
im|pala
△ im|pa|las *or*
im|pala
im|pale
△ im|pales
△ im|paled
△ im|pa|ling
im|pale|ment
im|pal|pa|bil|ity
im|palp|able
im|palp|ably
im|panel
△ im|pan|els
△ im|pan|elled
△ im|pan|el|ling
im|part
△ im|parts
△ im|par|ted

△ im|part|ing
im|par|ta|tion
im|par|tial
im|par|ti|al|ity
im|par|tially
im|pas|sa|bil|ity

im|pass|able
not able to be
passed through,
travelled along,
etc
⚠impassible

im|pass|able|
ness
im|pass|ably
im|passe

im|pass|ible
not susceptible to
pain, injury, etc;
unmoved
⚠impassable

im|pas|sion
△ im|pas|sions
△ im|pas|sioned
△ im|pas|sion|
ing
im|pas|sioned
im|pas|sive
im|pas|sively
im|pas|sive|ness
im|pas|siv|ity
im|pasto
im|pa|tience
im|pa|ti|ens
im|pa|tient
im|pa|tiently
im|peach
△ im|pea|ches
△ im|peached
△ im|peach|ing
im|peach|able
im|peach|ment

im|pecc|able
im|pecc|ably
im|pe|cu|ni|ous
im|pe|cu|ni|
ously
im|pe|cu|ni|ous|
ness
im|ped|ance
im|pede
△ im|pedes
△ im|peded
△ im|ped|ing
im|ped|iment
im|pedi|menta
impel
△ im|pels
△ im|pelled
△ im|pel|ling
im|pend
△ im|pends
△ im|pen|ded
△ im|pend|ing
im|pend|ing
im|pen|et|ra|bil|
ity
im|pen|et|rable
im|pen|et|rably
im|pen|it|ence
im|pen|it|ent
im|pen|it|ently
im|per|at|ive
im|per|at|ively
im|per|cep|ti|bil|
ity
im|per|cep|tible
im|per|cep|tibly
im|per|fect
im|per|fec|tion
im|per|fectly
im|per|ial
im|peri|al|ism
im|peri|al|ist
im|peri|al|is|tic
im|peri|ally

im|peril
　△ im|per|ils
　△ im|per|illed
　△ im|peril|ling
im|per|il|ment
im|peri|ous
im|peri|ously
im|peri|ous|ness
im|per|ish|able
im|per|man|ence
im|per|man|ency
im|per|man|ent
im|per|me|ab|il|ity
im|per|me|able
im|per|miss|ible
im|per|sonal
im|per|son|al|ity
im|per|son|ally
im|per|son|ate
　△ im|per|son|ates
　△ im|per|son|ated
　△ im|per|son|ating
im|per|son|ation
im|per|son|ator
im|per|tin|ence
im|per|tin|ent
im|per|tin|ently
im|per|tur|ba|bil|ity
im|per|turb|able
im|per|turb|ably
im|per|vi|ous
im|per|vi|ously
im|per|vi|ous|ness
im|pe|tigo
im|petu|os|ity
im|petu|ous
im|petu|ous|ness
im|petu|ously

im|pe|tus
　△ im|pet|uses
impi
　△ impis or im|pies
im|pi|ety
　△ im|pi|et|ies
im|pinge
　△ im|pin|ges
　△ im|pinged
　△ im|pin|ging
im|pinge|ment
im|pi|ous
im|pi|ously
im|pi|ous|ness
imp|ish
imp|ishly
imp|ish|ness
im|pla|ca|bil|ity
im|plac|able
im|plac|able|ness
im|plac|ably
im|plant
　VERB
　△ im|plants
　△ im|plan|ted
　△ im|plant|ing
im|plan|ta|tion
im|plau|si|bil|ity
im|plaus|ible
im|plaus|ibly
im|ple|ment
　VERB
　△ im|ple|ments
　△ im|ple|men|ted
　△ im|ple|ment|ing
im|ple|men|ta|tion
im|pli|cate
　△ im|pli|cates
　△ im|pli|ca|ted

　△ im|pli|ca|ting
im|pli|ca|tion
im|pli|cit
im|pli|citly
im|pli|cit|ness
im|plied
im|plode
　△ im|plodes
　△ im|plo|ded
　△ im|plo|ding
im|plore
　△ im|plores
　△ im|plored
　△ im|plor|ing
im|plor|ing
im|plor|ingly
im|plo|sion
im|plo|sive
imply
　△ im|plies
　△ im|plied
　△ im|ply|ing
im|po|lite
im|po|litely
im|po|lite|ness
im|pol|itic
im|pon|der|able
im|port
　VERB
　△ im|ports
　△ im|por|ted
　△ im|port|ing
im|port|ance
Im|port|ance of Being Earn|est, The
im|port|ant
im|port|antly
im|por|ta|tion
im|por|ter
im|por|tu|nate
im|por|tu|nately
im|por|tune
　△ im|por|tunes

　△ im|por|tuned
　△ im|por|tu|ning
im|por|tu|nity
　△ im|por|tu|ni|ties
im|pose
　△ im|po|ses
　△ im|posed
　△ im|po|sing
im|po|sing
im|po|singly
im|po|si|tion
im|pos|si|bil|ity
　△ im|pos|si|bil|it|ies
im|poss|ible
im|poss|ibly
im|pos|tor
im|pos|ture
im|po|tence
im|po|tent
im|po|tently
im|pound
　△ im|pounds
　△ im|poun|ded
　△ im|pound|ing
im|pov|er|ish
　△ im|pov|er|ishes
　△ im|pov|er|ished
　△ im|pov|er|ish|ing
im|pov|er|ished
im|pov|er|ish|ment
im|prac|ti|ca|bil|ity

> im|prac|tic|able
> *that cannot be done or used*
> ⚠ impractical

im|prac|tic|ably

im|prac|ti|cal
*lacking common
sense*
⚠ impracticable

im|prac|ti|cal|ity
△ im|prac|ti|cal|
  it|ies
im|prac|ti|cally
im|pre|cate
△ im|pre|cates
△ im|pre|ca|ted
△ im|pre|ca|ting
im|pre|ca|tion
im|pre|ca|tory
im|pre|cise
im|pre|ci|sion
im|preg|na|bil|
  ity
im|preg|nable
im|preg|nably
im|preg|nate
△ im|preg|nates
△ im|preg|na|ted
△ im|preg|na|
  ting
im|preg|na|tion
im|pres|ario
im|press
  VERB
△ im|pres|ses
△ im|pressed
△ im|pres|sing

im|pres|sion
im|pres|sion|ab|
  il|ity
im|pres|sion|
  able
im|pres|sion|
  ably
Im|pres|sion|ism
Im|pres|sion|ist
im|pres|sion|is|
  tic
im|pres|sion|is|
  tic|ally
im|pres|sive
im|pres|sively
im|pres|sive|ness
im|pri|ma|tur
im|print
  VERB
△ im|prints
△ im|prin|ted
△ im|print|ing
im|print|ing
im|pri|son
△ im|pris|ons
△ im|pris|oned
△ im|pris|on|ing
im|pris|on|ment
im|prob|ab|il|ity
△ im|prob|ab|il|
  it|ies
im|prob|able
im|prob|ably

im|pro|bity
△ im|pro|bit|ies
im|promptu
im|proper
im|prop|erly
im|pro|pri|ety
△ im|pro|pri|et|
  ies
im|prove
△ im|proves
△ im|proved
△ im|pro|ving
im|prove|ment
im|prov|id|ence
im|prov|id|ent
im|prov|id|ently
im|pro|vi|sa|tion
im|pro|vise
△ im|pro|vi|ses
△ im|pro|vised
△ im|pro|vi|sing
im|pro|vi|ser
im|pru|dence
im|pru|dent
im|pru|dently
im|pu|dence
im|pu|dent
im|pu|dently
im|pugn
△ im|pugns
△ im|pugned
△ im|pugn|ing
im|pugn|able

im|pugn|ment
im|pulse
im|pul|sion
im|pul|sive
im|pul|sively
im|pul|sive|ness
im|pu|nity
im|pure
im|pur|ity
△ im|pur|it|ies
im|pu|ta|tion
im|pute
△ im|putes
△ im|pu|ted
△ im|pu|ting

in
  inside, during,
  wearing, at
  home,
  fashionable, etc
  ⚠ inn

in|ab|il|ity
△ in|ab|il|it|ies
in ab|sen|tia
in|ac|ces|si|bil|
  ity
in|ac|cess|ible
in|ac|cess|ibly
in|ac|cur|acy
△ in|ac|cur|acies
in|ac|cur|ate
in|ac|cur|ately

---

in-

The following types of words generally form negatives with **in-** rather than **un-**:

words ending in -ence or -ent, -ible, -ice, -ity, -tude, -uble: **independence, independent, inflexible, injustice, inequality, ingratitude, insoluble.**

Note also: **incapacitated, indisposed, inexperienced.** Most other participial adjectives in -ed form negatives with **un-**.

in- becomes **il-** when joined to words beginning with **l** (**illogical**), **ir-** when joined to words beginning with **r** (**irregular**), and **im-** when joined to words beginning with **b, p, m** (**imbalance, impartial, immature**).

in|ac|tion
in|ac|tive
in|ac|tively
in|ac|tiv|ity
in|ad|equacy
△ in|ad|equa|cies
in|ad|equate
in|ad|equately
in|ad|mis|si|bil|ity
in|ad|miss|ible
in|ad|miss|ibly
in|ad|vert|ence
in|ad|vert|ent
in|ad|vert|ently
in|ad|vis|ab|il|ity
in|ad|vis|able
in|ali|en|able

in|amor|ata
*woman who is
loved or in love*
⚠ inamorato

in|amor|ato
*man who is
loved or in love*
⚠ inamorata

inane
in|anely
in|an|im|ate
in|ani|tion
in|an|ity
△ in|an|it|ies
in|ap|plic|ab|il|ity
in|ap|plic|able
in|ap|plic|ably
in|ap|pos|ite
in|ap|pos|itely
in|ap|pos|ite|ness
in|ap|pro|pri|ate
in|ap|pro|pri|ately

in|ap|pro|pri|ate|ness

inapt
*unsuitable;
unqualified*
⚠ inept

in|aptly
in|apt|ness
in|ar|ti|cu|late
in|ar|ti|cu|lately
in|ar|ti|cu|late|ness
in|ar|tis|tic
in|ar|tis|tic|ally
in|as|much
in|at|ten|tion
in|at|tent|ive
in|at|tent|ively
in|at|tent|ive|ness
in|aud|ib|il|ity
in|aud|ible
in|aud|ibly
in|au|gural
in|au|gur|ate
△ in|au|gur|ates
△ in|au|gur|ated
△ in|au|gur|ating
in|au|gur|ation
in|au|gur|ator
in|aus|pi|cious
in|aus|pi|ciously
in|aus|pi|cious|ness
in-bet|ween
in|board
in|born
in|bound
in|bred
in|breed
△ in|breeds
△ in|bred
△ in|breed|ing

in|breed|ing
in|cal|cu|la|bil|ity
in|cal|cu|lable
in|cal|cu|lably
in cam|era
in|can|desce
△ in|can|des|ces
△ in|can|desced
△ in|can|des|cing
in|can|des|cence
in|can|des|cent
in|can|des|cently
in|can|ta|tion
in|can|ta|tory
in|ca|pa|bil|ity
in|ca|pable
in|ca|pably
in|ca|pa|ci|tate
△ in|ca|pa|ci|tates
△ in|ca|pa|ci|ta|ted
△ in|ca|pa|ci|ta|ting
in|ca|pa|ci|ta|ted
in|ca|pa|ci|ta|tion
in|ca|pa|city
△ in|ca|pa|ci|ties
incapsulate *see*
encapsulate
in|car|cer|ate
△ in|car|cer|ates
△ in|car|cer|ated
△ in|car|cer|ating
in|car|cer|ation
in|car|nate
VERB
△ in|car|nates
△ in|car|na|ted
△ in|car|na|ting

In|car|na|tion
of Christ
in|car|na|tion
*of any spirit etc;
person who
typifies a quality
etc*
Inca
in|cau|tious
in|cau|tiously
in|cau|tious|ness
in|cen|di|ar|ism
in|cen|di|ary
NOUN
△ in|cen|di|ar|ies
in|cense
VERB
△ in|cen|ses
△ in|censed
△ in|cen|sing
in|cent|ive
in|cep|tion
in|cer|ti|tude
in|ces|sant
in|ces|santly
in|cest
in|ces|tu|ous
in|ces|tu|ously
in|ces|tu|ous|ness
inch
NOUN
△ in|ches
VERB
△ in|ches
△ inched
△ inch|ing
in|cho|ate
in|cho|ately
in|ci|dence
in|ci|dent
in|ci|den|tal
in|ci|den|tally
in|cin|er|ate

△ in|cin|er|ates
△ in|cin|er|ated
△ in|cin|er|ating
in|cin|er|ation
in|cin|er|ator
in|ci|pi|ence
in|ci|pi|ency
in|ci|pi|ent
in|ci|pi|ently
in|cise
△ in|ci|ses
△ in|cised
△ in|ci|sing
in|ci|sion
in|ci|sive
in|ci|sive|ly
in|ci|sive|ness
in|ci|sor
in|cite
△ in|cites
△ in|ci|ted
△ in|ci|ting
in|cite|ment
in|ci|vil|ity
△ in|ci|vil|it|ies
in|clem|ency
in|clem|ent
in|cli|na|tion
in|cline
VERB
△ in|clines
△ in|clined
△ in|cli|ning
in|clude
△ in|cludes
△ in|clu|ded
△ in|clu|ding
in|clu|sion
in|clu|sive
in|clu|sive|ly
in|cog|nito
in|cog|ni|zance
in|cog|ni|zant
in|co|her|ence

in|co|her|ent
in|co|her|ently
in|com|bust|ible
in|come
in|comer
in|com|ing
in|com|men|sur|
  ab|il|ity
in|com|men|sur|
  able
in|com|men|sur|
  ate
in|com|men|sur|
  ately
in|com|men|sur|
  ate|ness
in|com|mode
△ in|com|modes
△ in|com|mo|
  ded
△ in|com|mo|
  ding
in|com|mo|di|
  ous
in|com|mo|di|
  ously
in|com|mo|di|
  ous|ness
in|com|mu|ni|
  cado
in|com|par|ab|il|
  ity
in|com|par|able
in|com|par|able|
  ness
in|com|par|ably
in|com|pa|ti|bil|
  ity
in|com|pat|ible
in|com|pat|ibly
in|com|pet|ence
in|com|pet|ent
in|com|pet|ently
in|com|plete

in|com|pletely
in|com|plete|
  ness
in|com|pre|hen|
  si|bil|ity
in|com|pre|hens|
  ible
in|com|pre|hens|
  ibly
in|com|pre|hen|
  sion
in|con|ceiv|ab|il|
  ity
in|con|ceiv|able
in|con|ceiv|ably
in|con|clu|sive
in|con|clu|sively
in|con|clu|sive|
  ness
in|con|gru|ity
△ in|con|gru|it|
  ies
in|con|gru|ous
in|con|gru|ously
in|con|gru|ous|
  ness
in|con|se|quent
in|con|se|quen|
  tial
in|con|se|quen|
  ti|al|ity
in|con|se|quen|
  ti|ally
in|con|sid|er|
  able
in|con|sid|er|
  ably
in|con|sid|er|ate
in|con|sid|er|
  ately
in|con|sid|er|ate|
  ness
in|con|sid|er|
  ation

in|con|sis|tency
△ in|con|sis|ten|
  cies
in|con|sis|tent
in|con|sis|tently
in|con|so|lable
in|con|so|lably
in|con|spi|cu|ous
in|con|spi|cu|
  ously
in|con|spi|cu|
  ous|ness
in|con|stancy
in|con|stant
in|con|test|ab|il|
  ity
in|con|test|able
in|con|test|ably
in|con|tin|ence
in|con|tin|ency
in|con|tin|ent
in|con|tro|vert|
  ible
in|con|tro|vert|
  ibly
in|con|veni|ence
VERB
△ in|con|veni|en|
  ces
△ in|con|veni|
  enced
△ in|con|veni|en|
  cing
in|con|veni|ent
in|con|veni|ently
in|cor|por|ate
VERB
△ in|cor|por|ates
△ in|cor|por|ated
△ in|cor|por|
  ating
in|cor|por|ation
in|cor|por|eal
in|cor|por|eally

in|cor|por|eity
in|cor|rect
in|cor|rectly
in|cor|rect|ness
in|cor|ri|gi|bil|ity
in|cor|ri|gible
in|cor|ri|gibly
in|cor|rup|ti|bil|ity
in|cor|rupt|ible
in|cor|rupt|ibly
in|crease
  VERB
  △ in|crea|ses
  △ in|creased
  △ in|creas|ing
in|creas|ingly
in|cred|ib|il|ity
in|cred|ible
in|cred|ibly
in|cre|du|lity
in|cred|ulous
in|cred|ulously
in|cred|ulous|ness
in|cre|ment
in|cre|men|tal
in|cre|ment|ally
in|crim|in|ate
  △ in|crim|in|ates
  △ in|crim|in|ated
  △ in|crim|in|ating
in|crim|in|ating
in|crim|in|ation
in|crim|in|atory
incrust see
  encrust
in|cu|bate
  △ in|cu|bates
  △ in|cu|ba|ted
  △ in|cu|ba|ting
in|cu|ba|tion
in|cu|ba|tive

in|cu|ba|tor
in|cu|ba|tory
in|cu|bus
  △ in|cu|buses or
  in|cubi
in|cul|cate
  △ in|cul|cates
  △ in|cul|ca|ted
  △ in|cul|ca|ting
in|cul|ca|tion
in|cul|pate
  △ in|cul|pates
  △ in|cul|pa|ted
  △ in|cul|pa|ting
in|cum|bency
  △ in|cum|ben|cies
in|cum|bent
in|cu|nab|ulum
  △ in|cu|nab|ula
incur
  △ in|curs
  △ in|curred
  △ in|cur|ring
in|cur|ab|il|ity
in|cur|able
in|cur|ably
in|curi|ous
in|curi|ously
in|cur|sion
in|cur|sive
incus
  △ in|cu|des
in|daba
in|debted
in|debt|ed|ness
in|de|cency
  △ in|de|cen|cies
in|de|cent
in|de|cently
in|de|ci|pher|ab|il|ity
in|de|ci|pher|able

in|de|ci|pher|ably
in|de|ci|sion
in|de|ci|sive
in|de|ci|sively
in|de|ci|sive|ness
in|dec|or|ous
in|dec|or|ously
in|dec|or|ous|ness
in|de|corum
in|deed
in|de|fat|ig|able
in|de|fat|ig|ably
in|de|fen|si|bil|ity
in|de|fens|ible
in|de|fen|sibly
in|de|fin|able
in|de|fi|nably
in|def|in|ite
in|def|in|itely
in|def|in|ite|ness
in|de|his|cent
in|del|ible
in|del|ibly
in|deli|cacy
  △ in|deli|ca|cies
in|deli|cate
in|deli|cately
in|dem|ni|fi|ca|tion
in|dem|nify
  △ in|dem|ni|fies
  △ in|dem|ni|fied
  △ in|dem|ni|fy|ing
in|dem|nity
  △ in|dem|nit|ies
in|dent
  VERB
  △ in|dents
  △ in|den|ted
  △ in|dent|ing

in|den|ta|tion
in|den|tion
in|den|ture
  VERB
  △ in|den|tures
  △ in|den|tured
  △ in|den|tur|ing
in|de|pend|ence
in|de|pend|ent
in|de|pend|ently
in-depth
in|des|crib|able
in|des|crib|ably
in|de|struc|ti|bil|ity
in|de|struct|ible
in|de|struct|ibly
in|de|ter|min|able
in|de|ter|min|acy
in|de|ter|min|ate
in|de|ter|min|ately
in|de|ter|min|ate|ness
in|dex
  NOUN
  technical uses
  △ in|di|ces
  other senses
  △ in|dexes
  VERB
  △ in|dexes
  △ in|dexed
  △ in|dex|ing
in|dex|ation
in|dexer
Index Lib|rorum Pro|hi|bit|orum
index-linked
India
In|dia|man
  △ In|dia|men

In|dian
In|di|ana
Indic
in|di|cate
△ in|di|cates
△ in|di|ca|ted
△ in|di|ca|ting
in|di|ca|tion
in|dic|at|ive
in|di|ca|tor
in|di|ca|tory
in|di|ces
in|dict
△ in|dicts
△ in|dic|ted
△ in|dict|ing
in|dict|able
in|dict|ment
indie
in|dif|fer|ence
in|dif|fer|ent
in|dif|fer|ently
in|di|gence
in|di|gen|ous
in|di|gen|ously
in|di|gent
in|di|ges|ti|bil|ity
in|di|gest|ible
in|di|ges|tion
in|dig|nant
in|dig|nantly
in|dig|na|tion
in|dig|nity
△ in|dig|ni|ties
in|digo
△ in|di|gos or
   in|di|goes
in|di|rect
in|di|rectly
in|di|rect|ness
in|dis|cern|ible
in|dis|ci|pline
in|dis|ci|plined
in|dis|creet

in|dis|creetly
in|dis|cre|tion
in|dis|crim|in|ate
in|dis|crim|in|
   ately
in|dis|crim|in|
   ate|ness
in|dis|pen|sa|bil|
   ity
in|dis|pens|able
in|dis|pens|ably
in|dis|posed
in|dis|pos|ition
in|dis|put|able
in|dis|put|ably
in|dis|solu|bil|ity
in|dis|sol|uble
in|dis|sol|ubly
in|dis|tinct
in|dis|tinctly
in|dis|tinct|ness
in|dis|tin|guish|
   able
in|dis|tin|guish|
   ably
in|dium
in|di|vid|ual
in|di|vidu|al|ism
in|di|vidu|al|ist
in|di|vidu|al|is|
   tic|ally
in|di|vidu|al|ity
△ in|di|vidu|al|
   it|ies
in|di|vidu|al|iza|
   tion
in|di|vidu|al|ize
△ in|di|vidu|al|
   izes
△ in|di|vidu|al|
   ized
△ in|di|vidu|al|
   izing
in|di|vidu|ally

in|di|vis|ib|il|ity
in|di|vis|ible
in|di|vis|ibly
Indo-Aryan
in|doc|trin|ate
△ in|doc|trin|
   ates
△ in|doc|trin|
   ated
△ in|doc|trin|
   ating
in|doc|trin|ation
Indo-Euro|pean
Indo-Ira|nian
in|do|lence
in|do|lent
in|do|lently
in|dom|it|ab|il|
   ity
in|dom|it|able
in|dom|it|ably
In|do|ne|sia
In|do|nes|ian

in|door
ADJ.
⚠ indoors

in|doors
ADV.
⚠ indoor

Indo-Paci|fic
indorse see
   endorse
in|drawn
indri
in|du|bit|able
in|du|bit|ably
in|duce
△ in|du|ces
△ in|duced
△ in|du|cing
in|duce|ment
in|du|cible

in|duct
△ in|ducts
△ in|duc|ted
△ in|duct|ing
in|duct|ance
in|duc|tion
in|duct|ive
in|duct|ively
in|duc|tor
indue see endue
in|dulge
△ in|dul|ges
△ in|dulged
△ in|dul|ging
in|dul|gence
in|dul|gent
in|dul|gently
Indus
in|dus|trial
in|dus|tri|al|ism
in|dus|tri|al|ist
in|dus|tri|al|iza|
   tion
in|dus|tri|al|ize
△ in|dus|tri|al|
   izes
△ in|dus|tri|al|
   ized
△ in|dus|tri|al|
   izing
in|dus|tri|ally
in|dus|tri|ous
in|dus|tri|ously
in|dus|tri|ous|
   ness
in|dus|try
△ in|dus|tries
in|eb|ri|ate
VERB
△ in|eb|ri|ates
△ in|eb|ri|ated
△ in|eb|ri|ating
in|eb|ri|ation
in|eb|ri|ety

in|ed|ib|il|ity
in|ed|ible
in|edu|ca|bil|ity
in|educ|able
in|ef|fa|bil|ity
in|ef|fable
in|ef|fably
in|ef|fec|tive
in|ef|fec|tively
in|ef|fec|tive|
  ness
in|ef|fec|tual
in|ef|fec|tu|ally
in|ef|fec|tu|al|
  ness
in|ef|fi|ca|cious
in|ef|fi|ca|ciously
in|ef|fi|cacy
in|ef|fi|ciency
  △ in|ef|fi|cien|
  cies
in|ef|fi|cient
in|ef|fi|ciently
in|el|eg|ance
in|el|eg|ant
in|el|eg|antly
in|eli|gi|bil|ity
in|eli|gible
in|eluct|able
in|eluct|ably

---
inept
clumsy; silly
  ⚠ inapt
---

in|ep|ti|tude
in|eptly
in|ept|ness
in|equable
in|equal|ity
  △ in|equal|it|ies
in|equit|able
in|equit|ably
in|equity
  △ in|equi|ties

in|erad|ic|able
in|erad|ic|ably
inert
in|er|tia
in|er|tial
in|ertly
in|ert|ness
in|es|cap|able
in|es|cap|ably
in|es|sen|tial
in|es|tim|able
in|es|tim|ably
in|ev|it|ab|il|ity
in|ev|it|able
in|ev|it|ably
in|ex|act
in|ex|ac|ti|tude
in|ex|actly
in|ex|act|ness
in|ex|cus|able
in|ex|cus|ably
in|ex|haus|ti|bil|
  ity
in|ex|haust|ible
in|ex|haust|ibly
in|ex|or|ab|il|ity
in|ex|or|able
in|ex|or|ably
in|ex|pe|di|ence
in|ex|pe|di|ency
in|ex|pe|di|ent
in|ex|pen|sive
in|ex|pen|sively
in|ex|pen|sive|
  ness
in|ex|peri|ence
in|ex|peri|enced
in|ex|pert
in|ex|pertly
in|ex|pli|ca|bil|
  ity
in|ex|plic|able
in|ex|plic|ably
in|ex|pli|cit

in|ex|pli|citly
in|ex|press|i|ble
in|ex|press|ibly
in|ex|pres|sive
in|ex|tin|guish|
  able
in ex|tre|mis
in|ex|tric|able
in|ex|tric|ably
in|fal|li|bil|ity
in|fall|ible
in|fall|ibly
in|fa|mous
in|fa|mously
in|famy
  △ in|fa|mies
in|fancy
  △ in|fan|cies
in|fant

---
in|fanta
*eldest daughter
of king of Spain
or Portugal;
wife of an
infante*
  ⚠ infante

---
in|fante
*son of king of
Spain or
Portugal who is
not heir to
throne*
  ⚠ infanta
---

in|fan|ti|cide
in|fan|tile
in|fan|til|ism
in|fan|try
  NOUN
  △ in|fan|tries
in|fan|try|man
  △ in|fan|try|men
in|farc|tion

in|fatu|ate
  △ in|fatu|ates
  △ in|fatu|ated
  △ in|fatu|ating
in|fatu|ated
in|fatu|ation
in|fect
  △ in|fects
  △ in|fec|ted
  △ in|fect|ing
in|fec|tion
in|fec|tious
in|fec|tiously
in|fec|tious|ness
in|fe|li|ci|tous
in|fe|li|city
  △ in|fe|li|ci|ties
infer
  △ in|fers
  △ in|ferred
  △ in|fer|ring
in|fer|able
in|fer|ence
in|fer|en|tial
in|fer|en|tially
in|feri|or
in|feri|or|ity
in|fer|nal
in|fer|nally
in|ferno
inferrable *see*
  inferable
in|fer|tile
in|fer|til|ity
in|fest
  △ in|fests
  △ in|fes|ted
  △ in|fest|ing
in|fes|ta|tion
in|fi|del
in|fi|del|ity
  △ in|fi|del|it|ies
in|field
in|fielder

in-fight|ing
in|fill
  VERB
  △ in|fills
  △ in|filled
  △ in|fil|ling
in|fil|trate
  △ in|fil|trates
  △ in|fil|tra|ted
  △ in|fil|tra|ting
in|fil|tra|tion
in|fil|tra|tor
in|fin|ite
in|fin|itely
in|fin|ite|ness
in|fi|ni|tes|imal
in|fi|ni|tes|im|
  ally
in|fin|it|ive
in|fi|ni|tude
in|fin|ity
in|firm
in|firm|ary
  △ in|firm|ar|ies
in|firm|ity
  △ in|firm|it|ies
infix
  NOUN
  △ in|fixes
  VERB
  △ in|fixes
  △ in|fixed
  △ in|fix|ing
in|fix|ation
in flag|rante de|
licto
in|flame
  △ in|flames
  △ in|flamed
  △ in|fla|ming
in|flam|ma|bil|
  ity
in|flam|mable
in|flam|ma|tion

in|flam|ma|tory
in|flat|able
in|flate
  △ in|flates
  △ in|fla|ted
  △ in|fla|ting
in|fla|ted
in|fla|tion
in|fla|tion|ary
in|flect
  △ in|flects
  △ in|flec|ted
  △ in|flect|ing
in|flec|tion
in|flec|tional
in|flec|tive
in|flex|ib|il|ity
in|flex|ible
in|flex|ible|ness
in|flex|ibly
inflexion *see*
  inflection
inflexional *see*
  inflectional
in|flict
  △ in|flicts
  △ in|flic|ted
  △ in|flict|ing
in|flic|tion
in-flight
in|flor|es|cence
in|flow
in|flow|ing
in|flu|ence
  VERB
  △ in|flu|en|ces
  △ in|flu|enced
  △ in|flu|en|cing
in|flu|en|tial
in|flu|en|tially
in|flu|enza
in|flux
  △ in|fluxes
info

in|fo|mer|cial
in|form
  △ in|forms
  △ in|formed
  △ in|form|ing
in|for|mal
in|for|mal|ity
  △ in|for|mal|it|
  ies
in|form|ally
in|form|ant
in|for|ma|tion
in|for|ma|tional
in|form|at|ive
in|form|at|ively
in|form|at|ive|
  ness
in|formed
in|for|mer
in|fo|tain|ment
infra
in|frac|tion
infra dig
infra-red
in|fra|sonic
in|fra|sound
in|fra|struc|ture
in|fre|quency
in|frequent
in|frequently
in|fringe
  △ in|frin|ges
  △ in|fringed
  △ in|frin|ging
in|fringe|ment
in|fu|ri|ate
  △ in|fu|ri|ates
  △ in|fu|ri|ated
  △ in|fu|ri|ating
in|fu|ri|ating
in|fu|ri|atingly
in|fuse
  △ in|fu|ses
  △ in|fused

  △ in|fu|sing
in|fu|sion

---

in|geni|ous
  clever
    ⚠ ingenuous

---

in|geni|ously
in|geni|ous|ness
in|gé|nue
in|genu|ity

---

in|genu|ous
  naive
    ⚠ ingenious

---

in|genu|ously
in|genu|ous|ness
in|gest
  △ in|gests
  △ in|ges|ted
  △ in|gest|ing
in|gest|ible
in|ges|tion
ingle|nook
in|glori|ous
in|glori|ously
in|glori|ous|ness
in|go|ing
ingot
in|grained
In|grams
in|grate
in|gra|ti|ate
  △ in|gra|ti|ates
  △ in|gra|ti|ated
  △ in|gra|ti|ating
in|gra|ti|ating
in|gra|ti|atingly
in|gra|ti|tude
in|gre|di|ent
In|gres
in|gress
In|grid
in|grow|ing
in|grown

Inflection

Inflections of individual words are given at their places in the dictionary. Here, a few guidelines are offered to indicate the principles on which the regular inflection of words is based (although many others are irregular):

- Regular verbs add -s to form the third person singular, or -es when the verb ends in -s, -x, -z, -sh, or -ch as in **crunch**.

- Regular weak verbs add -ed to form the past tense and past participle, dropping a final e if present.

- Strong verbs change the vowel of the stem to form the past tense and past participle, eg **swim, swam, swum**. Irregular verbs sometimes do this; or change in other ways, eg **begin, began, begun**; **go, went, gone**; or do not change at all, eg **hit, hit, hit**.

- Regular verbs add -ing to form the present participle, usually dropping a final e if present, eg **look, looking; go, going; make, making**.

- Verbs ending in -y preceded by a consonant form endings in -ies, -ied, and -ying, eg **copy, copies, copied, copying**.

- Verbs ending in -ie form present participles in -ying, eg **die, dying; tie, tying**.

- Verbs ending in -c preceded by a vowel add -k in inflection, eg **magic, magicked, magicking; bivouac, bivouacked, bivouacking**.

- A final stressed syllable ending in a single consonant usually doubles the consonant, eg **batted, hitting, beginning**. But note **routeing** and **swingeing** (to preserve the sound and avoid confusion with **routing** and **swinging**).

- A final single consonant when not stressed (eg **budget** and **gallop**), is not normally doubled in inflection: **budgeted, galloping**. But note that final -l is always doubled, eg **quarrel, quarrelled, quarrelling**. Except: **paralleled**.

- Most nouns add -s to form plurals, eg **ants, books, tables, sofas**.

- They add -es when the noun ends in -s, -x, -z, -sh, or -ch as in **church**, eg **basses, boxes, minxes, buzzes, bushes, batches**.

- Nouns ending in -y preceded by a consonant form plurals in -ies, eg **baby, babies; granny, grannies**; but **journey, journeys; monkey, monkeys**.

- Nouns ending in -o form plurals in -os or -oes: see individual entries in the dictionary.

- Nouns ending in -f or -fe usually form plurals in -ves, eg: **beef, beeves** (animals); **calf, calves; elf, elves; hoof, hooves; knife, knives; leaf, leaves; life, lives; scarf, scarves; sheaf, sheaves; wharf, wharves**. Note: **dwarfs, roofs**; although **dwarves** and **rooves** are also found, the first under the influence of J R R Tolkien.

- Compound nouns usually form plurals on the second element, eg **house plants, filling-stations**. But note: **courts-martial, men-of-war**, and the phrase-based type **hangers-on** and **passers-by**.

- Some nouns remain unchanged in the plural, eg **biceps, forceps, innings, means, mews** (although **mewses** is sometimes used), **series, sheep, species**.

- Some names of animals can either remain unchanged in the plural, to denote an indeterminate number, eg **antelope, fish, wildebeest**; or add -s (or -es), to denote 'types of ...', eg **fishes** = 'types of fish' rather than 'several fish'.

- For nouns ending in -ful, see the panel at -ful.

- For plurals of non-naturalized words, and naturalized words which still follow the rules of the source language, see the panel at **Foreign words**.

- For -er and -est in adjectives, see the panel -er, -est.

in|ha|bit
△ in|hab|its
△ in|hab|ited
△ in|hab|it|ing
in|hab|it|able
in|hab|it|ant
in|ha|lant
in|ha|la|tion
in|hale
△ in|hales
△ in|haled
△ in|ha|ling
in|ha|ler
in|har|mo|ni|ous
in|har|mo|ni|
  ously
in|here
△ in|heres
△ in|hered
△ in|her|ing
in|her|ent
in|her|ently
in|herit
△ in|her|its
△ in|her|ited
△ in|her|it|ing
in|her|it|able
in|her|it|ance
in|her|itor
in|hi|bit
△ in|hib|its
△ in|hib|ited
△ in|hib|it|ing
in|hib|ited
in|hib|it|edly
in|hi|bi|tion
in|hib|itor
in|hos|pit|able
in|hos|pit|ably
in|hu|man
in|hu|mane
in|hu|manely
in|hu|man|ity
△ in|hu|man|it|ies

in|hu|manly
in|im|ical
in|im|ic|ally
in|im|it|able
in|im|it|ably
ini|quit|ous
ini|quit|ously
ini|quity
△ ini|qui|ties
ini|tial
VERB
△ ini|tials
△ ini|tialled
△ ini|tial|ling
ini|tially
ini|ti|ate
VERB
△ ini|ti|ates
△ ini|ti|ated
△ ini|ti|ating
ini|ti|ation
ini|tiat|ive
ini|ti|ator
in|ject
△ in|jects
△ in|jec|ted
△ in|ject|ing
in|jec|tion
in|ju|di|cious
in|ju|di|ciously
in|ju|di|cious|
  ness
in|junc|tion
in|junc|tive
in|jure
△ in|jures
△ in|jured
△ in|jur|ing
in|juri|ous
in|juri|ously
in|jury
△ in|jur|ies
in|jus|tice
ink

VERB
△ inks
△ inked
△ ink|ing
In|ka|tha
ink|blot
in|ki|ness
ink|ling
ink|pad
ink|stand
ink|well
inky
△ in|kier
△ in|ki|est
in|laid
in|land
in-law
in|lay
VERB
△ in|lays
△ in|laid
△ in|lay|ing
in|lay|ing
inlet
in loco pa|ren|tis
in|mate
in|most

> inn
> *pub*
> ⚠ in

in|nards
in|nate
in|nately
in|nate|ness
inner
in|ner|most

> in|ning
> *in baseball*
> ⚠ innings

> in|nings
> *sing. and pl.*

> *in cricket*
> ⚠ inning

inn|kee|per
in|no|cence
in|no|cent
in|no|cently
in|nocu|ous
in|nocu|ously
in|nocu|ous|ness
in|no|vate
△ in|no|vates
△ in|no|va|ted
△ in|no|va|ting
in|no|va|tion
in|no|va|tive
in|no|va|tor
in|no|va|tory
Inns|bruck
in|nu|endo
△ in|nu|en|dos
  or in|nu|en|
  does
In|nuit
in|nu|mer|able
in|nu|mer|ably
in|nu|mer|acy
in|nu|mer|ate
in|ocu|late
△ in|ocu|lates
△ in|ocu|la|ted
△ in|ocu|la|ting
in|ocu|la|tion
in|of|fen|sive
in|of|fen|sively
in|of|fen|sive|
  ness
in|oper|able
in|oper|at|ive
in|op|por|tune
in|op|por|tunely
in|or|din|ate
in|or|din|ately
in|or|ganic

in|or|gan|ic|ally
in-patient
input
  VERB
  △ in|puts
  △ input
  △ in|put|ting
in|quest
in|qui|et|ude
in|quire
  △ in|quires
  △ in|quired
  △ in|quir|ing
in|quirer
in|quir|ing
in|quir|ingly
in|quiry
  △ in|quir|ies
In|qui|si|tion
  papal tribunal
in|qui|si|tion
  intensive
  investigation
in|qui|si|tional
in|quis|it|ive
in|quis|it|ively
in|quis|it|ive|
  ness
in|quis|itor
in|quis|it|or|ial
in|quis|it|ori|ally
in re
in|road
in|rush
  △ in|rushes
in|sa|lu|bri|ous
in|sane
  NOUN
  sing. and pl.
  ADJ.
  △ in|sa|ner
  △ in|sa|nest
in|sanely
in|san|it|ari|ness

in|san|it|ary
in|san|ity
  △ in|san|it|ies
in|sa|ti|ab|il|ity
in|sa|ti|able
in|sa|ti|ably
in|scribe
  △ in|scribes
  △ in|scribed
  △ in|scri|bing
in|scrip|tion
in|scrip|tional
in|scru|ta|bil|ity
in|scrut|able
in|scrut|ably
in|sect
In|secta
in|sec|ti|ci|dal
in|sec|ti|cide
in|sec|ti|vore
in|sec|tiv|or|ous
in|se|cure
in|se|curely
in|se|cur|ity
  △ in|se|cur|it|ies
in|sem|in|ate
  △ in|sem|in|ates
  △ in|sem|in|ated
  △ in|sem|in|
  ating
in|sem|in|ation
in|sen|sate
in|sen|sately
in|sen|sate|ness
in|sen|si|bil|ity
in|sens|ible
in|sens|ibly
in|sen|sit|ive
in|sen|sit|ively
in|sen|si|tiv|ity
in|se|par|ab|il|ity
in|se|par|able
in|se|par|ably
in|sert

VERB
  △ in|serts
  △ in|ser|ted
  △ in|sert|ing
in|ser|tion
in-ser|vice
inset
  VERB
  △ in|sets
  △ inset
  △ in|set|ting
in|shore
in|side
in|si|der
in|si|di|ous
in|si|di|ously
in|si|di|ous|ness
in|sight
in|sight|ful
in|sig|nia
  △ in|sig|nia *or*
  in|sig|nias
in|sig|ni|fi|cance
in|sig|ni|fi|cant
in|sig|ni|fi|cantly
in|sin|cere
in|sin|cerely
in|sin|cer|ity
  △ in|sin|cer|it|ies
in|si|nu|ate
  △ in|si|nu|ates
  △ in|si|nu|ated
  △ in|si|nu|ating
in|si|nu|at|ingly
in|si|nu|ation
in|si|pid
in|sip|idly
in|sip|id|ness
in|sist
  △ in|sists
  △ in|sis|ted
  △ in|sist|ing
in|sist|ence
in|sist|ent

in|sist|ently
in situ
in|so|far
in|sole
in|so|lence
in|so|lent
in|so|lently
in|so|lu|bil|ity
in|sol|uble
in|sol|vency
in|sol|vent
in|som|nia
in|som|niac
in|so|much
in|sou|ci|ance
in|sou|ci|ant
in|spect
  △ in|spects
  △ in|spec|ted
  △ in|spect|ing
in|spec|tion
in|spec|tor
in|spec|tor|ate
In|spec|tor Calls,
  An
in|spi|ra|tion
in|spi|ra|tional
in|spire
  △ in|spires
  △ in|spired
  △ in|spir|ing
in|spired
in|spir|ing
in|spir|ingly
in|sta|bil|ity
in|stall
  △ in|stalls
  △ in|stalled
  △ in|stal|ling
in|stal|la|tion
in|stal|ment
in|stance
in|stant
in|stan|ta|ne|ous

in|stan|ta|ne|
  ously
in|stan|tly
in|star
in|stead
in|step
in|sti|gate
  △ in|sti|gates
  △ in|sti|ga|ted
  △ in|sti|ga|ting
in|sti|ga|tion
in|sti|ga|tor
in|stil
  △ in|stils
  △ in|stilled
  △ in|stil|ling
in|stil|la|tion
in|stil|ler
in|stil|ment
in|stinct
in|stinct|ive
in|stinct|ively
in|sti|tute
  VERB
  △ in|sti|tutes
  △ in|sti|tu|ted
  △ in|sti|tu|ting
in|sti|tu|tion
in|sti|tu|tional
in|sti|tu|tion|al|
  ism
in|sti|tu|tion|al|
  ize
  △ in|sti|tu|tion|
  al|izes
  △ in|sti|tu|tion|
  al|ized
  △ in|sti|tu|tion|
  al|izing
in|struct
  △ in|structs
  △ in|struc|ted
  △ in|struct|ing
in|struc|tion

in|struct|ive
in|struct|ively
in|struct|ive|ness
in|struc|tor
in|struct|ress
  △ in|struct|res|
  ses
in|stru|ment
  VERB
  △ in|stru|ments
  △ in|stru|men|
  ted
  △ in|stru|ment|
  ing
in|stru|men|tal
in|stru|men|tal|
  ist
in|stru|men|tally
in|stru|men|ta|
  tion
in|sub|or|din|ate
in|sub|or|din|
  ately
in|sub|or|din|
  ation
in|sub|stan|tial
in|sub|stan|ti|al|
  ity
in|sub|stan|tially
in|suf|fer|able
in|suf|fer|ably
in|suf|fi|ciency
in|suf|fi|cient
in|suf|fi|ciently
in|su|lar
in|su|lar|ity
in|su|late
  △ in|su|lates
  △ in|su|la|ted
  △ in|su|la|ting
in|su|la|tion
in|su|la|tor
in|su|lin
in|sult

VERB
  △ in|sults
  △ in|sul|ted
  △ in|sult|ing
in|sult|ing
in|sult|ingly
in|su|per|ab|il|ity
in|su|per|able
in|su|per|ably
in|sup|port|able
in|sur|able
in|sur|ance

in|sure
take out
insurance policy
  △ in|sures
  △ in|sured
  △ in|sur|ing
  ⚠ensure

in|sured
in|surer
in|sur|gence
in|sur|gency
in|sur|gent
in|sur|mount|ab|
  il|ity
in|sur|mount|
  able
in|sur|rec|tion
in|sur|rec|tion|
  ist
in|tact
in|taglio
in|take
in|tan|gi|bil|ity
in|tan|gible
in|tan|gibly
in|te|ger
in|teg|ral
in|teg|rand
in|teg|rate
  △ in|teg|rates
  △ in|teg|ra|ted

  △ in|teg|ra|ting
in|teg|ra|tion
in|teg|rity
in|tegu|ment
in|tegu|men|tal
in|tegu|ment|ary
in|tel|lect
in|tel|lec|tual
in|tel|lec|tu|al|ize
  △ in|tel|lec|tu|al|
  izes
  △ in|tel|lec|tu|al|
  ized
  △ in|tel|lec|tu|al|
  izing
in|tel|lec|tu|ally
in|tel|li|gence
in|tel|li|gent
in|tel|li|gently
in|tel|li|gent|sia
in|tel|li|gi|bil|ity
in|tel|li|gible
in|tel|li|gibly
in|tem|per|ance
in|tem|per|ate
in|tem|per|ately
in|tend
  △ in|tends
  △ in|ten|ded
  △ in|tend|ing
in|ten|ded
in|tense
in|tensely
in|ten|si|fi|ca|
  tion
in|ten|si|fier
in|ten|sify
  △ in|ten|si|fies
  △ in|ten|si|fied
  △ in|ten|si|fy|ing
in|ten|sity
  △ in|ten|si|ties
in|ten|sive
in|ten|sively

in|ten|sive|ness
in|tent
in|ten|tion
in|ten|tional
in|ten|tion|ally
in|tently
in|tent|ness
inter
△ in|ters
△ in|terred
△ in|ter|ring
in|ter|act
△ in|ter|acts
△ in|ter|ac|ted
△ in|ter|act|ing
in|ter|ac|tion
in|ter|act|ive
in|ter|act|ively
inter alia
in|ter|breed
△ in|ter|breeds
△ in|ter|bred
△ in|ter|breed|
 ing
in|ter|breed|ing
in|ter|cal|ary
in|ter|cede
△ in|ter|cedes
△ in|ter|ceded
△ in|ter|ceding
in|ter|cel|lu|lar
in|ter|cept
△ in|ter|cepts
△ in|ter|cep|ted
△ in|ter|cept|ing
in|ter|cep|tion
in|ter|cept|ive
in|ter|cep|tor
in|ter|ces|sion
in|ter|ces|sional
in|ter|ces|sor
in|ter|change
 VERB
△ in|ter|changes

△ in|ter|changed
△ in|ter|
 changing
in|ter|change|ab|
 il|ity
in|ter|change|
 able
in|ter|change|
 ably
in|ter|city
in|ter|com
in|ter|com|mu|
 ni|cate
△ in|ter|com|
 mu|ni|cates
△ in|ter|com|
 mu|ni|ca|ted
△ in|ter|com|
 mu|ni|ca|ting
in|ter|com|mu|
 ni|ca|tion
in|ter|con|nect
△ in|ter|con|
 nects
△ in|ter|con|nec|
 ted
△ in|ter|con|
 nect|ing
in|ter|con|nec|
 tion
in|ter|con|ti|nen|
 tal
in|ter|course
in|ter|crop|ping
in|ter|de|nomi|
 na|tional
in|ter|de|part|
 men|tal
in|ter|de|pend|
 ence
in|ter|de|pend|
 ent
in|ter|de|pend|
 ently

in|ter|dict
△ in|ter|dicts
△ in|ter|dic|ted
△ in|ter|dict|ing
in|ter|dic|tion
in|ter|dict|ory
in|ter|dis|ci|plin|
 ary
in|ter|est
 VERB
△ in|ter|ests
△ in|ter|es|ted
△ in|ter|est|ing
in|ter|es|ted
in|ter|est|edly
in|ter|est|ing
in|ter|est|ingly
in|ter|face
 VERB
△ in|ter|fa|ces
△ in|ter|faced
△ in|ter|fa|cing
in|ter|fa|cing
in|ter|fere
△ in|ter|feres
△ in|ter|fered
△ in|ter|fer|ing
in|ter|fer|ence
in|ter|fer|ing
in|ter|fer|om|
 eter
in|ter|feron
in|ter|fuse
△ in|ter|fu|ses
△ in|ter|fused
△ in|ter|fu|sing
in|ter|fu|sion
in|ter|ga|lac|tic
in|terim
in|ter|ior
in|ter|ject
△ in|ter|jects
△ in|ter|jec|ted
△ in|ter|ject|ing

in|ter|jec|tion
in|ter|jec|tional
in|ter|lace
△ in|ter|la|ces
△ in|ter|laced
△ in|ter|la|cing
in|ter|lace|ment
in|ter|lard
△ in|ter|lards
△ in|ter|lar|ded
△ in|ter|lard|ing
in|ter|leaf
△ in|ter|leaves
in|ter|leave
△ in|ter|leaves
△ in|ter|leaved
△ in|ter|leav|ing
in|ter|leu|kin
in|ter|line
△ in|ter|lines
△ in|ter|lined
△ in|ter|li|ning
in|ter|lin|ear
in|ter|lin|ea|tion
in|ter|li|ning
in|ter|link
△ in|ter|links
△ in|ter|linked
△ in|ter|link|ing
in|ter|lock
 VERB
△ in|ter|locks
△ in|ter|locked
△ in|ter|lock|ing
in|ter|lock|ing
in|ter|lo|cu|tion
in|ter|locu|tor
in|ter|locu|tory
in|ter|lo|per
in|ter|lude
in|ter|mar|riage
in|ter|marry
△ in|ter|mar|ries
△ in|ter|mar|ried

△ in|ter|mar|ry|
ing
in|ter|me|di|ary
△ in|ter|me|di|
ar|ies
in|ter|me|di|ate
VERB
△ in|ter|me|di|
ates
△ in|ter|me|di|
ated
△ in|ter|me|di|
ating
in|ter|me|di|
ately
in|ter|me|di|
ation

in|ter|ment
burial
⚠ internment

in|ter|mezzo
△ in|ter|mez|zos
or in|ter|mezzi
in|ter|min|able
in|ter|min|able|
ness
in|ter|min|ably
in|ter|min|gle
△ in|ter|min|gles
△ in|ter|min|
gled
△ in|ter|min|
gling
in|ter|mis|sion
in|ter|mit|tence
in|ter|mit|tent
in|ter|mit|tently
in|tern
VERB
△ in|terns
△ in|terned
△ in|tern|ing
in|ter|nal

in|ter|nal|iza|
tion
in|ter|nal|ize
△ in|ter|nal|izes
△ in|ter|nal|ized
△ in|ter|nal|izing
in|tern|ally
in|ter|na|tional
In|ter|na|tion|ale,
L'
in|ter|na|tion|al|
ism
in|ter|na|tion|al|
ist
in|ter|na|tion|al|
ity
in|ter|na|tion|al|
iza|tion
in|ter|na|tion|al|
ize
△ in|ter|na|tion|
al|izes
△ in|ter|na|tion|
al|ized
△ in|ter|na|tion|
al|izing
in|ter|na|tion|
ally
interne *see*
intern
in|ter|necine
in|ter|nee
In|ter|net

in|tern|ment
imprisonment etc
⚠ interment

in|ter|node
in|tern|ship
in|ter|pel|late
△ in|ter|pel|lates
△ in|ter|pel|la|ted
△ in|ter|pel|la|
ting

in|ter|pel|la|tion
in|ter|pel|la|tor
in|ter|pen|et|rate
△ in|ter|pen|et|
rates
△ in|ter|pen|et|
ra|ted
△ in|ter|pen|et|
ra|ting
in|ter|pen|et|ra|
tion
in|ter|per|sonal
in|ter|phase
in|ter|plan|et|ary
in|ter|play
In|ter|pol
in|ter|po|late
△ in|ter|po|lates
△ in|ter|po|lated
△ in|ter|po|la|
ting
in|ter|po|la|tion
in|ter|pose
△ in|ter|po|ses
△ in|ter|posed
△ in|ter|po|sing
in|ter|po|si|tion
in|ter|pret
△ in|ter|prets
△ in|ter|preted
△ in|ter|pret|ing
in|ter|pret|ation
in|ter|pret|at|ive
in|ter|pret|at|
ively
in|ter|pre|ter
in|ter|pret|ive
in|ter|pret|ively
in|ter|ra|cial
in|ter|ra|cially
in|ter|reg|num
△ in|ter|reg|
nums *or* in|
ter|regna

in|ter|re|late
△ in|ter|re|lates
△ in|ter|re|la|ted
△ in|ter|re|la|
ting
in|ter|re|la|ted
in|ter|re|la|tion
in|ter|re|la|tion|
ship
in|ter|ro|gate
△ in|ter|ro|gates
△ in|ter|ro|ga|
ted
△ in|ter|ro|ga|
ting
in|ter|ro|ga|tion
in|ter|rog|at|ive
in|ter|rog|at|
ively
in|ter|ro|ga|tor
in|ter|rog|at|ory
NOUN
△ in|ter|rog|at|
or|ies
in|ter|rupt
△ in|ter|rupts
△ in|ter|rup|ted
△ in|ter|rupt|ing
in|ter|rup|ter
in|ter|rup|tion
in|ter|rupt|ive
in|ter|sect
△ in|ter|sects
△ in|ter|sec|ted
△ in|ter|sect|ing
in|ter|sec|tion
in|ter|sec|tional
in|ter|space
VERB
△ in|ter|spa|ces
△ in|ter|spaced
△ in|ter|spa|cing
in|ter|sperse
△ in|ter|sper|ses

△ in|ter|spersed
△ in|ter|sper|
  sing
in|ter|sper|sion
in|ter|state
in|ter|stel|lar
in|ter|stice
in|ter|twine
△ in|ter|twines
△ in|ter|twined
△ in|ter|twi|ning
in|ter|val
in|ter|vene
△ in|ter|venes
△ in|ter|vened
△ in|ter|ven|ing
in|ter|ven|tion
in|ter|ven|tion|
  ism
in|ter|ven|tion|
  ist
in|ter|view
  VERB
△ in|ter|views
△ in|ter|viewed
△ in|ter|view|ing
in|ter|viewee
in|ter|viewer
in|ter|weave
△ in|ter|weaves
△ in|ter|wove
△ in|ter|weav|
  ing
△ in|ter|wo|ven
in|tes|tacy
in|tes|tate
in|tes|ti|nal
in|tes|tine
in|ti|fada
in|ti|macy
△ in|ti|ma|cies
in|ti|mate
  VERB
△ in|ti|mates

△ in|ti|ma|ted
△ in|ti|ma|ting
in|ti|mately
in|ti|ma|tion
in|tim|id|ate
△ in|tim|id|ates
△ in|tim|id|ated
△ in|tim|id|ating
in|tim|id|ating
in|tim|id|ation
in|tim|ism
into
in|tol|er|able
in|tol|er|ably
in|tol|er|ance
in|tol|er|ant
in|tol|er|antly
in|ton|ate
△ in|ton|ates
△ in|ton|ated
△ in|ton|ating
in|ton|ation
in|tone
△ in|tones
△ in|toned
△ in|ton|ing
in toto
in|tox|ic|ant
in|toxi|cate
△ in|toxi|cates
△ in|toxi|ca|ted
△ in|toxi|ca|ting
in|toxi|ca|ting
in|toxi|ca|tion
in|tra|cel|lu|lar
in|trac|ta|bil|ity
in|tract|able
in|tract|ably
in|tra|mu|ral
in|tra|mur|ally
in|tran|si|gence
in|tran|si|gent
in|tran|si|gently
in|tran|sit|ive

in|tran|sit|ively
in|tra|pre|neur
in|tra|uter|ine
in|tra|ven|ous
in|tra|ven|ously
intravert *see*
  introvert
in|tre|pid
in|tre|pid|ity
in|trep|idly
in|tri|cacy
△ in|tri|ca|cies
in|tri|cate
in|tri|cately
in|trigue
  VERB
△ in|trigues
△ in|trigued
△ in|tri|guing
in|tri|guing
in|tri|guingly
in|trin|sic
in|trin|sic|ally
intro
in|tro|duce
△ in|tro|du|ces
△ in|tro|duced
△ in|tro|du|cing
in|tro|du|cible
in|tro|duc|tion
in|tro|duc|tor|ily
in|tro|duc|tory
in|troit
in|tron
in|tro|spec|tion
in|tro|spect|ive
in|tro|spect|ively
in|tro|ver|sion
in|tro|vert
  VERB
△ in|tro|verts
△ in|tro|ver|ted
△ in|tro|vert|ing
in|trude

△ in|trudes
△ in|tru|ded
△ in|tru|ding
in|tru|der
in|tru|sion
in|tru|sive
in|tru|sively
in|tru|sive|ness
intrust *see*
  entrust
in|tuit
△ in|tu|its
△ in|tu|ited
△ in|tu|it|ing
in|tu|ition
in|tu|it|ive
in|tu|it|ively
in|tu|it|ive|ness
Inuit
Inuk|ti|tut
in|un|date
△ in|un|dates
△ in|un|da|ted
△ in|un|da|ting
in|un|da|tion
inure
△ in|ures
△ in|ured
△ in|ur|ing
in|ure|ment
in|vade
△ in|vades
△ in|va|ded
△ in|va|ding
in|va|der
in|va|lid
  VERB
△ in|va|lids
△ in|va|li|ded
△ in|va|li|ding
in|val|id|ate
△ in|val|id|ates
△ in|val|id|ated
△ in|val|id|ating

in|val|id|ation
In|va|lides,
  Hôtel des
in|va|lid|ity
in|val|idly
in|valu|able
in|valu|ably
in|vari|able
in|vari|ably
in|vari|ant
in|va|sion
in|va|sive
in|vect|ive
in|veigh
  △ in|veighs
  △ in|veighed
  △ in|veigh|ing
in|vei|gle
  △ in|vei|gles
  △ in|vei|gled
  △ in|veig|ling
in|veigle|ment
in|vent
  △ in|vents
  △ in|ven|ted
  △ in|vent|ing
in|ven|tion
in|vent|ive
in|vent|ive|ness
in|ven|tor
in|ven|tory
  NOUN
  △ in|ven|tor|ies
  VERB
  △ in|ven|tor|ies
  △ in|ven|tor|ied
  △ in|ven|tory|ing
In|ver|ness
in|verse
in|versely
in|ver|sion
in|vert
  △ in|verts
  △ in|ver|ted

△ in|vert|ing
in|ver|tase
in|ver|teb|rate
in|vest
  △ in|vests
  △ in|ves|ted
  △ in|vest|ing
in|ves|ti|gate
  △ in|ves|ti|gates
  △ in|ves|ti|ga|ted
  △ in|ves|ti|ga|
    ting
in|ves|ti|ga|tion
in|ves|ti|gat|ive
in|ves|ti|ga|tor
in|ves|ti|ga|tory
in|ves|ti|ture
in|vest|ment
in|ves|tor
in|vet|er|ate
in|vet|er|ately
in|vi|di|ous
in|vi|di|ously
in|vi|di|ous|ness
in|vi|gil|ate
  △ in|vi|gil|ates
  △ in|vi|gil|ated
  △ in|vi|gil|ating
in|vi|gil|ation
in|vi|gil|ator
in|vig|or|ate
  △ in|vig|or|ates
  △ in|vig|or|ated
  △ in|vig|or|ating
in|vig|or|ating
in|vig|or|ation
in|vin|ci|bil|ity
in|vin|cible
in|vin|cible|ness
in|vin|cibly
in|vi|ol|ab|il|ity
in|vi|ol|able
in|vi|ol|ably
in|vi|ol|ate

in|vi|si|bil|ity
in|vis|ible
In|vis|ible Man,
  The
in|vis|ibly
in|vi|ta|tion
in|vite
  VERB
  △ in|vites
  △ in|vi|ted
  △ in|vi|ting
in|vi|ting
in|vi|tingly
in vitro
in vivo
in|vo|ca|tion
in|voc|at|ory
in|voice
  VERB
  △ in|voi|ces
  △ in|voiced
  △ in|voi|cing
in|voke
  △ in|vokes
  △ in|voked
  △ in|vo|king
in|vol|un|tar|ily
in|vol|un|tary
in|volve
  △ in|volves
  △ in|volved
  △ in|vol|ving
in|volved
in|volve|ment
in|vul|ner|ab|il|
  ity
in|vul|ner|able
in|vul|ner|ably
in|ward
in|wardly
inwards *see*
  inward
in-your-face
Io

iod|ide
iod|ine
iod|ize
  △ iod|izes
  △ iod|ized
  △ iod|izing
ion
Iona
Ion|esco
Ionia
Ionic
ionic
ion|iza|tion
ion|ize
  △ ion|izes
  △ ion|ized
  △ ion|izing
ion|izer
iono|mer
iono|sphere
iono|spheric
Ios
iota
Iowa
ipe|ca|cu|anha
Iphi|ge|neia
ipso facto
Ip|swich
Iran
Iran|gate
Ira|nian
Iraq
iras|ci|bil|ity
iras|cible
iras|cibly
irate
irately
irate|ness
ire
ire|ful
Ire|land
Irene
Ire|ton
iri|des|cence

iri|des|cent
iri|des|cen|tly
irid|ium
Iris
iris
△ iri|ses *or* iri|
 des
Irish
Irish|man
△ Irish|men
Irish|wo|man
△ Irish|wo|men
irk
△ irks
△ irked
△ irk|ing ——
irk|some
irk|somely
Ir|kutsk
iron
 VERB
△ irons
△ ironed
△ iron|ing
Iron|bridge
iron|clad
iron-grey
ironic
iron|ical
iron|ic|ally
iron|ing
iron|mas|ter
iron|mon|ger
iron|mon|gery
△ iron|mon|ger|
 ies
Irons
Iron|sides
iron|stone
iron|ware
iron|work
irony
△ iron|ies
Iro|quois

ir|ra|di|ate
△ ir|ra|di|ates
△ ir|ra|di|ated
△ ir|ra|di|ating
ir|ra|di|ation
ir|ra|tional
ir|ra|tion|al|ity
ir|ra|tion|ally
ir|re|con|cil|ab|il|
 ity
ir|re|con|cil|able
ir|re|con|cil|ably
ir|re|cov|er|able
ir|re|cov|er|ably
ir|re|deem|able
ir|re|deem|ably
ir|re|dent|ism
ir|re|dent|ist
ir|re|du|cible
ir|re|du|cibly
ir|re|fut|able
ir|re|fut|ably
ir|re|gu|lar
ir|re|gu|lar|ity
△ ir|re|gu|lar|it|
 ies
ir|re|gu|larly
ir|re|lev|ance
ir|re|lev|ancy
△ ir|re|lev|an|cies
ir|re|lev|ant
ir|re|lev|antly
ir|re|li|gion
ir|re|li|gious
ir|re|me|di|able
ir|re|me|di|ably
ir|re|mov|able
ir|re|mov|ably
ir|re|par|ab|il|ity
ir|re|par|able
ir|re|par|ably
ir|re|place|able
ir|re|place|ably
ir|re|pres|si|bil|ity

ir|re|press|ible
ir|re|press|ibly
ir|re|proach|able
ir|re|proach|ably
ir|res|is|ti|bil|ity
ir|res|ist|ible
ir|res|ist|ible|ness
ir|res|ist|ibly
ir|res|ol|ute
ir|re|sol|utely
ir|re|sol|ute|ness
ir|re|so|lu|tion
ir|res|pect|ive
ir|res|pon|si|bil|
 ity
ir|res|pons|ible
ir|res|pons|ibly
ir|re|triev|able
ir|re|triev|ably
ir|rev|er|ence
ir|rev|er|ent
ir|rev|er|ently
ir|re|vers|ible
ir|re|vers|ibly
ir|re|vo|ca|bil|ity
ir|re|voc|able
ir|re|voc|ably
ir|rig|able
ir|ri|gate
△ ir|ri|gates
△ ir|ri|ga|ted
△ ir|ri|ga|ting
ir|ri|ga|tion
ir|rit|ab|il|ity
ir|rit|able|ness
ir|rit|able
ir|rit|ably
ir|rit|ant
ir|ri|tate
△ ir|ri|tates
△ ir|ri|ta|ted
△ ir|ri|ta|ting
ir|ri|ta|ting
ir|ri|ta|tingly

ir|ri|ta|tion
ir|rupt
△ ir|rupts
△ ir|rup|ted
△ ir|rupt|ing
ir|rup|tion
ir|rup|tive
Ir|ving
is
Isaac
Isa|bel
Isaiah, Book of
isch|aemia
Ish|er|wood
Ish|mael
is|in|glass
Isis
Isla
Islam
Is|la|ma|bad
Is|lamic
Is|la|mi|cist
Is|la|mi|ci|za|
 tion
Is|la|mi|cize
△ Is|la|mi|ci|zes
△ Is|la|mi|cized
△ Is|la|mi|ci|zing
Is|lam|iza|tion
Is|lam|ize
△ Is|lam|izes
△ Is|lam|ized
△ Is|lam|izing
is|land
is|lan|der

└&boxhr;&boxhr;┘
isle
island
 △aisle
┌&boxhr;&boxhr;┐

Isle of Man
Isle of Wight
islet
ism
Is|maili

isn't
iso|bar
iso|baric
Iso|bel
iso|chro|nal
iso|chron|ous
iso|late
 △ iso|lates
 △ iso|la|ted
 △ iso|la|ting
iso|la|ted
iso|la|tion
iso|la|tion|ism
iso|la|tion|ist
iso|leu|cine
iso|mer
iso|meric
iso|met|ric
iso|met|rics
 sing. and pl.
iso|morph
iso|mor|phic
iso|morph|ism
iso|morph|ous
iso|prene
isos|ce|les
iso|stasy

iso|therm
iso|tonic
iso|tope
iso|to|pic
iso|tro|pic
Israel
Is|raeli
Is|rael|ite
Is|si|go|nis
issue
 VERB
 △ is|sues
 △ is|sued
 △ is|su|ing
Is|tan|bul
isth|mus
 △ isth|muses
it
Ital|ian
Ital|ian|ate
italic
ita|li|ci|za|tion
ital|icize
 △ ital|ici|zes
 △ ital|icized
 △ ital|ici|zing
Italy

itch
 NOUN
 △ it|ches
 VERB
 △ it|ches
 △ itched
 △ itch|ing
it|chi|ness
itchy
 △ itch|ier
 △ it|chi|est
it'd
item
item|iza|tion
item|ize
 △ item|izes
 △ item|ized
 △ item|izing
it|er|ate
 △ it|er|ates
 △ it|er|ated
 △ it|er|ating
it|er|ation
it|er|at|ive
itin|er|ant
itin|er|ary
 △ itin|er|ar|ies

it'll

> its
> *of it*
> ⚠ it's

> it's
> *it is*
> ⚠ its

it|self
itsy-bitsy
itty-bitty
Ivan
Ivan|hoe
I've
Iviza *see* Ibiza
Ivor
ivory
 NOUN
 △ ivor|ies
Ivory Coast
Ivy
ivy
 △ ivies
ixia
Ixion
Izmir

-ize / -ise

This suffix represents the Greek verbal ending **-izo**. With many English verbs either form is permissible, and choice is often a question of personal preference or house style. However, once a choice is made, it should be applied consistently to all words of this type. The preference in this book is for **-ize**. **-ize** is also more common in North America, although it is not an Americanism.

Note that some words are derived from a root **-cise**, **-prise**, or **-vise**, or from some other fixed form that is not connected with Greek **-izo**. These have to be spelt **-ise**:

advertise	comprise	enfranchise	incise	reprise
advise	compromise	enterprise	merchandise	supervise
apprise	demise	excise	premise	surmise
arise	despise	exercise	prise (= ease	surprise
chastise	devise	franchise	open)	televise
circumcise	disguise	improvise	promise	

J

jam
*conserve of
boiled fruit and
sugar; cram;
stick*
VERB
△ jams
△ jammed
△ jam|ming
⚠ jamb

Ja|maica

jamb
*side-post of door
etc*
⚠ jam

jam|boree
James
James, Letter
of
Jame|son
James|town
jammy
△ jam|mier
△ jam|mi|est
jam-packed
Janá|ček
Jane
Jane Eyre
JANET
Janet
jan|gle
△ jan|gles
△ jan|gled
△ jang|ling
jangly
△ jang|lier
△ jang|li|est
Jan|ice
jan|is|sary
△ jan|is|sar|ies

jan|itor
Jan|sen
Jan|sen|ism
Janu|ary
Janus
Japan
japan
VERB
△ japans
△ ja|panned
△ ja|pan|ning
Jap|an|ese
jape
Japh|eth
Ja|po|nais|erie
ja|pon|ica
jar
VERB
△ jars
△ jarred
△ jar|ring
jar|di|ni|ère
jar|gon
Jar|man
jar|ring
jar|ringly
Jar|row
Jarry
Ja|ru|zel|ski
Jas|min
Jas|mine
jas|mine
Jason
jas|per
jaun|dice
jaun|diced
jaunt
VERB
△ jaunts
△ jaun|ted
△ jaunt|ing
jaun|tily
jaun|ti|ness
jaunty

△ jaun|tier
△ jaun|ti|est
Java
Ja|van|ese
jav|elin
jaw
VERB
△ jaws
△ jawed
△ jaw|ing
jaw|bone
jay
Jaya|war|dene
jay|walk
△ jay|walks
△ jay|walked
△ jay|walk|ing
jay|walker
jay|walk|ing
jazz
VERB
△ jaz|zes
△ jazzed
△ jazz|ing
jazz|ily
Jazz Singer, The
jazzy
△ jaz|zier
△ jaz|zi|est
J-curve
jeal|ous
jeal|ously
jeal|ousy
△ jeal|ous|ies
Jean
Jean de Flor|ette
jeans
Jed|dah
Jeep
jeer
VERB
△ jeers
△ jeered
△ jeer|ing

Jef|fer|son
Jef|freys
jehad *see* jihad
Je|ho|vah
je|june
je|ju|num

jell
set; take shape
△ jells
△ jelled
△ jell|ing
⚠ gel

Jel|li|coe
jel|lied
jelly
△ jel|lies
jel|ly|fish
△ jel|ly|fish *or*
jel|ly|fi|shes
Je|mima
jemmy
△ jem|mies
Jen|kins
Jen|ni|fer
jenny
△ jen|nies
jeo|pard|ize
△ jeo|pard|izes
△ jeo|pard|ized
△ jeo|pard|izing
jeo|pardy
jerbil *see* gerbil
jer|boa
je|re|miad
Je|re|miah,
Book of
Jer|emy
Jer|icho
jerk
VERB
△ jerks
△ jerked
△ jerk|ing

jerk|ily
jer|kin
jerky
je|ro|boam
Jer|ome
Jerry
△ Jer|ries
jerry
△ jer|ries
jerry-buil|der
jerry-build|ing
jerry-built
Jer|sey
jer|sey
Je|ru|sa|lem
Jesse
Jes|sica
jest
jes|ter
jest|ingly
Jes|uit
jesu|it|ical
jesu|it|ic|ally
Jesus
jet
    VERB
    △ jets
    △ jet|ted
    △ jet|ting
jet-black
jet|foil
jet-lagged
jet-pro|pelled
jet|sam
jet-set|ter
jet-set|ting
jet|ti|son
    △ jet|ti|sons
    △ jet|ti|soned
    △ jet|ti|son|ing
jetty
    △ jet|ties
Jew
jewel

jew|elled
jew|el|ler
jew|el|lery
Jew|ess
    △ Jew|es|ses
Jew|ish
Jew of Malta,
    The
Jewry
Jez|ebel
Jiang Jie|shi
Jiang Qing
jib
    VERB
    △ jibs
    △ jibbed
    △ jib|bing
jibe *see* gibe
jibe *see* gybe
Jiddah *see*
    Jeddah
jiffy
    △ jif|fies
Jiffy bag
jig
    VERB
    △ jigs
    △ jigged
    △ jig|ging
jig|ger
jig|gered
jig|gery-pokery
jig|gle
    VERB
    △ jig|gles
    △ jig|gled
    △ jig|gling
jig|saw
jihad
jilt
    △ jilts
    △ jil|ted
    △ jilt|ing

Jim Crow
jim|jams
jin|gle
    VERB
    △ jin|gles
    △ jin|gled
    △ jin|gling
jin|go|ism
jin|go|ist
jin|go|is|tic
jinja
jink
    VERB
    △ jinks
    △ jinked
    △ jink|ing
jinni
    △ jinn
jinx
    NOUN
    △ jinxes
    VERB
    △ jinxes
    △ jinxed
    △ jinx|ing
jit|ter
    VERB
    △ jit|ters
    △ jit|tered
    △ jit|ter|ing
jit|ter|bug
    VERB
    △ jit|ter|bugs
    △ jit|ter|bugged
    △ jit|ter|bug|
        ging
jit|tery
jiu-jitsu *see*
    jujitsu
Jiulong *see*
    Kowloon
jive
    VERB
    △ jives

△ jived
△ ji|ving
Joan
Joan of Arc
Job, Book of
job
    VERB
    △ jobs
    △ jobbed
    △ job|bing
job|ber
job|bery
job|less
job-shar|ing
Jo|casta
Jo|ce|lyn
Jock
jockey
    VERB
    △ jock|eys
    △ jock|eyed
    △ jock|ey|ing
jock|strap
jo|cose
jo|cosely
jo|cos|ity
jocu|lar
jo|cu|lar|ity
jocu|larly
joc|und
jo|cun|dity
jodh|purs
Jod|rell Bank
Joel, Book of
jog
    VERB
    △ jogs
    △ jogged
    △ jog|ging
jog|ger
jog|gers
jog|ging
jog|gle

VERB
△ jog|gles
△ jog|gled
△ jog|gling
jog-trot
Jo|han|nes|burg
John
John, Gos|pel
  ac|cord|ing to
John, Let|ters
  of
john
John Bull
johnny
△ john|nies
Johns Hop|kins
John|son
joie de vivre
join
  VERB
  △ joins
  △ joined
  △ join|ing
joiner
join|ery
joint
  VERB
  △ joints
  △ join|ted
  △ joint|ing
jointly
join|ture
  VERB
  △ join|tures
  △ join|tured
  △ join|tur|ing
joist
jo|joba
joke
  VERB
  △ jokes
  △ joked
  △ jo|king
joker

jokey
△ jo|kier
△ jo|ki|est
jo|ki|ness
jo|kingly
jol|li|fi|ca|tion
jol|li|ness
jol|lity
△ jol|li|ties
jolly
  VERB
  △ jol|lies
  △ jol|lied
  △ jol|ly|ing
  ADJ.
  △ jol|lier
  △ jol|li|est
jol|ly|boat
Jol|son
jolt
  VERB
  △ jolts
  △ jol|ted
  △ jolt|ing
Jonah, Book of
Jonah
Jon|athan
Jones
jon|quil
Jon|son
Jop|lin
Jor|dan
Jo|seph
Jo|seph of Ari|
  ma|thea
Jo|seph An|
  drews
Jo|sé|phine
  wife of Napoleon;
  French Christian
  name
Jo|seph|ine
  British Christian
  name

josh
  NOUN
  △ joshes
  VERB
  △ joshes
  △ joshed
  △ josh|ing
Joshua
Joshua, Book of
joss-stick
jos|tle
  VERB
  △ jos|tles
  △ jos|tled
  △ jos|tling
jot
  VERB
  △ jots
  △ jot|ted
  △ jot|ting
jot|ter
jot|ting
joule
jour|nal
jour|nal|ese
jour|nal|ism
jour|nal|ist
jour|nal|is|tic
Jour|nal of a
  Tour to the
  Heb|ri|des, The
Jour|nal of the
  Plague Year,
  A
jour|ney
  VERB
  △ jour|neys
  △ jour|neyed
  △ jour|ney|ing
jour|ney|man
  △ jour|ney|men
journo
  △ jour|nos *or*
  jour|noes

joust
  VERB
  △ jousts
  △ jous|ted
  △ joust|ing
Jove
jo|vial
jo|vi|al|ity
jo|vi|ally
jowl
Joy
joy
Joyce
joy|ful
joy|fully
joy|less
joy|ous
joy|ously
joy|ous|ness
joy|ride
  VERB
  △ joy|rides
  △ joy|rode
  △ joy|ri|ding
  △ joy-rid|den
joy|ri|der
joy|stick
ju|bi|lant
ju|bi|lantly
ju|bi|la|tion
ju|bi|lee
Judah
Ju|daic
Ju|da|ism
Judas
Judas Is|car|iot
jud|der
  VERB
  △ jud|ders
  △ jud|dered
  △ jud|der|ing
Jude
Jude, Let|ter of
Judea

*Jude the Ob|
scure*
judge
  VERB
△ jud|ges
△ judged
△ jud|ging
judge|ment
judge|men|tal
Jud|ges, Book
  of
ju|di|ca|ture
ju|di|cial
ju|di|ci|ally
ju|di|ci|ary
△ ju|di|ci|ari|es
ju|di|cious
ju|di|ciously
ju|di|cious|ness
Ju|dith
Ju|dith, Book of
judo
jug
  VERB
△ jugs
△ jugged
△ jug|ging
jug|ful
jug|ger|naut
jug|gle
△ jug|gles
△ jug|gled
△ jug|gling
jug|gler
Jugoslavia *see*
  Yugoslavia
jugu|lar
juice
jui|ci|ness

juicy
△ jui|cier
△ jui|ci|est
ju|jitsu
juju
ju|jube
juke|box
△ juke|boxes
julep
Jules et Jim
Julia
Ju|lian
Ju|li|ana
Julie
Ju|liet
Ju|lius Cae|sar
July
Jum|blat
jum|ble
  VERB
△ jum|bles
△ jum|bled
△ jum|bling
jumbo
jump
  VERB
△ jumps
△ jumped
△ jump|ing
jumped-up
jum|per
jump|ily
jum|pi|ness
jump-off
jump-start
△ jump-starts
△ jump-star|ted
△ jump-start|ing
jump|suit

jumpy
△ jum|pier
△ jum|pi|est
junc|tion
junc|ture
June
Jung
Jung|frau
jun|gle
*Jun|gle Book,
The*
jungle|fowl
jun|gly
△ jun|glier
△ jun|gli|est
ju|nior
ju|ni|per
junk
jun|ket
  VERB
△ jun|kets
△ jun|keted
△ jun|ket|ing
jun|kie
△ junk|ies
Juno
*Juno and the
Pay|cock*
junta
Ju|pi|ter
'Ju|pi|ter' Sym|
  phony
Jura
Jur|as|sic
ju|rid|ical
ju|ris|dic|tion
ju|ris|pru|dence
ju|ris|pru|den|
  tial

jur|ist
jur|is|tic
juror
jury
△ jur|ies
jury-box
△ jury-boxes
just
jus|tice
jus|ti|ci|ary
△ jus|ti|ci|ari|es
jus|ti|fi|able
jus|ti|fi|ably
jus|ti|fi|ca|tion
jus|tify
△ jus|ti|fies
△ jus|ti|fied
△ jus|ti|fy|ing
Jus|tin
Jus|tin|ian
justly
just|ness
Just So Stor|ies
jut
△ juts
△ jut|ted
△ jut|ting
Jute
jute
Jut|land
Ju|venal
ju|ven|ile
ju|ven|ilia
jux|ta|pose
△ jux|ta|po|ses
△ jux|ta|posed
△ jux|ta|po|sing
jux|ta|po|si|tion

K

Kaba
ka|baddi
Kab|ba|lah
Kab|bal|ist
Ka|buki
Kabul
kach|ina
Kádr
Kad|dish
kadi *see* cadi
Kaf|fir
Kafka
kaftan *see* caftan
Kai|ser
title of Prussian
kings 1870–1914
kai|ser
an emperor of
Germany,
Austria, or the
Holy Roman
Empire
ka|ke|mono
Ka|la|hari
ka|lan|choe
ka|lash|ni|kov
kale
kal|ei|do|scope
kal|ei|do|scopic
kal|ei|do|scop|ic|
ally
kal|ends
Ka|le|vala (Land
of Her|oes)
kale|yard
Kama Sutra
ka|mi|kaze
Kam|pala
Kampuchea *see*
Cambodia
kana
Kanchenjunga

see
Kangchenjunga
Kandy
kan|ga|roo
Kang|chen|
junga
Kan|sas
Kant
kao|lin
kao|lin|ite
Kapil Dev
kapok
kappa
kaput
Ka|ra|chi
Ka|rad|zic
Kara|jan
kara|kul
Ka|ra|man|lis
ka|ra|oke
ka|rate
kar|bo|van|ets
  △ kar|bo|vantsi
Karen
Kar|loff
Kar|lovy Vary
Karls|ruhe
karma
Kar|nak
kart
ka|ryo|type
kas|bah
Kash|mir
Kas|parov
Kas|sel
Ka|tha|kali
Kath|ar|ine
Kath|er|ine
Kath|mandu
ka|ty|did
Ka|unda
kauri
Ka|wa|saki
kayak

Kaye
Ka|zakh|stan
Kazan
Ka|zan|tzakis
kazoo
Kean
Keat|ing
Kea|ton
Keats
kebab
Keble
kedge
VERB
  △ ked|ges
  △ kedged
  △ ked|ging
ked|geree
keek
VERB
  △ keeks
  △ keeked
  △ keek|ing
keel
VERB
  △ keels
  △ keeled
  △ keel|ing
keel|haul
  △ keel|hauls
  △ keel|hauled
  △ keel|haul|ing
keelson *see*
kelson
keen
VERB
  △ keens
  △ keened
  △ keen|ing
ADJ.
  △ keener
  △ keen|est
keenly
keen|ness
keep

VERB
  △ keeps
  △ kept
  △ keep|ing
kee|per
keep-fit
keep|ing
keep|sake
keg
Keith
Kelly
Kelms|cott
kelp
kel|pie
kel|son
Kelt *see* Celt
kelt
kel|vin
Kemble
ken
VERB
  △ kens
  △ kent *or*
    kenned
  △ ken|ning
Ken|dal
kendo
Ken|il|worth
Ken|nedy
ken|nel
VERB
  △ ken|nels
  △ ken|elled
  △ ken|el|ling
Ken|neth
Ken|sing|ton
Kent
Ken|tucky
Kenya
Ken|yatta
kepi
Kep|ler
kept
Ker|ala

kera|tin

kerb
*edging to
pavement etc*
⚠curb

kerb-craw|ler
kerb-crawl|ing
kerb|stone
ker|chief
ker|fuf|fle
Ker|mit
Kern
ker|nel
kero|sene
Ker|ouac
Kerry
ke|rygma
kes|trel
Kes|wick
ketch
  △ ket|ches
ket|chup
ke|tone
ket|tle
kettle|drum
Kevin
Kew

key
*thing to open
lock etc; switch;
musical system;
island or reef;
enter electronic
data; harmonize*
VERB
  △ keys
  △ keyed
  △ key|ing
  ⚠quay

key|board
VERB
  △ key|boards

  △ key|boar|ded
  △ key|board|ing
key|boar|der
key|board|ist
key|hole
Keynes
Keynes|ian
key|note
key-ring
key|stone
key|stroke
key|word
khaki
khalif *see* caliph
Khan
khan
Khar|toum
Khat|cha|tur|ian
khe|dive
Khmer
Khmer Rouge
Khoi|san
Kho|meini
Khrush|chev
Khy|ber
kib|butz
  △ kib|but|zim
ki|bosh
  △ ki|boshes
kick
VERB
  △ kicks
  △ kicked
  △ kick|ing
kick|back
kicker
kick-off
kick-start
VERB
  △ kick-starts
  △ kick-star|ted
  △ kick-start|ing
kid

VERB
  △ kids
  △ kid|ded
  △ kid|ding
Kidd
kid|der
Kid|der|min|ster
kid|die
Kid|dush
kid|nap
VERB
  △ kid|naps
  △ kid|napped
  △ kid|nap|ping
Kid\napped
kid|ney
Kiel
Kieran
Kier|ke|gaard
kie|sel|guhr
Kie|sin|ger
Kiev
Ki|gali
Ki|kuyu
Kil|dare
Ki|li|man|jaro
Kil|kenny
kill
VERB
  △ kills
  △ killed
  △ kill|ing
Kil|lar|ney
kil|ler
kil|li|fish
sing. and pl.
kill|ing
kill|ingly
kill|joy
Kil|mar|nock
kiln
kilo
ki|lo|byte
ki|lo|cal|orie

ki|lo|cycle
ki|lo|gram
ki|lo|hertz
sing. and pl.
ki|lo|litre
ki|lo|metre
ki|lo|ton
ki|lo|watt
kilt
kil|ted
Kim
Kim|ber|ley
Kim Il-sung
ki|mono
kin
kind
ADJ.
  △ kinder
  △ kind|est
kin|der|gar|ten
kind-hearted
kind-heart|edly
kind-heart|ed|ness
*Kind Hearts
and Co|ro|nets*
kin|dle
  △ kin|dles
  △ kin|dled
  △ kind|ling
kind|li|ness
kind|ling
kindly
  △ kind|lier
  △ kind|li|est
kind|ness
  △ kind|nes|ses
kind|red
kine
ki|ne|matic
ki|ne|mat|ics
kin|es|ics
kin|esis
  △ kin|eses
kin|etic

kin|et|ic|ally
kin|et|ics
King
king
king|cup
king|dom
king|fi|sher
King Kong
King Lear
king|li|ness
kingly
△ king|lier
△ king|li|est
king|ma|ker
king|pin
king|post
King Priam
Kings, Books of
king|ship
king-size
Kings|ley
King's Lynn
Kings|ton
Kings|ton-
  upon-Hull
Kings|town
kinin
kink
  VERB
  △ kinks
  △ kinked
  △ kink|ing
kin|ki|ness
kinky
  △ kin|kier
  △ kin|ki|est
Kin|nock
kin|nor
Kin|sey
kins|folk
Kins|hasa
kin|ship
kins|man
  △ kins|men

kins|wo|man
  △ kins|wo|men
Kin|tyre
kiosk
kip
  VERB
  △ kips
  △ kipped
  △ kip|ping
Kip|ling
kip|per
  VERB
  △ kip|pers
  △ kip|pered
  △ kip|per|ing
Kir|bi|grip
Kir|ghi|zia
Ki|ri|bati
Kirk
kirk
Kirk|caldy
Kirk|cud|bright
Kirk|wall
Kirov
kirsch
Kish|inev
kis|met
Kiss, The
kiss
  NOUN
  △ kis|ses
  VERB
  △ kis|ses
  △ kissed
  △ kiss|ing
kiss|able
kis|ser
Kis|sin|ger
kis|so|gram
kit
  VERB
  △ kits
  △ kit|ted
  △ kit|ting

kit|bag
Kit-cat
kit|chen
Kitch|ener
kit|chen|ette
Kit|chen-Sink
kite
Kite|mark
kith
kith|ara
kitsch
kit|schy
  △ kit|schier
  △ kit|schi|est
kit|ten
kit|ten|ish
kit|ti|wake
kitty
  △ kit|ties
kiwi
Kiyev *see* Kiev
klaxon
Klee
Klein
Klem|perer
klep|to|ma|nia
klep|to|ma|niac
Klimt
klip|sprin|ger
Klop|stock
Klos|ters
knack
knacker
  VERB
  △ knack|ers
  △ knackered
  △ knack|er|ing
knap|sack
knap|weed

knave
  *scoundrel; jack
  at Cards*
  ⚠ nave

kna|very
  △ kna|ver|ies
kna|vish
kna|vishly

knead
  *squeeze with
  fingers*
  △ kneads
  △ knea|ded
  △ knead|ing
  ⚠ need

knee
  VERB
  △ knees
  △ kneed
  △ knee|ing
knee-bree|ches
knee|cap
  VERB
  △ knee|caps
  △ knee|capped
  △ knee|cap|ping
knee|cap|ping
knee-deep
knee-high
knee-jerk
kneel
  △ kneels
  △ knelt *or*
    kneeled
  △ kneel|ing
  △ knelt *or*
    kneeled
knee-length
knee|ler
knees-up
knell
  VERB
  △ knells
  △ knelled
  △ knell|ing
knelt
Knes|set

knew
knick¦er¦bock¦
  ers
knick|ers
knick-knack
knife
  NOUN
  △ knives
  VERB
  △ knifes
  △ knifed
  △ knifing
knife-edge

knight
*medieval
warrior; man
who has been
granted title of
'Sir' before his
first name*
VERB
△ knights
△ knigh¦ted
△ knight|ing
⚠ night

knight|hood
knightly
  △ knight¦lier
  △ knight¦li|est

knit
*make garments
etc with knitting
needles; united*
△ knits
△ knit¦ted *or*
  knit
△ knit|ting
⚠ nit

knit|ter
knit|ting
knit|ting-needle
knit|wear

knives
knob
knob¦bly
  △ knob|blier
  △ knob¦bli|est
knobby
  △ knob¦bier
  △ knob¦bi|est
knock
  VERB
  △ knocks
  △ knocked
  △ knock|ing
knock|about
knock|down
knocker
knock¦ing-shop
knock-kneed
knock-on
knock|out
knoll
Knos|sos

knot
*looped tie in
string etc;
tangle,
complexity; hard
patch in wood;
unit of water
speed*
VERB
△ knots
△ knot¦ted
△ knot|ting
⚠ not

*Knot Gar¦den,
The*
knot|grass
knot|hole
knotty
  △ knot¦tier
  △ knot¦ti|est
knot|weed

know
*understand; be
aware of;
recognize*
△ knows
△ knew
△ know|ing
△ known
⚠ no

know|able
know-all
know-how
know|ing
know|ingly
know¦ing|ness
know|ledge
know|ledge|able
know|ledge|ably
known
Knox
knuckle
knuckle-dus¦ter
koala
Koblenz *see*
  Coblenz
Kö¦chel
Ko¦dály
Koest|ler
Kofun
Kohl
kohl
kohl|rabi
kola *see* cola
kolk|hoz
  △ kolk|ho¦zes
Kom|so|mol
Kon Tiki
kook
koo¦ka|burra
kooky
  △ koo¦kier
  △ koo¦ki|est
ko¦peck

Koran
Kor|anic
Kordestan *see*
  Kurdistan
kore
  △ korai
Korea
Korean
kosher
Ko¦sy|gin
kou¦ros
  △ kou¦roi
Kow|loon
kow¦tow
  VERB
  △ kow|tows
  △ kow|towed
  △ kow¦tow|ing
kraal
krai
Kra¦ków
krem|lin
Kreon *see*
  Creon
krill
kris
  △ kri¦ses
Krishna

krona
*Swedish
currency unit*
△ kronor
*Icelandic
currency unit*
△ kronur
⚠ krone

krone
*Danish and
Norwegian
currency unit*
△ kroner
⚠ krona

Kronos *see*
Cronus
Kru¦ger
kru¦ger|rand
△ kru¦ger|rand
or kru¦ger|
rands
krumm|horn
Krupp

kryp|ton
Kuala Lum¦pur
Kubla Khan
Kub|rick
Ku|ching
kudos
Ku Klux Klan
kukri
kulak

ku¦m¦mel
kum|quat
kung fu
Kur¦dis|tan
Kurd
Ku¦ro|sawa
Kush
Ku|wait
kvass

△ kvas¦ses
kwa¦shi|or¦kor
Kyd
Kyle
kyle
Kyoto
Kyrie elei|son

L

la
lab
label
  VERB
  △ la¦bels
  △ la¦belled
  △ la¦bel¦ling
la¦bial
la¦bi¦ate
la¦bile
la¦bium
  △ labia
la¦bor¦at¦ory
  △ la¦bor¦at¦or¦ies
la¦bori¦ous
la¦bori¦ously
La¦bour
  politics
la¦bour
  work
  VERB
  △ la¦bours
  △ la¦boured
  △ la¦bour¦ing
la¦boured
la¦bourer
la¦bour-inten¦sive
la¦bour-saving
Lab¦ra¦dor
la¦bur¦num
laby¦rinth
la¦by¦rinth¦ine
lac
lace
  VERB
  △ laces
  △ laced
  △ la¦cing
La¦ce¦dae¦mon
la¦cer¦ate
  △ la¦cer¦ates

△ la¦cer¦ated
△ la¦cer¦ating
la¦cer¦ation
lace-up
Lach¦lan
lach¦ry¦mal
lach¦ry¦mose
lack
  VERB
  △ lacks
  △ lacked
  △ lack¦ing
lacka¦dai¦si¦cal
lacka¦dai¦si¦cally
lackey
lack¦ing
lack¦lustre
La¦co¦nia
la¦conic
la¦con¦ic¦ally
lac¦quer
  VERB
  △ lac¦quers
  △ lac¦quered
  △ lac¦quer¦ing
lacrimal *see*
  lachrymal
la¦crosse
lac¦tar¦ian
lac¦tate
  △ lac¦tates
  △ lac¦ta¦ted
  △ lac¦ta¦ting
lac¦ta¦tion
lac¦tic
lac¦tose
lac¦to¦ve¦ge¦tar¦ian
la¦cuna
  △ la¦cu¦nae *or*
    la¦cu¦nas
lacy
  △ la¦cier
  △ la¦ci¦est

lad
lad¦der
  VERB
  △ lad¦ders
  △ lad¦dered
  △ lad¦der¦ing
lad¦die
laden
la-di-da
la¦dies
la¦ding
la¦dle
  VERB
  △ la¦dles
  △ la¦dled
  △ ladling
ladle¦ful
lady
  △ la¦dies
la¦dy¦bird
Lady Chat¦ter¦
  ley's Lover
lady-in-wait¦ing
  △ la¦dies-in-
    wait¦ing
lady-kil¦ler
la¦dy¦like
Lady Mac¦beth
  of Mtsensk
  (Ledi Mak¦bet
  Mtsens¦kovo
  uyezda)
Lady of Sha¦
  lott, The
Lady of the
  Lake, The
Lady¦ship
Lady's Not for
  Burn¦ing, The
lady's-slip¦per
Lady Win¦der¦
  mere's Fan
La Fon¦taine
lag

VERB
△ lags
△ lagged
△ lag¦ging
lager
lag¦gard
lag¦ging
la¦goon
Lagos
lah *see* la
Lahore
laid

lain
  past participle of
  lie
  ⚠lane

Laing

lair
  animal's den;
  hiding-place
  ⚠layer

laird
lais¦sez-faire
laity
  △ lai¦ties
lake

lam
  beat
  △ lams
  △ lammed
  △ lam¦ming
  ⚠lamb

lama
  Buddhist monk
  ⚠llama

La¦ma¦ism
La¦marck
La¦marck¦ism
Lamb

lamb
young sheep;
give birth to this
VERB
△ lambs
△ lambed
△ lamb|ing
⚠ lam

lam|bada
lam|baste
  △ lam|bastes
  △ lam|bas|ted
  △ lam|bast|ing
lam|bency
lam|bent
Lam|beth
lamb|ing
lamb|skin
lambs|wool
lame
  VERB
  △ lames
  △ lamed
  △ la|ming
lamé
la|mella
  △ la|mel|lae
lamely
lame|ness
la|ment
  VERB
  △ la|ments
  △ la|men|ted
  △ la|ment|ing
lam|ent|able
lam|ent|ably
la|men|ta|tion
La|men|ta|tions,
  Book of
la|men|ted
lam|ina
  △ lam|inae
lam|in|ate

△ lam|in|ates
△ lam|in|ated
△ lam|in|ating
lam|in|ated
lam|in|ation
Lam|mas
lam|mer|geyer
Lam|ont
lamp
lamp|black
Lam|pe|dusa
lam|poon
  VERB
  △ lam|poons
  △ lam|pooned
  △ lam|poon|ing
lam|pooner
lam|poon|ist
lamp|post
lam|prey
lamp|shade
Lan|ark
Lan|ca|shire
Lan|cas|ter
Lan|cas|trian
Lance
lance
  VERB
  △ lan|ces
  △ lanced
  △ lan|cing
Lan|ce|llot
lan|ceo|late
lan|cer
lan|cet
land
  VERB
  △ lands
  △ lan|ded
  △ land|ing
lan|dau
lan|ded
land|fall
land-girl

land|ing
land|ing-craft
land|ing-gear
land|ing-stage
land|lady
  △ land|la|dies
land|locked
land|lord
land|lub|ber
land|mark
land|mass
  △ land|mas|ses
Lan|dor
land|ow|ner
land|race
Land|ro|ver
land|scape
Land|seer
land|slide
land|slip
land|ward

lane
minor road;
track; regular
path of ships or
aircraft
⚠ lain

Lang
Lange
Lang|land
Lang|try
lan|guage
Lan|gue|doc
lan|guid
lan|guidly
lan|guish
  △ lan|gui|shes
  △ lan|guished
  △ lan|guish|ing
lan|guish|ing
lan|guor
lan|guor|ous
lank

△ lan|ker
△ lank|est
lan|ki|ness
lank|ness
lanky
  △ lan|kier
  △ lan|ki|est
lano|lin
lan|tern
lan|tern-jawed
lan|than|ide
lan|tha|num
lan|yard
Lanza
Lao|coon
Laos
lap
  VERB
  △ laps
  △ lapped
  △ lap|ping
lap|aro|scope
La Paz
lap|dog
lapel
lap|id|ary
  △ lap|id|ar|ies
lapis laz|uli
Lap|ith
Lap|land
La Plante
Lapp
lap|pet
Lapp|lan|der
lapse
  VERB
  △ lap|ses
  △ lapsed
  △ lap|sing
lapsed
lap|top
lap|wing
Lara
lar|cen|ist

lar|ceny
△ lar|cen|ies
larch
△ lar|ches
lard
VERB
△ lards
△ lar|ded
△ lard|ing
lar|der
Lares
large
△ lar|ger
△ lar|gest
largely
large|ness
lar|gesse
largo
lar|iat
lark
VERB
△ larks
△ larked
△ lark|ing
Lar|kin
'Lark' Quartet
(Ler|chen|
quar|tett)
lark|spur
Lar|naca
La Roche|fou|
cauld
La|rousse
larva
△ lar|vae
lar|val
la|ryn|geal
la|ryn|gi|tis
larynx
La-sa *see* Lhasa
la|sagne
La Scala
Las|caux
las|ci|vi|ous

las|ci|vi|ously
laser
lash
NOUN
△ la|shes
VERB
△ la|shes
△ lashed
△ lash|ing
lash|ing
Laski
Las Pal|mas
lass
△ las|ses

lassi
yoghurt drink
⚠ lassie

lassie
young girl
⚠ lassi

las|si|tude
lasso
NOUN
△ las|sos *or* las|
soes
VERB
△ las|soes
△ las|soed
△ las|so|ing
last
VERB
△ lasts
△ las|ted
△ last|ing
last-ditch
last|ing
lastly
last-min|ute
*Last of Eng|
land, The*
*Last of the Mo|
hi|cans, The*

*Last Year at
Ma|ri|en|bad
(L'An|née der|
ni|ère à Ma|ri|
en|bad)*
Las Vegas
latch
NOUN
△ lat|ches
VERB
△ lat|ches
△ latched
△ latch|ing
latch|key
late
△ later
△ la|test
la|teen
lately
la|tency
late|ness
la|tent
later
lat|eral
lat|er|al|ity
lat|er|al|iza|tion
lat|er|ally
Lat|eran
lat|er|ite
la|test
latex
△ la|texes *or* la|
ti|ces

lath
strip of wood
⚠ lathe

lathe
cutting machine
⚠ lath

la|ther
VERB
△ la|thers

△ la|thered
△ la|ther|ing
lath|ery
Latin

La|tina
*Latin American
woman*
⚠ Latino

La|tino
*Latin American
man*
⚠ Latina

la|ti|tude
la|ti|tu|di|nal
la|ti|tu|di|nally
La|tium
lat|rine
lat|ter
lat|ter-day
lat|terly
lat|tice
lat|ticed
Lat|via
Lat|vian
laud
VERB
△ lauds
△ lau|ded
△ laud|ing
laud|abil|ity
laud|able
laud|ably
laud|anum
laud|at|ory
Lauder
lauds
laugh
VERB
△ laughs
△ laughed
△ laugh|ing
laugh|able

laugh|ably
laugh|ing
Laugh|ing Ca|va|lier, The
laugh|ingly
laugh|ing-stock
laugh|ter
Laugh|ton
Laun|ces|ton
launch
  NOUN
  △ laun|ches
  VERB
  △ laun|ches
  △ launched
  △ launch|ing
laun|cher
launch|ing-pad
laun|der
  △ laun|ders
  △ laun|dered
  △ laun|der|ing
laun|der|ette
laun|dress
  △ laun|dres|ses
laun|dry
  △ laun|dries
Laura
Laur|asia
laur|eate
Lau|rel
lau|rel
Laur|ence
Lau|sanne
lav
lava
la|va|tor|ial
lava|tory
  △ lava|tor|ies
lav|en|der
La|ven|gro
Laver
laver
La|vinia

lav|ish
  VERB
  △ lavi|shes
  △ lav|ished
  △ lav|ish|ing
lav|ishly
lav|ish|ness
La|vois|ier
law
law-abi|ding
law|court
law|ful
law|fully
law|ful|ness
law|less
law|lessly
law|less|ness
lawn
lawn|mower
Law|rence
law|ren|cium
law|suit
law|yer
lax
  △ laxer
  △ lax|est
laxa|tive
lax|ity
laxly
lax|ness
lay
  VERB
  △ lays
  △ laid
  △ lay|ing
lay|about
Lay|amon
lay-by

> layer
> *covering; person or thing that lays; sort of plant shoot; use layers*
> VERB
> △ layers
> △ layered
> △ layer|ing
> ⚠ lair

lay|ette
lay|man
  △ lay|men
lay-off
lay|out
lay|per|son
lay|wo|man
  △ lay|wo|men
Laz|ar|ist
Laz|arus
laze
  VERB
  △ lazes
  △ lazed
  △ la|zing
la|zily
la|zi|ness
lazy
  △ la|zier
  △ la|zi|est
lazy-bones

> lea
> *field*
> ⚠ lee

lea
arable land temporarily under grass see ley

> leach
> *seep through*
> △ lea|ches
> △ leached
> △ leach|ing
> ⚠ leech

leach|ing
lead

  VERB
  △ leads
  △ led
  △ lead|ing
leaded
leaden
lea|der
lead|er|ship
lead-in
lead|ing
lead-up
leaf
  NOUN
  △ leaves
  VERB
  △ leafs
  △ leafed
  △ leaf|ing
leaf|age
leaf|cut|ter
leaf|less
leaf|let
  VERB
  △ leaf|lets
  △ leaf|leted
  △ leaf|let|ing
leafy
  △ lea|fier
  △ lea|fi|est
league
  VERB
  △ leagues
  △ leagued
  △ lea|guing

> leak
> *escape of liquid or gas; hole etc for this; divulging of secrets; escape; allow to escape*
> VERB
> △ leaks

△ leaked
△ leak|ing
⚠leek

leak|age
lea|ki|ness
leaky
△ lea|kier
△ lea|ki|est
Leam|ing|ton
Lean
lean
VERB
△ leans
△ leant *or*
leaned
△ lean|ing
ADJ.
△ leaner
△ lean|est
Le|an|der
lean|ing
lean|ness
leant
lean-to
leap
VERB
△ leaps
△ leapt *or*
leaped
△ leap|ing
leap-frog
VERB
△ leap-frogs
△ leap-frogged
△ leap-frog|ging
learn
△ learns
△ learnt *or*
learned
△ learn|ing
learned
learn|edly
learner

learn|ing
lease
VERB
△ lea|ses
△ leased
△ leas|ing
lease|back
lease|hold
lease|hol|der
leash
NOUN
△ lea|shes
VERB
△ lea|shes
△ leashed
△ leash|ing
least
leather
VERB
△ leath|ers
△ leathered
△ leath|er|ing
leather-jacket
leath|ery
leave
VERB
△ leaves
△ left
△ leav|ing
leaven
VERB
△ leav|ens
△ leavened
△ leav|en|ing
leaves
leav|ings
Lea|vis
Leb|anon
Le|bens|raum
Le Carré
lecher
lech|er|ous
lech|er|ously
lech|ery

le|ci|thin
lec|tern
lec|ture
VERB
△ lec|tures
△ lec|tured
△ lec|tur|ing
lec|turer
lec|ture|ship
lec|tur|er|ship
led
Leda
ledge
ledger
Lee

lee
shelter
⚠lea

leech
sort of worm;
parasite
△ lee|ches
⚠leach

Leeds

leek
vegetable
⚠leak

leer
VERB
△ leers
△ leered
△ leer|ing
leer|ing
leer|ingly
leery
△ leer|ier
△ leeri|est
lees
leet
lee|ward
lee|way

left
left-field
left-hand
left-han|ded
left-han|dedly
left-han|ded|
ness
left-han|der
left|ism
left|ist

left-over
ADJ.
⚠leftovers

left|overs
NOUN
⚠left-over

left-wing
left-winger
lefty
△ left|ies
leg
VERB
△ legs
△ legged
△ leg|ging
leg|acy
△ leg|acies
legal
le|gal|ism
le|gal|ist
le|gal|is|tic
le|gal|ity
le|gal|iza|tion
le|gal|ize
△ le|gal|izes
△ le|gal|ized
△ le|gal|izing
le|gally
leg|ate
le|ga|tee
le|ga|tion
le|gato

legend
legen|dary
leger|de|main
leg|gings
leggy
△ leg|gier
△ leg|gi|est
Leg|horn
le|gi|bil|ity
le|gible
le|gibly
le|gion
le|gion|ary
△ le|gion|ar|ies
Lé|gion d' Hon|
neur
le|gion|naire
Le|gion|naires'
dis|ease
legis|late
△ legis|lates
△ legis|la|ted
△ legis|la|ting
le|gis|la|tion
legis|la|tive
legis|la|tor
legis|la|ture
le|git|im|acy
le|git|im|ate
VERB
△ le|git|im|ates
△ le|git|im|ated
△ le|git|im|ating
le|git|im|ately
le|gi|ti|mi|za|tion
le|git|im|ize
△ le|git|im|izes
△ le|git|im|ized
△ le|git|im|izing
leg|less
Lego
Lego|land
leg-pull
leg|room

leg|ume
le|gu|min|ous
Lehár
Le Havre
Leh|mann
lei
Leib|niz
Lei|ces|ter
Lei|ces|ter|shire
Leiden *see*
   Leyden
Leif Eriks|son
Leigh
Leila
Leip|zig
leis|ure
leis|ured
leis|urely
leit|mo|tiv
Lei|trim
Le Mans
lem|ming
Lem|nos
lemon
lem|on|ade
lemur
lend
△ lends
△ lent
△ lend|ing
len|der
Lendl
length
lengthen
△ length|ens
△ lengthened
△ length|en|ing
length|ily
lengthi|ness
length|ways
length|wise
lengthy
△ length|ier
△ lengthi|est

le|ni|ence
le|ni|ency
le|ni|ent
le|ni|ently
Lenin
len|ity
Len|non
lens
Lent
lent
Len|ten
len|ti|cel
len|til
lento
Lenya
Leo
Leo|nard
Leo|nardo da
   Vinci
Leon|ca|vallo
leo|nine
Leo|nora
Leo|pard, The
   (Il gat|to|
   pardo)
leo|pard
leo|pard|ess
△ leo|pard|es|ses
Leo|pold
leo|tard
leper
Le|pi|dop|tera
le|pi|dop|ter|ist
le|pi|dop|ter|ous
lep|re|chaun
lep|rosy
lep|rous
lep|ton
lep|to|tene
Ler|ner
Ler|wick
les|bian
les|bi|an|ism
Les|bos

lese-majesty
le|sion
Les|ley
   usually female
Les|lie
   usually male
Le|so|tho
less
les|see

les|sen
   diminish
△ les|sens
△ les|sened
△ les|sen|ing
⚠ lesson

Les|seps
les|ser
Les|sing

les|son
   teaching;
   reading in
   church
⚠ lessen

les|sor
lest
Les|ter
let
VERB
△ lets
△ let
△ let|ting
Letch|worth
let-down
le|thal
le|thally
le|thar|gic
le|thar|gic|ally
leth|argy
Lethe
let|ter
VERB
△ let|ters

△ let|tered
△ let|ter|ing
let|ter|box|ing
let|tered
let|ter|head
let|ter|ing
let|ter|press
let|tuce
leu|cine
leu|co|cyte
leuk|ae|mia
Le|vant
Le|van|tine
levee
level
  VERB
△ lev|els
△ lev|elled
△ lev|el|ling
level-headed
lev|el|ness
lever
  VERB
△ le|vers
△ le|vered
△ le|ver|ing
le|ver|age
lev|eret
Levi
le|vi|athan
Le|vi|athan
Levis
Lévi-Strauss
le|vi|tate
△ le|vi|tates
△ le|vi|ta|ted
△ le|vi|ta|ting
le|vi|ta|tion
Le|vite
Le|vi|ti|cus,
  Book of
levy
  NOUN
△ lev|ies

VERB
△ lev|ies
△ lev|ied
△ levy|ing
lewd
△ lew|der
△ lewd|est
lewdly
lewd|ness
Lewes
Lewis
Lewis
lex|eme
lex|ical
lex|ic|ally
lexi|co|gra|pher
lexi|co|gra|phic
lexi|co|gra|phy
lexi|col|ogy
lex|icon
Lex|ing|ton
lexis
ley
Ley|den
Lhasa
li|abil|ity
△ li|abil|it|ies
li|able
li|aise
△ li|ai|ses
△ li|aised
△ li|ais|ing
li|ai|son
liana

liar
person who tells lies
△ lyre

lib
li|ba|tion
libel
  VERB
△ li|bels
△ li|belled

△ li|bel|ling
li|bel|lous
li|bel|lously
Lib|eral
  politics
lib|eral
  generous
lib|er|al|ism
li|ber|al|ity
li|ber|al|iza|tion
lib|er|al|ize
△ lib|er|al|izes
△ lib|er|al|ized
△ lib|er|al|izing
lib|er|ally
lib|er|ate
△ lib|er|ates
△ lib|er|ated
△ lib|er|ating
lib|er|ated
lib|er|ation
lib|er|ator
Li|beria
li|ber|tari|an|ism
lib|er|tine
lib|erty
△ lib|er|ties
li|bi|di|nal
li|bi|din|ous
li|bido
Libra
Lib|ran
lib|rar|ian
lib|rar|ian|ship
lib|rary
△ lib|rar|ies
lib|ret|tist
lib|retto
△ lib|retti *or* lib|
  ret|tos
Li|bre|ville
Libya
lice
li|cence

NOUN
li|cense
  VERB
△ li|cen|ses
△ li|censed
△ li|cen|sing
li|censed
li|cen|see
li|cen|ti|ate
li|cen|tious
li|cen|tiously
li|cen|tious|ness
lichee *see* lychee
li|chen *or* lichen
  according to
  pronunciation
Lich|field
lich|gate
licit
li|citly
lick
  VERB
△ licks
△ licked
△ lick|ing
licorice *see*
  liquorice
lic|tor
lid
lid|ded
lido
lie
  untruth; tell this
  VERB
△ lies
△ lied
△ lying
lie
  situation; be
  positioned
△ lies
△ lay
△ lying
△ lain

Liech|ten|stein
lied
△ lie|der
lie-down
Lied von der Erde, Das (The Song of the Earth)
Liège
liege
lie-in
lien
lieu
lieu|ten|ancy
△ lieu|ten|an|cies
lieu|ten|ant
life
△ lives
Life and Death of Colo|nel Blimp, The
life|belt
life|blood
life|boat
life|buoy
life cy|cle
life|guard
life-jacket
life|less
life|lessly
life|less|ness
life|like
life|line
life|long
Life of Ga|li|leo, The
Life of Sam|uel John|son, The
lifer
life-saver
life-sav|ing
life-size
life-sized

life|style
life-sup|port
life|time
Lif|fey
lift
VERB
△ lifts
△ lif|ted
△ lift|ing
lift-off
li|ga|ment
li|ga|ture
VERB
△ li|ga|tures
△ li|ga|tured
△ li|ga|tur|ing
Li|geti
light
VERB
△ lights
△ lit *or* ligh|ted
△ light|ing
ADJ.
△ ligh|ter
△ light|est
ligh|ten
△ ligh|tens
△ ligh|tened
△ ligh|ten|ing
ligh|ter
ligh|ter-than-air
light-fin|gered
light-headed
light-head|edly
light-head|ed|ness
light-hearted
light-heart|edly
light-heart|ed|ness
light|house
light|ing
lightly
light|ness

light|ning
lights
light|ship
light|weight
light-year
lig|ne|ous
lig|nin
lig|nite
like
VERB
△ likes
△ liked
△ li|king
like|able
like|li|hood
likely
like-minded
liken
△ li|kens
△ li|kened
△ li|ken|ing
like|ness
△ like|nes|ses
like|wise
li|king
lilac
Lille
Lil|lie
Lil|li|pu|tian
Lilo
Li|lon|gwe
lilt
VERB
△ lilts
△ lil|ted
△ lilt|ing
lilt|ing
lily
△ lil|ies
lily-liv|ered
lily-of-the-val|ley
△ lil|ies-of-the-val|ley

lily-white
Lima
Li|mas|sol
limb
limbed
lim|ber
VERB
△ lim|bers
△ lim|bered
△ lim|ber|ing
limb|less
Limbo
limbo
lime
VERB
△ limes
△ limed
△ li|ming
lime|kiln
lime|light
Lim|er|ick
lim|er|ick
lime|stone
limey
limit
VERB
△ lim|its
△ lim|ited
△ lim|it|ing
li|mi|ta|tion
lim|ited
lim|it|less
limn|ing *or* lim|ning
according to pronunciation
limo
Li|moges
li|mon|ite
li|mou|sine
limp
VERB
△ limps
△ limped

△ limp|ing
ADJ.
△ lim|per
△ limp|est
lim|pet
lim|pid
lim|pid|ity
lim|pidly
lim|pid|ness
limp|ing
limp|ingly
limply
limp|ness
Lim|popo
limy
△ li|mier
△ li|mi|est
lin|age
linch|pin
Lin|coln
Lin|coln|shire
linc|tus
△ linc|tuses
Linda
Lind|bergh
lin|den
Lin|dis|farne
Lind|say
line
VERB
△ lines
△ lined
△ li|ning
lin|eage
lin|eal
lin|eally

lin|ea|ment
facial etc feature
⚠ liniment

lin|ear
lin|ear|ity
li|nea|tion
lined

line-engra|ving
Lin|eker
linen
liner
lines|man
△ lines|men
lines|wo|man
△ lines|wo|men
line-up
ling
fish
△ ling *or* lings
heather
△ lings
linga
lin|ger
△ lin|gers
△ lin|gered
△ lin|ger|ing
lin|gerer
lin|gerie
lin|ger|ing
lin|ger|ingly
lingo
lin|gua franca
△ lin|gua fran|
    cas
lin|gual
lin|gually
lin|guist
lin|guis|tic
lin|guis|tic|ally
lin|guis|tics
lingum *see* linga

lin|iment
medicinal cream
⚠ lineament

li|ning
link
VERB
△ links
△ linked
△ link|ing

link|age
Link|la|ter
links
link-up
Lin|lith|gow
Lin|naeus
lin|net
lino
li|no|cut
li|no|leum
lin|seed
lint
lin|tel
lion
Lio|nel
lion|ess
△ lion|es|ses
lion-hearted
lion|ize
△ lion|izes
△ lion|ized
△ lion|izing
lip
li|pase
lipid
li|po|gram
li|po|sculp|ture
li|po|some
li|po|suc|tion
lipped
lip-read
△ lip-reads
△ lip-read
△ lip-read|ing
lip-rea|der
lip-read|ing
lip-ser|vice
lip|stick
li|que|fac|tion
li|quefy
△ li|que|fies
△ li|que|fied
△ li|que|fy|ing

liqueur
*sweet drink of
flavoured spirits*
⚠ liquor

li|quid
li|qui|date
△ li|qui|dates
△ li|qui|da|ted
△ li|qui|da|ting
li|qui|da|tion
li|qui|da|tor
li|qui|dize
△ li|qui|di|zes
△ li|qui|dized
△ li|qui|di|zing
li|qui|di|zer

li|quor
liquid
⚠ liqueur

li|quor|ice
lira
△ lire *or* liras
Lis|bon
lisle
LISP
lisp
VERB
△ lisps
△ lisped
△ lisp|ing
lisp|ingly
lis|som
list
VERB
△ lists
△ lis|ted
△ list|ing
lis|ten
VERB
△ lis|tens
△ lis|tened
△ lis|ten|ing

lis|tener
Lis|ter
lis|teria
list|less
list|lessly
list|less|ness
Liszt
lit
lit|any
△ lit|an|ies
litchi *see* lychee
liter *see* litre
lit|er|acy
lit|eral
lit|er|al|ism
lit|er|al|ist
lit|er|ally
lit|er|al|ness
lit|er|ary
lit|er|ate
lit|er|ati
lit|era|ture
lith|arge
lithe
△ li|ther
△ li|thest
lithely
lithe|ness
li|thi|fi|ca|tion
lith|ium
litho
VERB
△ li|thoes
△ li|thoed
△ li|tho|ing
li|tho|graph
VERB
△ li|tho|graphs
△ li|tho|graphed
△ li|tho|graph|ing
li|tho|gra|pher
li|tho|gra|phic
li|tho|graph|ic|
ally

li|tho|gra|phy
li|tho|sphere
Li|thu|ania
Li|thu|an|ian
li|ti|gant
li|ti|gate
△ li|ti|gates
△ li|ti|ga|ted
△ li|ti|ga|ting
li|ti|ga|tion
li|ti|gious
li|ti|giously
lit|mus
li|to|tes
litre
lit|ter
VERB
△ lit|ters
△ lit|tered
△ lit|ter|ing
lit|ter|bug
lit|ter-lout
lit|tle
Lit|tle Dor|rit
Lit|tle Lord
Faunt|leroy
Lit|tle Rock
Lit|tle Women
Little|wood
lit|toral
li|tur|gi|cal
li|tur|gi|cally
lit|urgy
△ lit|ur|gies
live
VERB
△ lives
△ lived
△ liv|ing
live|able
lived-in
live-in
live|li|hood
live|li|ness

live|long
lively
△ live|lier
△ live|li|est
liven
△ li|vens
△ li|vened
△ li|ven|ing
liver
liv|er|ied
liv|er|ish
Liv|er|pool
Liv|er|pud|lian
liv|er|wort
liv|ery
△ liv|er|ies
liv|ery|man
△ liv|ery|men
lives
live|stock
live|ware
livid
liv|ing
liv|ing-room

Liv|ing|stone
explorer
⚠ Livingston

Liv|ing|ston
town
⚠ Livingstone

Livy
liz|ard
Ljub|ljana

llama
animal like
camel
⚠ lama

Llan|fair|pwll|
gwyn|gyll
Llan|gefni
Llan|gol|len

lla|nos
Lle|we|lyn
Lloyd
Lloyd-George
Lloyd's
Lloyd Webber
lo
loach
△ loa|ches

load
burden; fill
VERB
△ loads
△ loa|ded
△ load|ing
⚠ lode

loa|ded
loa|der
loadstar *see*
lodestar
loadstone *see*
lodestone
loaf
NOUN
△ loaves
VERB
△ loafs
△ loafed
△ loaf|ing
loa|fer
loam
loamy
△ loa|mier
△ loa|mi|est

loan
lend; thing lent
VERB
△ loans
△ loaned
△ loan|ing
⚠ lone

loan|word

loath
unwilling
⚠ loathe

loathe
hate
△ loathes
△ loathed
△ loa|thing
⚠ loath

loa|thing
loath|some
loaves
lob
  VERB
  △ lobs
  △ lobbed
  △ lob|bing
lobar
lo|bate
lobby
  NOUN
  △ lob|bies
  VERB
  △ lob|bies
  △ lob|bied
  △ lob|by|ing
lob|by|ing
lob|by|ist
lobe
lobed
lo|belia
lo|bot|omy
  △ lo|bot|om|ies
lob|ster

local
belonging to this area
⚠ locale

locale
place
⚠ local

lo|cal|ity
  △ lo|cal|it|ies
lo|cal|iza|tion
lo|cal|ize
  △ lo|cal|izes
  △ lo|cal|ized
  △ lo|cal|izing
lo|cal|ized
lo|cally
lo|cate
  △ lo|cates
  △ lo|ca|ted
  △ lo|ca|ting
lo|ca|tion
loch
loci
lock
  VERB
  △ locks
  △ locked
  △ lock|ing
lock|able
Locke
locker
Lock|er|bie
locket
lock|jaw
lock|out
lock|smith
lock|up
loco
lo|co|mo|tion
lo|co|mo|tive
lo|co|mo|tor
lo|co|mo|tory
locum
locus
  △ loci
lo|cust
lo|cu|tion

lode
ore-bearing rock
⚠ load

lode|star
lode|stone
lodge
  VERB
  △ lod|ges
  △ lodged
  △ lod|ging
lod|ger
lod|ging
loess
Loewe
loft
  VERB
  △ lofts
  △ lof|ted
  △ loft|ing
lof|tily
lof|ti|ness
lofty
  △ lof|tier
  △ lof|ti|est
log
  VERB
  △ logs
  △ logged
  △ log|ging
lo|gan|berry
  △ lo|gan|ber|ries
log|arithm
log|arith|mic
log|arith|mic|
  ally
log|book
log|ger|head
log|gia
log|ging
logic
lo|gi|cal
lo|gi|cal|ity
lo|gi|cally
lo|gi|cian
lo|gis|tic
lo|gis|ti|cal
lo|gis|ti|cally

lo|gis|tics
logo
lo|go|graph
lo|go|gram
Lo|hen|grin
loin
loin|cloth
Loire
loi|ter
  △ loi|ters
  △ loi|tered
  △ loi|ter|ing
loi|terer
Lola
Lo|lita
loll
  △ lolls
  △ lolled
  △ loll|ing
Lol|lard
lol|li|pop
lol|lop
  △ lol|lops
  △ lol|loped
  △ lol|lop|ing
lolly
  △ lol|lies
Lom|bard
Lom|bardy
Lomé
Lo|mond
Lon|don
Lon|don|derry

lone
alone
⚠ loan

lone|li|ness
lonely
  △ lone|lier
  △ lone|li|est
loner
lone|some
long

VERB
△ longs
△ longed
△ long|ing
ADJ.
△ lon|ger
△ lon|gest
long|boat
long|bow
*Long Day's
Jour|ney into
Night*
long-dis|tance
long-drawn-out
lon|gev|ity
Long|fel|low
long|hand
long|ing
long|ingly
lon|gi|tude
lon|gi|tu|di|nal
lon|gi|tu|di|nally
long-lived
Long|man
long-play|ing
long-range
long|ship
long|shore
long|shore|man
△ long|shore|men
long-sigh|ted
long-sigh|ted|
ness
long-stand|ing
long-suf|fer|ing
long-term
long|time
long|ways
long-win|ded
long-win|dedly
long-win|ded|
ness
loo
loo|fah

look
VERB
△ looks
△ looked
△ look|ing
look|alike
*Look Back in
Anger*
looker
looker-on
look-in
look|ing-glass
△ look|ing-glas|
ses
look|out
look-see
loom
VERB
△ looms
△ loomed
△ loom|ing
loon
loony
NOUN
△ loon|ies
ADJ.
△ loo|nier
△ loo|ni|est
loony-bin
loop
VERB
△ loops
△ looped
△ loop|ing
loop|hole
loopy
△ loo|pier
△ loo|pi|est

loose
*not tight or tied
up; untie*
VERB
△ loo|ses

△ loosed
△ loo|sing
ADJ.
△ loo|ser
△ loo|sest
⚠ lose

loose-leaf
loosely
loo|sen
△ loo|sens
△ loo|sened
△ loo|sen|ing
loose|ness
Loot

loot
booty; plunder
VERB
△ loots
△ loo|ted
△ loot|ing
⚠ lute

loo|ter
loot|ing
lop
△ lops
△ lopped
△ lop|ping
lope
VERB
△ lopes
△ loped
△ lo|ping
lop-eared
lop|si|ded
lo|qua|cious
lo|qua|ciously
lo|qua|cious|ness
lo|qua|city
Lorca
lord
Lord Jim
lord|li|ness

lordly
△ lord|lier
△ lord|li|est
Lord of the Flies
*Lord of the
Rings, The*
lords-and-ladies
Lord|ship
lore
Lo|re|lei
Loren
lorg|nette
loris
△ lori|ses
Lorna
Lorna Doone
Lor|raine
lorry
△ lor|ries
Los An|ge|les

lose
*mislay; be
deprived of*
△ loses
△ lost
△ losing
△ lost
⚠ loose

loser
Losey
losing
loss
△ los|ses
Los|sie|mouth
loss-lea|der
lost
Lot
lot
loth *see* loath
Lo|thian
lo|tion
lot|tery
△ lot|ter|ies

lotto
lotus
△ lo|tuses
lotus-eater
louche
△ loucher
△ louch|est
loud
△ lou|der
△ loud|est
loud|hai|ler
loudly
loud-mouthed
loud|ness
loud|spea|ker
lough
Lough|bor|ough
Louis
Lou|isi|ana
lounge
  VERB
△ loun|ges
△ lounged
△ loun|ging
loun|ger
lour
△ lours
△ loured
△ lour|ing
Lourdes
lour|ing
louse
  insect
△ lice
  nasty person
△ lou|ses
  VERB
△ lou|ses
△ loused
△ lous|ing
lous|ily
lousi|ness
lousy
△ lous|ier

△ lousi|est
lout
Louth
lout|ish
Louvre
louvre
louvred
lov|able
lov|age
love
  VERB
△ loves
△ loved
△ lov|ing
love|bird
love-child
△ love-chil|dren
Love for Love
love-in-a-mist
Love|lace
love|less
love-let|ter
love-lies-bleed|
  ing
love|li|ness
love|lorn
lovely
  NOUN
△ love|lies
  ADJ.
△ love|lier
△ love|li|est
love-making
love-match
△ love-mat|ches
lover
love|sick
Love|song of J
Al|fred Pru|
frock, The
lovey-dovey
lov|ing
loving-cup
lov|ingly

low
  VERB
△ lows
△ lowed
△ low|ing
  ADJ.
△ lower
△ low|est
low-born
low|brow
low-down
Low|ell
lower
  less high; make
  less high
  VERB
△ low|ers
△ low|ered
△ low|er|ing
lower
  become dark or
  threatening see
  lour
lower-case
lower-class
lowering
  threatening see
  louring
Low|es|toft
low-key

> low|land
> *low-lying land;*
> *belonging to this*
> ⚠Lowlands

> Low|lands, the
> *less mountainous*
> *area of S and E*
> *Scotland*
> ⚠lowland

Low|lan|der
  dweller in the
  Lowlands

low|lan|der
  lowland dweller
low|li|ness
lowly
△ low|lier
△ low|li|est
low|ness
low-pitched
low-pres|sure
Lowry
low-spir|ited
loyal
loy|al|ist
loy|ally
loy|alty
△ loy|al|ties
loz|enge
L-plate
Lu|anda
lub|ber
lub|berly
Lü|beck
Lu|bitsch
lu|bri|cant
lu|bri|cate
△ lu|bri|cates
△ lu|bri|ca|ted
△ lu|bri|ca|ting
lu|bri|ca|tion
lu|bri|ca|tor
lu|bri|cious
lu|bri|city
Lu|cerne
lu|cerne
Lucia di Lam|
mer|moor
lucid
lu|cid|ity
lu|cidly
Lu|ci|fer
Lu|cius
luck
luck|ily
lucki|ness

luck|less
Luck|now
lucky
  △ luck|ier
  △ lucki|est
Lucky Jim
lu|cra|tive
lu|cra|tively
lucre
Lu|cre|tius
Lud
Lud|dite
lu|di|crous
lu|di|crously
Lud|low
ludo
luff
  △ luffs
  △ luffed
  △ luff|ing
Luft|waffe
lug
  VERB
  △ lugs
  △ lugged
  △ lug|ging
Lu|gano
luge
  VERB
  △ luges
  △ luged
  △ lu|ging
Luger
lug|gage
lug|ger
lug|hole
lu|gu|bri|ous
lu|gu|bri|ously
lug|worm
Lu|kács
Luke
Luke, Gos|pel
  ac|cord|ing to
luke|warm

luke|warmly
lull
  VERB
  △ lulls
  △ lulled
  △ lull|ing
lul|laby
  △ lul|la|bies
Lully
lum|bago

> lum|bar
> *of the lower*
> *back*
>   ⚠ lumber

> lum|ber
> *disused furniture*
> *etc; felled*
> *timber; fell*
> *timber; burden*
> *with; blunder*
> *about*
> VERB
> △ lum|bers
> △ lum|bered
> △ lum|ber|ing
>   ⚠ lumbar

lum|ber|ing
lum|ber|jack
lumen
  △ lu|mina *or* lu|
    mens
Lu|mi|ère
lu|mi|naire
lu|min|ance
lu|min|ary
  △ lu|min|ar|ies
lu|min|es|cence
lu|min|es|cent
Lu|min|ism
lu|min|os|ity
lu|min|ous
lu|min|ously

lump
  VERB
  △ lumps
  △ lumped
  △ lump|ing
lump|ec|tomy
  △ lump|ec|tom|
    ies
lump|fish
  sing. and pl.
lump|ily
lum|pi|ness
lump|ish
lump|sucker
lumpy
  △ lum|pier
  △ lum|pi|est
lu|nacy
  △ lu|na|cies
lunar
lu|nate
lu|na|tic
lunch
  NOUN
  △ lun|ches
  VERB
  △ lun|ches
  △ lunched
  △ lunch|ing
lun|cheon
lunch|time
Lundy
lung
lunge
  VERB
  △ lun|ges
  △ lunged
  △ lun|ging
lung|fish
  sing. and pl.
lupin
lu|pine
lupus
lurch

NOUN
  △ lur|ches
VERB
  △ lur|ches
  △ lurched
  △ lurch|ing
lur|cher
lure
  VERB
  △ lures
  △ lured
  △ lur|ing
lurid
lur|idly
lur|id|ness
lurk
  △ lurks
  △ lurked
  △ lurk|ing
Lu|saka
lus|cious
lus|ciously
lus|cious|ness
lush
  NOUN
  △ lushes
  ADJ.
  △ lusher
  △ lush|est
lush|ness
lust
  VERB
  △ lusts
  △ lus|ted
  △ lust|ing
lust|ful
lust|fully
lust|ful|ness
lus|tily
lus|ti|ness
lustre
lus|trous
lus|trously
lusty

△ lus|tier
△ lus|ti|est

lute
*guitar-like
instrument*
⚠ loot

lu|tein|ize
△ lu|tein|izes
△ lu|tein|ized
△ lu|tein|izing
lu|ten|ist
lu|te|tium
Lu|ther
Luth|eran
Luth|er|an|ism
Luton
Lut|yens
lux
△ luxes

Lux|em|bourg
state
⚠ Luxemburg

Lux|em|burg
revolutionary
⚠ Luxembourg

Luxor
lux|uri|ance
lux|uri|ant
lux|uri|antly
lux|uri|ate
△ lux|uri|ates
△ lux|uri|ated
△ lux|uri|ating
lux|uri|ous
lux|uri|ously
lux|uri|ous|ness
lux|ury
△ lux|ur|ies
lyc|an|thropy
ly|ceum
ly|chee
lychgate *see*
lichgate
Ly|ci|das

Lycra
Lydia
lye
lying
Lyly
Lym|ing|ton
lymph
lym|pha|tic
lym|pho|cyte
lym|phoma
lynch
△ lyn|ches
△ lynched
△ lynch|ing
lynch|ing
Lyn|ette
Lynn Regis *see*
King's Lynn
lynx
△ lynxes
lynx-eyed
Lyons
lyo|phi|lic

lyo|pho|bic

lyre
sort of harp
⚠ liar

lyre-bird
lyric
lyr|ical
Lyr|ical Bal|lads
lyr|ic|ally
lyri|cism
lyri|cist
ly|ser|gic
ly|sine
lysis
△ lyses
Ly|sis|trata
ly|so|some
ly|so|zyme
Lytham St
Anne's
Lyt|tel|ton

-ly

This suffix is used to form adjectives (**earthly, leisurely**), and adverbs (**badly, happily**). The following spelling points should be noted:

- Words ending in **-ll** become **-lly**, eg **full, fully**.

- Words ending in **-le** preceded by a consonant drop the final e and become **-ly**, eg **single, singly; terrible, terribly**.

- Words ending in **-y** preceded by a consonant become **-ily**, eg **dry, drily; funny, funnily**; but **coyly, shyly, slyly, spryly, wryly**.

- Words of more than one syllable ending in **-ey** become **-ily**, eg **matey, matily**.

- Words of more than one syllable ending in **-ic** become **-ically**, eg **basic, basically; music, musically**.
  Except: **publicly**.

- Note also: **daily, duly, gaily, truly, wholly**.

M

ma
ma'am
Maasai *see*
  Masai
Maas|tricht
Maa|zel
Ma|bi|no|gion,
  The
mac
ma|cabre
mac|adam
mac|adam|ize
  △ mac|adam|izes
  △ mac|adam|
    ized
  △ mac|adam|
    izing
Macao
ma|caque
ma|ca|roni
  △ ma|ca|ro|nis
    or ma|ca|ro|
    nies
ma|ca|roon
Mac|Art|hur
Ma|cau|lay
macaw
Mac|beth
Mac|ca|bees
Maccles|field
Mac|Di|ar|mid
Mac|Don|ald
  prime minister
Mac|don|ald
  Scottish heroine
mace
Ma|ce|do|nia
ma|cer|ate
  △ ma|cer|ates
  △ ma|cer|ated
  △ ma|cer|ating
ma|cer|ation

Mac|gil|ly|
  cuddy's Reeks
Mach
ma|chete
Ma|chia|velli
Ma|chia|vel|lian
Ma|chia|vel|li|
  an|ism
mach|in|ate
  △ mach|in|ates
  △ mach|in|ated
  △ mach|in|ating
mach|in|ation
ma|chine
  VERB
  △ ma|chines
  △ ma|chined
  △ ma|chin|ing
ma|chine-gun
  VERB
  △ ma|chine-guns
  △ ma|chine-
    gunned
  △ ma|chine-gun|
    ning
ma|chin|ery
ma|chin|ist
mach|ismo
macho
macintosh *see*
  mackintosh
mack
Mac|ken|zie
mack|erel
  △ mack|er|els *or*
    mack|erel
Mack|in|tosh
mack|in|tosh
  △ mack|in|
    toshes
Mac|lean
Mac|Leish
Mac|Leod
Mac|mil|lan

Mac|Neice
Mâcon
Ma|con|chy
mac|ram
macro
mac|ro|bi|otic
mac|ro|bi|ot|ics
mac|ro|ceph|aly
mac|ro|cosm
mac|ro|eco|nom|
  ics
macro-instruc|
  tion
mac|ro|mol|
  ecule
mac|ron
mac|ro|pho|to|
  gra|phy
mac|ro|scopic
mac|ula
  △ macu|lae
mac|ule
mad
  △ mad|der
  △ mad|dest
Ma|da|gas|car
madam
  formal address to
  woman
  △ mesdames
  arrogant woman
  or girl; female
  brothel-keeper
  △ madams
Ma|dama But|
  ter|fly
Ma|dame
  △ Mes|dames
Ma|dame Bo|vary
mad|cap
mad|den
  △ mad|dens
  △ mad|dened
  △ mad|den|ing

mad|den|ing
mad|der

> **made**
> *past tense and*
> *past participle of*
> *make*
> ⚠ maid

Ma|deira
made-up
mad|house
Mad|hya Prad|
  esh
Ma|di|son
madly
mad|man
  △ mad|men
mad|ness
Ma|donna
Ma|dras
Ma|drid
mad|ri|gal
mad|wo|man
  △ mad|wo|men
mael|strom
mae|nad
mae|na|dic
maes|tro
  △ maes|tros *or*
    maes|tri
Mae|ter|linck
Maeve
Mae West
Ma|fe|king
Mafia
Ma|fi|oso
  △ Ma|fi|osi
mag
ma|ga|zine

> **Mag|da|len**
> *girl's name;*
> *Oxford college*
> ⚠ Magdalene

Mag¦da¦lene
saint's name;
Cambridge
college
△ Magdalen

Mag¦de¦burg
Ma¦gel¦lan
ma¦genta
mag¦got
mag¦goty
Magh¦reb
Magi
the 'three kings'
magi
pl. of magus
magic
 VERB
 △ magics
 △ ma¦gicked
 △ ma¦gick¦ing
ma¦gi¦cal
ma¦gi¦cally
Magic Flute,
 The (Die Zau¦
 ber¦flöte)
ma¦gi¦cian
Ma¦gi¦not
ma¦gis¦ter¦ial
ma¦gis¦teri¦ally
ma¦gis¦tracy
 △ ma¦gis¦tra¦
 cies
ma¦gis¦trate
mag¦lev
magma
 △ mag¦mas *or*
 mag¦mata
Magna Carta
mag¦na¦nim¦ity
mag¦nan¦im¦ous

mag¦nate
powerful or
high-ranking
person
△ magnet

mag¦ne¦sia
mag¦nes¦ite
mag¦nes¦ium

mag¦net
piece of metal
that attracts or
repels iron;
attractive person
etc
△ magnate

mag¦netic
mag¦net¦ic¦ally
mag¦net¦ism
mag¦net¦ite
mag¦net¦iza¦tion
mag¦net¦ize
 △ mag¦net¦izes
 △ mag¦net¦ized
 △ mag¦net¦izing
mag¦neto
mag¦ne¦to¦
 sphere
mag¦net¦ron
mag¦ni¦fi¦cat
mag¦ni¦fi¦ca¦
 tion
mag¦ni¦fi¦cence
mag¦ni¦fi¦cent
Mag¦ni¦fi¦cent
 Am¦ber¦sons,
 The
mag¦ni¦fi¦cently
Mag¦ni¦fi¦cent
 Seven, The
mag¦ni¦fier
mag¦nify
 △ mag¦ni¦fies
 △ mag¦ni¦fied
 △ mag¦ni¦fy¦ing

mag¦ni¦lo¦
 quence
mag¦ni¦lo¦quent
mag¦ni¦tude
mag¦no¦lia
mag¦num
Mag¦nus
Magog
mag¦pie
Ma¦gritte
magus
 △ magi
Mag¦yar
Ma¦ha\bha¦rata
ma¦ha¦rajah
ma¦ha¦rani
Ma¦ha¦ri¦shi
ma¦hatma
Ma¦ha¦yana
Mahdi
mahi-mahi
mah-jong
Mah¦ler
mahl¦stick
ma¦hog¦any
 NOUN
 △ ma¦hog¦an¦ies
Mahomet *see*
 Muhammad
ma¦hout
Mahratta *see*
 Maratha

maid
female servant;
unmarried woman
△ made

mai¦den
mai¦den¦hair
Mai¦den¦head
mai¦den¦head
mai¦den¦hood
maid¦ser¦vant
Maid¦stone

mail
postal system;
letters sent by
it; send by this
system; armour
 VERB
 △ mails
 △ mailed
 △ mail¦ing
△ male

mail¦bag
mailed
Mai¦ler
mail¦merge
mail-order
mail¦shot
 VERB
 △ mail¦shots
 △ mail¦shot
 △ mail¦shot¦ting
maim
 △ maims
 △ maimed
 △ maim¦ing

main
chief; chief pipe
etc in a system;
the open sea;
strength
△ mane

main¦brace
Maine
main¦frame
main¦land
main¦line
 △ main¦lines
 △ main¦lined
 △ main¦li¦ning
main¦li¦ner
main¦li¦ning
mainly
main¦sail

main|spring
main|stay
main|stream
main|stream|ing
main|tain
  △ main|tains
  △ main|tained
  △ main|tain|ing
main|ten|ance
Main|te|non
Mainz
Mairi
mai|son|ette
maî|tre d'hôtel
  △ maî|tres d'hôtel

> **maize**
> sort of cereal
> ⚠ maze

Majahidin *see*
  Mujahadeen
ma|jes|tic
ma|jes|tic|ally
maj|esty
  △ maj|es|ties
Maj|lis
ma|jol|ica
Major
major
  VERB
  △ ma|jors
  △ ma|jored
  △ ma|jor|ing
Major Bar|bara
Ma|jorca
major-domo
ma|jor|ette
major-general
ma|jor|ity
  △ ma|jor|it|ies
Ma|kar|ios
make
  VERB
  △ makes

△ made
△ ma|king
make-believe
make-or-break
maker
make|shift
make-up
make|weight
ma|king
Ma|labo
mal|ab|sorp|tion
Ma|la|chi
ma|la|chite
Ma|lade Ima|gi|
  naire, Le (The
  Ima|gin|ary In|
  va|lid; The
  Hy|po|chon|
  driac)
mal|ad|jus|ted
mal|ad|just|ment
mal|ad|min|is|ter
  △ mal|ad|min|is|
    ters
  △ mal|ad|min|is|
    tered
  △ mal|ad|min|is|
    ter|ing
mal|ad|min|is|
  tra|tion
mal|ad|roit
mal|ad|roitly
mal|ad|roit|ness
mal|ady
  △ mal|ad|ies
Mál|aga
Ma|la|gasy
mal|aise
mal|ap|rop|ism
mal|aria
mal|arial
mal|ar|key
Ma|lawi
Malay

Ma|lay|sia
Mal|colm
mal|con|tent
Mal|dives
Malé

> **male**
> of or for men; a
> male person
> ⚠ mail

ma|le|dic|tion
ma|le|dic|tory
ma|le|fac|tion
ma|le|fac|tor
male|ness
ma|le|vo|lence
ma|le|vo|lent
mal|fea|sance
mal|fea|sant
mal|for|ma|tion
mal|formed
mal|func|tion
  VERB
  △ mal|func|tions
  △ mal|func|
    tioned
  △ mal|func|tion|
    ing
Mali
mal|ice
ma|li|cious
ma|lign
  △ ma|ligns
  △ ma|ligned
  △ ma|lign|ing
ma|lig|nancy
  △ ma|lig|nan|
    cies
ma|lig|nant
ma|lig|nity
ma|lin|ger
  △ ma|lin|gers
  △ ma|lin|gered
  △ ma|lin|ger|ing

ma|lin|gerer
mall
mal|lard
  △ mal|lard *or*
  mal|lards
Mal|larmé
mal|le|ab|il|ity
mal|le|able
mal|let
mal|leus
  △ mal|lei
mal|low
Malmo
malm|sey
mal|nu|tri|tion
mal|odor|ous
Mal|ory
mal|prac|tice
Mal|raux

> **malt**
> grain mixture
> used for brewing
> etc; malt
> whisky; make
> into, combine
> with, malt
> VERB
> △ malts
> △ mal|ted
> △ malt|ing
> ⚠ moult

Malta
mal|tase
Mal|tese
Mal|tese Fal|
  con, The
Mal|thus
Mal|thu|sian
malt|ose
mal|treat
  △ mal|treats
  △ mal|trea|ted
  △ mal|treat|ing

mal|treat|ment
Mal|vern
mal|ver|sa|tion
mama
mamba
mambo
Mamluk
mam|mal
Mam|ma|lia
mam|ma|lian
mam|mary
mam|mo|gra|
  phy
mam|mon
mam|moth
Man, Isle of
man
  NOUN
  △ men
  VERB
  △ mans
  △ manned
  △ man|ning
man-about-
  town
  △ men-about-
  town
man|acle
  VERB
  △ man|acles
  △ man|acled
  △ man|ac|ling
man|age
  △ man|ages
  △ man|aged
  △ man|aging
man|age|able
man|age|ment
man|ager
ma|na|ger|ess
  △ ma|na|ger|es|
  ses
ma|na|ger|ial
Ma|nagua

Ma|nama
mañ|ana
Man and Su|
  per|man
Ma|nas|seh,
  Tribe of
man-at-arms
  △ men-at-arms
ma|na|tee
Man|ches|ter
Man|churia
Man|cu|nian
man|dala
Man|da|lay
man|da|rin
man|date
  VERB
  △ man|dates
  △ man|da|ted
  △ man|da|ting
man|da|tory
Man|dela
Man|de|ville
man|dible
man|do|lin
man|drake
man|drel
  shaft or axle
man|drill
  baboon

┌─────────────────┐
│ **mane**   │
│ *hair on neck of* │
│ *horse etc;*   │
│ *person's long*   │
│ *hair*   │
│ ⚠ *main*   │
└─────────────────┘

man-eater
man|ège
Manet
man|ful
man|ful|ness
manga
man|gan|ese

mange
man|gel-wur|zel
man|ger
mange|tout
man|gily
man|gi|ness
man|gle
  VERB
  △ man|gles
  △ man|gled
  △ man|gling
mango
  △ man|gos *or*
  man|goes
man|grove
mangy
  △ man|gier
  △ man|gi|est
man|han|dle
  △ man|han|dles
  △ man|han|dled
  △ man|hand|ling
Man|hat|tan
man|hole
man|hood
man-hour
man|hunt
mania
ma|niac
ma|ni|acal
manic
manic-depres|
  sive
Ma|ni|chae|ism
Ma|ni|chae|an|
  ism
mani|cure
  VERB
  △ mani|cures
  △ mani|cured
  △ mani|cur|ing
mani|cur|ist
mani|fest

VERB
  △ mani|fests
  △ mani|fes|ted
  △ mani|fest|ing
ma|ni|fes|ta|tion
mani|festly
ma|ni|festo
  △ mani|fes|tos
  or mani|fes|
  toes
mani|fold
mani|kin
Ma|nila
  place
ma|nila
  paper
ma|ni|pu|late
  △ ma|ni|pu|lates
  △ ma|ni|pu|la|
  ted
  △ ma|ni|pu|la|
  ting
ma|ni|pu|la|tion
ma|ni|pu|la|tive
Ma|ni|toba
man|kind
manky
  △ man|kier
  △ man|ki|est
man|li|ness
manly
  △ man|lier
  △ man|li|est
man-made
Mann
manna
man|ne|quin

┌─────────────────┐
│ **man|ner**   │
│ *way;* pl.   │
│ *politeness*   │
│ ⚠ *manor*   │
└─────────────────┘

man|nered
man|ner|ism

man|ner|li|ness
man|nerly
mannikin *see*
  manikin
man|nish
man|oeuv|ra|bil|
  ity
man|oeuv|rable
man|oeuvre
  VERB
  △ man|oeuvres
  △ man|oeuvred
  △ man|oeuv|ring
man-of-war
  △ men-of-war
ma|no|meter
ma|no|met|ric

manor
  country house;
  land under
  control of lord
  etc
  ⚠ manner

ma|nor|ial
man|power
man|qué
man|sard
manse
Man|sell
man|ser|vant
  △ man|ser|vants
Mans|field
Mans|field Park
man|sion
man|slaugh|ter
Man|tegna
man|tel
man|tel|piece
man|tel|shelf
  △ man|tel|
    shelves
man|tilla
man|tis

△ man|ti|ses *or*
  man|tes
man|tissa
man|tle
  VERB
  △ man|tles
  △ man|tled
  △ mant|ling
man-to-man
man|tra
man|trap
Man|tua
man|ual
ma|nu|ally
ma|nu|fac|ture
  VERB
  △ ma|nu|fac|
    tures
  △ ma|nu|fac|
    tured
  △ ma|nu|fac|tur|
    ing
ma|nu|fac|turer
ma|nu|fac|tur|
  ing
ma|nu|mis|sion
ma|nu|mit
  △ ma|nu|mits
  △ ma|nu|mit|ted
  △ ma|nu|mit|
    ting
ma|nure
  VERB
  △ ma|nures
  △ ma|nured
  △ ma|nur|ing
ma|nu|script
Manx
Manx|man
  △ Manx|men
Manx|wo|man
  △ Manx|wo|men
many

ADJ.
  △ more
  △ most
Mao|ism
Mao|ist
Maori
  NOUN
  △ Maori *or* Ma|
    oris
map
  VERB
  △ maps
  △ mapped
  △ map|ping
ma|ple
Ma|puto
ma|quette
Ma|quis
mar
  △ mars
  △ marred
  △ mar|ring
ma|ra|bou
ma|raca
Ma|ra|dona
ma|ras|chino
Marat
Ma|ratha
Ma|rathi
ma|ra|thon
ma|raud
  △ ma|rauds
  △ ma|rau|ded
  △ ma|raud|ing
ma|rau|der
ma|raud|ing
Mar|bella
mar|ble
mar|bled
marc
mar|ca|site
mar|cato
Mar|ceau
March

march
  NOUN
  △ mar|ches
  VERB
  △ mar|ches
  △ marched
  △ march|ing
mar|cher
mar|chi|on|ess
  △ mar|chi|on|es|
    ses
Mar|ci|ano
Mar|coni
Mar|cos
Mar|cuse
Mardi Gras

mare
  female horse
  △ mares
  flat area on
  moon or Mars
  △ maria
  ⚠ mayor

Marey
marg
Mar|ga|ret
mar|gar|ine
Mar|gate
mar|gin
mar|gi|nal
mar|gin|ally
mar|guer|ite
Maria
Mar|ian
Ma|ri|gold
ma|ri|gold
ma|ri|ju|ana
ma|rimba
Ma|rina
ma|rina
ma|ri|nade
  VERB
  △ ma|ri|nades

△ ma¦ri¦na¦ded
△ ma¦ri¦na¦ding
ma¦ri¦nate
△ ma¦ri¦nates
△ ma¦ri¦na¦ted
△ ma¦ri¦na¦ting
ma¦rine
mar¦iner
Mar¦ion
ma¦ri¦on¦ette
mar¦ital
mar¦it¦ally
mari¦time
mar¦jo¦ram
Mark
Mark, Gos¦pel
  ac¦cord¦ing to
mark
  VERB
  △ marks
  △ marked
  △ mark¦ing
mark-down
marked
mark¦edly
mar¦ker
mar¦ket
  VERB
  △ mar¦kets
  △ mar¦ke¦ted
  △ mar¦ket¦ing
mar¦ket¦able
mar¦ket-gar¦den
mar¦ket-gar¦
  dener
mar¦ket¦ing
mar¦ket-place
mark¦ing
Mark¦ova
marks¦man
  △ marks¦men
marks¦man¦ship
Marks
mark-up

marl
  VERB
  △ marls
  △ marled
  △ marl¦ing
Marl¦bor¦ough
Mar¦lene
Mar¦ley
mar¦lin
  △ mar¦lin or
    mar¦lins
mar¦lin¦spike
Mar¦lowe
marly
Mar¦ma¦duke
mar¦ma¦lade
mar¦mor¦eal
mar¦mo¦set
mar¦mot
Marne
ma¦roon
  VERB
  △ ma¦roons
  △ ma¦rooned
  △ ma¦roon¦ing
marque
mar¦quee
mar¦quess
  △ mar¦ques¦ses
mar¦quetry
mar¦quis
  △ mar¦qui¦ses
mar¦quise
  △ mar¦qui¦ses
Mar¦ra¦kesh
mar¦ram
mar¦riage
mar¦riage¦ab¦il¦
  ity
mar¦riage¦able
mar¦riage¦able¦
  ness
*Mar¦riage of
  Fig¦aro, The*

*(Le nozze di
  Fi¦garo)*
mar¦ried
mar¦row
mar¦row¦bone
mar¦row¦fat
marry
  △ mar¦ries
  △ mar¦ried
  △ mar¦ry¦ing
Mar¦ryat
Mars
Mar¦sala
*Mar¦seil\laise,
  La*
Mar¦seilles
Marsh
marsh
  △ mar¦shes

mar¦shal
  *high officer in
  army etc;
  organise*
  VERB
  △ mar¦shals
  △ mar¦shalled
  △ mar¦shal¦ling
  ⚠ martial

mar¦shal¦ling-
  yard
Mar¦shall

marsh¦mal¦low
  sweet
  ⚠ marsh
    mallow

marsh mal¦low
  plant
  ⚠ marshmallow

mar¦shy
  △ mar¦shier
  △ mar¦shi¦est

Mar¦ston
mar¦su¦pial
mart
mar¦tello

mar¦ten
  *small animal
  that lives in
  trees*
  ⚠ martin

Mar¦tha
Mar¦tial

mar¦tial
  warlike
  ⚠ marshal

Mar¦tian
Mar¦tin

mar¦tin
  swallow-like bird
  ⚠ marten

*Mar¦tin
  Chuzzle\wit*
mar¦ti¦net
Mar¦tini
Mar¦ti¦nique
Mar¦tin¦mas
  △ Mar¦tin¦mases
mar¦tyr
  VERB
  △ mar¦tyrs
  △ mar¦tyred
  △ mar¦tyr¦ing
mar¦tyr¦dom
mar¦vel
  VERB
  △ mar¦vels
  △ mar¦velled
  △ mar¦vel¦ling
Mar¦vell
mar¦vel¦lous
mar¦vel¦lously
Marx

Marx|ism
Marx|ist
Mary
Ma|ry|land
Ma|ry|le|bone
Mary Rose
mar|zi|pan
Masai
Mas|cagni
mas|cara
mas|car|pone
mas|cot
mas|cu|line
mas|cu|lin|ity
Mase|field
maser
Ma|seru
mash
  NOUN
  △ ma|shes
  VERB
  △ ma|shes
  △ mashed
  △ mash|ing
ma|shie

---
mask
  disguise for face;
  disguise; conceal
  VERB
  △ masks
  △ masked
  △ mask|ing
  ▲ masque
---

masked
mask|ing
mas|och|ism
mas|och|ist
ma|soch|is|tic
mason
ma|sonic
ma|sonry
Mas|or|ete

---
masque
  17th-century
  dramatic
  entertainment
  ▲ mask
---

mas|quer|ade
  VERB
  △ mas|quer|ades
  △ mas|quer|aded
  △ mas|quer|
    ading
mass
  NOUN
  △ mas|ses
  VERB
  △ mas|ses
  △ massed
  △ mass|ing
Mas|sa|chu|setts
mas|sacre
  VERB
  △ mas|sacres
  △ mas|sacred
  △ mas|sacring
mas|sage
  VERB
  △ mas|sa|ges
  △ mas|saged
  △ mas|sa|ging
Mas|se|net
mas|seur
mas|seuse
mas|sif
Mas|sine
Mas|sin|ger
mas|sive
mas|sively
Massorete *see*
  Masorete
mass-pro|duce
  △ mass-pro|du|
    ces
  △ mass-pro|duced

  △ mass-pro|du|
    cing
mass-pro|duced
mass-pro|duc|
  tion
mast
mas|taba
mast|ec|tomy
  △ mast|ec|tom|
    ies
mas|ter
  VERB
  △ mas|ters
  △ mas|tered
  △ mas|ter|ing
mas|ter-at-arms
  △ mas|ters-at-
    arms
Mas|ter Buil|
der, The (Byg|
mes|ter Sol|
ness)
mas|ter|ful
mas|ter|fully
mas|ter|li|ness
mas|terly
mas|ter|mind
  VERB
  △ mas|ter|minds
  △ mas|ter|
    minded
  △ mas|ter|mind|
    ing
mas|ter|piece
mas|ter|stroke
mas|tery
mas|ter|work
mast|head
mas|tic
mas|ti|cate
  △ mas|ti|cates
  △ mas|ti|ca|ted
  △ mas|ti|ca|ting
mas|ti|ca|tion

mas|tiff
mas|ti|tis
mas|to|don
mas|toid
Mas|tro|ianni
mas|tur|bate
  △ mas|tur|bates
  △ mas|tur|ba|ted
  △ mas|tur|ba|
    ting
mas|tur|ba|tion
mas|tur|ba|tory

---
mat
  small carpet;
  tangle
  VERB
  △ mats
  △ mat|ted
  △ mat|ting
  ▲ matt
  ▲ matte

Ma|ta|be|le|land
mat|ador
match
  △ mat|ches
  VERB
  △ mat|ches
  △ matched
  △ match|ing
match|box
  △ match|boxes
match|ing
match|less
match|ma|ker
match|ma|king
match|stick
match|wood
mate
  VERB
  △ mates
  △ ma|ted
  △ ma|ting
maté

mater
ma|ter|ial
ma|teri|al|ism
ma|teri|al|ist
ma|teri|al|is|tic
ma|teri|al|iza|
tion
ma|teri|al|ize
△ ma|teri|al|izes
△ ma|teri|al|ized
△ ma|teri|al|
izing
ma|teri|ally
ma|ter|nal
ma|ter|nally
ma|ter|nity
matey
△ ma|tier
△ ma|ti|est
ma|the|mat|ical
ma|the|mat|ic|
ally
ma|the|ma|ti|
cian
ma|the|mat|ics
Mat|hilda
maths
ma|tily
mat|inée
mat|ins
Ma|tisse
Mat|lock
mat|ri|arch
mat|ri|ar|chal
mat|ri|ar|chy
△ mat|ri|ar|chies
ma|tric
mat|ri|ces
mat|ri|ci|dal
mat|ri|cide
mat|ri|cu|late
△ mat|ri|cu|lates
△ mat|ri|cu|la|
ted

△ mat|ri|cu|la|
ting
mat|ri|cu|la|tion
mat|ri|lin|eal
mat|ri|mo|nial
mat|ri|mony
△ mat|ri|mon|ies
· mat|rix
△ mat|ri|ces *or*
mat|rixes
mat|ron
mat|ronly

matt
not shiny
⚠ mat
⚠ matte

matte
*smelting by-
product; camera
mask*
⚠ mat
⚠ matt

mat|ted
mat|ter
VERB
△ mat|ters
△ mat|tered
△ mat|ter|ing
Mat|ter|horn
mat|ter-of-fact
mat|ter-of-
factly
mat|ter-of-fact|
ness
Mat|thew
Mat|thew, Gos|
pel ac|cord|ing
to
Mat|thews
mat|ting
mat|tock
mat|tress

△ mat|tres|ses
mat|ur|ate
△ mat|ur|ates
△ mat|ur|ated
△ mat|ur|ating
mat|ur|ation
ma|ture
VERB
△ ma|tures
△ ma|tured
△ ma|tur|ing
ma|tur|ity
maty *see* matey
Maud
Maud
maud|lin
Maud|ling
Maugham
maul
VERB
△ mauls
△ mauled
△ maul|ing
maulstick *see*
mahlstick
Mau Mau
maun|der
△ maun|ders
△ maun|dered
△ maun|der|ing
Maundy
Mau|pas|sant
Mau|riac
Maur|ice
Mau|ri|ta|nia
Mau|ri|tius
Mau|ser
mau|so|leum
△ mau|so|leums
mauve
mav|er|ick
maw
mawk|ish
max|illa

△ max|il|lae
max|il|lary
Maxim
maxim
max|imal
Maxi|mil|ian
max|im|iza|tion
max|im|ize
△ max|im|izes
△ max|im|ized
△ max|im|izing
maxi|mum
Max|well
Max|well Da|
vies
May
may
VERB
△ might
Maya
Maya|kovsky
maybe
May Day
public holiday
may|day
distress signal
Mayer
May|fair
May|flower
may|fly
△ may|flies
may|hem
mayn't
may|on|naise

mayor
*head of town
council etc*
⚠ mare

may|oral
may|or|alty
△ may|or|al|ties
may|or|ess
△ may|or|es|ses

*Mayor of Cas|
ter|bridge, The*
may|pole

---

maze
  *puzzling
network of
passages etc;
complicated
system etc*
   ⚠maize

---

ma|zurka
Mba|bane
Mc|Car|thy
Mc|Car|thy|ism
Mc|Cart|ney
Mc|Cor|mack
McCoy
Mc|En|roe
Mc|Gona|gall
Mc|Lu|han
Mc|Queen
me
  PRON.
me
  *sol-fah symbol
see* mi
mea culpa
Mead
mead
meadow
meadow|sweet
mea|gre
meal
mea|lie
meals-on-
  wheels
mealy
  △ mea|lier
  △ mea|li|est
mealy-mouthed

---

mean
  stingy; nasty;

*shabby; crafty;
intend; wish to
say; entail*
  VERB
  △ means
  △ meant
  △ mean|ing
  ADJ.
  △ meaner
  △ mean|est
   ⚠mien

---

me|an|der
  VERB
  △ me|an|ders
  △ me|an|dered
  △ me|an|der|ing
meanie
mean|ing
mean|ing|ful
mean|ing|fully
mean|ing|less
meanly
mean|ness
means
  sing. and pl.
means-test
  △ means-tests
  △ means-tes|ted
  △ means-test|ing
meant
mean|time
mean|while
meany *see*
  meanie
mea|sles
measly
  △ meas|lier
  △ meas|li|est
meas|ur|able
meas|ure
  VERB
  △ meas|ures
  △ meas|ured

△ meas|ur|ing
meas|ured
*Meas|ure for
Meas|ure*
meas|ure|ment

---

meat
  *animal flesh
used as food; the
essence*
   ⚠meet
   ⚠mete

---

meat|ball
mea|ti|ness
me|atus
  △ me|atuses
meaty
  △ mea|tier
  △ mea|ti|est
Mecca
mecca
me|chanic
me|chan|ical
me|chan|ic|ally
me|chan|ics
mech|an|ism
mech|an|is|tic
mech|an|iza|tion
mech|an|ize
  △ mech|an|izes
  △ mech|an|ized
  △ mech|an|izing
Med

---

medal
  *metal award for
bravery etc*
   ⚠meddle

---

me|dal|lion
med|al|list

---

med|dle
  interfere
  △ med|dles

△ med|dled
  △ med|dling
   ⚠medal

---

med|dler
meddle|some
Medea
Me|del|lín
Mede
media
mediaeval *see*
  medieval
mediaevalist *see*
  medievalist
me|dia|genic
me|dial
me|di|ally
me|dian
me|di|ate
  △ me|di|ates
  △ me|di|ated
  △ me|di|ating
me|di|ation
me|di|ator
medic
Med|ic|aid
med|ical
med|ic|ally
me|di|ca|ment
Medi|care
med|ic|ate
  △ med|ic|ates
  △ med|ic|ated
  △ med|ic|ating
me|di|ca|tion
Me|dici
me|di|ci|nal
me|di|ci|nally
me|di|cine
med|ico
me|di|eval
me|di|eval|ist
Me|dina
me|di|ocre

me¦di¦oc¦rity
　△ me¦di¦oc¦ri¦
　　ties
me¦di¦tate
　△ me¦di¦tates
　△ me¦di¦ta¦ted
　△ me¦di¦ta¦ting
me¦di¦ta¦tion
me¦di¦ta¦tive
Me¦di¦ter¦ra¦
　nean
me¦dium
　NOUN
　source of news etc
　△ media
　other senses
　△ me¦diums
med¦lar
med¦ley
Médoc
me¦dulla
　△ me¦dul¦lae *or*
　　me¦dul¦las
Me¦dusa
me¦dusa
　△ me¦du¦sae
Med¦way
meek
　△ mee¦ker
　△ meek¦est
meekly
meek¦ness
meer¦schaum

meet
　encounter;
　meeting for sport
　etc; suitable
　VERB
　△ meets
　△ met
　△ meet¦ing
　ADJ.
　△ mee¦ter
　△ meet¦est
　⚠ meat
　⚠ mete

meet¦ing
meetly
mega
me¦ga¦byte
me¦ga¦lith
me¦ga¦li¦thic
me¦ga¦lo¦ma¦nia
me¦ga¦lo¦ma¦
　niac
me¦ga¦phone
me¦ga¦struc¦ture
me¦ga¦ton
mei¦osis
　△ mei¦oses
Meis¦sen
Meis¦ter¦sin¦ger
　von Nürn¦berg,
　Die (The Mas¦
　ter¦sin¦gers of
　Nur¦em¦berg)
mela¦mine
mel¦an¦cho¦lia
mel¦an¦cholic
mel¦an¦choly
me¦lange
Mel¦anie
mel¦anin
mel¦an¦oma
　△ mel¦an¦omas
　or mel¦an¦
　omata
me¦la¦to¦nin
Melba
Mel¦bourne
Me¦le¦ager
melee
Me¦lissa
mel¦li¦flu¦ent
mel¦li¦flu¦ous
mel¦li¦flu¦ously

mel¦li¦flu¦ous¦
　ness
mel¦low
　VERB
　△ mel¦lows
　△ mel¦lowed
　△ mel¦low¦ing
　ADJ.
　△ mel¦lower
　△ mel¦low¦est
me¦lodic
me¦lod¦ic¦ally
me¦lo¦di¦ous
me¦lo¦di¦ous¦
　ness
me¦lo¦drama
me¦lo¦dra¦matic
me¦lo¦dra¦mat¦
　ics
mel¦ody
　△ mel¦od¦ies
melon
Melos
Mel¦po¦mene
melt
　△ melts
　△ mel¦ted
　△ melt¦ing
melt¦down
melt¦ing-pot
Mel¦ville
Mel¦vin
Mel¦vyn
mem¦ber
mem¦ber¦ship
mem¦brane
mem¦bran¦ous
me¦mento
　△ me¦men¦tos *or*
　　me¦men¦toes
me¦mento mori
memo
mem¦oir
mem¦or¦abi¦lia

mem¦or¦able
mem¦or¦ably
mem¦or¦an¦dum
　△ mem¦or¦an¦
　　dums *or*
　　mem¦or¦anda
me¦mor¦ial
mem¦or¦ize
　△ mem¦or¦izes
　△ mem¦or¦ized
　△ mem¦or¦izing
mem¦ory
　△ mem¦or¦ies
Mem¦phis
mem¦sahib
men
men¦ace
　VERB
　△ men¦aces
　△ men¦aced
　△ men¦acing
men¦acing
mé¦nage
mé¦nage à trois
me¦na¦gerie
Menai
Men¦an¦der
mend
　VERB
　△ mends
　△ men¦ded
　△ mend¦ing
men¦da¦cious
men¦da¦city
Men¦del
men¦de¦le¦vium
Men¦de¦lian
Men¦dels¦sohn
men¦di¦cant
Men¦dip
men¦folk
Men¦gistu
men¦hir
me¦nial

men|in|gi|tis
men|inx
△ men|in|ges
men|is|cus
△ men|is|cuses
or men|isci
Men|non|ite
me|no|pau|sal
me|no|pause
men|orah
me|nor|rha|gia
Men|otti
Mensa
men|ses
men|strual
men|stru|ate
△ men|stru|ates
△ men|stru|ated
△ men|stru|ating
men|stru|ation
men|sur|ation
men|tal
men|tal|ity
△ men|tal|it|ies
men|tally
men|thol
men|tho|la|ted
men|tion
  VERB
△ men|tions
△ men|tioned
△ men|tion|ing
men|tor
menu
Me|nu|hin
Me|phis|toph|
  eles
mer|can|tile
mer|can|til|ism
Mer|ca|tor
mer|cen|ary
  NOUN
△ mer|cen|ar|ies
Mer|cer

mer|cer|ize
△ mer|cer|izes
△ mer|cer|ized
△ mer|cer|izing
mer|cer|ized
mer|chan|dise
  VERB
△ mer|chan|di|
  ses
△ mer|chan|
  dised
△ mer|chan|di|
  sing
mer|chant
Mer|chant of
  Ven|ice, The
Mer|cia
mer|ci|ful
mer|ci|fully
mer|ci|less
mer|ci|lessly
Mer|couri
mer|cur|ial
Mer|cury
mer|cury
mercy
△ mer|cies
mere
Me|re|dith
merely
me|re|tri|cious
mer|gan|ser
merge
△ mer|ges
△ merged
△ mer|ging
mer|ger
me|rid|ian
me|ri|di|onal
Mé|ri|mée
me|ringue
me|rino
me|ri|stem
merit

  VERB
△ mer|its
△ mer|ited
△ mer|it|ing
me|ri|to|cracy
△ me|ri|to|cra|
  cies
me|ri|tori|ous
Mer, La (The
  Sea)
Mer|lin
mer|lin
mer|lon
mer|maid
mer|man
△ mer|men
Me|ro|vin|gian
Mer|rick
mer|rily
mer|ri|ment
merry
△ mer|rier
△ mer|ri|est
merry-go-round
mer|ry|ma|ker
mer|ry|ma|king
Merry Widow,
  The (Die Lus|
  tige Witwe)
Merry Wives of
  Wind|sor, The
Mer|sey
Mer|sey|side
Mer|vyn
mesa
més|al|li|ance
mes|cal
mes|ca|lin
mes|clun
mes|dames
mes|en|ceph|
  alon
mes|en|tery
mesh

  NOUN
△ meshes
  VERB
△ meshes
△ meshed
△ mesh|ing
mes|mer|ism
mes|mer|ist
mes|mer|ize
△ mes|mer|izes
△ mes|mer|ized
△ mes|mer|izing
mes|mer|izing
Me|so|ameri|can
me|so|derm
me|so|li|thic
meson
me|so|phyll
Me|so|po|ta|mia
me|so|sphere
Me|so|zoic
mess
  NOUN
△ mes|ses
  VERB
△ mes|ses
△ messed
△ mess|ing
mes|sage
mes|sen|ger
Mes|ser|schmitt
Mes|si|aen
Mes|siah
Mes|si|anic
Mes|si|an|ism
mes|sily
Mes|sina
messy
△ mes|sier
△ mes|si|est
mes|tiza
mes|tizo
Met
met

me¦ta¦bolic
me¦ta¦bo¦lism
me¦ta¦bo¦lite
me¦ta¦bo¦lize
△ me¦ta¦bo¦li¦zes
△ me¦ta¦bo¦lized
△ me¦ta¦bo¦li¦zing
me¦ta¦car¦pal
me¦ta¦car¦pus
△ me¦ta¦carpi

> metal
> *shiny hard
> substance; small
> stones for road-
> making; make or
> mend with these*
> VERB
> △ metals
> △ met¦alled
> △ met¦al¦ling
> ⚠metmettle

me¦tal¦lic
met¦al¦lize
△ met¦al¦li¦zes
△ met¦al¦lized
△ met¦al¦li¦zing
met¦al¦loid
me¦tal¦lur¦gist
me¦tal¦lurgy
met¦al¦work
met¦al¦wor¦ker
me¦ta¦mor¦phic
me¦ta¦mor¦phism
me¦ta¦mor¦phose
△ me¦ta¦mor¦pho¦ses
△ me¦ta¦mor¦phosed
△ me¦ta¦mor¦pho¦sing
Me¦ta¦mor¦pho¦ses

me¦ta¦mor¦pho¦sis
△ me¦ta¦mor¦pho¦ses
me¦ta¦phase
me¦ta¦phor
me¦ta¦phor¦ical
me¦ta¦phor¦ic¦ally
me¦ta¦phys¦ical
me¦ta¦phys¦ic¦ally
me¦ta¦phys¦ics
me¦ta¦sta¦sis
△ me¦ta¦sta¦ses
me¦ta¦tar¦sal
me¦ta¦tar¦sus
△ me¦ta¦tarsi
me¦ta¦theory
△ me¦ta¦theor¦ies
Me¦ta¦zoa
me¦ta¦zoan

> mete
> *dispense*
> △ metes
> △ meted
> △ me¦ting
> ⚠meat
> ⚠meet

me¦teor
me¦te¦oric
me¦te¦or¦ic¦ally
me¦te¦or¦ite
me¦te¦or¦oid
me¦te¦oro¦lo¦gi¦cal
me¦te¦oro¦lo¦gist
me¦te¦oro¦logy

> meter
> *measuring and
> recording device;
> measure by this*

VERB
△ meters
△ metered
△ me¦ter¦ing
⚠metre

meth¦adone
meth¦anal
me¦thane
me¦tha¦noic
meth¦anol
me¦thinks
VERB
△ me¦thought
me¦thi¦on¦ine
method
me¦thod¦ical
me¦thod¦ic¦ally
Meth¦od¦ism
Meth¦od¦ist
meth¦odo¦lo¦gi¦cal
meth¦odo¦logy
me¦thought
meths
Meth¦uen
Me¦thu¦se¦lah
me¦thyl
me¦thy¦la¦ted
me¦thy¦lene
me¦ti¦cu¦lous
me¦ti¦cu¦lous¦ness
met¦onymy
△ met¦ony¦mies
met¦ope

> metre
> *metric unit of
> length; rhythmic
> scheme of poetry
> etc*
> ⚠meter

met¦ric

met¦ri¦cal
met¦ri¦cally
met¦ri¦cate
△ met¦ri¦cates
△ met¦ri¦ca¦ted
△ met¦ri¦ca¦ting
met¦ri¦ca¦tion
metro
met¦ro¦nome
met¦ro¦plex
△ met¦ro¦plexes
Met¦ro¦po¦lis
met¦ro¦po¦lis
△ met¦ro¦pol¦ises
met¦ro¦pol¦itan
Met¦ter¦nich

> met¦tle
> *courage*
> ⚠metal

mettle¦some
Metz
Meuse
mew
VERB
△ mews
△ mewed
△ mew¦ing

> mews
> *stables etc now
> used as garages
> or flats*
> △ mews *or*
> mew¦ses
> ⚠muse

Mex¦ican
Mex¦ico
Mey¦er¦beer
Mey¦er¦hold
mez¦zan¦ine
mezzo
Mez¦zo¦giorno
mezzo-sop¦rano

mez|zo|tint
mi
Miami
miaow
  VERB
  △ miaows
  △ miaowed
  △ miaow|ing
mi|asma
  △ mi|as|mata *or*
  mi|as|mas
mi|as|mal
mica
Micah, Book of
mice
Mi|chael
Mich|ael|mas
  △ Mich|ael|mases
Mi|chel|an|gelo
Miche|lin
Mich|igan
mick
mickey
Mickey Finn
Mickey Mouse
micro
mi|crobe
mi|cro|bial
mi|cro|bic
mi|cro|bio|lo|gi|
  cal
mi|cro|bio|lo|gist
mi|cro|bio|logy
mi|cro|chip
mi|cro|cir|cuit
mi|cro|cli|mate
mi|cro|com|pu|ter
mi|cro|cosm
mi|cro|cos|mic
mi|cro|dot
mi|cro|eco|nom|
  ics
mi|cro|elec|
  tronic

mi|cro|elec|tron|
  ics
mi|cro|fiche
mi|cro|film
mi|cro|light
mi|cro|meter
mi|cron
Mi|cro|ne|sia
mi|cro|nu|tri|ent
micro-organ|ism
mi|cro|phone
mi|cro|pho|to|
  gra|phy
mi|cro|pro|ces|
  sor
mi|cro|pyle
mi|cro|scope
mi|cro|scopic
mi|cro|scop|ic|
  ally
mi|cro|sec|ond
mi|cro|sur|gery
mi|cro|teach|ing
mi|cro|tome
mi|cro|tu|bule
mi|cro|wave
  VERB
  △ mi|cro|waves
  △ mi|cro|waved
  △ mi|cro|wa|
  ving
micro|wave|able
mic|tur|ate
  △ mic|tur|ates
  △ mic|tur|ated
  △ mic|tur|ating
mic|tur|ition
mid
mid-air
Midas
mid|day
mid|den
mid|dle

  VERB
  △ mid|dles
  △ mid|dled
  △ mid|dling
middle-aged
middle|brow
middle|man
  △ middle|men
Middle|march
middle-of-the-
  road
Middles|brough
Middle|ton
middle|weight
mid|dling
midge
mid|get
midi
Mid|ian|ite
mid|iron
mid|land
Mid|lands
mid|most
mid|night
mid-on
mid|point
mid|rib
mid|riff
mid|ship|man
  △ mid|ship|men
Mid|ship|man
  Easy, Mr
mid|ships
midst
mid|stream
mid|sum|mer
Mid|sum|mer's
  Night's
  Dream, The
mid|term
mid|way
mid|week
Mid|west
Mid|wes|tern

mid-wicket
mid|wife
  △ mid|wives
mid|wif|ery
mid|win|ter

> **mien**
>   *appearance;*
>   *expression;*
>   *manner*
>   △ mean

miff
  VERB
  △ miffs
  △ miffed
  △ miff|ing
miffed
miffy
  △ mif|fier
  △ mif|fi|est

> **might**
>   *past of* may;
>   *strength*
>   △ mite

might|ily
migh|ti|ness
mightn't
mighty
  △ migh|tier
  △ migh|ti|est
mig|ma|tite
mi|graine
mi|grant
mi|grate
  △ mi|grates
  △ mi|gra|ted
  △ mi|gra|ting
mi|gra|tion
mi|gra|tory
mih|rab
mi|kado
Mi|kado, The
mike

Mi|ko|nos

mil

mi|lady

△ mi|la|dies

Milan

milch

mild

△ milder

△ mild|est

mil|dew

VERB

△ mil|dews

△ mil|dewed

△ mil|dew|ing

mil|dewed

Mil|dred

mile

mile|age

mile|ometer

miler

Miles

mile|stone

Mil|haud

mi|lieu

△ mi|lieux *or*
    mi|lieus

mil|it|ancy

mil|it|ant

mi|li|tar|ily

mil|it|ar|ism

mil|it|ar|ist

mi|li|tar|is|tic

mi|li|tar|iza|tion

mil|it|ar|ize

△ mil|it|ar|izes

△ mil|it|ar|ized

△ mil|it|ar|izing

mil|it|ary

mil|it|ate

△ mil|it|ates

△ mil|it|ated

△ mil|it|ating

mi|li|tia

mi|li|tia|man

△ mi|li|tia|men

milk

VERB

△ milks

△ milked

△ milk|ing

milk|i|ness

milk|maid

milk|man

△ milk|men

milk|shake

milk|sop

milky

△ milk|ier

△ milk|ki|est

Mill

mill

VERB

△ mills

△ milled

△ mill|ing

Mil|lais

mil|len|ar|ian

mil|len|ari|an|
    ism

mil|len|nial

mil|len|nium

△ mil|len|nia

millepede *see*
    millipede

Mil|ler

mil|ler

mil|les|imal

Mil|let

mil|let

mil|li|ard

mil|li|bar

Mil|li|gan

mil|li|gram

mil|li|litre

mil|li|metre

mil|li|ner

mil|lin|ery

mill|ing

mil|lion

after a number

△ mil|lion

other senses

△ mil|lions

mil|lion|aire

mil|lion|air|ess

△ mil|lion|air|es|
    ses

mil|lionth

mil|li|pede

Mill on the
    Floss, The

mill|pond

Mills

mill|stone

mill|wheel

Milne

milometer *see*
    mileometer

mi|lord

Mi|lo|šević

milt

Mil|ton

Mil|ton Keynes

Mil|wau|kee

mime

VERB

△ mimes

△ mimed

△ mi|ming

mi|meo|graph

VERB

△ mi|meo|
    graphs

△ mi|meo|
    graphed

△ mi|meo|graph|
    ing

mi|mesis

mi|metic

mimic

VERB

△ mim|ics

△ mim|icked

△ mim|ick|ing

mim|icry

mi|mosa

min

mina *see* myna

mi|na|ret

mi|na|tory

mince

VERB

△ min|ces

△ minced

△ min|cing

mince|meat

min|cing

min|cingly

MIND

mind

VERB

△ minds

△ minded

△ mind|ing

mind-blow|ing

mind-bog|gling

minded

minder

mind|ful

mind|ful|ness

mind|less

mind|lessly

mind-rea|der

mind-read|ing

mine

VERB

△ mines

△ mined

△ mi|ning

mine|field

miner
    mineworker
    ⚠ minor

min|eral

min|era|lo|gi|cal

min|er|al|ogist
min|er|al|ogy
Mi|nerva
mi|nes|trone
mine|swee|per
min|gi|ness
min|gle
△ min|gles
△ min|gled
△ min|gling
mingy
△ min|gier
△ min|gi|est
Mini
make of small
car
mini
small; small one
minia|ture
minia|tur|ist
minia|tur|ize
△ minia|tur|izes
△ minia|tur|ized
△ minia|tur|
izing
mi|ni|bus
mi|ni|cab
mi|ni|com|pu|ter
minim
min|imal
min|im|al|ism
min|im|al|ist
min|im|ally
min|im|ize
△ min|im|izes
△ min|im|ized
△ min|im|izing
mi|ni|mum
△ mi|ni|mums
or min|ima
mi|ning
min|ion
miniscule *see*
minuscule

mini-ser|ies
mi|ni|skirt
min|is|ter
VERB
△ min|is|ters
△ min|is|tered
△ min|is|ter|ing
mi|nis|ter|ial
mi|nis|tra|tion
min|is|try
△ min|is|tries
Mi|ni|tel
mink
sing. and pl.
Min|ne|apo|lis
min|ne|ola
Min|ne|sota
min|now
Mi|noan

minor
of little or less
size, importance,
etc; below adult
age; person of
this age; musical
scale; of this
scale
△miner

Mi|norca
mi|nor|ity
△ mi|nor|it|ies
Minos
Mi|no|taur
Minsk
min|ster
min|strel
min|strelsy
mint
VERB
△ mints
△ min|ted
△ mint|ing
Min|toff

Min|ton
minty
△ min|tier
△ min|ti|est
min|uet
minus
NOUN
△ mi|nuses
min|us|cule
min|ute
NOUN
△ min|utes
VERB
△ min|utes
△ minu|ted
△ minu|ting
mi|nute
ADJ.
mi|nutely
Min|ute|man
mi|nu|tiae
minx
△ minxes
Mio|cene
Mi|ra|bel
mir|acle
mi|ra|cu|lous
mi|rage
Mi|randa
MIRAS
mire
VERB
△ mires
△ mired
△ mir|ing
mirin
Miró
Mir|ren
mir|ror
VERB
△ mir|rors
△ mir|rored
△ mir|ror|ing
mirth

mirth|ful
mirth|less
mis|ad|ven|ture
mis|al|li|ance
mis|an|thrope
Mis|an|thrope, Le
(The Miser)
mis|an|thro|pic
mis|an|thro|pist
mis|an|thropy
mis|ap|pli|ca|
tion
mis|ap|ply
△ mis|ap|plies
△ mis|ap|plied
△ mis|ap|ply|ing
mis|ap|pre|hend
△ mis|ap|pre|
hends
△ mis|ap|pre|
hen|ded
△ mis|ap|pre|
hend|ing
mis|ap|pre|hen|
sion
mis|ap|pro|pri|
ate
△ mis|ap|pro|
pri|ates
△ mis|ap|pro|
pri|ated
△ mis|ap|pro|
pri|ating
mis|ap|pro|pri|
ation
mis|be|got|ten
mis|be|have
△ mis|be|haves
△ mis|be|haved
△ mis|be|ha|ving
mis|be|ha|viour
mis|cal|cu|late
△ mis|cal|cu|
lates

△ mis|cal|cu|la|
ted
△ mis|cal|cu|la|
ting
mis|cal|cu|la|tion
mis|car|riage
mis|carry
△ mis|car|ries
△ mis|car|ried
△ mis|car|ry|ing
mis|cast
△ mis|casts
△ mis|cast
△ mis|cast|ing
mis|ce|gen|ation
mis|cel|la|ne|ous
mis|cel|lany
△ mis|cel|lan|ies
mis|chance
mis|chief
mis|chiev|ous
mis|chiev|ously
mis|chiev|ous|
ness
mis|ci|bil|ity
mis|cible
mis|con|ceive
△ mis|con|ceives
△ mis|con|
ceived
△ mis|con|ceiv|
ing
mis|con|cep|tion
mis|con|duct
mis|con|struc|
tion
mis|con|strue
△ mis|con|strues
△ mis|con|
strued
△ mis|con|stru|
ing
mis|cre|ant
mis|date

VERB
△ mis|dates
△ mis|da|ted
△ mis|da|ting
mis|deal
VERB
△ mis|deals
△ mis|dealt
△ mis|deal|ing
mis|deed
mis|de|mean|our
mis|di|rect
△ mis|di|rects
△ mis|di|rec|ted
△ mis|di|rect|ing
mis|di|rec|tion
*Mid|sum|mer
Mar|riage, The*
mise-en-scène
miser
mis|er|able
Mi|sér|ables, Les
mis|er|ably
misère
mi|seri|cord
mi|ser|li|ness
mi|serly
mis|ery
△ mis|er|ies
mis|fire
VERB
△ mis|fires
△ mis|fired
△ mis|fir|ing
mis|fit
mis|for|tune
mis|giv|ing
mis|gui|ded
mis|guid|edly
mis|han|dle
△ mis|han|dles
△ mis|han|dled
△ mis|hand|ling
mis|hap

mis|hear
△ mis|hears
△ mis|heard
△ mis|hear|ing
Mish|ima
mis|hit
VERB
△ mis|hits
△ mis|hit
△ mis|hit|ting
mish|mash
△ mish|ma|shes
Mish|nah
mis|in|form
△ mis|in|forms
△ mis|in|formed
△ mis|in|form|
ing
mis|in|for|ma|
tion
mis|in|ter|pret
△ mis|in|ter|
prets
△ mis|in|ter|pre|
ted
△ mis|in|ter|
pret|ing
mis|in|ter|pret|
ation
mis|judge
△ mis|jud|ges
△ mis|judged
△ mis|jud|ging
mis|judge|ment
mis|key
△ mis|keys
△ mis|keyed
△ mis|key|ing
mis|lay
△ mis|lays
△ mis|laid
△ mis|lay|ing
mis|lead
△ mis|leads

△ mis|led
△ mis|lead|ing
mis|lead|ing
mis|man|age
△ mis|man|ages
△ mis|man|aged
△ mis|man|aging
mis|man|age|
ment
mis|match
NOUN
△ mismat|ches
VERB
△ mis|mat|ches
△ mis|matched
△ mis|match|ing
mis|name
△ mis|names
△ mis|named
△ mis|na|ming
mis|no|mer
miso
mi|so|gy|nist
mi|so|gy|nous
mi|so|gyny
mis|place
△ mis|pla|ces
△ mis|placed
△ mis|pla|cing
mis|print
VERB
△ mis|prints
△ mis|prin|ted
△ mis|print|ing
mis|pri|sion
mis|pro|nounce
△ mis|pro|noun|
ces
△ mis|pro|
nounced
△ mis|pro|noun|
cing
mis|pro|nun|ci|
ation

mis|quo|ta|tion
mis|quote
△ mis|quotes
△ mis|quo|ted
△ mis|quo|ting
mis|read
△ mis|reads
△ mis|read
△ mis|read|ing
mis|rep|re|sent
△ mis|rep|re|
  sents
△ mis|rep|re|sen|
  ted
△ mis|rep|re|
  sent|ing
mis|rep|re|sen|
 ta|tion
mis|rule
  VERB
△ mis|rules
△ mis|ruled
△ mis|ru|ling
miss
  NOUN
△ mis|ses
  VERB
△ mis|ses
△ missed
△ miss|ing

mis|sal
mass book
⚠ missile

mis|sel-thrush
mis|sha|pen

mis|sile
flying bomb
⚠ missal

miss|ing
mis|sion
mis|sion|ary
△ mis|sion|ar|ies

missis *see*
 missus
Mis|sis|sippi
mis|sive
Miss Julie (Fro|
 |ken Julie)
Mis|souri
mis|spell
△ mis|spells
△ mis|spelt *or*
  mis|spelled
△ mis|spell|ing
mis|spend
△ mis|spends
△ mis|spent
△ mis|spend|ing
mis|sus
△ mis|suses
missy
△ mis|sies
mist
  VERB
△ mists
△ mis|ted
△ mist|ing
mis|take
  VERB
△ mis|takes
△ mis|took
△ mis|ta|king
△ mis|ta|ken
mis|ta|ken
mis|ta|kenly
mis|ter
mis|tily
mis|time
△ mis|times
△ mis|timed
△ mis|ti|ming
mis|ti|ness
mistle-thrush
△ mistle-
  thrushes
mistle|toe

mis|took
mis|tral
mis|treat
△ mis|treats
△ mis|trea|ted
△ mis|treat|ing
mis|treat|ment
mis|tress
△ mis|tres|ses
mis|trial
mis|trust
  VERB
△ mis|trusts
△ mis|trus|ted
△ mis|trust|ing
mis|trust|ful
misty
△ mis|tier
△ mis|ti|est
mis|un|der|stand
△ mis|un|der|
  stands
△ mis|un|der|
  stood
△ mis|un|der|
  stand|ing
mis|un|der|
 stand|ing
mis|un|der|stood
mis|use
  VERB
△ mis|uses
△ mis|used
△ mis|using
Mit|chell

mite
tiny creature,
thing, etc
⚠ might

Mit|ford
mi|ti|gate
△ mi|ti|gates
△ mi|ti|ga|ted

△ mi|ti|ga|ting
mi|to|chon|drion
△ mi|to|chon|
  dria
mi|to|sis
mitre
  VERB
△ mitres
△ mitred
△ mi|tring
mitt
mit|ten
Mit|ter|rand
mix
  NOUN
△ mixes
  VERB
△ mixes
△ mixed
△ mix|ing
mixed
mixed-abil|ity
mixed-up
mixer
mix|ture
mix-up
miz|zen|mast
M'Nagh|ten
mne|monic
mne|mon|ic|ally
mo
△ mos
moa
Mo|ab|ite
moan
  VERB
△ moans
△ moaned
△ moan|ing
moaner

moat
defensive trench
⚠ mote

mob
  VERB
  △ mobs
  △ mobbed
  △ mob|bing
mo|bile
mo|bil|ity
mo|bil|iza|tion
mo|bil|ize
  △ mo|bil|izes
  △ mo|bil|ized
  △ mo|bil|izing
mob|ster
Moby Dick
moc|ca|sin
mocha
mock
  VERB
  △ mocks
  △ mocked
  △ mock|ing
mock|ers
mock|ery
  △ mock|er|ies
mock|ing
mock|ing|bird
mock-up
Mod
mod

> modal
>   *of modes*
>   ⚠model
>   ⚠module

mo|dal|ity
mode

> model
>   *small replica;*
>   *person who sits*
>   *to artist etc;*
>   *person wearing*
>   *clothes for*
>   *buyers to*

inspect; make or
do these things
  VERB
  △ mod|els
  △ mod|elled
  △ mod|el|ling
    ⚠modal
    ⚠module

mod|el|ling
mo|dello
  △ mo|delli
modem
mod|er|ate
  VERB
  △ mod|er|ates
  △ mod|er|ated
  △ mod|er|ating
mod|er|ately
mod|er|ation
mod|er|ato
mod|er|ator
mod|ern
Mod|ern|ism
Mod|ern|ist
mod|ern|is|tic
mo|der|nity
mod|ern|iza|tion
mod|ern|ize
  △ mod|ern|izes
  △ mod|ern|ized
  △ mod|ern|izing
mod|est
mod|estly
mod|esty
mod|icum
mo|di|fi|ca|tion
mo|di|fier
mod|ify
  △ mo|di|fies
  △ mo|di|fied
  △ mo|di|fy|ing
Mo|di|gli|ani
mo|dish

mo|diste
mo|du|lar
mo|du|late
  △ mo|du|lates
  △ mo|du|la|ted
  △ mo|du|la|ting
mo|du|la|tion
mo|du|la|tor

> mod|ule
>   *unit forming*
>   *part of space*
>   *vehicle etc*
>   ⚠modal
>   ⚠model

mod|ulus
  △ mod|uli
modus oper|andi
modus vi|vendi
mog
Mo|ga|di|shu
moggy
  △ mog|gies
mogul
mo|hair
Mohammed *see*
  Muhammad
Mo|ham|medan
Mohave *see*
  Mojave
Mo|hawk
mo|hi|can
moi|ety
  △ moi|et|ies
moire
moiré
moist
  △ mois|ter
  △ moist|est
moisten
  △ moist|ens
  △ moist|ened
  △ moist|en|ing
moist|ness

mois|ture
mois|tur|ize
  △ mois|tur|izes
  △ mois|tur|ized
  △ mois|tur|izing
mois|tur|izer
Mo|jave
moke
molar
mo|lar|ity
mo|las|ses
Mold
Mol|da|via
mole
mo|lecu|lar
mo|le|cule
mole|hill
mole|skin
mo|lest
  △ mo|lests
  △ mo|les|ted
  △ mo|lest|ing
mo|les|ta|tion
Mo|li|ère
moll
Moll Flan|ders
mol|li|fi|ca|tion
mol|lify
  △ mol|li|fies
  △ mol|li|fied
  △ mol|li|fy|ing
mol|lusc
Mol|lusca
mol|ly|coddle
  △ mol|ly|coddles
  △ mol|ly|
    coddled
  △ mol|ly|cod|
    dling
Mo|loch
mol|ten
molto
mo|lyb|denum
mom

Mom|basa
mo|ment
mo|men|tar|ily
mo|men|tary
mo|men|tous
mo|men|tous|
  ness
mo|men|tum
mommy
  △ mom|mies
Mona
Mon|aco
Mon|aco-Ville
monad
Mona Lisa
mon|an|drous
mon|an|dry
mon|arch
mon|ar|chic
mon|ar|chi|cal
mon|arch|ism
mon|arch|ist
Mon|arch of the
  Glen
mon|ar|chy
  △ mon|ar|chies
mon|as|tery
  △ mon|as|ter|ies
mon|as|tic
mon|as|tic|ally
mon|as|ti|cism
Mon|day
Mon|drian
Monet
mon|et|ar|ism
mon|et|ar|ist
mon|et|ary
money
mon|ey|bags
money-changer
mon|eyed
money-grub|ber
money-grub|bing
mon|ey|len|der

mon|ey|ma|ker
money-making
mon|gol
Mon|go|lia
Mon|go|lian
mon|gol|ism
Mon|gol|oid
mon|gol|oid
Mon|gols
mon|goose
mon|grel
Mon|ica
mon|ied
mon|ism
mon|ist
mon|is|tic
mon|ition
mon|itor
  VERB
  △ mon|it|ors
  △ mon|it|ored
  △ mon|it|or|ing
mon|it|ory
monk
mon|key
  NOUN
  △ mon|keys
  VERB
  △ mon|keys
  △ mon|keyed
  △ mon|key|ing
monk|fish
sing. and pl.
monk|ish
monks|hood
Mon|mouth
mono
mo|no|chro|
  matic
mo|no|chrome
mon|ocle
mo|no|clo|nal
mo|no|coty|le|
  don

mon|ocu|lar
mo|no|cul|ture
mon|odic
mon|ody
  △ mon|od|ies
mon|oe|cious
mo|no|ga|mous
mo|no|gamy
mo|no|gram
  VERB
  △ mo|no|grams
  △ mo|no|
    grammed
  △ mo|no|gram|
    ming
mo|no|graph
mo|no|hybrid
mo|no|lin|gual
mo|no|lith
mo|no|lithic
mo|no|logue
mo|no|ma|nia
mo|no|ma|niac
mo|no|mer
mo|no|nuc|le|
  osis
mo|no|phonic
mo|no|plane
mo|no|pol|ist
mo|no|pol|is|tic
mo|no|pol|iza|
  tion
mo|no|pol|ize
  △ mo|no|pol|izes
  △ mo|no|pol|ized
  △ mo|no|pol|
    izing
Mo|no|poly
mo|no|poly
  △ mo|no|pol|ies
mon|op|sony
mo|no|rail
mo|no|sac|char|
  ide

mo|no|so|dium
mo|no|syl|labic
mo|no|syl|lable
mo|no|the|ism
mo|no|the|ist
mo|no|the|is|tic
mo|no|tone
mo|not|on|ous
mo|not|on|ously
mo|not|ony
mo|no|treme
mo|no|type
mo|no|va|lent
mon|ox|ide
Mon|roe
Mon|ro|via
Mons
Mon|sig|nor
  △ Mon|sig|nors
  or Mon|sig|
    nori
mon|soon
mon|ster
mon|stera
mon|strance
mon|stros|ity
  △ mon|stros|it|
    ies
mon|strous
mon|strously
mon|tage
Mon|ta|gue
Mon|taigne
Mon|tana
Mont Blanc
mont|bre|tia
Monte Carlo
Mon|te|negro
Mon|tes|quieu
Mon|tes|sori
Mon|te|verdi
Mon|te|vi|deo
Mon|te|zuma
Mont|fort

Mont|gol|fier
Mont|gom|ery
month
Month in the
 Coun|try, A
monthly
  NOUN
  △ month|lies
mont|mo|ril|lon|
ite

Mont|pel|ier
city in USA
 ⚠Montpellier

Mont|pel|lier
city in France
 ⚠Montpelier

Mon|treal
Mon|treux
Mont-Saint-
 Michel
monu|ment
monu|men|tal
moo
  VERB
  △ moos
  △ mooed
  △ moo|ing
mooch
  VERB
  △ moo|ches
  △ mooched
  △ mooch|ing
mood
mood|ily
moo|di|ness
Moody
moody
  △ moo|dier
  △ moo|di|est
moon
  VERB
  △ moons

△ mooned
△ moon|ing
moon|beam
Moonie
moon|light
  VERB
  △ moon|lights
  △ moon|ligh|ted
  △ moon|light|
   ing
moon|ligh|ter
moon|light|ing
'Moonlight'
 Sonata
moon|lit
moon|shine
moon|stone
Moon|stone, The
moon|struck
moony
  △ moo|nier
  △ moo|ni|est
Moor
moor
  VERB
  △ moors
  △ moored
  △ moor|ing
Moore
moor|hen
moor|ing
Moor|ish
moor|land

moose
sort of deer
sing. and pl.
 ⚠mouse
 ⚠mousse

moot
  VERB
  △ moots
  △ moo|ted
  △ moot|ing

mop
  VERB
  △ mops
  △ mopped
  △ mop|ping
mope
  VERB
  △ mopes
  △ moped
  △ mo|ping
moped
mop|pet
mo|quette
Morag
mo|raine

moral
to do with right
and wrong; wise
saying
 ⚠morale

mo|rale
level of
confidence,
optimism, etc
 ⚠moral

mor|al|ist
mor|al|is|tic
mor|al|ity
  △ mor|al|it|ies
mor|al|ize
  △ mor|al|izes
  △ mor|al|ized
  △ mor|al|izing
mor|al|izer
mo|rass
  △ mor|as|ses
mo|ra|tor|ium
  △ mo|ra|toria
Mo|ra|via
moray
mor|bid
mor|bid|ity

mor|dant
Mor|de|cai
More
more
More|cambe
morel
mor|ello
more|over
mores
Mor|gan
mor|gan|atic
Mor|gan le Fay
morgue
mori|bund
Mor|ley
Mor|mon
Mor|mon|ism
morn
mor|nay
morn|ing
Mo|rocco
mo|rocco
moron
Mo|roni
mor|onic
mo|rose
mo|rose|ness
Mor|peth
mor|pheme
mor|phine
morph|ing
mor|pho|gen|
 esis
mor|pho|lo|gi|cal
mor|phol|ogy
Mor|ris
mor|ris
mor|row
Morse
mor|sel
mor|tal
mor|tal|ity
mor|tar

VERB
△ mor|tars
△ mor|tared
△ mor|tar|ing
mor|tar|board
Morte d'Ar|thur
by Tennison
Morte D'Ar|
thur, Le
by Mallory
mort|gage
VERB
△ mort|ga|ges
△ mort|gaged
△ mort|ga|ging
mor|tice
mor|ti|cian
mor|ti|fi|ca|tion
mor|tify
△ mor|ti|fies
△ mor|ti|fied
△ mor|ti|fy|ing
Mor|ti|mer
mor|tise
VERB
△ mor|ti|ses
△ mor|tised
△ mor|ti|sing
Mor|ton
mor|tu|ary
△ mor|tu|ar|ies
Mo|saic
mo|saic
Mos|cow

Mosel
river
⚠ moselle

mo|selle
wine
⚠ Mosel

Moses
Moses and

Aaron (Moses
und Aron)
mosey
△ mo|seys
△ mo|seyed
△ mo|sey|ing
mosh|ing
Moslem *see*
Muslim
Mos|ley
mosque
mos|quito
△ mos|qui|tos *or*
mos|qui|toes
Moss
moss
△ mos|ses
MOS|SAD
mossy
△ mos|sier
△ mos|si|est
most
Mos|tar
mostly

mote
speck
⚠ moat

motel
motet
moth
moth|ball
moth-eaten
mother
VERB
△ moth|ers
△ moth|ered
△ moth|er|ing
mother|board
Mother Cour|age
and her Chil|
dren (Mut|ter
Cou|rage und
ihre Kin|der)

moth|er|ese
moth|er|hood
Moth|er|ing
Sun|day
mother-in-law
△ moth|ers-in-
law
moth|er|land
moth|erly
mother-of-pearl
Moth|er's Day
Moth|er|well
moth|proof
VERB
△ moth|proofs
△ moth|proofed
△ moth|proof|
ing

motif
repeated element
in a design etc
⚠ motive

mo|tile
mo|tion
VERB
△ mo|tions
△ mo|tioned
△ mo|tion|ing
mo|tion|less
mo|ti|vate
△ mo|ti|vates
△ mo|ti|va|ted
△ mo|ti|va|ting
mo|ti|va|tion

mo|tive
cause of, or
causing, action
⚠ motif

mot|ley
mo|to|cross
motor

VERB
△ mo|tors
△ mo|tored
△ mo|tor|ing
mo|tor|bike
mo|tor|cade
mo|tor|cycle
mo|tor|cyclist
mo|tor|ing
mo|tor|ist
mo|tor|ize
△ mo|tor|izes
△ mo|tor|ized
△ mo|tor|izing
mo|tor|way
Mo|town
motte
mot|tled
motto
△ mot|tos *or*
mot|toes
mould
VERB
△ moulds
△ moul|ded
△ mould|ing
moul|der
△ moul|ders
△ moul|dered
△ moul|der|ing
mould|ing
mouldy
△ moul|dier
△ moul|di|est
Mou|lin Rouge

moult
shed hair etc;
this process
VERB
△ moults
△ moul|ted
△ moult|ing
⚠ malt

mound
mount
  VERB
  △ mounts
  △ moun|ted
  △ mount|ing
moun|tain
moun|tain|eer
  VERB
  △ moun|tain|eers
  △ moun|tain|
    eered
  △ moun|tain|eer|
    ing
moun|tain|eer|ing
moun|tain|ous
Mount|bat|ten
moun|te|bank
moun|ted
Moun|tie
mourn
  △ mourns
  △ mourned
  △ mourn|ing
mourner
mourn|ful
mourn|fully
mourn|ing
Mourn|ing Be|
comes Elec|tra

mouse
  small rodent;
  computer input
  device; hunt
  mice
  NOUN
  △ mice
  VERB
  △ mou|ses
  △ moused
  △ mous|ing
    ⚠ moose
    ⚠ mousse

mouse-milk|ing
mou|ser
mouse|trap
mou|si|ness
mous|saka

mousse
  creamed food etc
  ⚠ moose
  ⚠ mouse

Moussorgsky
see
Mussorgsky
mous|tache
mousy
  △ mou|sier
  △ mou|si|est
moun|tain|eer|
  ing
mouth
  VERB
  △ mouths
  △ mouthed
  △ mouth|ing
mouth|feel
mouth|ful
mouth|piece
mouth-to-
  mouth
mouth|wash
  △ mouth|wa|
    shes
mouth-water|
  ing
mov|able
move
  VERB
  △ moves
  △ moved
  △ mov|ing
move|ment
mover
movie
Mo|vie|tone

mov|ing
mow
  VERB
  △ mows
  △ mowed
  △ mow|ing
mower
moxa
moxi|bus|tion
Mo|zam|bique
Moz|art
moz|za|rella
Mu|barak
much
  ADJ.
  △ more
  △ most
Much Ado
  about Noth|ing
much|ness
mu|ci|lage
mu|ci|la|gin|ous
muck
  VERB
  △ mucks
  △ mucked
  △ muck|ing
muck-rake
  △ muck-rakes
  △ muck-raked
  △ muck-raking
muck-raker
muck-raking
mucky
  △ muck|ier
  △ mucki|est

mu|cous
  ADJ.
  ⚠ mucus

mucus
  NOUN
  ⚠ mucous

mud
mud|bath
mud|di|ness
mud|dle
  VERB
  △ mud|dles
  △ mud|dled
  △ mud|dling
mud|dled
muddle-headed
muddy
  VERB
  △ mud|dies
  △ mud|died
  △ mud|dy|ing
  ADJ.
  △ mud|dier
  △ mud|di|est
mud|flat
mud|guard
mud|hop|per
mud|pack
mud|puppy
  △ mud|pup|pies
mud|skip|per
mud-slin|ger
mud-sling|ing
mud|stone
muesli
mu|ez|zin
muff
  VERB
  △ muffs
  △ muffed
  △ muff|ing
muf|fin
muffle
  △ muffles
  △ muffled
  △ muff|ling
muff|ler
mufti
mug

VERB
△ mugs
△ mugged
△ mug|ging
Mu|gabe
mug|ful
mug|ger
Mug|ger|idge
mug|gi|ness
mug|ging
mug|gins
△ mug|gin|ses
muggy
△ mug|gier
△ mug|gi|est
Mug|hal
mug|shot
mug|wump
Mu|ham|mad
Mu|har|ram
Mu|ja|ha|deen
mu|latto
△ mu|lat|tos or
mu|lat|toes
mul|berry
△ mul|ber|ries
mulch
NOUN
△ mul|ches
VERB
△ mul|ches
△ mulched
△ mulch|ing
mulct
VERB
△ mulcts
△ mulc|ted
△ mulct|ing
mule
mu|let|eer
mu|lish
Mull
mull

VERB
△ mulls
△ mulled
△ mull|ing
mul|lah
mulled
mul|let
mul|li|ga|tawny
mul|lion
mul|lioned
Mul|roney
mul|ti|cel|lu|lar
mul|ti|col|oured
mul|ti|cul|tural
mul|ti|fari|ous
mul|ti|form
mul|ti|lat|eral
mul|ti|lin|gual
mul|ti|me|dia
mul|ti|mil|lion|
aire
mul|ti|na|tional
mul|ti|par|ous
mul|tiple
mul|tiple-choice
mul|ti|plex
mul|ti|plic|and
mul|ti|pli|ca|tion
mul|ti|pli|city
VERB
△ mul|ti|pli|ci|
ties
mul|ti|plier
mul|ti|ply
△ mul|ti|plies
△ mul|ti|plied
△ mul|ti|ply|ing
mul|ti|pro|gram|
ming
mul|ti|pur|pose
mul|ti|ra|cial
mul|ti|storey
mul|ti|task|ing
mul|ti|tude
mul|ti|tu|din|ous

mul|ti|user
mum
mum|ble
VERB
△ mum|bles
△ mum|bled
△ mum|bling
mumbo-jumbo
mum|mer
mum|mery
△ mum|mer|ies
mum|mi|fi|ca|
tion
mum|mify
△ mum|mi|fies
△ mum|mi|fied
△ mum|mi|fy|ing
mum|ming
mummy
△ mum|mies
mumps
Munch
munch
△ mun|ches
△ munched
△ munch|ing
Mu|nch|hau|sen
mun|chies
mun|dane
Mungo
Mu|nich
mu|ni|ci|pal
mu|ni|ci|pal|ity
△ mu|ni|ci|pal|it|
ies
mu|ni|ci|pally
mu|ni|fi|cence
mu|ni|fi|cent
mu|ni|ments
mu|ni|tions

Mun|ster
Irish province
⚠ Münster

Mün|ster
German city
⚠ Munster

mun|tin
munt|jac
muon
mural
mur|al|ist
mur|der
△ mur|ders
△ mur|dered
△ mur|der|ing
mur|derer
mur|der|ess
△ mur|der|es|ses
*Mur|der in the
Ca|thed|ral*
mur|der|ous
*Mur|ders in the
Rue Morgue,
The*
Murdo
Mur|doch
Mur|iel
murk
mur|ki|ness
murky
△ mur|kier
△ mur|ki|est
Mur|mansk
mur|mur
VERB
△ mur|murs
△ mur|mured
△ mur|mur|ing
mur|mur|ous
mur|rain
Mur|ray
Mur|ray|field
Mus|ca|det
Mus|cat
mus|cat
mus|ca|tel

mus|cle
body tissue that
produces
movement;
strength
⚠ mussel

muscle-bound
muscle|man
Mus|co|vite
mus|co|vite
mus|cu|lar
mus|cu|lar|ity
mus|cu|la|ture
Muse

muse
ponder
△ muses
△ mused
△ mus|ing
⚠ mews

mu|seum
mu|seum-piece
mush
  NOUN
△ mushes
  VERB
△ mushes
△ mushed
△ mush|ing
mush|room
  VERB
△ mush|rooms
△ mush|roomed
△ mush|room|
   ing
mush|room-
  cloud
mushy
△ mush|ier
△ mushi|est
music
mu|si|cal

mu|si|cal|ity
mu|sic|ally
mu|si|cian
mu|si|cian|ship
mu|si|col|ogist
mu|si|col|ogy
mus|ings
musk
mus|ket
mus|ket|eer
mus|ketry
mus|ki|ness
musk|rat
musky
△ mus|kier
△ mus|ki|est
Mus|lim
mus|lin
mus|quash
△ mus|qua|shes
muss
△ mus|ses
△ mussed
△ muss|ing

mus|sel
sort of shellfish
⚠ muscle

Mus|so|lini
Mus|sorg|sky
must
mus|ta|chio
mus|ta|chi|oed
mus|tang
mus|tard
mus|ter
  VERB
△ mus|ters
△ mus|tered
△ mus|ter|ing
mus|ti|ness
mustn't
musty
△ mus|tier

△ mus|ti|est
mu|ta|bil|ity
mu|table
mu|ta|gen
mu|tant
mu|tate
△ mu|tates
△ mu|ta|ted
△ mu|ta|ting
mu|ta|tion
mu|ta|tis mu|tan|
dis
mute
  VERB
△ mutes
△ muted
△ mu|ting
muted
mu|ti|late
△ mu|ti|lates
△ mu|ti|la|ted
△ mu|ti|la|ting
mu|ti|la|tion
mu|tin|eer
mu|tin|ous
mu|tiny
  NOUN
△ mu|ti|nies
  VERB
△ mu|ti|nies
△ mu|ti|nied
△ mu|ti|ny|ing
mutt
mut|ter
  VERB
△ mut|ters
△ mut|tered
△ mut|ter|ing
mut|ton
mut|ton|chops
mut|ton|head
mu|tual
mu|tu|al|ism
mu|tu|al|ity

mu|tu|ally
Muy|bridge
Muzak
muz|zily
muz|zi|ness
muz|zle
  VERB
△ muz|zles
△ muz|zled
△ muz|zling
muzzy
△ muz|zier
△ muz|zi|est
my
my|al|gia
my|cel|ium
△ my|celia
My|cenae
My|cen|aean
my|col|ogy
my|co|toxin
my|elin
my|el|itis
my|el|oma
My|fanwy
Mykonos *see*
  Mikonos
my|lon|ite
myna
myo|car|diac
myo|car|dial
myo|car|di|tis
myo|car|dium
△ myo|car|dia
myo|fi|bril
myo|glo|bin
my|opia
my|opic
Myra
myr|iad
myr|mi|don
myrrh
Myrtle
myrtle

my|self
My|sore
mys|teri|ous
mys|teri|ously
mys|tery
△ mys|ter|ies

mys|tic
*person seeking
direct knowledge*

*of God; of such
knowledge or the
search for it*
▲ mystique

mys|ti|cal
mys|ti|cism
mys|ti|fi|ca|tion
mys|tify

△ mys|ti|fies
△ mys|ti|fied
△ mys|ti|fy|ing
mys|ti|fy|ing

mys|tique
*mysterious
quality*
▲ mystic

myth
myth|ical
myth|ic|ally
my|tho|lo|gi|cal
myth|ol|ogy
△ myth|olo|gies
myxo|ma|to|sis

N

NAAFI
nab
 △ nabs
 △ nabbed
 △ nab|bing
Nab|lus
nabob
Na|bo|kov
na|celle
nacho
nacre
na|cre|ous
Na|dine
nadir
nae|vus
 △ naevi
naff
 △ naf|fer
 △ naf|fest
nag
 VERB
 △ nags
 △ nagged
 △ nag|ging
Na|ga|saki
nag|ger
nag|ging
Na|gorno Ka|ra|
 bakh
Nagy
Nahum, Book
 of
naiad
 △ nai|ads or nai|
 ades
nail
 VERB
 △ nails
 △ nailed
 △ nail|ing
Nai|paul
Nai|robi

naïve
 △ naïver
 △ naïv|est
naïvely
naïv|ety
Na|ka|sone
naked
Naked and the
 Dead, The
na|kedly
na|ked|ness
naker
namby-pamby
name
 VERB
 △ names
 △ named
 △ na|ming
name-drop
 △ name-drops
 △ name-
 dropped
 △ name-drop|
 ping
name-drop|per
name-drop|ping
name|less
namely
name|plate
name|sake
Na|mi|bia
nan
Nana
nana
Nancy
nancy
 △ nan|cies
nanny
 NOUN
 △ nan|nies
 VERB
 △ nan|nies
 △ nan|nied
 △ nan|ny|ing

Nan|sen
Nantes
Nan|tucket
Naomi
nap
 VERB
 △ naps
 △ napped
 △ nap|ping
na|palm
 VERB
 △ na|palms
 △ na|palmed
 △ na|palm|ing
nape
na|pery
naph|tha
naph|tha|lene
nap|kin
Naples
Na|po|leon
Napoleon
Na|po|le|onic
nappe
nappy
 △ nap|pies
nar|cis|sism
nar|cis|sis|tic
nar|cis|sus
 △ nar|cis|suses
 or nar|cissi
nar|co|lepsy
nar|co|sis
 △ nar|co|ses
nar|co|ter|ror|
 ism
nar|cotic
nard
nares
nark
 VERB
 △ narks
 △ narked
 △ nark|ing

narky
 △ nar|kier
 △ nar|ki|est
nar|rate
 △ nar|rates
 △ nar|ra|ted
 △ nar|ra|ting
nar|ra|tion
nar|ra|tive
nar|ra|tor
nar|row
 VERB
 △ nar|rows
 △ nar|rowed
 △ nar|row|ing
 ADJ.
 △ nar|rower
 △ nar|row|est
nar|row|cast|ing
nar|row-gauge
nar|rowly
nar|row-minded
nar|row-mind|
 ed|ness
nar|row|ness
nar|thex
 △ nar|thexes
nar|whal
nasal
nas|al|ize
 △ nas|al|izes
 △ nas|al|ized
 △ nas|al|izing
nas|ally
nas|cent

Nash
architect; dandy
 ⚠ Nashe

Nashe
writer
 ⚠ Nash

Nash|ville

Nas|sau
Nas|ser
nas|tic
nas|tily
nas|ti|ness
nas|tur|tium
nasty
  NOUN
  △ nas|ties
  ADJ.
  △ nas|tier
  △ nas|ti|est
Natal
Na|talia
Na|than
Na|than|iel
na|tion
na|tional
na|tion|al|ism
national|ist
na|tion|al|is|tic
na|tion|al|is|tic|
  ally
na|tion|al|ity
  △ na|tion|al|it|ies
na|tion|al|iza|tion
na|tion|al|ize
  △ na|tion|al|izes
  △ na|tion|al|ized
  △ na|tion|al|
  izing
na|tion|ally
na|tion|wide
na|tive
na|tiv|ity
  △ na|tiv|it|ies
na|tron
nat|ter
  VERB
  △ nat|ters
  △ nat|tered
  △ nat|ter|ing
nat|ter|jack
nat|tily

natty
  △ nat|tier
  △ nat|ti|est
Na|tu|fian
nat|ural
nat|ur|al|ism
nat|ur|al|ist
nat|ur|al|is|tic
nat|ur|al|is|tic|
  ally
nat|ur|al|iza|tion
nat|ur|al|ize
  △ nat|ur|al|izes
  △ nat|ur|al|ized
  △ nat|ur|al|izing
nat|ur|ally
nat|ur|al|ness
na|ture
na|tur|ism
na|tur|ist
na|turo|pa|thy

naught
  nothing
  ⚠nought

naught|ily
naugh|ti|ness
naughty
  △ naugh|tier
  △ naugh|ti|est
Nauru
nau|sea
nau|se|ate
  △ nau|se|ates
  △ nau|se|ated
  △ nau|se|ating
nau|se|ating
nau|se|atingly
nau|se|ous
nau|ti|cal
nau|ti|cally
nau|ti|lus
  △ nau|ti|luses *or*
  nau|tili

Na|vajo

naval
  of the navy or
  ships
  ⚠navel

Na|varre

nave
  central part of
  church; hub of
  wheel
  ⚠knave

navel
  point on
  abdomen where
  umbilical cord
  was detached;
  any central point
  ⚠naval

na|vi|ga|bil|ity
nav|ig|able
na|vi|gate
  △ na|vi|gates
  △ na|vi|ga|ted
  △ na|vi|ga|ting
na|vi|ga|tion
na|vi|ga|tional
na|vi|ga|tor
Nav|ra|ti|lova
navvy
  △ nav|vies
navy
  △ na|vies
nawab
Naxos

nay
  no
  ⚠née
  ⚠neigh

Naz|ar|ene
Naz|ar|eth

Nazi
Naz|ism
N'Dja|mena
Ne|an|der|thal
neap
neap|tide
near
  VERB
  △ nears
  △ neared
  △ near|ing
  ADJ.
  △ nearer
  △ near|est
near|by
nearly
near|ness
near|side
near-sigh|ted
neat
  △ nea|ter
  △ neat|est
nea|ten
  △ neat|ens
  △ neatened
  △ neat|en|ing
neatly
neat|ness
Neb|raska
Ne|bu|chad|nez|
  zar
neb|ula
  △ neb|ulae *or*
  neb|ulas
neb|ular
ne|bu|lous
ne|bu|lously
ne|ces|sar|ily
ne|ces|sary
  △ ne|ces|sar|ies
ne|ces|si|tate
  △ ne|ces|si|tates
  △ ne|ces|si|ta|ted
  △ ne|ces|si|ta|ting

ne|ces|sity
△ ne|ces|si|ties
neck
VERB
△ necks
△ necked
△ neck|ing
neck|band
neck|er|chief
△ neck|er|chiefs
or neck|er|
chieves
neck|lace
neck|la|cing
neck|line
neck|tie
nec|ro|man|cer
nec|ro|mancy
nec|ro|philia
nec|ro|phil|iac
nec|ro|po|lis
△ nec|ro|pol|ises
nec|ro|sis
△ nec|ro|ses
nec|rotic
nec|tar
nec|tar|ine
nec|tary
△ nec|tar|ies

née
born with the name
⚠nay
⚠neigh

need
*require; be
obliged to; lack;
thing lacking*
VERB
△ needs
△ nee|ded
△ need|ing
⚠knead

need|ful
nee|dle
VERB
△ nee|dles
△ nee|dled
△ need|ling
needle|cord
needle|point
need|less
need|lessly
needle|wo|man
△ needle|wo|
men
needle|work
needn't
needs
needy
△ nee|dier
△ nee|di|est
ne|fari|ous
Ne|fer|titi
ne|gate
△ ne|gates
△ ne|ga|ted
△ ne|ga|ting
ne|ga|tion
neg|at|ive
VERB
△ neg|at|ives
△ neg|at|ived
△ neg|at|iv|ing
neg|at|ively
Negev
neg|lect
VERB
△ neg|lects
△ neg|lec|ted
△ neg|lect|ing
neg|lect|ful
nég|ligé
neg|li|gence
neg|li|gent
neg|li|gible
neg|li|gibly

ne|go|ti|able
ne|go|ti|ate
△ ne|go|ti|ates
△ ne|go|ti|ated
△ ne|go|ti|ating
ne|go|ti|ation
ne|go|ti|ator
Neg|ress
△ Neg|res|ses
Negro
△ Neg|roes
Neg|roid
Ne|he|miah,
Book of
Nehru

neigh
*cry of horse;
make this sound*
VERB
△ neighs
△ neighed
△ neigh|ing
⚠nay
⚠née

neigh|bour
neigh|bour|hood
neigh|bour|ing
neigh|bour|li|
ness
neigh|bourly
Neil
nei|ther
nek|ton
nelly
Nel|son
nel|son
Ne|ma|toda
ne|ma|tode
nem|esis
neo|clas|si|cal
Neo|clas|si|cism
neo-Dar|win|
ism

neo|dym|ium
Neo|ex|pres|
sion|ism
Neo-fas|cism
Neo|im|pres|
sion|ism
neo|li|thic
neo|lo|gism
neon
neo|na|tal
neo|nate
neo|phyte
neo|plasm
Neo|pla|ton|ism
Nepal
nephew
neph|rec|tomy
△ neph|rec|tom|
ies
neph|rite
neph|ri|tis
neph|rol|ogy
neph|ron
nep|ot|ism
ne|po|tis|tic
Nep|tune
nep|tu|nium
nerd
ner|eid
ner|ine
Nero
Ner|uda
nerve
VERB
△ nerves
△ nerved
△ ner|ving
nerve|less
nerve|lessly
nerve-rack|ing
ner|vily
ner|vi|ness
ner|vous
ner|vously

ner|vous|ness
nervy
 △ ner|vier
 △ ner|vi|est
Nes|bit
Ness
nest
 VERB
 △ nests
 △ nes|ted
 △ nest|ing
nes|tle
 △ nes|tles
 △ nes|tled
 △ nest|ling
nest|ling
net
 VERB
 △ nets
 △ net|ted
 △ net|ting
net|ball
nether
Neth|er|lands
neth|er|most
nett see net
net|ting
net|tle
 VERB
 △ net|tles
 △ net|tled
 △ net|tling
net|work
 VERB
 △ net|works
 △ net|worked
 △ net|work|ing
neural
neur|al|gia
neur|al|gic
neur|itis
neu|ro|lin|guis|
 tics
neur|ol|ogy

neur|one
neu|ro|psy|chol|
 ogy
neur|osis
 △ neur|oses
neur|otic
neu|ro|trans|mit|
 ter
neu|ter
 VERB
 △ neu|ters
 △ neu|tered
 △ neu|ter|ing
neut|ral
neut|ral|ity
neut|ral|iza|tion
neut|ral|ize
 △ neut|ral|izes
 △ neut|ral|ized
 △ neut|ral|izing
neut|rino
neut|ron
Ne|vada
never
nev|er|more
nev|er|the|less
Nev|ille
new
 ADJ.
 △ newer
 △ new|est
New|ark
new|born
New|bury
New|castle
New|castle
 under Lyme
new|comer
newel
new|fangled
New|found|
 land
New|gate

New Haven
American town
⚠Newhaven

New|haven
English town
⚠New
 Haven

newly
newly-weds
New|man
New|mar|ket
new|ness
New Orleans
New|port
New|quay
news
news|agent
news|cast
news|cas|ter
news|dealer
news|flash
 △ news|fla|shes
news|hound
news|let|ter
news|man
 △ news|men
news|mon|ger
news|pa|per
new|speak
news|print
news|reader
news|reel
news|room
news-ven|dor
news|wor|thy
newsy
 △ new|sier
 △ new|si|est
newt
New|ton
new|ton
New|to|nian

New York
New Zea|land
next
nexus
 △ nexus *or* nex|
 uses
ni|acin
Ni|ag|ara
nib
nib|ble
 VERB
 △ nib|bles
 △ nib|bled
 △ nib|bling
nib|bler
nib|lick
nibs
nicad
Ni|car|agua
Nice
nice
 △ nicer
 △ ni|cest
nicely
Ni|cene
nice|ness
ni|cety
 △ ni|cet|ies
niche
Ni|cho|las
Ni|chol|son
nick
 VERB
 △ nicks
 △ nicked
 △ nick|ing
nickel
nicker
 sing. and pl.
Nick|laus
nick-nack
nick|name
 VERB
 △ nick|names

△ nick|named
△ nick|na|ming
Ni|co|sia
ni|co|tine
ni|co|tinic
nic|ti|tate
△ nic|ti|tates
△ nic|ti|ta|ted
△ nic|ti|ta|ting
niece
ni|ello
△ ni|elli
niels|bohr|ium
Nie|mo|l|ler
Niépce
Nietz|sche
niff
VERB
△ niffs
△ niffed
△ niff|ing
niffy
△ nif|fier
△ nif|fi|est
nifty
△ nif|tier
△ nif|ti|est
Nigel
Niger
Ni|geria
Ni|ger-Congo
nig|gard
nig|gard|li|ness
nig|gardly
nig|ger
nig|gle
VERB
△ nig|gles
△ nig|gled
△ nig|gling
nig|gler
nig|gling
nigh

---

night
*period between
sunset and
sunrise*
⚠knight

night|cap
night|club
night|dress
△ night|dres|ses
night|fall
nigh|tie
Nigh|tin|gale
nigh|tin|gale
night|jar
night|life
night|long
nightly
night|mare
night|mar|ish
night|shade
night|shirt
night-time
*Night Watch,
The*
night|watch|
man
△ night|watch|
men
ni|hill|ism
ni|hill|ist
ni|hill|is|tic
Ni|jin|ska
Ni|jin|sky
Nijmegen
nil
Nile
Nill|giri
Nilo-Saharan
Nils|son
nim|ble
△ nim|bler
△ nim|blest
nimble|ness

---

nimbly
nim|bus
△ nim|buses *or*
nimbi
Nîmes
Nim|rod
nin|com|poop
nine
nine|fold
nine|pins
nine|teen
*Nine|teen Eighty
Four*
nine|teenth
nine|ties
nine|tieth
ninety
NOUN
△ nine|ties
Nin|eveh
ninja
△ ninja *or* nin|
jas
nin|jutsu
ninny
△ nin|nies
Nin|tendo
ninth
ninthly
ni|ob|ium
Nip
nip
VERB
△ nips
△ nipped
△ nip|ping
nip|per
nip|pi|ness
nip|ple
nippy
△ nip|pier
△ nip|pi|est
nir|vana
nisi

Nis|san
*car
manufacturer*
⚠Nissen

Nis|sen
sort of hut
⚠Nissan

---

nit
*young of louse;
fool*
⚠knit

---

nit-picker
nit-pick|ing
ni|trate
VERB
△ ni|trates
△ ni|tra|ted
△ ni|tra|ting
ni|tra|tion
nitre
ni|tric
ni|tride
ni|tri|fi|ca|tion
ni|trify
△ ni|tri|fies
△ ni|tri|fied
△ ni|tri|fy|ing
ni|trite
ni|tro|gen
ni|tro|gen|ous
ni|tro|gly|cer|ine
ni|trous
nitty-gritty
nit|wit
Niven
nix
Nixon
Nkomo
Nkru|mah
No *see* Noh
no

NOUN
△ noes
Noah
nob
no-ball
nob|ble
△ nob|bles
△ nob|bled
△ nob|bling
Nobel
no|bel|ium
no|bil|ity
no|ble
ADJ.
△ no|bler
△ no|blest
noble|man
△ noble|men
noble|ness
nob|lesse ob|lige
noble|wo|man
△ noble|wo|men
nobly
no|body
△ no|bod|ies
noc|tur|nal
noc|turn|ally
noc|turne
nod
VERB
△ nods
△ nod|ded
△ nod|ding
nodal
noddle
noddy

△ nod|dies
node
nod|ular
nod|ule
Noel
nog
nog|gin
Noh
nohow
noise
VERB
△ noises
△ noised
△ nois|ing
noise|less
noise|lessly
nois|ily
noisi|ness
noisome
noisy
△ nois|ier
△ noisi|est
nomad
no|madic
no|mad|ism
no-man's-land
nom-de-plume
△ *noms-de-plume*
no|men|cla|ture
nom|inal
nom|in|al|ism
nom|in|ally
nom|in|ate
△ nom|in|ates
△ nom|in|ated
△ nom|in|ating

no|mi|na|tion
nom|in|ative
nom|inee
Nona
non|age
no|na|gen|ar|ian
no|na|gon
non-aligned
non-align|ment
non-bel|li|ger|ent
nonce
nonce-word
non|chal|ance
non|chal|ant
non|chal|antly
non-com|bat|ant
non-com|mis|
  sioned
non-com|mit|tal
non-com|mit|
  tally
non com|pos
  men|tis
non-con|duc|tor
non|con|form|
  ism
non|con|form|ist
non|con|form|ity
non-con|tri|bu|
  tory
non-cus|to|dial
non-denom|in|
  ational
non|des|cript
none
non|en|tity

△ non|en|ti|ties
nones
none|the|less
non-event
non-fer|rous
non-fic|tion
non-flamm|able
non|in|ter|ven|
  tion
non-metal
no-no
non-obser|vance
no-non|sense
non|par|eil
non-per|son
non|plus
△ non|plus|ses
△ non|plussed
△ non|plus|sing
non-pro|lif|er|
  ation
non-renew|able
non|sense
non|sen|si|cal
non|sen|sic|ally
non sequi|tur
non-stan|dard
non-star|ter
non-stick
non-stop
non-U
non-union
non|ver|bal
non-voting
non-white
noo|dle

---

non-

non- is added to many kinds of words to form their opposites. Usually they have a hyphen, and a capital initial in the second element is retained: **non-alcoholic, non-believer, non-Christian, non-stick, non-violently**.

Note that **non-** is often used to form a negative with a neutral sense when a corresponding form in **un-** or **in-** has a special, usually unfavourable, meaning: **non-scientific** (compare *unscientific*), **non-sensitive** (compare *insensitive*).

nook
noon
no one
noose
nor
Nora
nor|ad|ren|al|ine
Nor|dic
Nor|folk
norm
Norma
nor|mal
nor|malcy
nor|mal|ity
nor|mal|iza|tion
nor|mal|ize
△ nor|mal|izes
△ nor|mal|ized
△ nor|mal|izing
nor|mally
Nor|man
Nor|mandy
nor|ma|tive
Norse
north
Nor|thamp|ton
Nor|thamp|ton|
  shire
North and South
Nor|than|ger Ab|
  bey
north|bound
north-east
north|eas|ter
north-east|erly
north-east|ern
North|east Pas|
  sage
nor|therly
  NOUN
  △ nor|ther|lies
nor|thern
nor|ther|ner
nor|thern|most

north-north-east
north-north-west
Nor|thum|ber|
  land
Nor|thum|bria
north|ward
north|wards
north-west
north-wes|ter
north-wes|terly
north-wes|tern
North|west Pas|
  sage
Nor|way
Nor|wegian
Nor|wich
nose
  VERB
  △ noses
  △ nosed
  △ no|sing ·
nose|bag
nose|bleed
nose|dive
  VERB
  △ nose|dives
  △ nose|dived
  △ nose|di|ving
nose|gay
nosey *see* nosy
*Nos|fer|atu
  (Nos|fera|tu,
  Eine Sym|pho|
  nie des Grau|
  ens)*
nosh
  NOUN
  △ noshes
  VERB
  △ noshes
  △ noshed
  △ nosh|ing
nosh-up
nos|tal|gia

nos|tal|gic
nos|tal|gic|ally
Nos|tra|da|mus
nos|tril
Nos|tromo
nos|trum
nosy
  △ no|sier
  △ no|si|est
nosy par|ker

not
  negatory adverb
  ▲knot

no|ta|bil|ity
no|table
no|tably
no|tar|ial
no|tary
  △ no|tar|ies
no|ta|tion
notch
  NOUN
  △ not|ches
  VERB
  △ not|ches
  △ notched
  △ notch|ing
note
  VERB
  △ notes
  △ no|ted
  △ no|ting
note|book
note|case
noted
note|let
note|pad
note|paper
note|wor|thi|
  ness
note|wor|thy
noth|ing
noth|ing|ness

no|tice
  VERB
  △ no|ti|ces
  △ no|ticed
  △ no|ti|cing
no|tice|able
no|tice|ably
no|tice-board
no|ti|fi|able
no|ti|fi|ca|tion
no|tify
  △ no|ti|fies
  △ no|ti|fied
  △ no|ti|fy|ing
no|tion
no|tional
no|to|chord
no|tori|ety
no|tori|ous
no|tori|ously
Notre Dame
Not|ting|ham
Not|ting|ham|
  shire
not|with|stand|ing
Nou|ak|chott

nou|gat
  sort of sweet
  ▲nugget

nought
  zero
  ▲naught

  NOUN
nour|ish
  △ nour|ishes
  △ nour|ished
  △ nour|ish|ing
nour|ish|ing
nour|ish|ment
nous
nou|veau riche
  △ *nou|veaux riches*

nou|velle cui|sine
Nou|velle
  Vague
nova
  △ novae
Nova Sco|tia
novel
nov|el|lette
nov|el|ist
no|vella
No|vello
nov|elty
  △ nov|el|ties
No|vem|ber
no|vena
Nov|gorod
nov|ice
no|vi|ci|ate
now
now|adays
No|well
no|where
nowt
noxi|ous
noxi|ously
noz|zle
nth
  as in to the nth
  degree
nu|ance
nub
Nubia
Nu|bian
nu|bile
nu|cel|lus
  △ nu|celli
nuc|lear
nuc|lear-free
nuc|le|ase
nuc|le|ate
  VERB
  △ nuc|le|ates
  △ nuc|le|ated
  △ nuc|le|ating

nuc|leo|lus
  △ nuc|leoli
nuc|leon
nuc|le|on|ics
nuc|leo|tide
nuc|leus
  △ nuc|lei
nuc|lide
nude
nudge
  VERB
  △ nud|ges
  △ nudged
  △ nud|ging
nu|dism
nu|dist
nu|dity
nuée ar\dente
Nuf|field
nu|ga|tory

---

nugget
*small lump (of
gold, etc)*
△nougat

---

nuis|ance
nuke
  VERB
  △ nukes
  △ nuked
  △ nu|king
Nu|ku'|alofa
null
nul|li|fi|ca|tion
null|ify
  △ nul|li|fies
  △ nul|li|fied
  △ nul|li|fy|ing
null|ity
numb
num|ber
  VERB
  △ num|bers
  △ num|bered

  △ num|ber|ing
num|ber-
  crunch|ing
num|ber|less
Num|bers,
  Book of
numbly
numb|ness
numbskull *see*
  numskull
nu|mer|acy
nu|meral
nu|mer|ate
nu|mer|ation
nu|mer|ator
nu|mer|ical
nu|mer|ic|ally
nu|mer|ol|ogy
nu|mer|ous
nu|mer|ously
nu|min|ous
nu|mis|ma|tic
nu|mis|mat|ics
nu|mis|ma|tist
num|skull
nun
nun|cio
Nun|ea|ton
Nunn
nun|nery
  △ nun|ner|ies
nup|tial
nup|ti|al|ity
Nur|em|berg
Nur|eyev
nurse
  VERB
  △ nur|ses
  △ nursed
  △ nur|sing
nurse|maid
nur|sery
  △ nur|ser|ies
nur|sery|man

  △ nur|sery|men
nur|sing
nur|ture
  VERB
  △ nur|tures
  △ nur|tured
  △ nur|tur|ing
nut
nu|ta|tion
nut|case
nut|cracker
*Nut\cracker,
  The (Shchel\
  kun\chik)*
nut|hatch
  △ nut|hat|ches
nut|house
nut|meg
nu|tri|ent
nu|tri|ment
nu|tri|tion
nu|tri|tional
nu|tri|tious
nu|tri|tive
nut|shell
nut|ter
nut|ti|ness
nutty
  △ nut|tier
  △ nut|ti|est
nux vom|ica
nuz|zle
  △ nuz|zles
  △ nuz|zled
  △ nuz|zling
Ny|er|ere
nylon
nymph
nym|phet
nym|pho
nym|pho|ma|nia
nym|pho|ma|
  niac
nys|ta|tin

O

oaf
oaf|ish
oaf|ishly
oaf|ish|ness
oak
oak-apple
oaken
Oak|ley
Oaks
oakum

oar
  *pole with flat
  blade for
  rowing; rower*
  ⚠ ore

oar|fish
  sing. and pl.
oars|man
  △ oars|men
oars|man|ship
oars|wo|man
  △ oars|wo|men
oasis
  △ oases
oast
oast-house
oat
oat|cake
oaten
Oates
oath
oat|meal
Oba|diah, Book
  of
Oban
ob|bli|gato
  NOUN
  △ ob|bli|ga|tos
    or ob|bli|gati
ob|dur|acy
ob|dur|ate

ob|dur|ately
ob|edi|ence
ob|edi|ent
ob|edi|ently
ob|ei|sance
ob|el|isk
ob|elus
  △ obeli
obese
obes|ity
obey
  △ obeys
  △ obeyed
  △ obey|ing
ob|fus|cate
  △ ob|fus|cates
  △ ob|fus|ca|ted
  △ ob|fus|ca|ting
ob|fus|ca|tion
ob|fus|ca|tory
obi|ter dic|tum
  △ *obi|ter dicta*
obi|tu|ary
  △ obi|tu|ar|ies
ob|ject
  VERB
  △ ob|jects
  △ ob|jec|ted
  △ ob|ject|ing
ob|jec|tion
ob|jec|tion|able
ob|jec|tion|ably
ob|jec|ti|val
ob|jec|tive
ob|jec|tively
ob|jec|tiv|ism
ob|jec|tiv|ity
ob|ject|less
ob|jec|tor
objet d'art
  △ *objets d'art*
objet trouvé
  △ *objets trouvés*
ob|last

ob|late
ob|la|tion
ob|li|gate
  △ ob|li|gates
  △ ob|li|ga|ted
  △ ob|li|ga|ting
ob|li|ga|tion
ob|li|ga|tor|ily
ob|li|ga|tori|ness
ob|liga|tory
ob|lige
  △ ob|li|ges
  △ ob|liged
  △ ob|li|ging
ob|li|ging
ob|li|gingly
ob|lique
ob|liquely
ob|lique|ness
ob|li|quity
ob|lit|er|ate
  △ ob|lit|er|ates
  △ ob|lit|er|ated
  △ ob|lit|er|ating
ob|lit|er|ation
ob|liv|ion
ob|li|vi|ous
ob|li|vi|ously
ob|li|vi|ous|ness
ob|long
ob|lo|quy
  △ ob|lo|quies
ob|noxi|ous
ob|noxi|ously
ob|nox|ious|ness
oboe
obo|ist
O'Brien
ob|scene
ob|scenely
ob|scen|ity
  △ ob|scen|it|ies
ob|scur|ant|ism
ob|scur|ant|ist

ob|scure
  VERB
  △ ob|scures
  △ ob|scured
  △ ob|scur|ing
ob|scurely
ob|scur|ity
  △ ob|scur|it|ies
ob|se|quies
ob|se|qui|ous
ob|se|qui|ously
ob|se|qui|ous|
  ness
ob|serv|able
ob|serv|ably
ob|ser|vance
ob|ser|vant
ob|ser|vantly
ob|ser|va|tion
ob|ser|va|tional
ob|ser|va|tory
  △ ob|ser|va|tor|
    ies
ob|serve
  △ ob|serves
  △ ob|served
  △ ob|ser|ving
ob|ser|ver
ob|sess
  △ ob|ses|ses
  △ ob|sessed
  △ ob|ses|sing
ob|ses|sion
ob|ses|sional
ob|ses|sive
ob|ses|sively
ob|ses|sive|ness
ob|sid|ian
ob|sol|es|cence
ob|sol|es|cent
ob|so|lete
ob|sta|cle
ob|stet|ric
ob|ste|tri|cian

ob|stet|rics
ob|sti|nacy
ob|sti|nate
ob|sti|nately
ob|strep|er|ous
ob|strep|er|ously
ob|strep|er|ous|
  ness
ob|struct
  △ ob|structs
  △ ob|struc|ted
  △ ob|struct|ing
ob|struc|tion
ob|struc|tion|
  ism
ob|struc|tion|ist
ob|struct|ive
ob|struct|ively
ob|struct|ive|
  ness
ob|tain
  △ ob|tains
  △ ob|tained
  △ ob|tain|ing
ob|tain|able
ob|trude
  △ ob|trudes
  △ ob|tru|ded
  △ ob|tru|ding
ob|tru|der
ob|tru|sion
ob|tru|sive
ob|tru|sively
ob|tru|sive|ness
ob|tuse
ob|tusely
ob|tuse|ness
ob|verse
ob|vi|ate
  △ ob|vi|ates
  △ ob|vi|ated
  △ ob|vi|ating
ob|vi|ous
ob|vi|ously

ob|vi|ous|ness
ocar|ina
O'Casey
Occam *see*
  Ockham
oc|ca|sion
  VERB
  △ oc|ca|sions
  △ oc|ca|sioned
  △ oc|ca|sion|ing
oc|ca|sional
oc|ca|sion|ally
Oc|ci|dent
oc|ci|den|tal
oc|cip|ital
oc|ci|put
oc|clude
  △ oc|cludes
  △ oc|clu|ded
  △ oc|clu|ding
oc|clu|sion
oc|cult
oc|cul|ta|tion
oc|cult|ism
oc|cult|ist
oc|cu|pancy
  △ oc|cu|pan|cies
oc|cu|pant
oc|cu|pa|tion
oc|cu|pa|tional
oc|cu|pa|tion|
  ally
oc|cu|pier
oc|cupy
  △ oc|cu|pies
  △ oc|cu|pied
  △ oc|cu|py|ing
occur
  △ oc|curs
  △ oc|curred
  △ oc|cur|ring
oc|cur|rence
ocean
ocean|ar|ium

ocean-going
Oceania
oceanic
ocean|og|ra|pher
oceano|gra|phic
ocean|og|ra|phy
oce|lot
och
och|one
ochre
ochre|ous
Ock|ham
o'clock
O'Con|nell
O'Con|nor
octad
oc|ta|gon
oc|tag|onal
oc|ta|hed|ral
oc|ta|hed|ron
  △ oc|ta|hedra *or*
    oc|ta|hed|rons
oc|tane
oct|ant
octaroon *see*
  octoroon
oc|tave
oc|tavo
octet
Oc|to|ber
Oc|to|brist
oc|to|gen|ar|ian
oc|to|pus
  △ oc|to|puses
oc|to|push
oc|to|roon
oc|to|syl|la|bic
oc|to|syl|lable
oc|tu|ple
ocu|lar
ocu|list
ocu|lus
  △ oculi
oda|lisque

odd
  △ odder
  △ od|dest
odd|ball
od|dity
  △ od|di|ties
oddly
odd|ments
odd|ness
odds
odds-on
ode
Ode on a Gre|
  cian Urn
Odessa
Ode to a Nigh|
  tin|gale
Ode to Au|tumn
Ode to the West
  Wind
Odets
odi|ous
odi|ously
odi|ous|ness
odium
odo|meter
odor|ifer|ous
odor|ous
odour
odour|less
Odys|seus
Odys|sey, The
odys|sey
oe|dema
  △ oe|de|mata *or*
    oe|de|mas
oe|de|mat|ous
Oe|di|pal
Oe|di|pus
Oe|di|pus Rex
o'er
oe|so|pha|geal
oe|so|pha|gus
  △ oe|so|phagi

oes|tra|diol
oes|tro|gen
oes|trus
of
off
Offa
offal
off|beat
off-Broad|way
off-col|our
off|cut
Of|fen|bach
of|fence
of|fend
△ of|fends
△ of|fen|ded
△ of|fend|ing
of|fen|ded
of|fen|der
of|fend|ing
of|fen|sive
of|fen|sively
of|fen|sive|ness
offer
VERB
△ of|fers
△ of|fered
△ of|fer|ing
of|fer|ing
of|fer|tory
△ of|fer|tor|ies
off|hand
off|han|ded
off|han|dedly
off|han|ded|ness
of|fice
of|fice-bearer
of|fice-block
of|fice-hol|der
of|fi|cer
of|fi|cial
of|fi|cial|dom
of|fi|cial|ese
of|fi|cially

of|fi|ci|ate
△ of|fi|ci|ates
△ of|fi|ci|ated
△ of|fi|ci|ating
of|fi|cious
of|fi|ciously
of|fi|cious|ness
off|ing
off-key
off-licence
off-lim|its
off-line
off|load
△ off|loads
△ off|loa|ded
△ off|load|ing
off-peak
off|print
off-put|ting
off-sea|son
off|set
VERB
△ off|sets
△ off|set
△ off|set|ting
off|shoot
off|shore
off|side
off|spring
off-stage
off-street
off-the-peg
off-white
oft
often
Ogam
Ogdon
ogee
ogle
△ ogles
△ ogled
△ ogling
O-grade
ogre

ogress
△ ogres|ses
ogrish
oh
Ohio
ohm
oho
ohone *see*
  ochone
oik
oil
VERB
△ oils
△ oiled
△ oil|ing
oil-cake
oil|cloth
oil-col|our
oiled
oil|field
oil-fired
oil|ily
oili|ness
oil-paint
oil-paint|ing
oil-rig
oil|seed
oil|skin
oil-tan|ker
oily
△ oil|ier
△ oili|est
oink
VERB
△ oinks
△ oinked
△ oink|ing
oint|ment
Oir|each|tas
Oisín *see* Ossian
okay
VERB
△ okays
△ okayed

△ okay|ing
okapi
△ oka|pis *or*
  okapi
okey-dokey
Ok|la|homa
okra
Olav
old
ADJ.
△ older
△ old|est
Old Bai|ley
Old|castle
*Old Cu|ri|os|ity
  Shop, The*
olden
old-fashioned
Old|ham
oldie
old-maid|ish
Old Mortality
Old Nick
old|ster
old-time
old-timer
Old Traf|ford
Old Vic
*Old Wives'
  Tale, The*
old-woman|ish
ole|agin|ous
ole|an|der
ole|fin
oleo|graph
O-Level
ol|fac|tory
Olga
ol|ig|arch
ol|ig|archic
ol|ig|arch|ical
ol|ig|archy
△ ol|ig|arch|ies
Oli|go|cene

oli|go|poly
Olive
olive
Oli|ver
Oli|ver Twist
Oli|vetti
Olivia
Oliv|ier
oliv|ine
Olwen
Olym|pia
Olym|piad
Olym|pian
Olym|pic
Olym|pus
Om
Oman
Omar
Omar Khay|
　yám
om|buds|man
　△ om|buds|men
omega
om|elette
omen
om|in|ous
om|in|ously
om|in|ous|ness

omis|sion
*thing left out;
doing this*
　⚠ emission

omit
　VERB
　△ omits
　△ omit|ted
　△ omit|ting
om|ni|bus
　△ om|ni|buses
OMNI|MAX
om|ni|po|tence
om|ni|po|tent
om|ni|po|tently

om|ni|pres|ence
om|ni|pres|ent
om|nis|ci|ence
om|nis|ci|ent
om|nis|ci|ently
om|ni|vore
om|ni|vor|ous
om|ni|vor|ously
om|ni|vor|ous|
　ness
Omsk
on
on|ager
onan|ism
On|as|sis
once
*Once and Fu|
　ture King, The*
once-over
on|co|gene
on|colo|gist
on|col|ogy
on|com|ing
on|co|vi|rus
ondes Mar|
　tenot
one
*One Day in the
　Life of Ivan
　De|ni|so|vich*
*One Flew Over
　the Cuckoo's
　Nest*
100 Soup Cans
O'Neill
one-liner
one|ness
one-off
on|er|ous
on|er|ously
on|er|ous|ness
one|self
one-sided
one-sidedly

one-sided|ness
One Thou|sand
　Guin|eas
one-time
one-to-one
one-up
one-upman|ship
one-way
on|go|ing
onion
oniony
on-line
on|looker
only
on-off
ono|mas|ti|con
ono|mas|tics
ono|ma|to|poeia
ono|ma|to|poeic
on|rush
on|screen
onset
on|shore
on|side
on|slaught
on-stage
on-stream
On|tario
On the Town
*On the Wa|ter|
　front*
onto
on|to|geny
on|to|lo|gi|cal
on|to|lo|gi|cally
on|tol|ogy
onus
　△ onuses
on|ward
onyx
oo|cyte
oodles
oo|gamy
oo|gen|esis

ooh
oö|lite
oom|pah
oomph
oops
oops-a-daisy
oo|spore
Oost|ende
ooze
　VERB
　△ oo|zes
　△ oozed
　△ ooz|ing
oozy
　△ oo|zier
　△ oo|zi|est
op
opa|city
opal
opal|es|cence
opal|es|cent
opaque
opaquely
opaque|ness
Op Art
open
　VERB
　△ opens
　△ opened
　△ open|ing
open-and-shut
open|cast
open-ended
opener
open-han|ded
open-han|dedly
open-han|ded|
　ness
open-hearted
open-heart|edly
open-heart|ed|
　ness
open|ing
openly

open-minded
open-mind|edly
open-mind|ed|
  ness
open|ness
open-plan
opera
op|er|abil|ity
op|er|able
opera buffa
opéra-comique
opera-glass
△ opera-glas|ses
opera-hat
opera-house
op|er|ate
△ op|er|ates
△ op|er|ated
△ op|er|ating
op|er|atic
op|er|at|ic|ally
op|era|tion
op|era|tional
op|era|tion|ally
op|era|tive
op|er|ator
oper|cu|lum
△ oper|cula
op|er|etta
op|eron

Ophelia
Ophir
oph|thal|mia
oph|thal|mic
oph|thal|mo|lo|
  gist
oph|thal|mo|logy
oph|thal|mo|
  scope
Ophuls
opi|ate
opine
△ opines
△ opined
△ opi|ning
opin|ion
opin|ion|ated
opium
Oporto
opos|sum
op|po|nent
op|por|tune
op|por|tunely
op|por|tune|ness
op|por|tun|ism
op|por|tun|ist
op|por|tun|is|tic
op|por|tun|ity
△ op|por|tun|it|
  ies

op|pose
△ op|po|ses
△ op|posed
△ op|po|sing
op|po|ser
op|po|sing
op|pos|ite
op|po|si|tion
op|press
△ op|pres|ses
△ op|pressed
△ op|press|ing
op|pres|sion
op|pres|sive
op|pres|sively
op|pres|sive|ness
op|pres|sor
op|pro|bri|ous
op|pro|bri|ously
op|pro|brium
op|pugn
△ op|pugns
△ op|pugned
△ op|pugn|ing
opt
△ opts
△ opted
△ opt|ing
optic
op|ti|cal

op|ti|cally
op|ti|cian
op|tics
op|ti|mal
op|ti|mism
op|ti|mist
op|ti|mis|tic
op|ti|mis|tic|ally
op|ti|mize
△ op|ti|mi|zes
△ op|ti|mized
△ op|ti|mi|zing
op|ti|mum
△ op|ti|mums *or*
  op|tima
op|tion
op|tional
op|tion|ally
op|tom|et|rist
opu|lence
opu|lent
opu|lently
Opüls *see*
  Ophuls
opus
△ opuses *or*
  opera
or
ora|cle
or|ac|ular

-er / -or

These suffixes are used to form agent nouns denoting people or things that do some action, eg **manager, opener**. The form **-or** is a less active suffix in English; the following are the most common nouns of this type ending in **-or**:

accelerator	conqueror	editor	negotiator	senator
actor	contractor	elevator	operator	solicitor
adaptor	contributor	excavator	possessor	spectator
adjudicator	councillor	generator	professor	sponsor
aggressor	creator	governor	projector	successor
agitator	defector	impersonator	protector	supervisor
auditor	dictator	interrogator	reactor	surveyor
benefactor	director	inventor	rector	translator
calculator	distributor	jailor	regulator	vendor
collector	doctor	liberator	sailor	visitor
competitor	donor	mediator	sculptor	

oracy

oral
*spoken; for the
mouth; spoken
test etc*
⚠ aural

or|ally
orange
orange|ade
Orange|man
△ Orange|men
orangery
△ oranger|ies
orangey
orang utan
ora|tion
ora|tor
ora|tor|ial
ora|tor|ical
ora|tor|ic|ally
ora|torio
ora|tory
△ ora|tor|ies
orb
orbit
VERB
△ or|bits
△ or|bi|ted
△ or|bit|ing
or|bi|tal
Or|ca|dian
or|chard
or|ches|tra
or|ches|tral
or|ches|trate
△ or|ches|trates
△ or|ches|tra|ted
△ or|ches|tra|ting
or|ches|tra|tion
or|ches|tra|tor
or|chid
Orczy

or|dain
△ or|dains
△ or|dained
△ or|dain|ing
or|dained
or|dain|ment
or|deal
order
VERB
△ or|ders
△ or|dered
△ or|der|ing
or|dered
or|der|li|ness
or|derly
NOUN
△ or|der|lies
or|di|nal
or|din|ance
or|din|and
or|din|ar|ily
or|din|ari|ness
or|din|ary
NOUN
△ or|din|ar|ies
or|din|ate
or|di|na|tion
ord|nance
Or|do|vi|cian
or|dure

ore
*rock etc from
which metal can
be extracted*
⚠ oar

or|eg|ano
Ore|gon
oreographic *see*
orographic
Or|es|teia
Orff
organ
or|gan|die

or|gan|elle
organ-grinder
or|ganic
or|gan|ic|ally
or|gan|ism
or|gan|ist
or|gan|iza|tion
or|gan|iza|tional
or|gan|iza|tion|
ally
or|gan|ize
△ or|gan|izes
△ or|gan|ized
△ or|gan|izing
or|gan|izer
or|ganza
or|gasm
VERB
△ or|gasms
△ or|gasmed
△ or|gas|ming
or|gas|mic
or|gi|as|tic
orgy
△ or|gies
oriel-win|dow
ori|ent
VERB
△ ori|ents
△ ori|en|ted
△ ori|ent|ing
Ori|en|tal
NOUN
ori|en|tal
ADJ.
Ori|en|tal|ist
ori|en|tate
△ ori|en|tates
△ ori|en|ta|ted
△ ori|en|ta|ting
ori|en|ta|ted
ori|en|ta|tion
ori|en|ted
ori|en|teer|ing

Ori|ent-Express
ori|fice
ori|gami
ori|gin
ori|ginal
ori|gin|al|ity
ori|gin|ally
ori|gin|ate
△ ori|gin|ates
△ ori|gin|ated
△ ori|gin|ating
ori|gin|ation
ori|gin|ator
ori|ole
Orion
Ork|ney
Or|lando
Or|lando Fu|ri|
oso

Orleans
French town
⚠ Orléans

Orléans
*French royal
dukedom*
⚠ Orleans

orlop
or|molu
or|na|ment
VERB
△ or|na|ments
△ or|na|men|ted
△ or|na|ment|ing
or|na|men|tal
or|na|men|tally
or|na|men|ta|
tion
or|nate
or|nately
or|nate|ness
or|nith|ine
or|ni|tho|lo|gi|cal

or|ni|tho|lo|gic|
  ally
or|ni|tho|lo|gist
or|ni|thol|ogy
oro|gen|esis
oro|geny
oro|gra|phic
oro|tund
oro|tund|ity
or|phan
  VERB
△ or|phans
△ or|phaned
△ or|phan|ing
or|phan|age
Or|pheus
Or|pheus and
  Eu|ry|dice
  (Orfeo ed Eu|
  ri|dice)
Orph|ism
or|rery
△ or|rer|ies
or|ris
or|ris-root
or|tho|don|tic
or|tho|don|tics
or|tho|don|tist
Or|tho|dox
  of the Orthodox
  Church or of
  strict Judaism
or|tho|dox
  following
  established
  opinions etc
or|tho|doxy
△ or|tho|dox|ies
or|tho|go|nal
or|tho|gra|phic
or|tho|graph|ical
or|tho|graph|ic|
  ally
or|tho|gra|phy

△ or|tho|graph|
  ies
or|tho|pae|dic
or|tho|paed|ics
or|tho|paed|ist
orth|op|tics
or|to|lan
Orton
Orwell
oryx
△ oryx or oryxes
Osaka
Os|borne
Oscar
os|cil|late
△ os|cil|lates
△ os|cil|la|ted
△ os|cil|la|ting
os|cil|la|tion
os|cil|la|tor
os|cil|lo|graph
os|cil|lo|scope
osier
Osi|ris
Oslo
os|mir|id|ium
os|mium
os|mo|regu|la|
  tion
os|mo|sis
△ os|mo|ses
os|mo|tic
os|mot|ic|ally
os|prey
os|se|ous
Os|sian
os|si|fi|ca|tion
os|si|fied
os|sify
△ os|si|fies
△ os|si|fied
△ os|si|fy|ing
Oss|ory
Ost|end

os|ten|si|bil|ity
os|tens|ible
os|tens|ibly
os|ten|sive
os|ten|ta|tion
os|ten|ta|tious
os|ten|ta|tiously
os|ten|ta|tious|
  ness
os|teo|arth|ri|tis
os|teo|ma|la|cia
os|teo|path
os|teo|pa|thic
os|teo|pa|thy
os|teo|por|osis
ost|ler
Ost|mark
Ost|po|li|tik
ost|ra|cism
ost|ra|cize
△ ost|ra|ci|zes
△ ost|ra|cized
△ ost|ra|ci|zing
ost|rich
△ ost|riches
Os|tro|goth
Os|wald
Os|wes|try
Otello (Oth|
  ello)
  opera by Verdi
Oth|ello, the
  Moor of Ven|
  ice
  play by
  Shakespeare
other
oth|er|wise
other|world|li|
  ness
other|worldly
otic
oti|ose
ot|itis

Otley
O'Toole
ot|tava rima
Ot|tawa
otter
Otto
Ot|to|man
  inhabitant of the
  Ottoman
  Empire; of this
  empire or its
  inhabitants
ot|to|man
  sort of sofa
Otway
Oua|ga|dou|gou
oub|li|ette
ouch
Ou|den|aarde

> ought
>   should
>   ⚠ aught

Ouija
ounce
our
Ouranus see
  Uranus
Our Mu|tual
  Friend
ours
our|selves
Our Town
ousel see ouzel
Ouse
oust
△ ousts
△ ous|ted
△ oust|ing
out
  VERB
△ outs
△ outed
△ out|ing

out|age
out-and-out
out|back
out|bal|ance
△ out|bal|an|ces
△ out|bal|anced
△ out|bal|an|
    cing
out|bid
△ out|bids
△ out|bid
△ out|bid|ding
out|board
out|bound
out|break
out|breed|ing
out|build|ing
out|burst
out|cast
out|caste
out|class
△ out|clas|ses
△ out|classed
△ out|class|ing
out|come
out|crop
out|cry
△ out|cries
out|da|ted
out|dis|tance
△ out|dis|tan|ces
△ out|dis|tanced
△ out|dis|tan|
    cing
outdo
△ out|does
△ out|did
△ out|do|ing
△ out|done
out|door
out|doors
outer
out|er|most
out|face

△ out|fa|ces
△ out|faced
△ out|fa|cing
out|fall
out|field
out|fiel|der
out|fight
△ out|fights
△ out|fought
△ out|fight|ing
out|fit
VERB
△ out|fits
△ out|fit|ted
△ out|fit|ting
out|fit|ter
out|flank
△ out|flanks
△ out|flanked
△ out|flank|ing
out|flow
out|fox
△ out|foxes
△ out|foxed
△ out|fox|ing
out|go|ing
out|grow
△ out|grows
△ out|grew
△ out|grow|ing
△ out|grown
out|growth
out|house
out|ing
out|land|ish
out|land|ishly
out|land|ish|ness
out|last
△ out|lasts
△ out|las|ted
△ out|last|ing
out|law
VERB
△ out|laws

△ out|lawed
△ out|law|ing
out|lawry
out|lay
out|let
out|line
VERB
△ out|lines
△ out|lined
△ out|lin|ing
out|live
△ out|lives
△ out|lived
△ out|liv|ing
out|look
out|ly|ing
out|man|oeuvre
△ out|man|
    oeuvres
△ out|man|
    oeuvred
△ out|man|oeuv|
    ring
out|mo|ded
out|num|ber
△ out|num|bers
△ out|num|
    bered
△ out|num|ber|
    ing
out|pace
△ out|pa|ces
△ out|paced
△ out|pa|cing
out|pa|tient
out|play
△ out|plays
△ out|played
△ out|play|ing
out|post
out|pour|ing
out|put
VERB
△ out|puts

△ out|put
△ out|put|ting
out|rage
VERB
△ out|ra|ges
△ out|raged
△ out|ra|ging
out|rage|ous
out|rage|ously
out|rage|ous|
    ness
out|rank
△ out|ranks
△ out|ranked
△ out|rank|ing
outré
out|ride
△ out|rides
△ out|rode
△ out|ri|ding
△ out|rid|den
out|ri|der
out|rig|ger
out|right
out|run
△ out|runs
△ out|ran
△ out|run|ning
△ out|run
out|sell
△ out|sells
△ out|sold
△ out|sell|ing
out|set
out|shine
△ out|shines
△ out|shone
△ out|shi|ning
out|side
out|si|der
*Out|sider, The
    (L'Ét|ran|ger)*
out|size
out|skirts

out|smart
  △ out|smarts
  △ out|smar¦ted
  △ out|smart|ing
out|spo¦ken
out|spo¦kenly
out|spo¦ken|ness
out|spread
out|stand|ing
out|stand|ingly
out|stare
  △ out|stares
  △ out|stared
  △ out|star¦ing
out|sta¦tion
out|stay
  △ out|stays
  △ out|stayed
  △ out|stay|ing
out|stretch
  △ out|stret¦ches
  △ out|stretched
  △ out|stretch|ing
out|stretched
out|strip
  △ out|strips
  △ out|stripped
  △ out|strip|ping
out|take
out-tray
out|vote
  △ out|votes
  △ out|vo¦ted
  △ out|vo¦ting
out|ward
out|wardly
out|weigh
  △ out|weighs
  △ out|weighed
  △ out|weigh|ing
out|wit
  △ out|wits
  △ out|wit¦ted
  △ out|wit|ting

out|with
out|work
out|wor¦ker
out|worn
ouzel
ouzo
ova
Oval
  London cricket
  ground
oval
  egg-shaped; this
  shape
ovar|ian
ovary
  △ ovar|ies
ova|tion
oven
oven|proof
oven-ready
oven|ware
over
over|act
  △ over|acts
  △ over|ac¦ted
  △ over|act|ing
over-age
over|all
over-anxi¦ous
over|arm
over|awe
  △ over|awes
  △ over|awed
  △ over|aw¦ing
over|bal¦ance
  △ over|bal¦an¦ces
  △ over|bal¦anced
  △ over|bal¦an¦
    cing
over|bear|ing
over|bear|ingly
over|blown
over|board
over|book

△ over|books
△ over|booked
△ over|book|ing
over|bur¦den
  △ over|bur¦dens
  △ over|bur¦
    dened
  △ over|bur¦den|
    ing
over|bur¦dened
over|cast
over|charge
  △ over|char¦ges
  △ over|charged
  △ over|char¦ging
over|cloud
  △ over|clouds
  △ over|clou¦ded
  △ over|cloud|ing
over|coat
over|come
  △ over|comes
  △ over|came
  △ over|com¦ing
  △ over|come
over-con¦fi¦dent
over|crowd
  △ over|crowds
  △ over|crow¦ded
  △ over|crowd|
    ing
over|crow¦ded
over|crowd|ing
over¦do
  △ over|does
  △ over|did
  △ over¦do|ing
  △ over|done
over|dose
  VERB
  △ over|do¦ses
  △ over|dosed
  △ over|do¦sing
over|draft

over|draw
  △ over|draws
  △ over|drew
  △ over|draw|ing
  △ over|drawn
over|drawn
over|dress
  △ over|dres¦ses
  △ over|dressed
  △ over|dress|ing
over|dressed
over|drive
over|due
over-emo¦tional
over|es¦ti|mate
  △ over|es¦ti|mates
  △ over|es¦ti|ma¦
    ted
  △ over|es¦ti|ma¦
    ting
over|es¦ti|ma¦
  tion
over|ex¦ert
  △ over|ex¦erts
  △ over|ex¦er¦ted
  △ over|ex¦ert|ing
over|ex¦er|tion
over|ex¦pose
  △ over|ex¦po¦ses
  △ over|ex¦posed
  △ over|ex¦po¦
    sing
over|ex¦po|sure
over|fish¦ing
over|flow
  △ over|flows
  △ over|flowed
  △ over|flow|ing
over|grown
over|hand
over|hang
  △ over|hangs
  △ over|hung
  △ over|hang|ing

over|haul
 △ over|hauls
 △ over|hauled
 △ over|haul|ing
over|head
over|hear
 △ over|hears
 △ over|heard
 △ over|hear|ing
over|heat
 △ over|heats
 △ over|hea¦ted
 △ over|heat|ing
over|hea¦ted
over|joyed
over|kill
over|la¦den
over|land
over|lap
 △ over|laps
 △ over|lapped
 △ over|lap|ping
over|lay
 △ over|lays
 △ over|laid
 △ over|lay|ing
over|leaf
over|lie
 △ over|lies
 △ over|lay
 △ over|ly|ing
 △ over|lain
over|load
 VERB
 △ over|loads
 △ over|loa¦ded
 △ over|load|ing
over|look
 △ over|looks
 △ over|looked
 △ over|look|ing
over|lord
overly
over|much

over|nice
over|night
over|pass
 △ over|pas¦ses
over|play
 △ over|plays
 △ over|played
 △ over|play|ing
over|power
 △ over|powers
 △ over|powered
 △ over|power|ing
over|power|ing
over|power|ingly
over|print
 △ over|prints
 △ over|prin¦ted
 △ over|print|ing
over|rate
 △ over|rates
 △ over|ra¦ted
 △ over|ra¦ting
over|reach
 △ over|rea¦ches
 △ over|reached
 △ over|reach|ing
over|re|act
 △ over|re|acts
 △ over|re|ac¦ted
 △ over|re|act|ing
over|re|ac¦tion
over|ride
 △ over|rides
 △ over|rode
 △ over|ri¦ding
 △ over|rid¦den
over|ri¦ding
over|rule
 △ over|rules
 △ over|ruled
 △ over|ru¦ling
over|run

 △ over|runs
 △ over|ran
 △ over|runn|ing
 △ over|run
over|seas
over|see
 △ over|sees
 △ over|saw
 △ over|see|ing
 △ over|seen
over|seer
over|sell
 △ over|sells
 △ over|sold
 △ over|sell|ing
over|sew
 △ over|sews
 △ over|sewed
 △ over|sew|ing
 △ over|sewn
over|sexed
over|sha¦dow
 △ over|shad|ows
 △ over|shad¦owed
 △ over|shad|ow|ing
over|shoe
over|shoot
 △ over|shoots
 △ over|shot
 △ over|shoot|ing
over|sight
over|sim¦pli|fi¦ca|tion
over|sim¦plify
 △ over|sim¦pli|fies
 △ over|sim¦pli|fied
 △ over|sim¦pli|fy¦ing
over|sleep
 △ over|sleeps

 △ over|slept
 △ over|sleep|ing
over|spend
 △ over|spends
 △ over|spent
 △ over|spend|ing
over|spill
over|state
 △ over|states
 △ over|sta¦ted
 △ over|sta¦ting
over|state|ment
over|stay
 △ over|stays
 △ over|stayed
 △ over|stay|ing
over|steer
 △ over|steers
 △ over|steered
 △ over|steer|ing
over|step
 △ over|steps
 △ over|stepped
 △ over|step|ping
over|stretched
over|strung
over|sub|scribe
 △ over|sub¦scribes
 △ over|sub¦scribed
 △ over|sub¦scri¦bing
over|sub|scribed
overt
over|take
 △ over|takes
 △ over|took
 △ over|ta¦king
 △ over|ta¦ken
over|tax
 △ over|taxes
 △ over|taxed
 △ over|tax|ing

over|throw
△ over|throws
△ over|threw
△ over|throw|
  ing
△ over|thrown
over|time
overtly
over|tone
over|ture
over|turn
△ over|turns
△ over|turned
△ over|turn|ing
over|view
over|ween|ing
over|weight
over|whelm
△ over|whelms
△ over|whelmed
△ over|whelm|
  ing
over|whelm|ing
over|whelm|
  ingly
over|work
△ over|works
△ over|worked
△ over|work|ing

over|worked
over|write
△ over|writes
△ over|wrote
△ over|wri|ting
△ over|writ|ten
over|wrought
Ovid
ovi|duct
ovi|form
ovine
ovi|par|ity
ovi|par|ous
ovi|pos|itor
ovoid
ovo|vi|vi|par|ous
ovu|late
△ ovu|lates
△ ovu|la|ted
△ ovu|la|ting
ovu|la|tion
ovule
ovum
△ ova
ow
owe
△ owes
△ owed
△ owing

Owen
Owens
owing
owl
owlet
owl|ish
owl|ishly
owl|ish|ness
own
  VERB
△ owns
△ owned
△ own|ing
owner
owner-occu|pier
ow|ner|ship
ox
△ oxen
ox|alic
Ox|bridge
oxen
oxeye
OXFAM
Ox|ford
Ox|ford|shire
ox|id|ant
ox|id|ase
oxi|da|tion
oxide

ox|id|iza|tion
ox|id|ize
△ ox|id|izes
△ ox|id|ized
△ ox|id|izing
oxlip
Oxon
Oxo|nian
ox|tail
oxy|acety|lene
oxy|gen
oxy|gen|ate
△ oxy|gen|ates
△ oxy|gen|ated
△ oxy|gen|ating
oxy|gen|ation
oxy|gen|ator
oxy|hae|mo|glo|
  bin
oxy|moron
oxy|to|cin
oyez
oys|ter
oy|ster|cat|cher
Oz
Oz|beck
ozone

P

Pabst
pace
  VERB
  △ paces
  △ paced
  △ pa¦cing
pace|ma|ker
pace|set|ter
Pa¦chel|bel
pa¦chisi
pa¦chy|derm
Pa¦ci¦fic
  ocean
pa¦ci¦fic
  peaceable
pa¦ci¦fi¦ca|tion
pa¦ci¦fier
pa¦ci¦fism
pa¦ci¦fist
pa¦cify
  △ pa¦ci¦fies
  △ pa¦ci¦fied
  △ pa¦ci¦fy¦ing
Pa¦cino
pack
  VERB
  △ packs
  △ packed
  △ pack|ing
pack|age
  VERB
  △ pack|ages
  △ pack|aged
  △ pack|aging
pack|aging
Packer
packet
pack|horse
pack|ing
pack|ing-case
pact
pad

VERB
△ pads
△ pad¦ded
△ pad¦ding
pad|ding
pad¦dle
  VERB
  △ pad¦dles
  △ pad¦dled
  △ pad¦dling
pad|dock
paddy
  △ pad¦dies
Pad|er|ew|ski
pad|lock
  VERB
  △ pad|locks
  △ pad|locked
  △ pad|lock|ing
padre
pad¦saw
Padua
paean
paederast *see*
  pederast
paederasty *see*
  pederasty
pae¦di|at|ric
pae¦di|at|ri|cian
pae¦di|at|rics
pae¦do|phile
pae¦do|philia
pa¦ella *or* paella
  according to
  pronunciation
Paes|tum
pagan
Pa¦ga|nini
pa¦gan|ism
page
  VERB
  △ pages
  △ paged
  △ pa¦ging

pa¦geant
pa¦gean|try
page|boy
pager
pa¦gin|ate
  △ pa¦gin|ates
  △ pa¦gin|ated
  △ pa¦gin|ating
pa¦gin|ation
pag¦li|acci, I
  (The Clowns)
pa¦goda
Pah|lavi
paid
paid-up

pail
  bucket
  ⚠ pale

pail|ful

pain
  hurt; trouble;
  cause these
  VERB
  △ pains
  △ pained
  △ pain|ing
  ⚠ pane

Paine
pained
pain|ful
pain|fully
pain|kil¦ler
pain|less
pain|lessly
pains|ta¦king
paint
  VERB
  △ paints
  △ pain¦ted
  △ paint|ing
paint|ball
paint|box

△ paint|boxes
paint|brush
  △ paint|bru¦shes
pain|ter
paint|ing

pair
  couple; make
  this
  VERB
  △ pairs
  △ paired
  △ pair|ing
  ⚠ pare
  ⚠ pear

pair-royal
Pais|ley
pajamas *see*
  pyjamas
Pa¦kis|tan
pa¦kora
pal
  VERB
  △ pals
  △ palled
  △ pal|ling
pal¦ace
Pal¦ach
pal|adin
pa|laeo|bot|any
Pa|laeo|cene
pa|laeo|ecol|ogy
pa|lae|og|ra|pher
pa|lae|og|ra|phy
pa|laeo|li¦thic
pa|lae|olo|gus
pa|lae|on|to|lo|
  gist
pa|lae|on|tol|ogy
Pa|laeo|si|ber|ian
Pa|laeo|zoic
pa|lan|quin
pal¦at|able

pal|ate
roof of mouth;
sense of taste
⚠palette
⚠pallet

pa|la|tial
Palau
pa|la|ver

pale
lacking colour or
vividness;
become thus
VERB
△ pales
△ paled
△ pa|ling
⚠pail

pale|face
palely
pale|ness
paleobotany *see*
    palaeobotany
paleoecology *see*
    palaeoecology
Pa|lermo
Pal|es|tine
Pal|es|tin|ian
Pal|es|trina

pal|ette
painter's board
for mixing
colours; range of
colours
⚠palate
⚠pallet

Pal|grave
Pa|li|kir
pal|imp|sest
pal|in|drome
pal|in|dromic
pa|ling

pa|li|sade
pall
    VERB
    △ palls
    △ palled
    △ pall|ing
Pal|la|di|an|ism
Pal|la|dio
pal|la|dium
pall-bearer

pal|let
mattress; base
for stacked
goods; potter's
tool
⚠palate
⚠palette

pal|li|asse
pal|li|ate
    △ pal|li|ates
    △ pal|li|ated
    △ pal|li|ating
pal|li|at|ive
pal|lid
pal|li|ness
Pal|liser nov|els,
    The
pal|lium
pal|lor
pally
    △ pal|li|er
    △ pal|li|est
palm
    VERB
    △ palms
    △ palmed
    △ palm|ing
Palma
palm|ate
Palmer
Palm|er|ston
pal|metto
palm|is|try

pal|mitic
palm|top
palmy
    △ palm|ier
    △ palmi|est
pa|lo|mino
pal|pable
pal|pably
pal|pate
    △ pal|pates
    △ pal|pa|ted
    △ pal|pa|ting
pal|pi|tate
    △ pal|pi|tates
    △ pal|pi|ta|ted
    △ pal|pi|ta|ting
pal|pi|ta|tion
palsy
    VERB
    △ pal|sies
    △ pal|sied
    △ pal|sy|ing
pal|tri|ness
pal|try
    △ pal|trier
    △ pal|tri|est
pa|lyn|ol|ogy
Pam|ela
pam|pas
pam|per
    △ pam|pers
    △ pam|pered
    △ pam|per|ing
pamph|let
Pan
pan
    VERB
    △ pans
    △ panned
    △ pan|ning
pan|acea
pan|ache
Pan-Afri|can|ism
Pan|ama

pan|ama
Pan-Amer|ican
pa|na|tella
pan|cake
Pan|chen
pan|chro|matic
pan|creas
panda
pan|demic
pan|de|mo|nium
pan|der
    △ pan|ders
    △ pan|dered
    △ pan|der|ing
Pan|dit
Pan|dora

pane
sheet of glass
⚠pain

pa|ne|gy|ric
panel
    VERB
    △ pan|els
    △ pan|elled
    △ pan|el|ling
panel-bea|ter
panel-beat|ing
pan|el|ling
pan|el|list
pang
Pan|gaea
pan|go|lin
pan|gram
Pan|handle
panic
    VERB
    △ pan|ics
    △ pan|icked
    △ pan|ick|ing
panic-buy
    △ panic-buys
    △ panic-bought
    △ panic-buy|ing

pan|icky
pan|icle
panic-stricken
Panjabi *see*
  Punjabi
pan|jan|drum
Pank|hurst
pan|nier
pan|oply
△ pan|op|lies
pan|or|ama
pan|or|amic
pan|or|amic|ally
pan|pipes
pansy
△ pan|sies
pant
  VERB
△ pants
△ pan|ted
△ pant|ing
pan|ta|loons
pan|tech|ni|con
pan|the|ism
pan|the|ist
pan|the|is|tic
pan|theon
pan|ther
pan|ties
pantihose *see*
  panty hose
pan|tile
panto
pan|to|graph
pan|to|mime
pan|to|thenic
pan|try
△ pan|tries
pants
panty hose
Panzer
pap
papa
pa|pacy

△ pa|pa|cies
papal
pa|pa|razzo
△ pa|pa|razzi
pa|paya
paper
  VERB
△ pa|pers
△ pa|pered
△ pa|per|ing
pa|per|back
pa|per|boy
pa|per|girl
paper mâché *see*
  papier mâché
pa|per|weight
pa|per|work
pa|pery
Paphos
pap|ier-mâché
pa|pilla
△ pa|pil|lae
pa|pil|loma
pa|pil|lon
pa|pist
pa|poose
pap|rika *or* pa|
  prika
  according to
  pronunciation
Papua New
  Gui|nea
pa|py|rus
△ pa|pyri *or* pa|
  py|ruses

par
normal standard
⚠parr

para
par|able
pa|ra|bola
pa|ra|bolic
Pa|ra|cel|sus

pa|ra|cet|amol
pa|ra|chute
  VERB
△ pa|ra|chutes
△ pa|ra|chu|ted
△ pa|ra|chu|ting
pa|ra|chu|ting
pa|ra|chu|tist
par|ade
  VERB
△ par|ades
△ par|aded
△ par|ading
pa|ra|digm
pa|ra|dig|ma|tic
pa|ra|dise
Pa|ra|dise Lost
Pa|ra|dise Re|
  gained
pa|ra|dox
△ pa|ra|doxes
pa|ra|dox|ical
pa|ra|dox|ic|ally
par|aes|the|sia
par|af|fin
pa|ra|gli|der
pa|ra|gli|ding
pa|ra|gon
pa|ra|graph
  VERB
△ pa|ra|graphs
△ pa|ra|graphed
△ pa|ra|graph|
  ing
Pa|ra|guay
pa|ra|keet
pa|ra|lan|guage
par|al|de|hyde
par|al|lax
△ par|al|laxes
par|al|lel
  VERB
△ par|al|lels
△ par|al|leled

△ par|al|lel|ing
par|al|lel|ism
par|al|lelo|gram
pa|ra|lym|pics
pa|ra|lyse
△ pa|ra|ly|ses
△ pa|ra|lysed
△ pa|ra|ly|sing
pa|ra|ly|sis
△ pa|ra|ly|ses
pa|ra|lytic
pa|ra|lyt|ic|ally
Pa|ra|ma|ribo
Pa|ra|me|cium
pa|ra|medic
pa|ra|med|ical
pa|ram|eter
pa|ra|mil|it|ary
pa|ra|mount
pa|ra|noia
pa|ra|noiac
pa|ra|noi|ac|ally
pa|ra|noid
pa|ra|nor|mal
pa|ra|pet
pa|ra|pher|na|lia
pa|ra|phrase
  VERB
△ pa|ra|phra|ses
△ pa|ra|phrased
△ pa|ra|phra|
  sing
pa|ra|ple|gia
pa|ra|ple|gic
pa|ra|psy|cho|lo|
  gi|cal
pa|ra|psy|cholo|
  gist
pa|ra|psy|chol|
  ogy
Pa|ra|quat
pa|ra|sail|ing
pa|ra|site
pa|ra|si|tic

pa|ra|sit|ical
pa|ra|sit|ic|ally
pa|ra|sit|ism
pa|ra|sit|ol|ogy
pa|ra|sol
pa|ra|sym|pa|
  thetic
pa|ra|thor|mone
pa|ra|thy|roid
pa|ra|troo|per
pa|ra|troops
pa|ra|ty|phoid
par|boil
  △ par|boils
  △ par|boiled
  △ par|boil|ing
par|cel
  VERB
  △ par|cels
  △ par|celled
  △ par|cel|ling
parch
  △ par|ches
  △ parched
  △ parch|ing
parch|ment
par|don
  △ par|dons
  △ par|doned
  △ par|don|ing
par|don|able
par|don|ably
par|doner

> pare
> *trim*
>   △ pares
>   △ pared
>   △ par|ing
>   ⚠ pair
>   ⚠ pear

par|en|chyma
par|ent

VERB
△ par|ents
△ par|en|ted
△ par|ent|ing
par|ent|age
par|en|tal
par|en|tally
par|en|thesis
  △ par|en|theses
par|en|thetic
par|en|thet|ical
par|en|thet|ic|ally
par|ent|hood
par|ent|ing
par ex|cel|lence
pa|riah *or* par|
  iah
  according to
  pronunciation
pa|ri|etal
Paris
par|ish
  △ par|ishes
par|ish|ioner
par|ity
  △ par|it|ies
park
  VERB
  △ parks
  △ parked
  △ park|ing
parka
park-and-ride
Par|ker
par|kin
par|king-lot
par|king-meter
par|king-ticket
Par|kin|son
par|kin|son|ism
park|land
park|way
parky
  △ par|kier

△ par|ki|est
par|lance
par|ley
  VERB
  △ par|leys
  △ par|leyed
  △ par|ley|ing
par|lia|ment
par|lia|men|tar|
  ian
par|lia|men|tary
par|lour
par|lous
Parma
Par|me|san
Par|nell
pa|ro|chial
pa|ro|chi|al|ism
pa|ro|chi|ally
par|od|ist
par|ody
  NOUN
  △ par|od|ies
  VERB
  △ par|od|ies
  △ par|od|ied
  △ par|ody|ing
pa|role
  VERB
  △ pa|roles
  △ pa|roled
  △ pa|ro|ling
Paros
par|ou|sia
par|ox|ysm
par|ox|ys|mal
par|quet
par|quetry
Parr

> parr
> *young salmon*
>   △ parr *or* parrs
>   ⚠ par

par|ri|ci|dal
par|ri|cide
par|rot
  VERB
  △ par|rots
  △ par|roted
  △ par|rot|ing
par|rot-fash|ion
par|rot|fish
  sing. and pl.
Parry
parry
  VERB
  △ par|ries
  △ par|ried
  △ par|ry|ing
  NOUN
  △ par|ries
parse
  △ par|ses
  △ parsed
  △ par|sing
par|sec
Par|see
Par|see|ism
par|ser
Par|si|fal
par|si|mo|ni|ous
par|si|mo|ni|ously
par|si|mony
pars|ley
pars|nip
par|son
par|son|age
part
  VERB
  △ parts
  △ par|ted
  △ part|ing
par|take
  △ par|takes
  △ par|took
  △ par|ta|king
  △ par|ta|ken

par|terre
par|theno|gen|
  esis
Par|thenon
Par|thian
par|tial
par|ti|al|ity
par|ti|ally
par|ti|ci|pant
par|ti|ci|pate
  △ par|ti|ci|pates
  △ par|ti|ci|pa|ted
  △ par|ti|ci|pa|
    ting
par|ti|ci|pa|tion
par|ti|ci|pa|tor
par|ti|ci|pa|tory
par|ti|cip|ial
par|ti|cipi|ally
par|ti|ciple
par|ti|cle
par|ti|col|oured
par|tic|ular
par|tic|ular|iza|
  tion
par|tic|ular|ize
  △ par|tic|ular|
    izes
  △ par|tic|ular|
    ized
  △ par|tic|ular|
    izing
par|tic|ularly
part|ing
par|ti|san
par|tis|an|ship
  or par|ti|san|
  ship
  according to
  pronunciation
par|tita
  △ par|tite *or*
    par|ti|tas
par|ti|tion

VERB
  △ par|ti|tions
  △ par|ti|tioned
  △ par|ti|tion|ing
par|ti|tive
par|ti|tively
partly
part|ner

VERB
  △ part|ners
  △ part|nered
  △ part|ner|ing
part|ner|ship
par|took
part|ridge
part-time
part-timer
par|turi|ent
par|tur|ition
party
  △ par|ties

par|venu
  vulgar newly-
  rich man
  ⚠parvenue

par|venue
  vulgar newly-
  rich woman
  ⚠parvenu

pas
  sing. and pl.
Pa|sa|dena
PAS|CAL
  computer
  language
Pas|cal
  French scholar;
  first name
pas|cal
  unit of pressure
pas|chal
pas de deux

  sing. and pl.
pasha
Pa|so|llini
pasque|flower
pass
VERB
  △ pas|ses
  △ passed
  △ pass|ing
pass|able
pass|ably
pas|sa|cag|lia
pas|sage
Pas|sage to
  India, A
pas|sage|way
pas|sata
pass|book
Pas|schen|daele
passé
pas|sen|ger
pas|ser-by
  △ pas|sers-by
pas|ser|ine
pas|sim
pass|ing
pas|sion
pas|sion|ate
pas|sion|ately
Pas|sion|ist
pas|sive
pas|sively
pas|sive|ness
pas|siv|ity
pass|key
Pass|over
pass|port
pass|word
past
pasta
paste
VERB
  △ pastes
  △ pas|ted

  △ pas|ting
paste|board

pas|tel
  sort of crayon;
  picture drawn
  with this; pale
  ⚠pastille

pas|tern
Pas|ter|nak
paste-up
Pas|teur
pas|teur|iza|tion
pas|teur|ize
  △ pas|teur|izes
  △ pas|teur|ized
  △ pas|teur|izing
pas|tiche

pas|tille
  sort of sweet;
  scent for room
  ⚠pastel

pas|time
pas|ti|ness
past|ing
Pas|ton Let|ters
pas|tor
pas|toral
pas|tor|ale
pas|tor|al|ism
'Pas|toral' Sym|
  phony
pas|tor|ate
pas|trami
pas|try
  △ pas|tries
pas|tur|age
pas|ture
VERB
  △ pas|tures
  △ pas|tured
  △ pas|tur|ing
pasty

pas|tier
△ pas|ti|est
pasty
△ pas|ties
pat
   VERB
△ pats
△ pat|ted
△ pat|ting
Pa|ta|go|nia
patch
   NOUN
△ pat|ches
   VERB
△ pat|ches
△ patched
△ patch|ing
patch|ily
pat|chi|ness
pat|chouli
patch|work
pat|chy
△ pat|chier
△ pat|chi|est
pate
pâté
pâté de foie
   gras
pa|tella
△ pa|tel|lae or
   pa|tel|las
paten
pa|tent or pat|
   ent
   according to
   pronunciation
   VERB
△ pa|tents or
   pat|ents
△ pa|ten|ted or
   pat|en|ted
△ pa|tent|ing or
   pat|ent|ing
pa|ten|tee or

pat|en|tee
   according to
   pronunciation
pa|tently or pat|
   ently
   according to
   pronunciation
Pater
pater
pa|ter|fa|mil|ias
pa|ter|nal
pa|ter|nal|ism
pa|ter|nal|is|tic
pa|ter|nally
pa|ter|nity
pat|er|nos|ter
path
Pathé
Pa|ther Pan|chali
   (Song of the
   Little Road)
pa|thetic
pa|thet|ic|ally
'Pa|thé|tique'
   Sonata
path|finder
pa|tho|gen
pa|tho|genic
pa|tho|gen|icity
pa|tho|lo|gi|cal
pa|tho|lo|gic|ally
pa|thol|ogist
pa|thol|ogy
pa|thos
pa|tience
pa|tient
pa|tiently
pat|ina
patio
pa|tis|serie
Pat|more
Pat|mos
Patna
pat|ois

sing. and pl.
Paton
pat|rial
pat|ri|al|ity
pat|ri|arch
pat|ri|ar|chal
pat|ri|arch|ate
pat|ri|ar|chy
△ pat|ri|arch|ies
Pa|tri|cia
pa|tri|cian
pat|ri|ci|dal
pat|ri|cide
Pat|rick
pat|ri|lin|eal
pat|ri|mo|nial
pat|ri|mony
△ pat|ri|mon|ies
pat|riot
pat|ri|otic
pat|ri|ot|ic|ally
pat|ri|ot|ism
Pat|roc|lus
pat|rol
   VERB
△ pat|rols
△ pat|rolled
△ pat|rol|ling
pat|rol|man
△ pat|rol|men
pat|ron
pat|ron|age
pat|ron|ize
△ pat|ron|izes
△ pat|ron|ized
△ pat|ron|izing
pat|ron|izing
pat|ron|izingly
pat|ro|nymic
pat|ten
pat|ter
   VERB
△ pat|ters
△ pat|tered

△ pat|ter|ing
pat|tern
   VERB
△ pat|terns
△ pat|terned
△ pat|tern|ing
pat|terned
Pat|ton
patty
△ pat|ties
pau|city
Paul
Paula
Pauli
Paul|ine
paunch
△ paun|ches
paun|chi|ness
paun|chy
△ paun|chier
△ paun|chi|est
pau|per
pau|per|ism
pause
   VERB
△ pau|ses
△ paused
△ paus|ing
pavan
Pa|va|rotti
pave
△ paves
△ paved
△ pa|ving
pave|ment
Pavia
pa|vil|ion
pa|ving
pa|ving-stone
Pav|lov
Pav|lova
   dancer
pav|lova
   pudding

paw
  VERB
  △ paws
  △ pawed
  △ paw|ing
pawk|ily
paw|ki|ness
pawky
  △ paw|kier
  △ paw|ki|est
pawl
pawn
  VERB
  △ pawns
  △ pawned
  △ pawn|ing
pawn|bro|ker
pawn|bro|king
pawn|shop
paw|paw
pay
  VERB
  △ pays
  △ paid
  △ pay|ing
pay|able
pay-as-you-earn
pay-bed
payee
payer
pay|load
pay|mas|ter
pay|ment
pay-off
pay|ola
pay|phone
pay|roll
Paz
pea

> peace
> *freedom from war; quiet*
> ⚠ piece

peace|able
peace|ably
peace|ful
peace|fully
peace|ful|ness
peace|ma|ker
peace|time
peach
  NOUN
  △ pea|ches
  VERB
  △ pea|ches
  △ peached
  △ peach|ing
pea|chy
  △ pea|chier
  △ pea|chi|est
Pea|cock
pea|cock
pea|hen

> peak
> *summit; maximum; reach maximum*
> VERB
> △ peaks
> △ peaked
> △ peak|ing
> ⚠ peek

Peake
pea|ki|ness
peaky
  △ pea|kier
  △ pea|ki|est

> peal
> *set of bells; their ringing; burst of noise; ring*
> VERB
> △ peals
> △ pealed
> △ peal|ing
> ⚠ peel

pea|nut

> pear
> *fruit; its tree*
> ⚠ pair
> ⚠ pare

Pearl

> pearl
> *jewellery bead found in oysters; precious thing; of or like pearl; grind barley*
> VERB
> △ pearls
> △ pearled
> △ pearl|ing
> ⚠ purl

Pearl Fish|ers, The (Les Pê|cheurs de perles)
Pearl Har|bor
pearl|ies
pearly
  △ pearl|ier
  △ pearli|est
Pears
peas|ant
peas|an|try
pease
pea-shoo|ter
pea-souper
peat
peaty
  △ pea|tier
  △ pea|ti|est
peb|ble
pebble|dash
peb|bly
  △ peb|blier
  △ peb|bli|est
pecan
pec|ca|dillo

pec|ca|dil|los
  or pec|ca|dil|loes
pec|cary
  △ pec|car|ies
peck
  VERB
  △ pecks
  △ pecked
  △ peck|ing
pecker
Peck|in|pah
peck|ish
Pécs
pec|tic
pec|tin
pec|toral
pe|cu|liar
pe|cu|li|ar|ity
pe|cu|li|arly
pe|cu|ni|ary
peda|go|gic
peda|go|gi|cal
peda|go|gic|ally
ped|agogue
ped|agogy

> pedal
> *foot-lever; work this*
> VERB
> △ ped|als
> △ ped|alled
> △ ped|al|ling
> ⚠ peddle

ped|alo
ped|ant
pe|dan|tic
pe|dan|tic|ally
ped|an|try

> ped|dle
> *act as a pedlar; sell illegally*

△ ped¦dles
△ ped¦dled
△ ped¦dling
△ pedal

ped¦dler
ped¦er¦ast
ped¦er¦asty
ped¦es¦tal
pe¦dest¦rian
pe¦dest¦ri¦an¦iza¦tion
pe¦dest¦ri¦an¦ize
　△ pe¦dest¦ri¦an¦izes
　△ pe¦dest¦ri¦an¦ized
　△ pe¦dest¦ri¦an¦izing
pediatrics *see*
　paediatrics
pedi¦cure
pedi¦gree
pedi¦ment
ped¦lar
ped¦ol¦ogy
pedo¦meter
ped¦uncle
pee
　VERB
　△ pees
　△ peed
　△ pee¦ing
Peebles

peek
　peep
　VERB
　△ peeks
　△ peeked
　△ peek¦ing
　△ peak

Peel

peel
　rind of fruit etc;
　strip off rind,
　clothes, etc
　VERB
　△ peels
　△ peeled
　△ peel¦ing
　△ peal

pee¦ler
peel¦ings
peep
　VERB
　△ peeps
　△ peeped
　△ peep¦ing
pee¦per
peep¦hole
peep¦show
peer
　VERB
　△ peers
　△ peered
　△ peer¦ing
peer¦age
peer¦ess
　△ peer¦es¦ses
Peer Gynt
peer¦less
peer¦lessly
peer¦less¦ness
peeve
　VERB
　△ peeves
　△ peeved
　△ peev¦ing
peeved
peev¦ish
peev¦ishly
peev¦ish¦ness
pee¦wit
peg

VERB
△ pegs
△ pegged
△ peg¦ging
Pe¦ga¦sus
peg¦ma¦tite
peig¦noir
Peiping *see*
　Beijing
pe¦jor¦at¦ive
pe¦jor¦at¦ively
peke
Pe¦kin¦ese
　sing. and pl.
Peking
　Chinese city see
　Beijing
Pe¦king Man
Pe¦king Opera
pekoe
pe¦la¦gic
pel¦ar¦go¦nium
Pelau *see* Palau
Pelé
Pe¦leus
peli¦can
　△ peli¦can *or*
　　peli¦cans
pel¦lagra
Pel¦léas et Mé¦li¦
　sande
pel¦let
pell-mell
pel¦lu¦cid
pel¦met
Pe¦lo¦pon¦nese
pe¦lota
pe¦lo¦ton
pelt
　VERB
　△ pelts
　△ pel¦ted
　△ pelt¦ing
pel¦vic

pel¦vis
　△ pel¦vises
Pem¦broke¦shire
pem¦mi¦can
pen
　VERB
　△ pens
　△ penned
　△ pen¦ning
penal
pe¦nal¦iza¦tion
pe¦nal¦ize
　△ pe¦nal¦izes
　△ pe¦nal¦ized
　△ pe¦nal¦izing
pe¦nally
pen¦alty
　△ pen¦al¦ties
pen¦ance
Pen¦ates
pence
pen¦chant
pen¦cil
　VERB
　△ pen¦cils
　△ pen¦cilled
　△ pen¦cil¦ling

pen¦dant
　NOUN
　△ pendent

pen¦dent
　ADJ.
　△ pendant

pend¦ing
pen¦du¦lous
pen¦du¦lously
pen¦du¦lum
Pe¦nel¦ope
pen¦et¦ra¦bil¦ity
pen¦et¦rable
pen¦et¦rate
　△ pen¦et¦rates

△ pen|et|ra|ted
△ pen|et|ra|ting
pen|et|ra|ting
pen|et|ra|tion
pen|friend
pen|pal
pen|guin
peni|cil|lin
pe|nile
pen|in|sula
pen|in|su|lar
penis
  △ pe|nises
peni|tence
peni|tent
peni|ten|tial
peni|ten|ti|ary
  △ peni|ten|ti|ar|
  ies
peni|tently
pen|knife
  △ pen|knives
pen|man|ship
Penn
pen|nant
pen|ni|less
Pen|nine
pen|non
Penn|syl|va|nia
penny
  △ pence *or* pen|
  nies
penny-half|
  penny
  △ penny-half|
  pence
penny-in-the-
  slot
penny-pin|cher
penny-pinch|ing
penny|worth
pe|no|lo|gi|cal
pe|nolo|gist
pe|nol|ogy

pen-pusher
pen-push|ing
Pen|rith
pen|sion
  VERB
  △ pen|sions
  △ pen|sioned
  △ pen|sion|ing
pen|sion|able
pen|sioner
pen|sive
pen|sively
pent
Pen|ta|gon
  US national
  military HQ
pen|ta|gon
  five-sided figure
pen|ta|go|nal
pen|ta|gram
pen|ta|meter
Pen|ta|teuch
Pen|ta|teu|chal
pent|ath|lon
pen|ta|tonic
pen|ta|va|lent
Pen|te|cost
Pen|te|cos|tal
Pen|te|cos|tal|
  ism
pent|house
pent-up
pen|ul|ti|mate
pen|um|bra
  △ pen|um|brae
  or pen|um|
  bras
pen|um|bral
pe|nuri|ous
pe|nuri|ously
pen|ury
Pen|zance
peon
peony

△ pe|on|ies
peo|ple
  VERB
  △ peo|ples
  △ peo|pled
  △ peop|ling
pep
  VERB
  △ peps
  △ pepped
  △ pep|ping
pep|lum
pep|per
  VERB
  △ pep|pers
  △ pep|pered
  △ pep|per|ing
pep|per|corn
pep|per|mill
pep|per|mint
pep|pery
pep|sin
pep|tic
pep|tide
Pepys
per
per|ad|ven|ture
per|am|bu|late
  △ per|am|bu|lates
  △ per|am|bu|la|
  ted
  △ per|am|bu|la|
  ting
per|am|bu|la|
  tion
per|am|bu|la|tor
per annum
per cap|ita
per|ceiv|able
per|ceive
  △ per|ceives
  △ per|ceived
  △ per|ceiv|ing
per cent

ADV.
per|cent
  NOUN
per|cent|age
per|cent|ile
per|cep|ti|bil|ity
per|cep|tible
per|cep|tibly
per|cep|tion
per|cep|tive
per|cep|tively
perch
  NOUN
  △ per|ches
  VERB
  △ per|ches
  △ perched
  △ perch|ing
per|chance
per|cipi|ent
Per|ci|val
per|co|late
  △ per|co|lates
  △ per|co|la|ted
  △ per|co|la|ting
per|co|la|tion
per|co|la|tor
per|cus|sion
per|cus|sion|ist
per|cus|sive
Percy
Per|dita
per|di|tion
per|eg|rin|ate
  △ per|eg|rin|ates
  △ per|eg|rin|ated
  △ per|eg|rin|
  ating
per|eg|rin|ation
per|eg|rine
Per|eg|rine
Pickle, The
Ad|ven|tures of
per|emp|tor|ily

per|emp|tory
per|en|nial
per|en|ni|ally
per|es|troika
Pérez de Cuél|
  lar
per|fect
  VERB
  △ per|fects
  △ per|fec|ted
  △ per|fect|ing
per|fec|ti|bil|ity
per|fect|ible
per|fec|tion
per|fec|tion|ism
per|fec|tion|ist
per|fectly
per|fi|di|ous
per|fi|di|ously
per|fidy
  △ per|fid|ies
per|for|ate
  △ per|for|ates
  △ per|for|ated
  △ per|for|ating
per|for|ation
per|force
per|form
  △ per|forms
  △ per|formed
  △ per|form|ing
per|form|ance
per|for|mer
per|fume
  VERB
  △ per|fumes
  △ per|fumed
  △ per|fu|ming
per|fu|mer
per|fu|mery
  △ per|fu|mer|ies
per|func|tor|ily
per|func|tory
per|fu|sion

per|gola
Per|go|lesi
per|haps
peri|anth
peri|car|dium
  △ peri|car|dia
peri|carp
Peri|cles
*Peri|cles, Prince
  of Tyre*
peri|dot|ite
peri|gee
Pé|ri|gord
peri|he|lion
  △ peri|he|lia
peril
per|il|ous
per|il|ously
per|im|eter
peri|na|tal
per|iod
peri|odic
peri|od|ical
peri|od|ic|ally
peri|odi|city
peri|od|on|ti|tis
peri|pa|tetic
peri|pa|tet|ic|ally
per|iph|eral
per|iph|ery
  △ per|iph|er|ies
per|iph|ra|sis
  △ per|iph|ra|ses
peri|phras|tic
peri|phras|tic|
  ally
peri|scope
peri|scopic
per|ish
  △ per|ishes
  △ per|ished
  △ per|ish|ing
per|ish|ab|il|ity
per|ish|able

per|ished
per|isher
per|ish|ing
per|ish|ingly
peri|stal|sis
peri|stal|tic
peri|style
peri|to|neal
peri|to|neum
  △ peri|to|nea *or*
  peri|to|neums
peri|to|ni|tis
peri|wig
peri|winkle
per|jure
  △ per|jures
  △ per|jured
  △ per|jur|ing
per|jurer
per|jury
  △ per|jur|ies
perk
  VERB
  △ perks
  △ perked
  △ perk|ing
perk|ily
per|ki|ness
perky
  △ per|kier
  △ per|ki|est
Perm
perm
  VERB
  △ perms
  △ permed
  △ perm|ing
per|ma|frost
per|ma|nence
per|ma|nency
per|ma|nent
per|ma|nently
per|man|gan|ate
per|meab|il|ity

per|meable
per|meate
  △ per|meates
  △ per|meated
  △ per|mea|ting
per|mea|tion
Per|mian
per|mis|si|bil|ity
per|miss|ible
per|mis|sion
per|mis|sive
per|mis|sively
per|mis|sive|ness
per|mit
  △ per|mits
  △ per|mit|ted
  △ per|mit|ting
per|mit|tiv|ity
per|mu|ta|bil|ity
per|mut|able
per|mu|ta|tion
per|mute
  △ per|mutes
  △ per|mu|ted
  △ per|mu|ting
per|mu|tate
  △ per|mu|tates
  △ per|mu|ta|ted
  △ per|mu|ta|ting
per|ni|cious
per|ni|ciously
per|nick|ety
Perón
per|ora|tion
per|ox|ide
  VERB
  △ per|ox|ides
  △ per|ox|ided
  △ per|oxi|ding
per|pen|dicu|lar
per|pen|di|cu|
  lar|ity
per|pen|dicu|
  larly

per|pet|rate
△ per|pet|rates
△ per|pet|ra|ted
△ per|pet|ra|ting
per|pet|ra|tion
per|pet|ra|tor
per|pet|ual
per|petu|ate
△ per|petu|ates
△ per|petu|ated
△ per|petu|ating
per|petu|ation
per|pe|tu|ity
△ per|pe|tu|it|ies
Per|pig|nan
per|plex
△ per|plexes
△ per|plexed
△ per|plex|ing
per|plex|edly
per|plex|ing
per|plex|ity
△ per|plex|it|ies
per|quis|ite
perry
△ per|ries
per se
per|se|cute
△ per|se|cutes
△ per|se|cu|ted
△ per|se|cu|ting
per|se|cu|tion
per|se|cu|tor
Per|se|phone
Per|seus
per|se|ver|ance
per|se|vere
△ per|se|veres
△ per|se|vered
△ per|se|ver|ing
Per|shing
Per|sia
Per|sian
per|si|flage

per|sim|mon
per|sist
△ per|sists
△ per|sis|ted
△ per|sist|ing
per|sist|ence
per|sist|ent
per|sist|ently
per|son
persona
△ per|so|nae *or*
  per|so|nas
per|son|able
per|son|ably
per|son|age
per|sonal
per|son|al|ity
△ per|son|al|it|
  ies
per|son|al|ize
△ per|son|al|izes
△ per|son|al|ized
△ per|son|al|
  izing
per|son|ally
*per|sona non
  grata*
△ *per|so|nae non
  gra|tae*
per|soni|fi|ca|
  tion
per|son|ify
△ per|soni|fies
△ per|soni|fied
△ per|soni|fy|ing
per|son|nel
per|spec|tive
Pers|pex
per|spi|ca|cious
per|spi|ca|
  ciously
per|spi|ca|city
per|spi|cu|ity
per|spicu|ous

per|spicu|ously
per|spir|ation
per|spire
△ per|spires
△ per|spired
△ per|spir|ing
per|suad|able
per|suade
△ per|suades
△ per|suaded
△ per|suad|ing
per|suader
per|suas|ible
Per|suas|ion
per|suas|ion
per|suas|ive
per|suas|ively
per|suas|ive|ness
pert
per|tain
△ per|tains
△ per|tained
△ per|tain|ing
Perth
per|ti|na|cious
per|ti|na|ciously
per|ti|na|city
per|tin|ence
per|tin|ency
per|tin|ent
pertly
pert|ness
per|turb
△ per|turbs
△ per|turbed
△ per|turb|ling
per|tur|ba|tion
per|turbed
per|tus|sis
Peru
Pe|ru|gia
pe|ruke
peru|sal
per|use

△ per|uses
△ per|used
peru|sing
per|vade
△ per|vades
△ per|va|ded
△ per|va|ding
per|va|sive
per|verse
per|versely
per|ver|sion
per|ver|sity
△ per|ver|si|ties
per|vert
VERB
△ per|verts
△ per|ver|ted
△ per|vert|ing
pe|seta
Pe|sha|war
pesk|ily
pesky
△ pes|kier
△ pes|ki|est
peso
pes|sary
△ pes|sar|ies
pes|sim|ism
pes|sim|ist
pes|sim|is|tic
pes|sim|is|tic|
  ally
pest
Pes|ta|lozzi
pes|ter
△ pes|ters
△ pes|tered
△ pes|ter|ing
pes|ti|cide
pes|ti|lence
pes|ti|lent
pes|ti|len|tial
pes|ti|lently
pes|tle

pesto

pet

  VERB

  △ pets

  △ pet|ted

  △ pet|ting

Pét|ain

petal

pe|tard

Peter

peter

  △ pe|ters

  △ pe|tered

  △ pe|ter|ing

Peter and the

  Wolf (Petya i

  volk)

Pe|ter|bor|ough

Pe|ter|head

Pe|ter|loo

Peter Pan

Pe|ters|burg

pe|ter|sham

pethi|dine

peti|ole

Pet|ipa

petit bour|geois

  △ *pet|its bour|*

  geois

pe|tite

pe|tite bour|geoisie

petit four

  △ pet|its fours

pe|ti|tion

  VERB

  △ pe|ti|tions

  △ pe|ti|tioned

  △ pe|ti|tion|ing

pe|ti|tioner

petit mal

petit point

Petit Prince, Le

  (The Little

  Prince)

Petra

Pet|rarch

> pet|rel
> *sort of bird*
> ⚠petrol

Petri-dish

  △ Petri-dishes

Pet|rie

pet|ri|fac|tion

pet|ri|fi|ca|tion

pet|rify

  △ pet|ri|fies

  △ pet|ri|fied

  △ pet|ri|fy|ing

pet|ro|chem|ical

pet|ro|chem|ic|

  ally

pet|ro|chem|is|

  try

pet|ro|cur|rency

pet|ro|dol|lar

> pet|rol
> *motor fuel*
> ⚠petrel

pet|ro|la|tum

pet|ro|leum

pet|ro|lo|gi|cal

pet|rolo|gist

pet|rol|ogy

Pet|rushka

pet|ti|coat

pet|ti|fog

  △ pet|ti|fogs

  △ pet|ti|fogged

  △ pet|ti|fog|ging

pet|ti|fog|ger

pet|ti|fog|ging

pet|tish

pet|tishly

pet|tish|ness

petty

  △ pet|tier

  △ pet|ti|est

petu|lance

petu|lant

petu|lantly

pe|tu|nia

Peu|geot

Pevs|ner

pew

pew|ter

pey|ote

Pfeif|fer

pfen|nig

pha|go|cyte

pha|go|cy|to|sis

phal|ange

pha|lan|ger

phal|anx

  △ phal|anxes *or*

  phal|an|ges

phal|ar|ope

phal|lic

phal|lus

  △ phal|luses *or*

  phalli

Phan|ero|zoic

phan|tasm

phan|tas|ma|

  goria

phan|tas|ma|

  goric

phan|tas|ma|gor|

  ical

phan|tas|mal

phantasy *see*

  fantasy

phan|tom

Phan|tom of the

  Opera

phar|aoh

Pha|ri|saic

Phar|isee

phar|ma|ceu|ti|

  cal

phar|ma|ceu|tics

phar|ma|cist

phar|ma|co|lo|gi|

  cal

phar|ma|colo|

  gist

phar|ma|col|ogy

phar|ma|co|

  poeia

phar|macy

  △ phar|ma|cies

pha|ryn|geal

pha|ryn|gi|tis

pha|rynx

  △ pha|ryn|xes

  △ pha|ryn|ges

phase

  VERB

  △ pha|ses

  △ phased

  △ pha|sing

pha|tic

pheas|ant

  △ pheas|ant *or*

  pheas|ants

phe|no|bar|bi|

  tone

phe|no|bar|bi|tal

phe|no|cryst

phe|nol

phe|nol|phtha|

  lein

phe|nom|enal

phe|nom|en|al|

  ism

phe|nom|en|ally

phe|nom|enon

  △ phe|nom|ena

phe|no|type

phe|nyl|al|an|ine

phe|nyl|ke|ton|

  uria

phero|mone

phew

phial

Phil|adel|phia
phil|adel|phus
phil|an|der
  △ phil|an|ders
  △ phil|an|dered
  △ phil|an|der|ing
phil|an|derer
phil|an|thropic
phil|an|thro|pist
phil|an|thropy
phi|la|telic
phi|lat|el|ist
phi|lat|ely
Philby
Phi|le|mon, Let|
  ter of Paul to
phil|har|monic
Philip
Phil|ippa
Phi|lippi
Phi|lip|pi|ans,
  Let|ter of Paul
  to the
phi|lip|pic
Phil|ip|pines
Phil|is|tine
  member of a
  biblical people,
  enemies of the
  Israelites; of this
  people
phil|is|tine
  uncultured,
  materialistic;
  such person
phil|is|tin|ism
phi|lo|lo|gi|cal
phi|lo|lo|gi|cally
phi|lo|lo|gist
phi|lo|logy
phi|lo|so|pher
phi|lo|soph|ical
phi|lo|soph|ic|
  ally

phi|lo|so|phize
  △ phi|lo|so|phi|
  zes
  △ phi|lo|so|
  phized
  △ phi|lo|so|phi|
  zing
phi|lo|so|phi|zer
phi|lo|so|phy
  △ phi|lo|so|phies
phil|tre
phle|bi|tis
phle|bot|omy
phlegm
phleg|matic
phleg|mat|ic|
  ally
phloem
phlo|gis|ton
phlox
Phnom Penh
pho|bia
pho|bic
Phoebe
Phoe|ni|cia
Phoe|ni|cian
Phoe|nix
  US city
phoe|nix
  mythical bird
phone
  △ phones
  △ phoned
  △ pho|ning
phone|card
phone-in
pho|neme
pho|ne|mic
pho|ne|mic|ally
pho|ne|mics
pho|netic
pho|net|ic|ally
pho|net|ics
pho|ney

△ pho|nier
△ pho|ni|est
pho|ney|ness
phonic *or* pho|
  nic
  according to
  pronunciation
phon|ic|ally *or*
  pho|nic|ally
  according to
  pronunciation
pho|ni|ness
pho|no|graph
pho|no|lo|gi|cal
pho|no|lo|gi|
  cally
pho|nolo|gist
pho|nol|ogy
  △ pho|nolo|gies
phony *see*
  phoney
phooey
phos|phate
phos|phor
phos|phor|esce
  △ phos|phor|es|
  ces
  △ phos|phor|
  esced
  △ phos|phor|es|
  cing
phos|phor|es|
  cence
phos|phor|es|
  cent
phos|phoric
phos|phorus
photo
pho|to|cell
pho|to|chem|is|
  try
pho|to|copi|able
pho|to|cop|ier
pho|to|copy

NOUN
  △ pho|to|cop|ies
VERB
  △ pho|to|cop|ies
  △ pho|to|cop|ied
  △ pho|to|copy|
  ing
pho|to|de|grad|
  able
pho|to|elec|tric
pho|to|elec|tric
pho|to|el|ec|tri|
  city
pho|to|en|gra|
  ving
Pho|to|fit
pho|to|genic
pho|to|gram|
  metry
pho|to|graph
VERB
  △ pho|to|graphs
  △ pho|to|
  graphed
  △ pho|to|graph|
  ing
pho|to|gra|pher
pho|to|gra|phic
pho|to|graph|ic|
  ally
pho|to|gra|phy
pho|to|gra|vure
pho|to|li|tho|gra|
  phy
pho|to|ly|sis
pho|to|metry
pho|to|mi|cro|
  graph
pho|to|mi|cro|
  gra|phy
pho|to|mon|tage
pho|to|mul|ti|
  plier
pho|ton

pho|to|peri|od|
ism
pho|to|pho|bia
Pho|to|real|ism
pho|to|re|cep|tor
pho|to|sen|si|tive
pho|to|sen|si|tiv|
ity
pho|to|sphere
Pho|to|stat
 NOUN
pho|to|stat
 VERB
 △ pho|to|stats
 △ pho|to|stat|ted
 △ pho|to|stat|
 ting
pho|to|syn|thesis
pho|to|syn|thes|
ize
 △ pho|to|syn|
 thes|izes
 △ pho|to|syn|
 thes|ized
 △ pho|to|syn|
 thes|izing
pho|to|syn|thetic
pho|to|taxis
pho|to|tro|pism
pho|to|type|set|
ter
phra|sal
phra|sally
phrase
 VERB
 △ phra|ses
 △ phrased
 △ phra|sing
phra|seo|lo|gi|cal
phra|seol|ogy
phreak|ing
phreno|lo|gi|cal
phren|olo|gist
phren|ol|ogy

phthi|sis
 △ phthi|ses
Phuket
phut
phy|col|ogy
phy|lac|tery
 △ phy|lac|ter|ies
Phyl|lis
phyl|lite
phyllo
phyl|lo|taxis
phyl|lo|taxy
phy|lo|geny
phy|lum
 △ phyla
physic
 VERB
 △ phys|ics
 △ phys|icked
 △ phys|ick|ing
phys|ical
phy|si|cal|ity
phys|ic|ally
phy|si|cian
phy|si|cist
phys|ics
physio
phy|si|og|nomy
 △ phy|si|og|
 nom|ies
phy|sio|lo|gi|cal
phy|si|olo|gist
phy|si|ol|ogy
phy|sio|ther|ap|
ist
phy|sio|ther|apy
phy|sique
phy|to|men|adi|
one
phy|to|pa|thol|
ogy
phy|to|plank|ton
pi
Pia|cenza

Piaf
Piaget
pia mater
 △ piae mat|res
pi|an|is|simo
pi|an|ist
piano
pi|ano|forte
Pi|an|ola
pi|azza
pib|roch
pic
 △ pics or pix
pica
pic|ador
Pic|ardy
pic|ar|esque
Pi|casso
pic|ca|lilli
pic|ca|ninny
 △ pic|ca|nin|nies
pic|colo
pick
 VERB
 △ picks
 △ picked
 △ pick|ing
pickaback see
 piggyback
pick|axe
picker
picket
 VERB
 △ pick|ets
 △ pick|eted
 △ pick|et|ing
Pick|ford
pick|ings
pickle
 VERB
 △ pickles
 △ pickled
 △ pick|ling
pickled

pick-me-up
pick|pocket
pick-up
Pick|wick Pa|
 pers, The
picky
 △ pick|ier
 △ picki|est
pic|nic
 VERB
 △ pic|nics
 △ pic|nicked
 △ pic|nick|ing
Pic|nic at Hang|
 ing Rock
pic|nicker
Pict
Pict|ish
pic|to|graph
pic|to|gram
pic|tor|ial
pic|tori|ally
pic|ture
 VERB
 △ pic|tures
 △ pic|tured
 △ pic|tur|ing
Pic|ture of Dor|
 ian Gray, The
Pic|tures at an
 Ex|hi|bi|tion
 (Kar|tinka s
 vys|tavki)
pic|tur|esque
pic|tur|esquely
pid|dle
 VERB
 △ pid|dles
 △ pid|dled
 △ pid|dling
pid|dling
pid|gin
pie
pie|bald

piece
portion; item;
trace; assemble
VERB
△ pieces
△ pieced
△ piecing
⚠ peace

pièce de ré|sis|
tance
△ *pièces de ré|sis|*
tance
piece|meal
piece of eight
△ pieces of
eight
piece|work
pied
pied-à-terre
△ pieds-à-terre
Pied|mont
Pied Piper of
Ham|elin
pie-dog *see* pye-
dog
pie-eyed
pier
pierce
△ pier|ces
△ pierced
△ pier|cing
pier|cing
Piero della
Fran|cesca
Pi|erre
Pi|er|rot
Piers
Piers Plow|man
pietà
pi|et|ism
pi|et|ist
pi|et|is|tic
piety

pi|ezo|elec|tric
pi|ezo|elec|tri|
city
pif|fle
pif|fling
pig
VERB
△ pigs
△ pigged
△ pig|ging
pi|geon
pi|geon|hole
VERB
△ pi|geon|holes
△ pi|geon|holed
△ pi|geon|ho|
ling
pi|geon-toed
pig|gery
△ pig|ger|ies
pig|gish
pig|gish|ness
Pig|gott
piggy
△ pig|gies
pig|gy|back
pig|headed
pig|head|edly
pig|head|ed|ness
pig-in-the-
middle
pig|let
pig|ment
VERB
△ pig|ments
△ pig|men|ted
△ pig|ment|ing
pig|men|ta|tion
pigmy *see*
pygmy
pig|skin
pig|sty
△ pig|sties
pig|swill

pig|tail
pika
pike
fish
△ pike *or* pikes
spear
△ pikes
pike|staff
pi|laff
pi|las|ter
Pi|late
pil|chard
pile
VERB
△ piles
△ piled
△ pi|ling
pile-dri|ver
pile-up
pil|fer
△ pil|fers
△ pil|fered
△ pil|fer|ing
pil|ferer
pil|grim
pil|grim|age
Pil|grim's Pro|
gress, The
Pi|li|pino
pill
pil|lage
VERB
△ pil|lages
△ pil|laged
△ pil|la|ging
pil|la|ger
pil|lar
pill|box
△ pill|boxes
pil|lion
pil|lory
NOUN
△ pil|lor|ies

VERB
△ pil|lor|ies
△ pil|lor|ied
△ pil|lory|ing
pil|low
VERB
△ pil|lows
△ pil|lowed
△ pil|low|ing
pil|low|case
pil|low|slip
pilot
VERB
△ pi|lots
△ pi|loted
△ pi|lot|ing
Pilt|down

pi|mento
allspice
⚠ pimiento

pi|mi|ento
red pepper
⚠ pimento

pimp
VERB
△ pimps
△ pimped
△ pimp|ing
pim|per|nel
pim|ple
pim|ply
△ pim|plier
△ pim|pli|est
PIN
pin
VERB
△ pins
△ pinned
△ pin|ning
pina|fore
pin|ball
pince-nez

pin|cers

pinch

   VERB

   △ pin|ches

   △ pinched

   △ pinch|ing

pinch|beck

pinched

   △ pincheder

   △ pinched|est

pin|cush|ion

Pin|dar

Pin|dus

Pine

   saxophonist

pine

   sort of tree; long

   for

   VERB

   △ pines

   △ pined

   △ pi|ning

pi|neal

pine|apple

Pine|apple Poll

Pi|nero

ping

   VERB

   △ pings

   △ pinged

   △ ping|ling

ping-pong

pin|head

pin|ion

   VERB

   △ pin|ions

   △ pin|ioned

   △ pin|ion|ing

pink

   VERB

   △ pinks

   △ pinked

   △ pink|ing

pin|kie

pink|ish

pinko

pinky

   pinkish

   △ pin|kier

   △ pin|ki|est

pinky

   little finger see

   pinkie

pinna

   △ pin|nae

pin|nace

pin|nacle

pin|nate

pinny

   △ pin|nies

Pi|no|chet

pi|nochle

pi|nole

pin|point

   △ pin|points

   △ pin|poin|ted

   △ pin|point|ing

pin|prick

pin|stripe

pint

pinta

pin|tail

Pin|ter

pin-up

pin|wheel

Pin|yin

pi|on|eer

   VERB

   △ pi|on|eers

   △ pi|on|eered

   △ pi|on|eer|ing

pious

pi|ously

pi|ous|ness

pip

   VERB

   △ pips

   △ pipped

   △ pip|ping

pipe

   VERB

   △ pipes

   △ piped

   △ pi|ping

pipe|clay

pipe-cleaner

pipe|line

Piper

piper

pip|ette

pi|ping

pi|pis|trelle

pipit

pip|pin

pip|squeak

pi|quancy

pi|quant

pique

   VERB

   △ piques

   △ piqued

   △ pi|quing

piqué

pi|quet

pi|racy

Pi|raeus

Pi|ran|dello

Pi|ra|nesi

pi|ranha

pi|rate

   VERB

   △ pi|rates

   △ pi|ra|ted

   △ pi|ra|ting

Pi|rates of Pen|

zance

pi|rat|ical

pi|rou|ette

   VERB

   △ pi|rou|ettes

   △ pi|rou|et|ted

   △ pi|rou|et|ting

Pisa

Pis|ca|tor

pis|ca|tor|ial

Pis|cean

Pis|ces

pis|ci|cul|ture

pis|cina

piss

   VERB

   △ pis|ses

   △ pissed

   △ piss|ing

Pis|sarro

pissed

pis|ta|chio

piste

---

pis|til

   part of flower

   ⚠pistol

Pis|toia

---

pis|tol

   hand gun

   ⚠pistil

---

pis|ton

pit

   VERB

   △ pits

   △ pit|ted

   △ pit|ting

pit-a-pat

Pit|cairn

pitch

   VERB

   △ pit|ches

   △ pitched

   △ pitch|ing

pitch-black

pitch|blende

pitch-dark

pit|cher

pitch|fork

pit|eous

pit|fall
pith
pit|head
pithy
△ pith|ier
△ pithi|est
pi|ti|able
pi|ti|ful
pi|ti|fully
pi|ti|less
Pit|man
piton
pit|stop
Pitt
pitta
pit|tance
pit|ter-pat|ter
Pitti
Pitts|burgh
pi|tu|it|ary
△ pi|tu|it|ar|ies
pity
VERB
△ pit|ies
△ pit|ied
△ pi|ty|ing
pi|ty|ing
pi|ty|ingly
Pius
pivot
VERB
△ piv|ots
△ piv|oted
△ piv|ot|ing
piv|otal
pix
pixel
pixie
Piz|arro
pizza
piz|zazz
piz|zeria
piz|zi|cato
plac|ard

VERB
△ plac|ards
△ plac|ar|ded
△ plac|ard|ing
pla|cate
△ pla|cates
△ pla|ca|ted
△ pla|ca|ting
pla|ca|tion
pla|ca|tory

place
point, position,
or area; put
VERB
△ pla|ces
△ placed
△ pla|cing
△ plaice

pla|cebo
place|man
△ place|men
place|ment
place-name
pla|centa
△ pla|cen|tae *or*
pla|cen|tas
pla|cid
pla|cid|ity
pla|cidly
pla|giar|ism
pla|giar|ist
pla|giar|ize
△ pla|giar|izes
△ pla|giar|ized
△ pla|giar|izing
plague
VERB
△ plagues
△ plagued
△ pla|guing

plaice
sort of fish

sing. and pl.
△ place

plaid
Plaid Cymru

plain
flat country;
knitting stitch;
simple; utterly
ADJ.
△ plai|ner
△ plain|est
△ plane

plain|chant
plainly
plain|ness
plain|song
plain-spo|ken
plaint

plain|tiff
aggrieved party
in civil lawsuit
△ plaintive

plain|tive
sad
△ plaintiff

plain|tively

plait
interlaced hair
etc; make this
VERB
△ plaits
△ plai|ted
△ plait|ing
△ plate

plan
VERB
△ plans
△ planned
△ plan|ning

Planck

plane
aeroplane; flat
surface; tool for
making this; sort
of tree; flat;
skim or soar like
aeroplane;
smooth wood
with plane.
VERB
△ planes
△ planed
△ pla|ning
△ plain

planet
pla|net|ar|ium
△ pla|net|aria *or*
pla|net|ari|
ums
plan|et|ary
pla|net|ol|ogy
Plan|ets, The
plan|gency
plan|gent
plan|gently
pla|ni|meter
plank
VERB
△ planks
△ planked
△ plank|ing
plank|ing
plank|ton
plan|ner
plan|ning
pla|no|gra|phic
plant
VERB
△ plants
△ planted
△ plant|ing
Plan|ta|genet

plan|tain
plan|ta|tion
planter
plan|ti|grade
plaque
plasma
plas|mid
Plas|mo|dium
plas|ter
  VERB
  △ plas|ters
  △ plas|tered
  △ plas|ter|ing
plas|ter|board
plas|tered
plas|terer
plas|tic
Plas|ti|cine
plas|ti|city
plas|ti|ci|zer
plas|tid
Plate

plate
  shallow dish;
  flat sheet of
  metal etc; coat
  with plate(s)
  VERB
  △ plates
  △ pla|ted
  △ pla|ting
  △ plait

plat|eau
  △ plat|eaux *or*
  plat|eaus
plate|ful
plate|layer
plate|let
platen
plat|form
Plath
pla|ting
plat|inum

plat|inum-blond
  ADJ.
plat|inum
  blonde
  NOUN
pla|ti|tude
pla|ti|tu|din|ous
Plato
Pla|tonic
pla|ton|ic|ally
Pla|ton|ism
pla|toon
plat|ter
pla|ty|pus
  △ pla|ty|puses
plau|dit
plaus|ibil|ity
plaus|ible
plaus|ibly
Plau|tus
play
  VERB
  △ plays
  △ played
  △ play|ing
play|able
play-act
  △ play-acts
  △ play-acted
  △ play-act|ing
play-act|ing
play|back
play|bill
play|boy
Play|boy of the
  West|ern
  World, The
Player
player
play|fel|low
play|ful
play|fully
play|ful|ness
play|ground

play|group
play|house
play|ing-card
play|ing-field
play|mate
play-off
play|pen
play|school
play|thing
play|time
play|wright
plaza
plea
plead
  △ pleads
  △ plea|ded
  △ plead|ing
plead|ing
plead|ingly
pleas|ant
pleas|antly
pleas|ant|ness
pleas|an|try
  △ pleas|ant|ries
please
  VERB
  △ plea|ses
  △ pleased
  △ pleas|ing
pleased
pleas|ing
pleas|ingly
plea|sur|able
plea|sur|ably
plea|sure
  VERB
  △ plea|sures
  △ plea|sured
  △ plea|sur|ing
pleat
  VERB
  △ pleats
  △ plea|ted
  △ pleat|ing

plea|ted
pleb
ple|beian
ple|bis|cite
plec|trum
pled
pledge
  VERB
  △ pled|ges
  △ pledged
  △ pled|ging

Pléiade, La
  French literary
  group
  △ Pleiades

Pleiades
  group of stars
  △ Pléiade, La

plein air
Pleio|cene
Pleis|to|cene
ple|nary
ple|ni|po|ten|ti|
  ary
  △ ple|ni|po|ten|
  ti|ar|ies
pleni|tude
plen|te|ous
plen|te|ously
plen|te|ous|ness
plen|ti|ful
plen|ti|fully
plenty
ple|on|asm
ple|on|as|tic
ple|on|as|tic|ally
pleth|ora
pleura
pleur|isy
plexus
  △ plexus *or*
  plex|uses

pli|abil|ity
pli|able
pli|ably
pli|ancy
pli|ant
pli|ers
plight
  VERB
△ plights
△ pligh|ted
△ plight|ing
plim|soll
Plim|soll line
plinth
Pliny
Plio|cene
plod
  VERB
△ plods
△ plod|ded
△ plod|ding
plod|der
ploidy
plonk
  VERB
△ plonks
△ plonked
△ plonk|ing
plop
  VERB
△ plops
△ plopped
△ plop|ping
plo|sive
plot
  VERB
△ plots
△ plot|ted
△ plot|ting
plot|ter
plough
  VERB
△ ploughs
△ ploughed

△ plough|ing
*Plough and the
Stars, The*
plough|man
△ plough|men
plough|share
plover
plow *see* plough
ploy
pluck
  VERB
△ plucks
△ plucked
△ pluck|ing
pluck|ily
plucki|ness
plucky
△ pluck|ier
△ plucki|est
plug
  VERB
△ plugs
△ plugged
△ plug|ging
plug|hole

> plum
> *sort of fruit;
> tree on which it
> grows; the best*
> ⚠plumb

plu|mage

> plumb
> *lead weight;
> straight;
> exactly; measure*
> △ plumbs
> △ plumbed
> △ plumb|ing
> ⚠plum

plum|bago
plumber
plumb|ing

plumb|line
plume
  VERB
△ plumes
△ plumed
△ plu|ming
plum|met
  VERB
△ plum|mets
△ plum|meted
△ plum|met|ing
plummy
△ plum|mier
△ plum|mi|est
plump
  VERB
△ plumps
△ plumped
△ plump|ing
  ADJ.
△ plump|per
△ plump|est
plumply
plump|ness
plu|mule
plumy
△ plu|mier
△ plu|mi|est
plun|der
  VERB
△ plun|ders
△ plun|dered
△ plun|der|ing
plun|derer
plunge
  VERB
△ plun|ges
△ plunged
△ plun|ging
plun|ger
plu|per|fect
plu|ral
plu|ral|ism
plu|ral|ist

plu|ral|is|tic
plu|ral|ity
△ plu|ral|it|ies
plus
  NOUN
△ pluses
plush
plushy
△ plush|ier
△ plushi|est
Plu|tarch
Pluto
plu|to|cracy
△ plu|to|cra|cies
plu|to|crat
plu|to|cratic
plu|tonic
plu|to|nium
ply
  NOUN
△ plies
  VERB
△ plies
△ plied
△ ply|ing
Ply|mouth
ply|wood
pneu|matic
pneu|mat|ic|ally
pneu|mo|nia
Po
po
poa
poach
△ poa|ches
△ poached
△ poach|ing
poa|cher
poach|ing
Po|ca|hon|tas

> poch|ade
> *sketch*
> ⚠pochard

poch|ard
sort of duck
⚠pochade

pock
pocket
  VERB
  △ pock|ets
  △ pock|eted
  △ pock|et|ing
pock|et|book
pock|et|ful
pock|mark
pock|marked
pod
  VERB
  △ pods
  △ pod|ded
  △ pod|ding
podgy
  △ pod|gier
  △ pod|gi|est
po|di|at|rist
po|di|atry
po|dium
  △ po|diums *or*
    podia
pod|sol
Poe
poem
poesy
poet
po|et|ess
  △ po|et|es|ses
po|etic
po|et|ical
po|et|ic|ally
poet laur|eate
  △ poets laur|eate
    or poet laur|
    eates
po|etry
po-faced
pogo

pog|rom
poign|ancy
poign|ant
poign|antly
poi|ki|lo|ther|
  mic
poin|set|tia
point
  VERB
  △ points
  △ poin|ted
  △ point|ing
point-blank
poin|ted
point|edly
point|ed|ness
poin|ter
Poin|til|lism
Poin|til|list
point|ing
point|less
point|lessly
point-to-point
poise
  VERB
  △ poi|ses
  △ poised
  △ pois|ing
poised
poi|son
  VERB
  △ poi|sons
  △ poi|soned
  △ poi|son|ing
poi|soner
poi|son|ous
poi|son|ously
Poit|iers
Poi|tou
poke
  △ pokes
  △ poked
  △ po|king
poke|berry

poker
poker-faced
poke|weed
po|ki|ness
poky
  △ po|kier
  △ po|ki|est
Po|land
Po|lan|ski
polar
po|lari|metry
Po|laris
po|lar|ity
  △ po|lar|it|ies
po|lar|iza|tion
po|lar|ize
  △ po|lar|izes
  △ po|lar|ized
  △ po|lar|izing
Po|lar|oid
pol|der
Pole
pole
pole|axe
  NOUN
  △ pole|axes
  VERB
  △ pole|axes
  △ pole|axed
  △ pole|ax|ing
pole|cat
po|lemic
po|lem|ic|ally
po|lemi|cist
po|lem|ics
po|lenta
pole-vaul|ter
po|lice
  VERB
  △ po|li|ces
  △ policed
  △ po|li|cing
po|lice|man
  △ po|lice|men

po|lice|woman
police|wo|men
pol|icy
  △ poli|cies
pol|icy-hol|der
polio
po|lio|my|el|itis
Po|lish
pol|ish
  VERB
  △ pol|ishes
  △ pol|ished
  △ pol|ish|ing
pol|isher
pol|it|buro
po|lite
  △ po|li|ter
  △ po|li|test
po|litely
po|lite|ness
poli|tic
  VERB
  △ poli|tics
  △ poli|ticked
  △ poli|tick|ing
po|lit|ical
po|lit|ic|ally
po|li|ti|cian
po|li|ti|ci|za|tion
po|li|ti|cize
  △ po|li|ti|ci|zes
  △ po|li|ti|cized
  △ po|li|ti|ci|zing
po|lit|ico
  △ po|li|ti|cos *or*
    po|li|ti|coes
pol|it|ics
pol|ity
  △ pol|it|ies
polka
  VERB
  △ pol|kas
  △ pol|kaed
  △ pol|ka|ing

poll
  VERB
  △ polls
  △ polled
  △ poll|ing
pol|lack
  △ pol|lack or
    pol|lacks
pol|lard
  VERB
  △ pol|lards
  △ pol|lar|ded
  △ pol|lard|ing
pol|len
pol|lin|ate
  △ pol|lin|ates
  △ pol|lin|ated
  △ pol|lin|ating
pol|lin|ation
pol|ling-booth
pol|ling-sta|tion
Pol|lock
poll|ster
pol|lu|tant
pol|lute
  △ pol|lutes
  △ pol|lu|ted
  △ pol|lu|ting
pol|lu|tion
Pol|lux
Polo
  explorer
polo
  game
po|lo|naise
po|lo|nium
po|lony
  △ po|lo|nies
Pol Pot
pol|ter|geist
pol|troon
poly
po|ly|am|ide
po|ly|and|rous

po|ly|an|dry
po|ly|an|thus
  △ po|ly|an|
    thuses
po|ly|ar|chy
po|ly|car|bon|ate
po|ly|cen|trism
po|ly|chro|matic
po|ly|chromy
po|ly|es|ter
po|ly|ethy|lene
po|ly|gam|ist
po|ly|gam|ous
po|ly|gam|ously
po|ly|gamy
po|ly|glot
po|ly|gon
po|ly|go|nal
po|ly|graph
po|ly|gyny
po|ly|hed|ral
po|ly|hed|ron
  △ po|ly|hed|rons
  or po|ly|hedra
po|ly|math
po|ly|mer
po|ly|meric
po|ly|mer|iza|
  tion
po|ly|mer|ize
  △ po|ly|mer|izes
  △ po|ly|mer|ized
  △ po|ly|mer|
    izing
po|ly|mor|phic
po|ly|morph|ism
po|ly|mor|phous
polyp
Po|ly|phe|mus
po|ly|phonic
po|ly|phony
po|ly|ploidy
po|ly|pous
po|ly|pro|pene

po|ly|pro|py|lene
po|lyp|tych
po|ly|sac|char|ide
po|ly|sty|rene
po|ly|syl|labic
po|ly|syl|lable
po|ly|syn|thetic
po|ly|tech|nic
po|ly|the|ism
po|ly|the|ist
po|ly|the|is|tic
poly|thene
po|ly|un|sat|ur|
  ated
po|ly|ur|eth|ane
po|ly|vi|nyl
pom
pom|ace
po|made
po|man|der
pome
pom|egran|ate
pom|elo
Pom|er|an|ian
pom|fret
pom|mel
  VERB
  △ pom|mels
  △ pom|melled
  △ pom|mel|ling
pommy
  △ pom|mies
pomp
Pom|pa|dour
Pomp and Cir|
  cum|stance
Pom|peii
Pom|pey
Pom|pi|dou
pom|pom
  ball of cut wool
  etc
pom-pom
  machine gun

pom|pos|ity
pom|pous
pom|pously
ponce
  VERB
  △ pon|ces
  △ ponced
  △ pon|cing
pon|cho
pond
pon|der
  △ pon|ders
  △ pon|dered
  △ pon|der|ing
pon|der|ous
pon|der|ously
pon|der|ous|ness
pong
  VERB
  △ pongs
  △ ponged
  △ pong|ing
pongy
  △ pong|ier
  △ pongi|est
pon|iard
pons
  △ pon|tes
Pon|te|fract
Ponte Vec|chio
pon|tiff
pon|ti|fi|cal
pon|ti|fi|cals
pon|ti|fi|cate
  △ pon|ti|fi|cates
  △ pon|ti|fi|ca|ted
  △ pon|ti|fi|ca|
    ting
pon|toon
pony
  △ po|nies
po|ny|tail
pony-trek|king
poo|dle

poof
pooh
pooh-pooh
△ pooh-poohs
△ pooh-poohed
△ pooh-pooh¦
ing
pool
VERB
△ pools
△ pooled
△ pool¦ing
Poole
poop
VERB
△ poops
△ pooped
△ poop¦ing
poo¦per

poor
lacking money;
not very good
△ poorer
△ poor|est
⚠ pore
⚠ pour

poor|house
Poor Laws
poorly
poor|ness
pop
VERB
△ pops
△ popped
△ pop¦ping
pop|corn
Pope
pope
po¦pery
pop-eyed
pop¦gun
pop¦in¦jay
po¦pish

pop¦lar
pop¦lin
pop¦pa¦dum
pop¦per
pop¦pet
pop¦ping-crease
poppy
△ pop¦pies
pop¦py¦cock
popsy
△ pop¦sies
popu¦lace
popu¦lar
popu¦lar¦ity
popu¦lar¦iza¦tion
popu¦lar¦ize
△ popu¦lar¦izes
△ popu¦lar¦ized
△ popu¦lar¦izing
popu¦larly
popu¦late
△ popu¦lates
△ popu¦la¦ted
△ popu¦la¦ting
popu¦la¦tion
popu¦lism
popu¦list
popu¦lous
pop-up
por¦beagle
por¦ce¦lain
porch
△ por¦ches
por¦cine
por¦cu¦pine

pore
small opening in
skin etc; study
closely
VERB
△ pores
△ pored
△ por¦ing

⚠ poor
⚠ pour

Porgy and Bess
pork
por¦ker
porky
△ por¦kier
△ por¦ki¦est
porn
porno
por¦nog¦ra¦pher
por¦no¦gra¦phic
por¦no¦graph¦ic¦
ally
por¦nog¦ra¦phy
por¦os¦ity
por¦ous
por¦phy¦ritic
por¦phyry
por¦poise
por¦ridge
por¦rin¦ger
Por¦sche
port
VERB
△ ports
△ por¦ted
△ port¦ing
por¦ta¦bil¦ity
port¦able
port¦age
VERB
△ port¦ages
△ port¦aged
△ port¦aging
por¦tal
Port-au-Prince
port¦cul¦lis
por¦tend
△ por¦tends
△ por¦ten¦ded
△ por¦tend¦ing
por¦tent

por¦ten¦tous
Por¦ter
por¦ter
por¦ter¦house
port¦fo¦lio
port¦hole
por¦tico
△ por¦ti¦cos *or*
por¦ti¦coes
por¦tion
VERB
△ por¦tions
△ por¦tioned
△ por¦tion¦ing
Por¦tis¦head
Port¦land
Port Louis
portly
△ port¦lier
△ port¦li¦est
port¦man¦teau
△ port¦man¦
teaus *or* port¦
man¦teaux
Port Moresby
Port Natal *see*
Durban
Port of Spain
Por¦ton Down
Porto Novo
por¦trait
Por¦trait of a
Lady, The
Por¦trait of the
Ar¦tist as a
Young Man,
A
por¦trai¦ture
por¦tray
△ por¦trays
△ por¦trayed
△ por¦tray¦ing
por¦trayal
Por¦tree

Port Said
Port San Car|
  los
Ports|mouth
Por|tu|gal
Por|tu|guese
Por|tu|guese
  man-of-war
Port-Vila
pose
  VERB
  △ poses
  △ posed
  △ po|sing
Po|sei|don

poser
difficult problem
⚠poseur

pos|eur
insincere person
⚠poser

posh
  VERB
  △ poshes
  △ poshed
  △ posh|ing
  ADJ.
  △ posher
  △ posh|est
posit
  △ pos|its
  △ pos|ited
  △ pos|it|ing
po|si|tion
  VERB
  △ po|si|tions
  △ po|si|tioned
  △ po|si|tion|ing
po|si|tional
pos|it|ive
pos|it|ively
pos|it|ive|ness

pos|it|iv|ism
pos|it|iv|ist
pos|it|ron
poss
posse
pos|sess
  △ pos|ses|ses
  △ pos|sessed
  △ pos|ses|sing
pos|sessed
pos|ses|sion
pos|ses|sive
pos|ses|sively
pos|ses|sive|ness
pos|ses|sor
pos|si|bil|ity
  △ pos|si|bil|it|ies
poss|ible
poss|ibly
pos|sum
post
  VERB
  △ posts
  △ pos|ted
  △ post|ing
post|age
pos|tal
post|bag
post|box
post|card
post|code
post|date
  △ post|dates
  △ post|da|ted
  △ post|da|ting
pos|ter
poste res|tante
pos|ter|ior
pos|ter|ity
pos|tern
post-free
post|gra|du|ate
post|haste
post|house

post|hu|mous
post|hu|mously
pos|til|ion
Post|im|pres|
  sion|ism
post|man
post|mark
post|mas|ter
Post|mas|ter
  Gen|eral
  △ Post|mas|ters
  Gen|eral
post|mer|id|ian
post me|rid|iem
post|mis|tress
  △ post|mis|tres|
  ses
Post-Mod|ern|
  ism
post-mor|tem
post|na|tal
post-oper|at|ive
post-paid
post|par|tum
post|pone
  △ post|pones
  △ post|poned
  △ post|po|ning
post|pone|ment
post|pran|dial
post-pro|duc|
  tion
post|script
post-trau|matic
pos|tu|lancy
pos|tu|lant
pos|tu|late
  △ pos|tu|lates
  △ pos|tu|la|ted
  △ pos|tu|la|ting
pos|tu|la|tion
pos|tural
pos|ture

  VERB
  △ pos|tures
  △ pos|tured
  △ pos|tur|ing
pos|turer
post|vi|ral
post|war
post|wo|man
  △ post|wo|men
posy
  △ po|sies
pot
  VERB
  △ pots
  △ pot|ted
  △ pot|ting
po|table
Pot|ala
pot|ash
po|tas|sium
po|ta|tion
po|tato
pot-bel|lied
pot-belly
  △ pot-bel|lies
pot|boiler
pot|bound
po|teen
po|tency
  △ po|ten|cies
po|tent
po|ten|tate
po|ten|tial
po|ten|tially
po|ten|tilla
po|ten|ti|om|eter
pot|herb
pot|hole
pot|ho|ler
pot|ho|ling
pot|hook
po|tion
pot|pourri
pot|sherd

pot-shot
Pot|ter
pot|ter
  VERB
  △ pot|ters
  △ pot|tered
  △ pot|ter|ing
Pot|ter|ies, the
pot|tery
  △ pot|ter|ies
pot|ti|ness
pot|ting-shed
potty
  NOUN
  △ pot|ties
  ADJ.
  △ pot|tier
  △ pot|ti|est
pouch
  △ pou|ches
pouffe
Pou|lenc
poul|terer
poul|tice
poul|try
pounce
  VERB
  △ poun|ces
  △ pounced
  △ poun|cing
Pound
pound
  VERB
  △ pounds
  △ poun|ded
  △ pound|ing
pound|age

> pour
> *flow, or make to*
> *flow, downwards*
> △ pours
> △ poured
> △ pour|ing

> ⚠ poor
> ⚠ pore

pour|boire
pourer
Pous|sin
pout
  VERB
  △ pouts
  △ pou|ted
  △ pout|ing
pou|ter
pov|erty
pov|erty-
  stricken
pow|der
  VERB
  △ pow|ders
  △ pow|dered
  △ pow|der|ing
pow|dery
Pow|ell
power
  VERB
  △ powers
  △ powered
  △ power|ing
Power and the
Glory, The
power-assis|ted
power|boat
power|ful
power|fully
power|house
power|less
pow|wow
  VERB
  △ pow|wows
  △ pow|wowed
  △ pow|wow|ing
Powys
pox
prac|ti|ca|bil|ity

> prac|tic|able
> *able to be done*
> *or used*
> ⚠ practical

prac|tic|ably

> prac|ti|cal
> *sensible;*
> *efficient; not*
> *theoretical*
> ⚠ practicable

prac|ti|cal|ity
  △ prac|ti|cal|it|ies
prac|ti|cally

> prac|tice
> NOUN
> ⚠ practise

> prac|tise
> VERB
> △ prac|ti|ses
> △ prac|tised
> △ prac|tis|ing
> ⚠ practice

prac|tised
prac|ti|tioner
Prado
prae|tor
prae|tor|ian
Prae|tor|ius
prag|matic
prag|ma|tism
prag|ma|tist
Prague
prahu *see* proa
Praia
prairie
praise
  VERB
  △ prai|ses
  △ praised
  △ prais|ing

praise|wor|thily
praise|wor|thi|
  ness
praise|wor|thy
pra|line
pram
prance
  △ pran|ces
  △ pranced
  △ pran|cing
prang
  VERB
  △ prangs
  △ pranged
  △ prang|ing
prank
prank|ster
pra|seo|dym|ium
prat
prate
  △ prates
  △ pra|ted
  △ pra|ting
prat|tle
  VERB
  △ prat|tles
  △ prat|tled
  △ prat|tling
prat|tler
prau *see* proa
prawn

> pray
> *address God or*
> *a god; entreat;*
> *used in ironical*
> *request*
> VERB
> △ prays
> △ prayed
> △ pray|ing
> ⚠ prey

prayer
pray|ing

preach
△ prea|ches
△ preached
△ preach|ing
pre|amble
pre|ar|range
△ pre|ar|ran|ges
△ pre|ar|ranged
△ pre|ar|ran|
  ging
pre|ar|range|
  ment
preb|end
preb|en|dal
preb|end|ary
△ preb|end|ar|
  ies
Pre|cam|brian
pre|can|cer|ous
pre|cari|ous
pre|cari|ously
pre|cari|ous|ness
pre|cast
pre|cau|tion
pre|cau|tion|ary
pre|cede
  go before
△ pre|cedes
△ pre|ceded
△ pre|ceding
pre|ced|ence
pre|ced|ent
pre|cen|tor
pre|cept
pre|ces|sion
pre|ces|sional
pre|cinct
pre|ci|os|ity
pre|cious
pre|ciously
pre|cious|ness
pre|ci|pice
pre|ci|pi|tate

VERB
△ pre|ci|pi|tates
△ pre|ci|pi|ta|ted
△ pre|ci|pi|ta|ting
pre|ci|pi|tately
pre|ci|pi|ta|tion
pre|ci|pi|tous
pré|cis
NOUN
sing. and pl.
VERB
△ pré|cises
△ pré|cised
△ pré|cis|ing
pre|cise
pre|cisely
pre|cise|ness
pre|ci|sion
pre|clude
△ pre|cludes
△ pre|clu|ded
△ pre|clu|ding
pre|clu|sion
pre|co|cious
pre|co|ciously
pre|co|city
pre|cog|ni|tion
pre|cog|ni|tive
pre|co|lum|bian
pre|con|ceive
△ pre|con|ceives
△ pre|con|ceived
△ pre|con|ceiv|
  ing
pre|con|cep|tion
pre|con|di|tion
pre|cur|sor
pre|da|cious
pre-date
△ pre-dates
△ pre-dated
△ pre-dating
pred|ator
pred|at|ori|ness

pred|at|ory
pre|de|cease
△ pre|de|cea|ses
△ pre|de|ceased
△ pre|de|ceas|
  ing
pre|de|ces|sor
pre|della
pre|des|ti|na|tion
pre|des|tine
△ pre|des|tines
△ pre|des|tined
△ pre|des|tin|ing
pre|de|ter|min|
  ation
pre|de|ter|mine
△ pre|de|ter|
  mines
△ pre|de|ter|
  mined
△ pre|de|ter|
  min|ing
pre|di|ca|ment
pre|di|cate
VERB
△ pre|di|cates
△ pre|di|ca|ted
△ pre|di|ca|ting
pre|di|ca|tion
pre|di|ca|tive
pre|di|ca|tively
pre|dict
△ pre|dicts
△ pre|dic|ted
△ pre|dict|ing
pre|dict|abil|ity
pre|dict|able
pre|dict|ably
pre|dic|tion
pre|di|lec|tion
pre|dis|pose
△ pre|dis|po|ses
△ pre|dis|posed
△ pre|dis|po|sing

pre|dis|po|si|tion
pre|dom|in|ance
pre|dom|in|ant
pre|dom|in|antly
pre|dom|in|ate
△ pre|dom|in|
  ates
△ pre|dom|in|
  ated
△ pre|dom|in|
  ating
pre-emin|ence
pre-emin|ent
pre-emin|ently
pre-empt
△ pre-empts
△ pre-emp|ted
△ pre-empt|ing
pre-emp|tion
pre-emp|tive
preen
△ preens
△ preened
△ preen|ing
pre|fab
pre|fab|ri|cate
△ pre|fab|ri|cates
△ pre|fab|ri|ca|
  ted
△ pre|fab|ri|ca|
  ting
pre|fab|ri|ca|tion
pre|face
VERB
△ pre|fa|ces
△ pre|faced
△ pre|fa|cing
pre|fa|tory
pre|fect
pre|fec|ture
pre|fer
△ pre|fers
△ pre|ferred
△ pre|fer|ring

pref|er|able
pref|er|ably
pref|er|ence
pref|er|en|tial
pre|fer|ment
pre|fi|gur|ation
pre|fig|ure
△ pre|fig|ures
△ pre|fig|ured
△ pre|fig|ur|ing
pre|fix
NOUN
△ pre|fixes
VERB
△ pre|fixes
△ pre|fixed
△ pre|fix|ing
pre|fron|tal
preg|nancy
△ preg|nan|cies
preg|nant
pre|heat
△ pre|heats
△ pre|hea|ted
△ pre|heat|ing
pre|hen|sile
pre|his|toric
pre|his|tor|ic|ally
pre|his|tory
pre|judge
△ pre|jud|ges
△ pre|judged
△ pre|jud|ging
pre|judge|ment
pre|ju|dice
VERB
△ pre|ju|di|ces
△ pre|ju|diced
△ pre|ju|di|cing
pre|ju|di|cial
prel|acy
△ prel|acies
prel|ate
pre|lim|in|ary

NOUN
△ pre|lim|in|ar|ies
pre|lims
Pre|lude, The
pre|lude
Pré|lude à l'après-midi d'un faune
pre|mar|ital
pre|ma|ture
pre|ma|turely
pre|med
pre|me|di|ca|tion
pre|medi|tate
△ pre|medi|tates
△ pre|medi|ta|ted
△ pre|medi|ta|ting
pre|men|strual

premier
prime minister; leading
⚠ première

pre|mi|ère
opening performance; give this
VERB
△ pre|mi|ères
△ pre|mi|èred
△ pre|mi|èr|ing
⚠ premier

prem|ier|ship
Prem|in|ger

prem|ises
a building and its grounds; in a legal document, preliminary

matter or items previously mentioned
⚠ premiss

prem|iss
preliminary assumption in logic etc
△ prem|is|ses
⚠ premises

pre|mium
pre|mo|lar
pre|mon|ition
Pre|mon|stra|ten|sian
pre|na|tal
pre|oc|cu|pa|tion
pre|oc|cu|pied
pre|oc|cupy
△ pre|oc|cu|pies
△ pre|oc|cu|pied
△ pre|oc|cu|py|ing
pre|or|dain
△ pre|or|dains
△ pre|or|dained
△ pre|or|dain|ing
prep
pre|pack
△ pre|packs
△ pre|packed
△ pre|pack|ing
pre|par|ation
pre|par|at|ory
pre|pare
△ pre|pares
△ pre|pared
△ pre|par|ing
pre|pared
pre|pay
△ pre|pays

△ pre|paid
△ pre|pay|ing
pre|pay|ment
pre|pon|der|ance
pre|pon|der|ant
pre|pon|der|ate
△ pre|pon|der|ates
△ pre|pon|der|ated
△ pre|pon|der|ating
pre|po|si|tion
pre|po|si|tional
pre|pos|sess
△ pre|pos|ses|ses
△ pre|pos|sessed
△ pre|pos|sess|ing
pre|pos|sess|ing
pre|pos|ter|ous
pre|pos|ter|ously
pre|puce
pre|quel
Pre-Raph|ael|ite
pre|re|cord
△ pre|re|cords
△ pre|re|cor|ded
△ pre|re|cord|ing
pre|re|quis|ite
pre|rog|ative
pres|age
NOUN
pres|age *or* pre|sage
VERB
△ pres|ages *or* pre|sages
△ pres|aged *or* pre|sages
△ pres|aging *or* pre|sa|ging
according to pronunciation

pres|by|opia
pres|by|ter
pres|by|ter|ian
pres|by|ter|ian|
  ism
pres|by|tery
  pres|by|ter|ies
pre-school
pres|ci|ence
pres|ci|ent
pre|scribe
  △ pre|scribes
  △ pre|scribed
  △ pre|scri|bing
pre|script
pre|scrip|tion
pre|scrip|tive
pre|scrip|tiv|ism
pres|ence
pres|ent
  NOUN
  ADJ.
pre|sent
  VERB
  △ pre|sents
  △ pre|sen|ted
  △ pre|sent|ing
pre|sent|ab|il|ity
pre|sent|able
pre|sent|ably
pre|sen|ta|tion
pres|ent-day
pre|sen|ter
pre|sen|ti|ment
pres|ently
pre|ser|va|tion
pre|ser|va|tive
pre|serve
  △ pre|serves
  △ pre|served
  △ pre|ser|ving
pre|ser|ver
pre|set
  △ pre|sets

△ pre|set
△ pre|set|ting
pre|side
  △ pre|sides
  △ pre|si|ded
  △ pre|si|ding
presi|dency
  △ presi|den|cies
presi|dent
presi|den|tial
pres|id|ium
  △ pres|id|iums
  or pres|idia
Pres|ley
Pre|so|cratic
press
  NOUN
  △ pres|ses
  VERB
  △ pres|ses
  △ pressed
  △ press|ing
pressed
press|gang
  VERB
  △ press|gangs
  △ press|ganged
  △ press|gang|ing
press|ing
press|man
  △ press|men
press-up
pres|sure
  VERB
  △ pres|sures
  △ pres|sured
  △ pres|sur|ing
pres|sur|ize
  △ pres|sur|izes
  △ pres|sur|ized
  △ pres|sur|izing
press|wo|man
  △ press|wo|men
Pres|ter John

pres|ti|di|gi|ta|
  tion
pres|ti|di|gi|ta|
  tor
pres|tige
pres|ti|gious
presto
Pres|ton
Pres|ton|pans
pre-stressed
Prest|wick
pre|sum|ably
pre|sume
  △ pre|sumes
  △ pre|sumed
  △ pre|sum|ing
pre|sump|tion
pre|sump|tive
pre|sump|tu|ous
pre|sump|tu|
  ously
pre|sup|pose
  △ pre|sup|po|ses
  △ pre|sup|posed
  △ pre|sup|po|
  sing
pre|sup|pos|ition
pre|tence
pre|tend
  △ pre|tends
  △ pre|ten|ded
  △ pre|tend|ing
pre|ten|der
pre|ten|sion
pre|ten|tious
pre|ten|tiously
pre|ten|tious|
  ness
pret|er|ite
pre|ter|nat|ural
pre|ter|nat|ur|
  ally
pre|text
Pre|toria

Pre|tor|ius
pret|ti|fi|ca|tion
pret|tify
  △ pret|ti|fies
  △ pret|ti|fied
  △ pret|ti|fy|ing
pret|tily
pret|ti|ness
pretty
  △ pret|tier
  △ pret|ti|est
pretty-pretty
pret|zel
pre|vail
  △ pre|vails
  △ pre|vailed
  △ pre|vail|ing
pre|val|ence
pre|val|ent
pre|val|ently
pre|va|ri|cate
  △ pre|va|ri|cates
  △ pre|va|ri|ca|ted
  △ pre|va|ri|ca|
  ting
pre|va|ri|ca|tion
pre|va|ri|ca|tor
pre|vent
  △ pre|vents
  △ pre|ven|ted
  △ pre|vent|ing
pre|vent|able
pre|ven|ta|tive
pre|ven|tion
pre|vent|ive
pre|view
  VERB
  △ pre|views
  △ pre|viewed
  △ pre|view|ing
Previn
pre|vi|ous
pre|vi|ously
Pré|vost

pre-war

> **prey**
> *victim; seize*
> *upon; exploit*
> VERB
> △ preys
> △ preyed
> △ prey|ing
> ⚠pray

prial
Priam
pri|ap|ism
price
  VERB
△ pri|ces
△ priced
△ pri|cing
price-fix|ing
price|less
pri|cey
△ pri|cier
△ pri|ci|est
prick
  VERB
△ pricks
△ pricked
△ prick|ing
prickle
  VERB
△ prickles
△ prickled
△ prick|ling
prick|li|ness
prickly
△ prick|lier
△ prick|li|est
pride
  VERB
△ prides
△ pri|ded
△ pri|ding
Pride and Pre|
ju|dice

priest
priest|ess
priest|es|ses
priest|hood
Priest|ley
priestly
△ priest|lier
△ priest|li|est
prig
prig|gish
prig|gishly
prig|gish|ness
prim
△ prim|mer
△ prim|mest
prima bal|ler|ina
pri|macy
△ pri|ma|cies
prima donna
primaeval *see*
  primeval
prima facie
pri|mal
pri|mar|ily
pri|mary
△ pri|mar|ies
pri|mate
Pri|ma|vera
  (Spring)
prime
  VERB
△ primes
△ primed
△ pri|ming
Prime of Miss
Jean Brodie,
The
pri|mer
pri|meval
pri|mi|grav|ida
prim|it|ive
prim|it|ively
prim|it|ive|ness
prim|it|iv|ism

primly
prim|ness
pri|mo|geni|ture
pri|mor|dial
pri|mor|di|ally
primp
△ primps
△ primped
△ primp|ing
Prim|rose
prim|rose
prim|ula
△ prim|ulae *or*
  prim|ulas
Pri|mus
△ Pri|muses
prince
prince|dom
princely
prin|cess
△ prin|ces|ses
Prince|ton

> **prin|ci|pal**
> *chief*
> ⚠principle

prin|ci|pal|ity
prin|ci|pally

> **prin|ciple**
> *rule*
> ⚠principal

prin|cipled
prink
△ prinks
△ prinked
△ prink|ing
print
△ prints
△ prin|ted
△ print|ing
print|able
prin|ter
print|ing

print|ing-press
△ print|ing-pres|
  ses
print|out
prior
pri|or|ess
△ pri|or|es|ses
pri|or|it|ize
△ pri|or|it|izes
△ pri|or|it|ized
△ pri|or|it|izing
pri|or|ity
△ pri|or|it|ies
pri|ory
△ pri|or|ies
Pris|cilla

> **prise**
> *lever (open etc)*
> △ pri|ses
> △ prised
> △ pri|sing
> ⚠prize

prism
pris|matic
pri|son
pris|oner
pris|sily
pris|si|ness
prissy
△ pris|sier
△ pris|si|est
pris|tine
pri|vacy
pri|vate
pri|va|teer
Pri|vate Lives
pri|vately
pri|va|tion
pri|vat|iza|tion
pri|vat|ize
△ pri|vat|izes
△ pri|vat|ized
△ pri|vat|izing

pri|vet
pri|vi|lege
pri|vi|leged
priv|ily
privy
  NOUN
  △ priv|ies
Prix de Rome
Prix Gon|court

prize
  reward; thing
  captured; best;
  value highly
  VERB
  △ pri|zes
  △ prized
  △ pri|zing
  ⚠prise

prize
  lever open etc see
  prise
prize-figh|ter
prize-fight|ing
pro
proa
pro|act|ive
pro-am
prob|ab|il|ity
prob|able
prob|ably
pro|band
pro|bate
pro|ba|tion
pro|ba|tion|ary
pro|ba|tioner
probe
  VERB
  △ probes
  △ probed
  △ pro|bing
pro|bity
prob|lem
prob|lem|atic

prob|lem|at|ical
prob|lem|at|ic|
  ally
pro|bos|cis
procaryote *see*
  prokaryote
pro|ce|dural
pro|ce|dur|ally
pro|ce|dure

pro|ceed
  go forward
  △ pro|ceeds
  △ pro|cee|ded
  △ pro|ceed|ing
  ⚠precede

pro|ceed|ing
pro|ceeds
pro|cess
  NOUN
  △ pro|ces|ses
  VERB
  △ pro|ces|ses
  △ pro|cessed
  △ pro|cess|ing
pro|ces|sion
pro|ces|sor
pro-choice
pro|claim
  △ pro|claims
  △ pro|claimed
  △ pro|claim|ing
pro|cla|ma|tion
pro|cliv|ity
  △ pro|cliv|it|ies
pro|cras|ti|nate
  △ pro|cras|ti|
  nates
  △ pro|cras|ti|na|
  ted
  △ pro|cras|ti|na|
  ting
pro|cras|ti|na|
  tion

pro|cras|ti|na|tor
proc|re|ate
  △ proc|re|ates
  △ proc|re|ated
  △ proc|re|ating
proc|re|ation
Pro|crus|tes
proc|tor
pro|cur|acy
  △ pro|cur|acies
pro|cur|ator
pro|cur|ator|ship
pro|cure
  △ pro|cures
  △ pro|cured
  △ pro|cur|ing
pro|cure|ment
pro|curer
pro|cur|ess
prod
  VERB
  △ prods
  △ prod|ded
  △ prod|ding
prod|igal
pro|di|gal|ity
prod|ig|ally
pro|di|gious
pro|di|giously
prod|igy
  △ prod|igies
pro|duce
  VERB
  △ pro|du|ces
  △ pro|duced
  △ pro|du|cing
pro|du|cer
pro|du|cible
prod|uct
pro|duc|tion
pro|duc|tive
pro|duc|tively
pro|duc|tiv|ity
proem

prof
pro|fan|ation
pro|fane
  VERB
  △ pro|fanes
  △ pro|faned
  △ pro|fa|ning
pro|fanely
pro|fan|ity
pro|fess
  △ pro|fes|ses
  △ pro|fessed
  △ pro|fess|ing
pro|fessed
pro|fes|sedly
pro|fes|sion
pro|fes|sional
pro|fes|sion|ally
pro|fes|sor
pro|fes|sor|ial
pro|fes|sor|ship
prof|fer
  △ prof|fers
  △ prof|fered
  △ prof|fer|ing
pro|fi|ciency
pro|fi|cient
pro|fi|ciently
pro|file

profit
  excess of income
  over expenses;
  benefit
  VERB
  △ prof|its
  △ prof|ited
  △ prof|it|ing
  ⚠prophet

prof|it|ab|il|ity
prof|it|able
prof|it|ably
pro|fit|eer

VERB
△ pro|fit|eers
△ pro|fit|eered
△ pro|fit|eer|ing
pro|fit|er|ole
pro|fit-shar|ing
prof|li|gacy
prof|li|gate
prof|li|gately
pro forma
pro|found
pro|foundly
Pro|fumo
pro|fund|ity
△ pro|fund|it|ies
pro|fuse
pro|fusely
pro|fu|sion
pro|gen|itor
pro|geny
pro|ges|ter|one
prog|no|sis
△ prog|no|ses
prog|nos|ti|cate
△ prog|nos|ti|cates
△ prog|nos|ti|ca|ted
△ prog|nos|ti|ca|ting
prog|nos|ti|ca|tion
prog|nos|ti|ca|tor

program
set of
instructions for
computer; write
this; instruct
computer by it;
schedule
electronic process
by means of a
program

VERB
△ pro|grams
△ pro|grammed
△ pro|gram|ming
A programme

pro|gram|mable

pro|gramme
plan of
performance etc;
the performance
etc itself;
arrange the
items in a
performance
VERB
△ pro|grammes
△ pro|grammed
△ pro|gram|ming
A program

pro|gram|mer
pro|gress
VERB
△ pro|gres|ses
△ pro|gressed
△ pro|gress|ing
pro|gres|sion
pro|gres|sive
pro|gres|sively
pro|hibit
△ pro|hib|its
△ pro|hib|ited
△ pro|hib|it|ing
Pro|hi|bi|tion
pro|hi|bi|tion
pro|hi|bi|tion|ist
pro|hib|it|ive
pro|hib|it|ory
pro|ject
VERB
△ pro|jects

△ pro|jec|ted
△ pro|ject|ing
pro|jec|tile
pro|jec|tion
pro|jec|tion|ist
pro|jec|tor
pro|ka|ry|ote
Pro|kof|iev
pro|lac|tin
pro|lapse
prole
pro|let|ar|ian
pro|let|ar|iat
pro-life
pro|lif|er|ate
△ pro|lif|er|ates
△ pro|lif|er|ated
△ pro|lif|er|ating
pro|lif|er|ation
pro|lific
pro|lif|ic|ally
pro|line
pro|lix
pro|lix|ity
△ pro|lix|it|ies
PRO|LOG
pro|logue
pro|long
△ pro|longs
△ pro|longed
△ pro|long|ing
pro|lon|ga|tion
PROM
prom
prom|en|ade
VERB
△ prom|en|ades
△ prom|en|aded
△ prom|en|ading
prom|en|ader
Pro|me|theus
pro|meth|ium
prom|in|ence
prom|in|ent

prom|in|ently
pro|mis|cu|ity
pro|mis|cu|ous
pro|mis|cu|ously
prom|ise
△ prom|ises
△ prom|ised
△ prom|is|ing
prom|is|ing
prom|is|ingly
prom|is|sory
prom|on|tory
△ prom|on|tor|ies
pro|mote
△ pro|motes
△ pro|mo|ted
△ pro|mo|ting
pro|mo|ter
pro|mo|tion
pro|mo|tional
prompt
VERB
△ prompts
△ promp|ted
△ prompt|ing
ADJ.
△ promp|ter
△ prompt|est
promp|ter
promp|ti|tude
promptly
prompt|ness
pro|mul|gate
△ pro|mul|gates
△ pro|mul|ga|ted
△ pro|mul|ga|ting
pro|mul|ga|tion
pro|mul|ga|tor
prone
prone|ness
prong
prong|buck

pronged
prong|horn
pronk|ing
pro|nom|inal
pro|nom|in|ally
pro|noun
pro|nounce
△ pro|noun|ces
△ pro|nounced
△ pro|noun|cing
pro|nounce|able
pro|nounced
pro|noun|cedly
pro|nounce|
   ment
pronto
pro|nun|ci|ation
proof
   VERB
△ proofs
△ proofed
△ proof|ing
proof-read
△ proof-reads
△ proof-read
△ proof-read|ing
proof-rea|der
prop
   VERB
△ props
△ propped
△ prop|ping
pro|pa|ganda
pro|pa|gand|ist
pro|pa|gand|ize
△ pro|pa|gand|
   izes
△ pro|pa|gand|
   ized
△ pro|pa|gand|
   izing
pro|pa|gate
△ pro|pa|gates
△ pro|pa|ga|ted

△ pro|pa|ga|ting
pro|pa|ga|tion
pro|pa|ga|tor
pro|pane
pro|pel
△ pro|pels
△ pro|pelled
△ pro|pel|ling

pro|pel|lant
   NOUN
   ⚠ propellent

pro|pel|lent
   ADJ.
   ⚠ propellant

pro|pel|ler
pro|pel|ling-pen|
   cil
pro|pen|sity
△ pro|pen|si|ties
proper
prop|erly
prop|er|tied
Pro|per|tius
prop|erty
△ prop|er|ties
prop|fan
pro|phase

proph|ecy
   NOUN
   △ proph|ecies
   ⚠ prophesy

proph|esy
   VERB
   △ proph|esies
   △ proph|esied
   △ proph|esying
   ⚠ prophecy

prophet
   predictor of

future events;
spokesman
   NOUN
   △ prophets
   ⚠ profit

proph|et|ess
pro|phetic
pro|phet|ic|ally
pro|phy|lac|tic
pro|phy|laxis
pro|pin|quity
pro|pi|ti|able
pro|pi|ti|ate
△ pro|pi|ti|ates
△ pro|pi|ti|ated
△ pro|pi|ti|ating
pro|pi|ti|ation
pro|pi|ti|ator
pro|pi|ti|atory
pro|pi|tious
pro|pi|tiously
pro|po|nent
pro|por|tion
   VERB
△ pro|por|tions
△ pro|por|tioned
△ pro|por|tion|
   ing
pro|por|tional
pro|por|tion|ally
pro|por|tion|ate
pro|por|tion|ately
pro|po|sal
pro|pose
△ pro|po|ses
△ pro|posed
△ pro|po|sing
pro|po|ser
pro|po|si|tion
   VERB
△ pro|po|si|tions
△ pro|po|si|
   tioned

△ pro|po|si|tion|
   ing
pro|pound
△ pro|pounds
△ pro|poun|ded
△ pro|pound|ing
prop|ran|olol
pro|pri|et|ary
pro|pri|etor
pro|pri|et|or|ial
pro|pri|et|ress
△ pro|pri|et|res|ses
pro|pri|ety
△ pro|pri|et|ies
prop|rio|cep|tor
pro|pul|sion
pro|pul|sive
pro|py|laeum
△ pro|py|laea
pro|py|lon
△ pro|pyla
pro rata
pro|ro|ga|tion
pro|rogue
△ pro|rogues
△ pro|rogued
△ pro|roguing
pro|saic
pro|sa|ic|ally
pros|cen|ium
△ pros|ceni|ums
△ pros|cenia
pros|ciutto
pros|cribe
△ pros|cribes
△ pros|cribed
△ pros|cri|bing
pros|crip|tion
pros|crip|tive
prose
pro|se|cute
△ pro|se|cutes
△ pro|se|cuted
△ pro|se|cu|ting

pro|se|cu|tion
pro|se|cu|tor
pros|elyte
pros|elyt|ism
pros|elyt|ize
△ pros|elyt|izes
△ pros|elyt|ized
△ pros|elyt|izing
Pros|er|pine
pros|odic
pros|od|ics
pros|od|ist
pros|ody
pros|pect
  VERB
△ pros|pects
△ pros|pec|ted
△ pros|pect|ing
pros|pect|ive
pros|pec|tor
pros|pec|tus
△ pros|pec|tuses
pros|per
△ pros|pers
△ pros|pered
△ pros|per|ing
pros|per|ity
pros|per|ous
pros|per|ously
Prost
pros|ta|glan|din

pros|tate
  gland
   ⚠ prostrate

pros|thesis
△ pros|theses
pros|ti|tute
  VERB
△ pros|ti|tutes
△ pros|ti|tu|ted
△ pros|ti|tu|ting
pros|ti|tu|tion

pros|trate
  lying flat;
  exhausted; throw
  oneself down
  flat; exhaust
  VERB
△ pros|trates
△ pros|tra|ted
△ pros|tra|ting
  ⚠ prostate

pros|tra|tion
prosy
△ pro|sier
△ pro|si|est
pro|tac|tin|ium
pro|tag|on|ist
pro|tea
pro|tean
pro|te|ase
pro|tect
△ pro|tects
△ pro|tec|ted
△ pro|tect|ing
pro|tec|tion
pro|tec|tion|ism
pro|tec|tion|ist
pro|tect|ive
pro|tect|ively
pro|tect|ive|ness
pro|tec|tor
Pro|tec|tor|ate
  system of
  government in
  England under
  O. and R. Crom-
  well, 1653–9
pro|tec|tor|ate
  office or rule of
  a protector;
  protectorship
  over weak or
  backward
  country

pro|tect|ress

pro|tégé
  man under
  guidance etc
  ⚠ protégée

pro|té|gée
  woman under
  guidance etc
  ⚠ protégé

pro|tein
pro tem
Pro|tero|zoic
pro|test
  VERB
△ pro|tests
△ pro|tes|ted
△ pro|test|ing
Prot|es|tant
Pro|test|ant|ism
pro|tes|ta|tion
pro|tes|ter
pro|throm|bin
Pro|tista
pro|to|col
Pro|to|cols of the
  El|ders of Zion
Proto-Indo-
  Euro|pean
pro|ton
pro|to|plasm
pro|to|type
Pro|to|zoa

pro|to|zoan
  NOUN
  ADJ.
  ⚠ protozoon

pro|to|zoon
  NOUN
  ⚠ protozoan

pro|tract

△ pro|tracts
△ pro|trac|ted
△ pro|tract|ing
pro|trac|ted
pro|trac|tor
pro|trude
△ pro|trudes
△ pro|tru|ded
△ pro|tru|ding
pro|tru|sion
pro|tru|sive
pro|tu|ber|ance
pro|tu|ber|ant
proud
△ prou|der
△ proud|est
Proud|hon
proudly
Proust
prov|able
prove
△ proves
△ proved
△ prov|ing
prov|en|ance
Pro|ven|çal
Pro|vence
prov|en|der
prov|erb
pro|ver|bial
pro|ver|bi|ally
Pro|verbs, Book
  of
pro|vide
△ pro|vides
△ pro|vi|ded
△ pro|vi|ding
pro|vi|ded
pro|vi|dence
pro|vi|dent
pro|vi|den|tial
pro|vi|den|tially
pro|vi|dently
pro|vi|der

prov|ince
pro|vin|cial
pro|vin|cial|ism
pro|vin|cially
proving-ground
pro|vi|sion
 VERB
 △ pro|vi|sions
 △ pro|vi|sioned
 △ pro|vi|sion|ing
pro|vi|sional
pro|vi|sion|ally
pro|viso
pro|vi|sory
pro|vo|ca|teur
pro|vo|ca|tion
pro|voc|at|ive
pro|voc|at|ively
pro|voke
 △ pro|vokes
 △ pro|voked
 △ pro|vo|king
pro|vo|king
prov|ost
prow
prow|ess
prowl
 VERB
 △ prowls
 △ prowled
 △ prowl|ing
prow|ler
prox|emics
prox|imal
prox|im|ate
prox|im|ity
proxy
 △ prox|ies
prude
Pru|dence
pru|dence
pru|dent
pru|den|tial
pru|dently

pru|dery
pru|dish
pru|dishly
pru|dish|ness
prune
 VERB
 △ prunes
 △ pruned
 △ pru|ning
pru|ning-hook
pru|ri|ence
pru|ri|ent
pru|ri|ently
prur|itis
Prus|sia
Prus|sian
prus|sic
pry
 VERB
 △ pries
 △ pried
 △ pry|ing
psalm
psalm|ist
psalm|ody
Psalms, Book of
psal|ter
psal|tery
pse|pho|lo|gi|cal
pseph|olo|gist
pseph|ol|ogy
pseud
Pseud|epig|
 rapha
pseudo
pseu|do|carp
pseu|do|nym
pseud|ony|mous
pseu|do|po|dium
 △ pseu|do|po|dia
psit|ta|co|sis
pso|ri|asis
psych

VERB
 △ psychs
 △ psyched
 △ psych|ing
Psy|che
psy|che
psy|che|delic
psy|chi|at|ric
psy|chi|at|rist
psy|chi|atry
psy|chic
Psy|cho
psy|cho
psy|cho|ana|lyse
 △ psy|cho|ana|
 ly|ses
 △ psy|cho|ana|
 lysed
 △ psy|cho|ana|
 ly|sing
psy|cho|an|aly|
 sis
psy|cho|ana|lyst
psy|cho|ana|lytic
psy|cho|ana|lyt|
 ical
psy|cho|babble
psy|cho|drama
psy|cho|lo|gi|cal
psy|cho|lo|gic|
 ally
psy|cholo|gist
psy|chol|ogy
psy|cho|met|rics
psy|cho|path
psy|cho|pa|thic
psy|cho|path|ic|
 ally
psy|cho|pa|thol|
 ogy
psy|cho|pa|thy
psy|cho|sis
 △ psy|cho|ses
psy|cho|so|matic

psy|cho|so|mat|
 ic|ally
psy|cho|sur|gery
psy|cho|ther|ap|
 ist
psy|cho|ther|apy
psy|chotic
psy|chot|ic|ally
Ptah
ptar|mi|gan
pter|ido|phyte
ptero|dac|tyl
ptero|saur
Ptol|emy
pto|maine
pty|alin
pub
pu|berty
pubes
 sing. and pl.
pu|bes|cence
pu|bes|cent
pubic
pubis
 △ pubes
pub|lic
pub|li|can
pub|li|ca|tion
pub|li|city
pub|li|cize
 △ pub|li|ci|zes
 △ pub|li|cized
 △ pub|li|ci|zing
pub|lic|ly
pub|lic-spir|ited
pub|lish
 △ pub|li|shes
 △ pub|lished
 △ pub|lish|ing
pub|lisher
pub|lish|ing
Puc|cini
puce
puck

pucker
  VERB
  △ puck|ers
  △ puck|ered
  △ puck|er|ing
puck|ish
pud|ding
pud|dle
  VERB
  △ pud|dles
  △ pud|dled
  △ pud|dling
pud|dling
pu|denda
pudgy
  △ pud|gier
  △ pud|gi|est
Pu|dov|kin
pu|eblo
pu|er|ile
pu|er|il|ity
pu|er|peral
pu|er|per|ium
Pu|erto Rico
puff
  VERB
  △ puffs
  △ puffed
  △ puff|ing
puff|ball
puf|fer
puf|fin
puf|fi|ness
puffy
  △ puf|fier
  △ puf|fi|est
pug
pu|gil|ism
pu|gil|ist
Pugin
pug|na|cious
pug|na|ciously
pug|na|city
pug-nosed

puis|sance
puis|sant
puke
  VERB
  △ pukes
  △ puked
  △ pu|king
pukka
pul|chri|tude
Pu|lit|zer
pull
  VERB
  △ pulls
  △ pulled
  △ pull|ing
pul|let
pul|ley
pull-out
pull|over
pul|lu|late
  △ pul|lu|lates
  △ pul|lu|la|ted
  △ pul|lu|la|ting
pul|lu|la|tion
pul|mon|ary
pulp
  VERB
  △ pulps
  △ pulped
  △ pulp|ing
pul|pit
pulpy
  △ pul|pier
  △ pul|pi|est
pul|sar
pul|sate
  △ pul|sates
  △ pul|sa|ted
  △ pul|sa|ting
pul|sa|tion
pulse
  VERB
  △ pul|ses
  △ pulsed

△ pul|sing
pul|ver|iza|tion
pul|ver|ize
  △ pul|ver|izes
  △ pul|ver|ized
  △ pul|ver|izing
puma
pum|ice
pum|mel
  △ pum|mels
  △ pum|melled
  △ pum|mel|ling
pump
  VERB
  △ pumps
  △ pumped
  △ pump|ing
pum|per|nickel
pump|kin
pun
  VERB
  △ puns
  △ punned
  △ pun|ning
Punch
  △ Pun|ches
punch
  NOUN
  △ pun|ches
  VERB
  △ pun|ches
  △ punched
  △ punch|ing
punch-bag
punch-ball
punch-drunk
punch|line
punch-up
pun|chy
  △ pun|chier
  △ pun|chi|est
punc|tilio
punc|tili|ous
punc|tili|ously

punc|tual
punc|tu|al|ity
punc|tu|ally
punc|tu|ate
  △ punc|tu|ates
  △ punc|tu|ated
  △ punc|tu|ating
punc|tu|ation
punc|ture
  VERB
  △ punc|tures
  △ punc|tured
  △ punc|tur|ing
pun|dit
pun|gency
pun|gent
pun|gently
Punic
pun|ish
  △ pun|ishes
  △ pun|ished
  △ pun|ish|ing
pun|ish|able
pun|ish|ing
pun|ish|ment
pu|nit|ive
pu|nit|ively
Pun|jab
Pun|jabi
punk
pun|net
pun|ster
punt
  VERB
  △ punts
  △ pun|ted
  △ punt|ing
pun|ter
puny
  △ pu|nier
  △ pu|ni|est
pup
  VERB
  △ pups

△ pupped
△ pup|ping
pupa
△ pupae *or* pupas
pupal
pupil
pup|pet
pup|pet|eer
pup|petry
puppy
△ pup|pies
Pu|rana
pur|blind
Pur|cell
pur|chase
VERB
△ pur|cha|ses
△ pur|chased
△ pur|chas|ing
pur|cha|ser
pur|dah
pure
△ purer
△ pur|est
pure-bred
purée
VERB
△ pur|ées
△ pur|éed
△ purée|ing
purely
pure|ness
pur|ga|tive
pur|ga|tory
purge
VERB
△ pur|ges
△ purged
△ pur|ging
puri
puri|fi|ca|tion
puri|fier
pur|ify
△ puri|fies

△ puri|fied
△ puri|fy|ing
Purim
pur|ine
pur|ism
pur|ist
pur|itan
puri|tan|ical
Puri|tan|ism
pur|ity

---

purl
*stitch in knitting
etc; make this;
flow with
murmuring
sound; swirl*
VERB
△ purls
△ purled
△ purl|ing
⚠ pearl

---

pur|lieu
pur|lin
pur|loin
△ pur|loins
△ pur|loined
△ pur|loin|ing
pur|ple
Pur|ple Heart
*US military
medal*
pur|ple heart
stimulant pill
pur|port
VERB
△ pur|ports
△ pur|por|ted
△ pur|port|ing
pur|pose
VERB
△ pur|po|ses
△ pur|posed
△ pur|pos|ing

pur|pose-built
pur|pose|ful
pur|pose|fully
pur|pose|less
pur|posely
pur|pos|ive
purr
△ purrs
△ purred
△ purr|ing
purse
VERB
△ pur|ses
△ pursed
△ purs|ing
pur|ser
pur|su|ance
pur|sue
△ pur|sues
△ pur|sued
△ pur|su|ing
pur|suer
pur|suit
pur|sui|vant
puru|lence
puru|lent
pur|vey
△ pur|veys
△ pur|veyed
△ pur|vey|ing
pur|vey|ance
pur|veyor
pur|view
pus
Pusey
push
VERB
△ pushes
△ pushed
△ push|ing
push|bike
push-chair
pusher
Push|kin

push|over
pushy
△ push|ier
△ pushi|est
pu|sil|lan|im|ity
pu|sil|lan|im|ous
pu|sil|lan|im|ously
puss
pussy
△ pus|sies
pus|sy|foot
△ pus|sy|foots
△ pus|sy|footed
△ pus|sy|foot|ing
pus|tu|lar
pus|tule

---

put
place
△ puts
△ put
△ put|ting
⚠ putt

---

pu|ta|tive
put-down
put-on
pu|tre|fac|tion
pu|trefy
△ pu|tre|fies
△ pu|tre|fied
△ pu|tre|fy|ing
pu|tres|cent
pu|trid
putsch
△ putsches

---

putt
*strike golf ball
gently; such stroke*
VERB
△ putts
△ put|ted
△ put|ting
⚠ put

---

put|ter
put|ting
put|ting-green
putty
  △ put|ties
put-upon
puz|zle
  VERB
  △ puz|zles
  △ puz|zled
  △ puz|zling
puzzle|ment
puz|zler
puz|zling
py|aemia

pye-dog
Pyg|ma|lion
pygmy
  △ pyg|mies
py|ja|mas
pylon
Pylos
Pym
Pyong|yang
pyor|rhoea
pyra|mid
py|ram|id|al
pyre
Py|ren|ean
Py|ren|ees

py|reth|rum
py|retic
Pyrex
py|rexia *or* pyr|
  exia
  according to
  pronunciation
pyr|id|ine
pyr|id|ox|ine
pyr|im|id|ine
py|rite
py|ro|clast
py|ro|lu|site
py|ro|ly|sis
py|ro|ma|nia

py|ro|meter
py|ro|tech|nics
py|rox|ene
Pyr|rhic
py|ru|vic
Py|thag|oras
py|thag|or|ean|
  ism
py|thon
pyx
pzazz *see*
  pizzazz

Q

Qaddafi *see*
Gaddafi
Qan|tas
Qatar
qi
qi gong
qua
quack
  VERB
  △ quacks
  △ quacked
  △ quack|ing
quack|ery
quad
Quad|ra|ges|ima
quad|ran|gle
quad|rant
quad|ra|phonic
quad|ra|phon|ics
quad|ra|phony
quad|rat
quad|rate
quad|ratic
quad|ren|nial
quad|ren|ni|ally
quad|ri|lat|eral
quad|rille
quad|ri|ple|gia
quad|ri|ple|gic
quad|ru|ped
quad|ruple
  △ quad|ruples
  △ quad|rupled
  △ quad|ru|pling
quad|ru|plet
quad|ru|pli|cate
  △ quad|ru|pli|
    cates
  △ quad|ru|pli|ca|
    ted
  △ quad|ru|pli|ca|
    ting

quad|ruply
quaff
  △ quaffs
  △ quaffed
  △ quaff|ing
quagga
quag|mire
quaich
  △ quai|ches
Quai d'Orsay
quail
  NOUN
  △ quail *or* quails
  VERB
  △ quails
  △ quailed
  △ quail|ing
quaint
  △ quain|ter
  △ quaint|est
quake
  VERB
  △ quakes
  △ quaked
  △ qua|king
Qua|ker
qual|ifi|ca|tion
qual|ifier
qual|ify
  △ qual|ifies
  △ qual|ified
  △ qual|ify|ing
qual|it|at|ive
qual|ity
  △ qual|it|ies
qualm
quand|ary
  △ quand|ar|ies
quango
Quant
quan|tify
  △ quan|ti|fies
  △ quan|ti|fied
  △ quan|ti|fy|ing

quan|ti|ta|tive
quan|tity
  △ quan|ti|ties
quant|ize
  △ quant|izes
  △ quant|ized
  △ quan|ti|zing
quan|tum
  △ quanta
quar|an|tine
  VERB
  △ quar|an|tines
  △ quar|an|tined
  △ quar|an|ti|
    ning
quark
quar|rel
  VERB
  △ quar|rels
  △ quar|relled
  △ quar|rel|ling
quar|rel|some
quarry
  NOUN
  △ quar|ries
  VERB
  △ quar|ries
  △ quar|ried
  △ quar|ry|ing
quart
quar|ter
  VERB
  △ quar|ters
  △ quar|tered
  △ quar|ter|ing
quar|ter|back
quar|ter|deck
quar|ter-final|ist
quar|ter|ing
quar|ter|light
quar|terly
  △ quar|ter|lies
quar|ter|mas|ter
quar|ter|staff

quar|tet
quarto
quartz
quartz|ite
qua|sar
quash
  △ quashes
  △ quashed
  △ quash|ing
quas|sia
qua|ter|nary
  NOUN
  △ qua|ter|nar|ies
quat|rain
quat|re|foil
quat|tro|cento
qua|ver
  VERB
  △ qua|vers
  △ qua|vered
  △ qua|ver|ing
qua|very

quay
wharf
⚠ key

Quayle
queas|ily
quea|si|ness
queasy
  △ quea|sier
  △ quea|si|est
Que|bec
Que|chua
Queen
queen
  VERB
  △ queens
  △ queened
  △ queen|ing
Queen Chris|tina
queenly
Queens|berry
Queens|land

queer
queerly
queer|ness
quell
△ quells
△ quelled
△ quell|ing
quench
△ quen|ches
△ quenched
△ quench|ing
que|nelle
quern
que|ru|lous
query
NOUN
△ quer|ies
VERB
△ quer|ies
△ quer|ied
△ query|ing
quest
VERB
△ quests
△ ques|ted
△ quest|ing
ques|tion
VERB
△ ques|tions
△ ques|tioned
△ ques|tion|
ing
ques|tion|able
ques|tioner
ques|tion|
naire

queue
line of waiting
people or things;
make this
VERB
△ queues
△ queued

△ queue|ing *or*
queu|ing
⚠ cue

quib|ble
VERB
△ quib|bles
△ quib|bled
△ quib|bling
quiche
quick
△ quicker
△ quick|est
quicken
△ quick|ens
△ quick|ened
△ quick|en|ing
quick-freeze
△ quick-free|zes
△ quick-froze
△ quick-freez|
ing
△ quick-fro|zen
quickie
quick|lime
quickly
quick|ness
quick|sand
quick|set
quick|sil|ver
quick|step
quid
pound sterling
after a number
△ quid
other uses
△ quids
tobacco
△ quids
quid|dity
△ quid|di|ties
quid pro quo
△ *quid pro quos*
qui|es|cence

qui|es|cent
quiet
VERB
△ qui|ets
△ qui|eted
△ qui|et|ing
qui|eten
△ qui|et|ens
△ qui|et|ened
△ qui|et|en|ing
qui|et|ism
qui|et|ist
qui|etly
qui|et|ness
qui|etude
qui|etus
quiff
△ quiffs
quill
Quil|ler-Couch
quilt
VERB
△ quilts
△ quil|ted
△ quilt|ing
quil|ted
quin
quince
quin|cen|ten|ary
△ quin|cen|ten|
ar|ies
quin|cunx
△ quin|cunxes
quin|ine *or* qui|
nine
according to
pronunciation
qui|noa
quin|ol|ine
Quin|qua|ges|
ima
quin|quen|nial
quin|quen|ni|
ally

quin|que|reme
quinsy
△ quin|sies
quin|tal
quint|es|sence
quint|es|sen|tial
quint|es|sen|ti|
ally
quin|tet
Quin|tin
quin|tuple
VERB
△ quin|tuples
△ quin|tupled
△ quin|tu|pling
quin|tup|let
quip
VERB
△ quips
△ quipped
△ quip|ping
quipu

quire
paper measure
⚠ choir

quirk
quirky
△ quir|kier
△ quir|ki|est
quis|ling
quit
VERB
△ quits
△ quit|ted *or*
quit
△ quitting
quitch
quite
Quito
quits
quit|tance
quit|ter
quiver

VERB

△ quiv|ers

△ quiv|ered

△ quiv|er|ing

quix|otic

quiz

  NOUN

△ quiz|zes

  VERB

△ quiz|zes

△ quizzed

△ quiz|zing

quiz|mas|ter

quiz|zi|cal

quiz|zi|cally

Qum|ran

quod

quoin

quoit

quon|dam

quor|ate

Quorn

quorum

quota

quo|table

quo|ta|tion

quote

VERB

△ quotes

△ quoted

△ quo|ting

quoth

quo|tid|ian

quo|tient

Qur'an *see* Koran

qwerty

R

Ra *see* Re
Rabat
rab|bet
  VERB
  △ rab|bets
  △ rab|beted
  △ rab|bet|ing
rabbi
rab|bin|ical
rab|bit
  VERB
  △ rab|bits
  △ rab|bi|ted
  △ rab|bit|ing
rab|ble
rabble-rouser
rabble-rous|ing
Rab|elais
Rab|elai|sian
rabid
ra|bid|ity
ra|bidly
ra|bid|ness
ra|bies
rac|coon
race
  VERB
  △ races
  △ raced
  △ ra|cing
race|card
race|course
race|horse
ra|ceme
racer
Ra|chel
ra|chis
Rach|man|inov
ra|cial
ra|cial|ism
ra|cially
ra|cily

Ra|cine
ra|ci|ness
ra|cing
ra|cism
ra|cist
rack
  VERB
  △ racks
  △ racked
  △ rack|ing
racket
rack|et|eer
  VERB
  △ rack|et|eers
  △ rack|et|eered
  △ rack|et|eer|ing
rack|et|eer|ing
rack|ets
Rack|ham
racon|teur
racoon *see*
  raccoon
racquet *see*
  racket
racy
  △ ra|cier
  △ ra|ci|est
rad
radar
Rad|cliffe
rad|dled
ra|dial
ra|di|ally
ra|dian
ra|di|ance
ra|di|ant
ra|di|antly
ra|di|ate
  VERB
  △ ra|di|ates
  △ ra|di|ated
  △ ra|di|ating
ra|di|ation
ra|di|ator

rad|ical
rad|ic|al|ism
rad|ic|ally
rad|ic|al|ness
ra|dicchio
rad|icle
radii
radio
  VERB
  △ ra|dios
  △ ra|di|oed
  △ ra|dio|ing
ra|dio|act|ive
ra|dio|ac|tiv|ity
ra|dio|bi|ol|ogy
ra|dio|car|bon
ra|dio|chem|is|
  try
ra|dio|gram
ra|dio|graph
ra|di|og|ra|pher
ra|di|og|ra|phy
ra|dio|iso|tope
ra|dio|lo|gi|cal
ra|di|olo|gist
ra|di|ol|ogy
radio-pager
radio-paging
ra|dio|phonic
ra|dio|scopic
ra|dio|scopy
ra|dio|ther|apy
rad|ish
  △ rad|ishes
ra|dium
ra|dius
  △ radii *or* ra|di|
    uses
radon
raf|fia
raf|fish
raf|fishly
raf|fish|ness
raf|fle

VERB
  △ raf|fles
  △ raf|fled
  △ raf|fling
raft
  VERB
  △ rafts
  △ raf|ted
  △ raft|ing
raf|ter
*Raft of the
  Medusa, The*
rag
  VERB
  △ rags
  △ ragged
  △ rag|ging
raga
ra|ga|muf|fin
rag-bag
rage
  VERB
  △ rages
  △ raged
  △ ra|ging
ragga
rag|ged
rag|gedly
rag|ged|ness
ra|ging
Ra|ging Bull
Rag|lan
rag|lan
ra|gout
rag|time
rag|wort
rai
raid
  VERB
  △ raids
  △ rai|ded
  △ raid|ing
rai|der
Raikes

rail
  VERB
  △ rails
  △ railed
  △ rail|ing
rail|car
rail|card
rail|head
rail|ing
rail|lery
rail|road
  VERB
  △ rail|roads
  △ rail|roaded
  △ rail|road|ing
rail|way
rai|ment

rain
  water droplets
  falling from
  clouds; do this
  VERB
  △ rains
  △ rained
  △ rain|ing
  ⚠ reign
  ⚠ rein

Rain|bow, The
rain|bow
rain|coat
rain|fall
rain|for|est
Rain|ier
Rain, Steam
  and Speed
rainy
  △ rai|nier
  △ rai|ni|est

raise
  lift; increase;
  rear; act of
  lifting

VERB
  △ rai|ses
  △ raised
  △ rais|ing
  ⚠ raze

rai|sin
rai|son d'être
  △ *rai|sons d'être*
raita
Raj
rajah
rake
  VERB
  △ rakes
  △ raked
  △ ra|king
rake-off
Rake's Pro|gress,
  A
  set of paintings
  by Hogarth
Rake's Pro|gress,
  The
  opera by
  Stravinsky
ra|kish
ra|kishly
ra|kish|ness
Rakhmaninov
  see
  Rachmaninov
raku
Ra|leigh
ral|len|tando
  △ ral|len|tan|dos
  or ral|len|
  tandi
rally
  NOUN
  △ ral|lies
  VERB
  △ ral|lies
  △ ral|lied

△ ral|ly|ing
ral|ly|cross
Ralph
RAM
ram
  VERB
  △ rams
  △ rammed
  △ ram|ming
Ra|ma|dan
Ram|bert
ram|ble
  VERB
  △ ram|bles
  △ ram|bled
  △ ram|bling
ram|bler
ram|bling
ram|blingly
ram|bu|tan
Ra|meau
ram|ekin
ra|mi|fi|ca|tion
ram|ify
  △ ra|mi|fies
  △ ra|mi|fied
  △ ra|mi|fy|ing
ram|jet
ramp
  VERB
  △ ramps
  △ ramped
  △ ramp|ing
ram|page
  VERB
  △ ram|pa|ges
  △ ram|paged
  △ ram|pa|ging
ramp|ant
ramp|antly
ram|part
ramp|ing
ram-raid

VERB
  △ ram-raids
  △ ram-rai|ded
  △ ram-raid|ing
ram-raid|ing
ram|rod
Ram|say
Rams|gate
ram|shackle
ram|sons
ran
ranch
  NOUN
  △ ran|ches
  VERB
  △ ran|ches
  △ ranched
  △ ranch|ing
ran|cher
ran|cid
ran|cid|ity
ran|cid|ness
ran|cor|ous
ran|cor|ously
ran|cour
rand
  △ rand *or* rands
Ran|dal
ran|dily
ran|di|ness
ran|dom
ran|domly
ran|dom|ness
randy
  △ ran|dier
  △ ran|di|est
ranee *see* rani
rang
range
  VERB
  △ ran|ges
  △ ranged
  △ ranging
range|finder

ranger
Ran|goon
rangy
△ ran|gier
△ ran|gi|est
rani
Rank
rank
VERB
△ ranks
△ ranked
△ rank|ing
ADJ.
△ ran|ker
△ rank|est
ran|ker
ran|kle
△ ran|kles
△ ran|kled
△ rank|ling
rankly
rank|ness
ran|sack
△ ran|sacks
△ ran|sacked
△ ran|sack|ing
ran|som
VERB
△ ran|soms
△ ran|somed
△ ran|som|ing
Ran|some
ran|somer
rant
VERB
△ rants
△ ran|ted
△ rant|ing
ran|ter
rant|ing
Rao

rap
sharp tap;
blame; sort of
music; make or
give these; the
least bit
VERB
△ raps
△ rapped
△ rap|ping
⚠ wrap

ra|pa|cious
ra|pa|ciously
ra|pa|cious|ness
ra|pa|city
rape
VERB
△ rapes
△ raped
△ ra|ping
Rape of Eu|ropa
Rape of Lu|
crece, The
Rape of the
Lock, The
Ra|phael
rapid
ra|pid|ity
rap|idly
ra|pid|ness
ra|pier
ra|pine
ra|pist
rap|per
rap|port
rap|proche|ment
rap|scal|lion
rapt
rap|tor
rap|tor|ial
rap|ture
rap|tur|ous
rare
△ rarer
△ rar|est

rarebit *use*
rabbit
rar|efied
rar|efy
△ rar|efies
△ rar|efied
△ rar|efy|ing
rarely
rar|ing
rar|ity
△ rar|it|ies
ras|cal
ras|cally
rase *see* raze
rash
NOUN
△ ra|shes
ADJ.
△ rasher
△ rash|est
ra|sher
rashly
rash|ness
Ra|sho|mon
rasp
VERB
△ rasps
△ rasped
△ rasp|ing
rasp|berry
△ rasp|ber|ries
ras|per
rasp|ing
rasp|ingly
Ras|pu|tin
raspy
△ ras|pier
△ ras|pi|est
Ras|se|las
Ras Shamra
Rasta
Ras|ta|far|ian
rat

VERB
△ rats
△ rat|ted
△ rat|ting
ratable *see*
rateable
ra|ta|fia
ratan *see* rattan
rat-a-tat-tat
ra|ta|touille
rat|bag
rat|chet
rate
VERB
△ rates
△ ra|ted
△ ra|ting
rate|able
rate-cap
△ rate-caps
△ rate-capped
△ rate-cap|ping
rate-cap|ping
rate|payer
ra|ther
ra|ti|fi|ca|tion
rat|ify
△ rat|ifies
△ rat|ified
△ rat|ify|ing
ra|ting
ratio
ra|tion
VERB
△ ra|tions
△ ra|tioned
△ ra|tion|ing
ra|tional
ra|tion|ale
ra|tion|al|ism
ra|tion|al|ist
ra|tion|al|is|tic
ra|tion|al|ity
ra|tion|al|iza|tion

ra|tion|al|ize
△ ra|tion|al|izes
△ ra|tion|al|ized
△ ra|tion|al|izing
ra|tion|al|ly
ra|tion|ing
rat|pack
rat|tan
rat|ter
Rat|ti|gan
Rat|tle
rattle
 VERB
△ rattles
△ rattled
△ rat|tling
rat|tler
rattle|snake
rattle|trap
rat|tling
rat|tly
ratty
△ rat|tier
△ rat|ti|est
rau|cous
rau|cously
rau|cous|ness
raunch|ily
raun|chy
△ raun|chier
△ raun|chi|est
rav|age
 VERB
△ rav|ages
△ rav|aged
△ rav|aging
rave
 VERB
△ raves
△ raved
△ ra|ving
Ravel
ravel

 VERB
△ ravels
△ rav|elled
△ rav|el|ling
raven
rav|en|ing
Ra|venna
rav|en|ous
rav|en|ously
rav|en|ous|ness
raver
rave-up
ra|vine
ra|ving
ra|vi|oli
rav|ish
△ rav|ishes
△ rav|ished
△ rav|ish|ing
rav|ish|ing
rav|ish|ingly
raw
△ rawer
△ raw|est
raw|boned
raw|hide
Raw|lings
raw|ness
Ray
ray
Ray-Bans
ray-gun
Ray|mond
Ray|naud
rayon

raze
 destroy
 completely
 △ ra|zing
 ⚠raise

razor
ra|zor|bill
raz|zle

razzle-dazzle
razz|ma|tazz
Re
re
reach
 NOUN
△ rea|ches
 VERB
△ rea|ches
△ reached
△ reach|ing
reach|able
reach-me-down
react
△ re|acts
△ re|ac|ted
△ re|act|ing
re|act|ance
re|ac|tion
re|ac|tion|ary
 NOUN
△ re|ac|tion|aries
re|ac|ti|vate
△ re|ac|ti|vates
△ re|ac|ti|va|ted
△ re|ac|ti|va|ting
re|ac|ti|va|tion
re|act|ive
re|ac|tor

read
 understand
 print, writing
 etc; this activity
 VERB
△ reads
△ read
△ read|ing
 ⚠reed

read|ab|il|ity
read|able
read|able|ness
Reade
rea|der

read|er|ship
read|ily
readi|ness
Read|ing
read|ing
read-out
ready
 NOUN
△ readies
 VERB
△ read|ies
△ read|ied
△ ready|ing
 ADJ.
△ readier
△ readi|est
ready-made
ready-to-wear
re|af|for|est
△ re|af|for|ests
△ re|af|for|es|ted
△ re|af|for|est|
 ing
re|af|for|es|ta|
 tion
Rea|gan
Rea|ga|nom|ics
re|agent

real
 genuine
 ⚠reel

re|align
△ re|aligns
△ re|aligned
△ re|align|ing
re|align|ment
real|ism
real|ist
real|is|tic
real|is|tic|ally
re|al|ity
△ re|al|it|ies
real|iz|able

real|iza|tion
real|ize
△ real|izes
△ real|ized
△ real|izing
really
realm
re|al|po|li|tik
real-time
re|al|tor
re|alty
ream
reap
△ reaps
△ reaped
△ reap|ing
rea|per
re|ap|ply
△ re|ap|plies
△ re|ap|plied
△ re|ap|ply|ing
rear
VERB
△ rears
△ reared
△ rear|ing
rear|guard
rearm
△ re|arms
△ re|armed
△ re|arm|ing
re|ar|ma|ment
rear|most
rear|ward
rea|son
VERB
△ rea|sons
△ rea|soned
△ rea|son|ing
rea|son|able
rea|son|able|ness
rea|son|ably
rea|son|ing
re|as|sur|ance

re|as|sure
△ re|as|sures
△ re|as|sured
△ re|as|sur|ing
re|as|sur|ing
re|as|sur|ingly
Ré|au|mur
re|bate
Re|becca
rebel
VERB
△ re|bels
△ re|belled
△ re|bel|ling
re|bel|lion
re|bel|li|ous
re|bel|li|ously
re|bel|li|ous|ness
Rebel With|out
a Cause
re|birth
re|birth|ing
re|boot
△ re|boots
△ re|boo|ted
△ re|boot|ing
re|bore
VERB
△ re|bores
△ re|bored
△ re|bor|ing
re|born
re|bound
VERB
△ re|bounds
△ re|boun|ded
△ re|bound|ing
re|buff
VERB
△ re|buffs
△ re|buffed
△ re|buff|ing
re|build

VERB
△ re|builds
△ re|built
△ re|build|ing
re|buke
VERB
△ re|bukes
△ re|buked
△ re|bu|king
rebus
△ re|buses
rebut
△ re|buts
△ re|but|ted
△ re|but|ting
re|but|tal
re|cal|cit|rance
re|ca|lcit|rant
re|call
VERB
△ re|calls
△ re|called
△ re|call|ing
re|cant
△ re|cants
△ re|can|ted
△ re|cant|ing
re|can|ta|tion
recap
VERB
△ re|caps
△ re|capped
△ re|cap|ping
re|ca|pit|ulate
△ re|ca|pit|ulates
△ re|ca|pit|ula|ted
△ re|ca|pit|ula|
   ting
re|ca|pit|ula|tion
re|cap|ture
VERB
△ re|cap|tures
△ re|cap|tured
△ re|cap|tur|ing

recce
VERB
△ rec|ces
△ rec|ced *or* rec|
   ceed
△ rec|ce|ing
re|cede
△ re|cedes
△ re|ce|ded
△ re|ced|ing
re|ced|ing
re|ceipt
re|ceive
△ re|ceives
△ re|ceived
△ re|ceiv|ing
re|ceived
re|cei|ver
re|ceiv|er|ship
re|cent
re|cently
re|cep|tacle
re|cep|tion
re|cep|tion|ist
re|cep|tive
re|cep|tively
re|cep|tive|ness
re|cep|tiv|ity
re|cep|tor
re|cess
NOUN
△ re|ces|ses
VERB
△ re|ces|ses
△ re|cessed
△ re|cess|ing
re|cess|ion
re|ces|sional
re|ces|sive
re|check
VERB
△ re|checks
△ re|checked
△ re|check|ing

re|cher|ché
re|chip|ping
re|cid|iv|ism
re|cid|iv|ist
recipe
re|cipi|ent
re|cip|ro|cal
re|cip|ro|cally
re|cip|ro|cate
△ re|cip|ro|cates
△ re|cip|ro|ca|
ted
△ re|cip|ro|ca|
ting
re|cip|ro|ca|tion
re|ci|pro|city
re|ci|tal
re|ci|tal|ist
re|ci|ta|tion
re|ci|ta|tive
re|cite
△ re|cites
△ re|ci|ted
△ re|ci|ting
reck|less
reck|lessly
reck|less|ness
reckon
△ reck|ons
△ reck|oned
△ reck|on|ing
reck|on|ing
re|claim
△ re|claims
△ re|claimed
△ re|claim|ing
re|claim|able
re|clam|ation
re|cline
△ re|clines
△ re|clined
△ re|cli|ning
re|cli|ner
re|cluse

re|cog|ni|tion
re|cog|niz|able
re|cog|niz|ably
re|cog|ni|zance
re|cog|nize
△ re|cog|ni|zes
△ re|cog|nized
△ re|cog|ni|zing
re|coil
VERB
△ re|coils
△ re|coiled
△ re|coil|ing
re|col|lect
△ re|col|lects
△ re|col|lec|ted
△ re|col|lect|ing
re|col|lec|tion
re|com|bin|ant
re|com|bi|na|
tion
re|com|mend
△ re|com|mends
△ re|com|men|
ded
△ re|com|mend|
ing
re|com|mend|
able
re|com|men|da|
tion
re|com|pense
VERB
△ re|com|pen|ses
△ re|com|pensed
△ re|com|pen|
sing
re|con|cile
△ re|con|ciles
△ re|con|ciled
△ re|con|ci|ling
re|con|ci|li|ation
re|con|ci|li|at|ory
re|con|dite

re|con|di|tion
△ re|con|di|tions
△ re|con|di|
tioned
△ re|con|di|tion|
ing
re|con|di|tioned
re|con|nais|sance
re|con|noitre
△ re|con|noitres
△ re|con|noitred
△ re|con|noit|
ring
re|con|sider
△ re|con|sid|ers
△ re|con|sid|ered
△ re|con|sid|er|
ing
re|con|sid|er|
ation
re|cons|ti|tute
△ re|con|sti|tutes
△ re|con|sti|tu|
ted
△ re|con|sti|tu|
ting
re|con|sti|tu|tion
re|con|struct
△ re|con|structs
△ re|con|struc|
ted
△ re|con|struct|
ing
re|con|struc|tion
rec|ord
NOUN
re|cord
VERB
△ re|cords
△ re|cor|ded
△ re|cord|ing
re|cor|der
re|cord|ing
rec|ord-player

re|count
tell (story etc)
△ re|counts
△ re|coun|ted
△ re|count|ing
⚠ re-count

re-count
*count again; this
activity*
VERB
△ re-counts
△ re-coun|ted
△ re-count|ing
⚠ recount

re|coup
△ re|coups
△ re|couped
△ re|coup|ing
re|coup|ment
re|course

re|cover
*get again; get
back*
△ re|cov|ers
△ re|cov|ered
△ re|cov|er|ing
⚠ re-cover

re-cov|er
cover again
△ re-cov|ers
△ re-cov|ered
△ re-cov|er|ing
⚠ recover

re|cov|er|ab|il|ity
re|cov|er|able
re|cov|ery
△ re|cov|er|ies
rec|re|ant
re|cre|ate
△ re|cre|ates

△ re|cre|ated
△ re|cre|ating
rec|re|ation
rec|re|ational
re|cri|min|ation
re|crim|in|at|ory
re|cru|desce
△ re|cru|des|ces
△ re|cru|desced
△ re|cru|des|cing
re|cru|des|cence
re|cru|des|cent
re|cruit
  VERB
△ re|cruits
△ re|crui|ted
△ re|cruit|ing
re|cruit|ment
re|crys|tal|li|za|
  tion
recta
rec|tal
rect|angle
rect|an|gu|lar
rec|ti|fi|able
rec|ti|fi|ca|tion
rec|ti|fier
rect|ify
△ rec|ti|fies
△ rec|ti|fied
△ rec|ti|fy|ing
rec|ti|lin|ear
rec|ti|tude
recto
rec|tor
rec|tor|ial
rec|tor|ship
rec|tory
△ rec|tor|ies
rec|tum
△ recta *or* rec|
  tums
re|cum|bent
re|cu|per|able

re|cu|per|ate
△ re|cu|per|ates
△ re|cu|per|ated
△ re|cu|per|ating
re|cu|per|ation
re|cu|per|ative
recur
△ recurs
△ re|curred
△ re|cur|ring
re|cur|rence
re|cur|rent
re|cur|rently
re|cu|sancy
re|cu|sant
re|cyc|lable
re|cy|cle
△ re|cy|cles
△ re|cy|cled
△ re|cyc|ling
re|cyc|ling
red
  ADJ.
△ red|der
△ red|dest
red-blooded
red-blood|ed|
  ness
red|breast
red|brick
Red|car
red|coat
red|cur|rant
red|den
△ red|dens
△ red|dened
△ red|den|ing
red|dish
Red|ditch
re|deem
△ re|deems
△ re|deemed
△ re|deem|ing
re|deem|able

re|deemer
re|deem|ing
re|demp|tion
re|demp|tive
re|de|ploy
△ re|de|ploys
△ re|de|ployed
△ re|de|ploy|ing
re|de|ploy|ment
re|de|velop
△ re|de|vel|ops
△ re|de|vel|oped
△ re|de|vel|op|
  ing
re|de|vel|oper
re|de|vel|op|
  ment
Red|ford
Red|grave
red-han|ded
red|head
red|headed
red-hot
re|dial
△ re|di|als
△ re|di|alled
△ re|di|al|ling
red-lining
red|ness
redo
△ re|does
△ redid
△ re|do|ing
△ re|done
red|ol|ence
red|ol|ent
red|ol|ently
re|dou|ble
△ re|dou|bles
△ re|dou|bled
△ re|doub|ling
re|doubt
re|doubt|able
re|doubt|ably

re|dound
△ re|dounds
△ re|doun|ded
△ re|dound|ing
redox
re|dress
  VERB
△ re|dres|ses
△ re|dressed
△ re|dress|ing
red|shank
red|shift
Red Shoes, The
red|skin
red|start
re|duce
△ re|du|ces
△ re|duced
△ re|du|cing
re|du|cer
re|du|ci|bil|ity
re|du|cible
re|du|cing
re|duc|tase
re|duc|tio ad ab|
  sur|dum
re|duc|tion
re|dund|ancy
△ re|dund|an|
  cies
re|dund|ant
re|du|pli|cate
△ re|du|pli|cates
△ re|du|pli|ca|
  ted
△ re|du|pli|ca|
  ting
re|du|pli|ca|tion
red|wood
Reed

reed
sort of grass
that grows in

water; vibrating strip of metal etc in some wind instruments

▲ read

reed|ily
ree|di|ness
reed|mace
reedy
△ ree|dier
△ ree|di|est
reef
VERB
△ reefs
△ reefed
△ reef|ing
ree|fer
reef|ing-jacket
reek
VERB
△ reeks
△ reeked
△ reek|ing

reel
cylinder for winding up thread, etc; sort of dance; wind up; dance; stagger
VERB
△ reels
△ reeled
△ reel|ing
▲ real

re-entry
△ re-ent|ries
Rees-Mogg
reeve
VERB
△ reeves
△ rove *or* reeved

△ reev|ing
△ reeved
ref
re|fect|ory
△ re|fect|or|ies
refer
△ re|fers
△ re|ferred
△ re|fer|ring
re|fer|able *or* ref|er|able
according to pronunciation
ref|eree
VERB
△ ref|er|ees
△ ref|er|eed
△ ref|er|ee|ing
ref|er|ence
ref|er|en|dum
△ ref|er|en|dums *or* ref|er|enda
ref|er|en|tial
re|fer|ral
re|ferred
re|fill
VERB
△ re|fills
△ re|filled
△ re|fill|ing
re|fill|able
re|fine
△ re|fines
△ re|fined
△ re|fi|ning
re|fined
re|fine|ment
re|fi|nery
△ re|fi|ner|ies
re|fi|ning
refit
VERB
△ re|fits
△ re|fit|ted

△ re|fit|ting
re|flag
△ re|flags
△ re|flagged
△ re|flag|ging
re|flate
△ re|flates
△ re|fla|ted
△ re|fla|ting
re|fla|tion
re|fla|tion|ary
re|flect
△ re|flects
△ re|flec|ted
△ re|flect|ing
re|flect|ance
re|flec|tion
re|flect|ive
re|flect|ively
re|flec|tor
re|flex
NOUN
△ re|flexes
re|flex|ive
re|flex|ively
re|flex|olo|gist
re|flex|ol|ogy
re|flux
△ re|fluxes
re|form
VERB
△ re|forms
△ re|formed
△ re|form|ing
re|form|able
re|for|ma|tion
re|form|at|ive
re|form|at|ory
△ re|form|at|or|ies
re|for|mer
re|form|ism
re|fract
△ re|fracts

△ re|frac|ted
△ re|fract|ing
re|frac|tion
re|fract|ive
re|frac|tor
re|frac|tor|iness
re|fract|ory
NOUN
△ re|frac|tor|ies
re|frain
VERB
△ re|frains
△ re|frained
△ re|frain|ing
re|fran|gi|bil|ity
re|fran|gible
re|fresh
△ re|freshes
△ re|freshed
△ re|fresh|ing
re|fresher
re|fresh|ing
re|fresh|ingly
re|fresh|ment
re|fri|ger|ant
re|fri|ger|ate
△ re|fri|ger|ates
△ re|fri|ger|ated
△ re|fri|ger|ating
re|fri|ger|ation
re|fri|ger|ator
re|fuel
△ re|fuels
△ re|fu|elled
△ re|fu|el|ling
ref|uge
re|fu|gee
re|ful|gence
re|ful|gent
re|fund
VERB
△ re|funds
△ re|fun|ded
△ re|fund|ing

re|fund|able
re|fur|bish
  △ re|fur|bi|shes
  △ re|fur|bished
  △ re|fur|bish|ing
re|fur|bish|ment
re|fu|sal
re|fuse
  △ re|fu|ses
  △ re|fused
  △ re|fu|sing
re|fuse|nik
re|fu|table
re|fu|ta|tion
re|fute
  △ re|futes
  △ re|fu|ted
  △ re|fu|ting
re|gain
  △ re|gains
  △ re|gained
  △ re|gain|ing
regal
re|gale
  △ re|gales
  △ re|galed
  △ re|ga|ling
re|ga|lia
re|gal|ity
re|gally
re|gard
  △ re|gards
  △ re|gar|ded
  △ re|gard|ing
re|gard|ful
re|gard|ing
re|gard|less
re|gard|lessly
re|gatta
Re|gency
  political regime
  in Britain 1811–
  20, or in France
  1715–23

re|gency
  position of,
  government by, a
  regent
  △ re|gen|cies
re|gen|er|ate
  VERB
  △ re|gen|er|ates
  △ re|gen|er|ated
  △ re|gen|er|ating
re|gen|er|ation
re|gen|er|at|ive
re|gen|er|ator
re|gent
reg|gae
Reg|gio di Ca|
  lab|ria
Reg|gio
  nell'Emi|lia
re|gi|cide
regime
regi|men
regi|ment
  VERB
  △ regi|ments
  △ regi|men|ted
  △ regi|ment|ing
regi|men|tal
regi|men|ta|tion
regi|men|ted
Re|gina
Re|gi|nald
re|gion
re|gional
re|gion|ally
regis|ter
  VERB
  △ regis|ters
  △ regis|tered
  △ regis|ter|ing
regis|tered
regis|trar
regis|tra|tion
regis|try

△ regis|tries
Re|gius
Règle du jeu, La
  (The Rules of
  the Game)
re|grade
  △ re|grades
  △ re|gra|ded
  △ re|gra|ding
re|gress
  VERB
  △ re|gres|ses
  △ re|gressed
  △ re|gress|ing
re|gres|sion
re|gres|sive
re|gres|sively
re|gret
  VERB
  △ re|grets
  △ re|gret|ted
  △ re|gret|ting
re|gret|ful
re|gret|fully
're|gret|table
re|gret|tably
re|group
  △ re|groups
  △ re|grouped
  △ re|group|ing
regu|lar
regu|lar|ity
regu|lar|iza|tion
regu|lar|ize
  △ regu|lar|izes
  △ regu|lar|ized
  △ regu|lar|izing
regu|larly
regu|late
  △ regu|lates
  △ regu|la|ted
  △ regu|la|ting
regu|la|tion
regu|la|tor

reg|ulo
re|gur|gi|tate
  △ re|gur|gi|tates
  △ re|gur|gi|ta|
    ted
  △ re|gur|gi|ta|
    ting
re|gur|gi|ta|tion
re|ha|bil|it|ate
  △ re|ha|bil|it|
    ates
  △ re|ha|bil|it|
    ated
  △ re|ha|bil|it|
    ating
re|ha|bil|it|ation
re|hash
  NOUN
  △ re|ha|shes
  VERB
  △ re|ha|shes
  △ re|hashed
  △ re|hash|ing
re|hear|sal
re|hearse
  △ re|hearses
  △ re|hearsed
  △ re|hears|ing
re|heat
  △ re|heats
  △ re|hea|ted
  △ re|heat|ing
re|house
  △ re|hou|ses
  △ re|housed
  △ re|hous|ing
Reich
Reichs|tag
Rei|gate

reign
  duration of rule
  of sovereign etc;
  be sovereign

VERB
△ reigns
△ reigned
△ reign|ing
⚠ rain
⚠ rein

reign|ing
reiki
re|im|burse
△ re|im|bur|ses
△ re|im|bursed
△ re|im|bur|sing
re|im|burse|
  ment

rein
*strap to control
horse; pull this;
control*
VERB
△ reins
△ reined
△ rein|ing
⚠ rain
⚠ reign

re|in|car|nate
VERB
△ re|in|car|nates
△ re|in|car|na|
  ted
△ re|in|car|na|
  ting
re|in|car|na|tion
rein|deer
△ rein|deer *or*
  rein|deers
re|in|force
△ re|in|for|ces
△ re|in|forced
△ re|in|for|cing
re|in|force|ment
Rein|hardt
re|in|state

△ re|in|states
△ re|in|sta|ted
△ re|in|sta|ting
re|in|state|ment
re|is|sue
VERB
△ re|is|sues
△ re|is|sued
△ re|is|su|ing
re|it|er|ate
△ re|it|er|ates
△ re|it|er|ated
△ re|it|er|ating
re|it|er|ation
Reith
re|ject
VERB
△ re|jects
△ re|jec|ted
△ re|ject|ing
re|jec|tion
rejig
△ re|jigs
△ re|jigged
△ re|jig|ging
re|joice
△ re|joi|ces
△ re|joiced
△ re|joi|cing
re|joi|cer
re|joi|cing
re|join
△ re|joins
△ re|joined
△ re|join|ing
re|join|der
re|ju|ven|ate
△ re|ju|ven|ates
△ re|ju|ven|ated
△ re|ju|ven|ating
re|ju|ven|ation
re|lapse
VERB
△ re|lap|ses

△ re|lapsed
△ re|lap|sing
re|late
△ re|lates
△ re|la|ted
△ re|la|ting
re|la|ted
re|la|tion
re|la|tion|ship
rel|at|ive
rel|at|ively
rel|at|iv|ism
re|la|tiv|ity
relax
△ re|laxes
△ re|laxed
△ re|lax|ing
re|lax|ant
re|lax|ation
re|laxed
re|lax|ing
relay
VERB
△ re|lays
△ re|layed
△ re|lay|ing
re|lease
VERB
△ re|lea|ses
△ re|leased
△ re|leas|ing
re|le|gate
△ re|le|gates
△ re|le|ga|ted
△ re|le|ga|ting
re|le|ga|tion
re|lent
△ re|lents
△ re|len|ted
△ re|lent|ing
re|lent|less
re|lent|lessly
re|lent|less|ness
relet

△ re|lets
relet
△ re|let|ting
rele|vance
rele|vancy
rele|vant
re|li|ab|il|ity
re|li|able
re|li|ably
re|li|ance
re|li|ant
relic
rel|ict
re|lief
re|lieve
△ re|lieves
△ re|lieved
△ re|liev|ing
re|lieved
re|li|gion
re|li|gious
NOUN
sing. and pl.
re|li|giously
re|li|gious|ness
re|lin|quish
△ re|lin|qui|shes
△ re|lin|quished
△ re|lin|quish|
  ing
re|lin|quish|
  ment
re|li|quary
△ re|li|quar|ies
rel|ish
VERB
△ rel|ishes
△ rel|ished
△ rel|ish|ing
re|live
△ re|lives
△ re|lived
△ re|liv|ing
re|load

△ re|loads
△ re|loa|ded
△ re|load|ing
re|lo|cate
△ re|lo|cates
△ re|lo|ca|ted
△ re|lo|ca|ting
re|lo|ca|tion
re|luct|ance
re|luct|ant
re|luct|antly
rely
△ re|lies
△ re|lied
△ re|ly|ing
re|main
△ re|mains
△ re|mained
△ re|main|ing
re|main|der
VERB
△ re|main|ders
△ re|main|dered
△ re|main|der|
ing
re|mains
re|make
VERB
△ re|makes
△ re|made
△ re|ma|king
re|mand
VERB
△ re|mands
△ re|man|ded
△ re|mand|ing
re|mark
VERB
△ re|marks
△ re|marked
△ re|mark|ing
re|mark|able
re|mark|ably
Re|marque

re|marry
△ re|mar|ries
△ re|mar|ried
△ re|mar|ry|ing
Rem|brandt
re|me|di|able
re|me|dial
re|me|di|ally
rem|edy
NOUN
△ rem|edies
VERB
△ rem|ed|ies
△ rem|ed|ied
△ rem|edy|ing
re|mem|ber
△ re|mem|bers
△ re|mem|bered
△ re|mem|ber|
ing
re|mem|brance
re|mind
△ re|minds
△ re|minded
△ re|mind|ing
re|minder
re|mi|nisce
△ re|mi|nis|ces
△ re|mi|nisced
△ re|mi|nis|cing
re|mi|nis|cence
re|mi|nis|cent
re|miss
re|mis|sion
re|missly
re|miss|ness
remit
VERB
△ re|mits
△ re|mit|ted
△ re|mit|ting
re|mit|tance
re|mit|tent
remix

NOUN
△ re|mixes
VERB
△ re|mixes
△ re|mixed
△ re|mix|ing
rem|nant
re|mon|strance
rem|on|strate
△ rem|on|strates
△ rem|on|stra|
ted
△ rem|on|stra|
ting
re|mon|stra|tion
re|morse
re|morse|ful
re|morse|fully
re|morse|less
re|morse|lessly
re|mote
re|mote-con|
trolled
re|motely
re|mote|ness
re|mould
VERB
△ re|moulds
△ re|moul|ded
△ re|mould|ing
re|mount
VERB
△ re|mounts
△ re|moun|ted
△ re|mount|ing
re|mov|able
re|moval
re|move
VERB
△ re|moves
△ re|moved
△ re|mov|ing
re|moved
re|mover

re|mu|ner|ate
△ re|mu|ner|ates
△ re|mu|ner|ated
△ re|mu|ner|
ating
re|mu|ner|ation
re|mu|ner|ative
Remus

Re|nais|sance
*revival of arts
etc in 14–16c
Europe*
   ⚠ renaissance
   ⚠ renascence

---

re|nais|sance
*rebirth; revival,
esp. cultural*
   ⚠ Renaissance
   ⚠ renascence

---

renal
re|name
△ re|names
△ re|named
△ re|na|ming

---

re|nas|cence
being born again
   ⚠ Renaissance
   ⚠ renaissance

---

re|nas|cent
rend
△ rends
△ rent
△ rend|ing
Ren|dell
ren|der
△ ren|ders
△ ren|dered
△ ren|der|ing
ren|der|ing
ren|dez|vous

NOUN
sing. and pl.
VERB
△ ren|dez|vous
△ ren|dez|
   voused
△ ren|dez|vous|
   ing
ren|di|tion
rend|zina
Rene
ren|egade
re|nege
△ re|ne|ges
△ re|neged
△ re|ne|ging
re|ne|ger
renew
△ re|news
△ re|newed
△ re|new|ing
re|new|able
re|newal
re|newer
renin
ren|net
ren|nin
Reno
Ren|oir
re|nounce
△ re|noun|ces
△ re|nounced
△ re|noun|cing
re|nounce|ment
re|noun|cer
re|no|vate
△ re|no|vates
△ re|no|va|ted
△ re|no|va|ting
re|no|va|tion
re|no|va|tor
re|nown
re|nowned
rent

VERB
△ rents
△ ren|ted
△ rent|ing
ren|tal
re|nun|ci|ation
re|open
△ re|opens
△ re|opened
△ re|open|ing
re|or|der
△ re|or|ders
△ re|or|dered
△ re|or|der|ing
rep
re|paint
VERB
△ re|paints
△ re|pain|ted
△ re|paint|ing
re|pair
VERB
△ re|pairs
△ re|paired
△ re|pair|ing

> re|pair|able
> *that can be*
> *repaired*
> ⚠ reparable

> rep|ar|able
> *that can be put*
> *right*
> ⚠ repairable

re|par|ation
re|par|tee
re|past
re|pat|ri|ate
△ re|pat|ri|ates
△ re|pat|ri|ated
△ re|pat|ri|ating
re|pat|ri|ation
repay

△ re|pays
△ re|paid
△ re|pay|ing
re|pay|able
re|pay|ment
re|peal
VERB
△ re|peals
△ re|pealed
△ re|peal|ing
re|peal|able
re|peat
VERB
△ re|peats
△ re|pea|ted
△ re|peat|ing
re|peat|able
re|pea|ted
re|peat|edly
re|pea|ter
repel
△ re|pels
△ re|pelled
△ re|pel|ling
re|pel|lence
re|pel|lent
re|pel|lently
re|pent
△ re|pents
△ re|pen|ted
△ re|pent|ing
re|pent|ance
re|pent|ant
re|per|cus|sion
re|per|cus|sive
rep|er|toire
rep|er|tory
△ rep|er|tor|ies
re|pe|ti|tion
re|pe|ti|tious
re|pe|ti|tiously
re|pe|ti|tious|
   ness
re|pet|it|ive

re|pet|it|ively
re|pet|it|ive|ness
re|pine
△ re|pines
△ re|pined
△ re|pi|ning
re|place
△ re|pla|ces
△ re|placed
△ re|pla|cing
re|place|able
re|place|ment
re|plant
△ re|plants
△ re|plan|ted
△ re|plant|ing
re|play
VERB
△ re|plays
△ re|played
△ re|play|ing
re|plen|ish
△ re|plen|ishes
△ re|plen|ished
△ re|plen|ish|ing
re|plen|ish|ment
re|plete
re|plete|ness
re|ple|tion
rep|lica
rep|lic|able
rep|li|cate
△ rep|li|cates
△ rep|li|ca|ted
△ rep|li|ca|ting
reply
NOUN
△ re|plies
VERB
△ re|plies
△ re|plied
△ re|ply|ing
re|point
△ re|points

△ re|poin|ted
△ re|point|ing
re|port
  VERB
△ re|ports
△ re|por|ted
△ re|port|ing
re|port|edly
re|por|ter
re|pose
  VERB
△ re|po|ses
△ re|posed
△ re|po|sing
re|pos|it|ory
△ re|pos|it|or|ies
re|pos|sess
△ re|pos|ses|ses
△ re|pos|sessed
△ re|pos|sess|ing
re|pos|ses|sion
rep|re|hend
△ rep|re|hends
△ rep|re|hen|ded
△ rep|re|hend|
  ing
rep|re|hen|sible
rep|re|hen|sibly
rep|re|sent
△ rep|re|sents
△ rep|re|sen|ted
△ rep|re|sent|ing
rep|re|sen|ta|tion
rep|re|sen|ta|
  tional
rep|re|sen|ta|tive
rep|re|sen|ta|
  tively
rep|re|sen|ta|
  tive|ness
re|press
△ re|pres|ses
△ re|pressed
△ re|press|ing

re|pres|sion
re|pres|sive
re|pres|sive|ness
re|pres|sor
re|prieve
  VERB
△ re|prieves
△ re|prieved
△ re|priev|ing
rep|ri|mand
△ rep|ri|mands
△ rep|ri|man|
  ded
△ rep|ri|mand|
  ing
re|print
  VERB
△ re|prints
△ re|prin|ted
△ re|print|ing
re|pri|sal
re|prise
  VERB
△ re|pri|ses
△ re|prised
△ re|pri|sing
re|proach
△ re|proa|ches
△ re|proached
△ re|proach|ing
re|proach|ful
re|proach|fully
rep|ro|bate
re|pro|duce
△ re|pro|du|ces
△ re|pro|duced
△ re|pro|du|cing
re|pro|du|cible
re|pro|duc|tion
re|pro|duc|tive
re|pro|duc|tively
re|proof
re|prove
△ re|proves

△ re|proved
△ re|prov|ing
re|prov|ing
re|prov|ingly
rep|tile
rep|til|ian
Rep|ton
Re|pub|lic, The
re|pub|lic
re|pub|li|can
re|pub|li|can|ism
re|pu|di|ate
△ re|pu|di|ates
△ re|pu|di|ated
△ re|pu|di|ating
re|pu|di|ation
re|pug|nance
re|pug|nant
re|pug|nantly
re|pulse
  VERB
△ re|pul|ses
△ re|pulsed
△ re|pul|sing
re|pul|sion
re|pul|sive
re|pul|sively
re|pul|sive|ness
reput|able
reput|ably
re|pu|ta|tion
re|pute
  VERB
△ re|putes
△ re|pu|ted
△ re|pu|ting
re|pu|tedly
re|quest
  VERB
△ re|quests
△ re|ques|ted
△ re|quest|ing
requiem
re|quire

△ re|quires
△ re|quired
△ re|quir|ing
re|quire|ment
re|quis|ite
re|qui|si|tion
  VERB
△ re|qui|si|tions
△ re|qui|si|
  tioned
△ re|qui|si|tion|
  ing
re|qui|tal
re|quite
△ re|quites
△ re|qui|ted
△ re|qui|ting
rere|dos
△ rere|doses
re|route
△ re|routes
△ re|routed
△ re|route|ing
rerun
  VERB
△ re|runs
△ reran
△ re|run|ning
△ rerun
res|cind
△ res|cinds
△ res|cin|ded
△ res|cind|ing
res|cind|ment
re|scis|sion
res|cue
  VERB
△ res|cues
△ res|cued
△ res|cu|ing
res|cuer
re|search
  NOUN
△ re|sear|ches

VERB
△ re|sear|ches
△ re|searched
△ re|search|ing
re|sear|cher
re|sem|blance
re|sem|ble
△ re|sem|bles
△ re|sem|bled
△ re|sem|bling
resent
△ re|sents
△ re|sen|ted
△ re|sent|ing
re|sent|ful
re|sent|fully
re|sent|ful|ness
re|sent|ment
res|er|va|tion
re|serve
VERB
△ re|serves
△ re|served
△ re|ser|ving
re|served
re|serv|ist
res|er|voir
re|shuffle
VERB
△ re|shuffles
△ re|shuffled
△ re|shuf|fling
re|side
△ re|sides
△ re|si|ded
△ re|si|ding
resi|dence
resi|dency
△ resi|den|cies
resi|dent
re|si|den|tial
re|sid|ual
resi|due
re|sign

△ re|signs
△ re|signed
△ re|sign|ing
res|ig|na|tion
re|signed
re|sign|edly
re|si|li|ence
re|si|li|ency
re|si|li|ent
resin
res|in|ous
re|sist
△ re|sists
△ re|sis|ted
△ re|sist|ing
re|sist|ance
re|sist|ant
re|sist|ible
re|sis|tiv|ity
re|sis|tor
Res|nais
re|so|cial|iza|tion
re|sol|uble
reso|lute
re|so|lutely
reso|lute|ness
re|so|lu|tion
re|solve
VERB
△ re|solves
△ re|solved
△ re|sol|ving
re|solved
res|on|ance
res|on|ant
res|on|antly
res|on|ate
△ res|on|ates
△ res|on|ated
△ res|on|ating
res|on|ator
re|sort
VERB
△ re|sorts

△ re|sor|ted
△ re|sort|ing
re|sound
△ re|sounds
△ re|soun|ded
△ re|sound|ing
re|sound|ing
re|sound|ingly
re|source
re|source|ful
re|source|fully
re|source|ful|
   ness
re|spect
VERB
△ re|spects
△ re|spec|ted
△ re|spect|ing
re|spec|ta|bil|ity
re|spect|able
re|spect|ably
re|spect|ful
re|spect|fully
re|spect|ful|ness
re|spect|ing
re|spect|ive
re|spect|ively
re|spell
△ re|spells
△ re|spelled *or*
re|spelt
△ re|spell|ing
Res|pighi
res|pir|ation
res|pir|ator
res|pir|at|ory
re|spire
△ re|spires
△ re|spired
△ re|spir|ing
res|pite
VERB
△ res|pites
△ res|pi|ted

△ res|pit|ing *or*
   res|pi|ting
   according to
   pronunciation
re|splend|ence
re|splend|ent
re|splend|ently
re|spond
△ re|sponds
△ re|spon|ded
△ re|spond|ing
re|spond|ent
re|sponse
re|spon|si|bil|ity
△ re|spon|si|bil|
   it|ies
re|spon|sible
re|spon|sibly
re|spon|sive
re|spon|sively
re|spon|sive|ness
re|spray
VERB
△ re|sprays
△ re|sprayed
△ re|spray|ing

---

rest
sleep;
relaxation; enjoy
these; remainder
VERB
△ rests
△ res|ted
△ rest|ing
⚠ wrest

---

res|taur|ant
res|tau|ra|teur
rest|ful
rest|fully
rest|ful|ness
res|ti|tu|tion
rest|ive
rest|ively

rest|ive|ness
rest|less
rest|lessly
rest|less|ness
re|stor|able
Res|tor|ation
  return of the
  Stuarts to the
  English throne
  (1660)
res|tor|ation
  giving back;
  reconstruction;
  return to previous
  circumstances etc
re|stor|at|ive
re|store
  △ re|stores
  △ re|stored
  △ re|stor|ing
re|storer
re|strain
  △ re|strains
  △ re|strained
  △ re|strain|ing
re|strained
re|straint
re|strict
  △ re|stricts
  △ re|stric|ted
  △ re|strict|ing
re|stric|ted
re|stric|tion
re|strict|ive
re|strict|ively
re|sult
  VERB
  △ re|sults
  △ re|sul|ted
  △ re|sult|ing
re|sul|tant
re|sume
  △ re|sumes
  △ re|sumed

△ re|su|ming
ré|sumé
re|sump|tion
re|sur|gence
re|sur|gent
re|sur|rect
  △ re|sur|rects
  △ re|sur|rec|ted
  △ re|sur|rect|ing
re|sur|rec|tion
Re|sur|rec|tion:
  Cook|ham, The
re|sus|ci|tate
  △ re|sus|ci|tates
  △ re|sus|ci|ta|ted
  △ re|sus|ci|ta|
    ting
re|sus|ci|ta|tion
re|tail
  VERB
  △ re|tails
  △ re|tailed
  △ re|tail|ing
re|tailer
re|tain
  △ re|tains
  △ re|tained
  △ re|tain|ing
re|tainer
re|take
  VERB
  △ re|takes
  △ re|took
  △ re|ta|king
  △ re|ta|ken
re|ta|li|ate
  △ re|ta|li|ates
  △ re|ta|li|ated
  △ re|ta|li|ating
re|ta|li|ation
re|ta|li|atory
re|tard
  △ re|tards
  △ re|tar|ded

△ re|tard|ing
re|tard|ant
re|tar|da|tion
re|tar|ded

---

retch
  strain to vomit
  NOUN
  △ ret|ches
  VERB
  △ ret|ches
  △ retched
  △ retch|ing
  ⚠ wretch

---

re|ten|tion
re|ten|tive
re|ten|tively
re|ten|tive|ness
re|tex|ture
  △ re|tex|tures
  △ re|tex|tured
  △ re|tex|tur|ing
re|think
  VERB
  △ re|thinks
  △ re|thought
  △ re|think|ing
re|ti|cence
re|ti|cent
re|ti|cu|late
  VERB
  △ re|ti|cu|lates
  △ re|ti|cu|la|ted
  △ re|ti|cu|la|ting
re|ti|cule
ret|ina
ret|inal
ret|inol
ret|inue
re|tiral
re|tire
  △ re|tires
  △ re|tired
  △ re|tir|ing

re|tired
re|tire|ment
re|tir|ing
re|tir|ingly
re|tort
  VERB
  △ re|torts
  △ re|tor|ted
  △ re|tort|ing
re|touch
  VERB
  △ re|touches
  △ re|touched
  △ re|touch|ing
re|trace
  △ re|tra|ces
  △ re|traced
  △ re|tra|cing
re|tract
  △ re|tracts
  △ re|trac|ted
  △ re|tract|ing
re|tract|able
re|tract|ile
re|trac|tion
re|train
  △ re|trains
  △ re|trained
  △ re|train|ing
re|tread
  VERB
  △ re|treads
  △ re|trod
  △ re|tread|ing
  △ re|trod|den
re|treat
  VERB
  △ re|treats
  △ re|trea|ted
  △ re|treat|ing
re|trench
  △ re|tren|ches
  △ re|trenched
  △ re|trench|ing

re|trench|ment
re|trial
ret|ri|bu|tion
re|tri|bu|tive
re|triev|able
re|trieval
re|trieve
△ re|trieves
△ re|trieved
△ re|triev|ing
re|trie|ver
ret|ro|ac|tive
ret|ro|ac|tively
ret|ro|ac|tiv|ity
ret|ro|grade
VERB
△ ret|ro|grades
△ ret|ro|gra|ded
△ ret|ro|gra|ding
ret|ro|gress
△ ret|ro|gres|ses
△ ret|ro|gressed
△ ret|ro|gress|
ing
ret|ro|gres|sion
ret|ro|gres|sive
retro-rocket
ret|ro|spect
ret|ro|spec|tion
ret|ro|spect|ive
ret|ro|spect|ively
re|troussé
ret|ro|vi|rus
retry
△ re|tries
△ re|tried
△ re|try|ing
ret|sina
re|turn
VERB
△ re|turns
△ re|turned
△ re|turn|ing
re|turn|able

Re|turn of the
Na|tive, The
Reu|ben
re|union
re|unite
△ re|unites
△ re|uni|ted
△ re|uni|ting
Reu|ter
rev
VERB
△ revs
△ revved
△ rev|ving
re|value
△ re|val|ues
△ re|val|ued
△ re|valu|ing
re|vamp
△ re|vamps
△ re|vamped
△ re|vamp|ing
re|veal
△ re|veals
△ re|vealed
△ re|veal|ing
re|veal|ing
re|veille
revel
△ rev|els
△ rev|elled
△ rev|el|ling
re|vela|tion
Re|vela|tion of
John, The
re|vela|tory
rev|el|ler
rev|elry
△ rev|el|ries
re|venge
VERB
△ re|ven|ges
△ re|venged
△ re|ven|ging

re|venge|ful
rev|enue
re|ver|ber|ate
△ re|ver|ber|ates
△ re|ver|ber|ated
△ re|ver|ber|
ating
re|ver|ber|ation
re|vere
△ re|veres
△ re|vered
△ re|ver|ing
rev|er|ence
rev|er|end
rev|er|ent
rev|er|en|tial
rev|er|en|tially
rev|er|ently
rev|erie
re|vers
sing. and pl.
re|ver|sal
re|verse
VERB
△ re|ver|ses
△ re|versed
△ re|ver|sing
re|versed
re|ver|sible
re|ver|sion
re|vert
△ re|verts
△ re|ver|ted
△ re|vert|ing

re|view
inspect;
examine; re-
examine; write
an evaluation
of; these
activities
VERB
△ re|views

△ re|viewed
△ re|view|ing
⚠ revue

re|viewer
re|vile
△ re|viles
△ re|viled
△ re|vi|ling
re|vile|ment
re|viler
re|vise
△ re|vi|ses
△ re|vised
△ re|vi|sing
re|vi|ser
re|vi|sion
re|vi|sion|ism
re|vi|sion|ist
re|vi|tal|ize
△ re|vi|tal|izes
△ re|vi|tal|ized
△ re|vi|tal|izing
re|vi|val
re|vi|val|ism
re|vi|val|ist
re|vive
△ re|vives
△ re|vived
△ re|vi|ving
re|vi|vi|fi|ca|tion
re|viv|ify
△ re|vi|vi|fies
△ re|vi|vi|fied
△ re|vi|vi|fy|ing
re|vo|cable
re|vo|ca|tion
re|voke
VERB
△ re|vokes
△ re|voked
△ re|vo|king
re|volt

VERB
△ re|volts
△ re|vol|ted
△ re|volt|ing
re|vol|ted
re|volt|ing
re|volt|ingly
re|vo|lu|tion
re|vo|lu|tion|ary
NOUN
△ re|vo|lu|tion|
aries
re|vo|lu|tion|ize
△ re|vo|lu|tion|
izes
△ re|vo|lu|tion|
ized
△ re|vo|lu|tion|
izing
re|vol|vable
re|volve
△ re|volves
△ re|volved
△ re|vol|ving
re|vol|ver
re|vol|ving

revue
variety show
⚠review

re|vul|sion
re|ward
VERB
△ re|wards
△ re|war|ded
△ re|ward|ing
re|ward|ing
re|wind
△ re|winds
△ re|wound
△ re|wind|ing
re|wire
△ re|wires
△ re|wired

△ re|wir|ing
re|word
△ re|words
△ re|wor|ded
△ re|word|ing
re|write
VERB
△ re|writes
△ re|wrote
△ re|wri|ting
Rex
Reyk|ja|vík
Rey|nolds
rhachis *see*
rachis
Rha|da|man|
thus
Rhae|tian
rhap|sodic
rhap|sod|ical
rhap|sod|ic|ally
rhap|sod|ize
△ rhap|sod|izes
△ rhap|sod|ized
△ rhap|sod|izing
rhap|sody
△ rhap|so|dies
*Rhap|sody in
Blue*
rhea
Rheims
*Rhein|gold, Das
(The Rhine|
gold)*
rhe|nium
rhe|ol|ogy
rheo|stat
rhe|sus
rhet|oric
rhe|tor|ical
rheum
rheu|ma|tic
rheu|ma|tism
rheu|ma|toid

Rhi|an|non
Rhine
rhine|stone
rhi|ni|tis
rhino
rhi|no|ceros
△ rhi|no|cer|oses
or rhi|no|ceros
rhi|no|virus
rhi|zoid
rhi|zome
Rhoda
Rhode Island
Rhodes
rho|dium
rho|do|den|dron
rho|dop|sin
rhom|boid
rhom|bus
△ rhom|buses *or*
rhombi
Rhona
Rhondda
Rhône
rhu|barb
Rhyl

rhyme
verse; make this
VERB
△ rhymes
△ rhymed
△ rhym|ing
⚠rime

rhy|ol|ite
Rhys
rhythm
rhyth|mic
rhyth|mi|cal
rhyth|mic|ally
ria
Ri|alto
rib

VERB
△ ribs
△ ribbed
△ rib|bing
rib|ald
rib|aldry
rib|and
ribbed
Rib|ben|trop
rib|bing
rib|bon
ri|bo|fla|vin
ri|bo|nu|cleic
ri|bose
ri|bo|some
Riccio *see*
Rizzio
rice
rich
△ richer
△ rich|est
Rich|ard
Rich|ards
Rich|ard|son
Riche|lieu
riches
richly
Rich|mond
rich|ness
Rich|ter
rick
VERB
△ ricks
△ ricked
△ rick|ing
rick|ets
rick|ety
rick-rack
rick|shaw
ri|co|chet
VERB
△ ri|co|chets
△ ri|co|cheted *or*
ri|co|chet|ted

△ ri|co|chet|ing
or ri|co|chet|
  ting
rid
△ rids
△ rid
△ rid|ding
rid|dance
rid|den
rid|dle
  VERB
△ rid|dles
△ rid|dled
△ rid|dling
ride
  VERB
△ rides
△ rode
△ rid|ding
△ rid|den
rider
ridge
  VERB
△ rid|ges
△ ridged
△ rid|ging
ridged
ridge|pole
Ridge|way
ri|di|cule
  VERB
△ ri|di|cules
△ ri|di|culed
△ ri|di|cu|ling
ri|dicu|lous
ri|dicu|lously
ri|dicu|lous|ness
ri|ding
Rid|ley
Rie|fens|tahl
Ries|ling
rife
riff
rif|fle

△ rif|fles
△ rif|fled
△ rif|fling
riff-raff
ri|fle
  VERB
△ ri|fles
△ ri|fled
△ ri|fling
rift
  VERB
△ rifts
△ rif|ted
△ rift|ing
rig
  VERB
△ rigs
△ rigged
△ rig|ging
Riga
rig|ging

right
  opposite of left;
  suitable;
  privilege etc that
  cannot be
  denied;
  completely;
  immediately
  VERB
△ rights
△ righ|ted
△ right|ing
  ⚠rite
  ⚠write

right-angled
right|eous
right|eously
right|eous|ness
right|ful
right|fully
right|ful|ness
right-hand

right-han|ded
right-han|ded|
  ness
right-han|der
right|ism
right|ist
rightly
right-minded
right|ward
right-wing
right-winger
rigid
ri|gid|ity
rigidly
rig|id|ness
rig|ma|role
Ri|go|letto
rigor mor|tis
rig|or|ous
rig|or|ously
rig|or|ous|ness
rig|our
rig-out
Rijks|mu|seum
rile
△ riles
△ riled
△ ri|ling
Rilke

rill
  stream
  ⚠rille

rille
  moon valley
  ⚠rill

rim
  VERB
△ rims
△ rimmed
△ rim|ming
Rim|baud

rime
  frost; cover with
  frost
  VERB
△ rimes
△ rimed
△ ri|ming
  ⚠rhyme

rime
  verse; make this
  see rhyme
Rime of the An|
  cient Mar|iner,
  The
rim|less
rimmed
Rim|sky-Kor|sa|
  kov
rimy
△ ri|mier
△ ri|mi|est
rind
  VERB
△ rinds
△ rinded
△ rind|ing

ring
  VERB
△ rings
  put ring on
△ ringed
  sound bell etc
△ rang
△ ring|ing
  sound bell etc
△ rung
  ⚠wring

ring|bolt
Ring des Ni|be|
lun|gen, Der
(The Ni|bel|
ung's Ring)

ringed
ringer
ring|lea|der
ring|let
ring|mas|ter
ring-pull
ring|side
ring|way
ring|worm
rink
rinse
  VERB
  △ rin|ses
  △ rinsed
  △ rins|ing
rin|ser
Rio de Ja|neiro
Rio Grande
Rioja
riot
  VERB
  △ riots
  △ rioted
  △ riot|ing
ri|oter
ri|ot|ous
ri|ot|ously
ri|ot|ous|ness
rip
  VERB
  △ rips
  △ ripped
  △ rip|ping
ri|par|ian
rip|cord
ripe
  △ riper
  △ ri|pest
ripen
  △ ri|pens
  △ ri|pened
  △ ri|pen|ing
ripe|ness
ri|pi|eno

△ ri|pi|eni or ri|
  pi|enos
rip-off
Ripon
ri|poste
  VERB
  △ ri|postes
  △ ri|pos|ted
  △ ri|post|ing
rip|per
rip|ple
  VERB
  △ rip|ples
  △ rip|pled
  △ rip|pling
rip|pling
rip|ply
  △ rip|plier
  △ rip|pli|est
rip-roar|ing
rip|saw
Rip Van Winkle
rise
  VERB
  △ rises
  △ rose
  △ ri|sing
  △ risen
riser
ris|ib|il|ity
ris|ible
ri|sing
risk
  VERB
  △ risks
  △ risked
  △ risk|ing
risk|ily
risky
  △ ris|kier
  △ ris|ki|est
Ri|sor|gi|mento
ris|otto
ris|qué

ris|sole
ri|tard|ando
  NOUN
  △ ri|tard|an|dos
  or ri|tard|andi

┌─────────────────┐
│ rite   │
│   *ceremony*   │
│   ⚠ right   │
│   ⚠ write   │
└─────────────────┘

Rite of Spring,
  The (Vesna
  Svyash|chen|
  naya)
rit|ual
ritu|al|ism
ritu|al|ist
ritu|al|is|tic
ritu|al|is|tic|ally
ritu|ally
ritzy
  △ rit|zier
  △ rit|zi|est
rival
  VERB
  △ ri|vals
  △ ri|valled
  △ ri|val|ling
ri|valry
  △ ri|val|ries
Ri|vals, The
riven
river
riv|er|ine
rivet
  VERB
  △ rivets
  △ riv|eted
  △ riv|et|ing
riv|eter
riv|et|ing
ri|vi|era
ri|vu|let
Riyadh

Riz|zio
Roach
roach
  fish
  sing. and pl.
  other senses
  △ roa|ches

┌─────────────────────┐
│ road   │
│   *way for vehicles etc* │
│   ⚠ rode   │
│   ⚠ rowed   │
└─────────────────────┘

road|bed
road|block
road-hog
road|hold|ing
road|house
roadie
road|side
road|stead
road|ster
road|way
road|work
road|wor|thi|ness
road|wor|thy
roam
  VERB
  △ roams
  △ roamed
  △ roam|ing
roamer
roan
roar
  VERB
  △ roars
  △ roared
  △ roar|ing
roar|ing
roast
  VERB
  △ roasts
  △ roas|ted
  △ roast|ing
roas|ter

roast|ing
rob
△ robs
△ robbed
△ rob|bing
Robbe-Gril|let
rob|ber
rob|bery
△ rob|ber|ies
Rob|bins
robe
VERB
△ robes
△ robed
△ ro|bing
Rob|ert
Rob|erts
Robe|son
Robes|pi|erre
Robey
Robin
robin
Robin Good|
fellow
Robin Hood
Rob|in|son
*Rob|in|son Cru|
soe*
robot
ro|botic
ro|bot|ics
Rob Roy
Rob|son
ro|bust
ro|bustly
ro|bust|ness
roc
Roch|dale
Ro|ches|ter
rochet
rock
VERB
△ rocks
△ rocked

△ rock|ing
rocka|billy
rock 'n' roll
rock-bottom
Rocke|fel|ler
rocker
rock|ery
△ rock|er|ies
rocket
VERB
△ rock|ets
△ rock|eted
△ rock|et|ing
rock|ily
rocki|ness
rock|rose
rocky
△ rock|ier
△ rocki|est
ro|coco
rod

| rode |
| *past tense of* |
| *ride* |
| ⚠road |
| ⚠rowed |

ro|dent
rodeo
Rod|er|ick
Rod|er|ick Ran|
dom, The Ad|
ven|tures of
Rod|gers
Rodin
Rod|ney
ro|do|mon|tade
VERB
△ ro|do|mon|
tades
△ ro|do|mon|ta|
ded
△ ro|do|mon|ta|
ding

| roe |
| *fish eggs or* |
| *sperm; sort of* |
| *deer* |
| ⚠row |

roentgen *see*
röntgen
ro|ga|tion
Roger
roger
VERB
△ ro|gers
△ ro|gered
△ ro|ger|ing
Ro|gers
Roget
rogue
ro|guery
△ ro|guer|ies
ro|guish
ro|guishly
ro|guish|ness
rois|ter
△ rois|ters
△ rois|tered
△ rois|ter|ing
rois|terer
Rokeby Venus,
The
Ro|land

| role |
| *part in play etc* |
| ⚠roll |

Rolf
roll
cylindrical
object; list; turn
like a cylinder
VERB
△ rolls
△ rolled
△ roll|ing

Rol|land
roll-call
rol|ler
Rol|ler|blades
rol|ler|coas|ter
rol|ler-skate
△ rol|ler-skates
△ rol|ler-ska|ted
△ rol|ler-ska|ting
rol|ler-ska|ter
rol|ler-ska|ting
rol|lick|ing
rol|ling
rol|ling-pin
Rol|ling Stones
roll|mop
roll|neck
roll-on
roll-off
Rolls
Rolls-Royce
roll-top
roll-up
roly-poly
NOUN
△ roly-polies
Roman
roman-à-clef
△ ro|mans-à-clef
ro|mance
VERB
△ ro|man|ces
△ ro|manced
△ ro|man|cing
Roman de la
Rose
Ro|man|esque
roman fleuve
Ro|ma|nia
Ro|ma|nian
Ro|man|ist
Ro|man|iza|tion
assimilation of
Roman culture

ro|man|iza|tion
use of roman
alphabet
Ro|manov
Ro|mans, Let|
ter of Paul to
the
ro|man|tic
ro|man|tic|ally
Ro|man|ti|cism
Ro|man|ti|cist
ro|man|ti|cize
  VERB
  △ ro|man|ti|ci|
  zes
  △ ro|man|ti|
  cized
  △ ro|man|ti|ci|
  zing
Ro|many
  △ Ro|man|ies
Rome
Romeo
Romeo and
Juliet
Rom|ish
Rom|mel
romp
  VERB
  △ romps
  △ romped
  △ romp|ing
rom|pers
Romu|lus
ron|deau
  △ ron|deaux
rondo
  △ ron|dos
Ron|sard
rönt|gen
rood
roof
  VERB
  △ roofs

△ roofed
△ roof|ing
roof|ing
roof|top
rook
  VERB
  △ rooks
  △ rooked
  △ rook|ing
rook|ery
  △ rook|er|ies
rookie
room
  VERB
  △ rooms
  △ roomed
  △ room|ing
Room at the
Top
room|ful
roo|mi|ness
room|mate
roomy
  △ roo|mier
  △ roo|mi|est
Roose|velt
roost
  VERB
  △ roosts
  △ roos|ted
  △ roost|ing
roos|ter
root
  VERB
  △ roots
  △ roo|ted
  △ root|ing
roo|ted
root|less
Roots
root|stock
rope
  VERB
  △ ropes

△ roped
△ ro|ping
rope|able
rope|way
ropy
  △ ro|pier
  △ ro|pi|est
Roque|fort
ro-ro
ror|qual
Ror|schach
Rory
ro|sa|ceous
Rosa|lind
Rosa|mund
ro|sary
  △ ro|sar|ies
Ros|cius
Rose
rose
rosé
ro|seate
Ro|seau
rose|bay wil|
  low|herb
Rose|bery
rose-col|oured
rose|hip
Rose|mary
rose|mary
Ro|sen|crantz
  and Guil|den|
  stern are Dead
Ro|sen|ka|va|lier,
  Der (The
  Knight of the
  Rose)
Roses, Wars of
  the
rose-tin|ted
Ro|setta Stone
ro|sette
rose|wood
Rosh Ha|sha|nah

Ro|si|cru|cian
ro|sily
rosin
  VERB
  △ ros|ins
  △ ros|ined
  △ ros|in|ing
ro|si|ness
Ros|kilde
Ross
Ros|sel|lini
Ros|setti
Ros|sini
Ross|lare
Ros|tand
ros|ter
  VERB
  △ ros|ters
  △ ros|tered
  △ ros|ter|ing
ros|tral
Ros|tro|po|vich
ros|trum
  △ ros|trums *or*
  ros|tra
rosy
  △ ro|sier
  △ ro|si|est
rot
  VERB
  △ rots
  △ rot|ted
  △ rot|ting
rota
Ro|tar|ian
Ro|tary
club
ro|tary
revolving on
axle; thing that
does this
  NOUN
  △ ro|tar|ies
ro|tate

△ ro|tates
△ ro|ta|ted
△ ro|ta|ting
ro|ta|tion
Rotavator *see*
  Rotovator

rote
  parrot-learning
  ⚠ wrote

rot|gut
Roth
Roth|er|ham
Roth|er|mere
Roths|child
roti
ro|ti|fer
ro|tis|serie
rotor
Ro|to|va|tor
rot|ten
rot|ten|ness
rot|ter
Rot|ter|dam
Rott|weiler
ro|tund
ro|tunda
ro|tund|ity
ro|tundly
ro|tund|ness
Rou|bil|iac
rou|ble
roué
Rouen
rouge
  VERB
  △ rouges
  △ rouged
  △ rou|ging
Rouge et le noir,
  Le (The Red
  and the Black)
Rou|get de
  Lisle

rough
  not smooth; not
  gentle;
  approximate;
  thug
  ADJ.
  △ rougher
  △ rough|est
  ⚠ ruff

rough|age
rough-and-
  ready
rough-and-
  tumble
rough|cast
  VERB
  △ rough|casts
  △ rough|cas|ted
  △ rough|cast|ing
  △ rough|cast
roughen
  △ rough|ens
  △ rough|ened
  △ rough|en|ing
rough-hew
  △ rough-hews
  △ rough-hewed
  △ rough-hew|
    ing
rough-hewn
rough|house
roughly
rough|neck
rough|ness
rough|shod
rou|lette
Roumania *see*
  Romania
round
  VERB
  △ rounds
  △ roun|ded
  △ round|ing

ADJ.
△ roun|der
△ round|est
round|about
roun|ded
roun|del
roun|de|lay
round|ers
Round|head
roundly
round|ness
round-shoul|
  dered
round-up
round|worm
rouse
  △ rou|ses
  △ roused
  △ rous|ing
rous|ing
Rous|seau
roust|about
rout
  VERB
  △ routs
  △ rou|ted
  △ rout|ing
route
  VERB
  △ routes
  △ routed
  △ route|ing
rou|tine
rou|tinely
Rout|ledge
roux
  sing. and pl.
rove
  △ roves
  △ roved
  △ ro|ving
rover
ro|ving

row
  propel by oars;
  this activity;
  argue;
  argument; things
  arranged in a
  line
  VERB
  △ rows
  △ rowed
  △ row|ing
  ⚠ roe

rowan
row|boat
row|dily
row|di|ness
rowdy
  NOUN
  △ row|dies
  ADJ.
  △ row|dier
  △ row|di|est
row|dy|ism
Rowe

rowed
  past tense of row
  ⚠ road
  ⚠ rode

rowel
Row|ena
rower
row|ing
Row|land|son
row|lock
Rown|tree
Roy
royal
Royal Hunt of
  the Sun, The
roy|al|ism
roy|al|ist
roy|ally

roy|alty
△ roy|al|ties
Royce
roz|zer
rub
 VERB
 △ rubs
 △ rubbed
 △ rub|bing
Ru|bái|yt of
 Omar Khay|
 yám, The
ru|bato
 NOUN
 △ ru|bati *or* ru|
  ba|tos
rub|ber
rub|ber|ize
 △ rub|ber|izes
 △ rub|ber|ized
 △ rub|ber|izing
rub|ber|neck
 VERB
 △ rub|ber|necks
 △ rub|ber|
  necked
 △ rub|ber|neck|
  ing
rub|ber-stamp
 △ rub|ber-
  stamps
 △ rub|ber-
  stamped
 △ rub|ber-
  stamp|ing
rub|bery
rub|bing
rub|bish
 VERB
 △ rub|bi|shes
 △ rub|bished
 △ rub|bish|ing
rub|bishy
rub|ble

Rub|bra
rub-down
ru|bella
Ru|bens
Ru|bi|con
ru|bi|cund
ru|bid|ium
Ru|bik
Ru|bin|stein
ruble *see* rouble
rub|ric
Ruby
ruby
 NOUN
 △ ru|bies
ruche
ruched
ruck
 VERB
 △ rucks
 △ rucked
 △ ruck|ing
ruck|sack
ruc|tion
rudd
rud|der
rud|der|less
ruddy
 △ rud|dier
 △ rud|di|est
rude
 △ ruder
 △ ru|dest
rudely
rude|ness
ru|di|ment
ru|di|men|tary
Ru|dolf
rue
 VERB
 △ rues
 △ rued
 △ ruing *or* rue|
  ing

rue|ful
rue|fully
rue|ful|ness

> ruff
> *frill; trump at*
> *cards*
> VERB
> △ ruffs
> △ ruffed
> △ ruff|ing
> △ rough

ruf|fian
ruf|fi|anly
ruf|fle
 VERB
 △ ruf|fles
 △ ruf|fled
 △ ruf|fling
ru|fous
Rufus
rug
Rugby
rug|ged
rug|gedly
rug|ged|ness
rug|ger
Ruhr
ruin
 VERB
 △ ruins
 △ ru|ined
 △ ru|in|ing
ru|in|ation
ru|in|ous
ru|in|ously
Ruis|dael
rule
 VERB
 △ rules
 △ ruled
 △ ru|ling
ruler
ru|ling

rum
 ADJ.
 △ rum|mer
 △ rum|mest
Rumania *see*
 Romania
Rumanian *see*
 Romanian
rumba
rum|ble
 VERB
 △ rum|bles
 △ rum|bled
 △ rum|bling
rum|bling
rum|bus|tious
ru|men
 △ ru|mina
ru|min|ant
ru|min|ate
 △ ru|min|ates
 △ ru|min|ated
 △ ru|min|ating
ru|min|ation
ru|min|at|ive
rum|mage
 VERB
 △ rum|ma|ges
 △ rum|maged
 △ rum|ma|ging
rummy
ru|mour
 VERB
 △ ru|mours
 △ ru|moured
 △ ru|mour|ing
rump
rum|ple
 VERB
 △ rum|ples
 △ rum|pled
 △ rump|ling
rum|pled
rum|pus

△ rum|puses
rumpy-pumpy
run
  VERB
  △ runs
  △ ran
  △ run|ning
  △ run
run|about
run|away
Run|cie
Run|corn
run-down
rune

> rung
> *step on ladder;*
> *past tense of*
> *ring*
> ⚠ wrung

runic
run-in
run|nel
run|ner
run|ner-up
run|ning
run|ning-board
runny
  △ run|nier

△ run|ni|est
Run|ny|mede
run-off
run-of-the-mill
runt
run-through
run-up
run|way
Run|yon
rupee
Ru|pert
rup|ture
  VERB
  △ rup|tures
  △ rup|tured
  △ rup|tur|ing
rural
Rural Rides
ruse
rush
  NOUN
  △ rushes
Rush|die
rushy
Rusk
rusk
Rus|kin
Rus|sell

rus|set
Rus|sia
Rus|sian
rust
  VERB
  △ rusts
  △ rus|ted
  △ rust|ing
rus|tic
rus|tic|ally
rus|ti|cate
  △ rus|ti|cates
  △ rus|ti|ca|ted
  △ rus|ti|ca|ting
rus|ti|city
rust|ily
rus|ti|ness
rus|tle
  VERB
  △ rus|tles
  △ rus|tled
  △ rust|ling
rust|ler
rust|proof
rusty
  △ rus|tier
  △ rus|ti|est
rut

VERB
△ ruts
△ rut|ted
△ rut|ting
Ruth
Ruth, Book of
ru|then|ium
Ruth|er|ford
ruth|er|ford|ium
ruth|less
ruth|lessly
ruth|less|ness
ru|tile
Rut|land
rut|ted
  △ rut|teder
  △ rut|ted|est
Ruysdael *see*
  Ruisdael
Rwanda
Ryan
Ryder

> rye
> *sort of grain;*
> *whisky made*
> *from this*
> ⚠ wry

Ryle

S

Saar
Sabah
Sab|bath
sab|bat|ical
sa|ble
sabot
sa|bo|tage
VERB
△ sa|bo|ta|ges
△ sa|bo|taged
△ sa|bo|ta|ging
sa|bo|teur
sabre
sabre-rat|tling
sabre|tooth
sac
sac|cade
sac|char|ide
sac|charin
Sac|charo|my|
ces
sa|cer|do|tal
Sacha
sa|chet
sack
VERB
△ sacks
△ sacked
△ sack|ing
sack|but
sack|cloth
sack|ful
sack|ing
Sack|ville
Sack|ville-West
sacra
sac|ral
sac|ra|ment
sac|ra|men|tal
Sac|ra|mento
sac|red
sac|ri|fice

VERB
△ sac|ri|fi|ces
△ sac|ri|ficed
△ sac|ri|fi|cing
sac|ri|fi|cial
sac|ri|lege
sac|ri|legi|ous
sac|rist
sac|ris|tan
sac|risty
△ sac|ris|ties
sac|ro|sanct
sac|ro|sanc|tity
sac|rum
△ sacra
sad
△ sad|der
△ sad|dest
Sadat
sad|den
△ sad|dens
△ sad|dened
△ sad|den|ing
sad|dle
VERB
△ sad|dles
△ sad|dled
△ sad|dling
saddle|back
saddle|backed
sad|dler
sad|dlery
△ sad|dler|ies
Sad|du|cee
Sade
sadhu
sa|dism
sa|dist
sa|dis|tic
Sad|ler's Wells
sadly
sad|ness
sado-mas|och|
ism

sado-mas|och|ist
sado-mas|och|is|
tic
sa|fari
safe
ADJ.
△ safer
△ sa|fest
safe-con|duct
safe-deposit
safe|guard
VERB
△ safe|guards
△ safe|guar|ded
△ safe|guard|ing
safe|keep|ing
safely
safety
safety-lamp
saf|flower
saf|fron
sag
VERB
△ sags
△ sagged
△ sag|ging
saga
sa|ga|cious
sa|ga|city
Sagan
sage
ADJ.
△ sager
△ sagest
sage|brush
sag|gar
saggy
△ sag|gier
△ sag|gi|est
Sa|git|tar|ian
Sa|git|tar|ius
sago
Sa|hara
sahib

said
Sai|gon

sail
ship's canvas
sheet to catch
wind; trip in
boat; arm of
windmill; travel
by boat
NOUN
after number
△ sail
other senses
△ sails
VERB
△ sails
△ sailed
△ sail|ing
⚠ sale

sail|board
sail|board|ing
sail|cloth
sail|fish
sail|ing
sai|lor
sain|foin
Sains|bury
saint
St Al|bans
St Chris|to|
pher-Nevis
St Cyr
St David's

Saint-Denis
theatre director
⚠ St-Denis

St-Denis
Paris suburb
⚠ Saint-
Denis

sain|ted

Saint-Exu|péry
St Gal|len
St George's
St Gott|hard

St Hel|ena
Atlantic island
⚠St Helens

St Hel|ens
English town
⚠St Helena

St Hel|ier
saint|hood
St Ives
Saint Joan
St John's
Saint-Just
St Kilda
St Kitts-Nevis
see St
Christopher-
Nevis
Saint Laur|ent
St Leger
saint|li|ness
St-Lô
St Louis
St Lucia
saintly
St-Malo
St Moritz
St Pe|ters|burg
Saint-Sae|ns
St-Simon
St-Tropez
Saint Vin|cent
and the Gre|
na|dines
Saint Vi|tus's
dance
saith
sake
Sak|harov

sal
sa|laam
VERB
△ sa|laams
△ sa|laamed
△ sa|laam|ing
salable *see*
saleable
sa|la|cious
sa|la|cious|ness
salad
Sa|la|din
Sa|la|manca
sa|la|man|der
sa|lami
Sala|mis
sal|ar|ied
sal|ary
△ sal|ar|ies
Sa|la|zar
Sale

sale
*selling; cheap
offer; on cheap
offer*
⚠sail

sale|able
Salem
Sa|lerno
sale|room
sales|man
△ sales|men
sales|man|ship
sales|per|son
sales|wo|man
△ sales|wo|men
Sal|ford
Salic
sa|li|cy|lic
sa|li|ent
Sa|li|eri
sa|line
Sal|in|ger

sa|lin|ity
Salis|bury
sa|liva
sa|li|vary *or* sal|
iv|ary
*according to
pronunciation*
sa|li|vate
△ sa|li|vates
△ sa|li|va|ted
△ sa|li|va|ting
sa|li|va|tion
Salk
sal|low
VERB
△ sal|lows
△ sal|lowed
△ sal|low|ing
ADJ.
△ sal|lower
△ sal|low|est
sally
NOUN
△ sal|lies
VERB
△ sal|lies
△ sal|lied
△ sal|ly|ing
sal|mon
△ sal|mon *or* sal|
mons
sal|mon|ella
△ sal|mon|el|lae
Sa|lome
Salon
art exhibition

salon
*hairdresser's etc
shop; drawing
room*
⚠saloon

Salon d'Au|
tomne

Salon des In|dé|
pen|dants
Salon des Re|fu|
sés
Sa|lon|ica

sa|loon
*public room;
bar; sort of car*
⚠salon

Salop
sa|lop|ettes
sal|ping|ec|
tomy
salsa
sal|sify
△ sal|si|fies
SALT
salt
VERB
△ salts
△ salted
△ salt|ing
salted
salti|ness
salt|petre
salty
△ salt|ier
△ salti|est
sa|lu|bri|ous
sa|luki
sa|lu|tar|ily
sa|lu|tary
sa|lu|ta|tion
sa|lu|ta|tory
sa|lute
VERB
△ sa|lutes
△ sa|lu|ted
△ sa|lu|ting
Sal|va|dor
sal|vage
VERB
△ sal|va|ges

△ sal|vaged

△ sal|va|ging

sal|vage|able

sal|va|tion

salve

  VERB

△ salves

△ salved

△ sal|ving

sal|ver

sal|via

salvo

△ sal|vos *or* sal|

  voes

sal vo|la|tile

Sal|yut

Salz|burg

Sa|man|tha

Sa|maria

Sa|mar|itan

sa|mar|ium

Sam|ar|kand

samba

same

same|ness

samey

sam|iz|dat

Samos

sa|mosa

Sa|mo|thrace

samo|var

sam|pan

sam|phire

sam|ple

  VERB

△ sam|ples

△ sam|pled

△ samp|ling

samp|ler

samp|ling

Sam|son

Sam|uel

Sam|uel, Books

  of

sa|murai

  sing. and pl.

San'a

San An|dreas

  Fault

sa|na|tor|ium

△ sa|na|tori|ums

  or sa|na|toria

sanc|ti|fi|ca|tion

sanc|tify

△ sanc|ti|fies

△ sanc|ti|fied

△ sanc|ti|fy|ing

sanc|ti|mo|ni|ous

sanc|ti|mo|ni|

  ous|ness

sanc|tion

  VERB

△ sanc|tions

△ sanc|tioned

△ sanc|tion|ing

sanc|tity

sanc|tu|ary

△ sanc|tu|ar|ies

sanc|tum

△ sanc|tums *or*

  sancta

Sand

sand

  VERB

△ sands

△ san|ded

△ sand|ing

san|dal

san|dal|wood

sand|bag

  VERB

△ sand|bags

△ sand|bagged

△ sand|bag|ging

sand|bank

sand|blast

  VERB

△ sand|blasts

△ sand|blas|ted

△ sand|blast|ing

sand|boy

sand|castle

san|der

sand|hop|per

San Diego

San|dino

sand|man

San|down

sand|pa|per

  VERB

△ sand|pa|pers

△ sand|pa|pered

△ sand|pa|per|

  ing

sand|pi|per

sand|pit

sand|stone

sand|storm

Sand|wich

sand|wich

  NOUN

△ sand|wiches

  VERB

△ sand|wiches

△ sand|wiched

△ sand|wich|ing

sandy

△ san|dier

△ san|di|est

sane

△ saner

△ sa|nest

sanely

San Fran|cisco

sang

sang|froid

san|gria

san|guin|ary

san|guine

San|hed|rin

san|it|ary

sa|ni|ta|tion

san|it|iza|tion

san|it|ize

△ san|it|izes

△ san|it|ized

△ san|it|izing

san|ity

sank

San Ma|rino

san|pro

San Sal|va|dor

sans-culottes

San Se|bas|tian

san|serif

Sans|krit

Sans Souci

Santa Claus

Santa Fe

Santa Sophia

  see Hagia

  Sophia

San|tay|ana

San|ti|ago

Santo Do|

  mingo

San|tor|ini

Saône

São Paulo

São Tomé and

  Prín|cipe

sap

  VERB

△ saps

△ sapped

△ sap|ping

sa|pi|ence

sa|pi|ent

sap|ling

sa|poni|fi|ca|tion

Sap|per

sap|per

sap|phic

sap|phire

Sap|pho

sap|pi|ness

sappy
sap|ro|lite
sap|ro|phyte
sa|ra|band
Sa|ra|cen
Sarah
Sarah Sid|dons
as the Tra|gic
Muse
Sa|ra|jevo
Sa|ra|wak
sar|casm
sar|cas|tic
sar|cas|tic|ally
sar|coma
△ sar|co|mas *or*
sar|co|mata
sar|coph|agus
△ sar|coph|agi
or sar|coph|
ag|uses
sar|dine
Sar|dinia
Sar|din|ian
sar|donic
sard|onyx
Sar|dou
sar|gasso
seaweed
△ sar|gas|sos *or*
sar|gas|soes
Sar|gasso
sea
sarge
Sar|gent
sari
Sark
sarky
△ sar|kier
△ sar|ki|est
sar|nie
sa|rong
sar|sa|pa|rilla
Sarto

sar|tor|ial
Sartre
sash
△ sa|shes
Sas|kat|che|wan
sas|sa|fras
Sas|sen|ach
Sas|soon
sat
Satan
sa|tanic
Sa|tan|ism
Sa|tan|ist
sat|chel
sate
△ sates
△ sated
△ sa|ting
sat|el|lite
sati *see* suttee
sa|ti|ab|il|ity
sa|ti|able
sa|ti|ate
△ sa|ti|ates
△ sa|ti|ated
△ sa|ti|ating
sa|ti|ation
Satie
sa|ti|ety
satin
sat|in|wood
sat|iny
sat|ire
sa|tir|ical
sat|ir|ist
sat|ir|iza|tion
sat|ir|ize
△ sat|ir|izes
△ sat|ir|ized
△ sat|ir|izing
sat|is|fac|tion
sat|is|fac|tor|ily
sat|is|fac|tory
sat|is|fied

sat|isfy
△ sat|is|fies
△ sat|is|fied
△ sat|is|fy|ing
sat|is|fy|ing
sat|rap
sat|suma
sat|ur|ate
△ sat|ur|ates
△ sat|ur|ated
△ sat|ur|ating
sat|ura|tion
Sat|ur|day
Sat|ur|day
Night and
Sun|day Morn|
ing
Sat|urn
sa|tur|na|lia
sa|tur|nine
satyr
sauce
VERB
△ sau|ces
△ sauced
△ sau|cing
sauce|pan
sau|cer
sau|ci|ness
saucy
△ sau|cier
△ sau|ci|est
Saudi Ara|bia
sauer|kraut
Saul
sauna
saun|ter
VERB
△ saun|ters
△ saun|tered
△ saun|ter|ing
saur|ian
saus|age
Saus|sure

sauté
VERB
△ sau|tés
△ sau|téd *or* sau|
téed
△ sau|té|ing *or*
sau|tée|ing
sav|age
VERB
△ sav|ages
△ sav|aged
△ sav|aging
sav|agely
sav|age|ness
sav|agery
△ sav|age|ries
sa|van|nah

sav|ant
learned man
⚠ savante

sav|ante
learned woman
⚠ savant

save
VERB
△ saves
△ saved
△ sa|ving
sa|ve|loy
Sav|ile
sa|ving
sa|vi|our
sav|oir-faire
Sa|vo|na|rola

sa|vory
aromatic plant
△ sa|vor|ies
⚠ savoury

sa|vour
VERB
△ sa|vours

△ sa|voured
△ sa|vour|ing
sa|vouri|ness

sa|voury
sharp-tasting;
pleasant; sharp-
tasting dish
NOUN
△ sa|vour|ies
⚠ savory

savoy
savvy
VERB
△ sav|vies
△ sav|vied
△ sav|vy|ing
saw
VERB
△ saws
△ sawed
△ saw|ing
saw|dust
saw|fish
sing. and pl.
saw|fly
△ saw|flies
saw|mill
saw|yer
sax
△ saxes
sax|horn
saxi|frage
Saxon
Sax|ony
saxo|phone
saxo|phon|ist
say
VERB
△ says
△ said
△ say|ing
Say|ers
say|ing

say-so
scab
VERB
△ scabs
△ scabbed
△ scab|bing
scab|bard
scab|bi|ness
scabby
△ scab|bier
△ scab|bi|est
sca|bies
sca|bi|ous
sca|brous
Sca|fell
scaf|fold
scaf|fold|ing
Scala, La
sca|lar
scald
VERB
△ scalds
△ scal|ded
△ scald|ing
scale
VERB
△ scales
△ scaled
△ sca|ling
sca|lene
scal|lion
scal|lop
VERB
△ scal|lops
△ scal|loped
△ scal|lop|ing
scal|ly|wag
scalp
VERB
△ scalps
△ scalped
△ scalp|ing
scal|pel
scaly

△ sca|lier
△ sca|li|est
scam
scamp
scam|per
VERB
△ scam|pers
△ scam|pered
△ scam|per|ing
scampi
scan
VERB
△ scans
△ scanned
△ scan|ning
scan|dal
scan|dal|ize
△ scan|dal|izes
△ scan|dal|ized
△ scan|dal|izing
scan|dal|mon|
ger
scan|dal|ous
scan|dal|ously
Scan|di|na|via
Scan|di|na|vian
scan|dium
scan|ner
scan|sion
scant
scan|tily
scan|ti|ness
scanty
△ scan|tier
△ scan|ti|est
Scapa Flow
scape|goat
scap|ula
△ scap|ulae *or*
scap|ulas
scap|ular
scar
VERB
△ scars

△ scarred
△ scar|ring
sca|rab
Scar|bor|ough
scarce
ADJ.
△ scar|cer
△ scar|cest
scarcely
scar|city
△ scar|cit|ies
scare
VERB
△ scares
△ scared
△ scar|ing
scare|crow
scare|mon|ger
scare|mon|ger|
ing
scarf
NOUN
clothing
△ scarves
woodwork
△ scarfs
VERB
△ scarfs
△ scarfed
△ scarf|ing
Scarfe
Scar|gill
sca|ri|fi|ca|tion
scar|ify
△ sca|ri|fies
△ sca|ri|fied
△ sca|ri|fy|ing
scar|la|tina
Scar|latti
scar|let
Scar|man
scarp
scar|per
△ scar|pers

△ scar|pered
△ scar|per|ing
scarves
scary
△ scar|ier
△ scari|est
scat
VERB
△ scats
△ scat|ted
△ scat|ting
sca|thing
sca|thingly
sca|to|lo|gi|cal
sca|tol|ogy
scat|ter
VERB
△ scat|ters
△ scat|tered
△ scat|ter|ing
scat|ter|brain
scat|ter|brained
scat|ter|ing
scatty
△ scat|tier
△ scat|ti|est
scav|enge
△ scav|en|ges
△ scav|enged
△ scav|en|ging
scav|en|ger
Scawfell see
Scafell
scen|ario
scene
scenery
scenic

scent
smell
VERB
△ scents
△ scen|ted
△ scent|ing

⚠ cent
⚠ sent

scep|tic
doubter
⚠ septic

scep|ti|cal
scep|ti|cism
sceptre
sched|ule
VERB
△ sched|ules
△ sched|uled
△ sched|uling
schema
△ sche|mata
sche|matic
sche|mat|iza|
tion
sche|mat|ize
△ sche|mat|izes
△ sche|mat|ized
△ sche|mat|
izing
scheme
VERB
△ schemes
△ schemed
△ sche|ming
sche|mer
scherzo
△ scher|zos or
scherzi
Schil|ler
schil|ling
schism
schis|matic
schist
schis|to|so|mi|
asis
schizo
schiz|oid
schi|zo|phre|nia

schi|zo|phrenic
or schi|zo|
phre|nic
according to
pronunciation
Schle|gel
Schlei|er|
macher
schlep
VERB
△ schleps
△ schlepped
△ schlep|ping
Schles|in|ger
Schles|wig-Hol|
stein
Schlie|mann
schlock
schmaltz
schmaltzy
△ schmalt|zier
△ schmalt|zi|est
schnapps
Schnau|zer
Schnei|der
schnit|zel
Schoen|berg
scholar
schol|arly
schol|ar|ship
schol|as|tic
schol|as|ti|cism
Schö|ne Mül|
lerin, Die (The
Fair Maid of
the Mill)
school
VERB
△ schools
△ schooled
△ school|ing
school|child
△ school|chil|
dren

School for Scan|
dal, The
school|house
school|ing
school-lea|ver
school|marm
school|marm|ish
school|mas|ter
school|mis|tress
△ school|mis|
tres|ses
school|tea|cher
schoo|ner
Scho|pen|hauer
schot|tische
Schu|bert
Schu|mann
schwa
Schwar|zen|eg|
ger
Schwarz|kopf
Schweit|zer
sci|atic
sci|at|ica
sci|ence
sci|en|ti|fic
sci|en|tif|ic|ally
sci|en|tist
sci-fi
sci|li|cet
Scilly
sci|mi|tar
scin|tilla
scin|til|late
△ scin|til|lates
△ scin|til|la|ted
△ scin|til|la|ting
scin|til|la|ting
scin|til|la|tion
scion
Sci|pio
scis|sors
sclera
scler|osis

scler|otic

scoff

  VERB

  △ scoffs

  △ scoffed

  △ scof|fing

scof|fing

scold

  VERB

  △ scolds

  △ scol|ded

  △ scold|ing

scold|ing

scollop *see*

  scallop

sconce

scone

scoop

  VERB

  △ scoops

  △ scooped

  △ scoop|ing

scoot

  △ scoots

  △ scoo|ted

  △ scoot|ing

scoo|ter

scope

scor|bu|tic

scorch

  NOUN

  △ scor|ches

  VERB

  △ scor|ches

  △ scorched

  △ scorch|ing

scor|cher

scorch|ing

score

  VERB

  △ scores

  △ scored

  △ scor|ing

score|board

scorer

scorn

  VERB

  △ scorns

  △ scorned

  △ scorn|ing

scorn|ful

scorn|fully

Scor|pio

scor|pion

Scor|sese

Scot

Scotch

  NOUN

  △ Scot|ches

scotch

  NOUN

  △ scot|ches

  VERB

  △ scot|ches

  △ scotched

  △ scotch|ing

scot-free

Scot|land

Scots

Scots|man

  △ Scots|men

Scots|wo|man

  △ Scots|wo|men

Scott

Scot|tie

Scot|tish

scoun|drel

scour

  VERB

  △ scours

  △ scoured

  △ scour|ing

scourer

scourge

  VERB

  △ scour|ges

  △ scourged

  △ scour|ging

Scouse

Scou|ser

scout

  VERB

  △ scouts

  △ scou|ted

  △ scout|ing

Scou|ter

scow

scowl

  VERB

  △ scowls

  △ scowled

  △ scowl|ing

Scrab|ble

  game

scrab|ble

  VERB

  △ scrab|bles

  △ scrab|bled

  △ scrab|bling

scrag

  VERB

  △ scrags

  △ scragged

  △ scrag|ging

scrag|gi|ness

scraggy

  △ scrag|gier

  △ scrag|gi|est

scram

  △ scrams

  △ scrammed

  △ scram|ming

scramble

  VERB

  △ scrambles

  △ scrambled

  △ scram|bling

scram|bler

scram|jet

scrap

  VERB

  △ scraps

  △ scrapped

  △ scrap|ping

scrap|book

scrape

  VERB

  △ scrapes

  △ scraped

  △ scra|ping

scra|per

scra|per|board

scra|pie

scrap|pily

scrap|pi|ness

scrappy

  △ scrap|pier

  △ scrap|pi|est

scratch

  NOUN

  △ scrat|ches

  VERB

  △ scrat|ches

  △ scratched

  △ scratch|ing

scratch|board

scratch|ily

scrat|chi|ness

scrat|chy

  △ scrat|chier

  △ scrat|chi|est

scrawl

  VERB

  △ scrawls

  △ scrawled

  △ scrawl|ing

scrawly

  △ scraw|lier

  △ scraw|li|est

scraw|ni|ness

scrawny

  △ scraw|nier

  △ scraw|ni|est

scream

  VERB

  △ screams

△ screamed
△ scream|ing
Scream, The
scree
screech
  NOUN
△ scree|ches
  VERB
△ scree|ches
△ screeched
△ screech|ing
scree|chy
△ scree|chier
△ scree|chi|est
screed
screen
  VERB
△ screens
△ screened
△ screen|ing
screen|play
screen-saver
screw
  VERB
△ screws
△ screwed
△ screw|ing
screw|ball
screw|dri|ver
screwed-up
screwy
△ screw|ier
△ screwi|est
Scri|abin
scrib|ble
  VERB
△ scrib|bles
△ scrib|bled
△ scrib|bling
scrib|bler
scrib|bly
△ scrib|blier
△ scrib|bli|est
scribe

Scrib|ner
scrim
scrim|mage
  VERB
△ scrim|ma|ges
△ scrim|maged
△ scrim|ma|ging
scrimp
△ scrimps
△ scrimped
△ scrimp|ing
scrimpy
△ scrim|pier
△ scrim|pi|est
scrim|shank
△ scrim|shanks
△ scrim|shanked
△ scrim|shank|ing
scrim|shan|ker
scrip
script
  VERB
△ scripts
△ scrip|ted
△ script|ing
scrip|tural
Scripture
  the Bible
scrip|ture
  sacred writings
script|wri|ter
scriv|ener
scrof|ula
scro|fu|lous
scroll
  VERB
△ scrolls
△ scrolled
△ scroll|ing
Scrooge
scro|tal
scro|tum
△ scrota *or* scro|
   tums

scrounge
△ scroun|ges
△ scrounged
△ scroun|ging
scroun|ger
scrub
  VERB
△ scrubs
△ scrubbed
△ scrub|bing
scrub|ber
scrubby
△ scrub|bier
△ scrub|bi|est
scrub|land
scruff
scruf]fily
scruf]fi|ness
scruffy
△ scruf]fier
△ scruf]fi|est
scrum
  VERB
△ scrums
△ scrummed
△ scrum|ming
scrum|mage
  VERB
△ scrum|ma|ges
△ scrum|maged
△ scrum|ma|ging
scrummy
△ scrum|mier
△ scrum|mi|est
scrump|tious
scrumpy
△ scrum|pies
scrunch
  NOUN
△ scrun|ches
  VERB
△ scrun|ches
△ scrunched
△ scrunch|ing

scrunch-dry
△ scrunch-dries
△ scrunch-dried
△ scrunch-dry|ing
scru|ple
  VERB
△ scru|ples
△ scru|pled
△ scru|pling
scru|pu|lous
scru|pu|lously
scru|tin|eer
scru|tin|ize
△ scru|tin|izes
△ scru|tin|ized
△ scru|tin|izing
scru|tiny
△ scru|tin|ies
scuba
Scud
  missile
scud
  move quickly;
  cloud, spray, etc
  driven by wind
  VERB
△ scuds
△ scud|ded
△ scud|ding
scuff
  VERB
△ scuffs
△ scuffed
△ scuff|ing
scuf]fle
  VERB
△ scuffles
△ scuffled
△ scuf]fling

scull
  sort of oar; sort
  of boat; propel
  with such oar(s)

VERB
△ sculls
△ sculled
△ scull|ing
⚠ skull

scul|ler
scul|lery
△ scul|ler|ies
sculpt
△ sculpts
△ sculp|ted
△ sculpt|ing
sculp|tor
sculp|tural
sculp|ture
VERB
△ sculp|tures
△ sculp|tured
△ sculp|tur|ing
sculp|tured
scum
VERB
△ scums
△ scummed
△ scum|ming
scum|bag
scum|bling
scummy
△ scum|mier
△ scum|mi|est
Scun|thorpe
scup|per
VERB
△ scup|pers
△ scup|pered
△ scup|per|ing
scurf
scurfy
△ scur|fier
△ scur|fi|est
scur|ril|ity
scur|ril|ous
scurry

NOUN
△ scur|ries
VERB
△ scur|ries
△ scur|ried
△ scur|ry|ing
scurvy
ADJ.
△ scur|vier
△ scur|vi|est
scut
scu|tel|lum
scut|tle
VERB
△ scut|tles
△ scut|tled
△ scut|tling
scuzzy
△ scuz|zier
△ scuz|zi|est
Scylla
scythe
VERB
△ scythes
△ scythed
△ scyth|ing
Scyth|ian

sea
*large expanse of
salt water*
⚠ see

sea|board
sea|bor|gium
sea|farer
sea|far|ing
sea|food
sea|going
Sea|gull, The
sea|gull
seal
VERB
△ seals
△ sealed

△ seal|ing
seal|ant
seal|ing-wax
△ seal|ing-waxes
seal|skin
Sea|ly|ham

seam
*join between
edges; layer of
coal etc; scar;
join edges; make
scar*
VERB
△ seams
△ seamed
△ seam|ing
⚠ seem

sea|man
△ sea|men
sea|man|ship
Sea|mas
sea|mer
sea|mi|ness
seam|less
seam|stress
seam|stres|ses
Sea|mus
seamy
△ sea|mier
△ sea|mi|est
Sean
sé|ance
sea|plane
sea|port

sear
*scorch-mark;
scorch; wither*
VERB
△ sears
△ seared
△ sear|ing
⚠ seer

search
NOUN
△ searches
VERB
△ searches
△ searched
△ search|ing
search|ing
search|light
sear|ing
Searle
sea|scape
sea|shell
sea|shore
sea|sick
sea|sick|ness
sea|side
sea|son
VERB
△ sea|sons
△ sea|soned
△ sea|son|ing
sea|son|able
sea|sonal
sea|soned
sea|son|ing
*Sea|sons, The
(Die Jah|res|
zei|ten)*
Sea|speak
*Sea Sym|phony,
A*
seat
VERB
△ seats
△ sea|ted
△ seat|ing
seat|ing
Se|attle
sea|ward
sea|weed
sea|wor|thi|ness
sea|wor|thy
se|ba|ceous

Se|bas|tian
Se|bas|to|pol
sebum
sec
se|cant *or* sec|ant
  according to
  pronunciation
se|ca|teurs
se|cede
  △ se|cedes
  △ se|ce|ded
  △ se|ce|ding
se|ces|sion
se|clude
  △ se|cludes
  △ se|clu|ded
  △ se|clu|ding
se|clu|ded
se|clu|sion
Se|combe
se|cond
  transfer
  △ se|conds
  △ se|con|ded
  △ se|cond|ing
sec|ond
  other senses
  VERB
  △ sec|onds
  △ sec|on|ded
  △ sec|ond|ing
sec|on|dary
sec|ond-degree
sec|on|der
sec|ondly
se|cond|ment
sec|ond-rate
se|crecy

se|cret
  ADJ.
    △ secrete

Se|cret Agent, The
sec|re|taire

sec|re|tar|ial
sec|re|tar|iat
sec|re|tary
  △ sec|re|tar|ies
sec|re|tary-bird
sec|re|tary-gen|
eral

se|crete
  VERB
    △ se|cretes
    △ se|cre|ted
    △ se|cre|ting
    △ secret

Se|cret Gar|den,
The
se|cre|tion
se|cret|ive
se|cret|ive|ness
Se|cret Life of
Wal|ter Mitty,
The
se|cretly
se|cre|tory
sect
sect|ar|ian
sect|ari|an|ism
sec|tion
  VERB
    △ sec|tions
    △ sec|tioned
    △ sec|tion|ing
sec|tional
sec|tor
sec|ular
sec|ular|ism
sec|ular|ist
sec|ular|ize
  △ sec|ular|izes
  △ sec|ular|ized
  △ sec|ular|izing
se|cure
  VERB
    △ se|cures

△ se|cured
△ se|cur|ing
ADJ.
△ se|curer
△ se|cur|est
se|curely
se|cur|ity
  △ se|cur|it|ies
sedan
se|date
  VERB
    △ se|dates
    △ se|da|ted
    △ se|da|ting
  ADJ.
    △ se|da|ter
    △ se|da|test
se|dately
se|da|tion
sed|at|ive
sed|en|tary
sedge
Sedge|moor
sedi|ment
se|di|men|tary
se|di|men|ta|tion
se|di|tion
se|di|tious
se|duce
  △ se|du|ces
  △ se|duced
  △ se|du|cing
se|duc|tion
se|duct|ive
se|duct|ively
se|duct|ive|ness
se|du|lity
sed|ulous
sedum

see
  perceive with the
  eyes;
  understand;

  speak to;
  imagine;
  bishopric
  VERB
    △ sees
    △ saw
    △ see|ing
    △ seen
    △ sea

seed
  NOUN
    △ seeds *or* seed
  VERB
    △ seeds
    △ see|ded
    △ seed|ling
seed|bed
see|ded
seed|head
seed|less
seed|ling
seed-pearl
seed-potato
  △ seed-pota|toes
seedy
  △ see|dier
  △ see|di|est
See|ger
see|ing
seek
  △ seeks
  △ sought
  △ seek|ing

seem
  appear (to be,
  etc)
    △ seems
    △ seemed
    △ seem|ing
    △ seam

seem|ing
seem|ingly

seemly
seen
seep
△ seeps
△ seeped
△ seep|ing
seep|age

seer
prophet
⚠ sear

seer|sucker
see|saw
VERB
△ see|saws
△ see|sawed
△ see|saw|ing
seethe
△ seethes
△ seethed
△ seeth|ing
seeth|ing
see-through
seg|ment
VERB
△ seg|ments
△ seg|men|ted
△ seg|ment|ing
seg|men|ta|tion
Se|go|via
seg|re|gate
△ seg|re|gates
△ seg|re|ga|ted
△ seg|re|ga|ting
seg|re|ga|ted
seg|re|ga|tion
seg|re|ga|tional
sei|gneur
Seine
seine
VERB
△ seines
△ seined
△ sein|ing

seis|mic
seis|mo|graph
seis|mog|raphy
seis|mo|lo|gi|cal
seis|molo|gist
seis|mol|ogy
seize
△ sei|zes
△ seized
△ seiz|ing
seiz|ure
sel|dom
se|lect
VERB
△ se|lects
△ se|lec|ted
△ se|lect|ing
se|lec|tion
se|lect|ive
se|lec|tiv|ity
se|lect|ness
se|lec|tor
sel|en|ite
se|len|ium
Seles
self
△ selves
self-abuse
self-addressed
self-appoin|ted
self-asser|tion
self-asser|tive
self-assur|ance
self-assured
self-cater|ing
self-centred
self-col|oured
self-con|fessed
self-con|fi|dence
self-con|fi|dent
self-con|scious
self-con|scious|
ness
self-con|tained

self-con|trol
self-con|trolled
self-defence
self-denial
self-deter|min|
ation
self-drive
self-efface|ment
self-effa|cing
self-employed
self-esteem
self-evi|dent
self-explan|at|
ory
self-ful|fil|ling
self-gov|ern|ing
self-gov|ern|
ment
self-harm|ing
self-heal
self-help
self-impor|tance
self-impor|tant
self-imposed
self-indul|gence
self-indul|gent
self-inflic|ted
self|ing
self-inter|est
self-inter|es|ted
self|ish
self|ish|ness
self|less
self|less|ness
self-made
self-opin|ion|
ated
self-pity
self-pol|lina|tion
self-pos|sessed
self-pos|ses|sion
self-pre|ser|va|
tion
self-rais|ing

self-reli|ance
self-reli|ant
self-respect
self-respect|ing
self-restraint
Sel|fridge
self-right|eous
self-right|eous|
ness
self-sac|ri|fice
self-sac|ri|fi|cing
self|same
self-sat|is|fac|
tion
self-sat|is|fied
self-seal|ing
self-see|ker
self-seek|ing
self-ser|vice
self-ser|ving
self-star|ter
self-styled
self-suf|fi|ciency
self-suf|fi|cient
self-sup|port|ing
self-willed
Selina
sell
VERB
△ sells
△ sold
△ sell|ing
Sel|la|field

sel|ler
one who sells
⚠ cellar

Sel|lers
Sel|lo|tape
VERB
△ Sel|lo|tapes
△ Sel|lo|taped
△ Sel|lo|ta|ping
sell-out

sell-through

sel|vage

selves

Sel|wyn

Sel|wyn-Lloyd

Selz|nick

se|man|tic

se|man|tic|ally

se|man|tics

se|ma|phore

VERB

△ se|ma|phores

△ se|ma|phored

△ se|ma|phor|
ing

sem|blance

semen

se|mes|ter

semi

semi-auto|matic

semi|breve

semi|cir|cle

semi|cir|cu|lar

semi|co|lon

semi|con|duc|tor

semi-detached

semi-final

semi-final|ist

sem|inal

sem|in|ally

sem|inar

sem|in|ar|ian

sem|in|ary

△ sem|in|ar|ies

se|min|ifer|ous

se|mi|ol|ogy

se|mi|otic

se|mi|ot|ics

semi-per|me|
able

semi-pre|cious

semi-pro|fes|
sional

semi|qua|ver

semi-skilled

Se|mite *or* Sem|
ite
according to
pronunciation

Sem|itic

semi|tone

semi-trop|ical

semi|vowel

semo|lina

Sem|tex

sen|ate

sen|ator

sena|tor|ial

send

△ sends

△ sent

△ send|ing

sen|der

Sen|dero Lu|mi|
noso (Shi|ning
Path)

send-off

send-up

Sen|eca

Se|ne|gal
state
⚠ Sénégal

Sé|né|gal
river
⚠ Senegal

Se|ne|gam|bia

sen|es|cence

sen|es|cent

sen|es|chal

se|nile

sen|il|ity

se|nior

se|ni|or|ity

Senna

senna

Sen|nett

sen|sa|tion

sen|sa|tional

sen|sa|tion|al|
ism

sen|sa|tion|al|ist

sen|sa|tion|ally

sense

VERB

△ sen|ses

△ sensed

△ sens|ing

Sense and Sen|
si|bil|ity

sense-datum

△ sense-data

sense|less

sense|lessly

sense|less|ness

sen|si|bil|ity

△ sen|si|bil|it|ies

sen|sible

sen|sibly

sen|si|tive

sen|si|tively

sen|si|tiv|ity

sen|si|ti|za|tion

sen|si|tize

△ sen|si|ti|zes

△ sen|si|tized

△ sen|si|ti|zing

sen|sor

sen|sory

sen|sual

sen|su|al|ity

sen|su|ous

sen|su|ously

sen|su|ous|ness

sent
past tense and
past participle of
send
⚠ cent
⚠ scent

sen|tence

VERB

△ sen|ten|ces

△ sen|tenced

△ sen|ten|cing

sen|ten|tious

sen|ten|tious|
ness

sen|tience

sen|tient

sen|ti|ment

sen|ti|men|tal

sen|ti|men|tal|
ism

sen|ti|men|tal|ist

sen|ti|men|tal|ity

sen|ti|men|tal|ize

△ sen|ti|men|tal|
izes

△ sen|ti|men|tal|
ized

△ sen|ti|men|tal|
izing

Sen|ti|men|tal
Jour|ney, A

sen|ti|men|tally

sen|ti|nel

sen|try

△ sen|tries

sentry-box

△ sentry-boxes

Seoul

sepal

sep|ar|abil|ity

sep|ar|able

sep|ar|ate

VERB

△ sep|ar|ates

△ sep|ar|ated

△ sep|ar|ating

sep|ar|ate|ness

Sep|ar|ate Ta|
bles

se|par|ation

sep|ar|at|ism
sep|ar|at|ist
sep|ar|ator
sepek tak|raw
Seph|ardi
  △ Seph|ar|dim
sepia
sepoy
sep|sis
  △ sep|ses
sept
septa
Sep|tem|ber
sep|ten|nial
sep|tet

> sep|tic
> contaminated;
> putrefying
> ⚠ sceptic

sep|ti|cae|mia
sep|tua|gen|ar|
  ian
Sep|tua|ges|ima
Sep|tua|gint
sep|tum
  △ septa
sep|tu|ple
  VERB
  △ sep|tu|ples
  △ sep|tu|pled
  △ sep|tu|pling
sep|tu|plet
se|pul|chral
se|pul|chre
  VERB
  △ sep|ul|chres
  △ sep|ulchred
  △ sep|ul|chring
se|quel
se|quence
se|quen|cing
se|quen|tial
se|ques|ter

△ se|ques|ters
△ se|ques|tered
△ se|ques|ter|ing
se|ques|trate
△ se|ques|trates
△ se|ques|tra|ted
△ se|ques|tra|ting
se|ques|tra|tion
se|ques|tra|tor
se|quin
se|quined
se|quoia
ser|ag|lio
ser|aph
  △ ser|aphs or
  sera|phim
ser|aphic
Ser|bia
Serbo-Croat
Ser|ena
ser|en|ade
  VERB
  △ ser|en|ades
  △ ser|en|aded
  △ ser|en|ading
ser|en|dip|it|ous
ser|en|dip|ity
ser|ene
ser|enely
Ser|en|geti
ser|en|ity
serf
serf|dom
serge

> ser|geant
> army etc non-
> commissioned
> officer
> ⚠ serjeant

ser|geant-at-
  arms
  △ ser|geants-at-
  arms

ser|geant-major

> ser|ial
> of or in a series
> ⚠ cereal

seri|al|ism
seri|al|iza|tion
seri|al|ize
  △ seri|al|izes
  △ seri|al|ized
  △ seri|al|izing
ser|ies
  sing. and pl.
serif
seri|graph
ser|ine
serio|comic
seri|ous
seri|ously
seri|ous|ness

> ser|jeant
> title of certain
> legal etc officials
> ⚠ sergeant

ser|mon
ser|mon|ize
  △ ser|mon|izes
  △ ser|mon|ized
  △ ser|mon|izing
ser|ol|ogy
sero|pos|it|ive
sero|tonin
ser|ous
ser|pent
ser|pen|tine
ser|ra|ted
ser|ra|tion
ser|ried
serum
  △ sera
ser|vant
serve

VERB
  △ serves
  △ served
  △ serving
ser|ver
ser|vice
  VERB
  △ ser|vi|ces
  △ ser|viced
  △ ser|vi|cing
ser|vice|abil|ity
ser|vice|able
ser|vice|man
  △ ser|vice|men
ser|vice|wo|man
  △ ser|vice|wo|
  men
ser|vi|ette
ser|vile
ser|vil|ity
ser|ving
ser|vi|tude
servo
ser|vo|mech|an|
  ism
ses|ame
ses|sile
ses|sion
ses|sional
ses|tet
Set
set
  VERB
  △ sets
  △ set
  △ set|ting
set-aside
set|back
Seth
set|tee
set|ter
set|ting
set|tle

VERB
△ set¦tles
△ set¦tled
△ set¦tling
settle|ment
set|tler
set-to
set-up
Seu|rat
seven
sev¦en|fold
*Seven Sam|urai
(Shi|chi|nin
No Sam|urai)*
sev¦en|teen
sev¦en|teenth
sev|enth
sev|enthly
*Sev|enth Seal,
The (Det
Sjunde In|seg|
let)*
sev¦en|ties
sev¦en|tieth
sev|enty
△ sev¦en|ties
sever
△ sev¦ers
△ sev¦ered
△ sev¦er|ing
sev|eral
sev¦er|ally
sev¦er|ance
se|vere
Sev¦ered Head, A
se|verely
se|ver|ity
Sev|ern
Se|ville
Sèvres

sew
  *stitch with
  thread*

△ sews
△ sewed
△ sew|ing
△ sewn
⚠ so
⚠ sow

sew|age
Sew|ell
sewer
sew¦er|age
sew|ing
sew|ing-
  machine
sex
  NOUN
  △ sexes
  VERB
  △ sexes
  △ sexed
  △ sex|ing
sexa|gen¦ar|ian
Sexa|ges¦ima
sexed
sex¦ily
sexi|ness
sex|ism
sex|ist
sex|less
sex|olo¦gist
sex|ol¦ogy
sex|ploi¦ta|tion
sext
sex|tant
sex|tet
sex|ton
sex|tuple
  VERB
  △ sex|tuples
  △ sex|tupled
  △ sex|tu|pling
sex|tu|plet
sex|ual
sexu|al¦ity

sexy
△ sex¦ier
△ sexi|est
Sey|chelles
Sey|mour
Sforza
sforz|ando
sfu|mato
sgraf|fito
△ sgraf|fiti
sh
shab|bily
shab¦bi|ness
shabby
△ shab¦bier
△ shab¦bi|est
Sha|bu|oth
shack
  VERB
  △ shacks
  △ shacked
  △ shack|ing
shackle
  VERB
  △ shackles
  △ shackled
  △ shack|ling
Shackle|ton
shad
△ shad *or* shads
shade
  VERB
  △ shades
  △ sha|ded
  △ sha|ding
sha¦di|ness
sha|ding
sha|doof
shadow
  VERB
  △ shad|ows
  △ shad|owed
  △ shad|ow|ing
shadow-box

△ shadow-boxes
△ shadow-boxed
△ shadow-box¦
  ing
shadow-box|ing
shad|owy
shaduf *see*
  shadoof
Shad|well
shady
△ sha¦dier
△ sha¦di|est
Shaf|fer
shaft
Shaftes|bury
shag
  VERB
  △ shags
  △ shagged
  △ shag|ging
shag¦gi|ness
shaggy
△ shag¦gier
△ shag¦gi|est
sha|green
Shah
shah
shake
  VERB
  △ shakes
  △ shook
  △ sha|king
  △ sha|ken
shake|down
shake-out
Sha|ker
  *member of
  religious sect*
sha|ker
  one who shakes
Shakes|peare
Shake|spear|ean
shake-up
sha|kily

sha|ki|ness
shako
△ sha|kos *or*
sha|koes
shaky
△ sha|kier
△ sha|ki|est
shale
shall
△ shall
△ should
shal|lot
shal|low
△ shal|lower
△ shal|low|est
sha|lom
shalt
shaly
sham
VERB
△ shams
△ shammed
△ sham|ming
sha|man
sha|man|ism
sha|man|is|tic
sham|ble
VERB
△ sham|bles
△ sham|bled
△ sham|bling
shambles
sham|bling
sham|bolic
shame
VERB
△ shames
△ shamed
△ sha|ming
shame|faced
shame|facedly
shame|ful
shame|fully
shame|less

shame|lessly
shame|less|ness
shammy
△ sham|mies
sham|poo
VERB
△ sham|poos
△ sham|pooed
△ sham|poo|ing
sham|rock
shandy
△ shan|dies
Shane
Shang|hai
shang|hai
△ shang|hais
△ shang|haied
△ shang|hai|ing
shank
Shan|kar
Shank|lin
shan't
shan|tung
shanty
△ shan|ties
shape
VERB
△ shapes
△ shaped
△ sha|ping
shape|less
shape|less|ness
shape|li|ness
shapely
△ shape|lier
△ shape|li|est
shard
share
VERB
△ shares
△ shared
△ shar|ing
share|hol|der
share-out

share|ware
Sha|ri'ah
shark
shark|skin
Sharon
Sharp
sharp
△ shar|per
△ sharp|est
shar|pen
△ sharp|ens
△ sharp|ened
△ sharp|en|ing
sharp|ener
shar|per
Sharpe|ville
sharply
sharp|ness
sharp|shoo|ter
sharp|shoot|ing
shat|ter
△ shat|ters
△ shat|tered
△ shat|ter|ing
shat|tered
shat|ter|ing
shave
VERB
△ shaves
△ shaved
△ sha|ving
sha|ven
sha|ver
sha|ving
Shavuot *see*
Shabuoth
Shavuoth *see*
Shabuoth
Shaw
shawl
she
sheaf
NOUN
△ sheaves

VERB
△ sheafs
△ sheafed
△ sheaf|ing

shear
*cutter; breaking
of metal etc
under strain; cut
off; twist or
break*
VERB
△ shears
△ sheared
△ shear|ing
△ shorn
⚠ sheer

shearer
shear|wa|ter

sheath
NOUN
⚠ sheathe

sheathe
VERB
△ sheathes
△ sheathed
△ sheath|ing
⚠ sheath

sheave *see* sheaf
Sheba
she|bang
shed
VERB
△ sheds
△ shed
△ shed|ding
she'd
sheen
Sheena
sheep
sing. and pl.
sheep-dip

sheep|dog
sheep|ish
sheep|ishly
sheep|ish|ness
sheep|shank
sheep|skin

sheer
  swerve; absolute;
  vertical;
  transparent;
  completely;
  vertically
  VERB
  △ sheers
  △ sheered
  △ sheer|ing
  ⚠ shear

Sheer|ness
sheet
  VERB
  △ sheets
  △ shee|ted
  △ sheet|ing
sheet-anchor
sheet|ing
Shef|field
sheikh
sheikh|dom
Sheila
sheila
shekel
Shek|inah
shel|drake
shel|duck
shelf
  △ shelves
shelf-life
shell
  VERB
  △ shells
  △ shelled
  △ shell|ing
she'll

shel|lac
  VERB
  △ shel|lacs
  △ shel|lacked
  △ shel|lack|ing
Shel|ley
shell|fish
  sing. and pl.
shell|ing
shell-shock
shell-shocked
Shel|ter
shel|ter
  VERB
  △ shel|ters
  △ shel|tered
  △ shel|ter|ing
shel|tered
shelve
  △ shelves
  △ shelved
  △ shel|ving
shelves
shel|ving
Shem
Shema
Shen|an|doah
she|nan|igans
shep|herd
  VERB
  △ shep|herds
  △ shep|her|ded
  △ shep|herd|ing
shep|herd|ess
  △ shep|herd|es|
    ses
Shera|ton
sher|bet
sherd see shard
Sher|idan
sher|iff
Sherpa
sherry
  △ sher|ries

Sher|wood
She Stoops to
  Con|quer, or
  The Mis|takes
  of a Night
Shet|land
Shia
shi|atsu
shib|bo|leth
shield
  VERB
  △ shields
  △ shiel|ded
  △ shield|ing
shift
  VERB
  △ shifts
  △ shif|ted
  △ shift|ing
shift|ily
shif|ti|ness
shift|less
shifty
  △ shif|tier
  △ shif|ti|est
Shi|ite
shil|ling
shilly-shally
  △ shilly-shal|lies
  △ shilly-shal|lied
  △ shilly-shal|ly|
    ing
Shil|ton
shim
  VERB
  △ shims
  △ shimmed
  △ shim|ming
shim|mer
  VERB
  △ shim|mers
  △ shim|mered
  △ shim|mer|ing
shim|mery

shin
  VERB
  △ shins
  △ shinned
  △ shin|ning
shin|bone
shin|dig
shine
  VERB
  △ shines
  △ shone
  △ shi|ning
shi|ner
shin|gle
  VERB
  △ shin|gles
  △ shin|gled
  △ shing|ling
shingly
Shi|ning Path
Shinto
Shin|to|ism
Shin|to|ist
shinty
  △ shin|ties
Shin|well
shiny
  △ shi|nier
  △ shi|ni|est
ship
  VERB
  △ ships
  △ shipped
  △ ship|ping
ship|board
ship|mate
ship|ment
ship|ping
ship|shape
ship|wreck
  VERB
  △ ship|wrecks
  △ ship|wrecked
  △ ship|wreck|ing

ship|wright
ship|yard
Shi|raz
shire
shirk
  △ shirks
  △ shirked
  △ shirk|ing
shir|ker
Shir|ley
shirt
shirt|sleeve
shirt-tail
shirt|wais|ter
shirty
  △ shir|tier
  △ shir|ti|est
shish
shit
  VERB
  △ shits
  △ shit *or* shit|
    ted *or* shat
  △ shit|ting
shitty
  △ shit|tier
  △ shit|ti|est
Shiva
shiver
  VERB
  △ shiv|ers
  △ shiv|ered
  △ shiv|er|ing
shiv|ery
shoal
  VERB
  △ shoals
  △ shoaled
  △ shoal|ing
shock
  VERB
  △ shocks
  △ shocked
  △ shock|ing

shock|ing
shod
shod|dily
shod|di|ness
shoddy
  △ shod|dier
  △ shod|di|est

shoe
  *foot-covering; fit
  this*
  VERB
  △ shoes
  △ shod *or* shoed
  △ shoeing
  ⚠ shoo

shoe|horn
shoe|lace
shoe|string
shogi
Sho|gun
Shol|ok|hov
Shona
shone

shoo
  *noise to chase
  away; chase
  with this noise*
  VERB
  △ shoos
  △ shooed
  △ shoo|ing
  ⚠ shoe

shook

shoot
  *move or cause to
  move quickly; fire
  gun etc, operate
  camera; produce
  new plant
  growth; new
  plant growth;*

*hunting expedition
with guns*
  VERB
  △ shoots
  △ shot
  △ shoot|ing
  ⚠ chute

shoo|ter
shoot|ing-stick
shop
  VERB
  △ shops
  △ shopped
  △ shop|ping
shop|keeper
shop|lift
  △ shop|lifts
  △ shop|lif|ted
  △ shop|lift|ing
shop|lif|ter
shop|lift|ing
shop|per
shop|ping
shop-soiled
shop|walker

shore
  *edge of sea etc;
  prop up*
  VERB
  △ shores
  △ shored
  △ shor|ing
  ⚠ sure

shore|line
shorn
short
  VERB
  △ shorts
  △ shor|ted
  △ short|ing
  ADJ.
  △ shor|ter

  △ short|est
short|age
short|bread
short|cake
short-change
  △ short-chan|ges
  △ short-changed
  △ short-chan|
    ging
short-cir|cuit
  △ short-cir|cuits
  △ short-cir|
    cuited
  △ short-cir|cuit|
    ing
short|com|ing
shor|ten
  △ shor|tens
  △ shor|tened
  △ shor|ten|ing
shor|ten|ing
short|fall
short|hand
short-han|ded
short|horn
shor|tie
short|list
  VERB
  △ short|lists
  △ short|lis|ted
  △ short|list|ing
short-lived
shortly
short|ness
shorts
short-sigh|ted
short-sigh|ted|
  ness
short-tem|pered
short-term
short-win|ded
shorty
  △ shor|ties
Shos|ta|ko|vich

shot
shot|gun
shot-put|ter
should
shoul|der
  VERB
  △ shoul|ders
  △ shoul|dered
  △ shoul|der|ing
shouldn't
shout
  VERB
  △ shouts
  △ shou|ted
  △ shout|ing
shove
  VERB
  △ shoves
  △ shoved
  △ shov|ing
shovel
  VERB
  △ shov|els
  △ shov|elled
  △ shov|el|ling
shov|el|board
shov|el|ler
show
  VERB
  △ shows
  △ showed
  △ show|ing
  △ shown
show|biz
show|case
show|down
shower
  VERB
  △ showers
  △ showered
  △ shower|ing
showery
showi|ness
show|ing

show|jum|per
show|jump|ing
show|man
  △ show|men
show|man|ship
shown
show-off
show|piece
show|room
showy
  △ show|ier
  △ showi|est
shoyu
shrank
shrap|nel
shred
  VERB
  △ shreds
  △ shred|ded
  △ shred|ding
shred|der
shrew
shrewd
  △ shrew|der
  △ shrewd|est
shrewdly
shrewd|ness
shrew|ish
Shrews|bury
shriek
  VERB
  △ shrieks
  △ shrieked
  △ shriek|ing
shrift
shrike
shrill
  VERB
  △ shrills
  △ shrilled
  △ shrill|ing
  ADJ.
  △ shril|ler
  △ shril|lest

shrill|ness
shrimp
  VERB
  △ shrimps
  △ shrimped
  △ shrimp|ing
shrimp|ing
shrine
shrink
  VERB
  △ shrinks
  △ shrank
  △ shrink|ing
  △ shrunk
  AS ADJ.
  △ shrun|ken
shrink|age
shrink-wrap
  △ shrink-wraps
  △ shrink-
    wrapped
  △ shrink-wrap|
    ping
shrivel
  △ shriv|els
  △ shriv|elled
  △ shriv|el|ling
Shrop|shire
Shrop|shire Lad, A
shroud
  VERB
  △ shrouds
  △ shrou|ded
  △ shroud|ing
Shrove Tues|
  day
shrub
shrub|bery
  △ shrub|ber|ies
shrubby
  △ shrub|bier
  △ shrub|bi|est
shrug
  VERB

  △ shrugs
  △ shrugged
  △ shrug|ging
shrunk
shrun|ken
shud|der
  VERB
  △ shud|ders
  △ shud|dered
  △ shud|der|ing
shuf|fle
  VERB
  △ shuf|fles
  △ shuf|fled
  △ shuf|fling
shuffle|board
shufti
shun
  △ shuns
  △ shunned
  △ shun|ning
shunt
  VERB
  △ shunts
  △ shun|ted
  △ shunt|ing
shush
  VERB
  △ shushes
  △ shushed
  △ shush|ing
shut
  VERB
  △ shuts
  △ shut
  △ shut|ting
shut|down
Shute
shut|eye
shut|ter
  VERB
  △ shut|ters
  △ shut|tered
  △ shut|ter|ing

shuttle
  VERB
  △ shuttles
  △ shuttled
  △ shut|tling
shuttle|cock
shy
  NOUN
  △ shies
  VERB
  △ shies
  △ shied
  △ shy|ing
  ADJ.
  △ shyer *or* shier
  △ shy|est *or* shi|
    est
shyly
shy|ness
shy|ster
si
sial
Siam
Si|am|ese
  NOUN
  native of Siam
  sing. and pl.
Sian
Si|bel|ius
Si|beria
sib|il|ance
sib|il|ancy
sib|il|ant
sib|ling
sibyl
si|byl|line
sic
Si|cil|ian
Si|cily
sick
  VERB
  △ sicks
  △ sicked
  △ sick|ing

ADJ.
  △ sicker
  △ sick|est
sick-bay
sicken
  △ sick|ens
  △ sick|ened
  △ sick|en|ing
sick|en|ing
sick|en|ingly
Sick|ert
sickle
sick-leave
sickle-cell
sickly
  △ sick|lier
  △ sick|li|est
sick|ness
Sid|dons
side
  VERB
  △ sides
  △ sided
  △ si|ding
side|board
side|burn
side|car
side|kick
side|light
side|line
side|long
si|der|eal
sid|er|ite
side-saddle
side|show
side|spin
side-split|ting
side-step
  VERB
  △ side-steps
  △ side-stepped
  △ side-step|
    ping
side|swipe

side|track
  △ side|tracks
  △ side|tracked
  △ side|track|ing
side|walk
side|ways
side|winder
si|ding
si|dle
  △ si|dles
  △ si|dled
  △ si|dling
Sid|mouth
Sid|ney
Sidon
Sieff
siege
Sieg|fried
sie|mens
  sing. and pl.
Siena
Si|en|ese
Sien|kie|wicz
si|enna
si|erra
Si|erra Leone
Si|erra Ne|vada
si|esta
sieve
  VERB
  △ sieves
  △ sieved
  △ siev|ing
sie|vert
sift
  △ sifts
  △ sif|ted
  △ sift|ing
sigh
  VERB
  △ sighs
  △ sighed
  △ sigh|ing

---

sight
  power of seeing;
  thing seen;
  opinion; espy;
  aim
  VERB
  △ sights
  △ sigh|ted
  △ sight|ing
    ⚠ cite
    ⚠ site

---

sigh|ted
sight|less
sight-read
  △ sight-reads
  △ sight-read
  △ sight-read|
    ing
sight-read|ing
sight-screen
sight|see
  △ sight|sees
  △ sight|saw
  △ sight|see|ing
sight|see|ing
sight|seer
sig|il|log|raphy
sign
  VERB
  △ signs
  △ signed
  △ sign|ing
sig|nal
  VERB
  △ sig|nals
  △ sig|nalled
  △ sig|nal|ling
sig|nal-box
  △ sig|nal-boxes
sig|nal|ize
  △ sig|nal|izes
  △ sig|nal|ized
  △ sig|nal|izing

sig|nally
sig|nal|man
△ sig|nal|men
sig|na|tory
△ sig|na|tor|ies
sig|na|ture

sig|net
small seal
⚠cygnet

sig|net-ring
sig|ni|fi|cance
sig|ni|fi|cant
sig|ni|fi|cantly
sig|nify
△ sig|ni|fies
△ sig|ni|fied
△ sig|ni|fy|ing
sign|post
VERB
△ sign|posts
△ sign|pos|ted
△ sign|post|ing
Sig|urd
Sikh
Sikh|ism
Sik|kim
si|lage
Silas
Sil|bury
Sil|ches|ter
si|lence
VERB
△ si|len|ces
△ si|lenced
△ si|len|cing
si|len|cer
si|lent
si|lently
Si|lenus
Si|lesia
sil|hou|ette
VERB
△ sil|hou|ettes

△ sil|hou|et|ted
△ sil|hou|et|ting
sil|ica
si|li|cate
si|li|con
si|li|cone
si|li|co|sis
silk
sil|ken
sil|ki|ness
silk-screen
silk|worm
silky
△ sil|kier
△ sil|ki|est
sill
sillabub *see*
syllabub
sil|lily
sil|li|ness
Sil|li|toe
silly
NOUN
△ sil|lies
ADJ.
△ sil|lier
△ sil|li|est
silo
silt
VERB
△ silts
△ sil|ted
△ silt|ing
Si|lur|ian
sil|van
sil|ver
VERB
△ sil|vers
△ sil|vered
△ sil|ver|ing
sil|ver|fish
sing. and pl.
sil|ver-pla|ted
sil|ver|side

sil|ver|smith
Sil|ver|stone
sil|very
sil|vi|cul|ture
sima
Si|menon
Sim|eon
sim|ian
sim|ilar
si|mi|lar|ity
△ si|mi|lar|it|ies
si|mi|larly
sim|ile
si|mil|it|ude
Simla
sim|mer
VERB
△ sim|mers
△ sim|mered
△ sim|mer|ing
Sim|nel
sim|nel
Simon
si|mony
sim|per
VERB
△ sim|pers
△ sim|pered
△ sim|per|ing
sim|ple
△ simp|ler
△ simp|lest
simple-minded
simple-mind|ed|
ness
simple|ton
sim|pli|city
sim|pli|fi|ca|tion
sim|plify
△ sim|pli|fies
△ sim|pli|fied
△ sim|pli|fy|ing
sim|plis|tic
sim|plis|tic|ally

Sim|plon
simply
si|mu|late
△ si|mu|lates
△ si|mu|la|ted
△ si|mu|la|ting
si|mu|la|ted
si|mu|la|tion
si|mu|la|tor
sim|ul|cast
sim|ul|ta|neous
sim|ul|ta|neously
sin
VERB
△ sins
△ sinned
△ sin|ning
Sinai
Sin|an|thro|pus
Si|natra
since
sin|cere
sin|cerely
sin|cer|ity
Sin|clair
Sind
sine
Sin|ead
si|ne|cure
sine die
sine qua non
sinew
sin|ewy
sin|fo|ni|etta
sin|ful
sing
△ sings
△ sang
△ sing|ing
△ sung
Sin|ga|pore
singe
VERB
△ sin|ges

△ singed
△ singe|ing
Singer
singer
sing|ing
*Singin' in the
  Rain*
single
  VERB
  △ singles
  △ singled
  △ sing|ling
single-breas|ted
single-fig|ure
single-han|ded
single-han|dedly
single-minded
single-mind|
  edly
single-mind|ed|
  ness
singles
sing|let
sin|gle|ton
singly
sing|song
Sing|spiel
sin|gu|lar
sin|gu|lar|ity
  △ sin|gu|lar|it|ies
sin|gu|larly
Sin|hal|ese
  NOUN
  sing. and pl.
sin|is|ter
Si|nitic
sink
  VERB
  △ sinks
  △ sank
  △ sink|ing
  △ sunk
  AS ADJ.
  △ sun|ken

sin|ker
sin|ner
Sinn Féin
Si|nolo|gist
Si|nol|ogy
Sino-Ti|betan
si|nu|os|ity
sinu|ous
sinu|ous|ness
sinus
  △ si|nuses
si|nus|itis
Siob|han
Sion
Sioux
sip
  VERB
  △ sips
  △ sipped
  △ sip|ping
si|phon
  VERB
  △ si|phons
  △ si|phoned
  △ si|phon|ing
sir
sire
  VERB
  △ sires
  △ sired
  △ sire|ing
Siren
  *mythological
  creature*
siren
  *hooter making
  long wailing
  noise; seductress*
Sir|ius
sir|loin
si|rocco
sis
  △ sis|ses
sisal

sis|kin
Sis|ley
sissy
  △ sis|sies
sis|ter
sis|ter|hood
sis|ter-in-law
  △ sis|ters-in-law
sis|ter|li|ness
sis|terly
Sis|tine
Si|sy|phus
sit
  △ sits
  △ sat
  △ sit|ting
sitar
sit|com
sit-down

site
  place; position
  VERB
  △ sites
  △ sited
  △ si|ting
  ▲ cite
  ▲ sight

Sit|hole
sit-in
sit|ter
sit|ting
sit|ting-room
situ|ate
  △ situ|ates
  △ situ|ated
  △ situ|ating
si|tu|ation
sit-up
Sit|well
six
  NOUN
  △ sixes
Six, Les

*Six Char|ac|ters
  in Search of an
  Au|thor (Sei
  per|son|aggi in
  cerca d'au|tore)*
sixer
six|fold
six-pack
six|pence
six|penny
six|teen
six|teenth
sixth
sixth-for|mer
sixthly
six|ties
six|tieth
sixty
  NOUN
  △ six|ties
size
  VERB
  △ sizes
  △ sized
  △ si|zing
size|able
Size|well
siz|zle
  VERB
  △ siz|zles
  △ siz|zled
  △ siz|zling
ska
Skag|er|rak
skate
  NOUN
  ice-slide
  △ skates
  fish
  △ skate *or* skates
  VERB
  △ skates
  △ ska|ted
  △ ska|ting

skate|board

  VERB

  △ skate|boards

  △ skate|boar|ded

  △ skate|board|
    ing

ska|ter

ska|ting

ske|daddle

  △ ske|daddles

  △ ske|daddled

  △ ske|dad|dling

Skeg|ness

skein

skel|etal

skel|eton

Skel|mers|dale

Skel|ton

sketch

  NOUN

  △ sket|ches

  VERB

  △ sket|ches

  △ sketched

  △ sketch|ing

sketch|ily

sket|chi|ness

sketchy

  △ sket|chier

  △ sket|chi|est

skew

  VERB

  △ skews

  △ skewed

  △ skew|ing

skew|bald

skewer

  VERB

  △ skew|ers

  △ skew|ered

  △ skew|er|ing

skew|ness

skew-whiff

ski

VERB

  △ skis

  △ skied *or* ski'd

  △ ski|ing

Skia|thos

skid

  VERB

  △ skids

  △ skid|ded

  △ skid|ding

Skid|daw

skier

skiff

ski|ing

skil|ful

skil|fully

skill

skilled

skil|let

skim

  △ skims

  △ skimmed

  △ skim|ming

skim|mer

skimp

  △ skimps

  △ skimped

  △ skimp|ing

skimp|ily

skim|pi|ness

skimpy

  △ skim|pier

  △ skim|pi|est

skin

  VERB

  △ skins

  △ skinned

  △ skin|ning

skin-deep

skin-diver

skin-diving

skin|flint

skin|ful

skin|head

skink

skinny

  △ skin|nier

  △ skin|ni|est

skinny-dip

  △ skinny-dips

  △ skinny-dipped

  △ skinny-dip|
    ping

skinny-dip|ping

skint

skin-tight

skip

  VERB

  △ skips

  △ skipped

  △ skip|ping

skip|per

  VERB

  △ skip|pers

  △ skip|pered

  △ skip|per|ing

skip|ping-rope

skirl

  VERB

  △ skirls

  △ skirled

  △ skirl|ing

skir|mish

  NOUN

  △ skir|mi|shes

  VERB

  △ skir|mi|shes

  △ skir|mished

  △ skir|mish|ing

Ski|ros

skirt

  VERB

  △ skirts

  △ skir|ted

  △ skirt|ing

skit

skit|tish

skit|tle

skive

  VERB

  △ skives

  △ skived

  △ ski|ving

skiver

skivvy

  NOUN

  △ skiv|vies

  VERB

  △ skiv|vies

  △ skiv|vied

  △ skiv|vy|ing

Skopje

skua

skul|dug|gery

skulk

  △ skulks

  △ skulked

  △ skulk|ing

skull
bony case of head
△ scull

skull|cap

skunk

sky

  NOUN

  △ skies

  VERB

  △ skies

  △ skied

  △ sky|ing

sky-blue

sky-diver

sky-diving

Skye

sky-high

sky|jack

  △ sky|jacks

  △ sky|jacked

  △ sky|jack|ing

Sky|lab

sky|lark

VERB
△ sky|larks
△ sky|larked
△ sky|lark|ing
sky|light
sky|line
sky|scra|per
sky|ward
sky|way
slab
VERB
△ slabs
△ slabbed
△ slab|bing
slack
VERB
△ slacks
△ slacked
△ slack|ing
ADJ.
△ slacker
△ slack|est
slacken
△ slack|ens
△ slack|ened
△ slack|en|ing
slacker
slacks
slag
VERB
△ slags
△ slagged
△ slag|ging
slain
slake
△ slakes
△ slaked
△ sla|king
sla|lom
slam
VERB
△ slams
△ slammed
△ slam|ming

slammer
slan|der
VERB
△ slan|ders
△ slan|dered
△ slan|der|ing
slan|der|ous
slang
VERB
△ slangs
△ slanged
△ slang|ing
slangy
△ slang|ier
△ slangi|est
slant
VERB
△ slants
△ slan|ted
△ slant|ing
slant|ing
slap
VERB
△ slaps
△ slapped
△ slap|ping
slap-bang
slap|dash
slap-happy
slap|stick
slap-up
slash
NOUN
△ sla|shes
VERB
△ sla|shes
△ slashed
△ slash|ing
slat
slate
VERB
△ slates
△ slated
△ sla|ting

sla|ting
slat|ted
slat|tern
slat|tern|li|ness
slat|ternly
slaugh|ter
VERB
△ slaugh|ters
△ slaugh|tered
△ slaugh|ter|ing
slaugh|ter|house
Slav
slave
VERB
△ slaves
△ slaved
△ sla|ving
slave-dri|ver
sla|ver
    one who trades
    in slaves
slaver
    spittle; dribble
VERB
△ slav|ers
△ slav|ered
△ slav|er|ing
sla|very
Slavic
sla|vish
sla|vishly
Sla|vonic

┌─────────────────┐
slay
    kill
VERB
△ slays
△ slew
△ slay|ing
△ sleigh
└─────────────────┘

slayer
sleaze
slea|zi|ness
sleazy

△ slea|zier
△ slea|zi|est
sled
VERB
△ sleds
△ sled|ded
△ sled|ding
sledge
VERB
△ sled|ges
△ sledged
△ sled|ging
sledge|ham|mer
sleek
VERB
△ sleeks
△ sleeked
△ sleek|ing
ADJ.
△ slee|ker
△ sleek|est
sleep
VERB
△ sleeps
△ slept
△ sleep|ing
slee|per
sleep|ily
slee|pi|ness
sleep|ing-bag
Sleep|ing
    Beauty, The
    (Spyash\chaya
    kra|sa|vitsa)
sleep|less
sleep|walk
△ sleep|walks
△ sleep|walked
△ sleep|walk|ing
sleep|walker
sleep|walk|ing
sleepy
△ slee|pier
△ slee|pi|est

slee|py|head

sleet
VERB
△ sleets
△ slee|ted
△ sleet|ing

sleety
△ slee|tier
△ slee|ti|est

sleeve

sleeve|less

sleigh
sledge; travel in this
VERB
△ sleighs
△ sleighed
△ sleigh|ing
⚠slay

sleight

slen|der
△ slen|derer
△ slen|der|est

slept

sleuth
VERB
△ sleuths
△ sleuthed
△ sleuth|ing

slew
VERB
△ slews
△ slewed
△ slew|ing
also past tense of slay

slewed

slice
VERB
△ sli|ces
△ sliced
△ sli|cing

sli|cer

slick
VERB
△ slicks
△ slicked
△ slick|ing
ADJ.
△ slicker
△ slick|est

slick|en|side

slicker

slide
VERB
△ slides
△ slid
△ sli|ding

slide-rule

slight
VERB
△ slights
△ sligh|ted
△ slight|ing
ADJ.
△ sligh|ter
△ slight|est

slightly

Sligo

slily *see* slyly

slim
VERB
△ slims
△ slimmed
△ slim|ming
ADJ.
△ slim|mer
△ slim|mest

slime

sli|mily

sli|mi|ness

slim|mer

slim|ming

slimy
△ sli|mier
△ sli|mi|est

sling

VERB
△ slings
△ slung
△ sling|ing

sling|back

sling|shot

slink
△ slinks
△ slunk
△ slink|ing

slink|ily

slin|ki|ness

slinky
△ slin|kier
△ slin|ki|est

slip
VERB
△ slips
△ slipped
△ slip|ping

slip-knot

slip-on

slip|per

slip|pered

slip|peri|ness

slip|pery

slippy
△ slip|pier
△ slip|pi|est

slip|shod

slip|stream

slip-up

slip|way

slit
VERB
△ slits
△ slit
△ slit|ting

sli|ther
VERB
△ slith|ers
△ slith|ered
△ slith|er|ing

slith|ery

sliver
VERB
△ sliv|ers
△ sliv|ered
△ sliv|er|ing

sli|vo|vitz
△ sli|vo|vit|zes

Sloane

slob
VERB
△ slobs
△ slobbed
△ slob|bing

slob|ber
VERB
△ slob|bers
△ slob|bered
△ slob|ber|ing

slob|bish

slobby
△ slob|bier
△ slob|bi|est

sloe
blackthorn
⚠slow

slog
VERB
△ slogs
△ slogged
△ slog|ging

slo|gan

sloop

slop
VERB
△ slops
△ slopped
△ slop|ping

slope
VERB
△ slopes
△ sloped
△ slo|ping

slop|pily

slop|pi|ness
sloppy
△ slop|pier
△ slop|pi|est
slosh
NOUN
△ sloshes
VERB
△ sloshes
△ sloshed
△ slosh|ing
sloshed
slot
VERB
△ slots
△ slot|ted
△ slot|ting
sloth
sloth|ful
slouch
NOUN
△ slou|ches
VERB
△ slou|ches
△ slouched
△ slouch|ing
Slough
slough
VERB
△ sloughs
△ sloughed
△ slough|ing
Slo|vak
Slo|va|kia
sloven
Slo|venia
slov|en|li|ness
slov|enly

slow
*not fast; become
this*
VERB
△ slows
△ slowed
△ slow|ing
ADJ.
△ slower
△ slow|est
ADV.
△ slower
△ slow|est
⚠ sloe

slow|coach
△ slow|coa|ches
slowly
slow|ness
slow-worm
sludge
△ slud|ges
sludgy
△ slud|gier
△ slud|gi|est
slug
VERB
△ slugs
△ slugged
△ slug|ging
slug|gard
slug|gish
sluice
VERB
△ sluices
△ sluiced
△ sluicing
slum
VERB
△ slums
△ slummed
△ slum|ming
slum|ber
VERB
△ slum|bers
△ slum|bered
△ slum|ber|ing
slum|ber|ing
slum|ber|ous

slummy
△ slum|mier
△ slum|mi|est
slump
VERB
△ slumps
△ slumped
△ slump|ing
slung
slunk
slur
VERB
△ slurs
△ slurred
△ slur|ring
slurp
VERB
△ slurps
△ slurped
△ slurp|ing
slurry
△ slur|ries
slush
△ slushes
slushy
△ slush|ier
△ slushi|est
slut
slut|tish
sly
△ slyer
△ sly|est
slyly
smack
VERB
△ smacks
△ smacked
△ smack|ing
smacker
small
ADJ.
△ smal|ler
△ small|est
small|hol|der

small|hold|ing
small-minded
small|ness
small|pox
small-time
smarm
VERB
△ smarms
△ smarmed
△ smarm|ing
smarm|ily
smar|mi|ness
smarmy
△ smar|mier
△ smar|mi|est
smart
VERB
△ smarts
△ smar|ted
△ smart|ing
ADJ.
△ smar|ter
△ smart|est
smart alec
smart-alecky
smar|ten
△ smar|tens
△ smar|tened
△ smar|ten|ing
smartly
smart|ness
smash
NOUN
△ sma|shes
VERB
△ sma|shes
△ smashed
△ smash|ing
smash-and-grab
smashed
sma|sher
smash|ing
smash-up
smat|ter|ing

smear
  VERB
  △ smears
  △ smeared
  △ smear|ing
smeary
  △ smear|ier
  △ smeari|est
smegma
smell
  VERB
  △ smells
  △ smelled *or*
    smelt
  △ smell|ing
smel|li|ness
smel|ling-salts
smelly
  △ smel|lier
  △ smel|li|est
smelt
  NOUN
  △ smelts *or*
    smelt
  VERB
  △ smelts
  △ smel|ted
  △ smelt|ing
  also past tense
  and past
  participle of
  smell
smel|ter
Smet|ana
smid|gen
smile
  VERB
  △ smiles
  △ smiled
  △ smi|ling
Smiles
smirch
  NOUN
  △ smir|ches

VERB
  △ smir|ches
  △ smirched
  △ smirch|ing
smirk
  VERB
  △ smirks
  △ smirked
  △ smirk|ing
smite
  △ smites
  △ smote
  △ smi|ting
  △ smit|ten
Smith
smith
smi|ther|eens
Smith|field
Smith|so|nian
smithy
  △ smith|ies
smit|ten
smock
  VERB
  △ smocks
  △ smocked
  △ smock|ing
smock|ing
smog
smoggy
  △ smog|gier
  △ smog|gi|est
smoke
  VERB
  △ smokes
  △ smoked
  △ smo|king
smoked
smoke|less
smo|ker
smoke|screen
smoke|stack
smo|ki|ness
smo|king

smoky
  △ smo|kier
  △ smo|ki|est
Smol|lensk
Smol|lett
smolt
smooch
  NOUN
  △ smoo|ches
  VERB
  △ smoo|ches
  △ smooched
  △ smooch|ing
smoochy
  △ smoo|chier
  △ smoo|chi|est
smooth
  VERB
  △ smooths
  △ smoothed
  △ smooth|ing
  ADJ.
  △ smoo|ther
  △ smooth|est
smoo|thie
smoothly
smooth|ness
smooth-talk|ing
smooth-tongued
smor|gas|bord
smote
smother
  △ smoth|ers
  △ smoth|ered
  △ smoth|er|ing
smoul|der
  VERB
  △ smoul|ders
  △ smoul|dered
  △ smoul|der|ing
smudge
  VERB
  △ smud|ges
  △ smudged

△ smud|ging
smudgy
  △ smud|gier
  △ smud|gi|est
smug
  △ smug|ger
  △ smug|gest
smug|gle
  △ smug|gles
  △ smug|gled
  △ smug|gling
smug|gler
smug|gling
smugly
smug|ness
smut
  VERB
  △ smuts
  △ smut|ted
  △ smut|ting
Smuts
smut|ti|ness
smutty
  △ smut|tier
  △ smut|ti|est
Smyrna
snack
snaf|fle
  VERB
  △ snaf|fles
  △ snaf|fled
  △ snaf|fling
snag
  VERB
  △ snags
  △ snagged
  △ snag|ging
snail
snake
  VERB
  △ snakes
  △ snaked
  △ sna|king
snake|bite

snake-char|mer
sna|kily
snaky
△ sna|kier
△ sna|ki|est
snap
VERB
△ snaps
△ snapped
△ snap|ping
snap|dra|gon
snap|per
snap|pily
snap|pi|ness
snappy
△ snap|pier
△ snap|pi|est
snap|shot
snare
VERB
△ snares
△ snared
△ snar|ing
snarl
VERB
△ snarls
△ snarled
△ snarl|ing
snarl-up
snatch
NOUN
△ snat|ches
VERB
△ snat|ches
△ snatched
△ snatch|ing
snaz|zily
snazzy
△ snaz|zier
△ snaz|zi|est
Snead
sneak
VERB
△ sneaks

△ sneaked
△ sneak|ing
sneak|ers
sneak|ily
sneak|ing
sneaky
△ snea|kier
△ snea|ki|est
sneer
VERB
△ sneers
△ sneered
△ sneer|ing
sneer|ing
sneeze
VERB
△ snee|zes
△ sneezed
△ sneez|ing
snick
VERB
△ snicks
△ snicked
△ snick|ing
snicker *see*
snigger
snide
sniff
VERB
△ sniffs
△ sniffed
△ sniff|ing
sniff|ily
snif|fle
VERB
△ snif|fles
△ snif|fled
△ snif|fling
sniffy
△ snif|fier
△ snif|fi|est
snif|ter
snig|ger

VERB
△ snig|gers
△ snig|gered
△ snig|ger|ing
snip
VERB
△ snips
△ snipped
△ snip|ping
snipe
NOUN
bird
sing. and pl.
other senses
△ snipes
VERB
△ snipes
△ sniped
△ sni|ping
sni|per
snip|pet
snitch
NOUN
△ snit|ches
VERB
△ snit|ches
△ snitched
△ snitch|ing
snit|cher
snivel
VERB
△ sniv|els
△ sniv|elled
△ sniv|el|ling
snob
snob|bery
snob|bish
snob|bish|ness
snobby
△ snob|bier
△ snob|bi|est
snog
VERB
△ snogs

△ snogged
△ snog|ging
snood
snook
snoo|ker
VERB
△ snoo|kers
△ snoo|kered
△ snoo|ker|ing
snoop
VERB
△ snoops
△ snooped
△ snoop|ing
snoo|per
snoot|ily
snoo|ti|ness
snooty
△ snoo|tier
△ snoo|ti|est
snooze
VERB
△ snoo|zes
△ snoozed
△ snooz|ing
snore
VERB
△ snores
△ snored
△ snor|ing
snor|kel
VERB
△ snor|kels
△ snor|kelled
△ snor|kel|ling
Snorri Stur|
luson
snort
VERB
△ snorts
△ snor|ted
△ snort|ing
snot
snot|tily

snot|ti|ness

snotty

△ snot|tier

△ snot|ti|est

snout

Snow

snow

VERB

△ snows

△ snowed

△ snow|ing

snow|ball

VERB

△ snow|balls

△ snow|balled

△ snow|ball|ing

snow|berry

△ snow|ber|ries

snow-blind

snow|board

VERB

△ snow|boards

△ snow|boar|ded

△ snow|board|ing

snow|board|ing

snow|bound

snow|cap

snow-capped

Snow|don

Snow|do|nia

snow|drift

snow|drop

snow|fall

snow|flake

snow|line

snow|man

△ snow|men

snow|mo|bile

snow|plough

snow|shoe

Snow White and the Seven Dwarfs

snowy

△ snow|ier

△ snowi|est

snub

VERB

△ snubs

△ snubbed

△ snub|bing

snuff

VERB

△ snuffs

△ snuffed

△ snuff|ing

snuff|box

△ snuff|boxes

snuf|fle

VERB

△ snuf|fles

△ snuf|fled

△ snuf|fling

snug

△ snug|ger

△ snug|gest

snug|gery

△ snug|ger|ies

snug|gle

△ snug|gles

△ snug|gled

△ snug|gling

snugly

Snyder

---

so

in this way; to this extent; in order that

⚠ sew

⚠ sow

---

soak

VERB

△ soaks

△ soaked

△ soak|ing

soaked

soak|ing

so-and-so

Soane

soap

VERB

△ soaps

△ soaped

△ soap|ing

soap|box

△ soap|boxes

soap|stone

soapy

△ soa|pier

△ soa|pi|est

---

soar

glide; rise sharply

△ soars

△ soared

△ soar|ing

⚠ sore

---

sob

VERB

△ sobs

△ sobbed

△ sob|bing

sober

VERB

△ so|bers

△ so|bered

△ so|ber|ing

so|ber|ing

So|bers

so|bri|ety

so|bri|quet

sob-story

△ sob-stor|ies

soca

so-called

soc|cer

so|ci|abil|ity

so|ci|able

so|ci|able|ness

so|ci|ably

so|cial

so|cial|ism

so|cial|ist

so|cial|ite

so|cial|iza|tion

so|cial|ize

△ so|cial|izes

△ so|cial|ized

△ so|cial|izing

so|ci|ally

so|ci|ety

△ so|ci|et|ies

so|cio|bi|ol|ogy

so|cio|gram

so|cio|lin|guis|tics

so|cio|lo|gi|cal

so|ci|olo|gist

so|ci|ology

so|ci|om|etry

sock

VERB

△ socks

△ socked

△ sock|ing

socket

so|cle

Soc|ra|tes

So|cratic

sod

VERB

△ sods

△ sod|ded

△ sod|ding

soda

sod|den

sod|ding

so|dium

Sodom

sod|om|ite

sod|om|ize

△ sod|om|izes

△ sod|om|ized

△ sod|om|izing

sod¦omy

Sod's law

Soekarno *see*
  Sukarno

sofa

sof¦fit

Sofia

soft
  ADJ.
  △ sof¦ter
  △ soft¦est

soft¦ball

soft-boiled

soften
  △ soft¦ens
  △ soft¦ened
  △ soft¦en¦ing

soft¦ener

soft-hearted

sof¦tie

soft-pedal
  △ soft-ped¦als
  △ soft-ped¦alled
  △ soft-ped¦al¦
    ling

soft-soap
  △ soft-soaps
  △ soft-soaped
  △ soft-soap¦ing

soft-spo¦ken

soft¦ware

soft¦wood

softy
  △ sof¦ties

sog¦gily

sog¦gi¦ness

soggy
  △ sog¦gier
  △ sog¦gi¦est

soh

Soul *see* Seoul

Soho

soil

VERB
△ soils
△ soiled
△ soil¦ing

soirée

so¦journ
VERB
△ so¦journs
△ so¦journed
△ so¦journ¦ing

sol

sola

sol¦ace
VERB
△ sol¦aces
△ sol¦aced
△ sol¦acing

sol¦ace¦ment

solar

so¦lar¦ium
  △ so¦lar¦iums *or*
    so¦laria

sold

sol¦der
VERB
△ sol¦ders
△ sol¦dered
△ sol¦der¦ing

sol¦der¦ing-iron

sol¦dier
VERB
△ sol¦diers
△ sol¦diered
△ sol¦dier¦ing

sol¦dierly

sole
  bottom of foot;
  sort of fish; put
  soles on; only
  NOUN
  fish
  △ sole *or* soles
  other senses

△ soles
VERB
△ soles
△ soled
△ so¦ling
⚠ soul

so¦le¦cism

so¦le¦cis¦tic

solely

sol¦emn

so¦lem¦nity
  △ so¦lem¦ni¦ties

sol¦em¦ni¦za¦tion

sol¦em¦nize
  △ sol¦em¦ni¦zes
  △ sol¦em¦nized
  △ sol¦em¦ni¦zing

sol¦emnly

so¦len¦oid

So¦lent

sol-fa

so¦li¦cit
  △ so¦li¦cits
  △ so¦li¦ci¦ted
  △ so¦li¦cit¦ing

so¦li¦ci¦ta¦tion

so¦li¦ci¦tor

so¦li¦ci¦tor-advo¦
  cate

So¦li¦ci¦tor-Gen¦
  eral

so¦li¦ci¦tous

so¦li¦ci¦tously

so¦li¦ci¦tude

solid
  ADJ.
  △ sol¦ider
  △ sol¦id¦est

Soli¦dar¦ity
  Polish trade
  union

so¦li¦dar¦ity
  mutual support

so¦li¦di¦fi¦ca¦tion

so¦lid¦ify
  △ so¦lid¦ifies
  △ so¦lid¦ified
  △ so¦lid¦ify¦ing

so¦lid¦ity

sol¦idly

solid-state

sol¦idus
  △ sol¦idi

So¦li¦hull

so¦lilo¦quize
  △ so¦lilo¦qui¦zes
  △ so¦lilo¦quized
  △ so¦lilo¦qui¦zing

so¦lilo¦quy
  △ so¦lilo¦quies

sol¦ip¦sism

sol¦ip¦sist

so¦li¦taire

sol¦it¦ari¦ness

sol¦it¦ary
  △ sol¦it¦ar¦ies

sol¦itude

sol¦mi¦za¦tion

solo

so¦lo¦ist

Solo¦mon

Solo¦mon's seal

sol¦stice

Solti

solu¦bil¦ity

sol¦uble

sol¦ute

so¦lu¦tion

sol¦vable

sol¦va¦tion

solve
  △ solves
  △ solved
  △ sol¦ving

sol¦vency

sol¦vent

Sol¦way

Sol|zhen|it|syn
So|mali
So|ma|lia
so|ma|tic
so|ma|to|tro|
phin
som|bre
som|brely
som|brero
some
some|body
NOUN
△ some|bod|ies
some|day
some|how
*Some Like it
Hot*
some|one
som|er|sault
VERB
△ som|er|saults
△ somer|saul|ted
△ som|er|sault|
ing
Som|er|set
some|thing
some|time
some|times
some|what
some|where
Somme
somn|am|bu|
lism
somn|am|bu|list
som|no|lence
som|no|lent
So|moza

son
  *male child; sort
  of Cuban music*
  ⚠ sun

sonar
so|nata

so|na|tina
Sond|heim
son et lu|mi|ère
song
song|bird
Song of Solo|mon
Song of Songs
*Song of the
  Earth, The*
*Songs of In|no|
  cence and Ex|
  peri|ence*
song|ster
song|stress
△ song|stres|ses
*Songs with|out
  Words (Lie|der
  ohne Worte)*
sonic
son-in-law
△ sons-in-law
son|net
sonny
so|nor|ity
△ so|nor|it|ies
son|or|ous *or* so|
  nor|ous
  *according to
  pronunciation*
Sons and Lovers
soon
△ sooner
△ soon|est
soot
soothe
△ soothes
△ soothed
△ sooth|ing
sooth|ing
sooth|say
△ sooth|says
△ sooth|said
△ sooth|say|ing
sooth|sayer

sooty
△ soot|ier
△ sooti|est
sop
VERB
△ sops
△ sopped
△ sop|ping
Soper
So|phia
soph|ism
soph|ist
so|phis|ti|cate
VERB
△ so|phis|ti|cates
△ so|phis|ti|ca|
  ted
△ so|phis|ti|ca|
  ting
so|phis|ti|ca|ted
so|phis|ti|ca|tion
soph|istry
△ soph|is|tries
So|pho|cles
so|pho|more
sop|or|ific
sop|pily
sop|pi|ness
sop|ping
soppy
△ sop|pier
△ sop|pi|est
sop|rano
Sop|with
sor|bet
sor|bi|tol
Sor|bonne
sor|cerer
sor|cer|ess
△ sor|cer|es|ses
sor|cery
sor|did
sor|dino
△ sor|dini

sore
  *diseased spot;
  tender*
  ADJ.
  △ sorer
  △ sor|est
  ⚠ soar

sorely
sor|ghum
sor|or|ity
△ sor|or|it|ies
sor|rel
sor|row
VERB
△ sor|rows
△ sor|rowed
△ sor|row|ing
sor|row|ful
sor|row|fully
sorry
ADJ.
△ sor|rier
△ sor|ri|est
sort
VERB
△ sorts
△ sor|ted
△ sort|ing
sor|tie
VERB
△ sor|ties
△ sor|tied
△ sor|tie|ing
sorus
△ sori
so-so
sos|ten|uto
sot
Soth|eby
Sotho-Tswana
sot|tish
sotto voce
sou

soubrette 385 spar

sou|brette
soubriquet *see*
  sobriquet
souf|flé
sough
  VERB
  △ soughs
  △ soughed
  △ sough|ing
sought
sought-after
souk
sou|kous

soul
spirit; essence
  ⚠sole

soul-des|troy|
  ing
soul|ful
soul|fully
soul|less
soul-search|ing
sound
  VERB
  △ sounds
  △ soun|ded
  △ sound|ing
  ADJ.
  △ soun|der
  △ sound|est
*Sound and the
  Fury, The*
sound|bite
sound|board
sound-box
  △ sound-boxes
sound|ing
sound|ing-board
soundly
*Sound of Music,
  The*
sound|track
soup

soup|çon
soupy
  △ sou|pier
  △ sou|pi|est
sour
  VERB
  △ sours
  △ soured
  △ sour|ing
  ADJ.
  △ sourer
  △ sour|est
source
sourly
sour|puss
  △ sour|pus|ses
Sousa
souse
  VERB
  △ sou|ses
  △ soused
  △ sous|ing
soused
sou|tane
south
Sou|thamp|ton
south|bound
South|cott
south-east
South East Asia
south-east|er
south-east|erly
  NOUN
  △ south-east|er|
    lies
south-east|ern
South|end
south|erly
  NOUN
  △ south|er|lies
south|ern
south|er|ner
south|ern|most
Sou|they

south|paw
South|port
South Shields
south|ward
south|wards
South|wark
South|well
south-west
south|wes|ter
south-wes|terly
  NOUN
  △ south-wes|ter|
    lies
south-west|ern
sou|venir
sou'|wes|ter
sov|er|eign
sov|er|eignty
  △ sov|er|eign|
    ties
so|viet

sow
*put seed out to
grow; female pig*
  VERB
  △ sows
  △ sowed
  △ sow|ing
  △ sown *or*
    sowed
  ⚠sew
  ⚠so

So|weto
soy
soya
Soy|inka
soz|zled
spa
space
  VERB
  △ spa|ces
  △ spaced
  △ spa|cing

space|craft
  sing. and pl.
Space|lab
space|man
  △ space|men
space|wo|man
  △ space|wo|men
spa|cious
spa|cious|ness
spade
spade|work
spa|dix
  △ spa|di|ces
spa|ghetti
Spain
spake
Spam
span
  VERB
  △ spans
  △ spanned
  △ span|ning
Span|dex
span|drel
span|gle
  VERB
  △ span|gles
  △ span|gled
  △ span|gling
Span|glish
Span|iard
span|iel
Span|ish
*Span|ish Tra|
  gedy, The*
spank
  VERB
  △ spanks
  △ spanked
  △ spank|ing
span|ker
spank|ing
span|ner
spar

VERB
△ spars
△ sparred
△ spar|ring
spare
VERB
△ spares
△ spared
△ spar|ing
spar|ing
spar|ingly
Spark
spark
VERB
△ sparks
△ sparked
△ spark|ing
spar|kle
VERB
△ spar|kles
△ spar|kled
△ spark|ling
spark|ler
spark|ling
spar|row
sparrow-hawk
sparse
△ spar|ser
△ spar|sest
sparsely
sparse|ness
spar|sity
Sparta
Spar|ta|cist
Spar|ta|cus
spar|tan
spasm
spas|modic
spas|mod|ic|ally
spas|tic
spat
VERB
△ spats
△ spat|ted

△ spat|ting
also past tense
and past
participle of spit
spate
spathe
spa|tial
spat|ter
VERB
△ spat|ters
△ spat|tered
△ spat|ter|ing
spat|ula
spawn
VERB
△ spawns
△ spawned
△ spawn|ing
spay
△ spays
△ spayed
△ spay|ing
speak
△ speaks
△ spoke
△ speak|ing
△ spo|ken
speak|easy
△ speak|eas|ies
spea|ker
spear
VERB
△ spears
△ speared
△ spear|ing
spear|head
VERB
△ spear|heads
△ spear|headed
△ spear|head|ing
spear|mint
spec
spe|cial
spe|cial|ism

spe|cial|ist
spe|ci|al|ity
△ spe|ci|al|it|ies
spe|cial|iza|tion
spe|cial|ize
△ spe|cial|izes
△ spe|cial|ized
△ spe|cial|izing
spe|cial|ized
spe|cially
specialty *see*
speciality
spe|ci|ation
spe|cie
spe|cies
sing. and pl.
spe|cies|ism
spe|ci|fic
spe|cif|ic|ally
spe|ci|fi|ca|tion
specify
△ spe|ci|fies
△ spe|ci|fied
△ spe|ci|fy|ing
spe|ci|men
spe|ci|os|ity
spe|cious
spe|cious|ness
speck
speckle
VERB
△ speckles
△ speckled
△ speck|ling
speckled
specs
spec|ta|cle
spec|tacu|lar
spec|tacu|larly
spec|tate
△ spec|tates
△ spec|ta|ted
△ spec|ta|ting
spec|ta|tor

spec|tral
spectre
spec|tro|meter
spec|tro|scope
spec|trum
△ spec|tra *or*
spec|trums
spe|cu|late
△ spe|cu|lates
△ spe|cu|la|ted
△ spe|cu|la|ting
spe|cu|la|tion
spe|cu|la|tive
spe|cu|la|tor
spe|cu|lum
△ spec|ula
sped
speech
△ spee|ches
speech|ify
△ speech|ifies
△ speech|ified
△ speech|ify|ing
speech|less
speed
VERB
△ speeds
go fast
△ sped
break speed
limit; set or
increase speed of
engine etc
△ speeded
△ speed|ing
speed|boat
speed|ily
speedo
speed|ometer
speed|way
speed|well
speedy
△ spee|dier
△ spee|di|est

Speke
spe|lae|ol|ogy
spell
  VERB
  △ spells
  △ spelt *or*
    spelled
  △ spell|ing
spell|bind|ing
spell|bound
spell|ing
spelt
spe|lunk|ing
Spence
Spen|cer
spend
  △ spends
  △ spent
  △ spend|ing
Spen|der
spend|thrift
Spen|ser
spent
sperm
sper|ma|ceti
sper|ma|to|gen|
  esis
sper|ma|to|phyte
sper|ma|to|zoon
  △ sper|ma|to|zoa
sper|mi|cide
spew
  VERB
  △ spews
  △ spewed
  △ spew|ing
sphag|num
  △ sphagna
sphal|er|ite
sphere
spher|ical
spher|oid
sphinc|ter
sphinx

  △ sphinxes
sphyg|mo|ma|
  nom|eter
sphyg|mom|eter
spice
  VERB
  △ spi|ces
  △ spiced
  △ spi|cing
spicy
  △ spi|cier
  △ spi|ci|est
spi|der
spi|dery
spiel
Spiel|berg
spif|fing
spi|got
spike
  VERB
  △ spikes
  △ spiked
  △ spi|king
spike|let
spike|nard
spi|kily
spi|ki|ness
spiky
  △ spi|kier
  △ spi|ki|est
spill
  VERB
  △ spills
  △ spilt *or* spilled
  △ spill|ing
spill|age
Spil|lane
spilt
spin
  VERB
  △ spins
  △ spun
  △ spin|ning
spina bi|fida

spin|ach
spi|nal
spin|dle
spindly
  △ spin|dlier
  △ spin|dli|est
spin-drier
spin|drift
spin-dry
  △ spin-dries
  △ spin-dried
  △ spin-dry|ing
spin-dryer
spine
spine-chil|ler
spine-chill|ing
spine|less
spinet
spin|na|ker
spin|ner
spin|neret
spin|ney
spin|ning-jenny
  △ spin|ning-jen|
    nies
spin|ning-wheel
spin-off
Spi|noza
spin|ster
spin|ster|hood
spiny
  △ spi|nier
  △ spi|ni|est
Spion Kop
spir|acle
spir|aea
spi|ral
  VERB
  △ spi|rals
  △ spi|ralled
  △ spi|ral|ling
spi|rally
spire
spirit

  VERB
  △ spir|its
  △ spir|ited
  △ spir|it|ing
spir|ited
spirit-lamp
spir|it|ual
spir|itu|al|ism
spir|itu|al|ist
spir|itu|al|ity
spir|itu|ally
spir|itu|ous
spi|ro|chaete
spi|ro|gyra
spit
  VERB
  △ spits
  △ spat
  △ spit|ting
Spit|al|fields
spite
  VERB
  △ spites
  △ spi|ted
  △ spi|ting
spite|ful
spite|fully
spite|ful|ness
Spit|fire
  aeroplane
spit|fire
  bad-tempered
  person
Spits|ber|gen
spit|tle
spit|toon
spiv
spivvy
  △ spiv|vier
  △ spiv|vi|est
splash
  NOUN
  △ spla|shes

VERB
△ spla|shes
△ splashed
△ splash|ing
splash|down
splat
splat|ter
VERB
△ splat|ters
△ splat|tered
△ splat|ter|ing
splay
△ splays
△ splayed
△ splay|ing
spleen
splen|did
splen|didly
splen|di|fer|ous
splen|dour
splen|etic
splice
VERB
△ spli|ces
△ spliced
△ spli|cing
splint
splin|ter
VERB
△ splin|ters
△ splin|tered
△ splin|ter|ing
Split
split
VERB
△ splits
△ split
△ split|ting
split|ting
splodge
VERB
△ splod|ges
△ splod|ged
△ splod|ging

splurge
VERB
△ splur|ges
△ splurged
△ splur|ging
splut|ter
VERB
△ splut|ters
△ splut|tered
△ splut|ter|ing
Spock
Spode
spoil
VERB
△ spoils
△ spoilt *or*
    spoiled
△ spoil|ing
spoiler
Spoils of Poyn|
    ton, The
spoil|sport
spoke
spo|ken
spokes|man
△ spokes|men
spokes|per|son
spokes|wo|man
△ spokes|wo|
    men
Spo|leto
spo|li|ation
spon|daic
spon|dee
sponge
VERB
△ spon|ges
△ sponged
△ spon|ging
spon|ger
spongy
△ spon|gier
△ spon|gi|est
spon|sor

VERB
△ spon|sors
△ spon|sored
△ spon|sor|ing
spon|sored
spon|sor|ship
spon|ta|neity
spon|ta|neous
spoof
VERB
△ spoofs
△ spoofed
△ spoof|ing
spook
VERB
△ spooks
△ spooked
△ spook|ing
spooky
△ spoo|kier
△ spoo|ki|est
spool
spoon
VERB
△ spoons
△ spooned
△ spoon|ing
spoon|bill
Spoo|ner
spoo|ner|ism
spoon-feed
△ spoon-feeds
△ spoon-fed
△ spoon-feed|
    ing
spoon|ful
△ spoon|fuls
spoor
spor|adic
spor|ad|ic|ally
spor|an|gium
△ spor|an|gia
spore
sporo|phyll

sporo|phyte
spor|ran
sport
VERB
△ sports
△ spor|ted
△ sport|ing
sport|ing
sport|ingly
sport|ive
sports|man
△ sports|men
sports|man|like
sports|man|ship
sports|wo|man
△ sports|wo|men
sporty
△ spor|tier
△ spor|ti|est
spot
VERB
△ spots
△ spot|ted
△ spot|ting
spot|less
spot|lessly
spot|less|ness
spot|light
VERB
△ spot|lights
△ spot|lit *or*
    spot|ligh|ted
△ spot|light|ing
spot-on
spot|ted
spot|ter
spot|ti|ness
spotty
△ spot|tier
△ spot|ti|est
spouse
spout
VERB
△ spouts

△ spou|ted
△ spout|ing
sprain
  VERB
  △ sprains
  △ sprained
  △ sprain|ing
sprang
sprat
sprawl
  VERB
  △ sprawls
  △ sprawled
  △ sprawl|ing
spray
  VERB
  △ sprays
  △ sprayed
  △ spray|ing
spray-gun
spread
  VERB
  △ spreads
  △ spread
  △ spread|ing
spread-eagled
spread|sheet
spree
sprig
spright|li|ness
sprightly
spring
  VERB
  △ springs
  △ sprang
  △ spring|ing
  △ sprung
Spring Awa|
  ken|ing (Früh|
  lings Er|wa|
  chen)
spring|board
spring|bok
spring-clean

  VERB
  △ spring-cleans
  △ spring-
    cleaned
  △ spring-clean|
    ing
sprin|ger
sprin|gi|ness
Spring|steen
spring|tail
spring|time
springy
  △ sprin|gier
  △ sprin|gi|est
sprin|kle
  VERB
  △ sprin|kles
  △ sprin|kled
  △ sprink|ling
sprink|ler
sprink|ling
sprint
  VERB
  △ sprints
  △ sprin|ted
  △ sprint|ing
Sprin|ter
  sort of train
sprin|ter
  runner
sprit
sprite
sprit|sail
sprit|zer
sprocket
sprout
  VERB
  △ sprouts
  △ sprou|ted
  △ sprout|ing
spruce
  ADJ.
  △ spru|cer
  △ spru|cest

sprung
spry
  △ spryer
  △ spry|est
spryly
spry|ness
spud
spume
  VERB
  △ spumes
  △ spumed
  △ spu|ming
spumy
  △ spu|mier
  △ spu|mi|est
spun
spunk
spunky
  △ spun|kier
  △ spun|ki|est
spur
  VERB
  △ spurs
  △ spurred
  △ spur|ring
spurge
spu|ri|ous
spurn
  △ spurns
  △ spurned
  △ spurn|ing
spurt
  VERB
  △ spurts
  △ spur|ted
  △ spurt|ing
Sput|nik
sput|ter
  VERB
  △ sput|ters
  △ sput|tered
  △ sput|ter|ing
spu|tum
  △ sputa

spy
  NOUN
  △ spies
  VERB
  △ spies
  △ spied
  △ spy|ing
spy|glass
  △ spy|glas|ses
spy|hole
squab
squab|ble
  VERB
  △ squab|bles
  △ squab|bled
  △ squab|bling
squabby
  △ squab|bier
  △ squab|bi|est
squad
squaddy
  △ squad|dies
squad|ron
squalid
squall
  VERB
  △ squalls
  △ squalled
  △ squall|ing
squally
squalor
squan|der
  △ squan|ders
  △ squan|dered
  △ squan|der|ing
square
  VERB
  △ squares
  △ squared
  △ squar|ing
square-bash|ing
squarely
squash

NOUN
△ squa|shes
VERB
△ squa|shes
△ squashed
△ squash|ing
squashy
△ squa|shier
△ squa|shi|est
squat
VERB
△ squats
△ squat|ted
△ squat|ting
ADJ.
△ squat|ter
△ squat|test
squat|ter
squaw
squawk
VERB
△ squawks
△ squawked
△ squawk|ing
squawky
△ squaw|kier
△ squaw|ki|est
squeak
VERB
△ squeaks
△ squeaked
△ squeak|ing
squea|ki|ness
squeaky
△ squeak|ier
△ squeaki|est
squeal
VERB
△ squeals
△ squealed
△ squeal|ing
squealer
squeam|ish

squee|gee
*rubber-bladed
scraper*
⚠ squeegie

squeegie
*one who cleans
car windows in
traffic jams*
⚠ squeegee

squeeze
VERB
△ squee|zes
△ squeezed
△ squeez|ing
squeeze-box
△ squeeze-boxes
squeezer
squelch
NOUN
△ squel|ches
VERB
△ squel|ches
△ squelched
△ squelch|ing
squelchy
△ squel|chier
△ squel|chi|est
squib
squid
△ squid *or*
squids
squiffy
△ squif|fier
△ squif|fi|est
squiggle
squiggly
△ squig|glier
△ squig|gli|est
squinch
△ squin|ches
squint

VERB
△ squints
△ squin|ted
△ squint|ing
squire
squirm
VERB
△ squirms
△ squirmed
△ squirm|ing
squir|rel
squirt
VERB
△ squirts
△ squir|ted
△ squirt|ing
squish
NOUN
△ squi|shes
VERB
△ squi|shes
△ squished
△ squish|ing
Sreb|ren|ica
Sri-Jaya|war|
dena|pura
Sri Lanka
stab
VERB
△ stabs
△ stabbed
△ stab|bing
sta|bil|ity
sta|bil|iza|tion
sta|bil|ize
△ sta|bil|izes
△ sta|bil|ized
△ sta|bil|izing
sta|bil|izer
sta|ble
stac|cato
stack
VERB
△ stacks

△ stacked
△ stack|ing
sta|dium
△ sta|di|ums *or*
sta|dia
staff
NOUN
stick
△ staffs *or*
staves
other senses
△ staffs
VERB
△ staffs
△ staffed
△ staff|ing
Staf|ford
Staf|ford|shire
stag
stage
VERB
△ sta|ges
△ staged
△ sta|ging
stage|coach
△ stage|coa|ches
stage|hand
stage-man|age
△ stage-man|
ages
△ stage-man|
aged
△ stage-man|
aging
stage-struck
stag|fla|tion
stag|ger
VERB
△ stag|gers
△ stag|gered
△ stag|ger|ing
stag|ger|ing
sta|gi|ness
sta|ging

stag|nant

stag|nate

△ stag|nates

△ stag|na|ted

△ stag|na|ting

stag|na|tion

stagy

△ sta|gier

△ sta|gi|est

staid

△ stai|der

△ staid|est

stain

VERB

△ stains

△ stained

△ stain|ing

Staines

stair
step
⚠ stare

stair|case

stair|way

stair|well

stake
*post; money bet
or invested;
support with
stake; bet or
invest*
VERB
△ stakes
△ staked
△ sta|king
⚠ steak

stake-out

stal|ac|tite

stal|ag|mite

stale

△ staler

△ stalest

stale|mate

stale|ness

Sta|lin

Sta|lin|grad

Sta|lin|ism

stalk

VERB

△ stalks

△ stalked

△ stalk|ing

stal|ker

stalk|ing-horse

stall

VERB

△ stalls

△ stalled

△ stall|ing

stal|lion

stal|wart

sta|men

Stam|ford

stam|ina

stam|mer

VERB

△ stam|mers

△ stam|mered

△ stam|mer|ing

stamp

VERB

△ stamps

△ stamped

△ stamp|ing

stam|pede

VERB

△ stam|pedes

△ stam|peded

△ stam|peding

stamp|ing-
ground

stance

stanch *see*
staunch

stan|chion

stand

VERB

△ stands

△ stood

△ stand|ing

stan|dard

stan|dard-bearer

stan|dard|iza|
tion

stan|dard|ize

△ stan|dard|izes

△ stan|dard|ized

△ stan|dard|
izing

stand-by

stand-in

stand|ing

stand-off

stand-off|ish

stand|pipe

stand|point

St An|drews

stand|still

Stan|is|lav|sky

stank

Stan|ley

Stan|nar|ies

stanza

sta|pes
sing. and pl.

sta|phy|lo|coc|
cus

△ sta|phy|lo|
cocci

sta|ple

VERB

△ sta|ples

△ sta|pled

△ sta|pling

sta|pler

star

VERB

△ stars

△ starred

△ star|ring

star|board

starch

NOUN

△ star|ches

VERB

△ star|ches

△ starched

△ starch|ing

Star Chamber

starch|ily

star|chi|ness

starchy

△ star|chier

△ star|chi|est

star-crossed

star|dom

star|dust

stare
*long look; do
this*
VERB
△ stares
△ stared
△ star|ing
⚠ stair

star|fish
sing. and pl.

star|ga|zer

star|ga|zing

stark

ADJ.

△ star|ker

△ stark|est

stark|ers

stark-naked

star|let

star|light

star|ling

star|lit

starry

starry-eyed

star-spangled

star-stud|ded

START
talks
start
  VERB
  △ starts
  △ star|ted
  △ start|ing
star|ter
start|ing-block
star|tle
  △ star|tles
  △ star|tled
  △ start|ling
start|ling
star|va|tion
starve
  △ starves
  △ starved
  △ star|ving
stash
  NOUN
  △ sta|shes
  VERB
  △ sta|shes
  △ stashed
  △ stash|ing
Stasi
state
  VERB
  △ states
  △ stated
  △ sta|ting
state|less
state|li|ness
stately
  △ state|lier
  △ state|li|est
state|ment
Sta|ten
state|room
States Gen|eral
State|side
states|man
  △ states|men

states|man|like
states|man|ship
states|wo|man
  △ states|wo|men
sta|tic
stat|ics
station
  VERB
  △ sta|tions
  △ sta|tioned
  △ sta|tion|ing

sta|tion|ary
not moving
  ⚠ stationery

sta|tioner

sta|tion|ery
writing materials
  ⚠ stationary

sta|tion|mas|ter
sta|tis|ti|cal
sta|tis|ti|cally
sta|tis|ti|cian
sta|tis|tics
sta|tue
sta|tu|esque
sta|tu|ette
stat|ure
sta|tus
stat|ute
sta|tu|tor|ily
sta|tu|tory
staunch
  VERB
  △ staun|ches
  △ staunched
  △ staunch|ing
  ADJ.
  △ staun|cher
  △ staunch|est
stave
  VERB
  △ staves

△ stove *or*
  staved
△ sta|ving
staves
stay
  VERB
  △ stays
  △ stayed
  △ stay|ing
stay-at-home
stayer
stead
stead|fast
stead|fastly
stead|fast|ness
Steadi|cam
stead|ily
steadi|ness
steady
  VERB
  △ stead|ies
  △ stead|ied
  △ steady|ing
  ADJ.
  △ stead|ier
  △ steadi|est

steak
*best beef; slice of
meat or fish*
  ⚠ stake

steak|house

steal
*take away
dishonestly; a
bargain*
  VERB
  △ steals
  △ stole
  △ steal|ing
  △ stolen
  ⚠ steel

stealth

stealth|ily
stealthy
  △ stealth|ier
  △ stealthi|est
steam
  VERB
  △ steams
  △ steamed
  △ steam|ing
steam-boat
stea|mer
steam|rol|ler
  VERB
  △ steam|rol|lers
  △ steam|rol|lered
  △ steam|rol|ler|
    ing
steam|ship
steamy
  △ stea|mier
  △ stea|mi|est
steed
Steel

steel
*metal made of
iron and carbon;
made of or like
this*
  VERB
  △ steels
  △ steeled
  △ steel|ing
  ⚠ steal

Steele
steel|works
steely
  △ stee|lier
  △ steeli|est
steep
  VERB
  △ steeps
  △ steeped
  △ steep|ng

ADJ.
△ stee|per
△ steep|est
stee|pen
△ steep|ens
△ steep|ened
△ steep|en|ing
stee|ple
steeple|chase
  VERB
△ steeple|cha|
  ses
△ steeple|chased
△ steeple|cha|
  sing
steeple|cha|ser
steeple|jack
steeply
steep|ness
steer
  VERB
△ steers
△ steered
△ steer|ing
steer|age
steer|ing-wheel
ste|go|saurus
Stein
stein
Stein|beck
Stei|ner
Stein|way
stele
△ ste|lae
Stella
stel|lar
stem
  VERB
△ stems
△ stemmed
△ stem|ming
Sten
stench
△ sten|ches

sten|cil
  VERB
△ sten|cils
△ sten|cilled
△ sten|cil|ling
Stend|hal
ste|no|gra|pher
ste|no|gra|phic
ste|no|gra|phy
sten|tor|ian
Step
  exercise system

> step
> *pace; gait; unit of stair; walk*
> VERB
> △ steps
> △ stepped
> △ step|ping
> ⚠ steppe

step|bro|ther
step|child
△ step|chil|dren
step|daugh|ter
step|fa|ther
ste|pha|no|tis
Ste|phen
Ste|phen|son
step|lad|der
step-par|ent

> steppe
> *large plain*
> ⚠ step

Step|pen|wolf, Der
step|ping-stone
step|son
ste|ra|dian
ste|reo
ste|reo|chem|is|
  try
ste|reo|phonic

ste|reo|phon|ic|
  ally
ste|re|ophony
ste|reo|sco|pic
ste|reo|scop|ic|
  ally
ste|reo|type
  VERB
△ ste|reo|types
△ ste|reo|typed
△ ste|reo|typ|ing
ste|reo|typed
ster|ile
ster|il|ity
ster|il|iza|tion
ster|il|ize
△ ster|il|izes
△ ster|il|ized
△ ster|il|izing
ster|ling
stern
△ ster|ner
△ stern|est
ster|nal
Sterne
sternly
stern|ness
ster|num
△ ster|nums *or*
  sterna
ster|oid
sterol
ster|tor|ous
stet
△ stets
△ stet|ted
△ stet|ting
stetho|scope
stet|son
ste|ve|dore
Stev|en|age
Ste|vens
Ste|ven|son
stew

VERB
△ stews
△ stewed
△ stew|ing
stew|ard
  VERB
△ stew|ards
△ stew|ar|ded
△ stew|ard|ing
stew|ard|ess
△ stew|ard|es|ses
Stew|art
stewed
stick
  VERB
△ sticks
△ stuck
△ stick|ing
sticker
sticki|ness
stick|ing-plas|ter
stick-in-the-mud
stickle|back
stick|ler
sticky
△ stick|ier
△ sticki|est
sticky-fin|gered
stiff
  ADJ.
△ stif|fer
△ stif|fest
stif|fen
△ stif|fens
△ stif|fened
△ stif|fen|ing
stiffly
stiff-necked
stiff|ness
stiff|ware
sti|fle
△ sti|fles
△ sti|fled
△ sti|fling

sti⦙fling
stigma
stig|mata
stig⦙mat|iza|tion
stig⦙ma|tize
△ stig⦙ma|tizes
△ stig⦙ma|tized
△ stig⦙ma|ti⦙zing
stil|boes|trol

> stile
> *steps over fence*
> *etc*
> △ style

sti⦙letto
still
  VERB
△ stills
△ stilled
△ still|ing
  ADJ.
△ stil⦙ler
△ still|est
still
still⦙born
still|ness
stilt
stil⦙ted
Stil⦙ton
sti⦙mu|lant
sti⦙mu|late
△ sti⦙mu|lates
△ sti⦙mu|la⦙ted
△ sti⦙mu|la⦙ting
sti⦙mu|la⦙ting
sti⦙mu|la⦙tion
sti⦙mu|lus
△ stim|uli
sting
  VERB
△ stings
△ stung
△ sting|ing
stin⦙gily

stin⦙gi|ness
sting|ing
sting|ray
stingy
△ stin⦙gier
△ stin⦙gi|est
stink
  VERB
△ stinks
△ stank *or* stunk
△ stink|ing
△ stunk
stin⦙ker
stink|horn
stink|ing
stint
  VERB
△ stints
△ stin⦙ted
△ stint|ing
sti|pend
sti|pen⦙di|ary
△ sti|pen⦙di|ar⦙
  ies
stip⦙ple
  VERB
△ stip⦙ples
△ stip⦙pled
△ stip⦙pling
sti|pu|late
△ sti|pu|lates
△ sti|pu|la⦙ted
△ sti|pu|la⦙ting
sti|pu|la⦙tion
stir
  VERB
△ stirs
△ stirred
△ stir|ring
stir-crazy
stir-fry
  NOUN
△ stir-fries

  VERB
△ stir-fries
△ stir-fried
△ stir-fry|ing
Stir|ling
stir|rer
stir|ring
stir|rup
stitch
  NOUN
△ stit⦙ches
  VERB
△ stit⦙ches
△ stitched
△ stitch|ing
stitch|wort
stoat
stock
  VERB
△ stocks
△ stocked
△ stock|ing
stock|ade
  VERB
△ stock|ades
△ stock|aded
△ stock|ading
stock|bro⦙ker
stock|bro⦙king
Stock|hau⦙sen
Stock|holm
stock|ily
stocki|ness
stocki|net
stock|ing
stock|inged
stock-in-trade
stock|ist
stock|job⦙ber
stock|pile
  VERB
△ stock|piles
△ stock|piled
△ stock|pi⦙ling

Stock|port
stock|room
stock-still
stock|ta⦙king
Stock|ton-on-
  Tees
stocky
△ stock|ier
△ stocki|est
stock|yard
stodge
  VERB
△ stod|ges
△ stodged
△ stod|ging
stod⦙gi|ness
stodgy
△ stod|gier
△ stod|gi|est
stoic
sto|ical
sto|ic|ally
stoi⦙chi|om⦙etry
sto|icism
stoke
△ stokes
△ stoked
△ sto|king
stoke|hold
Stoke-on-Trent
Sto⦙ker
sto⦙ker
Sto⦙kow|ski
stole
sto⦙len
stolid
sto|lid|ity
stol|idly
stol|id|ness
sto⦙lon
stoma
△ sto|mata
stom|ach

VERB
△ stom|achs
△ stom|ached
△ stom|ach|ing
stom|ach-ache
stomata
sto|ma|tal
stomp
VERB
△ stomps
△ stomped
△ stomp|ing
stone
weight
△ stone
other senses
△ stones
VERB
△ stones
△ stoned
△ sto|ning
stone|chat
stone|crop
stoned
Stone|henge
stone|ma|son
stone|wall
△ stone|walls
△ stone|walled
△ stone|wall|ing
stone|ware
stone|washed
sto|nily
stony
△ sto|nier
△ sto|ni|est
stony-broke
stood
stooge
stool
stool|ball
stool-pigeon
stoop

VERB
△ stoops
△ stooped
△ stoop|ing
stoop
basin see stoup
stop
VERB
△ stops
△ stopped
△ stop|ping
stop|cock
Stopes
stop|gap
stop-off
stop-over
stop|page
Stop|pard
stop|per
stop|watch
△ stop|wat|ches
stor|age
store
VERB
△ stores
△ stored
△ stor|ing
store|house
Storey

storey
floor in building
⚠ story

stork
storm
VERB
△ storms
△ stormed
△ storm|ing
Stor|mont
storm|troo|per
stormy
△ stor|mier
△ stor|mi|est

Stor|no|way

story
narrative
△ stor|ies
⚠ storey

story|line
stoup
Stour|bridge
stout
ADJ.
△ stou|ter
△ stout|est
stout-hearted
stoutly
stout|ness
stove
stow
△ stows
△ stowed
△ stow|ing
stow|age
stow|away
Stowe
Stra|bane
stra|bis|mus
Strabo
Stra|chey
strad|dle
△ strad|dles
△ strad|dled
△ strad|dling
Stra|di|vari
strafe
△ strafes
△ strafed
△ stra|fing
Straf|ford
strag|gle
△ strag|gles
△ strag|gled
△ strag|gling
strag|gler
straggly

△ strag|glier
△ strag|gli|est

straight
not crooked
ADJ.
△ straigh|ter
△ straight|est
⚠ strait

straigh|ten
△ straight|ens
△ straight|ened
△ straight|en|ing
straight|for|
ward
strain
VERB
△ strains
△ strained
△ strain|ing
strained
strai|ner

strait
*narrow strip of
sea; hardship;
narrow; tight*
⚠ straight

strait|ened
strait|jacket
strait-laced
Straits Set|tle|
ments
strand
VERB
△ strands
△ stran|ded
△ strand|ing
strange
△ stranger
△ strangest
strangely
strange|ness
stranger

*Strangers and
Bro|thers*
stran|gle
△ stran|gles
△ stran|gled
△ stran|gling
strangle|hold
stran|gler
stran|gu|late
△ stran|gu|lates
△ stran|gu|la|ted
△ stran|gu|la|ting
stran|gu|la|tion
Stran|raer
strap
VERB
△ straps
△ strapped
△ strap|ping
strap|ped
strap|ping
Stras|bourg
strata
stra|ta|gem
stra|tegic
stra|tegic|ally
strat|egist
strat|egy
△ strat|egies
Strat|ford-
upon-Avon
strath
Strath|clyde
strath|spey
stra|ti|fi|ca|tion
strat|ify
△ stra|ti|fies
△ stra|ti|fied
△ stra|ti|fy|ing
stra|ti|gra|phy
stra|to|sphere
stra|to|spheric
stra|tum
△ strata

stra|tus
△ strati
Strauss
Stra|vin|sky
straw
straw|berry
△ straw|ber|ries
stray
VERB
△ strays
△ strayed
△ stray|ing
streak
VERB
△ streaks
△ streaked
△ streak|ing
streaked
strea|ker
strea|ki|ness
streaky
△ strea|kier
△ strea|ki|est
stream
VERB
△ streams
△ streamed
△ stream|ing
strea|mer
stream|ing
stream|line
△ stream|lines
△ stream|lined
△ stream|li|ning
stream|lined
stream|li|ning
Streep
street
street|car
*Street|car
Named De|sire,
A*
street|walker
street|wise

Strei|sand
strength
streng|then
△ streng|thens
△ streng|thened
△ streng|then|
ing
strenu|os|ity
strenu|ous
strenu|ously
strenu|ous|ness
strep|to|coc|cus
△ strep|to|cocci
strep|to|my|cin
stress
NOUN
△ stres|ses
VERB
△ stres|ses
△ stressed
△ stress|ing
stress|ful
stress-mark
stretch
NOUN
△ stret|ches
VERB
△ stret|ches
△ stretched
△ stretch|ing
stret|cher
stret|cher-bearer
stret|chi|ness
stret|chy
△ stret|chier
△ stret|chi|est
strew
△ strews
△ strewed
△ strew|ing
△ strewn
strewth
stria
△ striae

stri|ated
stri|ation
stricken
strict
△ stric|ter
△ strict|est
strictly
strict|ness
stric|ture
stride
VERB
△ strides
△ strode
△ stri|ding
△ strid|den
stri|dency
stri|dent
stri|dently
strife
stri|gil
strike
VERB
△ strikes
△ struck
△ stri|king
strike-breaker
stri|ker
stri|king
Strind|berg
string
VERB
△ strings
△ stringed
△ string|ing
△ strung
strin|gency
strin|gent
strin|gently
stringer
stringi|ness
stringy
△ string|ier
△ string|iest
strip

VERB
△ strips
△ stripped
△ strip|ping
stripe
  VERB
△ stripes
△ striped
△ stri|ping
striped
strip|ling
strip|per
strip-search
△ strip-searches
△ strip-searched
△ strip-search|ing
strip|tease
stripy
△ stri|pier
△ stri|pi|est
strive
△ strives
△ strove
△ stri|ving
△ stri|ven
strobe
stro|bi|lus
△ stro|bili
strobo-flash
△ strobo-fla|shes
stro|bo|scope
stro|bo|scopic
strode
Stroess|ner
stroke
  VERB
△ strokes
△ stroked
△ stro|king
stroll
  VERB
△ strolls
△ strolled
△ stroll|ing

Strong
strong
△ stronger
△ strong|est
strong|arm
  VERB
△ strong|arms
△ strong|armed
△ strong|arm|
  ing
strong|box
△ strong|boxes
strong|hold
strongly
strong|room
stron|tium
strop
  VERB
△ strops
△ stropped
△ strop|ping
stroppy
△ strop|pier
△ strop|pi|est
Stroud
strove
struck
struc|tural
struc|tur|al|ism
struc|tur|al|ist
struc|tur|ally
struc|ture
  VERB
△ struc|tures
△ struc|tured
△ struc|tur|ing
stru|del
strug|gle
  VERB
△ strug|gles
△ strug|gled
△ strug|gling
strum

VERB
△ strums
△ strummed
△ strum|ming
strum|pet
strung
strut
  VERB
△ struts
△ strut|ted
△ strut|ting
strych|nine
Stu|art
stub
  VERB
△ stubs
△ stubbed
△ stub|bing
stub|bi|ness
stub|ble
stubbly
stub|born
stub|bornly
stub|born|ness
Stubbs
stubby
△ stub|bier
△ stub|bi|est
stucco
  NOUN
△ stuc|cos or
  stuc|coes
  VERB
△ stuc|cos or
  stuc|coes
△ stuc|coed
△ stuc|co|ing
△ stuc|coed or
  stuc|co'd
stuck
stuck-up
stud
  VERB
△ studs

△ stud|ded
△ stud|ding
stu|dent
stud|ied
stu|dio
stu|di|ous
stu|di|ously
stu|di|ous|ness
study
  NOUN
△ stud|ies
  VERB
△ stud|ies
△ stud|ied
△ study|ing
stuff
  VERB
△ stuffs
△ stuffed
△ stuff|ing
stuf|fily
stuf|fi|ness
stuff|ing
stuffy
△ stuf|fier
△ stuf|fi|est
stul|tify
△ stul|ti|fies
△ stul|ti|fied
△ stul|ti|fy|ing
stul|ti|fy|ing
stum|ble
  VERB
△ stum|bles
△ stum|bled
△ stum|bling
stum|bling-
  block
stump
  VERB
△ stumps
△ stumped
△ stump|ing
stum|pi|ness

stumpy
△ stum|pier
△ stum|pi|est
stun
△ stuns
△ stunned
△ stun|ning
stung
stunk
stun|ner
stun|ning
stun|ningly
stunt
VERB
△ stunts
△ stun|ted
△ stunt|ing
stun|ted
stunt|man
△ stunt|men
stunt|wo|man
△ stunt|wo|men
stupa
stu|pe|fac|tion
stu|pefy
△ stu|pe|fies
△ stu|pe|fied
△ stu|pe|fy|ing
stu|pe|fy|ing
stu|pend|ous
stu|pend|ously
stu|pid
△ stu|pider
△ stu|pid|est
stu|pid|ity
stu|pidly
stu|por
stur|dily
stur|di|ness
sturdy
△ stur|dier
△ stur|di|est
stur|geon
Sturm und Drang

stut|ter
VERB
△ stut|ters
△ stut|tered
△ stut|ter|ing
Stutt|gart
Stuy|ves|ant

---

sty
pig kennel
△ sties
⚠ stye

---

stye
*swelling on
eyelid*
⚠ sty

---

style
*manner;
elegance; design*
VERB
△ styles
△ styled
△ styl|ing
⚠ stile

---

styl|ish
styl|ishly
styl|ist
styl|is|tic
styl|is|tic|ally
styl|is|tics
styl|ize
△ styl|izes
△ styl|ized
△ styl|izing
styl|ized
sty|lo|bate
sty|lo|met|rics
sty|lom|etry
sty|lus
△ styl|uses *or*
   styli
sty|mie

VERB
△ sty|mies
△ sty|mied
△ sty|mie|ing *or*
   sty|my|ing
styp|tic
Styx
suave
△ suaver
△ suav|est
suavely
suav|ity
sub
VERB
△ subs
△ subbed
△ sub|bing
sub|al|tern
sub|aqua
sub|at|omic
sub|con|scious
sub|con|sciously
sub|con|tin|ent
sub|con|tract
VERB
△ sub|con|tracts
△ sub|con|trac|ted
△ sub|con|tract|
   ing
sub|con|trac|tor
sub|cul|ture
sub|cu|ta|neous
sub|di|rect|ory
△ sub|di|rect|or|
   ies
sub|di|vide
△ sub|di|vides
△ sub|di|vi|ded
△ sub|di|vi|ding
sub|di|vi|sion
sub|due
△ sub|dues
△ sub|dued
△ sub|du|ing

sub|dued
sub|edit
△ sub|ed|its
△ sub|ed|ited
△ sub|ed|it|ing
sub|ed|itor
sub|fusc
su|bito
sub|ject
VERB
△ sub|jects
△ sub|jec|ted
△ sub|ject|ing
sub|jec|tion
sub|ject|ive
sub|ject|ively
sub ju|dice
sub|ju|gate
△ sub|ju|gates
△ sub|ju|ga|ted
△ sub|ju|ga|ting
sub|ju|ga|tion
sub|junct|ive
sub|let
△ sub|lets
△ sub|let
△ sub|let|ting
sub|li|mate
VERB
△ sub|li|mates
△ sub|li|ma|ted
△ sub|li|ma|ting
sub|li|ma|tion
sub|lime
VERB
△ sub|limes
△ sub|limed
△ sub|li|ming
sub|limely
sub|lim|inal
sub|lim|in|ally
sub|lim|ity
sub|ma|chine-
   gun

sub|mar|ine
sub|mar|iner
sub|merge
△ sub|mer|ges
△ sub|merged
△ sub|mer|ging
sub|mer|sible
sub|mer|sion
sub|mis|sion
sub|mis|sive
sub|mis|sively
sub|mis|sive|
ness
sub|mit
△ sub|mits
△ sub|mit|ted
△ sub|mit|ting
sub|nor|mal
sub|or|din|ate
VERB
△ sub|or|din|ates
△ sub|or|din|
ated
△ sub|or|din|
ating
sub|or|din|ation
sub|orn
△ sub|orns
△ sub|orned
△ sub|orn|ing
sub|plot
sub|poena
VERB
△ sub|poenas
△ sub|poenaed
or subpoena'd
△ sub|poena|ing
sub|rou|tine
sub|scribe
△ sub|scribes
△ sub|scribed
△ sub|scri|bing
sub|scri|ber
sub|script

sub|scrip|tion
sub|se|quent
sub|se|quently
sub|ser|vi|ence
sub|ser|vi|ent
sub|set
sub|side
△ sub|sides
△ sub|si|ded
△ sub|si|ding
sub|sid|ence or
sub|si|dence
according to
pronunciation
sub|si|di|ar|ity
sub|si|di|ary
NOUN
△ sub|si|di|ar|ies
sub|sid|ize
△ sub|sid|izes
△ sub|sid|ized
△ sub|sid|izing
sub|sidy
△ sub|sid|ies
sub|sist
△ sub|sists
△ sub|sis|ted
△ sub|sist|ing
sub|sist|ence
sub|soil
sub|sonic
sub|spe|cies
sing. and pl.
sub|stance
sub|stan|dard
sub|stan|tial
sub|stan|tially
sub|stan|ti|ate
△ sub|stan|ti|
ates
△ sub|stan|ti|
ated
△ sub|stan|ti|
ating

sub|stan|ti|ation
sub|stan|tive
sub|stan|tively
sub|sti|tute
VERB
△ sub|sti|tutes
△ sub|sti|tuted
△ sub|sti|tu|ting
sub|sti|tu|tion
sub|strate
sub|stra|tum
△ sub|strata
sub|sume
△ sub|sumes
△ sub|sumed
△ sub|su|ming
sub|sump|tion
sub|tend
△ sub|tends
△ sub|ten|ded
△ sub|tend|ing
sub|ter|fuge
sub|ter|ra|nean
sub|text
sub|title
subtle
△ subt|ler
△ subt|lest
sub|tlety
△ sub|tle|ties
subtly
sub|tract
△ sub|tracts
△ sub|trac|ted
△ sub|tract|ing
sub|trac|tion
sub|trop|ical
sub|urb
sub|ur|ban
sub|ur|bia
sub|ven|tion
sub|ver|sion
sub|ver|sive
sub|vert

△ sub|verts
△ sub|ver|ted
△ sub|vert|ing
sub|way
suc|ceed
△ suc|ceeds
△ suc|cee|ded
△ suc|ceed|ing
suc|cess
△ suc|ces|ses
suc|cess|ful
suc|cess|fully
suc|ces|sion
suc|ces|sive
suc|ces|sively
suc|ces|sor
suc|cinct
suc|cinctly
suc|cinct|ness
Succoth see
Sukkoth
suc|cour
VERB
△ suc|cours
△ suc|coured
△ suc|cour|ing
suc|cu|bus
△ suc|cubi
suc|cu|lence
suc|cu|lent
suc|cumb
△ suc|cumbs
△ suc|cumbed
△ suc|cumb|ing
such
such-and-such
such|like
suck
VERB
△ sucks
△ sucked
△ suck|ing
sucker
suckle

△ suckles
△ suckled
△ suck|ling
Suck|ling
suck|ling
su|crose
suc|tion
Sudan
sud|den
sud|denly
sud|den|ness
Su|deten
su|dor|ific
suds
sue
△ sues
△ sued
△ suing
suede
suet
Su|eto|nius
Suez
suf|fer
△ suf|fers
△ suf|fered
△ suf|fer|ing
suf|fer|ance
suf|ferer
suf|fer|ing
suf|fice
△ suf|fi|ces
△ suf|ficed
△ suf|fi|cing
suf|fi|ciency
△ suf|fi|cien|cies
suf|fi|cient
suf|fi|ciently
suf|fix
NOUN
△ suf|fixes
VERB
△ suf|fixes
△ suf|fixed
△ suf|fix|ing

suf|fo|cate
△ suf|fo|cates
△ suf|fo|ca|ted
△ suf|fo|ca|ting
suf|fo|ca|ting
suf|fo|ca|tion
Suf|folk
suf|fra|gan
suf|frage
suf|fra|gette
suf|fuse
△ suf|fu|ses
△ suf|fused
△ suf|fu|sing
suf|fu|sion
Sufi
Su|fism
Sugar
sugar
VERB
△ su|gars
△ su|gared
△ su|gar|ing
su|gar-beet
su|gared
su|gari|ness
su|gar-maple
su|gary
sug|gest
△ sug|gests
△ sug|ges|ted
△ sug|gest|ing
sug|gest|ible
sug|ges|tion
sug|gest|ive
sug|gest|ively
sui|ci|dal
sui|cide

suit
*set of clothes or
cards; lawsuit;
be appropriate
or acceptable*

VERB
△ suits
△ suited
△ suit|ing
△ suite

suit|ab|il|ity
suit|able
suit|ably
suit|case

suite
*set of rooms or
musical pieces;
attendants of
king etc*
△ suit

suitor
Su|karno
Suk|koth
Su|lai|man
sulk
VERB
△ sulks
△ sulked
△ sulk|ing
sulk|ily
sul|ki|ness
sulky
△ sul|kier
△ sul|ki|est
Sulla
sul|len
sul|lenly
sul|len|ness
Sul|li|van
Sul|lom Voe
sully
△ sul|lies
△ sul|lied
△ sul|ly|ing
sul|phate
sul|phide
sul|phon|am|ide

sul|phur
sul|phur|ous
sul|tan
sul|tana
sul|trily
sul|tri|ness
sul|try
△ sul|trier
△ sul|tri|est
sum
VERB
△ sums
△ summed
△ sum|ming
sumac
Su|ma|tra
sum|mar|ily
sum|mar|ize
△ sum|mar|izes
△ sum|mar|ized
△ sum|mar|izing

sum|mary
*outline; done in
outline*
NOUN
△ sum|mar|ies
△ summery

sum|ma|tion
sum|mer
sum|mer|house

sum|mer|time
*season of
summer*
△ summer
time

sum|mer time
*time one hour
ahead of normal
local time, used
in summer*
△ summertime

sum|mery
*of or like
summer*
⚠ summary

sum|ming-up
sum|mit
sum|mon
  △ sum|mons
  △ sum|moned
  △ sum|mon|ing
sum|mons
  NOUN
  △ sum|mon|ses
  VERB
  △ sum|mon|ses
  △ sum|monsed
  △ sum|mons|ing
sumo
sump
sump|tu|ary
sump|tu|ous
sun
  VERB
  △ suns
  △ sunned
  △ sun|ning
sun|bathe
  △ sun|bathes
  △ sun|bathed
  △ sun|ba|thing
sun|ba|thing
sun|beam
sun|bed
sun|burn

sun|dae
*ice cream topped
with fruit etc*
⚠ Sunday

Sun|day
first day of week
⚠ sundae

Sun|der|land
sun|dew
sun|dial
sun|down
sundry
  NOUN
  △ sun|dries
sun|fish
  sing. and pl.
sun|flower
  Sun| flowers
sung
sun|glas|ses
sunk
sun|ken
sun-lamp
sun|light
sun|lit
Sunni
Sun|nite
sunny
  △ sun|nier
  △ sun|ni|est
sun|rise
sun|roof
sun|set
sun|shade
sun|shine
sun|spot
sun|stroke
sun|tan
sun-tanned
sun|trap
sun-up
sup
  VERB
  △ sups
  △ supped
  △ sup|ping
super
su|per|an|nu|
ated
su|per|an|nu|
ation

su|perb
su|perbly
su|per|charge
  △ su|per|char|
ges
  △ su|per|
charged
  △ su|per|char|
ging
su|per|char|ger
su|per|ci|li|ous
su|per|ci|li|ously
su|per|ci|li|ous|
ness
su|per|con|duc|
tiv|ity
su|per|con|duc|
tor
su|per|cool|ing
su|per|ego
su|per|ero|ga|tion
su|per|fi|cial
su|per|fi|ci|al|ity
su|per|fi|cially
su|per|flu|id|ity
su|per|flu|ity
  △ su|per|flu|it|
ies
su|per|flu|ous
su|per|gi|ant
su|per|grass
  △ su|per|gras|ses
su|per|het|ero|
dyne
su|per|hu|man
su|per|im|pose
  △ su|per|im|po|
ses
  △ su|per|im|
posed
  △ su|per|im|po|
sing
su|per|im|po|si|
tion

su|per|in|tend
  △ su|per|in|
tends
  △ su|per|in|ten|
ded
  △ su|per|in|tend|
ing
su|per|in|tend|
ence
su|per|in|tend|
ent
su|per|ior
su|peri|or|ity
su|per|la|tive
su|per|man
  △ su|per|men
su|per|mar|ket
su|per|na|tant
su|per|na|tural
su|per|nova
  △ su|per|no|vae
  or su|per|no|
vas
su|per|nu|mer|
ary
  NOUN
  △ su|per|nu|mer|
ar|ies
su|per|ox|ide
su|per|phos|
phate
su|per|power
su|per|script
su|per|sede
  △ su|per|sedes
  △ su|per|seded
  △ su|per|seding
su|per|ses|sion
su|per|sonic
su|per|son|ic|ally
su|per|star
su|per|sti|tion
su|per|sti|tious
su|per|string

su|per|struc|ture
su|per|tax
△ su|per|taxes
su|per|ti|tle
su|per|vene
△ su|per|venes
△ su|per|vened
△ su|per|ven|ing
su|per|ven|tion
su|per|vise
△ su|per|vi|ses
△ su|per|vised
△ su|per|vi|sing
su|per|vi|sion
su|per|vi|sor
su|per|vi|sory
su|pine
sup|per
sup|plant
△ sup|plants
△ sup|plan|ted
△ sup|plant|ing
sup|ple
△ sup|pler
△ sup|plest
sup|ple|ly
sup|ple|ment
VERB
△ sup|ple|ments
△ sup|ple|men|
ted
△ sup|ple|ment|
ing
sup|ple|ment|ary
sup|ple|men|ta|
tion
sup|ple|ness
sup|pli|cant
sup|pli|cate
△ sup|pli|cates
△ sup|pli|ca|ted
△ sup|pli|ca|ting
sup|pli|ca|tion
sup|plier

sup|ply
NOUN
△ sup|plies
VERB
△ sup|plies
△ sup|plied
△ sup|ply|ing
sup|port
VERB
△ sup|ports
△ sup|por|ted
△ sup|port|ing
sup|por|ter
sup|port|ing
sup|port|ive
sup|pose
△ sup|po|ses
△ sup|posed
△ sup|po|sing
sup|posed
sup|po|sedly
sup|pos|ition
sup|pos|itional
sup|pos|itious
sup|pos|it|ory
△ sup|pos|it|or|
ies
sup|press
△ sup|pres|ses
△ sup|pressed
△ sup|pres|sing
sup|pres|sion
sup|pres|sor
sup|pur|ate
△ sup|pur|ates
△ sup|pur|ated
△ sup|pur|ating
sup|pur|ation
supra
su|pra|na|tional
su|prem|acy
su|preme
su|premely
su|premo

sura
sur|charge
VERB
△ sur|char|ges
△ sur|charged
△ sur|char|ging
surd

sure
  certain;
  certainly
  ADJ.
  △ surer
  △ sur|est
  ⚠ shore

sure-fire
sure-footed
surely
sure|ness
sur|ety
△ sur|et|ies
surf
VERB
△ surfs
△ surfed
△ surf|ing
sur|face
VERB
△ sur|fa|ces
△ sur|faced
△ sur|fa|cing
sur|fac|tant
surf|board
surf|cast|ing
sur|feit
VERB
△ sur|feits
△ sur|fei|ted
△ sur|feit|ing
sur|fer
surf|ing
surge
VERB
△ sur|ges

△ surged
△ sur|ging
sur|geon
sur|gery
△ sur|ger|ies
sur|gi|cal
sur|gic|ally
Suri|nam
sur|li|ness
surly
△ sur|lier
△ sur|li|est
sur|mise
VERB
△ sur|mi|ses
△ sur|mised
△ sur|mi|sing
sur|mount
△ sur|mounts
△ sur|moun|ted
△ sur|mount|ing
sur|mount|able
sur|name
sur|pass
△ sur|pas|ses
△ sur|passed
△ sur|pass|ing
sur|passed

sur|plice
  chorister's vestment
  ⚠ surplus

sur|plus
  remainder;
  remaining
  NOUN
  △ sur|pluses
  ⚠ surplice

sur|prise
VERB
△ sur|pri|ses
△ sur|prised
△ sur|pri|sing

sur|prised
'Sur|prise' Sym|
  phony
sur|pri|sing
sur|real
Sur|real|ism
Sur|real|ist
sur|real|is|tic
sur|ren|der
  VERB
  △ sur|ren|ders
  △ sur|ren|dered
  △ sur|ren|der|ing
sur|rep|ti|tious
sur|rep|ti|tiously
sur|rep|ti|tious|
  ness
Sur|rey
sur|ro|gacy
  △ sur|ro|ga|cies
sur|ro|gate
sur|round
  VERB
  △ sur|rounds
  △ sur|roun|ded
  △ sur|round|ing
sur|round|ing
sur|round|ings
sur|tax
  △ sur|taxes
Sur|tees
sur|ti|tle
sur|veil|lance
sur|vey
  VERB
  △ sur|veys
  △ sur|veyed
  △ sur|vey|ing
sur|veyor
sur|vi|val
sur|vive
  △ sur|vives
  △ sur|vived
  △ sur|vi|ving

sur|vi|ving
sur|vi|vor
sus *see* suss
Susan
sus|cep|ti|bil|ity
  △ sus|cep|ti|bil|
    it|ies
sus|cept|ible
sushi
sus|pect
  VERB
  △ sus|pects
  △ sus|pec|ted
  △ sus|pect|ing
sus|pend
  △ sus|pends
  △ sus|pen|ded
  △ sus|pend|ing
sus|pen|der-belt
sus|pen|ders
sus|pense
sus|pense|ful
sus|pen|sion
sus|pi|cion
sus|pi|cious
sus|pi|ciously
suss
  NOUN
  △ sus|ses
  VERB
  △ sus|ses
  △ sussed
  △ suss|ing
Sus|sex
sus|tain
  △ sus|tains
  △ sus|tained
  △ sus|tain|ing
sus|tained
sus|ten|ance
Suth|er|land
sut|tee
Sut|ton Cold|
  field

Sut|ton Hoo
su|ture
  VERB
  △ su|tures
  △ su|tured
  △ su|tur|ing
Suva
su|zer|ain
su|zer|ainty
svelte
  △ svel|ter
  △ svelt|est
swab
  VERB
  △ swabs
  △ swabbed
  △ swab|bing
swad|dle
  △ swad|dles
  △ swad|dled
  △ swad|dling
swad|dling-
  clothes
swag
  VERB
  △ swags
  △ swagged
  △ swag|ging
swag|ger
  VERB
  △ swag|gers
  △ swag|gered
  △ swag|ger|ing
swag|ger-stick
swag|man
  △ swag|men
Swa|hili
swain
swal|low
  VERB
  △ swal|lows
  △ swal|lowed
  △ swal|low|ing
swal|low|tail

swam
swami
swamp
  VERB
  △ swamps
  △ swamped
  △ swamp|ing
swampy
  △ swam|pier
  △ swam|pi|est
swan
  VERB
  △ swans
  △ swanned
  △ swan|ning
swank
  VERB
  △ swanks
  △ swanked
  △ swank|ing
swanky
  △ swan|kier
  △ swan|ki|est
Swan Lake (Le|
  be|di|noye oz|
  ero)
Swan|sea
swap
  VERB
  △ swaps
  △ swapped
  △ swap|ping
swarm
  VERB
  △ swarms
  △ swarmed
  △ swarm|ing
swar|thi|ness
swar|thy
  △ swar|thier
  △ swar|thi|est
swash|buck|ling
swas|tika
swat

VERB
△ swats
△ swat|ted
△ swat|ting
swatch
△ swat|ches

swath
strip of land, cut
grass, etc
⚠ swathe

swathe
bandage or
wrapping; wrap
or bind
VERB
△ swathes
△ swathed
△ swa|thing
⚠ swath

sway
VERB
△ sways
△ swayed
△ sway|ing
Swazi
Swa|zi|land
swear
△ swears
△ swore
△ swear|ing
swear-word
sweat
VERB
△ sweats
△ sweated *or*
sweat
△ sweat|ing
sweat|band
sweater
sweat|shirt
sweat|shop
sweat|suit

sweaty
△ sweat|ier
△ sweati|est
Swede
swede
Swe|den
Swe|den|borg
Swe|dish
sweep
VERB
△ sweeps
△ swept
△ sweep|ing
swee|per
sweep|ing
sweep|ingly
sweep|stake
sweet
ADJ.
△ swee|ter
△ sweet|est
sweet-and-sour
sweet|bread
sweet|corn
sweeten
△ sweet|ens
△ sweet|ened
△ sweet|en|ing
sweet|ener
sweet|heart
swee|tie
sweetly
sweet|meat
sweet|ness
sweet-talk
△ sweet-talks
△ sweet-talked
△ sweet-talk|ing
sweet-toothed
swell
VERB
△ swells
△ swelled
△ swell|ing

△ swol|len *or*
swelled
swell|ing
swel|ter
VERB
△ swel|ters
△ swel|tered
△ swel|ter|ing
swel|ter|ing
swept
swerve
VERB
△ swerves
△ swerved
△ swer|ving
Swift
swift
ADJ.
△ swif|ter
△ swift|est
swiftly
swift|ness
swig
VERB
△ swigs
△ swigged
△ swig|ging
swill
VERB
△ swills
△ swilled
△ swill|ing
swim
VERB
△ swims
△ swam
△ swim|ming
△ swum
swim|mer
swim|ming
swim|ming-bath
swim|ming-
costume
swim|mingly

swim|ming-pool
swim|suit
Swin|burne
swin|dle
VERB
△ swin|dles
△ swin|dled
△ swind|ling
swind|ler
Swin|don
swine
pig
△ swine
other senses
△ swines
swing
VERB
△ swings
△ swung
△ swing|ing
swing|boat
swinge|ing
swinger
swing|ing
swi|nish
swipe
VERB
△ swipes
△ swiped
△ swi|ping
swirl
VERB
△ swirls
△ swirled
△ swirl|ing
swish
NOUN
△ swi|shes
VERB
△ swi|shes
△ swished
△ swish|ing
Swiss

*Swiss Family
   Rob|in|son, The
   (Der schweiz|
   er|ische Rob|in|
   son)*
Switch
switch
   NOUN
   △ swit|ches
   VERB
   △ swit|ches
   △ switched
   △ switch|ing
switch|back
switch|board
switched-on
Swithin
Swit|zer|land
swivel
   VERB
   △ swiv|els
   △ swiv|elled
   △ swiv|el|ling
swizz
   △ swiz|zes
swizzle
   VERB
   △ swizzles
   △ swizzled
   △ swiz|zling
swizzle-stick
swol|len
swoon
   VERB
   △ swoons
   △ swooned
   △ swoon|ing
swoop
   VERB
   △ swoops
   △ swooped
   △ swoop|ing
swop *see* swap
sword

sword|fish
   sing. and pl.
sword|play
swords|man
   △ swords|men
swords|man|
      ship
sword|stick
sword|tail
swore
sworn
swot
   VERB
   △ swots
   △ swot|ted
   △ swot|ting
swum
swung
sy|bar|ite
sy|bar|itic
Sybil
sy|ca|more
sy|co|phancy
sy|co|phant
sy|co|phan|tic
Syd|ney
syl|lab|ary
   △ syl|lab|ar|ies
syl|labi
syl|labic
syl|la|bi|fi|ca|
      tion
syl|lab|ify
   △ syl|la|bi|fies
   △ syl|la|bi|fied
   △ syl|la|bi|fy|ing
syl|lable
syl|la|bub
syl|la|bus
   △ syl|la|buses *or*
      syl|labi
syl|lo|gism
syl|lo|gis|tic
sylph

*Syl|phides, Les
   (The Sylphs)*
sylph-like
syl|van
Syl|ves|ter
sym|bi|osis
   △ sym|bi|oses
sym|bi|otic

sym|bol
   *thing
   representing
   another*
   △ cymbal

sym|bolic
sym|bol|ic|ally
sym|bol|ism
sym|bol|ist
sym|bol|ize
   △ sym|bol|izes
   △ sym|bol|ized
   △ sym|bol|izing
sym|met|ri|cal
sym|met|ri|cally
sym|metry
   △ sym|met|ries
sym|pa|thetic
sym|pa|thet|ic|
      ally
sym|pa|thize
   △ sym|pa|thi|zes
   △ sym|pa|thized
   △ sym|pa|thi|
      zing
sym|pa|thi|zer
sym|pathy
   △ sym|pa|thies
sym|phonic
*Sym|pho|nie
   Fan|tas|tique*
sym|phony
   △ sym|phon|ies
*Sym|po|sium,
   The*

sym|po|sium
   △ sym|po|sia *or*
      sym|po|si|ums
symp|tom
symp|to|matic
syn|agogue
syn|apse
syn|ap|sis
synch
   VERB
   △ synchs
   △ synched
   △ synch|ing
syn|chro|mesh
   △ syn|chro|
      meshes
syn|chronic
syn|chron|ical
Syn|chron|ism
syn|chron|iza|
      tion
syn|chron|ize
   △ syn|chron|izes
   △ syn|chron|ized
   △ syn|chron|
      izing
syn|chron|ous
syn|chro|tron
syn|cline
syn|co|pate
   △ syn|co|pates
   △ syn|co|pa|ted
   △ syn|co|pa|ting
syn|co|pa|tion
syn|cope
syn|dic
syn|dic|al|ism
syn|di|cate
   VERB
   △ syn|di|cates
   △ syn|di|ca|ted
   △ syn|di|ca|ting
syn|di|ca|tion
syn|drome

syn|ec|do|che
syn|er|gism
syn|ergy
  △ syn|er|gies
Synge
synod
syno|nym
syn|ony|mous
syn|op|sis
  △ syn|op|ses
syn|op|tic
sy|no|via *or* syn|
  ovia
  according to
  pronunciation
sy|no|vial *or*
  syn|ovial

according to
pronunciation
syn|tac|tic
syn|tac|ti|cal
syn|tax
  △ syn|taxes
syn|the|sis
  △ syn|the|ses
syn|thes|ize
  △ syn|thes|izes
  △ syn|thes|ized
  △ syn|thes|izing
syn|thes|izer
syn|thetic
syn|thet|ic|ally
syph|ilis

syph|il|itic
syphon *see*
  siphon
Sy|ra|cuse
Syria
Syr|iac
sy|ringa
sy|ringe
  VERB
  △ sy|rin|ges
  △ sy|ringed
  △ sy|rin|ging
sy|rinx
  △ sy|rin|ges *or*
    sy|rinxes
syrup

syr|upy
sys|tem
sys|tem|atic
sys|tem|at|ic|ally
sys|tem|at|ics
sys|tem|at|iza|
  tion
sys|tem|at|ize
  △ sys|tem|at|izes
  △ sys|tem|at|ized
  △ sys|tem|at|
    izing
sys|temic
sys|tem|ic|ally
sys|tole
sys|tolic

T

ta
tab
　VERB
　△ tabs
　△ tabbed
　△ tab|bing
tab|ard
Ta|basco
tab|bou|leh
tabby
　△ tab|bies
tab|er|nacle
Tab|itha
tabla
tab|la|ture
ta|ble
　VERB
　△ ta|bles
　△ ta|bled
　△ ta|bling
tab|leau
　△ tab|leaux
table|cloth
table d'hôte
　△ tables d'hôte
table|land
table|spoon
table|spoon|ful
tab|let
table|ware
tab|loid
taboo
　VERB
　△ ta|boos
　△ ta|booed
　△ ta|boo|ing
tabor
tab|ular

ta|bu|late
　△ ta|bu|lates
　△ ta|bu|la|ted
　△ ta|bu|la|ting
ta|bu|la|tion
ta|bu|la|tor
ta|cho|graph
ta|cho|meter
ta|chy|car|dia
tacit
ta|citly
ta|cit|ness
ta|ci|turn
ta|ci|turn|ity
ta|ci|turnly
Ta|ci|tus
tack
　VERB
　△ tacks
　△ tacked
　△ tack|ing
tack|ily
tacki|ness
tackle
　VERB
　△ tackles
　△ tackled
　△ tack|ling
tacky
　△ tack|ier
　△ tacki|est
taco
tact
tact|ful
tact|fully
tact|ful|ness
tac|tic
tac|ti|cal
tac|tic|ally
tac|ti|cian

tac|tics
tac|tile
tact|less
tact|lessly
tact|less|ness
tad|pole
tae|kwondo
taf|feta
taff|rail
Taffy
　△ Taf|fies
tag
　VERB
　△ tags
　△ tagged
　△ tag|ging
Ta|ga|log
tag|lia|telle
Ta|gore
Tagus
ta|hini
Ta|hiti
Tai
t'ai chi
taiga

---

tail
*hindmost part of
animal etc; legal
limit on
inheritance;
follow closely;
pull stalks from
(fruit etc)*
　VERB
　△ tails
　△ tailed
　△ tail|ing
　⚠ tale

---

tail|back

tail|board
tail|coat
tailed
tail|gate
tail|less
tail-light
tailor
　VERB
　△ tail|ors
　△ tail|ored
　△ tail|or|ing
tailor-bird
tail|ored
tail|or|ess
　△ tail|or|es|ses
tailor-made
tail|piece
tail|plane
tail|spin
taint
　VERB
　△ taints
　△ tain|ted
　△ taint|ing
tain|ted
tai|pan
Tai|pei
Tai|wan
Ta|jik|is|tan
Taj Mahal
take
　VERB
　△ takes
　△ took
　△ taken
take|away
take-off
take|over
taker
take-up

-t
For verbs ending in **-ed / -t**, see **-ed**.

ta¦king
talc
tal¦cum

tale
story; lie
⚠tail

tale-bearer
tal¦ent
tal¦en¦ted
Tale of a Tub,
A
Tale of Two
Cit¦ies, A
Tales from the
Vi¦enna Woods
(Ge¦schich\ten
aus dem Wi¦en¦
er\wald)
Tales of Hoff
mann, The
(Les Contes
d'Hoff\mann)
Tali¦esin
tal¦is¦man
tal¦is¦ma¦nic
talk
  VERB
  △ talks
  △ talked
  △ talk¦ing
talk¦at¦ive
talker
talkie
talk¦ing-point
talk¦ing-shop
talk¦ing-to
tall
  △ taller
  △ tall¦est
tall¦boy
Tal¦linn
Tal¦lis
tall¦ness

tal¦low
tally
  NOUN
  △ tal¦lies
  VERB
  △ tal¦lies
  △ tal¦lied
  △ tal¦ly¦ing
tally-ho
tal¦ly¦man
  △ tal¦ly¦men
Tal¦mud
Tal¦mu¦dic
Tal¦mud¦ist
talon
talus
  △ tali
tame¦able
Tam¦ara
ta¦mari
ta¦ma¦rind
ta¦ma¦risk
Tambo
tam¦bour
tam¦bour¦ine
Tam¦bur\laine
  the Great
tame
  VERB
  △ tames
  △ tamed
  △ ta¦ming
  ADJ.
  △ tamer
  △ ta¦mest
tamely
tame¦ness
tamer
Tamil
Ta¦ming of the
  Shrew, The
tam-o'-shan¦ter
tam¦oxi¦fen
tamp

△ tamps
△ tamped
△ tamp¦ing
tam¦per
△ tam¦pers
△ tam¦pered
△ tam¦per¦ing
tam¦per-evi¦dent
tam¦pion
tam¦pon
  VERB
  △ tam¦pons
  △ tam¦poned
  △ tam¦pon¦ing
Tam¦sin
tam-tam
Tam¦worth
tan
  VERB
  △ tans
  △ tanned
  △ tan¦ning
Tananarive *see*
  Antananarivo
tan¦dem
tan¦doori
tang
Tan¦gan¦yika
tan¦gent
tan¦gen¦tial
tan¦gen¦tially
tan¦ger¦ine
tan¦gi¦bil¦ity
tan¦gible
tan¦gibly
Tan¦gier
tan¦gle
  VERB
  △ tan¦gles
  △ tan¦gled
  △ tang¦ling
tan¦gled
tango

VERB
△ tan¦goes
△ tan¦goed
△ tan¦go¦ing
tangy
△ tang¦ier
△ tan¦gi¦est
tank
  VERB
  △ tanks
  △ tanked
  △ tank¦ing
tank¦ard
tan¦ker
tank¦ful
tanned
tan¦ner
tan¦nery
  △ tan¦ner¦ies
Tann¦häuser
tan¦nic
tan¦nin
tan¦ning
Tan¦noy
tansy
  △ tan¦sies
tan¦tal¦iza¦tion
tan¦tal¦ize
  △ tan¦tal¦izes
  △ tan¦tal¦ized
  △ tan¦tal¦izing
tan¦tal¦izing
tan¦tal¦izingly
tan¦ta¦lum
Tan¦ta¦lus
tan¦ta¦lus
  △ tan¦ta¦luses
tan¦ta¦mount
Tan¦tra
tan¦trum
Tan¦za¦nia
Tao¦ism
Tao¦ist
tap

VERB
△ taps
△ tapped
△ tap|ping
tapa
tap-dance
VERB
△ tap-dan|ces
△ tap-danced
△ tap-dan|cing
tap-dan|cer
tap-dan|cing
tape
VERB
△ tapes
△ taped
△ ta|ping
tape-meas|ure

taper
candle;
increasing
thinness; make
or become
thinner
VERB
△ ta|pers
△ ta|pered
△ ta|per|ing
⚠ tapir

tape-record
△ tape-records
△ tape-recor|ded
△ tape-record|
ing
tape-record|ing
ta|pered
ta|per|ing
tap|es|tried
tap|es|try
△ tap|es|tries
tape|worm
ta|pi|oca

tapir
sort of animal
△ tapir *or* tapirs
⚠ taper

tap|pet
tap|room
tap|root
tar
VERB
△ tars
△ tarred
△ tar|ring
Tara
ta|ra|ma|sa|lata
tar|an|tella
tar|an|tula
tar|boosh
△ tar|boo|shes
tard|ily
tar|di|ness
tardy
△ tar|dier
△ tar|di|est

tare
sort of vetch;
weed; weight of
empty container,
vehicle, etc
⚠ tear

tar|get
VERB
△ tar|gets
△ tar|geted
△ tar|get|ing
Tar|gum
tar|iff
tar|la|tan
Tarl|ton
tar|mac
tar|mac|adam
tarn
tar|nish

NOUN
△ tar|ni|shes
VERB
△ tar|ni|shes
△ tar|nished
△ tar|nish|ing
tar|nish|able
taro
tarot
tar|pau|lin
Tar|quin
tar|ra|gon
tar|ri|ness
tarry
VERB
△ tar|ries
△ tar|ried
△ tar|ry|ing
ADJ.
△ tar|rier
△ tar|ri|est
tar|sal
Tar|sus
tar|sus
tart
VERB
△ tarts
△ tar|ted
△ tart|ing
tar|tan
Tar|tar
tar|tar
tar|taric
tartly
tart|ness
tar|tra|zine
Tar|tuffe, ou
L'Im|pos|teur
tarty
△ tar|tier
△ tar|ti|est
Tar|zan of the
Apes
Tash|kent

task
task-force
task|mas|ter
task|mis|tress
△ task|mis|tres|
ses
Tas|ma|nia
Tass
tassel
VERB
△ tas|sels
△ tas|selled
△ tas|sel|ling
Tasso
tast|able
taste
VERB
△ tastes
△ tas|ted
△ tast|ing
taste|ful
taste|fully
taste|ful|ness
taste|less
taste|lessly
taste|less|ness
taster
tast|ily
tasti|ness
tast|ing
tasty
△ tast|ier
△ tasti|est
tat
VERB
△ tats
△ tat|ted
△ tat|ting
ta-ta
Tatar *see* Tartar
Tate
Tati
tat|ter
tat|tered

tat|tily
tat|ti|ness
tat|ting
tat|tle
  VERB
  △ tat|tles
  △ tat|tled
  △ tat|tling
tat|tler
tat|too
  VERB
  △ tat|toos
  △ tat|tooed
  △ tat|too|ing
tat|tooer
tat|too|ist
tatty
  △ tat|tier
  △ tat|ti|est
Tatum

taught
past tense of
teach
  ⚠ taut

taunt
  VERB
  △ taunts
  △ taun|ted
  △ taunt|ing
taunt|ing
taunt|ingly
Taun|ton
taupe
Taur|ean
Tau|rus

taut
tight
  △ tauter
  △ taut|est
  ⚠ taught

tau|ten
  △ taut|ens

△ taut|ened
△ taut|en|ing
tau|to|lo|gi|cal
tau|tol|og|ous
tau|tol|ogy
  △ tau|tol|ogies
Tav|ener
tav|ern
ta|verna
taw|drily
taw|dri|ness
tawdry
  △ taw|drier
  △ taw|dri|est
tawny
  NOUN
  △ taw|nies
  ADJ.
  △ taw|nier
  △ taw|ni|est
taws
tax
  NOUN
  △ taxes
  VERB
  △ taxes
  △ taxed
  △ tax|ing
tax|able
tax|ation
tax-deduct|ible
tax-free
taxi
  VERB
  △ taxis
  △ taxied
  △ taxi|ing *or*
    taxy|ing
taxi|cab
taxi|derm|ist
taxi|dermy
Taxi Dri|ver
taxi|meter
tax|ing

taxis
taxo|nomic
tax|on|om|ist
tax|on|omy
tax|payer
Tay
Tay|lor
Tay|side
Tbil|isi
t-cell
Tchai|kov|sky
te *see* ti

tea
sort of drink;
leaf from which
it is made;
afternoon or
evening meal
  ⚠ tee

tea|cake
teach
  △ tea|ches
  △ taught
  △ teach|ing
teach|able
tea|cher
teach-in
teach|ing
tea-cosy
  △ tea-cosies
tea|cup
tea|cup|ful
tea|house
teak
teal
  sing. and pl.

team
group working
etc together;
form this
  VERB
  △ teams

△ teamed
△ team|ing
⚠ teem

team|ster
team-work
tea|pot

tear
drop of liquid
made when
crying; rip
  VERB
  △ tears
  △ tore
  △ tear|ing
  △ torn
  ⚠ tare
  ⚠ tier

tear|away
tear|drop
tear|ful
tear|fully
tear|ful|ness
tear|ing
tear-jer|ker
tear-jerk|ing
tear|less
tea|room
tear-stained
tease
  VERB
  △ tea|ses
  △ teased
  △ teas|ing
tea|sel
tea|ser
tea|shop
teas|ing
teas|ingly
tea|spoon
tea|spoon|ful
teat
teazel *see* teasel

teazle *see* teasel
Teb|bit
tec
tech
tech|ne|tium
tech|ni|cal
tech|ni|cal|ity
  △ tech|ni|cal|it|
  ies
tech|ni|cally
tech|ni|cian
Tech|ni|color
tech|nique
techno
tech|no|babble
tech|no|cracy
  △ tech|no|cra|cies
tech|no|crat
tech|no|cratic
tech|no|lo|gi|cal
tech|nol|ogist
tech|nol|ogy
  △ tech|nol|ogies
tec|ton|ics
Ted
Ted|der
teddy
  △ ted|dies
Teddy boy
Te Deum
te|di|ous
te|di|ously
te|di|ous|ness
te|dium

> tee
>   *letter* T;
>   *starting-place in*
>   *golf; place ball*
>   *on this; target*
>   *in quoits and*
>   *curling*
>   **VERB**
>   △ tees

  △ teed
  △ tee|ing
  ▲ tea

> teem
>   *be abundant*
>   △ teems
>   △ teemed
>   △ teem|ing
>   ▲ team

teen
teen|age
teen|ager
teensy
  △ teen|sier
  △ teen|si|est
teensy-weensy
teeny
  △ tee|nier
  △ tee|ni|est
teeny|bop|per
teeny-weeny
teepee *see* tepee
Tees
tee shirt *see* T-
shirt
Tees|side
tee|ter
  △ tee|ters
  △ tee|tered
  △ tee|ter|ing

> teeth
>   **PL. NOUN**
>   ▲ teethe

> teethe
>   **VERB**
>   △ teethes
>   △ teethed
>   △ teeth|ing
>   ▲ teeth

teeth|ing

tee|to|tal
tee|to|tal|ler
te|fil|len
Tef|lon
Te|gu|ci|galpa
Tehe|ran
Teil|hard de
  Char|din
Te Ka|nawa
tel *see* tell
Tel Aviv-Jaffa
tele-ad
tele|bank|ing
tele|cast
  VERB
  △ tele|casts
  △ tele|cast *or*
    tele|cas|ted
  △ tele|cast|ing
tele|cas|ter
tele|com|mu|ni|
  ca|tion
tele|com|mu|ter
tele|com|mu|
  ting
tele|con|fer|en|
  cing
tele|cot|tage
tele|gram
tele|graph
  VERB
  △ tele|graphs
  △ tele|graphed
  △ tele|graph|ing
tele|gra|pher
tele|graph|ese
tele|gra|phic
tele|graph|ic|ally
tele|graph|ist
tele|gra|phy
tele|kin|esis
tele|kin|etic
Te|lem|achus
Te|le|mann

tele|mar|ket|ing
Tele|mes|sage
tele|meter
tele|met|ric
tele|metry
teleo|lo|gi|cal
tele|olo|gist
tele|ol|ogy
tele|pa|thic
tele|path|ic|ally
tele|path|ist
tele|pa|thy
tele|phone
  VERB
  △ tele|phones
  △ tele|phoned
  △ tele|pho|ning
tele|phonic
teleph|on|ist
teleph|ony
tele|photo
tele|pho|to|gra|
  phic
tele|pho|to|gra|
  phy
tele|prin|ter
Tele|promp|ter
tele|sales
tele|scope
  VERB
  △ tele|scopes
  △ tele|scoped
  △ tele|sco|ping
tele|scopic
tele|scop|ic|ally
tele|shop|ping
tele|text
tele|thon
Tele|type
tel|evan|gel|ist
tele|vise
  △ tele|vi|ses
  △ tele|vised
  △ tele|vi|sing

tele|vi|sion
tele|vis|ual
tele|visu|ally
tele|work|ing
telex
  NOUN
  △ tel|exes
  VERB
  △ tel|exes
  △ tel|exed
  △ tel|ex|ing
Tel|ford
Tell
tell
  VERB
  △ tells
  △ told
  △ tell|ing
tel|ler
tell|ing
tell|ingly
tell|ing-off
tell|tale
tel|lur|ian
tel|lur|ium
telly
  △ tel|lies
te|lo|phase
Tel|star
Te|lugu
te|mer|ity
temp
  VERB
  △ temps
  △ temped
  △ temp|ing
tem|per
  VERB
  △ tem|pers
  △ tem|pered
  △ tem|per|ing
tem|pera
tem|pera|ment
tem|pera|men|tal

tem|pera|ment|
  ally
tem|per|ance
tem|per|ate
tem|per|ately
tem|per|ate|ness
tem|pera|ture
Tem|pest, The
tem|pest
tem|pes|tu|ous
tem|pes|tu|ously
tem|pes|tu|ous|
  ness
tempi
Temp|lar
tem|plate
Tem|ple
tem|ple
tempo
  △ tem|pos *or*
  tempi
tem|poral
tem|por|ally
tem|por|ar|ily
tem|por|ari|ness
tem|por|ary
  NOUN
  △ tem|por|ar|ies
tem|por|iza|tion
tem|por|ize
  △ tem|por|izes
  △ tem|por|ized
  △ tem|por|izing
tem|por|izer
tempt
  △ tempts
  △ temp|ted
  △ tempt|ing
temp|ta|tion
*Temp|ta|tion of
  St An|thony*
temp|ter
tempt|ing
tempt|ingly

temp|tress
  △ temp|tres|ses
tem|pura
ten
ten|ab|il|ity
ten|able
ten|acious
ten|aciously
ten|acious|ness
ten|acity
ten|ancy
  △ ten|an|cies
ten|ant
  VERB
  △ ten|ants
  △ ten|an|ted
  △ ten|ant|ing
ten|an|ted
ten|an|try
tench
  sing. and pl.
tend
  △ tends
  △ ten|ded
  △ tend|ing
ten|dency
  △ ten|den|cies
ten|den|tious
ten|den|tiously
ten|den|tious|ness
ten|der
  VERB
  △ ten|ders
  △ ten|dered
  △ ten|der|ing
  ADJ.
  △ ten|derer
  △ ten|der|est
ten|der|foot
  △ ten|der|feet *or*
  ten|der|foots
ten|der-hearted
ten|der-heart|
  edly

ten|der-heart|ed|
  ness
*Ten|der is the
  Night*
ten|der|ize
  △ ten|der|izes
  △ ten|der|ized
  △ ten|der|izing
ten|der|izer
ten|der|loin
ten|derly
ten|der|ness
ten|din|itis
ten|don
ten|dril
ten|drilled
ten|ement
Ten|er|ife
tenet
ten|fold
Teng Hsiao-
  p'ing *see* Deng
  Xiaoping

ten|ner
£10 note
⚠ tenor

Ten|nes|see
Ten|niel
ten|nis
Ten|ny|son
tenon
  VERB
  △ ten|ons
  △ ten|oned
  △ ten|on|ing

tenor
*high-voiced male
singer; tendency*
⚠ tenner

ten|pin
tense

VERB
△ ten|ses
△ tensed
△ tens|ing
ADJ.
△ ten|ser
△ ten|sest
tensely
tense|ness
ten|sile
ten|sil|ity
ten|sion
 VERB
 △ ten|sions
 △ ten|sioned
 △ ten|sion|ing
tent
 VERB
 △ tents
 △ ten|ted
 △ tent|ing
tent|acle
tent|acled
ten|tacu|lar
ten|ta|tive
ten|ta|tively
ten|ta|tive|ness
ten|ter
ten|ter|hook
tenth
tenthly
tenu|ous
tenu|ously
tenu|ous|ness
ten|ure
ten|ured
tepee
tephillin *see*
 tefillen
tepid
te|pid|ity
tep|idly
te|quila
te|ra|byte

te|ra|to|gen
ter|bium
terce
ter|cel
ter|cen|ten|ary
 △ ter|cen|ten|ar|
 ies
ter|cen|ten|nial
ter|cet
te|redo
Ter|ence
Ter|esa
ter|gi|ver|sate
 △ ter|gi|ver|sates
 △ ter|gi|ver|sa|
 ted
 △ ter|gi|ver|
 sating
ter|gi|ver|sa|tion
term
 VERB
 △ terms
 △ termed
 △ term|ing
ter|ma|gant
ter|min|ab|il|ity
ter|min|able
ter|minal
ter|min|ally
ter|min|ate
 △ ter|min|ates
 △ ter|min|ated
 △ ter|min|ating
ter|min|ation
ter|mi|no|lo|gi|cal
ter|mi|no|lo|gic|
 ally
ter|min|olo|gist
ter|min|ology
 △ ter|min|olo|
 gies
ter|mi|nus
 △ ter|mini *or*
 ter|min|uses

ter|mite
tern
tern|ary
ter|pene
Terp|si|chore
terp|si|chor|
 ean
ter|race
 VERB
 △ ter|ra|ces
 △ ter|raced
 △ ter|ra|cing
ter|ra|cotta
terra firma
ter|rain
ter|ra|pin
ter|rar|ium
 △ ter|raria *or*
 ter|rari|ums
ter|rest|rial
ter|rible
ter|ribly
ter|rier
ter|ri|fic
ter|rif|ic|ally
ter|ri|fied
ter|rify
 △ ter|ri|fies
 △ ter|ri|fied
 △ ter|ri|fy|ing
ter|ri|fy|ing
ter|rine
ter|ri|tor|ial
ter|ri|tory
 △ ter|ri|tor|ies
ter|ror
ter|ror|ism
ter|ror|ist
ter|ror|ize
 △ ter|ror|izes
 △ ter|ror|ized
 △ ter|ror|izing
ter|ror-stricken
Terry

terry
 △ ter|ries
terse
 △ ter|ser
 △ ters|est
tersely
terse|ness
ter|tiary
 NOUN
 △ ter|tiar|ies
Ter|tul|lian
Tery|lene
terza rima
tesla
TESSA
 savings scheme
Tessa
 woman's
 Christian name
tes|sel|late
 △ tes|sel|lates
 △ tes|sel|la|ted
 △ tes|sel|la|ting
tes|sel|la|ted
tes|sel|la|tion
tes|sera
 △ tes|serae
tes|si|tura
Tess of the
 D'Ur|ber|villes
test
 VERB
 △ tests
 △ tes|ted
 △ test|ing
testa
test|able
tes|ta|ceous
tes|ta|ment
tes|ta|ment|ary
test|ate
tes|ta|tor
tes|ta|trix
 △ tes|ta|trixes

test-drive
△ test-drives
△ test-drove
△ test-dri|ving
△ test-driven
tes|ter
tes|tes
tes|ti|cle
tes|ti|cu|lar
tes|tify
△ tes|ti|fies
△ tes|ti|fied
△ tes|ti|fy|ing
test|ily
tes|ti|mo|nial
tes|ti|mony
△ tes|ti|mon|ies
tes|ti|ness
test|ing
tes|tis
△ tes|tes
tes|tos|ter|one
testy
△ tes|tier
△ tes|ti|est
tet|anus
tetch|ily
tet|chi|ness
tetchy
△ tet|chier
△ tet|chi|est
tête-à-tête
tether
VERB
△ teth|ers
△ teth|ered
△ teth|er|ing
tetra
tet|ra|chloro|me|
  thane
tet|ra|cyc|line
tet|rad
tet|ra|gon

Tet|ra|gram|ma|
  ton
tet|ra|hed|ron
tet|ram|eter
tet|ra|pod
Teu|ton
Teu|tonic
Texas
Tex-Mex
text
text|book
tex|tile
tex|tual
tex|tu|ally
tex|tural
tex|ture
VERB
△ tex|tures
△ tex|tured
△ tex|tur|ing
tex|tured
tex|tur|ize
△ tex|tur|izes
△ tex|tur|ized
△ tex|tur|izing
Thack|eray
Thai
Thai|land
thal|amus
△ thal|ami
tha|las|saemia
tha|las|so|ther|
  apy
△ tha|las|so|ther|
  ap|ies
tha|lido|mide
thal|lium
thal|loid
thal|lus
△ thal|luses or
  thalli
Thames
than
tha|na|tol|ogy

thane
Tha|net
thank
VERB
△ thanks
△ thanked
△ thank|ing
thank|ful
thank|fully
thank|ful|ness
thank|less
thank|lessly
thank|less|ness
thanks|giv|ing
Thant
Tharp
that
ADJ.
△ those
PRONOUN
△ those
thatch
NOUN
△ that|ches
VERB
△ that|ches
△ thatched
△ thatch|ing
That|cher
that|cher
thaw
VERB
△ thaws
△ thawed
△ thaw|ing
the
Thea
theatre
theatre-in-the-
  round
the|at|ri|cal
the|at|ri|cal|ity
the|at|ri|cally
Thebes

thee
theft

> their
>   *of them*
>   ⚠there
>   ⚠they're

theirs
the|ism
the|ist
the|is|tic
Thelma
them
theme
them|selves
then
thence
thence|forth
thence|for|ward
theo|cracy
△ theo|cra|cies
theo|crat
theo|cra|tic
theo|crat|ic|ally
Theo|cri|tus
the|odo|lite
Theo|dora
Theo|dor|akis
Theo|dore
The|od|oric
theo|lin|guis|tics
theo|lo|gian
theo|lo|gi|cal
theo|lo|gic|ally
the|ol|ogy
△ the|olo|gies
the|orbo
the|orem
the|or|etic
the|or|et|ical
the|or|et|ic|ally
the|or|eti|cian
the|or|ist
the|or|ize

△ the|or|izes
△ the|or|ized
△ the|or|izing
the|ory
△ the|or|ies
theo|so|phic
theo|soph|ical
theo|soph|ic|ally
theo|soph|ist
theo|sophy
△ theo|soph|ies
thera|peu|tic
thera|peu|tic|ally
thera|peu|tics
ther|ap|ist
ther|apy
△ ther|ap|ies
Thera|vada

there
at that place
⚠ their
⚠ they're

there|abouts
there|af|ter
thereby
there|fore
therein
thereof
thereon
Ther|esa
thereto
there|un|der
there|upon
therm
ther|mal
Ther|ma|lite
therm|ally
Ther|mi|dor
ther|mion
ther|mi|onic
ther|mi|on|ics
ther|mis|tor
ther|mo|couple

ther|mo|dy|namic
ther|mo|dy|nam|ic|ally
ther|mo|dy|nam|ics
ther|mo|elec|tric
ther|mo|elec|tri|city
ther|mo|gra|phy
ther|mo|lu|min|es|cence
ther|mom|eter
ther|mo|nuc|lear
ther|mo|pile
ther|mo|plas|tic
Ther|mo|py|lae
Ther|mos
△ Ther|moses
ther|mo|set|ting
ther|mo|sphere
ther|mo|stat
ther|mo|static
ther|mo|stat|ic|ally
the|saurus
△ the|saur|uses
or the|sauri
these
The|seus
the|sis
△ the|ses
Thes|pian
Thes|sa|lo|ni|ans, Let|ters of Paul to the
Thes|saly
Thet|ford
they
they'd
they'll

they're
they are
⚠ their
⚠ there

they've
thi|am|ine
thick
ADJ.
△ thicker
△ thick|est
thicken
△ thick|ens
△ thick|ened
△ thick|en|ing
thick|en|ing
thicket
thick|head
thick-headed
thickly
thick|ness
thick|set
thick-skinned
thief
△ thieves
thieve
△ thieves
△ thieved
△ thiev|ing
thiev|ing
thiev|ish
thiev|ishly
thiev|ish|ness
thigh
thim|ble
thim|ble|ful
Thim|phu
thin
VERB
△ thins
△ thinned
△ thin|ning
ADJ.
△ thin|ner
△ thin|nest
thine
thing
thin|gummy
△ thin|gum|mies

thin|gummy|bob
thin|gummy|jig
think
VERB
△ thinks
△ thought
△ think|ing
Thin|ker, The (Le Pen|seur)
thin|ker
think|ing
thinly
thin|ner
thin|ness
thin-skinned
thio|sul|phate
third
thirdly
Third Man, The
thirst
VERB
△ thirsts
△ thirs|ted
△ thirst|ing
thirst|ily
thirs|ti|ness
thir|sty
△ thirs|tier
△ thirs|ti|est
thir|teen
thir|teenth
thir|ties
thir|tieth
thirty
NOUN
△ thir|ties
Thirty-Nine Steps, The
this
ADJ.
△ these
PRON.
△ these

this|tle
this|tle|down
thi|ther
thixo|tropy
tho'
thole
  VERB
  △ tholes
  △ tholed
  △ tho|ling
thole|pin
tholos
  △ tholoi
Thomas
Thom|ism
Thomp|son
Thom|son
thong
Thor
thor|acic
thorax
  △ thor|axes *or*
    thor|aces
Thor|eau
thor|ium
thorn
Thorn|dike
thorny
  △ thor|nier
  △ thor|ni|est
thor|ough
thor|ough|bred
thor|ough|fare
thor|ough|go|
  ing
thor|oughly
thor|ough|ness
Thorpe
those
thou
though
thought
thought|ful
thought|fully

thought|ful|ness
thought|less
thought|lessly
thought|less|
  ness
thou|sand
  NOUN
  after a number
  △ thousand
  other senses
  △ thousands
Thou|sand and
  One Nights,
  The
thou|sandth
Thrace
thrall

> thrash
> *beat person; this*
> *act; elaborate*
> *party*
> NOUN
> △ thra|shes
> VERB
> △ thra|shes
> △ thrashed
> △ thrash|ing
> ▲ thresh

thrash|ing
thread
  VERB
  △ threads
  △ threaded
  △ thread|ing
thread|bare
thread|worm
threat
threaten
  △ threat|ens
  △ threat|ened
  △ threat|en|ing
threat|en|ing
threat|en|ingly

three
three-di|men|
  sional
three|fold
Three Mus|ket|
  eers, The (Les
  Trois Mous|
  que|taires)
three|pence
three|penny
three-ply
three-quar|ter
Three Sis|ters,
  The (Tri ses|
  try)
three|some
thre|no|dial
thre|nodic
thren|od|ist
thren|ody
  △ thren|od|ies
thre|on|ine

> thresh
> *beat grain*
> △ thre|shes
> △ threshed
> △ thresh|ing
> ▲ thrash

thre|sher
thresh|old

> threw
> *past tense of*
> *throw*
> ▲ through

thrice
thrift
thrift|ily
thrif|ti|ness
thrift|less
thrifty
  △ thrif|tier
  △ thrif|ti|est

thrill
  VERB
  △ thrills
  △ thrilled
  △ thrill|ing
thrill|er
thrill|ing
thrill|ingly
thrips
  △ thrips *or*
    thrip|ses
thrive
  △ thrives
  △ throve *or* thrived
  △ thri|ving
  △ thri|ven *or*
    thrived
thri|ving
throat
throat|ily
throa|ti|ness
throaty
  △ throa|tier
  △ throa|ti|est
throb
  VERB
  △ throbs
  △ throbbed
  △ throb|bing

> throe
> *pain*
> ▲ throw

throm|bin
throm|bo|sis
  △ throm|bo|ses
throm|botic
throm|bus
  △ thrombi
throne
  VERB
  △ thrones
  △ throned
  △ thro|ning

throng
thros|tle
throt|tle
  VERB
  △ throt|tles
  △ throt|tled
  △ throt|tling

through
  from one end to
  the other;
  because of
   ⚠ threw

through|out
through|put
Through the
Look|ing-Glass

throw
  hurl
  VERB
  △ throws
  △ threw
  △ throw|ing
  △ thrown
   ⚠ throe

throw|away
throw|back
throw-in
thru
thrum
  VERB
  △ thrums
  △ thrummed
  △ thrum|ming
thrush
  △ thrushes
thrust
  VERB
  △ thrusts
  △ thrus|ted
  △ thrust|ing
Thu|cy|di|des
thud

VERB
△ thuds
△ thud|ded
△ thud|ding
thug
thug|gery
thug|gish
Thule
thu|lium
thumb
  VERB
  △ thumbs
  △ thumbed
  △ thumb|ing
thumb-nail
thumb|screw
thumb|tack
thump
  VERB
  △ thumps
  △ thumped
  △ thump|ing
thun|der
  VERB
  △ thun|ders
  △ thun|dered
  △ thun|der|ing
Thun|der|bird
thun|der|bolt
thun|der|clap
thun|der|cloud
thun|der|ing
thun|der|ous
thun|der|ously
thun|der|storm
thun|der|struck
thun|dery
Thur|ber
thur|ible
Thurs|day
Thurso
thus
Thut|mose
thwack

VERB
△ thwacks
△ thwacked
△ thwack|ing
thwart
  VERB
  △ thwarts
  △ thwar|ted
  △ thwart|ing
thy

thyme
  herb
   ⚠ time

thy|mine
thy|mus
  △ thymi
thy|roid
thy|rox|ine
thy|self
ti
Ti|an|an|men
tiara
Tiber

Ti|ber|ias
  town and lake in
  Israel
   ⚠ Tiberius

Ti|ber|ius
  Roman emperor
   ⚠ Tiberias

Tibet
Ti|betan
tibia
  △ tib|ias *or* tib|
   iae
Ti|bul|lus

tic
  nervous twitch
  etc
   ⚠ tick

tick
  sound of clock;
  mark of
  approval; make
  these; parasite
  on sheep etc;
  credit
  VERB
  △ ticks
  △ ticked
  △ tick|ing
   ⚠ tic

ticker
ticker-tape
ticket
  VERB
  △ tick|ets
  △ tick|eted
  △ tick|et|ing
tick|ing-off
tickle
  VERB
  △ tickles
  △ tickled
  △ tick|ling
tick|lish
tick|lish|ness
tick-tack
tidal
ti|dally
tidbit *see* titbit
tid|dler
tid|dly
  △ tid|dlier
  △ tid|dli|est
tid|dly|winks
tide
  VERB
  △ tides
  △ tided
  △ ti|ding
tide|mark
tide|way

ti|dily
ti|di|ness
ti|dings
tidy
  VERB
  △ ti|dies
  △ ti|died
  △ ti|dy|ing
  ADJ.
  △ ti|dier
  △ ti|di|est
tie
  VERB
  △ ties
  △ tied
  △ ty|ing
tie-break
tie-breaker
tie-clip
tie-dyed
tie-dye|ing
tie-in
tie-pin
Ti|epolo

tier
  vertical row;
  arrange thus
  VERB
  △ tiers
  △ tiered
  △ tier|ing
  ⚠ tear

tiercel see tercel
tiff
  VERB
  △ tiffs
  △ tiffed
  △ tiff|ing
Tif|fany
tif|fin
tig
tiger
ti|ger|ish

tight
  ADJ.
  △ tigh|ter
  △ tight|est
tigh|ten
  △ tight|ens
  △ tight|ened
  △ tight|en|ing
tight-fis|ted
tight-knit
tight-lipped
tightly
tight|ness
tight|rope
tights
Tig|ray
ti|gress
  △ ti|gres|ses
Ti|gris
tike
tikka
Til|bury
tilde
tile
  VERB
  △ tiles
  △ tiled
  △ ti|ling
tiler
ti|ling
till
  VERB
  △ tills
  △ tilled
  △ till|ing
till|able
till|age
til|ler
Til|ley
Tilly
tilt
  VERB
  △ tilts
  △ til|ted

  △ tilt|ing
tilth
tilt-ham|mer

tim|ber
  wood; provide
  this
  VERB
  △ tim|bers
  △ tim|bered
  △ tim|ber|ing
  ⚠ timbre

tim|bered

timbre
  sound quality
  ⚠ timber

tim|brel
Tim|buktu

time
  passage of days,
  hours, etc.;
  measurement of
  this; make this
  measurement
  VERB
  △ times
  △ timed
  △ ti|ming
  ⚠ thyme

time-hon|oured
time|kee|per
time|keep|ing
time|less
time|lessly
time|less|ness
time|li|ness
timely
  △ time|lier
  △ time|li|est
Time Ma|chine,
  The
time|piece

timer
Times, The
time-served
time|ser|ver
time-shar|ing
time|table
  VERB
  △ time|tables
  △ time|tabled
  △ time|tab|ling
time|worn
timid
tim|id|ity
tim|idly
ti|ming
tim|or|ous
tim|or|ously
tim|or|ous|ness
Tim|othy
Tim|othy, Let|
  ters of Paul to
tim|pani
tim|pan|ist
tin
  VERB
  △ tins
  △ tinned
  △ tin|ning
tinc|ture
  VERB
  △ tinc|tures
  △ tinc|tured
  △ tinc|tur|ing
Tindale see
  Tyndale
tin|der
tin|der-box
  △ tin|der-boxes
Tin Drum, The
  (Die Blech|
  trom|mel)
tine
tinea
tin|foil

tin|ful
ting
ting-a-ling
tinge
  VERB
△ tin|ges
△ tinged
△ tin|ging
tin|gle
  VERB
△ tin|gles
△ tin|gled
△ ting|ling
ting|ling
tingly
△ ting|lier
△ ting|li|est
ti|ni|ness
tin|ker
  VERB
△ tin|kers
△ tin|kered
△ tin|ker|ing
tin|kle
  VERB
△ tin|kles
△ tin|kled
△ tink|ling
tinkly
△ tink|lier
△ tink|li|est
tinned
tin|nily
tin|ni|ness
tin|ni|tus
tinny
△ tin|nier
△ tin|ni|est
tin-opener
tin|pot
tin|sel
tin|selly
tin|smith
tint

VERB
△ tints
△ tin|ted
△ tint|ing
Tin|tern
tin|tin|nabu|la|
  tion
Tin|tor|etto
tiny
△ ti|nier
△ ti|ni|est
tip
  VERB
△ tips
△ tipped
△ tip|ping
tip-off
tipped
Tip|per|ary
tip|pet
Tip|pett
Tipp-Ex
tip|ple
  VERB
△ tip|ples
△ tip|pled
△ tip|pling
tip|pler
tip|sily
tip|si|ness
tip|staff
△ tip|staffs or
  tip|staves
tip|ster
tipsy
△ tip|sier
△ tip|si|est
tip|toe
  VERB
△ tip|toes
△ tip|toed
△ tip|toe|ing
tip|top
tir|ade

Tir|ana

> tire
>   *make weary*
> △ tires
> △ tired
> △ tir|ing
> ⚠ tyre

tire
  rubber casing for
  wheel rim see *tyre*
tired
△ tireder
△ tired|est
tiredly
tired|ness
tire|less
tire|lessly
tire|less|ness
Ti|re|sias
tire|some
tire|somely
tire|some|ness
tir|ing
tiro
Tirol
'tis
tis|sue
tit
titan
Ti|tanic
ti|tanic
ti|ta|nium
tit|bit
tit|fer
tith|able
tithe
  VERB
△ tithes
△ tithed
△ tith|ing
Ti|tian
tit|il|late
△ tit|il|lates

△ tit|il|la|ted
△ tit|il|la|ting
tit|il|la|ting
ti|til|la|tion
titi|vate
△ titi|vates
△ titi|va|ted
△ titi|va|ting
ti|ti|va|tion
ti|tle
  VERB
△ ti|tles
△ ti|tled
△ ti|tling
titled
tit|mouse
△ tit|mice
Tito
ti|trate
△ ti|trates
△ ti|tra|ted
△ ti|tra|ting
ti|tra|tion
titre
tit|ter
  VERB
△ tit|ters
△ tit|tered
△ tit|ter|ing
tit|tle
tittle-tattle
  VERB
△ tittle-tattles
△ tittle-tattled
△ tittle-tat|tling
titty
△ tit|ties
tit|ular
tit|ularly
Titus
Titus, Let|ter
  of Paul to
tizzy
△ tiz|zies

T-junc|tion

> to
> *towards*
> ⚠ too
> ⚠ two

toad
toad|flax
toad-in-the-hole
toad|stool
toady
  NOUN
  △ toad|ies
  VERB
  △ toad|ies
  △ toad|ied
  △ toady|ing
toady|ish
toady|ism
toast
  VERB
  △ toasts
  △ toas|ted
  △ toast|ing
toas|ted
toas|ter
toast|ing-fork
toast|mas|ter
toast|mis|tress
  △ toast|mis|tres|
    ses
to|bacco
  △ to|bac|cos *or*
    to|bac|coes
to|bac|con|ist
To|bago
To|bias
to|bog|gan
  VERB
  △ to|bog|gans
  △ to|bog|ganed
  △ to|bog|gan|ing
to|bog|gan|ing
to|bog|ganer

to|bog|gan|ist
To|bruk
toc|cata
Toc H
to|co|pherol
toc|sin
tod
today
tod|dle
  VERB
  △ tod|dles
  △ tod|dled
  △ tod|dling
tod|dler
toddy
  △ tod|dies
to-do

> toe
> *digit at end of
> foot; touch with
> this*
> VERB
> △ toes
> △ toed
> △ toe|ing
> ⚠ tow

toe-cap
toe-hold
toe|nail
toe|rag
toff
tof|fee
tof|fee-apple
tof|fee-nosed
tofu
tog
  VERB
  △ togs
  △ togged
  △ tog|ging
toga
togaed
to|gether

to|geth|er|ness
tog|gle
  VERB
  △ tog|gles
  △ tog|gled
  △ tog|gling
Togo
toil
  VERB
  △ toils
  △ toiled
  △ toil|ing
toi|let
toil|etry
  △ toil|et|ries
toil|some
toil|worn
Tokay
token
to|ken|ism
Tokyo
tol|booth
told
To|ledo
tol|er|ab|il|ity
tol|er|able
tol|er|ably
tol|er|ance
tol|er|ant
tol|er|antly
tol|er|ate
  △ tol|er|ates
  △ tol|er|ated
  △ tol|er|ating
tol|er|ation
Tol|kien
toll
  VERB
  △ tolls
  △ tolled
  △ toll|ing
toll|gate
Tol|puddle
Tol|stoy

tolu|ene
Tom
tom
toma|hawk
to|mato
  △ to|ma|toes
tomb
tom|bola
tom|boy
*Tom Brown's
  School|days*
tomb|stone
tom|cat
tome
tom|fool
tom|fool|ery
  △ tom|fool|er|ies
*Tom Jones, The
  His|tory of*
Tommy
  △ Tom|mies
tom|my|gun
tommy-rot
to|mog|ra|phy
to|mor|row
tompion *see*
  tampion
*Tom Saw|yer,
  The Ad|ven|
  tures of*
Tomsk
Tom Thumb
tom|tit
tom-tom

> ton
> *20
> hundredweight*
> ⚠ tonne
> ⚠ tun

tonal
to|nal|ity
  △ to|nal|it|ies

Ton|bridge
*town in Kent 5
miles north of*
⚠ Tunbridge
Wells

tone
  VERB
  △ tones
  △ toned
  △ to|ning
tone-deaf
tone-deaf|ness
tone||less
tone||lessly
tong
Tonga
tongs
tongue
  VERB
  △ tongues
  △ tongued
  △ tonguing
tongue-tie
tongue-tied
tongue-twis|ter
tonguing
tonic
to|night
ton|nage

tonne
*1000
kilogrammes*
⚠ ton
⚠ tun

ton|ner
ton|sil
ton|sil|lec|tomy
  △ ton|sil|lec|
    tom|ies
ton|sil|li|tis
ton|sor|ial
ton|sure

VERB
△ ton|sures
△ ton|sured
△ ton|sur|ing
ton|sured
ton|tine
ton-up

too
also; excessively
⚠ to
⚠ two

took
tool
  VERB
  △ tools
  △ tooled
  △ tool|ing
tool|bag
tool|box
  △ tool|boxes
tool|kit
tool|ma|ker
tool|ma|king
toot
  VERB
  △ toots
  △ too|ted
  △ toot|ling
tooth
  NOUN
  △ teeth
  VERB
  △ tooths
  △ toothed
  △ tooth|ing
tooth|ache
tooth|brush
  △ tooth|bru|shes
tooth|ily
tooth|less
tooth|paste
tooth|pick
tooth|pow|der

tooth|some
toothy
  △ tooth|ier
  △ too|thi|est
too|tle
  VERB
  △ too|tles
  △ too|tled
  △ toot|ling
toot|sie
top
  VERB
  △ tops
  △ topped
  △ top|ping
topaz
  △ to|pazes
top|coat
top-dress
  △ top-dres|ses
  △ top-dressed
  △ top-dress|ing
top-dress|ing
tope
  VERB
  △ topes
  △ toped
  △ to|ping
toper
top-flight
top|gal|lant
top-heavy
topi
to|pi|ary
  △ to|pi|ar|ies
topic
top|ical
to|pi|cal|ity
top|ic|ally
top|knot
top|less
top|mast
top|most
top-notch

to|po|graph|ical
to|po|graph|ic|
  ally
to|pog|ra|phy
  △ to|pog|ra|
    phies
to|po|lo|gi|cal
to|po|lo|gic|ally
to|pol|ogy
To|pol|ski
top|per
top|ping
top|ple
  △ top|ples
  △ top|pled
  △ top|pling
top|sail
top-secret
top|side
top|soil
top|spin
topsy-tur|vily
topsy-tur|vi|ness
topsy-turvy
toque
tor
Torah
Tor|bay
torc
torch
  △ tor|ches
torch|light
tore
tor|ea|dor
tor|ero
torii
tor|ment
  VERB
  △ tor|ments
  △ tor|men|ted
  △ tor|ment|ing
tor|men|til
tor|men|tor
torn

Tor|nado
tor|nado
△ tor|na|does
Tor|ness
Tor|onto
tor|pedo
 NOUN
 △ tor|pe|dos *or*
  tor|pe|does
 VERB
 △ tor|pe|does
 △ tor|pe|doed
 △ tor|pe|do|ing
tor|pid
tor|pid|ity
tor|pidly
tor|por
Tor|quay
torque
Tor|quil
torr
tor|rent
tor|ren|tial
tor|rid
tor|sion
tor|sional
torso
tort
Tor|tel|ier
tor|tilla
tor|toise
tor|toise|shell
tor|tu|ous
tor|tu|ously
tor|tu|ous|ness
tor|ture
 VERB
 △ tor|tures
 △ tor|tured
 △ tor|tur|ing
tor|tur|ous
tor|tur|ously
torus
 △ tori

Tor|vill
Tory
 △ Tor|ies
Tory|ism
Tosca
Tos|ca|nini
toss
 NOUN
 △ tos|ses
 VERB
 △ tos|ses
 △ tossed
 △ toss|ing
toss-up
tot
 VERB
 △ tots
 △ tot|ted
 △ tot|ting
total
 VERB
 △ to|tals
 △ to|talled
 △ to|tal|ling
to|tal|it|ar|ian
to|tal|it|ari|an|
 ism
to|tal|ity
 △ to|tal|ities
To|tal|iza|tor
to|tal|ize
 △ to|tal|izes
 △ to|tal|ized
 △ to|tal|izing
to|tal|izer
to|tally
Tote
tote
 △ totes
 △ toted
 △ toting
totem
to|temic
to|tem|ism

To the Light\house
tot|ter
 VERB
 △ tot|ters
 △ tot|tered
 △ tot|ter|ing
tot|tery
tot|ting-up
tou|can
touch
 NOUN
 △ touches
 VERB
 △ touches
 △ touched
 △ touch|ing
touch|down
tou|ché
touched
touch|ily
touchi|ness
touch|ing
touch|ingly
touch|line
touch|pa|per
touch|stone
touch-type
 △ touch-types
 △ touch-typed
 △ touch-typ|ing
touch-typ|ing
touch-typ|ist
touch|wood
touchy
 △ touch|ier
 △ touchi|est
tough
 ADJ.
 △ tougher
 △ tough|est
toughen
 △ tough|ens
 △ tough|ened
 △ tough|en|ing

toughly
tough|ness
Tou|lon
Tou|louse
Tou|louse-Lau|
 trec
tou|pee
tour
 VERB
 △ tours
 △ toured
 △ tour|ing
Tour|aine
tour de force
 △ *tours de force*
Tour de France
Tour|ette
tour|ism
tour|ist
tour|isty
tour|ma|line
Tour|nai
tour|na|ment
tour|ne|dos
 sing. and pl.
Tour|neur
tour|ney
 VERB
 △ tour|neys
 △ tour|neyed
 △ tour|ney|ing
tour|ni|quet
Tours
*Tours of Dr
 Syn|tax, The*
tousle
 VERB
 △ tousles
 △ tousled
 △ tous|ling
Tous|saint
L'Ou|ver|ture
tout

VERB
△ touts
△ tou|ted
△ tout|ing

tow
*pull along
behind; this
action; thing so
pulled; hemp for
ropes*
VERB
△ tows
△ towed
△ tow|ing
⚠ toe

to|wards
tow|bar
tow-col|oured
towel
VERB
△ tow|els
△ tow|elled
△ tow|el|ling
tow|el|ling
tower
VERB
△ towers
△ tow|ered
△ tow|er|ing
tow|er|ing
tow-head
tow-headed
tow|line
tow|rope
town
townee
*Town Like
Alice, A*
town|scape
towns|folk
town|ship
towns|man
△ towns|men

towns|people
tow|path
tox|ae|mia
tox|ae|mic
toxic
tox|icity
△ tox|ici|ties
toxi|colo|gist
toxi|col|ogy
toxin
toxo|cara
tox|oid
toy
VERB
△ toys
△ toyed
△ toy|ing
Toyn|bee
Toy|ota
tra|be|ated
trace
VERB
△ tra|ces
△ traced
△ tra|cing
tra|cer
tra|cery
△ tra|cer|ies
Tra|cey
tra|chea
△ tra|cheae
tra|che|ot|omy
△ tra|che|ot|om|
ies
tra|che|os|tomy
△ tra|che|os|
tom|ies
tra|choma
tra|cing
tra|cing-paper
track
VERB
△ tracks
△ tracked

△ track|ing
track|ball
track|er|ball
track|ing
track|suit
tract
trac|ta|bil|ity
tract|able
tract|ably
Trac|tar|ian|ism
trac|tion
trac|tional
tract|ive
trac|tor
Tracy
trad
trade
VERB
△ trades
△ tra|ded
△ tra|ding
trade-in
trade|mark
trade|name
trade-off
tra|der
tra|des|can|tia
trades|man
△ trades|men
trades|people

**Trades Union
Congress**
⚠ trade union

trades|wo|man
△ trades|wo|men

trade union
⚠ Trades
Union
Congress

tra|di|tion
tra|di|tional
tra|di|tion|al|ism

tra|di|tion|al|ist
tra|di|tion|ally
tra|duce
△ tra|du|ces
△ tra|duced
△ tra|du|cing
tra|duce|ment
tra|du|cer
Tra|fal|gar
traf|fic
VERB
△ traf|fics
△ traf|ficked
△ traf|fick|ing
traf|ficker
tra|gedian
tra|gedi|enne
tra|gedy
△ tra|ged|ies
tra|gic
tra|gic|ally
tra|gi|com|edy
△ tra|gi|com|ed|
ies
tra|gi|comic
tra|gi|com|ic|ally
Tra|herne
trail
VERB
△ trails
△ trailed
△ trail|ing
trail|bla|zer
trail|bla|zing
trailer
train
VERB
△ trains
△ trained
△ train|ing
train-bearer
trained
train|ee
trainer

train|ing
train-spot|ter
train-spot|ting
traipse
 VERB
 △ traip|ses
 △ traipsed
 △ traip|sing

---
trait
feature of
character etc
 △tray

---

trai|tor
trai|tor|ous
trai|tor|ously
trait|ress
 △ trait|res|ses
Tra|jan
tra|ject|ory
 △ tra|ject|or|ies
Tra|lee
tram
tram|car
tram|line
tram|mel
 VERB
 △ tram|mels
 △ tram|melled
 △ tram|mel|ling
tramp
 VERB
 △ tramps
 △ tramped
 △ tramp|ing
tram|ple
 VERB
 △ tram|ples
 △ tram|pled
 △ tramp|ling
tram|po|line
 VERB
 △ tram|po|lines
 △ tram|po|lined

△ tram|po|li|ning
tram|way
trance
tran|nie
tran|quil
tran|quil|lity
tran|quil|lize
 △ tran|quil|li|zes
 △ tran|quil|lized
 △ tran|quil|li|zing
tran|quil|li|zer
tran|quilly
trans|act
 △ trans|acts
 △ trans|ac|ted
 △ trans|act|ing
trans|ac|tion
trans|ac|tor
trans|al|pine
trans|at|lan|tic
Trans|cau|ca|sia
trans|cei|ver
trans|cend
 △ trans|cends
 △ trans|cen|ded
 △ trans|cend|ing
trans|cend|ence
trans|cend|ency
trans|cend|ent
trans|cen|den|tal
trans|cen|den|tal|ism
trans|cen|dent|ally
trans|con|ti|nen|tal
tran|scribe
 △ tran|scribes
 △ tran|scribed
 △ tran|scri|bing
tran|script
tran|scrip|tion

Trans|da|nu|bia
trans|du|cer
tran|sept
trans|fer
 VERB
 △ trans|fers
 △ trans|ferred
 △ trans|fer|ring
trans|fer|able
trans|fer|ence
trans|fig|ur|ation
trans|fig|ure
 △ trans|fig|ures
 △ trans|fig|ured
 △ trans|fig|ur|ing
trans|fix
 △ trans|fixes
 △ trans|fixed
 △ trans|fix|ing
trans|fix|ion
trans|form
 △ trans|forms
 △ trans|formed
 △ trans|form|ing
trans|for|ma|tion
trans|for|ma|tional
trans|for|mer
trans|fuse
 △ trans|fu|ses
 △ trans|fused
 △ trans|fu|sing
trans|fu|sion
trans|genic
trans|gress
 △ trans|gres|ses
 △ trans|gressed
 △ trans|gress|ing
trans|gres|sion
trans|gres|sor
tranship *see*
 transship
trans|hu|mance

tran|si|ence
tran|si|ency
tran|si|ent
tran|si|ently
tran|sis|tor
tran|sis|tor|ize
 △ tran|sis|tor|izes
 △ tran|sis|tor|ized
 △ tran|sis|tor|izing
tran|sis|tor|ized
tran|sit
 VERB
 △ trans|its
 △ trans|ited
 △ trans|it|ing
trans|ition
trans|itional
trans|ition|ally
trans|ition|ary
trans|it|ive
trans|it|ively
trans|it|or|ily
trans|it|ori|ness
trans|it|ory
Trans|kei
trans|late
 △ trans|lates
 △ trans|la|ted
 △ trans|la|ting
trans|la|tion
trans|la|tional
trans|la|tor
trans|lit|er|ate
 △ trans|lit|er|ates
 △ trans|lit|er|ated
 △ trans|lit|er|ating
trans|lit|er|ation
trans|lo|ca|tion

trans|lu|cence
trans|lu|cency
trans|lu|cent
trans|lu|cently
trans|mi|grate
△ trans|mi|
  grates
△ trans|mi|gra|ted
△ trans|mi|gra|
  ting
trans|mi|gra|tion
trans|mis|sible
trans|mis|sion
trans|mit
△ trans|mits
△ trans|mit|ted
△ trans|mit|ting
trans|mit|ter
trans|mog|ri|fi|
  ca|tion
trans|mog|rify
△ trans|mog|ri|
  fies
△ trans|mog|ri|
  fied
△ trans|mog|ri|
  fy|ing
trans|mu|table
trans|mu|ta|tion
trans|mute
△ trans|mutes
△ trans|mu|ted
△ trans|mu|ting
tran|som
trans|par|ency
△ trans|par|en|
  cies
trans|par|ent
trans|par|ently
tran|spir|ation
trans|pire
△ trans|pires
△ trans|pired
△ trans|pir|ing

trans|plant
VERB
△ trans|plants
△ trans|plan|ted
△ trans|plant|ing
trans|plan|ta|
  tion
trans|port
VERB
△ trans|ports
△ trans|por|ted
△ trans|port|ing
trans|port|able
trans|por|ta|tion
trans|por|ter
trans|po|sable
trans|pose
△ trans|po|ses
△ trans|posed
△ trans|po|sing
trans|po|si|tion
trans|pu|ter
trans|sex|ual
trans|ship
△ trans|ships
△ trans|shipped
△ trans|ship|
  ping
trans|ship|ment
Trans-Siber|ian
tran|sub|stan|ti|
  ate
△ tran|sub|stan|
  ti|ates
△ tran|sub|stan|
  ti|ated
△ tran|sub|stan|
  ti|ating
tran|sub|stan|ti|
  ation
trans|ur|anic
Trans|vaal
trans|verse
trans|versely

trans|vest|ism
trans|vest|ite
Tran|syl|va|nia
trap
VERB
△ traps
△ trapped
△ trap|ping
trap|door
trapes see
  traipse
tra|peze
tra|pez|ium
△ tra|pezi|ums
  or tra|pezia
trap|ez|oid
trap|per
trap|pings
Trap|pist
trash
trash|can
trash|ily
tra|shi|ness
trashy
△ tra|shier
△ tra|shi|est
trat|toria
△ trat|tor|ias or
  trat|torie
trauma
△ trau|mas or
  trau|mata
trau|matic
trau|mat|ic|ally
trau|mat|ize
△ trau|mat|izes
△ trau|mat|ized
△ trau|mat|izing
trav|ail
VERB
△ trav|ails
△ trav|ailed
△ trav|ail|ing
travel

VERB
△ trav|els
△ trav|elled
△ trav|el|ling
travelator see
  travolator
trav|elled
trav|el|ler
trav|el|ogue
Traven
tra|ver|sal
tra|verse or trav|
  erse
VERB
△ tra|ver|ses or
  trav|er|ses
△ tra|versed or
  trav|ersed
△ tra|vers|ing or
  trav|ers|ing
according to
pronunciation
trav|esty
NOUN
△ trav|es|ties
VERB
△ trav|es|ties
△ trav|es|tied
△ trav|es|ty|ing
Tra|vi|ata, La
tra|vo|la|tor
trawl
VERB
△ trawls
△ trawled
△ trawl|ing
traw|ler

tray
flat piece of
wood etc with
rim, for carrying
things
△ trait

treach|er|ous
treach|er|ously
treach|er|ous|
  ness
treach|ery
  △ treach|er|ies
trea|cle
tread
  VERB
  △ treads
  △ trod
  △ tread|ing
  △ trod|den or
    trod
trea|dle
  VERB
  △ trea|dles
  △ trea|dled
  △ tread|ling
tread|mill
trea|son
trea|son|able
trea|son|ably
treas|ure
  VERB
  △ treas|ures
  △ treas|ured
  △ treas|ur|ing
Treas|ure Is|land
treas|urer
treas|ure-trove
treas|ury
  △ treas|ur|ies
treat
  VERB
  △ treats
  △ trea|ted
  △ treat|ing
treat|ise
treat|ment
treaty
  △ treat|ies
Treb|iz|ond
tre|ble

VERB
  △ tre|bles
  △ tre|bled
  △ treb|ling
trebly
tre|cento
tred|dle
Tree
tree
  VERB
  △ trees
  △ treed
  △ tree|ing
tree|less
tree|top
tre|foil
trek
  VERB
  △ treks
  △ trekked
  △ trek|king
trel|lis
  NOUN
  △ trel|li|ses
  VERB
  △ trel|li|ses
  △ trel|lised
  △ trel|lis|ing
trel|lised
trem|ble
  VERB
  △ trem|bles
  △ trem|bled
  △ trem|bling
trem|bling
trem|blingly
trembly
  △ trem|blier
  △ trem|bli|est
tre|mend|ous
tre|mend|ously
trem|olo
tremor
trem|ulous

trem|ulously
trem|ulous|ness
trench
  NOUN
  △ tren|ches
  VERB
  △ tren|ches
  △ trenched
  △ trench|ing
tren|chancy
tren|chant
tren|chantly
tren|cher
tren|cher|man
  △ tren|cher|men
trend
  VERB
  △ trends
  △ tren|ded
  △ trend|ing
trend|ily
trend|set|ter
trend|set|ting
trendy
  NOUN
  △ trend|ies
  ADJ.
  △ tren|dier
  △ tren|di|est
Trent
Trento
tre|pan
  VERB
  △ tre|pans
  △ tre|panned
  △ tre|pan|ning
tre|phine
  VERB
  △ tre|phines
  △ tre|phined
  △ tre|phi|ning
trep|id|ation
tres|pass

NOUN
  △ tres|pas|ses
  VERB
  △ tres|pas|ses
  △ tres|passed
  △ tres|pass|ing
tres|pas|ser
tress
  △ tres|ses
tres|tle
Tret|ya|kov
Tre|vel|yan
Treves
Tre|vith|ick
Trevor
trews
triad
tri|adic
Trial, The (Der
  Pro|zess)
trial
tri|an|gle
tri|an|gu|lar
tri|an|gu|lar|ity
tri|an|gu|larly
tri|an|gu|late
  △ tri|an|gu|lates
  △ tri|an|gu|la|ted
  △ tri|an|gu|la|
    ting
tri|an|gu|la|tion
Tri|as|sic
tri|ath|lete
tri|ath|lon
tri|bal
tri|bal|ism
tri|bally
tribe
tribes|man
  △ tribes|men
tribes|wo|man
  △ tribes|wo|men
tri|bu|la|tion
tri|bu|nal

trib|une
tri|bu|tary
△ tri|bu|tar|ies
trib|ute
tri|carb|oxy|lic
trice
tri|ceps
tri|cer|at|ops
trich|in|osis
tri|chloro|meth|
ane
trich|ol|ogy
trick
VERB
△ tricks
△ tricked
△ trick|ing
trick|ery
△ trick|er|ies
trick|ily
trick|iness
trickle
VERB
△ trickles
△ trickled
△ trick|ling
trick|ster
tricky
△ trick|ier
△ tricki|est
tri|col|our
tri|col|oured
tri|cot
tri|cy|cle
VERB
△ tri|cy|cles
△ tri|cy|cled
△ tri|cyc|ling
tri|cyc|list
Tri|dent
missile
tri|dent
fork-like weapon
Tri|den|tine *or*

Trid|ent|ine
according to
pronunciation
tried
tri|en|nial
tri|en|ni|ally
Trier
trier
Tri|este
tri|fle
VERB
△ tri|fles
△ tri|fled
△ tri|fling
tri|fling
trig
trig|ger
VERB
△ trig|gers
△ trig|gered
△ trig|ger|ing
trig|ger-happy
tri|gly|cer|ide
trig|lyph
tri|go|no|met|ric
tri|go|no|met|ri|cal
tri|go|nom|etry
trike
tri|lat|eral
tri|lat|er|ally
Trilby
trilby
△ tril|bies
tri|lin|gual
trill
VERB
△ trills
△ trilled
△ trill|ing
tril|lion
after number
△ trillion
other senses
△ trillions

tril|lionth
tri|lo|bite
tril|ogy
△ tril|ogies
trim
VERB
△ trims
△ trimmed
△ trim|ming
ADJ.
△ trim|mer
△ trim|mest
tri|ma|ran
trim|es|ter
trimly
trim|mer
trim|ming
trim|ness
Trin|idad and
To|bago
Trin|it|ar|ian
Trin|it|ar|ian|
ism
tri|ni|tro|tolu|
ene
trin|ity
△ trin|it|ies
trin|ket
trin|ketry
trio
trip
VERB
△ trips
△ tripped
△ trip|ping
tri|part|ite
tripe
tri|ple
VERB
△ tri|ples
△ tri|pled
△ trip|ling
trip|let
trip|li|cate

VERB
△ trip|li|cates
△ trip|li|ca|ted
△ trip|li|ca|ting
trip|li|ca|tion
triply
tri|pod
Trip|oli
tri|pos
△ tri|poses
trip|per
trip|tych
trip-wire
tri|reme
tri|sect
△ tri|sects
△ tri|sec|ted
△ tri|sect|ing
tri|sec|tion
Tris|tan and Is|
olde (Tris|tan
und Is|olde)
Tris|tan da
Cunha
Tris|tram
Tris|tram
Shandy, The
Life and Opin|
ions of
trite
△ tri|ter
△ tri|test
tritely
trite|ness
trit|ium
tri|ton
tri|umph
VERB
△ tri|umphs
△ tri|umphed
△ tri|umph|ing
tri|um|phal
tri|um|phant
tri|um|phantly

Tri|umph of the
Will (Tri|
umph des Wil|
lens)
tri|um|vir
△ tri|um|viri *or*
tri|um|virs
tri|um|vi|ral
tri|um|vir|ate
tri|va|lence
tri|va|lency
tri|va|lent
trivet
tri|via
triv|ial
tri|vi|al|ity
△ tri|vi|al|it|ies
tri|vi|al|iza|tion
tri|vi|al|ize
△ tri|vi|al|izes
△ tri|vi|al|ized
△ tri|vi|al|izing
tri|vi|ally
tro|chee
trod
trod|den
trog|lo|dyte
troika
Tro|ilus
*Tro|ilus and
Cres|sida*
opera by Walton
*Tro|ilus and Cri|
seyde*
poem by Chaucer
Tro|jan
troll
VERB
△ trolls
△ trolled
△ troll|ing
trol|ley
trol|lop
Trol|lope

trom|bone
trom|bo|nist
trompe l'oeil
Troon

troop
group (esp of
soldiers); move
in a crowd
VERB
△ troops
△ trooped
△ troop|ing
⚠troupe

troo|per
Troop|ing the
Col|our
troop-ship
trope
tro|phy
△ tro|phies
tropic
trop|ical
trop|ic|ally
tro|pism
tro|po|sphere
Trot
trot
VERB
△ trots
△ trot|ted
△ trot|ting
troth
Trot|sky
Trot|sky|ism
Trot|sky|ist
Trot|sky|ite
trot|ter
trou|ba|dour
trou|ble
VERB
△ trou|bles
△ trou|bled
△ troub|ling

trou|bled
trouble|ma|ker
trouble|shoo|ter
trouble|shoot|
ing
trouble|some
trouble|somely
troub|lous
trough
trounce
△ troun|ces
△ trounced
△ troun|cing
troun|cing

troupe
group of actors,
acrobats, etc
⚠troop

trou|per
trou|sers
trous|seau
△ trous|seaux *or*
trous|seaus
trout
△ trout *or* trouts
'Trout' Quintet
*Tro|va|tore, Il
(The Trou|ba|
dour)*
trove
Trow|bridge
trowel
Troy
troy
Troyes
tru|ancy
△ tru|an|cies
tru|ant
VERB
△ tru|ants
△ tru|an|ted
△ tru|ant|ing
truce

truck
VERB
△ trucks
△ trucked
△ truck|ing
trucker
truck|ing
truckle
VERB
△ truckles
△ truckled
△ truck|ling
truc|ulence
truc|ulency
truc|ulent
truc|ulently
trudge
VERB
△ trud|ges
△ trudged
△ trud|ging
true
VERB
△ trues
△ trued
△ tru|ing
ADJ.
△ truer
△ tru|est
true-blue
true-love
true|ness
Truf|faut
truf|fle
trug
tru|ism
truly
Tru|man
trump
VERB
△ trumps
△ trumped
△ trump|ing
trumped-up

trump|ery
△ trump|er|ies
trum|pet
  VERB
  △ trum|pets
  △ trum|peted
  △ trum|pet|ing
trum|peter
trun|cate
  VERB
  △ trun|cates
  △ trun|cated
  △ trun|ca|ting
trun|ca|tion
trun|cheon
trun|dle
  △ trun|dles
  △ trun|dled
  △ trund|ling
trunk
Truro
truss
  NOUN
  △ trus|ses
  VERB
  △ trus|ses
  △ trussed
  △ truss|ing
trust
  VERB
  △ trusts
  △ trus|ted
  △ trust|ing
trus|tee
trus|tee|ship
trust|ful
trust|fully
trust|ful|ness
trust|ily
trust|ing
trust|ingly
trus|ti|ness
trust|wor|thily
trust|wor|thi|ness

trust|wor|thy
trusty
  NOUN
  △ trust|ies
  ADJ.
  △ trus|tier
  △ trus|ti|est
truth
truth|ful
truth|fully
truth|ful|ness
try
  NOUN
  △ tries
  VERB
  △ tries
  △ tried
  △ try|ing
try|ing
try-on
try-out
tryp|sin
tryp|to|phan
try|sail
tryst
  VERB
  △ trysts
  △ trys|ted
  △ tryst|ing
tsar
tsar|ev|itch
  △ tsar|ev|it|ches
tsar|ina
tsetse
T-shirt
T-square
tsu|nami
Tu|areg
tua|tara
tub
tuba
tub|bi|ness
tubby
  △ tub|bier

△ tub|bi|est
tube
tube|less
tuber
tu|bercle
tu|ber|cu|lar
tu|ber|cu|lin
tu|ber|cu|lin-tes|ted
tu|ber|cu|lo|sis
tu|ber|cu|lous
tu|ber|ous
tub|ful
tu|bing
Tü|bin|gen
Tubruq *see*
  Tobruk
tub-thum|per
tub-thump|ing
tu|bu|lar
tu|bule
tuck
  VERB
  △ tucks
  △ tucked
  △ tuck|ing
tucker
Tuc|son
Tudor
Tues|day
tufa
tu|fa|ceous
tuff
tuf|fa|ceous
tuf|fet
tuft
tuf|ted
tufty
  △ tuf|tier
  △ tuf|ti|est
tug
  VERB
  △ tugs
  △ tugged
  △ tug|ging

tug|boat
tug-of-love
tug-of-war
Tuil|er|ies
tu|ition
tulip
Tull
tulle
tum
tum|ble
  VERB
  △ tum|bles
  △ tum|bled
  △ tum|bling
tum|ble|down
tumble-drier
tumble-dry
  △ tumble-dries
  △ tumble-dried
  △ tumble-dry|
    ing
tumble-dryer
tum|bler
tum|bler|ful
tumble|weed
tum|bling-bar|
  rel
tum|brel
tu|mes|cence
tu|mes|cent
tumid
tu|mid|ity
tu|midly
tummy
  △ tum|mies
tummy-but|ton
tu|mor|ous
tu|mour
tu|mu|lar
tu|mult
tu|mul|tu|ous
tu|mul|tu|ously
tu|mu|lus
  △ tu|muli

tun
barrel
⚠ ton
⚠ tonne

tuna
△ tuna *or* tunas
tunable *see*
tuneable

Tun|bridge
Wells
town in Kent 5
miles south of
⚠ Tonbridge

tun|dra
tune
VERB
△ tunes
△ tuned
△ tu|ning
tune|able
tune|ful
tune|fully
tune|ful|ness
tune|less
tune|lessly
tune|less|ness
tuner
tung|sten
tunic
tu|ning-fork
Tunis
Tu|nisia
tun|nel
VERB
△ tun|nels
△ tun|nelled
△ tun|nel|ling
tunny
△ tun|nies
tup
VERB
△ tups

△ tupped
△ tup|ping
tup|pence
tup|penny
Tu|ran|dot
Tur|an|ga|lîla-
  Sym|pho|nie
tur|ban
tur|baned
tur|bid
tur|bid|ity
tur|bidly
tur|bine
tur|bo|char|ger
tur|bo|fan
tur|bo|jet
tur|bo|prop
tur|bot
△ tur|bot *or* tur|
  bots
tur|bu|lence
tur|bu|lent
tur|bu|lently
turd
tur|een
turf
NOUN
△ turfs *or* turves
VERB
△ turfs
△ turfed
△ turf|ing
turfy
△ turf|ier
△ tur|fi|est
Tur|genev
tur|ges|cence
tur|ges|cent
tur|gid
tur|gid|ity
tur|gidly
Turin
Turk
Tur|key

tur|key
Tur|kic
Turk|ish
Turk|men|is|tan
tur|meric
tur|moil
turn
VERB
△ turns
△ turned
△ turn|ing
turn|about
turn|around
Turn|berry
turn|coat
Tur|ner
tur|ner
turn|ing
turn|ing-circle
turn|ing-point
tur|nip
turn|key
turn|off
Turn of the
  Screw, The
turn-on
turn-out
turn|over
turn|pike
turn|stile
turn|ta|ble
turn-up
tur|pen|tine
Tur|pin
tur|pi|tude
tur|quoise
tur|ret
tur|reted
tur|tle
tur|tle|dove
turtle-neck
turves
Tus|can
Tus|cany

tusk
tusked
tus|ker
Tus|saud
tus|sle
VERB
△ tus|sles
△ tus|sled
△ tus|sling
tus|sock
tus|socky
tut
VERB
△ tuts
△ tut|ted
△ tut|ting
Tu|tan|kha|men
tu|tel|age
tu|tel|ary
tutor
VERB
△ tu|tors
△ tu|tored
△ tu|tor|ing
tu|tor|ial
tu|tori|ally
tu|tor|ship
Tutsi
tutti
tutti-frutti
tut-tut
VERB
△ tut-tuts
△ tut-tut|ted
△ tut-tut|ting
tutu
Tu|valu
tu-whit tu-
  whoo
tux
△ tuxes
tux|edo
Tuzla
twad|dle

VERB
△ twad|dles
△ twad|dled
△ twad|dling
Twain
twain
twang
VERB
△ twangs
△ twanged
△ twang|ing
twangy
△ twan|gier
△ twan|gi|est
twat
tweak
VERB
△ tweaks
△ tweaked
△ tweak|ing
twee
Tweed
tweed
tweedy
△ twee|dier
△ twee|di|est
tweely
'tween
twee|ness
tweet
VERB
△ tweets
△ twee|ted
△ tweet|ing
twee|ter
tweez|ers
twelfth
twelfthly
*Twelfth Night,
or What You
Will*
twelve
twelve|fold
twelve|month

twelve-tone
twen|ties
twen|tieth
twenty
NOUN
△ twen|ties
twerp
twice
twid|dle
VERB
△ twid|dles
△ twid|dled
△ twid|dling
twid|dler
twid|dly
△ twid|dlier
△ twid|dli|est
twig
VERB
△ twigs
△ twigged
△ twig|ging
twiggy
twi|light
twi|lit
twill
VERB
△ twills
△ twilled
△ twill|ing
twilled
twill|ing
twin
VERB
△ twins
△ twinned
△ twin|ning
twine
VERB
△ twines
△ twined
△ twi|ning
twin-engined
twinge

VERB
△ twin|ges
△ twinged
△ twin|ging
twin|kle
VERB
△ twin|kles
△ twin|kled
△ twink|ling
twink|ling
twinkly
△ twink|lier
△ twink|li|est
twin|set
twirl
VERB
△ twirls
△ twirled
△ twirl|ing
twirly
twirp *see* twerp
twist
VERB
△ twists
△ twis|ted
△ twist|ing
twis|ted
twis|ter
twisty
△ twis|tier
△ twis|ti|est
twit
VERB
△ twits
△ twit|ted
△ twit|ting
twitch
NOUN
△ twit|ches
VERB
△ twit|ches
△ twitched
△ twitch|ing
twit|cher

twitch|ily
twit|chy
△ twit|chier
△ twit|chi|est
twit|ter
VERB
△ twit|ters
△ twit|tered
△ twit|ter|ing
twit|tery

two
the number 2;
this amount
⚠ to
⚠ too

two-bit
two-edged
two-faced
two|fold
*Two Gentle|men
of Ver|ona,
The*
two-handed
two|pence
two|penny
two-piece
two-ply
NOUN
△ two-plies
two-seater
two-sided
two|some
two-step
two-stroke
*2001: A Space
Odys|sey*
Two Thou|sand
Guin|eas
two-time
△ two-times
△ two-timed
△ two-timing
two-timer

two-tone
two-way
ty|coon
Tyger, The
tying
tyke
Tyler
tym|panic
tympani *see*
  timpani
tympanist *see*
  timpanist
tym|panum
  △ tym|pana *or*
  tym|pan|ums
Tynan
Tyn|dale
Tyne
Tyne and Wear
Tyne|side
Tyn|wald
type
  VERB
  △ types

△ typed
△ typing
type|cast
  VERB
  △ type|casts
  △ type|cast
  △ type|cast|ing
type|face
type|script
type|set
  △ type|sets
  △ type|set
  △ type|set|ting
type|set|ter
type|write
  △ type|writes
  △ type|wrote
  △ type|wri|ting
  △ type|writ|ten
type|wri|ter
type|wri|ting
ty|phoid
ty|phoon
ty|phus

typ|ical
typ|ic|ally
typ|ify
  △ typi|fies
  △ typi|fied
  △ typi|fy|ing
typ|ing
typ|ist
typo
ty|pog|ra|pher
ty|po|gra|phic
ty|po|graph|ical
ty|po|graph|ic|
  ally
ty|pog|ra|phy
ty|ran|ni|cal
ty|ran|nic|ally
tyr|an|nize
  △ tyr|an|ni|zes
  △ tyr|an|nized
  △ tyr|an|ni|zing
ty|ran|no|saur
ty|ran|no|saurus
tyr|an|nous

tyr|an|nously
tyr|anny
  △ tyr|an|nies
ty|rant
Tyre

---

tyre
  rubber casing for
  wheel rim
    ▲ tire

---

tyro *see* tiro
Tyrol *see* Tirol
ty|ro|sine
Tyr|rhen|ian
Tyson
tzar *see* tsar
tzarevitch *see*
  tsarevich
tzarina *see*
  tsarina
tzat|ziki
tzi|gane

U

ubi|quit|ous
ubi|quity
U-boat
Uc|cello
Udall
udder
Uf|fizi
ufol|ogy
Uganda
ugh
ugli
△ uglis *or* ug|lies
ugly
△ ug|lier
△ ug|li|est
Uh|len|beck
ukase
Ukraine
uku|lele
Ulan Bator
Ul|bricht
ulcer
ul|cer|ate
△ ul|cer|ates
△ ul|cer|ated
△ ul|cer|ating
ul|cer|ation
ul|cer|ous
Ul|la|pool
Ulls|water
Ulm
ulna
△ ulnae *or* ulnas
ulnar
Ulric
Ul|ster

Northern
Ireland; of
Northern
Ireland
ul|ster
overcoat
ul|ter|ior
ul|ti|mate
ul|ti|mately
ul|ti|ma|tum
△ ul|ti|ma|tums
or ul|ti|mata
ul|timo
ultra-high
ul|tra|ma|rine
ul|tra|mon|tane
Ul|tra|mon|tan|
ism
ul|tra|sonic
ul|tra|son|ic|ally
ul|tra|son|ics
ul|tra|sound
ul|tra|vi|olet
ulu|late
△ ulu|lates
△ ulu|la|ted
△ ulu|la|ting
ulu|la|tion
Ulys|ses
U-matic
umbel
um|bel|late
um|bel|li|fer|ous
umber
Um|berto
um|bil|ical
um|bil|icus *or*
um|bi|li|cus

△ um|bil|lici *or*
um|bi|lici *or*
um|bil|ic|uses
or um|bi|li|
cuses
according to
pronunciation
umbra
△ um|brae *or*
um|bras
um|brage
um|brella
Um|bria
um|laut
um|pire
VERB
△ um|pires
△ um|pired
△ um|pir|ing
ump|teen
ump|teenth
Una
un|able
un|ac|count|able
un|ac|count|ably
un|ac|cus|tomed
un|ad|op|ted
un|ad|ul|ter|ated
un|ad|vised
un|ad|vi|sedly
un|af|fec|ted
un|ali|en|able
un|al|loyed
un|an|im|ity
un|an|im|ous
un|an|swer|able
un|ap|proach|able
un|armed

un|asked
un|as|sail|able
un|as|su|ming
un|at|tached
un|at|ten|ded
un|av|ail|ing

| un|aware |
| ADJ. |
| ⚠ unawares |

| un|awares |
| ADV. |
| ⚠ unaware |

un|bal|anced
un|bear|able
un|bear|ably
un|be|com|ing
un|be|known
un|be|knownst
un|be|lief
un|be|liev|able
un|be|liev|ably
un|be|liever
un|be|liev|ing
un|bend
△ un|bends
△ un|bent
△ un|bend|ing
un|bend|ing
un|bid|den
un|block
un|blush|ing
un|born
un|bosom
△ un|bos|oms
△ un|bos|omed
△ un|bos|om|ing

un-

un- is an active prefix that can be added freely to many kinds of words to form their opposites (**unnatural, unperson, unhelpfully**). When added to verbs, it usually signifies reversal of the action rather than its opposite, eg: **unblock, undo, unwind**. Some words use **in-** and not **un-**: see the panel at **in-**.

un|boun|ded
un|bowed
un|bri|dled
un|bur|den
  △ un|bur|dens
  △ un|bur|dened
  △ un|bur|den|
    ing
un|called-for
un|can|nily
un|can|ni|ness
un|canny
un|cared-for
un|cere|mo|ni|
  ous
un|cere|mo|ni|
  ously
un|cer|tain
un|cer|tainty
  △ un|cer|tain|
    ties
un|char|ted
un|chris|tian
un|cial
un|cir|cum|cised
un|ci|vil
un|civ|illy
un|clasp
  △ un|clasps
  △ un|clasped
  △ un|clasp|ing
un|cle
un|clean
un|clear
Uncle Tom's
Cabin
Uncle Vanya
(Dya|dya
Vanya)
un|clothe
  △ un|clothes
  △ un|clothed
  △ un|clo|thing
un|com|fort|able

un|com|fort|ably
un|com|mon
un|com|monly
un|com|pro|mi|
  sing
un|com|pro|mi|
  singly
un|con|cern
un|con|cerned
un|con|cer|nedly
un|con|di|tional
un|con|di|tion|
  ally
un|cons|cion|
  able
un|cons|cious
un|cons|ciously
un|con|sti|tu|
  tional
un|con|sti|tu|
  tion|ally
un|cork
  △ un|corks
  △ un|corked
  △ un|cork|ing
un|cou|ple
  △ un|cou|ples
  △ un|cou|pled
  △ un|coup|ling
un|couth
un|cover
  △ un|cov|ers
  △ un|cov|ered
  △ un|cov|er|ing
un|crowned
unc|tion
unc|tu|ous
un|cured
un|cut
un|da|ted
un|de|ceive
  △ un|de|ceives
  △ un|de|ceived
  △ un|de|ceiv|ing

un|de|ci|ded
un|de|ni|able
un|de|ni|ably
under
un|der|achieve
  △ un|der|
    achieves
  △ un|der|
    achieved
  △ un|der|achiev|
    ing
un|der|achie|ver
un|der-age
un|der|arm
un|der|belly
  △ un|der|bel|lies
un|der|car|riage
un|der|charge
  △ un|der|char|
    ges
  △ un|der|
    charged
  △ un|der|char|
    ging
un|der|clothes
un|der|coat
  VERB
  △ un|der|coats
  △ un|der|coa|ted
  △ un|der|coat|
    ing
un|der|cover
un|der|cur|rent
un|der|cut
  △ un|der|cuts
  △ un|der|cut
  △ un|der|cut|
    ting
un|der|dog
un|der|done
un|der|em|
  ployed
un|der|em|ploy|
  ment

un|der|es|ti|mate
  △ un|der|es|ti|
    mates
  △ un|der|es|ti|
    ma|ted
  △ un|der|es|ti|
    ma|ting
un|der|felt
un|der|foot
un|der|gar|ment
un|der|go
  △ un|der|goes
  △ un|der|went
  △ un|der|go|ing
  △ un|der|gone
un|der|gra|du|ate
un|der|ground
un|der|growth
un|der|hand
un|der|han|ded
un|der|lay
  VERB
  △ un|der|lays
  △ un|der|laid
  △ un|der|lay|ing
un|der|lie
  △ un|der|lies
  △ un|der|lay
  △ un|der|ly|ing
  △ un|der|lain
un|der|line
  △ un|der|lines
  △ un|der|lined
  △ un|der|li|ning
un|der|ling
un|der|ly|ing
un|der|men|
  tioned
Under Milk
Wood
un|der|mine
  △ un|der|mines
  △ un|der|mined
  △ un|der|mi|ning

un|der|neath
un|der|pants
un|der|pass
△ un|der|pas|ses
un|der|pin
△ un|der|pins
△ un|der|pinned
△ un|der|pin|
ning
un|der|play
△ un|der|plays
△ un|der|played
△ un|der|play|
ing
un|der|pri|vi|
leged
un|der|pro|duce
△ un|der|pro|du|
ces
△ un|der|pro|
duced
△ un|der|pro|du|
cing
un|der|pro|duc|
tion
un|der|rate
△ un|der|rates
△ un|der|ra|ted
△ un|der|ra|ting
un|der|ra|ted
un|der|seal
VERB
△ un|der|seals
△ un|der|sealed
△ un|der|seal|ing
un|der-sec|re|
tary
△ un|der-sec|re|
tar|ies
un|der|sell
△ un|der|sells
△ un|der|sold
△ un|der|sel|ling
un|der|sexed

un|der|shoot
△ un|der|shoots
△ un|der|shot
△ un|der|shoot|
ing
un|der|side
un|der|signed
un|der|sized
un|der|skirt
un|der|staffed
un|der|stand
△ un|der|stands
△ un|der|stood
△ un|der|stand|
ing
un|der|stand|
able
un|der|stand|
ably
un|der|stand|ing
un|der|state
△ un|der|states
△ un|der|sta|ted
△ un|der|sta|ting
un|der|state|
ment
un|der|stood
un|der|study
NOUN
△ un|der|stud|
ies
VERB
△ un|der|stud|
ies
△ un|der|stud|
ied
△ un|der|study|
ing
un|der|take
△ un|der|takes
△ un|der|took
△ un|der|ta|king
△ un|der|ta|ken
un|der|ta|ker

un|der|ta|king
*Under the Vol|
cano*
un|der|tone
un|der|took
un|der|tow
un|der|value
△ un|der|val|ues
△ un|der|val|ued
△ un|der|valu|
ing
un|der|wa|ter
un|der|wear
un|der|went
un|der|world
un|der|write
△ un|der|writes
△ un|der|wrote
△ un|der|wri|
ting
△ un|der|writ|
ten
un|der|wri|ter
un|des|ir|able
un|des|ir|ably
undid
un|dies
undo
△ un|does
△ undid
△ un|do|ing
△ un|done
un|do|ing
un|done
un|doubted
un|doubtedly
un|dreamed-of
un|dreamt-of
un|dress
VERB
△ un|dres|ses
△ un|dressed
△ un|dress|ing
undue

un|du|lant
un|du|late
△ un|du|lates
△ un|du|la|ted
△ un|du|la|ting
un|du|la|tion
un|duly
un|dy|ing
un|earned
un|earth
△ un|earths
△ un|earthed
△ un|earth|ing
un|earth|li|ness
un|earthly
un|ease
un|eas|ily
un|ea|si|ness
un|easy
un|ea|ten
un|eco|nomic
un|eco|nom|ical
un|em|ployed
un|em|ploy|
ment
un|equal
un|equalled
un|equi|vo|cal
un|equi|vo|cally
un|er|ring
un|even
un|event|ful
un|event|fully
un|ex|ampled
un|ex|cep|tion|
able
un|ex|cep|tional
un|fail|ing
un|fail|ingly
un|fair
un|fairly
un|fair|ness
un|faith|ful
un|fath|om|able

un|fa|vour|able
un|fa|vour|ably
un|feel|ing
un|fet|tered
'Un|fin|ished'
  Sym|phony
unfit
un|fit|ted
un|flap|pa|bil|ity
un|flap|pable
un|flap|pably
un|fledged
un|flinch|ing
un|fold
  △ un|folds
  △ un|fol|ded
  △ un|fold|ing
un|for|given
un|for|giv|ing
un|for|tu|nate
un|for|tu|nately
un|foun|ded
un|freeze
  △ un|free|zes
  △ un|froze
  △ un|freez|ing
  △ un|fro|zen
un|frock
  △ un|frocks
  △ un|frocked
  △ un|frock|ing
un|funny
un|furl
  △ un|furls
  △ un|furled
  △ un|furl|ing
un|gain|li|ness
un|gainly
  △ un|gain|lier
  △ un|gain|li|est
Un|gar|etti
un|god|li|ness
un|godly
un|gov|ern|able

un|guar|ded
un|guard|edly
un|guent
un|gu|late
un|hand
  △ un|hands
  △ un|han|ded
  △ un|hand|ing
un|hap|pily
un|hap|pi|ness
un|happy
un|health|ily
un|healthi|ness
un|healthy
un|heard
un|heard-of
un|help|ful
un|help|fully
un|hinge
  △ un|hin|ges
  △ un|hinged
  △ un|hin|ging
un|hinged
un|holy
un|horse
  △ un|hor|ses
  △ un|horsed
  △ un|hors|ing
uni
uni|cam|eral
uni|cel|lu|lar
uni|corn
uni|cy|cle
uni|cyc|list
un|iden|ti|fied
uni|fi|ca|tion
uni|form
uni|formed
uni|for|mi|tar|
  ian|ism
uni|form|ity
uni|formly
unify
  △ uni|fies

  △ uni|fied
  △ uni|fy|ing
uni|lat|eral
uni|lat|er|al|ism
uni|lat|er|al|ist
uni|lat|er|ally
un|im|peach|
  able
un|in|spired
un|in|spir|ing
un|in|ter|es|ted
union
uni|on|ism
uni|on|ist
uni|on|iza|tion
uni|on|ize
  △ uni|on|izes
  △ uni|on|ized
  △ uni|on|izing
Union Jack
unique
uniquely
unique|ness
uni|sex
uni|son
unit
Uni|tar|ian
Uni|tar|ian|ism
unit|ary
unite
  △ unites
  △ uni|ted
  △ uni|ting
uni|ted
Uni|ted Arab
  Emir|ates
Uni|ted King|
  dom
Unity
unity
  △ uni|ties
uni|va|lency
uni|va|lent
uni|ver|sal

uni|ver|sal|ity
uni|ver|sally
uni|verse
uni|ver|sity
  △ uni|ver|si|ties
uni|vo|calic
un|kempt
un|kind
  △ un|kinder
  △ un|kind|est
un|known
un|la|den
un|leaded
un|learn
  △ un|learns
  △ un|learnt or
  un|learned
  △ un|learn|ing
un|learned
un|learnt
un|leash
  △ un|lea|shes
  △ un|leashed
  △ un|leash|ing
un|leav|ened
un|less
un|let|tered
un|like
un|like|li|hood
un|like|li|ness
un|likely
un|lim|ited
un|lined
un|lis|ted
unlit
un|load
  △ un|loads
  △ un|loa|ded
  △ un|load|ing
un|lock
  △ un|locks
  △ un|locked
  △ un|lock|ing
un|looked-for

un|loose
△ un|loo|ses
△ un|loosed
△ un|loos|ing
un|loo|sen
△ un|loos|ens
△ un|loos|ened
△ un|loos|en|ing
un|loved
un|luck|ily
un|lucky
un|made
un|make
△ un|makes
△ un|made
△ un|ma|king
unman
△ un|mans
△ un|manned
△ un|man|ning
un|manned
un|man|ner|li|ness
un|man|nerly
un|mar|ried
un|mask
△ un|masks
△ un|masked
△ un|mask|ing
un|men|tion|able
un|mer|ci|ful
un|mis|tak|able
un|mis|tak|ably
un|mi|ti|ga|ted
un|moved
un|named
un|na|tural
un|na|tur|ally
un|nerve
△ un|nerves
△ un|nerved
△ un|ner|ving
un|ner|ving

un|nil|pen|tium
un|nil|qua|dium
un|nil|sep|tium
un|num|bered
un|ob|tru|sive
un|ob|tru|sively
un|pack
△ un|packs
△ un|packed
△ un|pack|ing
un|paid
un|pa|ral|leled
un|par|lia|ment|ary
un|per|son
un|pick
△ un|picks
△ un|picked
△ un|pick|ing
un|pleas|ant
un|pleas|antly
un|pleas|ant|ness
un|plug
△ un|plugs
△ un|plugged
△ un|plug|ging
un|pop|ular
un|popu|lar|ity
un|prac|ti|cal
un|prac|tised
un|pre|ce|den|ted
un|pre|pos|ses|sing
un|prin|cipled
un|print|able
un|pro|fes|sional
un|put|down|able
un|quali|fied
un|ques|tion|able
un|ques|tion|ably

un|ques|tion|ing
un|ques|tion|ingly
un|quiet
un|quote
un|ravel
△ un|rav|els
△ un|rav|elled
△ un|rav|el|ling
un|read
un|read|able
un|ready
un|real
un|re|al|ity
un|re|lent|ing
un|re|mit|ting
un|re|qui|ted
un|re|served
un|re|ser|vedly
un|rest
un|ri|valled
un|roll
△ un|rolls
△ un|rolled
△ un|roll|ing
un|ruf|fled
un|ru|li|ness
un|ruly
△ un|ru|lier
△ un|ru|li|est
un|saddle
△ un|saddles
△ un|saddled
△ un|sad|dling
un|safe
un|said
un|sat|ur|ated
un|sa|voury
unsay
△ un|says
△ un|said
△ un|say|ing
un|scathed
un|scram|ble
△ un|scram|bles

△ un|scram|bled
△ un|scram|bling
un|screw
△ un|screws
△ un|screwed
△ un|screw|ing
un|scru|pu|lous
un|sea|son|able
un|seat
△ un|seats
△ un|sea|ted
△ un|seat|ing
un|seem|li|ness
un|seemly
un|seen
un|self|ish
un|self|ishly
un|self|ish|ness
un|set|tle
△ un|set|tles
△ un|set|tled
△ un|set|tling
un|set|tled
un|shak|able
un|sight|li|ness
un|sightly
un|skilled
un|so|ciable
un|so|cial
un|sold
un|so|phis|ti|ca|ted
un|sound
un|spar|ing
un|speak|able
un|speak|ably
un|spent
un|sta|ble
un|stint|ing
un|stop
△ un|stops
△ un|stopped
△ un|stop|ping

un|stop|pable
un|strung
un|stuck
un|stud|ied
un|sung
un|sure
un|swer|ving
un|tamed
un|tan|gle
△ un|tan|gles
△ un|tan|gled
△ un|tan|gling
un|taxed
un|think|able
un|think|ing
un|throne
△ un|thrones
△ un|throned
△ un|thro|ning
un|ti|dily
un|tidy
VERB
△ un|ti|dies
△ un|ti|died
△ un|ti|dy|ing
ADJ.
△ un|ti|dier
△ un|ti|di|est
untie
△ un|ties
△ un|tied
△ un|ty|ing
until
un|time|li|ness
un|timely
unto
un|told
un|touch|able
un|to|ward
un|tried
un|true
un|truth
un|truth|ful
un|used

un|usual
un|usu|ally
un|ut|ter|able
un|var|nished
un|veil
△ un|veils
△ un|veiled
△ un|veil|ing
un|veil|ing
un|voiced
un|waged
un|well
un|wiel|di|ness
un|wieldy
un|will|ing
un|will|ingly
un|will|ing|ness
un|wind
△ un|winds
△ un|wound
△ un|wind|ing
un|wise
un|wisely
un|wit|ting
un|wit|tingly
un|won|ted
un|wound
un|writ|ten
unzip
△ un|zips
△ un|zipped
△ un|zip|ping
up
VERB
△ ups
△ upped
△ up|ping
up-and-com|ing
Upani|shad
up|beat
up|braid
△ up|braids
△ up|brai|ded
△ up|braid|ing

up|bring|ing
up-country
up|date
VERB
△ up|dates
△ up|da|ted
△ up|da|ting
Up|dike
up-end
△ up-ends
△ up-ended
△ up-end|ing
up|front
up|grade
△ up|grades
△ up|gra|ded
△ up|gra|ding
up|heaval
up|held
Up-Helly-Aa
up|hill
up|hold
△ up|holds
△ up|held
△ up|hold|ing
up|hol|ster
△ up|hol|sters
△ up|hol|stered
△ up|hol|ster|ing
up|hol|stered
up|hol|sterer
up|hol|stery
up|keep
up|land
up|lift
VERB
△ up|lifts
△ up|lif|ted
△ up|lift|ing
up|lift|ing
up|load
△ up|loads
△ up|loa|ded
△ up|load|ing

up-mar|ket
up|most
upon
upper
up|per|cut
up|per|most
up|pish
up|pity
Upp|sala
up|right
up|ri|sing
up|roar
up|roari|ous
up|roari|ously
up|root
△ up|roots
△ up|roo|ted
△ up|root|ing
ups-a-daisy
up|scale
upset
VERB
△ up|sets
△ upset
△ up|set|ting
up|set|ting
up|shot

up|side
NOUN
⚠ upsides

up|sides
ADJ.
⚠ upside

up|stage
VERB
△ up|sta|ges
△ up|staged
△ up|sta|ging
up|stairs
up|stand|ing
up|start
up|stream

up|surge
upsy-daisy *see*
  ups-a-daisy
up|take
up|thrust
up|tight
up|turn
  VERB
  △ up|turns
  △ up|turned
  △ up|turn|ing
up|ward
up|wardly
up|wind
ura|cil
ur|ae|mia
Ural
Ur|alic
ur|an|in|ite
ur|an|ium
Ur|anus
Urban
urban
ur|bane
ur|ban|ity
ur|ban|iza|tion
ur|ban|ize
  △ ur|ban|izes
  △ ur|ban|ized
  △ ur|ban|izing
ur|chin
Urdu
urea
ur|eter

ur|ethra
  △ ur|eth|ras *or*
    ur|eth|rae
ur|eth|ri|tis
urge
  VERB
  △ urges
  △ urged
  △ ur|ging
ur|gency
  △ ur|gen|cies
ur|gent
ur|gently
uric
uri|nal
ur|in|ary
ur|in|ate
  △ ur|in|ates
  △ ur|in|ated
  △ ur|in|ating
ur|in|ation
urine
urn
ur|ol|ogy
urs|ine
Ur|sula
Ur|su|line
Uru|guay
us
us|able
usage
use
  VERB
  △ uses

△ used
△ using
used
use|ful
use|fully
use|ful|ness
use|less
use|lessly
use|less|ness
user
user-friendly
usher
  VERB
  △ ush|ers
  △ ush|ered
  △ ush|er|ing
ush|er|ette
Us|ti|nov
usual
usu|ally
us|urer
us|uri|ous
usurp
  △ usurps
  △ usurped
  △ usurp|ing
usur|pa|tion
usur|per
usury
Utah
uten|sil
uter|ine
uterus
  △ uteri

util|it|ar|ian
util|it|ar|ian|ism
util|ity
  △ util|it|ies
util|iza|tion
util|ize
  △ util|izes
  △ util|ized
  △ util|izing
ut|most
Uto|pia
uto|pia
uto|pian
Utrecht
utricle
Utrillo
utter
  VERB
  △ ut|ters
  △ ut|tered
  △ ut|ter|ing
ut|ter|ance
ut|terly
ut|ter|most
Ut|tley
U-turn
uvula
  △ uvu|las *or*
    uvu|lae
uvu|lar
ux|ori|ous
Uz|bek|is|tan

V

vac
va|cancy
  △ va|can|cies
va|cant
va|cantly
va|cate
  △ va|cates
  △ va|ca|ted
  △ va|ca|ting
va|ca|tion
  VERB
  △ va|ca|tions
  △ va|ca|tioned
  △ va|ca|tion|ing
vac|cin|ate
  △ vac|cin|ates
  △ vac|cin|ated
  △ vac|cin|ating
vac|cin|ation
vac|cine
va|cil|late
  △ va|cil|lates
  △ va|cil|la|ted
  △ va|cil|la|ting
va|cil|la|tion
va|cu|ity
  △ va|cu|it|ies
va|cu|ole
va|cu|ous
va|cu|ously
va|cuum
  NOUN
  in technical
  senses
  △ vacua
  other senses
  △ va|cu|ums
  VERB
  △ va|cu|ums
  △ va|cu|umed
  △ va|cu|um|ing
va|cuum-packed

vade-mecum
Vadim
Vaduz
va|ga|bond
va|gary
  △ va|gar|ies
va|gina
va|gi|nal
va|gin|is|mus
vag|rancy
vag|rant
vague
  △ va|guer
  △ va|guest
va|guely
vague|ness
vagus
  △ vagi

> **vain**
> *arrogant; futile*
> △ vai|ner
> △ vain|est
> ⚠ vane
> ⚠ vein

vain|glori|ous
vain|glory
vainly

> **val|lance**
> *fabric strip*
> ⚠ valence

> **vale**
> *valley*
> ⚠ veil

va|le|dic|tion
va|le|dict|ory

> **va|lence**
> *atom's combining*
> *power*
> ⚠ valance

Va|len|cia

va|lency
  △ va|len|cies
Val|en|tine
val|en|tine
Val|en|tino
val|er|ian
Val|erie
valet
  VERB
  △ val|ets
  △ val|eted
  △ val|et|ing
valeta *see* veleta
Valetta *see*
  Valletta
va|le|tu|din|ar|ian
Val|halla
va|li|ant
va|li|antly
valid
val|id|ate
  △ val|id|ates
  △ val|id|ated
  △ val|id|ating
val|id|ation
va|lid|ity
va|line
va|lise
Val|ium
Val|ky|rie
Val|la|dolid
Val|letta
val|ley
val|or|ous
val|our
Val|par|aíso
va|lu|able
va|lu|ably
va|lu|ation
value
  VERB
  △ val|ues
  △ val|ued
  △ va|lu|ing

val|ued
val|ue|less
val|uer
valve
val|vu|lar
va|moose
  △ va|moo|ses
  △ va|moosed
  △ va|moos|ing
vamp
  VERB
  △ vamps
  △ vamped
  △ vamp|ing
vam|pire
van
va|na|dium
Van Allen
Van|brugh
Vance
Van|cou|ver
Van|dal
  member of
  ancient
  Germanic tribe;
  of this tribe
van|dal
  destructive
  hooligan
van|dal|ism
van|dal|ize
  △ van|dal|izes
  △ van|dal|ized
  △ van|dal|izing
Van|der|bilt
Van der Post

> **vane**
> *weathervane;*
> *blade of*
> *propeller etc*
> ⚠ vain
> ⚠ vein

Van|essa

Van Eyck
Van Gogh
van|guard
va|nilla
van|ish
△ van|ishes
△ van|ished
△ van|ish|ing
van|ity
△ van|it|ies
Van|ity Fair
novel by
Thackeray
Van|ity Fair
place in
Bunyan's
Pilgrim's
Progress
van|quish
△ van|qui|shes
△ van|quished
△ van|quish|ing
vant|age
Va|nu|atu
vapid
va|pid|ity
va|por|iza|tion
va|por|ize
△ va|por|izes
△ va|por|ized
△ va|por|izing
va|pour
Var|èse
vari|ab|il|ity
vari|able
vari|ably
vari|ance
vari|ant
vari|ation
vari|col|oured
va|ri|cose
var|ied
vari|ega|ted
vari|ega|tion

va|ri|ety
△ va|ri|et|ies
vari|ous
vari|ously
var|let
var|mint
var|nish
NOUN
△ var|ni|shes
VERB
△ var|ni|shes
△ var|nished
△ var|nish|ing
Varro
var|sity
△ var|sit|ies
vary
△ var|ies
△ var|ied
△ vary|ing
vary|ing
vary|ingly
vas
△ vasa
vas|cu|lar
vas de|fer|ens
△ vasa de|fer|en|
tia
vase
vas|ec|tomy
△ vas|ec|tom|ies
Va|sel|ine
va|so|con|stric|tor
va|so|di|la|tor
va|so|pres|sin
vas|sal
vas|sal|age
vast
△ vas|ter
△ vast|est
vastly
vast|ness
VAT
tax

vat
large tank
Vat|ican
vat|man
△ vat|men
vau|de|ville
Vaughan
Vaughan Wil|liams
vault
VERB
△ vaults
△ vaul|ted
△ vault|ing
vault|ing
vault|ing-horse
vaunt
VERB
△ vaunts
△ vaun|ted
△ vaunt|ing
vaunt|ingly
veal
vec|tor
Veda
Ve|danta
Vedic
ve|duta
△ ve|dute
veer
VERB
△ veers
△ veered
△ veer|ing
veg
Vega
vegan
ve|gan|ism
vege|bur|ger
ve|get|able
ve|getal
ve|get|ar|ian
ve|get|ar|ian|ism
ve|get|ate
△ ve|get|ates

△ ve|get|ated
△ ve|get|ating
ve|get|ation
ve|get|at|ive
veg|gie
ve|hem|ence
ve|hem|ent
ve|hem|ently
vehi|cle
ve|hic|ular

veil
covering for woman's
face or head; thing
that covers or hides;
cover with these
VERB
△ veils
△ veiled
△ veil|ing
⚠ vale

vein
blood vessel;
thin layer; tone
⚠ vain
⚠ vane

veined
veiny
△ vein|ier
△ veini|est
Ve|láz|quez
Vel|cro
veld
ve|leta
vel|lum
ve|lo|city
△ ve|lo|ci|ties
ve|lour
vel|vet
vel|vet|een
vel|vety
vena cava
△ venae cavae

---

venal
bribable
⚠ venial

ve|nal|ity
ve|nally
ven|ation
vend
△ vends
△ ven|ded
△ vend|ing
ven|dee

---

ven|der
seller of goods in market etc
⚠ vendor

---

ven|detta

---

ven|dor
seller of house etc
⚠ vender

---

ven|eer
VERB
△ ven|eers
△ ven|eered
△ ven|eer|ing
ven|er|able
ven|er|ate
△ ven|er|ates
△ ven|er|ated
△ ven|er|ating
ven|er|ation
ven|er|eal
Ven|etia
Ven|etian
Ven|ez|uela
ven|geance
venge|ful

---

ve|nial
forgivable
⚠ venal

---

ve|ni|al|ity
Ven|ice
*Ven|ice Pre|
serv'd, or a
Plot Dis|cov|
ered*
ven|ison
venom
ven|om|ous
ve|nous
vent
VERB
△ vents
△ ven|ted
△ vent|ing
ven|ti|late
△ ven|ti|lates
△ ven|ti|la|ted
△ ven|ti|la|ting
ven|ti|la|tion
ven|ti|la|tor
Vent|nor
vent|ral
vent|rally
vent|ricle
ven|tric|ular
ven|tri|lo|quism
ven|tri|lo|quist
ven|tri|lo|quize
△ ven|tri|lo|qui|
zes
△ ven|tri|lo|
quized
△ ven|tri|lo|qui|
zing
ven|ture
VERB
△ ven|tures
△ ven|tured
△ ven|tur|ing
ven|turer
ven|ture|some
venue
ven|ule

Venus
Vera
ver|aci|ous

---

ver|ac|ity
truthfulness
⚠ voracity

---

ver|anda
verb
ver|bal
ver|bal|ism
ver|bal|ize
△ ver|bal|izes
△ ver|bal|ized
△ ver|bal|izing
verb|ally
ver|ba|tim
ver|bena
ver|bi|age
ver|bose
ver|bos|ity
verd|ancy
verd|ant
Verdi
ver|dict
ver|di|gris
ver|dure
verge
VERB
△ ver|ges
△ verged
△ ver|ging
ver|ger
veri|fi|able
veri|fi|ca|tion
ver|ify
△ veri|fies
△ veri|fied
△ veri|fy|ing
ver|ily
veri|sim|ili|tude
ver|it|able
ver|it|ably
Ver|ity

---

ver|ity
△ ver|it|ies
*Ver|klärte
Nacht (Trans|
fig|ured Night)*
Ver|laine
Ver|meer
ver|mi|celli
ver|mi|form
ver|mil|ion
ver|min
ver|min|ous
ver|mouth
ver|nacu|lar
ver|nal
ver|nal|iza|tion
ver|nally
Verne
ver|nier
Ver|non
Ver|ona
Ver|on|ese
Ver|on|ica
ver|on|ica
Ver|roc|chio
ver|ruca
△ ver|ru|cas *or*
ver|ru|cae
Ver|sailles
ver|sa|tile
ver|sa|til|ity
verse
versed
ver|si|fi|ca|tion
ver|si|fier
ver|sify
△ ver|si|fies
△ ver|si|fied
△ ver|si|fy|ing
ver|sion
verso
ver|sus
ver|tebra
△ ver|teb|rae

ver|teb|ral
ver|teb|rate

ver|tex
peak; tip
△ ver|texes *or*
ver|ti|ces
⚠ vortex

ver|ti|cal
ver|tic|ally
ver|ti|gin|ous
ver|tigo
Ve|ru|la|mium
ver|vain
verve
Ver|woerd
very
Very light
Ve|sa|lius
ve|si|cle
Ves|pa|sian
ves|pers
Ves|pucci
ves|sel
vest
   VERB
   △ vests
   △ ves|ted
   △ vest|ing
ves|tal
ves|ti|bule
ves|tige
ves|ti|gial
vest|ment
vestry
   △ vest|ries
Ve|su|vius
vet
   VERB
   △ vets
   △ vet|ted
   △ vet|ting
vetch
   △ vet|ches

vet|eran
vet|er|in|ar|ian
vet|er|in|ary
   NOUN
   △ vet|er|in|ar|ies
veto
   NOUN
   △ ve|toes
   VERB
   △ ve|toes
   △ ve|toed
   △ ve|to|ing
vex
   △ vexes
   △ vexed
   △ vex|ing
vex|ation
vex|atious
vexed
vex|ing
via
vi|ab|il|ity
vi|able
via|duct
vial
viands
vi|at|icum
   △ vi|at|ic|ums *or*
   vi|at|ica
vibes
vi|brancy
vi|brant
vi|brantly
vi|bra|phone
vi|bra|pho|nist
vi|brate
   △ vi|brates
   △ vi|bra|ted
   △ vi|bra|ting
vi|bra|tion
vi|brato
vi|bra|tor
vi|bra|tory
vicar

vic|ar|age
vicar-apos|tolic
vicar-gen|eral
vi|car|ial
vi|car|ious
*Vicar of Wake|
field*
vice
vice-chan|cel|lor
vice|ger|ency
vice|ger|ent
vice|regal
vice|roy
vice|roy|alty
vice|roy|ship
vice versa
Vichy
vi|cin|ity
   △ vi|cin|it|ies
vi|cious
vi|ciously
vi|cious|ness
vi|cis|si|tude
vic|tim
vic|tim|iza|tion
vic|tim|ize
   △ vic|tim|izes
   △ vic|tim|ized
   △ vic|tim|izing
Vic|tor
vic|tor
Vic|tor Em|
man|uel
Vic|toria
vic|toria
Vic|tor|ian
Vic|tori|ana
vic|tori|ous
Vic|tory, HMS
vic|tory
   △ vic|tor|ies
vic|tual
   VERB
   △ vic|tuals

   △ vic|tualled
   △ vic|tual|ling
vic|tual|ler
vi|cuña
Vidal
vide
vi|de|li|cet
video
   VERB
   △ vid|eos
   △ vid|eoed
   △ vid|eo|ing
vi|deo|cas|sette
vi|deo|tape
vi|deo|text
vie
   △ vies
   △ vied
   △ vying
Vi|enna
Vi|en|ti|ane
Viet Cong
Viet Minh
Viet|nam
Viet|nam|ese
view
   VERB
   △ views
   △ viewed
   △ view|ing
view|data
viewer
view|finder
*View from the
Bridge, A*
view|ing
view|point
vigil
vi|gil|ance

vi|gil|ant
watchful
⚠ vigilante

vi|gi|lante
*self-appointed
enforcer of law
and order*
⚠ vigilant

vign|ette
vig|or|ous
vig|or|ously
vig|our
vi|king
Vila *see* Port-
Vila
vile
△ viler
△ vi|lest
vi|li|fi|ca|tion
vil|ify
△ vili|fies
△ vili|fied
△ vili|fy|ing
villa
vil|lage
Vil|lage, The
vil|la|ger

vil|lain
wicked person
⚠ villein

vil|lain|ous
vil|lainy
△ vil|lain|ies
Villa-Lobos

vil|lein
feudal peasant
⚠ villain

vil|lein|age
Vil|lon
vil|lus
△ villi
Vil|nius
vim
Vimy

vi|nai|grette
Vin|cent
vin|di|cate
△ vin|di|cates
△ vin|di|ca|ted
△ vin|di|ca|ting
vin|di|ca|tion
vin|di|ca|tory
vin|dict|ive
vin|dict|ively
vin|dict|ive|ness
vine
vin|egar
vin|eg|ary
vine|yard
vingt-et-un
vi|ni|cul|ture
vi|ni|cul|tur|ist
Vín|land
vino
vi|nous
vin|tage
vint|ner
vinyl
viol
viola
vi|ol|ate
△ vi|ol|ates
△ vi|ol|ated
△ vi|ol|ating
vi|ol|ation
vi|ol|ator
vi|ol|ence
vi|ol|ent
vi|ol|ently
vi|olet
vio|lin
vio|lin|ist
viol|ist
Viol|let-Le-
Duc
vio|lon|cel|list
vio|lon|cello
viper

vi|rago
△ vi|ra|goes *or*
vi|ra|gos
viral
Vir|gil
vir|gin
vir|ginal
Vir|ginia
Vir|gini|ans, The
vir|gin|ity
Virgo
vir|ile
vi|ril|ity
viro|lo|gi|cal
vir|ol|ogy
vir|tual
vir|tu|ally
vir|tue
vir|tu|os|ity
vir|tu|oso
vir|tu|ous
vir|tu|ously
vi|ru|lence
vi|ru|lent
virus
△ vir|uses
visa
vis|age
vis-à-vis
NOUN
sing. and pl.
vis|ca|cha
vis|cera
vis|ceral
vis|cid
Vis|conti
vis|cose
vis|cos|ity
vis|count
vis|countcy
△ vis|count|cies
vis|count|ess
△ vis|count|es|
ses

vis|count|ship

vis|cous
*sticky; semi-
liquid*
⚠ viscus

vis|cus
*large internal
bodily organ*
△ vis|cera
⚠ viscous

Vishnu
vi|si|bil|ity
vis|ible
vis|ibly
Vi|si|goth
vi|sion
vi|sion|ary
NOUN
△ vi|sion|ar|ies
visit
VERB
△ vis|its
△ vis|ited
△ vis|it|ing
vis|it|ant
vi|si|ta|tion
vis|it|ing-card
vis|itor
visor
vista
vis|ual
vi|su|al|iza|tion
vi|su|al|ize
△ vi|su|al|izes
△ vi|su|al|ized
△ vi|su|al|izing
vi|su|ally
vital
vi|tal|ity
vi|tal|iza|tion
vi|tal|ize
△ vi|tal|izes

△ vi|tal|ized
△ vi|tal|izing
vi|tally
vi|ta|min *or* vit|
 amin
 according to
 pronunciation
Vitez
vi|ti|ate
 △ vi|ti|ates
 △ vi|ti|ated
 △ vi|ti|ating
vi|ti|ation
vi|ti|cul|ture
vit|re|ous
vit|ri|fi|ca|tion
vit|ri|fied
vit|rify
 △ vit|ri|fies
 △ vit|ri|fied
 △ vit|ri|fy|ing
vit|riol
vit|ri|olic
Vi|tru|vius
vi|tu|per|ate
 △ vi|tu|per|ates
 △ vi|tu|per|ated
 △ vi|tu|per|ating
vi|tu|per|ation
vi|tu|per|ative
viva
 VERB
 △ vivas
 △ vivaed
 △ viva|ing
vivace
vi|va|cious
vi|va|ciously
vi|va|city
Vi|valdi
vi|var|ium
 △ vi|vari|ums *or*
 vi|varia
viva voce

NOUN
 △ viva voces
Viv|ian
vivid
viv|idly
viv|id|ness
vi|vi|par|ity
vi|vi|par|ous
vi|vi|sect
 △ vi|vi|sects
 △ vi|vi|sec|ted
 △ vi|vi|sect|ing
vi|vi|sec|tion
vi|vi|sec|tion|ist
vixen
viz
vi|zier *or* viz|ier
 according to
 pronunciation
V-neck
V-necked
vocab
vo|cable
vo|ca|bu|lary
 △ vo|ca|bu|lar|
 ies
vocal
vo|cal|ist
vo|cal|iza|tion
vo|cal|ize
 △ vo|cal|izes
 △ vo|cal|ized
 △ vo|cal|izing
vo|cally
vo|ca|tion
vo|ca|tional
vo|ca|tion|ally
voc|at|ive
vo|ci|fer|ate
 △ vo|ci|fer|ates
 △ vo|ci|fer|ated
 △ vo|ci|fer|ating
vo|ci|fer|ous
vo|ci|fer|ously

vo|ci|fer|ous|
 ness
Vo|da|fone
vodka
vogue
voice
 VERB
 △ voi|ces
 △ voiced
 △ voi|cing
voice-box
 △ voice-boxes
voiced
voice|less
voice-over
void
 VERB
 △ voids
 △ voi|ded
 △ void|ing
voile
voi|vod|ship
vola|tile
vola|til|ity
vola|til|iza|tion
vo|lat|il|ize
 △ vo|lat|il|izes
 △ vo|lat|il|ized
 △ vo|lat|il|izing
vol-au-vent
vol|canic
vol|cano
 △ vol|ca|noes
vole
Volga
vo|li|tion
vo|li|tional
Volks|wa|gen
vol|ley
 VERB
 △ vol|leys
 △ vol|leyed
 △ vol|ley|ing
vol|ley|ball

Vol|pone, or The
 Fox
Vol|sun|ga|saga
volt
volt|age
Vol|taire
volte-face
volt|meter
volu|bil|ity
vol|uble
vol|ubly
vol|ume
volu|met|ric
vo|lu|min|ous
vol|un|tar|ily
vol|un|tary
 NOUN
 △ vol|un|tar|ies
vol|un|teer
 VERB
 △ vol|un|teers
 △ vol|un|teered
 △ vol|un|teer|ing
vo|lup|tu|ary
 NOUN
 △ vo|lup|tu|ar|
 ies
vo|lup|tu|ous
vo|lup|tu|ously
vo|lup|tu|ous|
 ness
vo|lute
vomit
 VERB
 △ vom|its
 △ vom|ited
 △ vom|it|ing
Von|ne|gut
Von Stern|berg
voo|doo
 VERB
 △ voo|doos
 △ voo|dooed
 △ voo|doo|ing

Voor|trek|ker
vor|acious
vor|aciously

vor|acity
greed; eagerness
⚠ veracity

Vor|ster

vor|tex
whirlpool
△ vor|texes *or*
vor|ti|ces
⚠ vertex

vor|ti|cal
Vor|ti|cism
Vor|ti|gern
vo|tary
△ vo|tar|ies
vote

VERB
△ votes
△ vo|ted
△ vo|ting
voter
vo|tive
vouch
△ vou|ches
△ vouched
△ vouch|ing
vou|cher
vouch|safe
△ vouch|safes
△ vouch|safed
△ vouch|sa|fing
vous|soir
VERB
△ vous|soirs
△ vous|soired
△ vous|soir|ing
VOW

VERB
△ vows
△ vowed
△ vow|ing
vowel
vox pop
vox pop|uli
voy|age
VERB
△ voy|ages
△ voy|aged
△ voy|aging
Voy|ager
voy|ager
voy|eur
voy|eur|ism
voy|eur|is|tic
V-sign
Vul|can
vul|can|ite
vul|can|iza|tion

vul|can|ize
△ vul|can|izes
△ vul|can|ized
△ vul|can|izing
vul|gar
vul|gar|ism
vul|gar|ity
△ vul|gar|it|ies
vul|gar|iza|tion
vul|gar|ize
△ vul|gar|izes
△ vul|gar|ized
△ vul|gar|izing
vul|garly
Vul|gate
vul|ner|ab|il|ity
vul|ner|able
vul|pine
vul|ture
vulva
vying

W

Wace
wacky
  △ wack|ier
  △ wacki|est
wad
wad|ding
wad|dle
  VERB
  △ wad|dles
  △ wad|dled
  △ wad|dling
wade
  △ wades
  △ waded
  △ wa|ding
wader
wadi
Wafd
wafer
waf|fle
  VERB
  △ waf|fles
  △ waf|fled
  △ waf|fling
waf|fler
waft
  VERB
  △ wafts
  △ waf|ted
  △ waft|ing
wag
  VERB
  △ wags
  △ wagged
  △ wag|ging
wage
  VERB
  △ wages
  △ waged
  △ wa|ging
wager

VERB
  △ wa|gers
  △ wa|gered
  △ wa|ger|ing
wag|gish
wag|gle
  VERB
  △ wag|gles
  △ wag|gled
  △ wag|gling
Wag|ner
wagon
wag|oner
Wah|habi
waif
waif-like
wail
  VERB
  △ wails
  △ wailed
  △ wail|ing
Wain
wains|cot
wains|cot|ing

waist
  *part of human
  body between
  ribs and hips*
  ⚠ waste

waist|band
waist|coat

wait
  *pause until
  expected event
  occurs*
  VERB
  △ waits
  △ wai|ted
  △ wait|ing
  ⚠ weight

Waite
wai|ter

*Wait|ing for
  Godot (En At|
  tend|ant
  Godot)*
wait|ing-list
wait|ing-room
wait|ress
  △ wait|res|ses

waive
  forgo
  △ waives
  △ waived
  △ waiv|ing
  ⚠ wave

wai|ver
Wajda
wake
  VERB
  △ wakes
  △ woke
  △ wa|king
  △ woken
Wake|field
wake|ful
wake|fully
waken
  △ wa|kens
  △ wa|kened
  △ wa|ken|ing
Walachia *see*
  Wallachia
Wal|cott
Wal|den
Wal|den|ses
Wal|den|sian
Wald|heim
Wald|ster|ben

wale
  *ridge on skin or
  cloth; planks at
  top of ship's side*
  ⚠ whale

Wales
Wa|esa
walk
  VERB
  △ walks
  △ walked
  △ walk|ing
walk|about
walker
walkie-talkie
walk|ing
walk|ing-stick
Walk|man
walk-on
walk|out
walk|over
*Wal|ku|re, Die
  (The Val|ky|
  rie)*
walk|way
wall
  VERB
  △ walls
  △ walled
  △ wall|ing
wal|laby
  △ wal|la|bies
Wal|lace
Wal|la|chia
wal|lah
Wal|la|sey
wall|bar
Wal|ler
wal|let
wall|eye
wall|eyed
wall|flower
Wal|lo|nia
Wal|loon
wal|lop
  VERB
  △ wal|lops
  △ wal|loped
  △ wal|lop|ing

wal|lop|ing
wal|low
△ wal|lows
△ wal|lowed
△ wal|low|ing
wall|pa|per
VERB
△ wall|pa|pers
△ wall|pa|pered
△ wall|pa|per|ing
Walls|end
wall-to-wall
wally
△ wal|lies
wal|nut
Wal|pole
wal|rus
△ wal|ruses *or*
wal|rus
Wal|rus and the
Car|pen|ter, The
Wal|sall
Wal|sing|ham
Wal|ter
Wal|ton
waltz
NOUN
△ waltzes
VERB
△ waltzes
△ waltzed
△ waltz|ing
wam|pum
wan
△ wan|ner
△ wan|nest
wand
wan|der
VERB
△ wan|ders
△ wan|dered
△ wan|der|ing
wan|derer
wan|der|lust

wane
VERB
△ wanes
△ waned
△ wa|ning
wan|gle
VERB
△ wan|gles
△ wan|gled
△ wang|ling
wank
VERB
△ wanks
△ wanked
△ wank|ing
Wan|kel
wan|ker
wanly
wan|nabe
wan|ness
want
VERB
△ wants
△ wan|ted
△ want|ing

wanted
needed; sought
for
⚠ wonted

want|ing
wan|ton
VERB
△ wan|tons
△ wan|toned
△ wan|ton|ing
wan|tonly
wan|ton|ness
wap|iti
war
VERB
△ wars
△ warred
△ war|ring

War and Peace
War|beck
war|ble
VERB
△ war|bles
△ war|bled
△ warb|ling
warb|ler
War|burg
ward
VERB
△ wards
△ war|ded
△ ward|ing
war|den
War|den, The
war|der
ward|ress
△ ward|res|ses
ward|robe
ward|room

ware
thing sold; type
of pottery etc
⚠ wear

ware|house
war|fare
war|farin
war|head
War|hol
war|horse
war|ily
wari|ness
war|like
war|lock
war|lord
warm
VERB
△ warms
△ warmed
△ warm|ing
ADJ.
△ war|mer

△ warm|est
warm-blooded
warm-hearted
warm|ing-pan
warmly
war|mon|ger
warmth
warm-up
warn
△ warns
△ warned
△ warn|ing
War|ner
warn|ing
warn|ingly
war|nog|ra|phy
War of the
Worlds, The
warp
VERB
△ warps
△ warped
△ warp|ing
war|paint
war|path
war|rant
VERB
△ war|rants
△ war|ran|ted
△ war|rant|ing
war|rant|able
war|ran|tor
war|ranty
△ war|rant|ies
War|ren
war|ren
War Re|quiem
War|ring|ton
war|rior
War|rior, HMS
War|saw
war|ship
wart
wart|hog

war|time
War|wick
War|wick|shire
wary
 △ war|ier
 △ wari|est
was
wash
 NOUN
 △ wa|shes
 VERB
 △ wa|shes
 △ washed
 △ wash|ing
Wash, The
wash|able
wash|ba|sin
wash|cloth
washed-out
washed-up
washer
wash|er|wo|man
 △ wash|er|wo|
 men
wash|hand
wash|house
wash|ing
wash|ing-
 machine
wash|ing-pow|
 der
Wash|ing|ton
*Wash|ing|ton
 Square*
wash|ing-up
wash|out
wash|room
wash|stand
washy
 △ wash|ier
 △ washi|est
wasn't
wasp
wasp|ish

Wasps, The
wasp-wais|ted
was|sail
wast
wast|age

> waste
> *squander; not
> wanted;
> abandoned or
> devastated area*
> VERB
> △ wastes
> △ wasted
> △ wast|ing
> ⚠ waist

waste|ful
waste|land
*Waste Land,
 The*
waster
wast|rel
watch
 NOUN
 △ wat|ches
 VERB
 △ wat|ches
 △ watched
 △ watch|ing
watch|dog
watch|ful
watch|fully
watch|ful|ness
watch|ma|ker
watch|man
 △ watch|men
watch|night
watch|tower
watch|word
water
 VERB
 △ wa|ters
 △ wa|tered
 △ wa|ter|ing

*Water-Babies,
 The*
wa|ter|borne
Wa|ter-car|rier
wa|ter|col|our
wa|ter-col|our|ist
wa|ter-cooled
wa|ter|course
wa|ter|cress
 △ wa|ter|cres|ses
wa|ter-divi|ner
wa|ter|fall
Wa|ter|ford
wa|ter|fowl
wa|ter|front
Wa|ter|gate
wa|ter|glass
wa|ter|hole
wa|ter|ing-can
wa|ter|ing-hole
wa|ter|ing-place
wa|ter|line
wa|ter|logged
Wa|ter|loo
wa|ter|mark
 VERB
 △ wa|ter|marks
 △ wa|ter|marked
 △ wa|ter|mark|ing
wa|ter|mill
Water Music
wa|ter|proof
 VERB
 △ wa|ter|proofs
 △ wa|ter|proofed
 △ wa|ter|proof|
 ing
wa|ter|shed
wa|ter|side
wa|ter-ski
 △ wa|ter-skis
 △ wa|ter-skied
 or wa|ter-ski'd
 △ wa|ter-ski|ing

wa|ter-ski|ing
wa|ter-soft|ener
wa|ter|spout
wa|ter|tight
wa|ter|way
wa|ter|wheel
wa|ter|works
wa|tery
Wat|ford
Watt
watt
wat|tage
Wat|teau
wattle
watt|meter
Waugh

> wave
> *moving ridge of
> water, air, etc;
> move hand as
> signal etc*
> VERB
> △ waves
> △ waved
> △ wa|ving
> ⚠ waive

wave|band
wave|length
waver
 △ wa|vers
 △ wa|vered
 △ wa|ver|ing
Wa|ver|ley
wavy
 △ wa|vier
 △ wa|vi|est
wax
 NOUN
 △ waxes
 VERB
 △ waxes
 △ waxed
 △ wax|ing

waxen
wax|wing
wax|work
waxy
△ wax|ier
△ waxi|est

> **way**
> *route; manner*
> ⚠ weigh

way|bill
way|farer
way|far|ing
Way|land
way|lay
△ way|lays
△ way|laid
△ way|lay|ing
way|leave
Wayne
*Way of All
   Flesh, The*
*Way of the
   World, The*
way-out
way|side
way|ward
wazir
we

> **weak**
> *not strong*
> △ wea|ker
> △ weak|est
> ⚠ week

wea|ken
△ weak|ens
△ weak|ened
△ weak|en|ing
weak-kneed
weak|ling
weak-minded
weak|ness
△ weak|nes|ses

weal
Weald
wealth
wealthy
△ wealth|ier
△ wealthi|est
wean
VERB
△ weans
△ weaned
△ wean|ing
weapon
weap|onry

> **wear**
> *clothes; use;
> damage caused
> by use; be
> dressed in;
> become or make
> broken or
> dispirited*
> VERB
> △ wears
> △ wore
> △ wear|ing
> △ worn
> ⚠ ware

wear|able
wearer
wear|ily
weari|ness
wear|ing
weari|some
weary
VERB
△ wear|ies
△ wear|ied
△ weary|ing
ADJ.
△ wear|ier
△ weari|est
wea|sel
wea|ther

VERB
△ weath|ers
△ weath|ered
△ weath|er|ing
weath|er|bea|ten
weath|er|board
weath|er|cock
weath|er|ing
weath|er|man
△ weath|er|men
weath|er|proof
weath|er|vane
weave
VERB
△ weaves
△ wove
△ weav|ing
△ woven
wea|ver
wea|ver|bird
web
Webb
webbed
web|bing
Weber
weber
We|bern
web-footed
Web|ster
web-toed
wed
△ weds
△ wed|ded *or* wed
△ wed|ding
we'd
wed|ded
Wed|dell
wed|ding
We|de|kind
wedge
VERB
△ wed|ges
△ wedged
△ wed|ging

Wedg|wood
wed|lock
Wed|nes|day
wee
VERB
△ wees
△ weed
△ wee|ing
ADJ.
△ weer
△ weest
weed
VERB
△ weeds
△ wee|ded
△ weed|ling
weed|kil|ler
weedy
△ wee|dier
△ wee|di|est

> **week**
> *seven days*
> ⚠ weak

week|day
week|end
weekly
NOUN
△ week|lies
weeny
△ wee|nier
△ wee|ni|est
weep
VERB
△ weeps
△ wept
△ weep|ling
weep|ing
weepy
NOUN
△ weep|ies
ADJ.
△ wee|pier
△ wee|pi|est

wee|vil
wee-wee
  VERB
  △ wee-wees
  △ wee-weed
  △ wee-wee|ing
weft

> weigh
> *find weight of*
> △ weighs
> △ weighed
> △ weigh|ing
> ⚠ way

weigh|bridge
weigh-in

> weight
> *heaviness; add*
> *weight or bias to*
> VERB
> △ weights
> △ weigh|ted
> △ weight|ing
> ⚠ wait

weight|ing
weight|less
weight|less|ness
weight|lif|ter
we:ght|lift|ing
weight-train|ing
weighty
  △ weigh|tier
  △ weigh|ti|est

> Weil
> *French*
> *philosopher*
> ⚠ Weill

> Weill
> *German*
> *composer*
> ⚠ Weil

Wei|mar
weir
weird
  △ weir|der
  △ weird|est
weirdly
weird|ness
weirdo
Weiss|mul|ler
Weiz|mann

> Welch
> *used only in the*
> *names of certain*
> *Welsh regiments*
> ⚠ Welsh

welch *see* Welsh
wel|come
  VERB
  △ wel|comes
  △ wel|comed
  △ wel|com|ing
weld
  VERB
  △ welds
  △ wel|ded
  △ weld|ing
wel|der
wel|fare
well
  VERB
  △ wells
  △ welled
  △ well|ing
  ADJ.
  △ bet|ter
  △ best
  ADV.
  △ bet|ter
  △ best
we'll
well|be|ing
Welles
well|head

Wel|ling|ton
wel|ling|ton
well-knit
well-known
well-nigh
well-off
Wells
well|spring
Well-Tem|pered
  Clav|ier, The
  (Das Wohl|tem|
  per|irte Kla|vier)
well-to-do
well-wisher
welly
  △ wel|lies

> Welsh
> *of Wales*
> ⚠ Welch

welsh
  △ wel|shes
  △ welshed
  △ welsh|ing
Welsh|man
  △ Welsh|men
Welsh|wo|man
  △ Welsh|wo|
    men
welt
  VERB
  △ welts
  △ wel|ted
  △ welt|ing
wel|ter
  VERB
  △ wel|ters
  △ wel|tered
  △ wel|ter|ing
wel|ter|weight
wel|wits|chia
Wel|wyn
Wem|bley
wen

Wen|ces|laus
wench
  NOUN
  △ wen|ches
  VERB
  △ wen|ches
  △ wenched
  △ wench|ing
wend
  △ wends
  △ wen|ded
  △ wend|ing
Wendy
went
wept
were
we're
weren't
were|wolf
  △ were|wolves
wert
Wes|ker
Wes|ley
Wes|leyan
Wes|sex
West
west
west|bound
wes|ter|ing
west|erly
  NOUN
  △ west|er|lies
west|ern
west|er|ner
west|ern|most
West|ern Samoa
West In|dian
West In|dies
West|meath
West Mid|lands
West|min|ster
West|mor|land
Wes|ton-super-
  Mare

West Point
West Side Story
West Sus|sex
west|ward
Westward Ho|
 novel by
 Kingsley
Westward Ho|
 village in Devon

wet
*not dry; make
thus*
VERB
△ wets
△ wet *or* wet|ted
△ wet|ting
ADJ.
△ wet|ter
△ wet|test
⚠ whet

wether
we've
Wex|ford
Wey|mouth
whack
 VERB
 △ whacks
 △ whacked
 △ whack|ing
whacked
whack|ing

whale
*large marine
mammal; hunt
this; large or
excellent
example (of)*
VERB
△ whales
△ whaled
△ whaling
⚠ wale

whale|bone
whaler
whaling
wharf
 △ wharfs *or*
  wharves
wharf|age
whar|fin|ger
what
what-d'you-
 call-it
what|ever
*What Mai|sie
 Knew*
what|not
what's-his-name
what|sit
what|so|ever
wheat
wheat|ear
whea|ten
wheat|meal
wheat|sheaf
whee|dle
 △ whee|dles
 △ whee|dled
 △ wheed|ling
wheed|ler
wheel
 VERB
 △ wheels
 △ wheeled
 △ wheel|ing
wheel|bar|row
wheel|base
wheel|chair
Whee|ler
wheeler-dealer
wheeler-deal|ing
wheel|house
whee|lie
wheel|wright
wheeze

VERB
 △ whee|zes
 △ wheezed
 △ wheez|ing
wheez|ily
wheezy
 △ whee|zier
 △ whee|zi|est
whelk
whelp
 VERB
 △ whelps
 △ whelped
 △ whelp|ing
when
whence
when|ever
when|so|ever
where
where|abouts
whereas
whereby
where|fore
wherein
whereof
whereon
where|so|ever
where|upon
wher|ever
where|wi|thal
wherry
 △ wher|ries

whet
sharpen
△ whets
△ whet|ted
△ whet|ting
⚠ wet

whe|ther
whet|stone
whew
whey
which

which|ever
Whicker
whiff
Whig
Whig|gery
Whig|gish
while
 VERB
 △ whiles
 △ whiled
 △ whi|ling
whilst
whim
whim|per
 VERB
 △ whim|pers
 △ whim|pered
 △ whim|per|ing
whim|si|cal
whim|si|cal|ity
whim|si|cally
whimsy
 △ whim|sies
whin
whine
 VERB
 △ whines
 △ whined
 △ whi|ning
whinge
 VERB
 △ whin|ges
 △ whinged
 △ whin|ging
whinny
 NOUN
 △ whin|nies
 VERB
 △ whin|nies
 △ whin|nied
 △ whin|ny|ing
whip
 VERB
 △ whips

△ whipped
△ whip|ping
whip|cord
whip|lash
  △ whip|la|shes
whip|per-in
  △ whip|pers-in
whip|per-snap|
  per
whip|pet
whip|ping-boy
whip|ping-top
whip|poor|will
whippy
  △ whip|pier
  △ whip|pi|est
whip-round
whip|stock
whirl
  VERB
  △ whirls
  △ whirled
  △ whirl|ing
whir|li|gig
whirl|pool
whirl|wind
whir|ly|bird
whirr
  VERB
  △ whirrs
  △ whirred
  △ whir|ring
whisk
  VERB
  △ whisks
  △ whisked
  △ whisk|ing
whis|ker
whis|kery
whisky
  △ whis|kies
whis|per
  VERB
  △ whis|pers

△ whis|pered
△ whis|per|ing
whist
whis|tle
  VERB
  △ whis|tles
  △ whis|tled
  △ whist|ling
Whist|ler
whistle-stop
Whit
  of Whitsun

> whit
> *the least bit*
> ⚠ wit

Whitby
White
white
  ADJ.
  △ whi|ter
  △ whi|test
white|bait
white-col|lar
White Devil,
The
white|fly
  △ white|flies
White|hall
white-hot
White House
white-knuckle
White|law
whi|ten
  VERB
  △ whi|tens
  △ whi|tened
  △ whi|ten|ing
whi|tener
white|ness
White Nile
white-out
white|wash

VERB
△ white|wa|shes
△ white|washed
△ white|wash|
  ing
white|wood
whi|ther
whi|ting
whi|tish
whit|low
Whit|man
Whit|sun
Whit|sun|tide
Whit|ting|ton
whit|tle
  △ whit|tles
  △ whit|tled
  △ whit|tling
whizz
  NOUN
  △ whiz|zes
  VERB
  △ whiz|zes
  △ whizzed
  △ whizz|ing
who
whoa
who'd
who|dunit
who|ever

> whole
> *complete; a*
> *complete unit*
> ⚠ hole

whole|hearted
whole|heart|edly
whole|meal
whole|ness
whole|sale
whole|saler
whole|some
whole|somely
whole|some|ness

VERB
white|wa|shes ...

wholly
whom
whom|ever
whom|so|ever

> whoop
> *cry of delight;*
> *cougher's gasp;*
> *make these*
> VERB
> △ whoops
> △ whooped
> △ whoop|ing
> ⚠ hoop

whoo|pee
whoo|per
whoop|ing
whoops
whop
  △ whops
  △ whopped
  △ whop|ping
whop|per
whop|ping

> whore
> *prostitute; act*
> *as, be client of,*
> *prostitute*
> VERB
> △ whores
> △ whored
> △ whor|ing
> ⚠ hoar

who're
whore|house
whorl
who's
who's
whose
who|so|ever
why
Whym|per
Wick
wick

wicked
△ wick|eder
△ wick|ed|est
wick|edly
wick|ed|ness
wicker
wick|er|work
wicket
wicket-kee|per
Wick|low
Wicliffe *see*
  Wycliffe
wide
  ADJ.
  △ wider
  △ wi|dest
widely
widen
  △ wi|dens
  △ wi|dened
  △ wi|den|ing
wide|ness
wide-ranging
wide|spread
widgeon *see*
  wigeon
wid|get
Wid|nes
widow
  VERB
  △ wid|ows
  △ wid|owed
  △ wid|ow|ing
wid|ower
width
width|ways
wield
  △ wields
  △ wiel|ded
  △ wield|ing
wife
  △ wives
wifely
wig

Wigan
wi|geon
wigged
wig|ging
wig|gle
  △ wig|gles
  △ wig|gled
  △ wig|gling
wig|gly
  △ wig|glier
  △ wig|gli|est
Wight, Isle of
wight
Wig|more
wig|wam
Wil|bye
wild
  ADJ.
  △ wilder
  △ wild|est
wild|cat
*Wild Duck, The
  (Vild\an|den)*
Wilde
wil|de|beest
  △ wil|de|beest *or*
    wil|de|beests
Wilder
wil|der|ness
wild|fire
wild|fowl
wild|fow|ler
wild|fowl|ing
wild|life
wildly
wild|ness
*Wild Straw\ber|
  ries (Smult|
  ron|stäl\let)*
wile
  VERB
  △ wiles
  △ wiled
  △ wi|ling

Wil|fred
wil|ful
wilfully
wil|ful|ness
wi|li|ness
Wil|kie
will
  VERB
  △ wills
  △ willed
  △ will|ing
Wil|liam
Wil|liams
*Wil\liam Tell
  (Guil\laume
  Tell)*
willie
  penis see willy
wil|lies
  anxiety
will|ing
will|ingly
will|ing|ness
will-o'-the-wisp
wil|low
wil|lowy
will|power
willy
  △ wil|lies
willy-nilly
Wil|son
wilt
  VERB
  △ wilts
  △ wil|ted
  △ wilt|ing
Wilt|shire
wily
  △ wi|lier
  △ wi|li|est
Wimble|don
wimp
  VERB
  △ wimps

△ wimped
△ wimp|ing
win
  VERB
  △ wins
  △ won
  △ win|ning
wince
  VERB
  △ win|ces
  △ winced
  △ win|cing
win|cey|ette
winch
  NOUN
  △ win|ches
  VERB
  △ win|ches
  △ winched
  △ winch|ing
Win|ches|ter
wind
  VERB
  deprive of breath
  △ winds
  △ winded
  △ wind|ing
  wrap; twist
  △ winds
  △ wound
  △ wind|ing
wind|bag
wind|break
wind|chea|ter
wind|chill
winder
Win|der|mere
wind|fall
wind|ing-sheet
*Wind in the
  Wil\lows, The*
wind|jam|mer
wind|lass
  △ wind|las|ses

wind|mill
win|dow
win|dow-dress|
  ing
win|dow-shop|
  ping
win|dow|sill
wind|pipe
Wind|scale
wind|screen
wind|screen-
  wiper
wind|shield
wind|sock
Wind|sor
wind|surf|ing
wind|swept
wind|ward
windy
  △ win|dier
  △ win|di|est
wine
wine|bib|ber
wi|nery
  △ wi|ner|ies
wine|skin
wing
  VERB
  △ wings
  △ winged
  △ wing|ing
winger
wing|less
wing|span
Wi|ni|fred
wink
  VERB
  △ winks
  △ winked
  △ wink|ing
win|ker
win|kle
  VERB
  △ win|kles

△ win|kled
△ wink|ling
winkle-picker
win|ner
Win|nie-the-
  Pooh
win|ning
win|ningly
win|ning-post
Win|ni|peg
win|now
  △ win|nows
  △ win|nowed
  △ win|now|ing
wino
Wins|low Boy, The
win|some
win|somely
win|some|ness
Win|ston
win|ter
  VERB
  △ win|ters
  △ win|tered
  △ win|ter|ing
win|ter|green
Win|ter's Tale,
  The
win|ter|time
win|tri|ness
win|try
winy
  △ wi|nier
  △ wi|ni|est
wipe
  VERB
  △ wipes
  △ wiped
  △ wi|ping
wiper
wire
  VERB
  △ wires
  △ wired

△ wir|ing
wire-haired
wire|less
  △ wire|les|ses
wire|tap
  △ wire|taps
  △ wire|tapped
  △ wire|tap|ping
wire|worm
wir|ing
wiry
  △ wi|rier
  △ wi|ri|est
Wis|con|sin
wis|dom
wise
  ADJ.
  △ wiser
  △ wi|sest
wise|acre
wise|crack
wisely
wish
  NOUN
  △ wi|shes
  VERB
  △ wi|shes
  △ wished
  △ wish|ing
wish|bone
wishy-washy
wisp
wispy
  △ wisp|ier
  △ wis|pi|est
wis|teria
wist|ful
wist|fully
wist|ful|ness

| wit |
| NOUN |
| *humour;* |
| *intelligence* |

| VERB |
| *know* |
| △ wot |
| △ wist |
| △ wit|ting |
| ⚠ whit |

witch
  △ wit|ches
witch|craft
witch|ery
with
wi|thal
with|draw
  △ with|draws
  △ with|drew
  △ with|draw|ing
  △ with|drawn
with|drawal
with|drawn
withe
wither
  △ with|ers
  △ with|ered
  △ with|er|ing
with|ered
with|er|ing
with|ers
with|hold
  △ with|holds
  △ with|held
  △ with|hold|ing
within
with|out
with|stand
  △ with|stands
  △ with|stood
  △ with|stand|ing
withy
  △ with|ies
wit|less
wit|ness
  NOUN
  △ wit|nes|ses

VERB
△ wit|nes|ses
△ wit|nessed
△ wit|ness|ing
wit|ness-box
△ wit|ness-boxes
wit|ness-stand
Witt|gen|stein
wit|ti|cism
wit|tily
wit|ti|ness
wit|tingly
witty
△ wit|tier
△ wit|ti|est
Wit|wa|ters|rand
wives
wiz|ard

Wiz|ard of Oz,
The
film
⚠ *Wonderful
Wizard of
Oz, The*

wiz|ened
woad
wob|ble
VERB
△ wob|bles
△ wob|bled
△ wob|bling
wob|bli|ness
wobbly
△ wob|blier
△ wob|bli|est
Wode|house
wodge

woe
misery; trouble
⚠ woo

woe|be|gone
woe|ful

woe|fully
woe|ful|ness
wog
wok
woke
woken
Wo|king
wold
wolf
NOUN
△ wolves
VERB
△ wolfs
△ wolfed
△ wolf|ing
wolf|cub
Wolfe
Wol|fen|den
wolf|ish
wolf|ishly
Wol|fit
wolf|ram
wolfs|bane
Woll|stone|craft
Wol|sey
Wol|ver|hamp|
ton
wol|ver|ine
woman
NOUN
△ women
wo|man|hood
wo|man|ish
wo|man|ize
△ wo|man|izes
△ wo|man|ized
△ wo|man|izing
wo|man|izer
wo|man|kind
wo|man|li|ness
wo|manly
womb
wom|bat
women

wo|men|folk
Women in Love
won
won|der
VERB
△ won|ders
△ won|dered
△ won|der|ing
won|der|ful
won|der|fully

Won|der|ful
Wizard of Oz,
The
book
⚠ *Wizard of
Oz, The*

won|der|land
won|der|ment
wond|rous
wond|rously
wonky
△ won|kier
△ won|ki|est

wont
*custom;
accustomed*
⚠ won't

won't
will not
⚠ wont

won|ted
accustomed
⚠ wanted

woo
court
△ woos
△ wooed
△ woo|ing
⚠ woe

Wood
wood
wood|bine
wood|chuck
wood|cock
wood|cut
wood|cut|ter
wooded
wooden
wooden-headed
wood|enly
wood|en|ness
wood|land
wood|louse
△ wood|lice
wood|pecker
wood|ruff
Wood|stock
wood|wind
wood|work
wood|worm
△ wood|worm *or*
wood|worms
woody
△ wood|ier
△ woodi|est
wooer
woof
VERB
△ woofs
△ woofed
△ woof|ing
woofer
Woo|key
wool
Woolf
wool-gath|er|ing
wool|len
Wool|ley
wool|li|ness
woolly
NOUN
△ wool|lies

ADJ.
△ wool|lier
△ wool|li|est
wool|sack
Wool|worth
woo|zily
woozy
△ woo|zier
△ woo|zi|est
wop
Wor|ces|ter
word
VERB
△ words
△ wor|ded
△ word|ing
word-blind|ness
word|class
△ word|clas|ses
Worde
word|ily
word|iness
word|ing
word-per|fect
word-pro|cess|ing
Words|worth
wordy
△ word|ier
△ wordi|est
wore
work
VERB
△ works
△ worked
△ work|ing
work|ab|il|ity
work|able
work|aday
worka|holic
work|bas|ket
work|bench
△ work|ben|ches
work|box
△ work|boxes

work|day
worker
work|force
work|house
work-in
work|ing
work|ing-party
△ work|ing-par|
  ties
Work|ing|ton
work|load
work|man
△ work|men
work|man|like
work|man|ship
work|mate
work|out
work|piece
work|place
work|shop
work|shy
work|top
work-to-rule
world
world-bea|ter
world-class
world-famous
world|li|ness
worldly
△ world|lier
△ world|li|est
worldly-wise
world-sha|king
world|weary
world|wide
worm
VERB
△ worms
△ wormed
△ worm|ing
worm|cast
worm-eaten
worm|hole
Worms

worm|wood
wormy
△ worm|ier
△ wormi|est
worn
wor|ried
wor|rier
wor|ri|some
worry
NOUN
△ wor|ries
VERB
△ wor|ries
△ wor|ried
△ wor|ry|ing
worse
wor|sen
△ wor|sens
△ wor|sened
△ wor|sen|ing
wor|ship
VERB
△ wor|ships
△ wor|shipped
△ wor|ship|ping
wor|ship|ful
wor|ship|per
worst
VERB
△ worsts
△ wors|ted
△ worst|ing
wors|ted
wort
worth
wor|thily
wor|thi|ness
Wor|thing
worth|less
worth|lessly
worth|less|ness
worth|while
worthy

NOUN
△ wor|thies
ADJ.
△ wor|thier
△ wor|thi|est
would
would-be
wouldn't
wound
VERB
△ wounds
△ woun|ded
△ wound|ing
also past tense
and past part. of
wind
wove
woven
wow
VERB
△ wows
△ wowed
△ wow|ing

Woz|zeck
opera by Berg
⚠ *Woyzeck*

Woy|zeck
play by Buchner
⚠ *Wozzeck*

wrack
wraith
wran|gle
VERB
△ wran|gles
△ wran|gled
△ wrang|ling

wrap
fold round;
cover; shawl
VERB
△ wraps

△ wrapped
△ wrap|ping
⚠ rap

wrap|around
wrap|per
wrap|ping
wrap|round
wrasse
wrath
wrath|ful
wrath|fully
wreak
△ wreaks
△ wreaked
△ wreak|ing
wreath
NOUN
wreathe
VERB
△ wreathes
△ wreathed
△ wrea|thing
wreck
VERB
△ wrecks
△ wrecked
△ wreck|ing
wreck|age
wrecker
Wreck of the
Deutsch|land,
The
Wren
wren
wrench
NOUN
△ wren|ches
VERB
△ wren|ches
△ wrenched
△ wrench|ing

wrest
wrench; grab
△ wrests
△ wres|ted
△ wrest|ing
⚠ rest

wres|tle
VERB
△ wres|tles
△ wres|tled
△ wrest|ling
wrest|ler
wrest|ling

wretch
unfortunate
person
△ wret|ches
⚠ retch

wret|ched
wretch|edly
wretch|ed|ness
Wrex|ham
wrick
wrig|gle
VERB
△ wrig|gles
△ wrig|gled
△ wrig|gling
wrig|gly
△ wrig|glier
△ wrig|gli|est
Wright
wright

wring
twist and
squeeze
△ wrings
△ wrung
△ wring|ing
⚠ ring

wringer
wrin|kle
VERB
△ wrin|kles
△ wrin|kled
△ wrink|ling
wrinkly
wrist
wrist|let
wrist|watch
△ wrist|wat|ches
writ

write
set down in
words etc;
compose
△ writes
△ wrote
△ wri|ting
△ writ|ten
⚠ right
⚠ rite

write-off
wri|ter
write-up
writhe
△ writhes
△ writhed
△ wri|thing
wri|ting
wri|ting-paper
writ|ten
Wroc|ław
wrong
VERB
△ wrongs
△ wronged
△ wrong|ing
wrong|doer
wrong|do|ing
wrong|foot

△ wrong|foots
△ wrong|footed
△ wrong|foot|ing
wrong|ful
wrong|fully
wrongly

wrote
past tense of
write
⚠ rote

wroth
wrought
wrought-up

wrung
past tense of
wring
⚠ rung

wry
twisted; ironic
△ wryer
△ wryest
⚠ rye

wryly
wry|neck
wurst
Wuth|er|ing
Heights
Wyatt
wych-elm
Wych|er|ley
Wyc|liffe
Wye
Wyler
Wynd|ham
Wy|om|ing
Wyss
Wys|zyn|ski

X

xan|thoma
△ xan|tho|mata
X-chro|mo|
  some
Xen|akis
Xeno|cra|tes
xeno|glos|sia
xeno|lith

xenon
Xeno|pha|nes
xeno|phobe
xeno|pho|bia
xeno|pho|bic
Xeno|phon
xero|gra|phic
xero|gra|phy
xero|phyte
Xerox

NOUN
△ Xer|oxes
VERB
△ Xer|oxes
△ Xer|oxed
△ Xer|ox|ing
Xer|xes
Xhosa
Xmas
△ Xmases

X-ray
VERB
△ X-rays
△ X-rayed
△ X-ray|ing
xylem
xy|lene
xylol
xy|lo|phone
xy|lo|phon|ist

Y

yacht
yacht|ing
yachts|man
△ yachts|men
yachts|wo|man
△ yachts|wo|men
yack
VERB
△ yacks
△ yacked
△ yack|ing
yah
yahoo
Yah|weh
yak
NOUN
△ yaks *or* yak
yak
VERB see *yack*
ya|ki|tori
Yale
Yalta
yam
yam|mer
VERB
△ yam|mers
△ yam|mered
△ yam|mer|ing
yang

Yang|tze
Yank
yank
VERB
△ yanks
△ yanked
△ yank|ing
Yan|kee
yap
VERB
△ yaps
△ yapped
△ yap|ping
yappy
△ yap|pier
△ yap|pi|est
yard
yard|age
yard-arm
Yar|die
yard|stick
Yar|mouth
yar|mulka
yarn
Yaro|slavl
yar|row
yash|mak
Yates
yaw
VERB
△ yaws

△ yawed
△ yaw|ing
yawl
yawn
VERB
△ yawns
△ yawned
△ yawn|ing
yawn|ing
yaws
Y-chro|mo|some
ye
yea
yeah
year
year-book
year|ling
yearly
yearn
△ yearns
△ yearned
△ yearn|ing
yearn|ing
yeast
yeasty
△ yeast|ier
△ yeas|ti|est
Yeats
yell
VERB

△ yells
△ yelled
△ yell|ing
yel|low
VERB
△ yel|lows
△ yel|lowed
△ yel|low|ing
ADJ.
△ yel|lower
△ yel|low|est
yel|low-bel|lied
yel|low|ham|mer
yel|low|ish
yel|low|ness
yelp
VERB
△ yelps
△ yelped
△ yelp|ing
Yemen
yen
NOUN
desire
△ yens
currency unit
△ yen
VERB
△ yens
△ yenned
△ yen|ning

-y / -ey / -ie

-y and **-ie** are used to form diminutive or pet forms of words, eg: **granny, panty, potty**. **-y** is more usual, but **-ie** is used in the following words: **auntie, birdie, budgie, cookie, dearie, girlie, goalie, junkie, laddie, lassie, movie, nightie, oldie, quickie, softie, zombie**; and **-ey** is added to words ending in **-e**: **limey, matey, nursey**.

-y and **-ey** are also used to form descriptive adjectives, both from other adjectives and from nouns, eg **bluey** (= somewhat blue), **buttery** (= like butter). Sometimes the resulting words develop special meanings, like **chancy** and **nosy**. Final **-e** is dropped in more common words, eg **bony, chancy, mousy, nosy**, but note: **cagey, cakey, dicey, pricey**.

Note also: **clayey, gooey**.

yeo¦man
△ yeo¦men
yeo|manry
△ yeo¦man¦ries
Yeo¦men of the Guard
Yeo¦vil
yep
Ye¦re¦van
yes
NOUN
△ yes¦ses
yes-man
△ yes-men
yes¦ter¦day
yes¦ter¦year
yet
yeti
Yev¦tu¦shenko

yew
sort of tree
⚠ewe

Y-fronts
Ygg¦dra¦sil
Yid
Yid¦dish
yield
VERB
△ yields
△ yielded
△ yield¦ing
yield¦ing

yin
yippee
ylang-ylang
yob
yobbo
yodel
VERB
△ yo¦dels
△ yo¦delled
△ yo¦del¦ling
yo¦del¦ler
yoga
yog¦hurt
yogi

yoke
*wooden
shoulder-frame
for pulling,
carrying, etc;
impose this*
VERB
△ yokes
△ yoked
△ yo¦king
⚠yolk

yokel
Yo¦ko¦hama

yolk
*yellow part of
egg*
⚠yoke

Yom Kip¦pur
yon
yon¦der
Yonge
yonks
yoo-hoo

yore
long ago
⚠your

York
yor¦ker
York¦ist
York¦shire
Yo¦ruba
you
you'd
you'll
Young
young
ADJ.
△ younger
△ young¦est
*Young Per¦son's
Guide to the
Or¦ches¦tra*
young¦ster

your
of you
⚠yore

you're
yours

your¦self
△ your¦selves
youth
youth¦ful
youth¦fully
youth¦ful¦ness
you've
yowl
VERB
△ yowls
△ yowled
△ yowl¦ing
yo-yo
VERB
△ yo-yoes
△ yo-yoed
△ yo-yo¦ing
Ypres
yt¦ter¦bium
yt¦trium
yucca
yucky
△ yuck¦ier
△ yucki¦est
Yugo¦sla¦via
Yukon
Yule
yummy
△ yum¦mier
△ yum¦mi¦est
yum-yum
yup¦pie
Yves

Z

za¦bag¦li¦one
Zacharias *see*
 Zechariah,
 Book of
Za¦greb
Zaire
zakat
Zam|bezi
Zam¦bia
Zam¦en|hof
ZANU
Zan¦uck
zany
 △ za¦nier
 △ za¦ni|est
Zan¦zi¦bar
zap
 △ zaps
 △ zapped
 △ zap|ping
zap¦per
ZAPU
Zara
zar|zu¦ela
zeal

Zea|land
 Danish island
 ▲Zeeland

zealot
zeal|ous
zeal|ously
zebra
 △ zeb¦ras *or*
  zebra
zebu

Ze¦char|iah,
 Book of
zed
zee
Zee|brugge

Zee|land
 province in
 Netherlands
 ▲Zealand

Zef¦fir|elli
Zeiss
Zen
Zend-Avesta
zen¦ith
Zeno
zeo|lite
Zeph¦an|jah,
 Book of
zephyr
Zep|pelin
Zer|matt
zero
 VERB
 △ zer¦oes
 △ zeroed
 △ zero|ing
zero-rated
zest
zest|ful
zest|fully
zeugma
Zeus
Zhou Enlai
Zia Ul-Haq
Zieg|feld
zig|gurat
zig¦zag

Ze¦char|iah,
 VERB
 △ zig|zags
 △ zig|zagged
 △ zig|zag|ging
zilch
zillion
Zim|babwe
Zim¦mer
zinc
zinc|ite
zine
zing
 VERB
 △ zings
 △ zinged
 △ zing|ing
zin|nia
Zi¦nov|iev
Zion
Zion|ism
Zion|ist
zip
 VERB
 △ zips
 △ zipped
 △ zip|ping
zip¦per
zippy
 △ zip|pier
 △ zip|pi|est
zir|con
zir|co¦nium
zi¦ther
zo|diac
Zoe
Zola
zom¦bie
zonal

zone
 VERB
 △ zones
 △ zoned
 △ zo|ning
zonked
zoo
zo|olo¦gi|cal
zo|olo|gic|ally
zo¦olo|gist
zo|ology
zoom
 VERB
 △ zooms
 △ zoomed
 △ zoom|ing
zo|ophyte
zo|oplank|ton
Zoro|as¦ter
Zoro|as|trian
Zoro|as¦trian|
  ism
zos¦ter
Zou|ave
zouk
zuc|chini
 △ zuc|chini *or*
  zuc|chi¦nis
Zui¦der Zee
Zu|leika Dob¦son
Zulu
Zur¦ich
Zwin|gli
Zwolle
zy¦gote
zy¦mase
zy|motic